CEDU쎄듀는 A **C**omprehensive **E**nglish e**DU**cation(**종합적 영어교육**)**의 약자입니다.**

펴낸이 김기훈 I 김진희
펴낸곳 (주)쎄듀 I 서울특별시 강남구 논현로 305 (역삼동)
발행일 2022년 4월 15일 제1개정판 1쇄
내용문의 www.cedubook.com
구입문의 콘텐츠 마케팅 사업본부
Tel. 02-6241-2007
Fax. 02-2058-0209
등록번호 제 22-2472호
ISBN 978-89-6806-251-3

쎈쓰업

듣기 모의고사

30회

S E N S E

저자

김기훈 現 ㈜ 쎄듀 대표이사

現 메가스터디 영어영역 대표강사

前 서울특별시 교육청 외국어 교육정책자문위원회 위원

저서 천일문 / 천일문 Training Book / 천일문 GRAMMAR / 어법끝 / 어휘끝

첫단추 / 쎈쓰업 / 파워업 / 빈칸백서 / 오답백서 / 독해비

쎄듀 본영어 / 문법의 골든룰 101 / Grammar Q

거침없이 Writing / ALL씀 서술형 / 수능실감 등

쎄듀 영어교육연구센터

쎄듀 영어교육센터는 영어 콘텐츠에 대한 전문지식과 경험을 바탕으로

최고의 교육 콘텐츠를 만들고자 최선의 노력을 다하는 전문가 집단입니다.

이혜경 전임연구원

마케팅	콘텐츠 마케팅 사업본부
영업	문병구
제작	정승호
인디자인 편집	올댓에디팅
디자인	쎄듀 디자인팀
영문교열	Stephen Daniel White

PREFACE

이 책을 펴내며

수능의 문제 유형에 익숙해졌다면, 이제는 수능 문제 풀이 감각을 길러야 할 때입니다.

수능을 대비하는 가장 중요한 과정 중 하나가 바로 모의고사 대비입니다. 모의고사를 대비하는 가장 좋은 방법은 그와 꼭 같은 형태의 문제를 실전처럼 풀어보는 것인데, 무엇보다도 자신의 실력에 맞는 문제로 풀이 훈련을 해야 합니다. 그런데 그냥 문제를 푸는 것만으로는 부족함을 느끼게 될 것입니다. 실제 시험장에서 실력을 제대로 발휘하려면 실전 감각이 있어야 합니다. 즉, 특정 문제 외에는 두 번 들려주지 않으므로 특히 집중해야 합니다. 간혹 놓치는 부분이 있더라도 당황하지 않고 침착하게 대처해야 합니다. 듣기만 잘해서는 안 되고 선택지도 동시에 바르게 이해해야 합니다.

실전에 필요한 이러한 감각은 충분한 양의 질 좋은 문제로 꾸준한 학습을 통해서만 길러질 수 있습니다.

학습 방법을 좀 더 구체적으로 제안하자면 다음과 같습니다.

<쎄듀 Sense Up 듣기 모의고사 30회>의 문제는 최신 수능 경향을 반영하면서 아직 수능 난이도의 문제를 소화하기는 어려운 학생들에게 문제 풀이 감각을 기를 수 있는 난이도로 구성하였습니다. 무엇보다 매회의 모의고사를 일정 시간에 맞춰 꾸준히 풀기를 권해 드립니다. 문제 풀이란 '복습'의 과정까지 포함하는 것으로서, 복습의 중요성은 아무리 강조해도 지나치지 않습니다.

문제 풀이 후 그것을 자기 것으로 소화하는 과정이 가장 중요합니다.

따라서 학습계획을 짤 때는 반드시 복습시간까지 계산에 넣도록 하십시오. 그리고 책에서 제시하는 '베스트 공부 방법'을 참고로 자기만의 복습 방법을 만들어 꾸준히 실천하세요!

경영학에 나오는 개념 중에는 **Plan(계획), Do(실천), See(평가)**가 있는데, 목표를 달성하려면 실천 가능한 계획을 세우고, 그대로 실천하고, 점검하는 이 3가지 단계를 반복해야 한다는 말입니다. 이것을 학습 단계에도 똑같이 적용해보세요. <쎄듀 Sense Up 듣기 모의고사 30회>는 이를 돕기 위해 Study Diary, 어휘리스트·어휘테스트와 같은 장치를 마련해 두었습니다.

이제 가장 중요한 것은 여러분의 실천입니다!

모쪼록 이 책을 통해 수능을 준비하는 모든 학생이 진정한 공부의 즐거움을 누리고 좋은 결과를 얻을 수 있기를 진심으로 기원합니다.

저자

ABOUT THIS BOOK

이 책의 구성과 특징

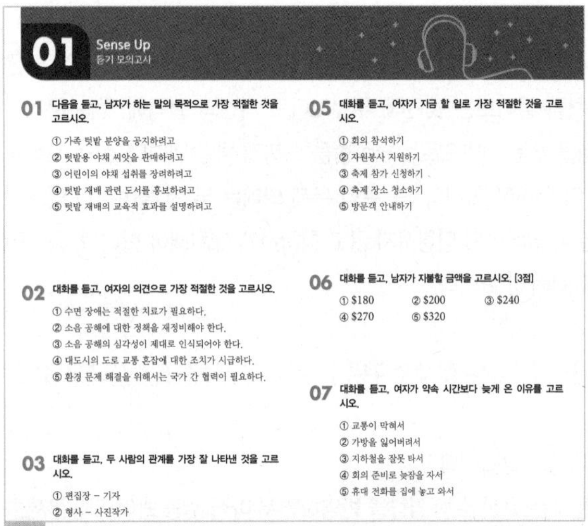

❶ 최신 수능 대비

최신 경향을 반영하여 실전에 대비할 수 있도록 엄선된 문제만을 수록했습니다.

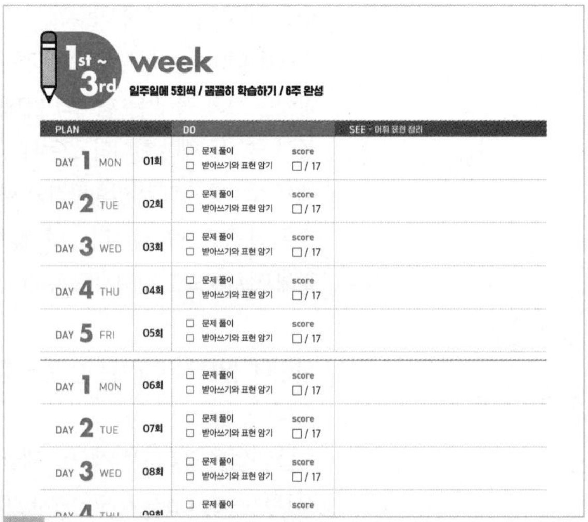

❷ Study Diary

계획적인 학습을 위해 마련했습니다. 공부한 내용을 기록하다 보면 내 실력이 커나가는 모습을 볼 수 있습니다.

❸ 정답 및 해설

혼자서 복습할 때도 어려움이 없도록 자세한 해설을 실었고 다양한 어휘의 중요 뜻을 수록했습니다.

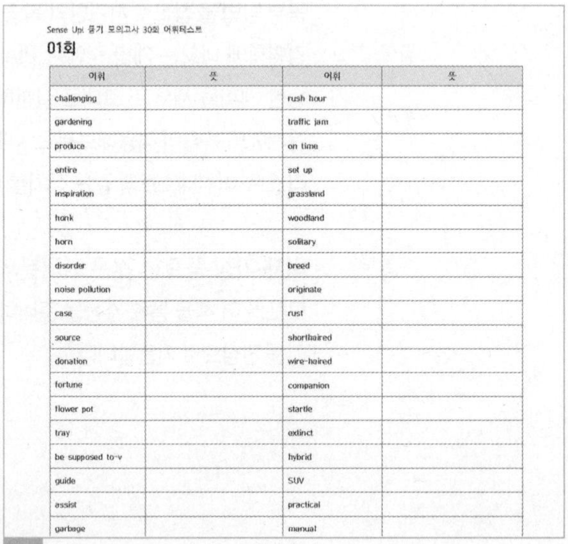

❹ 어휘리스트 · 어휘테스트

교재에 나온 중요 어휘를 모두 정리한 어휘리스트로 단어를 암기하고, 어휘테스트로 확인해보세요. **www.cedubook.com**에서 무료로 다운로드받으실 수 있습니다.

CONTENTS

수능 문제 풀이 감각을 키워주는 Sense Up

HOW TO?

쎈쓰업, 베스트 공부 방법

1 실전처럼 녹음을 들으며 문제를 푼다.

이해를 못한 부분이 있다고 해서 다시 듣거나 하지 말고 녹음에 맞춰 실전처럼 문제를 풉니다. 독해 문제와 달리 듣기 문제는 순식간에 흘러가 버리므로, 단서를 한순간에 놓쳐버리면 생각할 시간을 더 들인다고 해서 정답률을 높일 수 있는 것이 아닙니다. 듣기 문제는 이해했든 하지 못했든 바로바로 해결하고, 다음 문제를 푸는 데 절대 지장을 받지 않도록 해야 합니다. 또한, 실전의 경우처럼 약간의 소음이 있는 상태로 듣기 문제를 푸는 것을 권합니다. 되도록 이어폰을 사용하지 말고 녹음기에서 흘러나오는 소리를 들으면서 푸는 것이 더 도움이 됩니다. 속도 조절이 가능한 기기인 경우, 약간 빠르게 조절하여 문제를 푸는 것도 좋습니다.

2 정답에 맞춰 채점을 한다.

잘 이해하지 못했으나 우연히 맞은 것도 복습을 위해 표시를 합니다.

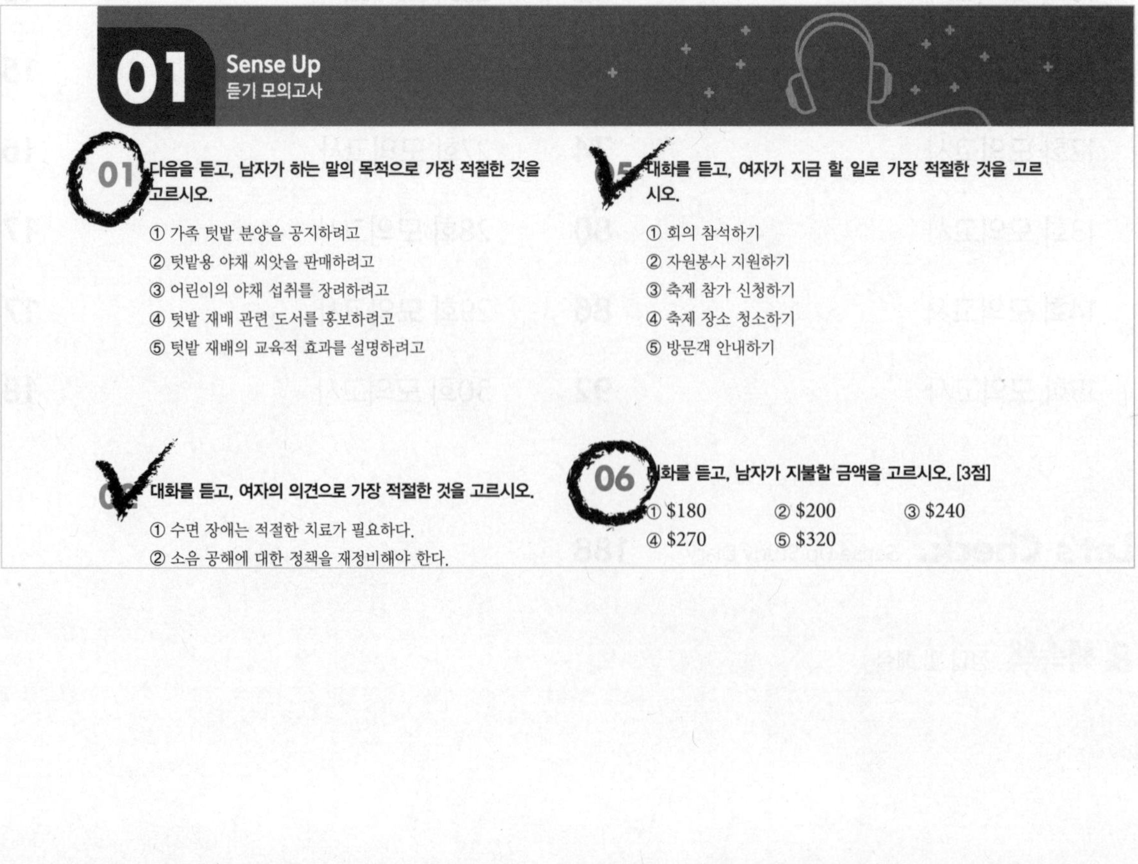
01 Sense Up
듣기 모의고사

01 다음을 듣고, 남자가 하는 말의 목적으로 가장 적절한 것을 고르시오.
① 가족 텃밭 분양을 공지하려고
② 텃밭용 야채 씨앗을 판매하려고
③ 어린이의 야채 섭취를 장려하려고
④ 텃발 재배 관련 도서를 홍보하려고
⑤ 텃밭 재배의 교육적 효과를 설명하려고

02 대화를 듣고, 여자의 의견으로 가장 적절한 것을 고르시오.
① 수면 장애는 적절한 치료가 필요하다.
② 소음 공해에 대한 정책을 재정비해야 한다.

05 대화를 듣고, 여자가 지금 할 일로 가장 적절한 것을 고르시오.
① 회의 참석하기
② 자원봉사 지원하기
③ 축제 참가 신청하기
④ 축제 장소 청소하기
⑤ 방문객 안내하기

06 대화를 듣고, 남자가 지불할 금액을 고르시오. [3점]
① $180 ② $200 ③ $240
④ $270 ⑤ $320

3 2에 표시한 문제를 포함하여 틀린 문제를 점검한다.

본인이 왜 틀렸는지를 아는 것이 진정한 실력을 늘리는 길입니다. 받아쓰기를 해보면 본인이 어휘나 표현을 잘 몰라 틀리는지, 연음 등을 잘 알아듣지 못하는지를 확인할 수 있습니다. 즉, 받아쓰기를 하고 나서 script와 틀린 부분을 대조해 봅니다. 원래 알고 있는 어휘나 표현인데 잘 받아쓰지 못했다면 연음 등 영어 특유의 발음에 익숙하지 못한 것입니다. 반대로 잘 알아듣기는 했는데 의미를 모른다면, 듣기 문제에 자주 등장하는 실용 어휘나 표현을 좀 더 익혀야 합니다.

4 학습 일지를 작성한다.

목표를 실천하기 위해서는 계획을 세우고(PLAN), 실천하고(DO), 점검해야(SEE)합니다. 이 중에서 혹시 잘못된 것이 있으면 다시 고쳐서 PLAN-DO-SEE를 반복합니다. 학습 일지를 적어보면서 계획적인 공부 습관을 만들어 보세요!

1st ~ 3rd week

일주일에 5회씩 / 꼼꼼히 학습하기 / 6주 완성

PLAN		DO		SEE - 어휘 표현 정리
DAY 1 MON	01회	□ 문제 풀이 □ 받아쓰기와 표현 암기	score □ / 17	
DAY 2 TUE	02회	□ 문제 풀이 □ 받아쓰기와 표현 암기	score □ / 17	
DAY 3 WED	03회	□ 문제 풀이 □ 받아쓰기와 표현 암기	score □ / 17	
DAY 4 THU	04회	□ 문제 풀이 □ 받아쓰기와 표현 암기	score □ / 17	

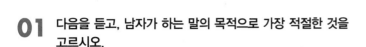

01 다음을 듣고, 남자가 하는 말의 목적으로 가장 적절한 것을 고르시오.

① 가족 텃밭 분양을 공지하려고
② 텃밭용 야채 씨앗을 판매하려고
③ 어린이의 야채 섭취를 장려하려고
④ 텃밭 재배 관련 도서를 홍보하려고
⑤ 텃밭 재배의 교육적 효과를 설명하려고

02 대화를 듣고, 여자의 의견으로 가장 적절한 것을 고르시오.

① 수면 장애는 적절한 치료가 필요하다.
② 소음 공해에 대한 정책을 재정비해야 한다.
③ 소음 공해의 심각성이 제대로 인식되어야 한다.
④ 대도시의 도로 교통 혼잡에 대한 조치가 시급하다.
⑤ 환경 문제 해결을 위해서는 국가 간 협력이 필요하다.

03 대화를 듣고, 두 사람의 관계를 가장 잘 나타낸 것을 고르시오.

① 편집장 – 기자
② 형사 – 사진작가
③ 작가 – 삽화가
④ 시장 – 사설탐정
⑤ 연구원 – 교수

04 대화를 듣고, 그림에서 대화의 내용과 일치하지 않는 것을 고르시오.

05 대화를 듣고, 여자가 지금 할 일로 가장 적절한 것을 고르시오.

① 회의 참석하기
② 자원봉사 지원하기
③ 축제 참가 신청하기
④ 축제 장소 청소하기
⑤ 방문객 안내하기

06 대화를 듣고, 남자가 지불할 금액을 고르시오. [3점]

① \$180 ② \$200 ③ \$240
④ \$270 ⑤ \$320

07 대화를 듣고, 여자가 약속 시간보다 늦게 온 이유를 고르시오.

① 교통이 막혀서
② 가방을 잃어버려서
③ 지하철을 잘못 타서
④ 회의 준비로 늦잠을 자서
⑤ 휴대 전화를 집에 놓고 와서

08 대화를 듣고, 사막솜꼬리토끼(desert cottontail)에 관해 언급되지 않은 것을 고르시오.

① 서식지 ② 단독 생활
③ 먹이 찾는 시간 ④ 번식 시기
⑤ 수명

09 Vizsla에 관한 다음 내용을 듣고, 일치하지 않는 것을 고르시오.

① 원산지가 헝가리이다.
② 털이 짧거나 뻣뻣할 수 있다.
③ 사냥개라서 가정에서 키우기에 적절하지 않다.
④ 주인을 잘 따라 훈련시키기 수월하다.
⑤ 거의 멸종될 뻔한 적이 있다.

10 다음 표를 보면서 대화를 듣고, 남자가 구입할 차량을 고르시오.

Enviro-Cars Hybrid Models 2022

Name	Number of doors	Gear shift	Seats	Mileage (miles/liter)	Full-electric capability
① Eclipse Minivan	4	Manual	8	39	✓
② Spring Coupe	2	Automatic	5	49	✓
③ Portland SUV	4	Manual	8	39	
④ Solaris Sedan	4	Automatic	5	54	✓
⑤ Sierra Coupe	4	Manual	4	54	

11 대화를 듣고, 남자의 마지막 말에 대한 여자의 응답으로 가장 적절한 것을 고르시오.

① I think we should delay our plan.
② Why don't we take a bus instead?
③ We should have brought raincoats.
④ Today's weather forecast was wrong.
⑤ Going mountain climbing will cheer us up.

12 대화를 듣고, 여자의 마지막 말에 대한 남자의 응답으로 가장 적절한 것을 고르시오.

① No, but the car is 10 years old now.
② I think I might have to buy a new car.
③ I might be able to recommend a better repair shop.
④ Yes, it could have happened in a better location.
⑤ The repair shop said it was a common problem.

13 대화를 듣고, 남자의 마지막 말에 대한 여자의 응답으로 가장 적절한 것을 고르시오. [3점]

▶ Woman : ______

① You can ask for a discount on your next visit.
② I'm sorry, but I need to know your brother's illness.
③ How much money do you have in this account?
④ You cannot return the sausages after the expiration date.
⑤ You are very kind to him. I will put together something nice.

14 대화를 듣고, 여자의 마지막 말에 대한 남자의 응답으로 가장 적절한 것을 고르시오.

▶ Man : ______

① OK. I'll give it a try for my waistline.
② Good. I'd love some spicy food tonight.
③ How much weight do you think I should lose?
④ I didn't know you knew how to speak Korean.
⑤ Of course, I love Korean food better than Chinese food.

15 다음 상황 설명을 듣고, Heather가 룸메이트들에게 할 말로 가장 적절한 것을 고르시오. [3점]

▶ Heather : ______

① It's your turn to cook dinner today.
② I'm tired of living in this dirty room.
③ I'm planning to move to a new dormitory.
④ Let's create a schedule and divide the cleaning.
⑤ Where do you want to go out to shop this Saturday?

[16~17] 다음을 듣고, 물음에 답하시오.

16 여자가 하는 말의 주제로 가장 적절한 것은?

① how to drive safely
② how to reduce traffic
③ how to control your car
④ how to stay alert while driving
⑤ how to improve driving confidence

17 운전 중 삼가야 할 행동으로 언급되지 않은 것은?

① 고속 주행
② 흡연
③ 식사
④ 차량용 TV 보기
⑤ 핸드폰 통화

01

M: Parents know ______________________________ to get kids to eat enough vegetables, but gardening may help. Research shows that when kids help grow vegetables, they are more likely to eat more produce and try different kinds, too. The benefits of gardening don't end there. It also is a great way to get the entire family outside for fresh air and physical activity. If you want to try ______________________________, Rena Brown's *Vegetable Gardens* will be a good guide to start. This delightful, newly published guide will get families excited about growing their own vegetables. In *Vegetable Gardens*, you'll get all the inspiration and knowledge you need to get out there and start planting. Order now, and you'll get an eco bag for free.

02

W: Minsu, you don't look good. What's up?

M: I ______________________________. The street noise bothers me at night. There are people laughing and shouting, honking horns, and loud music.

W: I can imagine ______________________________ to live near a busy street.

M: It is. A recent news story reported that many people, especially in cities, suffer from hearing loss and sleep disorders.

W: I saw that, too.

M: If only the government would take responsibility.

W: The news also said that many countries are now taking steps to reduce noise pollution.

M: Isn't the problem equally serious in our own country?

W: I think so, but so far we ______________________________ the issue.

M: You're right.

W: The government ______________________________ unless that changes.

03

M: Hey, Allison. ______________________________ at the moment?

W: I'm working on the case I told you about. But I only need a couple of days.

M: You know I ______________________________ because of your story?

W: It will be worth it! I promise.

M: Have you found something interesting?

W: According to my sources, a high-ranking government official accepted inappropriate donations!

M: Wow, that's big.

W: And his wife owns some land in Amherst. But only yesterday the local government announced a plan to build a new town in that region. They'll make a fortune.

M: You're right! This is ______________________________. It will be an interesting article.

W: Well, it's my job to get the facts and tell the readers.

04

W: Honey, ______________________________ our favorite comedy show? Let's watch!

M: Great idea! I love it because it's so funny. I'll just turn on the TV. Wait a minute, have you seen the remote control?

W: I think I saw it on the table next to the stairs.

M: I don't see it there. I thought I left it next to the heart-shaped cushion on the sofa. But it's gone.

W: Hmmm.... Have you checked next to the flower pot in front of the window?

M: I searched there already, but I didn't see it.

W: I remember I ______________________________ on the carpet.

M: Yeah, I was. But there's nothing on the carpet ______________________________.

W: That's strange.

M: Oh, I found it! It was under the newspaper. That's why I couldn't see it.

W: Honey, please leave the remote control in the tray next to the TV. ______________________________.

M: All right. I will next time.

정답 및 해설 p.2

05

M: Joyce, have you heard about our school festival?

W: Yes, I heard it'll begin next Friday. I'm looking forward to it.

M: It'll be great fun. By the way, ________________ ______________ at the festival.

W: Did you apply for it? What are you going to do there?

M: We'll help out with tasks such as guiding visitors, assisting with parking and picking up garbage.

W: Sounds great.

M: How about joining us? ____________________ __________________ in the festival, so we need more volunteers for such a large number of visitors.

W: All right. I'll do that. Please tell me how I can sign up.

M: You can do it at our school's website using your smartphone. The deadline is tomorrow.

W: Tomorrow? Then I'll do it right now.

M: I'm sure ______________________________. And there'll be a volunteer meeting at the student's union on Tuesday.

06

W: What are you looking at, Dad?

M: I'm looking at the summer course schedule of a language institute for you. I remember you said ________________________ to China during winter vacation.

W: That's right. Can I see?

M: Sure.

W: It says they have two lower-level courses. Chinese Grammar starts in July, and Chinese Speaking begins in August.

M: I see that. ____________________________?

W: Each course is $120. But if you sign up for a package that includes both of them, the price is $200.

M: OK, I'll register you for the package. We can save $40! And I heard that I can get a 10 percent discount ______________________________.

W: But look, we can see that packaged lectures are excluded from the discount, so we can't benefit from it.

M: I didn't see that, but you're right. Anyway, I'll register you for the package.

W: Thanks, Dad.

07

W: Hi, Jack. I'm terribly sorry I'm late again.

M: That's okay. I know ______________________ at rush hour.

W: Right. That's why I took the subway. I thought I could avoid any traffic jams.

M: Oh, then why are you late? You ______________ ______________, did you?

W: No. I even left my house on time.

M: Let me guess. You forgot your bag at home.

W: Almost. Actually, I forgot my phone at home. I had to go all the way back from the station to get it.

M: Anyway, you're here now. Let's get set up for the meeting.

W: Of course. I have the files in my bag. I prepared everything last night.

M: Great. We still __________________________.

08

M: What are you watching, Amy?

W: It's a nature documentary about desert cottontails. Aren't they cute?

M: Sure! I love rabbits. So, ____________________ ____________?

W: It was filmed in the animal's natural habitat, the deserts, grasslands, and woodlands of western North America.

M: I thought they would ________________, but this one is all alone.

W: Actually, they're mostly solitary animals. They live alone ____________________.

M: Interesting! It sure looks hot there!

W: That's why they search for food in the early morning or evening, when the sun is down.

M: Makes sense. It must be __________________ ____________, as well.

W: The show said they breed in the spring and the young leave the nest after only two weeks.

M: Wow, I never knew!

09

W: Do you want to get a dog? Then, here is a breed that you might want. The Vizsla is ____________ ____________________ in Hungary. The Vizsla is a medium-sized dog with a deep golden rust color and can be shorthaired or wire-haired. He is a natural hunter with an excellent nose in the field, and he is ____________________________. The Vizsla is generally shy, and may be startled by sudden noises. He loves to please his owner and is very easy to train. Sadly, this unique breed ____________________________ in Hungary during the years between the two World Wars. Luckily, the dogs survived and now are quite popular in the United States.

10

W: What are you looking at?

M: It's a catalogue of the latest hybrid cars.

W: You're buying a hybrid? I thought you loved your SUV.

M: Well, ____________________________. I never took it into the mountains anyway.

W: What is the main thing you are looking for?

M: Well, two doors is definitely out. My mom is ____ ______________ like that.

W: Don't you prefer to drive a manual transmission?

M: Yes, ____________________. And I need room for my wife, son, and my parents. Together there are 5 of us.

W: I guess it comes down to mileage and whether you want to drive purely on electricity.

M: I want a car that has full-electric capability. ____ ________________, mileage isn't that important.

11

M: Helen, ________________________ tomorrow's climb to the top of Mt. Seorak?

W: Not really. ______________________________ heavy rain and strong winds. I was going to call you.

M: No way! What should we do?

12

W: It's lucky that you were near a repair shop ______ ____________________.

M: I know, but I'm worried that it might become a regular problem.

W: Are you saying ____________________________ before?

13

M: Do you sell imported cheese and sausages here?

W: Yes, ____________________________________.

M: Great. I'm looking for a mixed selection to give as a gift.

W: We can choose a variety of sausages and some nice cheese for you.

M: Can you also ____________________________?

W: I think we can arrange that for you. What's the occasion?

M: My brother is in the hospital ______________ ______________.

W: I'm so sorry to hear that. I hope he gets well soon.

M: I'm sure he would appreciate that you said that.

W: How much would you like to spend?

M: I'm not worried about the cost when it involves my brother.

14

W: What kind of restaurant do you want to go to tonight?

M: Let's go to the new French restaurant. It'll be romantic.

W: Hmm... I was thinking of Korean food.

M: Korean food? ______________________________.

W: ______________________________. It's healthy and delicious.

M: Actually, I am trying to lose weight and eat healthy food.

W: Then Korean food ______________________________ ______________.

M: But if it's going to be Asian cuisine, you know I love Chinese food.

W: I know you do. But many of the dishes we love are really oily, like deep-fried noodles.

M: But Korean food is spicy.

W: Some things are, but others aren't so spicy. Remember it's really healthy, nutritious food.

15

M: Heather lives in a dormitory with two other roommates. She's been living with the same roommates for two years now, and they've all become good friends. On the weekends, they ______________________________ or eat together. All three of them usually get along with hardly any disagreements. Heather's very happy with the current situation ______________________________. It seems like she's always the one stuck with the cleaning. She rarely sees her roommates clean, so she wants to suggest that they somehow ______________________________ who cleaned the room. In this situation, what would Heather most likely say to her roommates?

16-17

W: Common sense and calm thinking are essential for smart drivers. For example, common sense says it's ______________________________ when you are running late. Why? Because doing this in city traffic saves you ______________________________, and greatly increases the risk of accidents. Next, it's absolutely important to keep a space of three seconds between your car and the vehicle ahead. This space gives you life-saving time to ______________________________. Most important of all, though, is to give your full attention to the job and never smoke or eat at the wheel. It's not illegal, but if it leads to careless driving it could land you in trouble with the law. ______________________________ while driving is illegal. Of course, some special systems allow you to talk without holding your phone. Similar to eating, drinking soft beverages at the wheel is not illegal, but it can carry the same careless-driving penalty. A study found that those who took a sip of a drink at the wheel were 22% ______________________________.

01 다음을 듣고, 여자가 하는 말의 목적으로 가장 적절한 것을 고르시오.

① 새로운 의료장비를 홍보하려고
② 환자를 돌볼 자원봉사자를 모집하려고
③ 아프가니스탄의 어려운 현실을 알리려고
④ 어린이병원을 위한 기부금을 요청하려고
⑤ 가난한 어린이들을 경제적으로 지원하려고

02 대화를 듣고, 남자의 의견으로 가장 적절한 것을 고르시오.

① 올바른 수면 습관에 관한 교육이 필요하다.
② 장시간의 낮잠은 불면증을 유발하므로 피해야 한다.
③ 허리 통증을 피하려면 딱딱한 곳에서 자는 것이 좋다.
④ 자투리 시간을 활용하여 부족한 수면을 보충해야 한다.
⑤ 편하게 낮잠을 잘 수 있는 공간을 교내에 마련해야 한다.

03 대화를 듣고, 두 사람의 관계를 가장 잘 나타낸 것을 고르시오.

① 교수 – 조교
② 미술품 수집가 – 판매업자
③ 상점 주인 – 고객
④ 미술 선생님 – 학생
⑤ 조각가 – 예술 비평가

04 대화를 듣고, 그림에서 대화의 내용과 일치하지 않는 것을 고르시오.

05 대화를 듣고, 남자가 할 일로 가장 적절한 것을 고르시오.

① 학교 도서관에 가기
② 연구 보고서 도와주기
③ 마지막 단락 작성하기
④ 친구 생일 파티에 가기
⑤ 백화점에서 선물 구입하기

06 대화를 듣고, 여자가 지불할 금액을 고르시오. [3점]

① $400 ② $420 ③ $450
④ $470 ⑤ $500

07 대화를 듣고, 남자의 딸이 피아노 교습에 참여할 수 없는 이유를 고르시오.

① 강사가 부족해서
② 신청 기간이 지나서
③ 대상 연령이 아니라서
④ 교습 기간이 너무 길어서
⑤ 피아노를 배운 적이 있어서

08 다음을 듣고, Nelson Mandela에 관해 언급되지 않은 것을 고르시오.

① 출생지 ② 출신 대학
③ 투옥 기간 ④ 수상 내역
⑤ 퇴임 후 활동

09 립스틱에 관한 다음 내용을 듣고, 일치하지 않는 것을 고르시오.

① 약 5,000년 전에 처음 사용되었다.
② 독성 때문에 죽음을 부르기도 했다.
③ Cleopatra는 곤충으로 만든 립스틱을 썼다.
④ 16세기 영국에서는 사용이 금지되었다.
⑤ 판매용은 파리에서 최초로 만들어졌다.

10 다음 표를 보면서 대화를 듣고, 여자가 선택할 아파트를 고르시오. [3점]

	Location	No. of bedrooms	Rent
① Green Lake Apartments	downtown	1	$1,100
② City View Apartments	downtown	2	$1,100
③ Tower Apartments	downtown	2	$1,300
④ Garden Estate Apartments	suburb	2	$700
⑤ Serenity Lanes Apartments	suburb	1	$600

11 대화를 듣고, 남자의 마지막 말에 대한 여자의 응답으로 가장 적절한 것을 고르시오.

① I don't think it will take much longer.
② That would be best. Thank you.
③ No thanks. I'm just looking.
④ I recommend the cheaper of the two.
⑤ Are you looking for any specific features?

12 대화를 듣고, 여자의 마지막 말에 대한 남자의 응답으로 가장 적절한 것을 고르시오.

① Yes, they usually deliver on time.
② No, I don't know who called me.
③ Well, I'll call you at another time.
④ I tried several times but the line was busy.
⑤ This is the first time we've ordered from that place.

13 대화를 듣고, 남자의 마지막 말에 대한 여자의 응답으로 가장 적절한 것을 고르시오. [3점]

▶ Woman : ______________________

① Please pick any flavor you want.
② I'm very sorry, but it is not available now.
③ You said you wanted strawberry, didn't you?
④ It is my favorite. You won't regret your choice.
⑤ I don't understand why you don't like Vanilla ice cream.

14 대화를 듣고, 여자의 마지막 말에 대한 남자의 응답으로 가장 적절한 것을 고르시오.

▶ Man : ______________________

① Don't worry, I will do all the talking.
② I'll take you to this place every month.
③ Take your time and relax. It will get better.
④ The restaurant closes soon. Finish off the food.
⑤ Why don't you just eat whatever he brought you?

15 다음 상황 설명을 듣고, Blair가 Susan에게 할 말로 가장 적절한 것을 고르시오. [3점]

▶ Blair : ______________________

① What time does the movie start tomorrow?
② Do you know any shortcuts to get there?
③ I'm really sorry that I didn't tell you.
④ Can you give me directions to your house?
⑤ What kind of movies do you prefer to watch?

[16~17] 다음을 듣고, 물음에 답하시오.

16 남자가 하는 말의 주제로 가장 적절한 것은?

① a guide to privacy in the workplace
② how to deal with an unfair labor practice
③ the importance of keeping personal space
④ the definition of healthy workplace hierarchy
⑤ relation between social status and private space

17 언급된 대상이 아닌 것은?

① 회사 상사
② 교사
③ 연예계 스타
④ 군대의 장군
⑤ 의사

01

W: My message to you is a very simple one. Our hospital helps the poorest children of Afghanistan. ______________________, to continue our work in caring for the sick and injured children of this country. To this end, your support ______________________. Our hospital urgently needs more beds and new medical equipment. A donation of as little as $20 will ______________________ to save at least 50 babies from death. Without your help, many of these children will have no hope. Open your wallets and your hearts. Give ______________________. Every single cent will be immediately put to use.

02

W: You look tired. Are you okay?

M: I haven't been getting enough sleep because I've been watching the Olympics.

W: I see. Sometimes I ______________ because I don't sleep well at night. When that happens, I nap during a break.

M: But it's uncomfortable and it hurts my back ______________________.

W: You're right. It's impossible to sleep soundly.

M: I wish we had another place to sleep.

W: It sounds like you want a room for napping.

M: Why not? In fact, just a few beds in the break room would be enough.

W: That would ______________, but shouldn't we spend our time in more productive ways?

M: Well, experts say that napping for 10 to 30 minutes ______________________.

W: I didn't know that.

03

W: That is really good! Your work ______________________.

M: Well, I owe it all to you. I never worked with clay before this class.

W: I ______________________. I think your true talent is coming out.

M: Well, I was inspired by your piece that was in the big show last year.

W: Ah, the one that you said looked like the moon ______________________?

M: Yes. Sorry I said that. That was before I understood art.

W: That's OK. I always tell the class that art is subjective.

M: So it's OK if I still think it looks like the moon?

W: I'll ______________________: I think it looks like the moon, too!

04

W: Now, I'll show you ______________________.

M: Okay, I'm ready.

W: First, check the mirror above the sink. If there's any dirt, you should get rid of it completely.

M: All right. I'll ______________________.

W: Next, two towels should be prepared.

M: Would you like me to hang them on the rack?

W: No. That used to be the policy, but now we ______________________ on the counter.

M: Okay. Where does the soap go, then?

W: It goes on the left side of the sink. Right in front of the tissue with the pyramid logo on it.

M: I see. What about the bathrobe?

W: The bathrobe should be on a hanger, and you ______________________. Now, that's all. Can you remember everything I told you?

M: No problem. I think I've got it.

05

W: Hey Andrew! How's the research paper going?

M: I just need to write the last paragraph. It will be done tomorrow.

W: Good for you! Maybe you can help me with mine next.

M: ____?

W: I'm writing about the effects of dams on the environment.

M: I'd love to help, but I don't know anything about that subject.

W: Well, that's okay. There are many reference books in the school library. Oh, by the way, aren't you supposed to go to Jack's birthday party today?

M: Yeah... but ____________________________ now. The party started twenty minutes ago.

W: Well, you know how the saying goes, "__________ ____________________."

M: Umm.... I guess you're right. I'd better head out.

W: Hey, don't forget your bag.

06

W: I need to pay for the work __________________ ______________.

M: OK. Do you have a membership card for our business?

W: Yes, I do. Here you are.

M: Great, that will ____________________________ right away.

W: Excellent. What is the total?

M: Well, before the discount it is $500.

W: Do you accept this coupon? I _______________ ____________________ from my card company.

M: Let me see. Oh yes, you can use this coupon. With this, any customer gets a $30 discount from the total service fee.

W: That means I only need to pay $420?

M: I'm sorry, no. We can offer only one kind of discount at a time. To get $30 off, you have to give up the 10 percent discount.

W: Then I'll definitely choose ___________________ ____________________.

07

W: How can I help you?

M: I heard your Piano Laboratory is looking for children to receive free piano lessons. I'd like to ____.

W: Do you know this is part of student teacher training?

M: Yes, I read it in this brochure.

W: Keyboard majors in our university will teach the children. How old is your child?

M: She's 8 years old. __________________________ children ages 7-9, right?

W: Yes. It's a three-month program beginning September 9.

M: Okay. My daughter ________________________ ______________ the piano. She took piano lessons for a year.

W: Really? I'm sorry, but she can't participate in this program. This is for children with no previous piano lessons.

M: Oh, I didn't know that. ____________________.

08

M: ____ is Nelson Mandela. Born in Transkei, South Africa in 1918, he was the son of the chief advisor of the Tembu tribe. As a young man, he moved to Johannesburg to study law. Later, he would join the African National Congress (ANC) party and ____ against the ruling party's racist agenda. In 1961, he helped establish the ANC's military, partly in response to the Sharpeville Massacre a year earlier. In 1964, he ________________________ ____________________, and he remained there until 1990. After being released from prison, Mandela became a symbol for peace. He won the Nobel Peace Prize in 1993 and became president of South Africa in 1994. After stepping down in 1999, ________________________________ and HIV/AIDS through the Nelson Mandela Foundation. Today, he is deeply respected in South Africa, where he is remembered as "the father of the nation."

09

W: Lipstick can be seen nearly everywhere, but do you know its history? Lipstick dates back at least 5,000 years to the ancient city of Ur, near Babylon. At that time, colorful stones ____________________ ____________________ to the lips for color. The ancient Egyptians also had a form of lipstick. Unfortunately, the chemicals it contained were poisonous and led to several deaths. Meanwhile, Cleopatra's lipstick was made from crushed insects such as beetles. During the 16th century, Queen Elizabeth I made lipstick popular among rich people in England. She introduced the trend of white faces ____________________ ____________________. In 1884, the first commercial lipstick was invented by perfumers in Paris, and by the end of the 19th century a French cosmetic company ____________________ ____________________.

10

W: Bill, I need some advice. I'm apartment hunting.
M: Show me your list of apartments.
W: Here.... I live in the suburbs now and I want to live downtown. But downtown apartments are too expensive and too small.
M: Really? You live in a suburban two-bedroom apartment, right?
W: Yes, ____________________.
M: I don't think it's cheap. It might be only $700 in rent but how much do you spend on gas driving downtown to work?
W: Over $400 a month.
M: And that's only gas. There are repairs and.... So, these downtown apartments aren't ____________________ ____________________.
W: But they are smaller.
M: Well, there's one downtown apartment ____________________ ____________________. It's no more expensive than living in suburbia if you include the gas.
W: You're right. I guess I should move downtown.
M: I think so.

11

M: These two TVs are the most popular on the market today.
W: Each is good ____________________. I don't know which to choose.
M: Why don't I give you ____________________ ____________________?

12

W: Is there something wrong, Robert?
M: Yes, I ordered a pizza an hour ago but ____________________ ____________________.
W: Did you call to find out ____________________?

13

M: I'd like to get a scoop of strawberry ice cream, please.
W: Yes, sir. Just one minute. I'm sorry, we're ____________________ ____________________.
M: Then how about a scoop of raspberry instead?
W: Sorry, sir. We are out of raspberry as well.
M: This isn't my lucky day. You ____________________ ____________________.
W: We've just had a large group of teenage customers. That's why. I'm sure we can find something that you like.
M: Tell me ____________________.
W: We have Banana Coconut, Vanilla, Walnut, Apple Mint, and Chocolate Chip available.
M: OK. I'll try something new today!
W: Thank you for understanding.
M: I'll try the first one. Give me one scoop of it, please.

14

W: Oh no! The waiter brought the wrong food. I ordered a burger with cheese and bacon.

M: We'll just call him back over and ____________ ________________.

W: No. I don't want to start trouble.

M: Don't be silly. It's his job to make sure we get what we ordered.

W: ________________________________.

M: But if you aren't going to enjoy your meal, you ________________________________.

W: I don't want to make him mad.

M: Like I said before, it's his job. He will feel worse if we don't say anything and he realizes it later.

W: I'm not sure. I ____________________________ about this.

15

W: Blair's friend, Mitchell, thought Blair would get along with Susan. So Mitchell arranged for Blair and Susan to go to a movie together. Susan lives in a neighborhood which Blair ________ ______________________. Before driving there, he looks at a map and takes the easiest route possible ______________________________. Not having driven there before means, however, that ______________________________________. He arrives at Susan's house 20 minutes late. Susan is not angry, as Blair phoned her from his car. Blair introduces himself and apologizes. Blair says they ______________________________. So they get in the car. Blair knows they are behind schedule and need to get to the theater quickly. In this situation, what would Blair most likely say to Susan?

16-17

M: I want you to imagine your dream job. Do you ____________________________? Without any clues about your personal goals, I'm willing to bet that for many of you the dream includes money, respect, and a large office. These are the common indicators of success across a variety of cultures. We don't find it surprising that people with higher status are generally given more space and privacy. For instance, we knock before entering our ____________________, but we walk into ________________________________ without hesitating. And we'd probably be quite surprised to find the head of our company working in a tiny office or somewhere open to distractions. Likewise, in many schools, teachers have offices, dining rooms, and even toilets that are private, but students do not have such special places. In the world of show business, stars receive ______________________ ____________________________________. These are places where they can prepare in peace for their big performances. Even in the military, this relation can be easily seen — new recruits practically sleep on top of each other, while ______________________ ______________________________________.

01 다음을 듣고, 여자가 하는 말의 목적으로 가장 적절한 것을 고르시오.

① 인증받은 불꽃놀이용 폭죽을 광고하려고
② 독립기념일 행사의 자원봉사자를 모집하려고
③ 불꽃놀이 할 때 안전 수칙 준수를 당부하려고
④ 축제 중 어린이 안전사고 방지를 촉구하려고
⑤ 독립기념일 축하 불꽃놀이 행사를 홍보하려고

02 대화를 듣고, 남자의 의견으로 가장 적절한 것을 고르시오.

① 용돈은 아이가 필요할 때마다 주어야 한다.
② 아이가 용돈기입장을 작성하게 해야 한다.
③ 아이가 용돈을 스스로 관리하게 해야 한다.
④ 용돈은 아이가 스스로 마련하게 해야 한다.
⑤ 용돈의 일정액을 의무적으로 저축하게 해야 한다.

03 대화를 듣고, 두 사람의 관계를 가장 잘 나타낸 것을 고르시오.

① 부동산 중개업자 – 의뢰인
② 티켓 판매원 – 고객
③ 역사학자 – 리포터
④ 여행 안내인 – 여행객
⑤ 역사 교사 – 학생

04 대화를 듣고, 그림에서 대화의 내용과 일치하지 않는 것을 고르시오.

05 대화를 듣고, 남자가 여자를 위해 할 일로 가장 적절한 것을 고르시오.

① 교과서 복사해주기
② 시험공부 도와주기
③ 교과서 대신 구해주기
④ 친구 전화번호 알려주기
⑤ 자신의 교과서 빌려주기

06 대화를 듣고, 여자가 지불할 금액을 고르시오. [3점]

① $28.00 ② $34.60 ③ $36.00
④ $43.20 ⑤ $48.00

07 대화를 듣고, 두 사람이 Bluehill 식당에 가지 못하는 이유를 고르시오.

① 가격이 너무 비싸서
② 예약을 하지 않아서
③ 위치가 너무 멀어서
④ 고객 평가가 좋지 않아서
⑤ 오늘 영업을 하지 않아서

08 대화를 듣고, 팀의 성공 요인에 관해 언급되지 않은 것을 고르시오.

① 공동의 목표 ② 팀원 간의 화합력
③ 적절한 자원 ④ 부단한 노력
⑤ 팀원의 의사 결정 권한

09 Kale에 관한 다음 내용을 듣고, 일치하지 않는 것을 고르시오.

① 기억력 향상에 도움이 된다.
② 기원전 600년경에 소아시아에서 유럽으로 전해졌다.
③ 잎의 크기가 작은 것을 사는 것이 좋다.
④ 보관할 때는 봉지를 묶지 않는 것이 좋다.
⑤ 오래 보관하면 쓴맛이 강해진다.

10 다음 표를 보면서 대화를 듣고, 두 사람이 구매할 코트 걸이를 고르시오.

Coat Racks				
Model	Height	Weight	Material	Price
① A	160 cm	5 kg	Wood	$80
② B	160 cm	3 kg	Metal	$40
③ C	180 cm	5 kg	Metal	$50
④ D	180 cm	8 kg	Wood	$40
⑤ E	200 cm	9 kg	Wood	$60

11 대화를 듣고, 남자의 마지막 말에 대한 여자의 응답으로 가장 적절한 것을 고르시오.

① Jessica is already at the museum.
② I'm eager to see the new exhibits.
③ I think the three of us can go together.
④ She's hoping to finish the painting tonight.
⑤ That depends on when she has to go home.

12 대화를 듣고, 여자의 마지막 말에 대한 남자의 응답으로 가장 적절한 것을 고르시오.

① I'm also interested in acting.
② Right. Your writing is incredible.
③ Oh, now I'm even more excited.
④ OK. Let's watch it one more time.
⑤ You always meet my expectations.

13 대화를 듣고, 남자의 마지막 말에 대한 여자의 응답으로 가장 적절한 것을 고르시오. [3점]

▶ Woman : ______________________

① Then I'll change it and put 6 first.
② Do I write my date of birth here?
③ Then I'm finished filling out this form.
④ Could you solve the problem with me?
⑤ The problem is I wasn't born in America.

14 대화를 듣고, 여자의 마지막 말에 대한 남자의 응답으로 가장 적절한 것을 고르시오. [3점]

▶ Man : ______________________

① My phone number is 3486-9274.
② It's on the memo pad by the phone.
③ Oh, you don't have to. Snacks are enough.
④ His address is 57 Coastal Highway, Ocean City.
⑤ Thanks. The drinks are right there in the fridge.

15 다음 상황 설명을 듣고, Nick이 Mike에게 할 말로 가장 적절한 것을 고르시오.

▶ Nick : ______________________

① Don't forget to take your books with you.
② I'd like to help with your work at the bakery.
③ I think you're trying to do too much at once.
④ Don't worry. I'll pay your library fines for you.
⑤ Do you want me to return these books to the library?

[16~17] 다음을 듣고, 물음에 답하시오.

16 남자가 하는 말의 주제로 가장 적절한 것은?

① the main cause of an upset stomach
② the nutritional value of bananas and rice
③ several foods that can ease an upset stomach
④ the best and worst foods to eat when you're sick
⑤ why food poisoning should be treated promptly

17 언급된 음식이 아닌 것은?

① 바나나 ② 쌀 ③ 감자
④ 블루베리 ⑤ 허브차

01

W: The Fourth of July is coming. It's common for families and friends to ________________________ ______________ the day. You can watch fireworks in your backyard on this day. There will be a public firework display near your home and it's the best way to enjoy the fireworks. Why? Every year, hundreds of fires are caused by home fireworks on the Fourth of July. If you want to ____________ __________________________ in your backyard, make sure you select legal "consumer" fireworks from a licensed store. It's also important to wear safety glasses when igniting fireworks. Never give fireworks to young children even if they are only sparklers and if an adult is nearby. ____________ ____________________ and make it a memorable Fourth of July this year.

02

W: Oliver, does your son receive an allowance?
M: Of course. Why?
W: Actually, I'm wondering about ______________ ____________________________________ as an allowance for my daughter.
M: Well, in my case, I give my son $20 every Monday.
W: Don't you think $20 a week is too much for a teenage boy?
M: ____________________________, but he usually takes care of all his needs with that money.
W: So, you never give him extra when he asks?
M: Right. I want my son to learn the value of money ________________________.
W: I see. That does seem like a good way for him to learn to manage money.
M: Hopefully, it will be better for him in the long run.
W: That's reasonable. Thanks for the advice.

03

W: Could everyone please follow me?
M: Excuse me, I didn't hear. When was this residence built?
W: It was built in 1847.
M: And you said it was built for some of the King's family to live in.
W: That's right.
M: It's very beautiful. Can ______________________ ____________________________?
W: No, I'm sorry. This palace ____________________ __________________________________.
M: OK, I understand.
W: Thank you. We're going to walk to the Palace's Secret Garden now. After the Secret Garden ____ ___________________________ a small museum detailing the history of the palace.
M: Oh? So I can learn more about the palace in the museum.
W: Yes, and you can even buy a book detailing the palace's history.
M: Good.

04

M: Amy, do you have time now? I'd like to show you ____.
W: Sure, I'm free. Oh, you put the title "Changing Seasons" on the top. That's nice.
M: Yes, ___________________ Gothic type to make it simple and powerful.
W: Good idea. I also like the two round circles in the middle.
M: I wanted to show what this book is about, so I put an important object in each circle.
W: That's an excellent idea. ____________________ _________________ reminds me of the apple tree in the story.
M: That's right. And the bird in the right circle is the one that escapes from the cage.
W: I see. And you put the author's picture ________ ____ __________________________. That's a good way to highlight such a famous author.
M: Thanks.

05

W: This is Linda speaking.

M: Hey, Linda. It's Jason. ____________________ ____________________ for your philosophy exam?

W: No, not yet.

M: But the exam is in two days!

W: I know, but ______________________________. I've looked everywhere for it. I even went to the bookstore to purchase a new one, but they're all sold out.

M: Oh no. Do you at least want ____________________ ______________?

W: It would be great if I could.

M: Actually, I have a better idea. A friend of mine has the textbook. He might be able to lend it to you.

W: ________________________ he doesn't need it?

M: Yes, he took the class last semester. I'll let you know immediately after I call and ask him.

W: Thanks a million. You're a lifesaver.

06

W: Let's take the kids and go see *Koala 2* this Saturday afternoon.

M: There is a sequel to *Koala*?

W: Yes, you and the kids loved the first one. __________ ________________________ on the Internet now.

M: OK. ____. Click there. It shows the price, $12 per ticket.

W: And three tickets for the children.

M: No, only Linda and Lisa can come. Derek is busy on Saturday afternoon. He is going to a birthday party for a friend.

W: OK. ________________________. Tickets for the children are $8 each. Wow! That's still expensive for children.

M: Yes, it's only a 30 percent discount from the adult price. But, honey, don't forget you'll get a 10 percent discount with your credit card.

W: Good!

07

W: Do you have any plans this evening, Bob?

M: No, I don't have anything planned. Why?

W: I want to ________________________. You always treat me so it's time for me to treat you for once.

M: You really don't have to.

W: I insist. There's a restaurant that recently got great reviews. I heard it's amazing. It's called Bluehill.

M: Oh, I've heard about that place. I've been wanting to go, too. But I hope their prices are not too high.

W: Don't worry about it! Remember, I'm paying tonight.

M: Thank you so much, Laura! Do you know _______ ______________________?

W: Let me check my phone to find their exact location. It's not very far. I'll make a reservation. Oh, dear!

M: What's wrong?

W: The website says same-day reservations _________ ____________________. I should have made the reservation yesterday.

M: Well, it's totally fine. We can go another time.

08

W: Please have a seat, Jim.

M: Okay. Is there a problem?

W: Not at all. In fact, I've decided to make you a team leader.

M: That's great! I can already think of several talented individuals I'd like to work with.

W: The skills of the team members are ___________ ____________________________________. But a successful team must also work together.

M: I see. So, they should have a common goal and personalities ________________________________?

W: Exactly. A team also needs the right resources to be successful.

M: I'll do my best to provide them with everything they need.

W: ______________________________. Finally, it's important for a team to feel effective.

M: Then, I should give them some freedom and power to make their own decisions?

W: I think you've got it. You're going to be great.

09

M: Kale, a vegetable with green or purple leaves, is a memory-enhancing food, ______________________ ______________, tuna, and spinach. It is a relative of the wild cabbage and comes in several varieties, ______________________________, texture, and appearance. Originally from Asia Minor, it was brought to Europe around 600 B.C. Kale is available throughout the year, although it is most widely available during its peak, from the middle of winter through the beginning of spring. ______________________, it's wise to choose ones with smaller-sized leaves since these tend to have a milder flavor. To store kale, place it in a plastic bag ______________________ ________. It will keep for up to 5 days but will grow increasingly bitter as the days pass.

10

W: Honey, do you remember talking about getting a coat rack for the hallway?

M: Sure, I remember. Why? ______________________ ______________________?

W: There are a few in this catalog. Why don't you take a look?

M: Let me see.... The largest one looks nice. But would it fit in our hall?

W: No, I measured this morning, and 180 cm is the largest we can get.

M: That's too bad. Oh, it says we can get free shipping on orders under 8 kg. ______________________ ______________________.

W: Okay. What about the material? Wood looks nice, don't you think?

M: Of course, but it's not very strong, and it's susceptible to scratches.

W: That leaves two, and I'm afraid ______________________ ______________________.

M: That's a good point. Let's get the more expensive one of the two.

W: Great. I'll place the order this afternoon.

11

M: I'm going to an art museum after school. __________ ______________________?

W: I would, but I ______________________________ with Jessica.

M: That's no problem. By the way, what are you going to do?

12

W: You are ______________________ from this movie, aren't you?

M: Yes. I heard the main actor did an excellent job.

W: Right. What's more, the movie ______________________ ______________ in the original novel.

13

M: ______________________________________ the application?

W: Actually, I have a question.

M: Yes?

W: Here it says, "Date of birth." I'm not sure ________ ______________________. I wrote down the day, the month, and then the year.

M: No, write down the month, the day, and then the year.

W: Oh? On this form I wrote down 10/6/1992 because I was born on the 10th of June in 1992.

M: In America we always put the month first.

W: Really? In my country ______________________ ______________________.

M: Not here. People here will think you were born in October.

14

W: Hi, Larry.

M: Hi, Cecilia. Come on in. You're a little late. The game ________________________.

W: Sorry. Thanks for inviting me to watch the soccer game at your house. Your house is nice.

M: Thank you. We usually all relax and watch TV there in the living room.

W: ____ ____________ the game?

M: Yes. By the way, do you know when James will be here?

W: ________________________ as quickly as he could. Oh.... I've bought potato chips and other snacks for everyone.

M: Thanks. I'll go into the kitchen and get some drinks. Let me take your jacket. And please have a seat.

W: ____.

M: It's OK. Would you call and tell James to hurry up?

W: But I don't have my cell phone, so I don't know his number.

15

W: Nick is a college student. He shares an apartment with two other students. One of the students, Mike, ________________________________. Mike has several reports to finish this week. He also has two final exams to take. ________________ ________, he works part time at a small bakery. Today, Nick notices some of Mike's library books in the living room. ______________________ ______________ today. Nick mentions this to Mike, but Mike says he's far too busy. He says that he only has a few minutes ____________ ________________________ at the bakery. Nick understands Mike's situation and he wants to help Mike avoid any library fines. In this situation, what would Nick most likely say to Mike?

16-17

M: Do you have an upset stomach? Sadly, your doctor may say that the best treatment is simply to wait until the symptoms disappear. However, choosing the right foods may ______________ ________________________. For example, bananas have been used for generations to soothe upset stomachs. They contain kalium, which you may need if you lost too much water from vomiting. Their sugars will also provide much needed calories at a time when you're probably not eating enough. Rice is another soothing food ________________________ ______________. In fact, potatoes or oats are also good. ________________________ ________________________ for a long time and they don't push your body to produce more acid. If you can't eat anything solid, herbal teas without caffeine can also help a troubled stomach. Chamomile is a favorite, but any herbal tea ________________________________ into your body. With the right choices and plenty of rest, you'll be feeling better in no time at all.

01 **다음을 듣고, 남자가 하는 말의 목적으로 가장 적절한 것을 고르시오.**

① 학습용 놀이 기구를 판매하려고
② 교육용 모바일 앱을 홍보하려고
③ 스마트폰의 순기능을 설명하려고
④ 학습 계획용 캘린더를 소개하려고
⑤ 학부모-교사 공유 사이트를 개설하려고

02 **대화를 듣고, 여자의 의견으로 가장 적절한 것을 고르시오.**

① 과다한 에너지 드링크 섭취는 유해하다.
② 청소년의 탈선 예방을 위한 대책이 필요하다.
③ 에너지 드링크보다 커피를 마시는 것이 낫다.
④ 밤샘 공부는 학업에 부정적인 영향을 미친다.
⑤ 성장기 어린이의 카페인 섭취를 제한해야 한다.

03 **대화를 듣고, 두 사람의 관계를 가장 잘 나타낸 것을 고르시오.**

① 식당 종업원 - 손님
② 간호사 - 입원 환자
③ 레스토랑 지배인 - 요리사
④ 호텔 지배인 - 호텔 투숙객
⑤ 구급차 운전기사 - 구조대원

04 **대화를 듣고, 그림에서 대화의 내용과 일치하지 않는 것을 고르시오.**

05 **대화를 듣고, 남자가 할 일로 가장 적절한 것을 고르시오.**

① 아침 식사 준비하기
② 병원 진료 예약하기
③ 딸의 잠자리 봐주기
④ 약국에서 약 사 오기
⑤ 딸을 병원에 데려가기

06 **대화를 듣고, 여자가 지불할 금액을 고르시오. [3점]**

① $120　② $162　③ $180
④ $198　⑤ $216

07 **대화를 듣고, 여자가 기숙사에서 살지 않으려는 이유를 고르시오.**

① 기숙사 비용이 올라서
② 방 크기가 너무 작아서
③ 사람들의 소음이 심해서
④ 신청이 이미 마감되어서
⑤ 룸메이트와 문제가 있어서

08 **대화를 듣고, Ivy League에 관해 언급되지 않은 것을 고르시오.**

① 소속 대학　② 위치
③ 이름의 유래　④ 창립자
⑤ 공식 창립연도

09 **Experience Spain에 관한 다음 내용을 듣고, 일치하지 않는 것을 고르시오.**

① 최대 세 개의 도시를 여행할 수 있다.
② 왕복 항공료가 포함되어 있다.
③ 수영장이 있는 호텔을 선택할 수 있다.
④ 온라인이나 전화로 신청할 수 있다.
⑤ 출발일로부터 최소 2주 전에 신청해야 한다.

10 다음 표를 보면서 대화를 듣고, 여자가 지원할 일자리를 고르시오.

CAPILANO SUSPENSION BRIDGE PARK
AVAILABLE POSITIONS

	Closing Date	Job Description	Benefit
① A	Nov. 26th	Making repairs	Scholarship opportunities
② B	Dec. 1st	Cleaning the grounds	Free admission for family members
③ C	Dec. 1st	Managing accounts	Free admission for family members
④ D	Dec. 12th	Guest services	Scholarship opportunities
⑤ E	Dec. 12th	Assisting the chef	Discounted food

11 대화를 듣고, 남자의 마지막 말에 대한 여자의 응답으로 가장 적절한 것을 고르시오.

① Actually, it's just above, on the fifth floor.
② Thanks for taking the time to meet with me.
③ We can talk as soon as I finish my experiments.
④ I'm there every night because of the presentation.
⑤ I'm surprised you've never been to the lab before.

12 대화를 듣고, 여자의 마지막 말에 대한 남자의 응답으로 가장 적절한 것을 고르시오.

① Everything looks so delicious.
② You can bring anyone you like.
③ Something to drink would be great.
④ I really appreciate your help with this.
⑤ Please put what you brought over there.

13 대화를 듣고, 남자의 마지막 말에 대한 여자의 응답으로 가장 적절한 것을 고르시오.

▶ Woman : ______________________

① If you keep walking on it, it will feel better.
② Why don't you put some ice on it?
③ It's better to be safe than sorry.
④ The basketball court is in a gymnasium.
⑤ I think Tom should pay for your doctor visit.

14 대화를 듣고, 여자의 마지막 말에 대한 남자의 응답으로 가장 적절한 것을 고르시오. [3점]

▶ Man : ______________________

① You got the wrong idea about healthy food.
② No, I think you should skip breakfast every day.
③ I think we could all ask for help at times like this.
④ Why don't we take your friends out to dinner too?
⑤ You know, it takes time and effort to slim down.

15 다음 상황 설명을 듣고, Alice가 Janice에게 할 말로 가장 적절한 것을 고르시오. [3점]

▶ Alice : ______________________

① I think it's more important to attend the study group.
② I'm worried that I don't have time for piano lessons.
③ I will have to meet you on the weekend instead.
④ I'm afraid I can't be part of the study group any more.
⑤ This study group has really helped me with chemistry.

[16~17] 다음을 듣고, 물음에 답하시오.

16 여자가 하는 말의 주제로 가장 적절한 것은?

① how to be a better listener
② various ways to make friends
③ the meaning of being a friend
④ hobbies to enjoy with other people
⑤ the value of long-lasting friendship

17 취미나 관심사로 언급되지 않은 것은?

① 요리 ② 음악 ③ 영화
④ 스포츠 ⑤ 수집

01

M: Often parents worry that their children ________ ______________________________. They are concerned that their children play too many games. However, there are ________________ ____________________ apps for students on smartphones. One of the best of them is Khan Academy. For kids, Khan Academy teaches simple math, reading, and languages in a fun way using cute animal characters. For high school students, there are more than 10,000 videos and explanations of math, science, economics, history, and so on. Additionally, they can ask teachers questions on the app. The most amazing thing is that it's all free. Download it today! Make your smartphone even smarter with this app. Khan Academy ________ __________________________.

02

W: Did you ______________________________ in time?

M: Barely. I had to stay up all night working on it. I must have had at least four energy drinks.

W: Whoa, you ______________________________ ____________________ if you can.

M: Why? They have less caffeine than a cup of coffee.

W: That's true for most of them, but they also contain many other harmful ingredients. I heard that some students ______________________________ from them and have even had to go to the hospital.

M: Really? I didn't know that.

W: The news said that kids who regularly consume energy drinks are more likely to engage in risky behavior and make poor life decisions.

M: I only drink them to stay awake, but maybe I should stop.

03

M: Good morning, Miss James, how are you feeling this morning?

W: Not so good. I ______________________________ ______________ last night.

M: Sorry to hear that! What was bothering you? We do have a bit of trouble with noise from the ambulances coming and going.

W: No, it wasn't noisy. Perhaps it was ______________ __________________ last night.

M: What did you have?

W: Nothing special; pumpkin soup, steamed rice, some fruit, that's all.

M: Did you have pain in your stomach?

W: Yes, quite a lot actually.

M: Well, that's to be expected after your operation. You know one of us __________________________; whenever you're in pain you should press the button next to your bed.

W: I don't want to cause you any trouble.

M: Miss James! ______________________________!

04

W: Have you finished packing for the trip yet, Mike?

M: I'm working on it now, Mom.

W: I washed the sneakers you asked for and _______ _________________________.

M: Yes, I saw them. Thanks, Mom.

W: No problem. Will you bring a backpack or a suitcase?

M: We might go hiking on the second day, so it will be ______________________________________. It's on the bed.

W: Okay. You know, the weather forecast said it'll be freezing. Why don't you bring ________________ ____________?

M: I already put them in my backpack.

W: Okay. Please make sure to bring your baseball cap, also.

M: I ______________________________ so that I'll remember to wear it tomorrow.

W: Well done. By the way, have you seen the dog? I haven't seen him all day.

M: He's right here, under the table. I think he wants to follow me.

05

W: I'm concerned about our daughter, honey. She looks really sick.

M: You're right. She already took some cold medicine, but ________________________________.

W: I think it's more serious than just a cold. I'd better make a doctor's appointment.

M: Good thinking. Do you want me to do it?

W: That's okay. I'll do it before I prepare her breakfast.

M: Is she feeling well enough to eat? Last night, she went straight to bed after her bath.

W: She needs to eat something, even if it's just a little soup. Also, ________________________________ from the living room?

M: I don't think there's any left. I'll get some more from the pharmacy.

W: Thank you. I'll ________________________ and then make her breakfast while you go to the pharmacy.

M: Sounds good. And don't worry too much. She'll be okay.

W: I hope ____________________________.

06

M: Wonderland Dream Park, Nathan speaking. How may I help you?

W: I'm a kindergarten teacher, and I'd like to bring my class to your amusement park. ___________ ______________________?

M: Tickets for children under 12 are $9 each. Older children and adults can enter for $15.

W: There will be a total of 4 adults and 20 children under the age of 12. Do you ________________________ ________________?

M: We do. You can purchase a pack of 10 child tickets for $60. Likewise, a pack of 10 adult tickets costs $100.

W: In that case, I'll need two 10-packs of children's tickets and ______________________________.

M: Great. How would you like to pay?

W: I'll pay by credit card, and I'll use my Smart Shopping card for an additional 10% off.

M: Okay. Great. Is there anything else I can do for you?

W: No, that's all. Thanks.

07

M: Hi, Madison! ______________________________ on the bulletin board?

W: I was looking for an apartment, but the rent is pretty high.

M: Why don't you stay in the dorm, then? _________ ______________________________ already?

W: No, it's due next week.

M: Oh, let me guess. The dorm room is a bit small. Do you want a more spacious room?

W: It's not that. I don't mind the size of the room.

M: You had some trouble with your roommate last semester, right?

W: No, my ex-roommate was a great person. But the people in the dorm make a lot of noise.

M: ______________________________. There are some people having parties and making noise even at midnight.

W: Yeah! They don't mind all the warnings and complaints. I'm a little sensitive to the noise, so I can't live there anymore.

M: I understand.

08

M: Hi, Yuna. How's your college search going?

W: Hi, Will. Umm... ____________________, I guess.

M: Yeah, me too. I spent last night reading about the Ivy League schools.

W: Ah, those are eight universities: Brown, Columbia, Cornell, Dartmouth, Harvard, Pennsylvania, Princeton, and Yale.

M: Right. They're located in the northeastern United States. My dad really ________________________ Brown.

W: It's a good school. By the way, do you know why it's called the "Ivy League"?

M: I read that those eight schools form a football league, meaning they play games against one another.

W: Oh, ______________________. And the name of "Ivy" is probably because the buildings are old and covered in ivy.

M: Right, but ______________________________ ____________________ until 1954. It's rather recent.

W: Interesting.

09

W: Best Tour, your first choice for traveling Europe, is currently offering a unique "Experience Spain" package. This is a one-week trip to Spain. It visits Madrid and Barcelona, and ____________ ______________________ in Toledo. There are several other options as well, so prices vary, but round-trip airfare and hotel accommodations are included. Each city has a choice of two hotels. And if you love to swim, hotels with indoor pools are ______________________________. To sign up, simply visit our website at www.besttour.com, fill out the form, and then call to confirm with us afterward. Please keep in mind that this package is likely to be extremely popular, so make sure to ______________________________________ of your trip.

10

M: Hey, are you still looking for a job?

W: Yeah, but I haven't found anything interesting. Why do you ask?

M: Capilano Suspension Bridge Park is looking for people. Check out this ad.

W: Oh, learning to make repairs would be interesting. But ______________________________.

M: The others don't close until December. How about sanitation work?

W: Frankly, ______________________________.

M: I guess you're not willing to clean the grounds then. What are you interested in?

W: Helping a chef sounds a lot better to me.

M: I always enjoy your cooking, but I'm sure the job will be ______________________________.

W: Yeah, you're right. So I guess ______________ ____________. Free admission for family members would be nice.

M: True, but a scholarship opportunity might be more valuable.

W: Hmm... I think you're right. I will apply for that one.

M: Good choice.

11

M: I think we need to meet and discuss our presentation.

W: Well, I'll be in the science lab tonight. ____________ ______________________________?

M: I think ______________________________. It's on the fourth floor, right?

12

W: Do you need any help ______________________ ____________________?

M: I don't think so. Everything is almost ready.

W: All right. Then is there ____________________ ____________________?

13

W: Why are you limping?

M: I fell playing basketball and Tom ____________ ____________________.

W: That sounds like a rough game.

M: It was just an accident. We were both going for a rebound.

W: Let me see your ankle. Ouch! It's as big as the basketball you were playing with!

M: Do you think it's broken?

W: I'm not sure. How does it feel ______________ ____________________?

M: Really bad.

W: If you don't get to the doctor soon, you may not play basketball for a long, long time.

M: Do you think I need the doctor? Maybe I could just ______________________________.

14

M: When are you going to come down and eat dinner? We are waiting for you.

W: I'm trying to lose weight, so ______________ ______________.

M: That's not healthy, and it's not the best way to lose weight.

W: Well, that's what my friends told me I should do.

M: Sorry to say this, but your friends are wrong. Remember, ______________________________.

W: Just let me try it my way, and ______________ ______________.

M: I can't let you do that. I'm your father, and I care about your well-being.

W: I hate being so fat!

M: Honey, you just need to exercise more and eat healthier foods.

W: I don't have time for exercise. And ____________ ____________________________.

15

M: Alice is a junior in high school. This semester, she is taking a particularly difficult chemistry class. ______________________________________, she and a few other students formed a study group. The group meets twice a week, on Mondays and Thursdays, and ___________________________ for Alice. Unfortunately, Alice's mom insists that Alice take piano lessons. Just yesterday, _______ ______________________________ for lessons that are the same time as her study group. Alice is not happy about giving up her study group, but she ______________________________________ the piano lessons. Now, Alice receives a call from Janice, one of the study-group members. Janice asks if Alice is ready for tonight's meeting. In this situation, what would Alice most likely say to Janice?

16-17

W: Let's talk a little bit about friendship. It means different things to different people, and every friendship is unique. Everybody has his or her own way to make friends, but there are a couple of things that you can do to become successful at it. First, ________________________________. Whether you're having dinner together or just hanging out, always be ready to listen. Secondly, ________________________________, and do things together. Any hobby can work, but some seem to be better for making friends than others. For example, many people love music, so you can make many friends by developing an active interest in it. Similarly, ____________________ ____________________ will give you plenty to talk about with most people. Likewise, playing a popular sport, such as soccer, will help you connect with others. But special hobbies, like collecting comic books, are also good. They often lead to more meaningful friendships, and they ____. As you can see, there are many ways. What has worked for you?

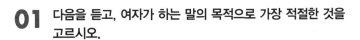

05 Sense Up 듣기 모의고사

01 **다음을 듣고, 여자가 하는 말의 목적으로 가장 적절한 것을 고르시오.**

① 투표 방법을 안내하려고
② 시장 선거 참여를 독려하려고
③ 시장 후보 지지를 호소하려고
④ 시장 후보의 공약을 설명하려고
⑤ 투표율을 높이는 대책을 논의하려고

02 **대화를 듣고, 남자의 의견으로 가장 적절한 것을 고르시오.**

① 멕시코 음식은 독특한 향이 강한 것이 특징이다.
② 멕시코 음식 엔칠라다는 체중 감량에 효과적이다.
③ 향신료는 식욕을 자극하며 음식에 풍미를 더한다.
④ 매운 음식은 건강에 긍정적인 효과를 줄 수 있다.
⑤ 너무 매운 음식은 특정 질병을 유발할 수도 있다.

03 **대화를 듣고, 두 사람의 관계를 가장 잘 나타낸 것을 고르시오.**

① 수의사 – 개 주인
② 회사 상사 – 회사 직원
③ 부동산 중개인 – 집 주인
④ 아파트 관리인 – 아파트 주민
⑤ 아래층 거주자 – 위층 거주자

04 **대화를 듣고, 그림에서 대화의 내용과 일치하지 않는 것을 고르시오.**

05 **대화를 듣고, 여자가 남자에게 부탁한 일로 가장 적절한 것을 고르시오.**

① 여자의 음악 밴드에 합류하기
② 밴드의 이름 지어주기
③ 함께 공연 보러 가기
④ 여자에게 키보드 빌려주기
⑤ 밴드 공연 관람권 구매하기

06 **대화를 듣고, 남자가 지불할 금액을 고르시오.**

① $19 ② $24 ③ $29
④ $30 ⑤ $32

07 **대화를 듣고, 여자가 이사를 가려는 이유를 고르시오.**

① 방이 좁아서
② 룸메이트와 싸워서
③ 이웃이 시끄러워서
④ 주인이 아파트를 매도해서
⑤ 기숙사 입주가 결정되어서

08 **대화를 듣고, 복사기에 관해 언급되지 않은 것을 고르시오.**

① 제품 번호 ② 문제점
③ 구입 시기 ④ 수리 기간
⑤ 수리 기사 방문일

09 **Red Valley National Park에 관한 다음 내용을 듣고, 일치하지 않는 것을 고르시오.**

① 지정된 등산로를 이용해야 한다.
② 야영은 지정된 장소에서 해야 한다.
③ 바비큐 후에 그릴을 닦아야 한다.
④ 음식물은 텐트 안에 보관해서는 안 된다.
⑤ 야영은 7월과 8월에만 허용된다.

10 다음 표를 보면서 대화를 듣고, 남자가 추천할 개를 고르시오.

The Best Dog For You				
	Shedding	Size	Character	Protection
① A	less	medium	gentle	○
② B	less	small	energetic	×
③ C	less	medium	energetic	×
④ D	less	medium	energetic	○
⑤ E	more	small	gentle	×

11 대화를 듣고, 여자의 마지막 말에 대한 남자의 응답으로 가장 적절한 것을 고르시오.

① "Sorry" isn't enough this time.
② You'd better start cleaning quickly.
③ I know I don't keep my promises often.
④ Tim invited me to his birthday party today.
⑤ When I came home, I had to finish my homework.

12 대화를 듣고, 남자의 마지막 말에 대한 여자의 응답으로 가장 적절한 것을 고르시오.

① Well, you've got the wrong person.
② Oh! I'm sorry I don't remember you.
③ What a coincidence! That's why I'm here.
④ Great! Your mother must be proud of you.
⑤ Right, are you still in touch with your classmates?

13 대화를 듣고, 여자의 마지막 말에 대한 남자의 응답으로 가장 적절한 것을 고르시오. [3점]

▶ Man : ______________________

① That's okay. I'll talk to your team members.
② Yes, you should have started playing earlier.
③ I'm sorry, but I don't have enough time.
④ You did a good job. I'm very proud of you.
⑤ Don't be upset. You can do better next time.

14 대화를 듣고, 남자의 마지막 말에 대한 여자의 응답으로 가장 적절한 것을 고르시오. [3점]

▶ Woman : ______________________

① Please help yourself. I hope you like Greek food.
② You're a wonderful husband. Your wife is very lucky.
③ This is delicious! Thanks for inviting me to dinner.
④ I'm sure she'll understand you. Don't get stressed.
⑤ Don't worry too much. I hope your wife gets better soon.

15 다음 상황 설명을 듣고, Robert가 택시 기사에게 할 말로 가장 적절한 것을 고르시오. [3점]

▶ Robert : ______________________

① Excuse me. I might be late for a meeting, so please hurry.
② I had a good laugh. I enjoyed talking with you.
③ Is something going on? Why is the traffic so bad?
④ If you don't hurry, I'm going to miss my flight.
⑤ I'm so relieved that you drive safely.

[16~17] 다음을 듣고, 물음에 답하시오.

16 남자가 하는 말의 주제로 가장 적절한 것은?

① the popularity of home cooking
② causes of conflicts within a family
③ effects of poor eating habits on health
④ ways of improving family relationships
⑤ home cooking for good family relationships

17 언급된 요리가 <u>아닌</u> 것은?

① 사과 파이 ② 피자
③ 팬케이크 ④ 푸딩
⑤ 구운 닭고기

01

W: Hello, my name is Julie Christen, president of the election committee. June 12th is the day ______ ______________________________ for Jay Valley. I hope all of you will take part in this election and vote for a person ______________________ ______________________ to be mayor of Jay Valley. It is everyone's right and duty to vote in this election. Unfortunately, the voting rate has been decreasing over the past twenty years. As a citizen, please ________________________________ for this community by voting. We hope to see you at the election booths on June 12th, between 9 a.m. and 6 p.m. Thank you.

02

M: Tracy, do you like Mexican food?

W: Yes, I love enchiladas. ______________________ ____________ enchiladas?

M: No, I heard they're very hot and spicy.

W: Yeah, I feel like I'm riding a roller coaster when I eat them.

M: I understand. Hot, spicy food _______________ ___________________.

W: Yeah, and it's good for weight loss. I heard an ingredient in hot, spicy food can _____________ ______________________ bonus calories.

M: That ingredient is capsaicin. I heard capsaicin also has the ability to kill some cancer cells.

W: Yes, I read that in the newspaper!

M: And it can protect against the buildup of cholesterol in the blood.

W: That's why I like enchiladas. Are you sure you don't want to try them?

M: I'm sure. My eyes ______________________ when I eat spicy food, and I can't control it.

03

W: Hello, Mr. Clarke. I want to speak to you about something.

M: Oh, Ms. Scot. Come on in. _______________ _____________ some coffee or tea?

W: I'm fine, thank you. I brought some homemade cookies for you.

M: They look delicious. Thank you.

W: I came here to talk about your dog. He ______ ____________________ when you're not home.

M: Really? My dog's very quiet and well-behaved when I'm home with him.

W: That may be true when someone is at home, but the minute you leave, he becomes a very different dog.

M: Oh, I can't believe it.

W: ____ for two days, he jumped up and down and barked all night.

M: Oh, that's awful.

W: I couldn't get any sleep for those two nights, since I live downstairs.

M: I'm terribly sorry about that. I will speak to a dog trainer and ______________________________.

04

M: Honey, take a look at this picture.

W: Oh, is that from your trip to the beach with your brother's family?

M: Yeah, we had a great time. Look at my nephew!

W: He's ____________________________, right? I'm impressed!

M: I was too. And on the left, you can see my brother's wife. She's ____________________________ under a parasol.

W: She's smart to avoid the sun. Hey, who are the two boys playing with a ball on the sand?

M: I'm not sure, actually. They were there with another family.

W: Well, I certainly recognize your niece. She's ____________________________!

M: Haha, right! She almost caught it, but then she fell in love with that giant sand sculpture on the right.

W: Oh, it looks like such a good time! __________ ____________________________.

05

M: Hello.
W: Hi, Travis. It's me, Mary.
M: Oh, hey, Mary. I ______________________________ ______________. What's up?
W: I just got back from a vacation and have started something new and exciting.
M: What's going on? Tell me.
W: Well, a few of my friends and I decided to start a band.
M: A band? You mean a music band? That sounds really cool!
W: It's a rock band, and we're calling ourselves, "Supersonic."
M: I really like the name. ______________________________ ____________________ we used to play together. Remember when you played guitar and I sang?
W: I'll never forget those days. Actually, we need a keyboard player and someone who can do the vocals, too. I was hoping ______________________ ______________________.
M: Oh, wow. That's a great offer, but I'm really busy these days.
W: Travis, we desperately need you. A club has already booked us for a performance, and ______________ ________________________.
M: Well, I need to think it over.

06

W: Welcome to The Chocolate Factory. How can I help you?
M: I'd like to buy a box of chocolates for my wife.
W: How sweet! ____________________________. What kind of chocolate does she like?
M: Well, truffles are her favorite.
W: We're ____________________________________ this weekend.
M: Sounds great. How much are they?
W: The truffles with a cream filling are $2 each, and the ones with nuts are $3.
M: In that case, I'll take four with the cream filling and three with nuts.
W: Okay. Four cream filling and three nuts. Is there ______________________________?
M: How much are these chocolate lollipops?
W: They're $2 each.
M: I'll take six.
W: All right. Shall I ______________________________ ______________?
M: Yes, please.

07

M: Hey, Crystal. Why are you checking out the classified ads?
W: I'm looking for ______________________________.
M: A new apartment? I thought you were happy with your roommate.
W: Debby and I ________________________________. We actually live in a nice two-bedroom apartment right now.
M: I thought so. Your place is near Riverside Park, right? I heard that's a great area. So what's the problem? ____________________________ your neighbors?
W: No, not at all. They're nice.
M: Then what is it?
W: Well, my landlord has recently sold the apartment building, and all the tenants __________________ __________________ by the end of next month.
M: Oh, that's too bad. Have you ever thought about living on campus? You could save a lot of time and money.
W: Hmm.... It's definitely something to think about.

08

M: Hello, you've reached Copymax. This is Allan Goldberg speaking. __________________________?
W: Hello, I'm calling from Mannington Company. ______________________________ out of order.
M: Could you give me the model number for the copier?
W: It's QM 4829.
M: ____?

W: All our copies are coming out with black dots and marks. And the paper often gets jammed.
M: May I ask when you purchased the machine?
W: I'm not sure, but it's definitely over five years old.
M: Your warranty is no longer valid, so you'll have to pay for the parts that are replaced. Will that be all right with you?
W: Sure.
M: I'll ______________________________ tomorrow morning.
W: Great. Thanks for your help.

09

M: Welcome to Red Valley National Park. While here, there are a few things you should keep in mind. We ask that you only ______________________________ ____________________ within the park. For those of you who are here to camp, you can do so only in the campsites. You are ______________ ______________________________ or eating outside the campsites as it can be dangerous. There are also a few precautions you must take within the campsites. Please ____________________ ____________________ the grill after a barbecue. Also, never store food inside your tent. All food should be stored in the steel containers located at each site. This is to prevent wildlife from entering the sites for food. Red Valley National Park _____ ____________________________. Peak season in the park is from July to September.

10

M: Hi. Are you here ______________________________?
W: Yes, I'd really like a companion for my daughter. She is 15 years old now.
M: What should I take into account ______________ ____?
W: My husband has a mild allergy to animal fur, so I need something that won't shed everywhere and that's easy to clean up after.
M: There are dogs that shed less, so I'd recommend ______________________________. What size dog are you looking for?
W: I'd like a medium size dog.
M: How much daily exercise will you give your dog? I mean, some energetic dogs need a lot of exercise.
W: Oh, I see. I'm hoping the dog will be a jogging companion for my daughter. So I want an active dog.
M: Okay. Do you want a dog that will protect your house? Do you want a dog ____________________ ______________________________?
W: No, I don't want a "Beware of Dog" dog. I just want a playful dog for my daughter.
M: Then, I know exactly which dog is good for you.

11

W: Michael, look at all this mess! Clean your room.
M: I'm sorry, Mom. I promise ____________________ tomorrow.
W: I want you to clean it up today. ______________ ____________________________ now?

12

M: Good afternoon, Professor Sherman. I'm not sure ______________________________. I'm Jim Bradley.
W: Oh, Jim. You were a student of my History class last year, weren't you?
M: No, you ______________________________ with someone else. I'm the son of your friend, Joyce Bradley.

13

M: How was your weekend, Sydney?
W: Don't ask. It was terrible ____________________ ____________________.
M: Oh, did you have a woman's soccer match at school?
W: Yeah, we trained so hard this time, and we ______________________________.
M: Oh, I'm sorry to hear that.

W: I had a few chances to score a goal but missed. Everyone ______________________________, and I let them down.
M: What was the score?
W: It was four to zero.
M: How disappointing for everyone on the team!
W: I don't know if I should continue playing. I ______________________________.

14

W: Hey, Ethan. What are you reading ______________________________?
M: Oh, Julia. I didn't know you were standing there.
W: Is it an interior decor magazine? Everything looks so colorful.
M: It's actually a Greek cookbook.
W: Why is a graphic designer reading a cookbook? I guess you want to get some visual ideas from the magazine. It has a really nice layout.
M: Actually, ______________________.
W: It isn't? Is this a secret hobby ______________________________? I had no idea you were a cook.
M: My wife is Greek and it's her birthday next week. I ______________________________ for my wife.

15

W: Robert just arrived at the Dallas International Airport for a business trip. He ______________________________ in the afternoon after his arrival. He ______________________________ and asks the driver to go downtown where his company's headquarters is located. Fortunately, it isn't rush hour, so ______________________________. His taxi driver seems friendly and quite talkative. Robert also notices that he is a cautious driver. In fact, he seems to drive a little too safely because he is driving very slowly. When Robert looks at his watch, he ______________________________ because he feels he might not make it to the meeting on time. In this situation, what would Robert most likely say to the taxi driver?

16-17

M: There is a saying that a family that eats together, stays together. With a busy lifestyle, people ______________________________ and not cooking at home. But this can break up the healthy dynamics of a family unit. So, it's important for a family to spend time cooking and eating together. Cooking at home can ______________________________ among family members. It brings the family together and opens up communication. It allows the family to share problems or issues in their everyday lives. In addition, cooking for your loved ones is an expression of love. A mother who bakes an apple pie or makes pancakes is sending the message that ______________________________ to make something delicious and wholesome for her family. A homemade pudding is filled with a parent's love and care, ______________________________. Also, the aroma of delicious food at home such as ribs, pasta, or baked chicken will certainly please anyone in the house and help everyone feel the true comforts of home. Clearly, home cooking is not only more delicious ______________________________ the relationships in a family.

01 다음을 듣고, 여자가 하는 말의 목적으로 가장 적절한 것을 고르시오.

① 화재 대피 훈련 시작을 알리려고
② 정기 소방 훈련 실시를 권유하려고
③ 화재 경보 오작동에 대해 사과하려고
④ 화재 경보와 긴급 대피를 공지하려고
⑤ 소방 훈련 시간과 방법을 안내하려고

02 대화를 듣고, 남자의 의견으로 가장 적절한 것을 고르시오.

① 여행지에 구급상자를 챙겨가는 것이 좋다.
② 외국에서는 개인 보안에 특히 주의해야 한다.
③ 해외여행 시 여행자 보험 가입이 필수적이다.
④ 여권 분실을 대비하여 서류를 미리 챙겨둬야 한다.
⑤ 공항에서의 출국 절차를 알면 시간을 아낄 수 있다.

03 대화를 듣고, 두 사람의 관계를 가장 잘 나타낸 것을 고르시오.

① 지원자 – 면접관
② 전화 교환원 – 사업가
③ 매장 매니저 – 구직자
④ 직업 소개인 – 인사 담당자
⑤ 컴퓨터 수리기사 – 사무직원

04 대화를 듣고, 그림에서 대화의 내용과 일치하지 않는 것을 고르시오.

05 대화를 듣고, 남자가 여자를 위해 할 일로 가장 적절한 것을 고르시오.

① 인터넷 URL 주소 알려 주기
② 인터넷 전용 방송프로그램 소개하기
③ 퀴즈 정답을 문자 메시지로 보내 주기
④ 인터넷을 이용한 영어 학습법 추천하기
⑤ 퀴즈 프로그램의 라디오 주파수 알려 주기

06 대화를 듣고, 두 사람이 지불할 금액을 고르시오. [3점]

① $75 ② $95 ③ $115
④ $135 ⑤ $150

07 대화를 듣고, 제품 시연이 연기된 이유를 고르시오.

① 자료 준비가 미흡해서
② 상사가 해외 출장 중이어서
③ 다른 팀이 준비가 되지 않아서
④ 시연 장소가 예약되지 않아서
⑤ 회사에 급한 회의가 있어서

08 다음을 듣고, 삵(leopard cat)에 관해 언급되지 않은 것을 고르시오.

① 생김새 ② 공격성
③ 먹이 습성 ④ 번식력
⑤ 평균 수명

09 Global Cyber Games에 관한 다음 내용을 듣고, 일치하지 않는 것을 고르시오.

① 올해로 7회째 열리고 있다.
② 각각 다른 도시에서 4년에 한 번 열린다.
③ 선수들은 모두 한 마을에서 머문다.
④ 선수들은 모두 자국에서 예선을 거친다.
⑤ 올해는 70개국에서 770명이 넘는 선수들이 모였다.

10 다음 표를 보면서 대화를 듣고, 두 사람이 선택할 식당을 고르시오.

		Children's Menu	Hours	Takes Reservations	Distance from Home
①	Bon Appetit	○	4 p.m. – 11 p.m.	○	5 miles
②	The Western Grill	○	10 a.m. – 10 p.m.	×	12 miles
③	Lucy's Steakhouse	○	10 a.m. – 10 p.m.	○	15 miles
④	Bistro 46	×	11 a.m. – 10 p.m.	×	20 miles
⑤	Ravioli	○	11 a.m. – 11 p.m.	○	25 miles

11 대화를 듣고, 남자의 마지막 말에 대한 여자의 응답으로 가장 적절한 것을 고르시오.

① Yes, I forgot to take it.
② Yes, these pants are ruined.
③ No, I threw it out by accident.
④ No, it's at home in my dresser.
⑤ Sure, the prices there are competitive.

12 대화를 듣고, 여자의 마지막 말에 대한 남자의 응답으로 가장 적절한 것을 고르시오.

① I don't trust this real estate agency.
② Luckily, we found this place quickly.
③ It's my day off, so we can go together.
④ I'll call a moving company later today.
⑤ We can help them find their new place.

13 대화를 듣고, 남자의 마지막 말에 대한 여자의 응답으로 가장 적절한 것을 고르시오. [3점]

▶ Woman : ______________________

① OK. I will phone her right now.
② Well, I'm fed up with her attitude.
③ I don't care what she thinks about you.
④ Thanks for returning my book, Carla.
⑤ She shouldn't have eaten lunch first.

14 대화를 듣고, 여자의 마지막 말에 대한 남자의 응답으로 가장 적절한 것을 고르시오.

▶ Man : ______________________

① Don't worry. It's not expensive.
② Don't worry. I will deliver them to your house.
③ Why don't you pick up your shirts right now?
④ I will ask if we can have some new ones made.
⑤ We are sorry. I will not charge you for your shirts.

15 다음 상황 설명을 듣고, Susan이 Carol에게 할 말로 가장 적절한 것을 고르시오. [3점]

▶ Susan : Carol, ______________________

① my mom said I could raise a dog.
② I can't because I'm going away next week.
③ have a great trip and say "hi" to Roger for me.
④ I want to, but I must get my mom's permission first.
⑤ I can take Roger for a walk every day if you want.

[16~17] 다음을 듣고, 물음에 답하시오.

16 남자가 하는 말의 주제로 가장 적절한 것은?

① the negative impact of games on learning
② ways to use games for educational purposes
③ proposals for reinventing higher education
④ a positive outlook on the space tourism industry
⑤ the necessity of developing various adult learning tools

17 언급된 기관이 아닌 것은?

① 소방서　② 대학
③ 군대　④ 항공 우주국
⑤ 기상청

01

W: May I have your attention, please. This is your emergency operator. A fire has been reported. Please ______________________________ through the nearest exit. This is not a drill. I repeat, this is not a drill. All persons shall ______________________________, walk down to the lobby and exit the building. DO NOT USE THE ELEVATORS! After you leave the building, please move away from the exits. Disabled persons should be taken to the closest smoke-free stairwell to await evacuation by the Fire Department. You will be notified when it is safe to re-enter the building. We will ______________________________.

02

M: Mia, how is the packing going?

W: ______________________________, Dad. I just need to pack my first-aid kit.

M: Okay. You're bringing sunscreen and a hat also, right?

W: Of course.

M: Hmm.... I see your passport here. By the way, did you get travel insurance?

W: I didn't. Why? Do you think it's necessary?

M: Yes, I do. Anything could happen in a foreign country. You ______________________________.

W: What's the benefit of having insurance?

M: It will cover you if you suddenly need to be hospitalized.

W: I guess ______________________________.

M: Right. Plus, insurance covers the loss of important items, like your passport.

W: That could be useful. ______________________________ at the airport.

M: I'd rather we look online first.

W: Okay. Let's do that.

03

M: Hello?

W: Hi! This is Judy Brown at Business Systems Incorporated.

M: Yes, Ms. Brown. How can I help you?

W: We're looking for an administrative assistant, someone who can use a computer, do some filing... ______________________________.

M: Oh, I'm sure we can find someone who's qualified. ______________________________ a little bit more about the job responsibilities?

W: We need someone to answer the phone and take messages. They must have a good telephone voice.

M: Uh-huh.

W: And someone who's willing to work evenings once in a while, when things get busy.

M: Weekends, too?

W: No, probably not.

M: Well, let me look through our files and find someone ______________________________. I'll call you tomorrow afternoon. Is that okay?

W: Okay. I'll be waiting for your call. Thanks.

04

M: Hi, I'm Sean's father.

W: Come on in, Mr. Nelson. Thank you for coming to the teacher/parent conference.

M: My pleasure. Wow! Did the children draw the trees and dinosaurs on the wall?

W: Yes, they did. Do you ______________________________ from the ceiling? Sean colored two of them.

M: Sean really loves birds. Are these photos of the students on the bulletin board on the right?

W: Yes, they're photos of children ______________________________ here at the kindergarten. There's a picture of Sean there, too. See if you can find him.

M: The children all look so happy. Thank you for taking such good care of them.

W: It's my pleasure. Let me find your name tag on the

table. The ribbon on the tag was made by the kids. Oh, here it is.

M: They're so cute!

W: The conference ______________________ on the second floor. Go past the balloon arch and up the stairs.

M: Wow, I really feel like I'm in a fairy tale.

05

M: Hey, Kara. Did you do this morning's English quiz?

W: The one in the newspaper?

M: No, the one on the *Let's Talk* radio program.

W: Oh, I've heard that's an excellent show.

M: It is. The quiz is really hard, but ______________ ________________________________ today!

W: Wow, I should listen to the show too. Where do I find it?

M: I subscribe to the Internet radio podcast and listen on my computer. I'll give you the URL address.

W: But I've got a clock radio. I'd like _____________ __________________________.

M: In that case, I'll send you the radio frequency number by text message.

W: Okay. What time is *Let's Talk* on?

M: Eight a.m., Monday through Friday.

W: Thanks, Ben.

06

W: What time is it?

M: It's 10:30. __________________________________.

W: Traffic was bad.

M: Now, should we get full-day ski passes?

W: Maybe not. Let's see, the full-day ski passes are $75, and the lift fee is $20.

M: Oh, I have two free lift coupons, so _____________ __________________________________.

W: That's nice.

M: What about the afternoon passes?

W: They're $40. But what will we do until 12:30?

M: I don't know.

W: Hmm, I guess we could shop for ski stuff.

M: Well, you know I ___________________________ ______________________. I really want to ski a lot. Let's get full-day passes.

W: You start without me then. You know I usually get tired after a few runs anyway. I'll buy an afternoon pass.

M: OK. I'll meet you at the top of the mountain at 1.

07

W: Hi, William. What are you working on?

M: I'm preparing the handouts for this afternoon's product demonstration. ____________________ ____________________?

W: Great, except for one thing. Didn't you see the email announcing the delay of the demonstration?

M: Oh, no! I guess the research-and-development team ______________________________________ ______________.

W: Actually, it is just because the conference room ____ ____________________. The demonstration will be tomorrow instead.

M: I'm a little embarrassed, but I suppose I can use the extra time to gather some more data.

W: Good thinking. Anyway, I have to hurry to a meeting with my team leader. He just returned from his business trip to London.

M: Okay. Good luck with that! Talk to you later.

08

W: The leopard cat is a small wildcat native to South and East Asia. ________________ its leopard-like spots, but its relation to the leopard is distant. Leopard cats are similar in size to house cats, but more slender with longer legs. Their feet are poorly-suited to walking on snow and they consequently avoid areas where snow depths exceed 10 cm. They eat meat, ________________ including lizards, birds, and insects. They give birth to between two and four kittens at a time, and the kittens remain in the cave until they are about one month old. In the wild, leopard cats have an average lifespan of approximately 4 years, but ________________ up to 20 years if raised by humans.

09

M: Welcome competitors, spectators, and viewers at home! This is the seventh Global Cyber Games. Even though it is our seventh year, few people outside the gaming world ________________. So let me tell you about the Global Cyber Games. The Global Cyber Games ________________ the Olympics. Every year a different city hosts the competition. And while at the games, the competitors all live together in one village. Moreover, all the competitors here have passed the qualifying round in their home country. This year we have over 770 competitors from 70 nations competing. I want to ________________!

10

M: ________________ where to go for Mom's birthday?

W: Well, I did some research online and found five restaurants that have very good reviews.

M: Okay. Let's take a look.... We need a restaurant that has a children's menu, so this one's out.

W: How about this restaurant?

M: Well, ________________, but they're not open for lunch.

W: You're right, and I guess that's a problem since we're planning to have lunch.

M: What about this one? They're open for lunch.

W: Yeah, but we also need to go somewhere ________________.

M: Right, almost all restaurants will be crowded at lunchtime. We're left with only two choices then. Why don't you pick?

W: Hmm.... Let's go to the one closer to home.

M: Sounds good to me!

11

M: These pants are too small. ________________ for me?

W: I don't know if the store will accept them.

M: I think they will. ________________?

12

W: Wow, I didn't realize ________________, did you?

M: No. We really need to hurry up and find a new place.

W: Exactly! ________________ a real estate agency?

13

M: Hi, Jenna. Is something wrong?

W: Not really. I am just waiting for Carla. We're supposed to go and eat lunch together.

M: What time ________________________________ ______________?

W: Fifteen minutes ago!

M: Oh?

W: I wish she were reliable like you.

M: Me?

W: When we make an appointment, you __________ ____________________. And when you borrow something, you always give it back before I ask you.

M: Let me guess — she borrowed something and didn't give it back.

W: That's right. It was a book, and I needed it for a test yesterday.

M: Well, if she's late right now, why don't you phone her?

W: She should phone me. She's _________________ _____________________.

M: I agree. It's like she doesn't care.

14

W: Hi. I'm here to pick up the shirts ____________ ______________________________ yesterday.

M: OK. Do you have your ticket?

W: No, but my last name is Stark.

M: Let me see... it looks like your shirts aren't going to be ready until 5 p.m.

W: But I was told they would be ready in 24 hours. That means 2 p.m.

M: I'm sorry, ma'am. That really means __________ ____________________________ the next day.

W: I'm leaving for the airport at 5 p.m. And I don't have anything to wear for the meeting in London. ____________________________________?

M: We have some spare shirts in your size that we can loan you.

W: OK, then. I should borrow some. Anyway, do I need to come here to pick up my shirts again?

15

W: Susan loves dogs, but when Susan asked her mom last year about having a dog, her mom said that a dog ________________________________ ________________. She also said Susan's father wouldn't agree to it. So, Susan doesn't have a dog. Next week Carol, a friend of Susan's, is going on a five-day trip for summer vacation with her family. Carol needs someone to take care of her pet puppy, Roger, so she asks Susan what she is doing next week. Susan says her dad is _________________ ___________________, so she and her mom are just staying home. Carol asks Susan __________ ____________________ Roger. In this situation, what would Susan most likely say to Carol?

16-17

M: Adults ______________________________ video games will do more good than harm. That's because they recognize the power of video games as educational tools. Gaming ________________ ______________________________ that help adults handle some of the world's most serious problems, and it's already being used in several important areas. For instance, firefighters _______ ____________________________ biochemical disasters. University administrators are using it to reinvent higher education. Military services are using it to prepare for battle. And even space agencies worldwide are using it to explore mission types. When the pressures are high and the choices fast-paced and complex, using games to explore the options can provide substantial advantages. But institutions like schools, universities, and governments ___________________________ ___________________ only when regular adults get comfortable with the tools of gaming.

01 다음을 듣고, 여자가 하는 말의 목적으로 가장 적절한 것을 고르시오.

① 물 절약 캠페인 동참을 호소하려고
② 수질 오염 방지 대책을 설명하려고
③ 수질 조사 결과에 대해 공지하려고
④ 수도관 공사로 인한 단수를 안내하려고
⑤ 소방 도로 주정차 금지 법안을 소개하려고

02 대화를 듣고, 남자의 의견으로 가장 적절한 것을 고르시오.

① 야생 동물 보호법을 강화해야 한다.
② 유기견 실태에 대한 많은 관심이 필요하다.
③ 유기견 입양은 신중을 기울여야 할 문제이다.
④ 청소년이 자원봉사 활동을 하는 것은 중요하다.
⑤ 동물 보호소는 유기견 보호에 중대한 역할을 한다.

03 대화를 듣고, 두 사람의 관계를 가장 잘 나타낸 것을 고르시오.

① 호텔 직원 – 손님
② 경찰 – 행인
③ 화가 – 작품 구매인
④ 미술관 직원 – 관람객
⑤ 배우 경호원 – 배우 팬

04 대화를 듣고, 그림에서 대화의 내용과 일치하지 않는 것을 고르시오.

05 대화를 듣고, 여자가 할 일로 가장 적절한 것을 고르시오.

① 예산 책정하기
② 도와줄 사람 찾기
③ 보고서 재검토하기
④ 회의 날짜 변경하기
⑤ 프로그램 오류 복구하기

06 대화를 듣고, 남자가 지불할 금액을 고르시오. [3점]

① $240 ② $252 ③ $360
④ $372 ⑤ $540

07 대화를 듣고, 여자가 다음 정류장에서 내리려는 이유를 고르시오.

① 쇼핑해야 해서
② 영화를 보기로 해서
③ 친구와 서점에 가야 해서
④ 엄마가 케이크를 사오라고 해서
⑤ 여동생의 휴대전화를 찾아야 해서

08 대화를 듣고, 지구본의 문제점에 관해 언급되지 않은 것을 고르시오.

① 작은 크기 ② 건전지 불량
③ 흐린 색깔 ④ 국가명 표기 오류
⑤ 비싼 가격

09 Hudson Talent Agency의 강습에 관한 다음 내용을 듣고, 일치하지 않는 것을 고르시오.

① 재능 있는 어린이를 뮤지컬 배우로 양성한다.
② 연기 경험이 있는 어린이를 대상으로 한다.
③ 2개월 동안 토요일마다 강습을 실시한다.
④ 뮤지컬 <Annie>의 오디션을 목표로 연습한다.
⑤ 신청은 선착순으로 받는다.

10 다음 표를 보면서 대화를 듣고, 여자가 선택할 운동 수업을 고르시오.

YMCA Fitness Class Schedule

Class	Time	Difficulty	Trainer	Price
① Kickboxing	4 p.m.	very challenging	Jordan	$80
② Pilates	7 p.m.	moderately challenging	Victoria	$40
③ Meditation	8 p.m.	not challenging	Anna	$30
④ Yoga	7 p.m.	moderately challenging	Thomas	$60
⑤ Water Aerobics	8 p.m.	not challenging	Jessica	$50

11 대화를 듣고, 여자의 마지막 말에 대한 남자의 응답으로 가장 적절한 것을 고르시오.

① Good, you did very well in history.
② Really? Then I did all that for nothing.
③ Yes, on one level I can understand that.
④ Don't worry. We all know it isn't your fault.
⑤ Well, whether he meant it or not, I don't know.

12 대화를 듣고, 남자의 마지막 말에 대한 여자의 응답으로 가장 적절한 것을 고르시오.

① It doesn't matter to me.
② But it's worth the price.
③ Now I'm almost bankrupt.
④ That's exactly what I want.
⑤ We have a lot more expensive ones.

13 대화를 듣고, 여자의 마지막 말에 대한 남자의 응답으로 가장 적절한 것을 고르시오. [3점]

▶ Man : ______________________

① It's always fun to play with other kids.
② You can't bring his kids to the concert.
③ You should have eaten dinner beforehand.
④ I understand why you wanted to earn your way.
⑤ Don't worry, the concert should end before then.

14 대화를 듣고, 남자의 마지막 말에 대한 여자의 응답으로 가장 적절한 것을 고르시오. [3점]

▶ Woman : ______________________

① Wow! You've changed a lot in the last two years!
② Stephanie is my best friend and she is my role model.
③ What a coincidence to meet you here! It's a small world!
④ I'm sorry, but you must be confusing me with someone else.
⑤ Please give my regards to your parents. Have a nice holiday!

15 다음 상황 설명을 듣고, Grace가 Megan에게 할 말로 가장 적절한 것을 고르시오.

▶ Grace : ______________________

① All my friends are already there.
② I'll promise to see you next month.
③ I'll be at your house in half an hour.
④ There is a doctor on call 24 hours a day.
⑤ I'm sorry, but I don't think I can make it tonight.

[16~17] 다음을 듣고, 물음에 답하시오.

16 남자가 하는 말의 주제로 가장 적절한 것은?

① the harmful effects of computer games
② the best computer game to boost creativity
③ various classroom games useful for teaching
④ the release of new educational computer games
⑤ controversies over playing games at an early age

17 언급된 과목이 아닌 것은?

① 역사 ② 수학 ③ 지리
④ 물리 ⑤ 문학

01

W: The Blue Bell Canyon County Water Company ______________________ to all Northville residents. We have good news for Northville residents ______________________ that flows through rusty water pipes. In order to provide you with cleaner water, we will undergo construction of new water pipes. Due to this major construction, water will be cut off from 10 a.m. to 5 p.m. on September 12th. We apologize for the inconvenience but ______________________ as we will provide you with cleaner water. We ask that you prepare a personal reservoir of water before the construction. For further information, please call 915-1121, or visit our website www.bluecanwater.com.

02

W: Scott, do you want to see a movie this Saturday?

M: Sounds fun, but I can't. I'll be at the animal shelter.

W: Oh, that's right. I forgot that you volunteer there. How is that going?

M: Well, it's alright. I love the dogs, and the other volunteers are great, but sometimes ______________________.

W: The animal shelter is doing great work. Is it really that bad?

M: Yes. There are so many dogs ______________________. People are so careless sometimes.

W: That is sad. At least there are people like you ______________________.

M: Thanks, but the number of abandoned dogs isn't going to decrease unless a lot more people get involved.

03

M: Excuse me, ma'am. You ______________________.

W: Why? My legs are killing me, so I just need to rest on this wall for a minute. I must have walked miles today. Do I have to ask permission first?

M: No, but I'm afraid it's not a wall.

W: What are you talking about?

M: That is ______________________. The title is right over there. It says, "2050 Fifth Avenue."

W: Oh, really? I'm so sorry. I just thought it was a decorative wall in the corner.

M: No, it's a sculpture from an up-and-coming young artist named James Spacy.

W: Really? Now I'd like to take a photo of it.

M: Hold on. You ______________________.

W: Oh, I'm sorry. I just want to have a photo of this piece as a souvenir.

M: You can purchase post cards at the shop near the entrance.

W: Okay. Thanks.

04

W: I found a picture of a porch that I really like. Here it is.

M: Let's take a look. There are plants ______________________ that lead to the door.

W: Yes, and look at the bird-shaped postbox.

M: You mean the postbox ______________________ next to the door? It looks so cute.

W: The porch also has two rocking chairs. You and I can sit on the chairs for a relaxing evening.

M: There's also a side table between the chairs. We can put drinks, like beer and wine, on it.

W: No way. I want to put a vase with flags on the table like ______________________.

M: Okay. When we ______________________ on the rocking chairs, we will be able to see the hanging potted plants on the ceiling.

W: All the greenery will ______________________
____________________.

M: Sounds good.

05

M: Can I talk to you for a minute?

W: Of course, Mr. Johnson.

M: ____________________________ your financial report for last quarter and the figures must be inaccurate.

W: Are you sure? I was very careful.

M: Based on our yearly budget, ________________
____________________ in the last quarter alone.

W: Let me take a look. Oh, it looks like I entered the wrong numbers into this column here. I'm so sorry.

M: That's alright. But ________________________
Ms. Thomson at the meeting tomorrow.

W: Right, that's at 10 a.m.

M: So, I just want you to check all the figures again and correct the errors. Can you do that?

W: Sure. No problem. I'll take care of it.

06

W: Good evening. How can I help you?

M: Hi, I'd like to buy some tickets for the musical, *Mamma Mia*. Do you ______________________
__________________________?

W: Yes. Where would you like to sit?

M: Where are the best seats ____________________
_______________?

W: Well, the best seats are in the orchestra section, in the center.

M: How much does it cost to be in the orchestra?

W: It costs 250 dollars per seat.

M: That's too expensive for us. What's the next best seating?

W: Up in the middle section of the theater, the seats are $180, but __________________________. We only have 120-dollar tickets and 80-dollar tickets.

M: Oh, then I'd like __________________________.
Three, please.

W: All right. Would you like to buy a program book? It's 12 dollars.

M: Yes, please. I'd like one.

07

W: Alright, I'll talk to you later. Arnie, ____________
______________________, and I can't go to the bookstore with you. I have to ________________
________________________.

M: Is something wrong? The next stop is the Cineplex. Are you going to see a movie?

W: It's not that. I just got off the phone with my sister and she said she lost her phone.

M: Oh, that's too bad. Does she know where it is?

W: Yeah, she said she left it at a store while she was shopping.

M: Did she tell you which store it was?

W: It happens that the store is next to the Cineplex, so
________________________________.

M: Oh, I see. Where is she?

W: She's already at home, so she ________________
________________________.

M: Well, why don't we get off together? I'll go to the bookstore tomorrow.

W: That's a great idea. There's also a place that has delicious cookies, so let's stop by there, too.

M: It's time to get off. Let's go.

08

M: Royal Globe. Is there anything I can help you with today?
W: Yes. I found ______________________________ that I bought the other day from your website.
M: I'm sorry to hear that. May I ask what the problem is?
W: The description said it was a desktop globe, but it's too small.
M: Oh, but ______________________________.
W: And it has a problem with the batteries. You said it has a glow-in-the-dark feature, but __________ __________________.
M: I'm sorry to hear that.
W: Also, the color of the sea should be blue, but it looks gray. And the worst problem is that the names of two countries are reversed.
M: Really?
W: Yeah! "Canada" is at the bottom and "United States" is on top. It should be ____________________ ____________.
M: Oh, no! That's a terrible mistake. I'm so sorry. I'd be happy to give you your money back.

09

M: Do you have a child ____________________ ____________? Hudson Talent Agency is looking for up-and-coming child actors. We are currently offering classes to help talented children become professional musical actors. No prior acting experience is required. Our classes are held every Saturday from 10 a.m. to noon, from May 5th to July 5th. All children who are enrolled in our program will have ______________________ ______________________ in the hit Broadway musical, *Annie*. Students will practice a number of songs and dance routines to prepare for the musical audition. Applications will be taken on a first come, ______________________. If you'd like more information regarding the program, contact our program director, Terry Theissen. Our number is 313-545-1500. Call us today.

10

W: Hello, I'd like to sign up for a fitness class, please.
M: Is this your first time taking a class at the YMCA, ma'am?
W: Yes, I just joined the gym last week, and now I'm ______________________________________!
M: Here's a schedule containing all of our classes. You'll need to take into account what time you want your class to be, first.
W: I work from 9 a.m. to 5 p.m., so I can't do anything in the morning or afternoon. What sorts of things do you offer in the evening?
M: How difficult would you like your class to be?
W: I want at least ______________________! I'm here to lose weight, after all.
M: Understood. A medium-level class might suit you just right, then. Which do you prefer, a male or female trainer?
W: I'm fine with either.
M: The last thing to consider would be the price of the classes. You'll want to ____________________ ____________________ when choosing a class.
W: I'm looking for something under $50. What do you ______________________?
M: I think I know exactly what class will be perfect for you.

11

W: What did you do last night?
M: ______________________ for today's history test. There were too many chapters to study!
W: Oh, no! Didn't you hear that several chapters ____________________?

12

M: This table ______________________________. How much is it?
W: It's 853 dollars plus tax.
M: Well, it's a bit expensive. It's out of my budget.

13

W: Hi! How are you, Alexis?

M: Pretty well. ______________________, though. What do you feel like doing?

W: Well, we could go to the lake and do some kayaking.

M: We did that last week. How about going to a concert? Do you like classical music?

W: Yes, I love it! You know I play the violin!

M: I read in the newspaper that the Blue County Philharmonic is playing at the new symphony hall tonight.

W: Sounds terrific. __________________________?

M: The concert starts at 4:30 p.m. How about meeting at 4?

W: I'd love to. Oh, no. I'm afraid I can't. __________ ____________________ if the concert goes late.

M: Why? Do you have another plan tonight?

W: Yes, I need to be at Mr. Albert's house by 8:00 p.m. ____ until 10:30.

14

M: Excuse me. Will you ____________________ ______________? My seat is 3C.

W: Sure. Go ahead.

M: Thanks. Oh, ____________________________?

W: Well, I'm not sure.

M: Weren't you at Stephanie's party last Saturday?

W: Yes, I was. Were you there, too?

M: Yeah. Now I remember. You're her friend, right? I'm her colleague, Joseph Whittier.

W: Nice to see you again. I'm Emily Nicholas. Are you going home for the Christmas holiday?

M: Yes, I'm from Denver, and my parents still live there.

W: Oh, really? I'm also from Denver. Joseph Whittier... Oh, ________________________________ __________ Lincoln Elementary School?

M: Yes, I did. Yeah! Now I remember your name. You're Emily!

15

W: Grace and Megan are best friends. Megan's ____________________________________, and naturally she invited Grace to her birthday party. It is going to be a sleepover, and Megan invites several of her closest friends. Grace told Megan that ________________________________, but this evening, on the night of the party, Grace's mother is very sick. Her mother has got a bad cold, so Grace ____________________________________. Her father is ________________________, and her brother is in New York to study. Now Grace picks up the phone and dials Megan's number. In this situation, what would Grace most likely say to Megan over the phone?

16-17

M: Are you overwhelmed with the increasing amount of schoolwork and discouraged about your poor performance at school? Do you ____________ ______________________ playing your favorite computer game that you forget what time it is? We have good news for you. We've come up with a variety of games to help you study __________ ______________________ you learn at school. For instance, a game called *The Unknown World* makes history come alive for you as you experience historical events through digital, real-time travel. With *Exciting Numbers*, you can learn math in a fun way while playing number games. Another, called *Wonderful Odyssey*, ________________ __________ countries, cities, rivers, mountains, and lakes through a ride on a helicopter and learn a lot about geography ____________________ ____________. *A Brilliant Storyteller* helps you learn a work of literature through quiz games ____________________________________. Please visit our website now and buy one of these new and exciting games. You'll see results almost immediately!

01 다음을 듣고, 남자가 하는 말의 목적으로 가장 적절한 것을 고르시오.

① 건강 체조를 알려주려고
② 헬스클럽을 광고하려고
③ 다이어트 방법을 알려주려고
④ 식이요법의 중요성을 설명하려고
⑤ 무료 상담 프로그램을 안내하려고

02 대화를 듣고, 여자의 의견으로 가장 적절한 것을 고르시오.

① 기사 작성을 글쓰기 교육의 일환으로 삼아야 한다.
② 기자가 되기 위해서는 설득력 있게 글을 써야 한다.
③ 기사 작성 시 분량을 지키고 독자를 생각해야 한다.
④ 학생들을 독자로 하는 기사 제목은 간략할수록 좋다.
⑤ 학교 잡지에 실리는 글은 유익한 내용을 담아야 한다.

03 대화를 듣고, 두 사람의 관계를 가장 잘 나타낸 것을 고르시오.

① 작가 – 영화감독
② 영화 평론가 – 리포터
③ 배우 – 에이전트
④ 부동산 중개인 – 고객
⑤ 구인 스카우트 전문가 – 구직자

04 대화를 듣고, 그림에서 대화의 내용과 일치하지 <u>않는</u> 것을 고르시오.

05 대화를 듣고, 여자가 남자를 위해 할 일로 가장 적절한 것을 고르시오.

① 스마트폰 빌려주기
② 다른 버스 알려주기
③ 저녁 식사 준비하기
④ 생일 선물 사다 주기
⑤ 버스 도착 시각 알아보기

06 대화를 듣고, 남자가 지불할 금액을 고르시오. [3점]

① $570 ② $620 ③ $1,020
④ $1,140 ⑤ $1,240

07 대화를 듣고, 여자가 친구 집에 가려는 이유를 고르시오.

① 친구 개를 찾아주려고
② 영화관에 함께 가려고
③ 쇼핑하러 가자고 권유하려고
④ 친구에게 케이크를 갖다주려고
⑤ 슬픔에 잠긴 친구를 위로하려고

08 대화를 듣고, 시합에 관해 언급되지 <u>않은</u> 것을 고르시오.

① 대결 선수 ② 코치
③ 후원사 ④ 시합 장소
⑤ 시합일

09 Kamo 고등학교의 영화제에 관한 다음 내용을 듣고, 일치하지 <u>않는</u> 것을 고르시오.

① 10월 첫 주에 시작한다.
② 개인 또는 그룹으로 참여할 수 있다.
③ 단편 영화는 5분~15분 길이여야 한다.
④ 수상자는 10월 5일에 발표된다.
⑤ 당선된 작품은 학교 콘서트홀에서 상영된다.

10 다음 표를 보면서 대화를 듣고, 남자가 대여하기로 한 자동차를 고르시오.

ACE RENT A CAR

Model	Type	Rental Fee (per day)	Insurance (per day)	GPS Navigation System	Drop-Offs at Different Locations
① A	SUV	$43	$3	○	×
② B	compact	$45	$4	×	×
③ C	SUV	$52	$5	○	○
④ D	SUV	$59	$7	○	○
⑤ E	SUV	$48	$5	×	○

11 대화를 듣고, 남자의 마지막 말에 대한 여자의 응답으로 가장 적절한 것을 고르시오.

① Thank you for being here tonight.
② No, it's not finished yet. Be patient.
③ It's delicious. You're really a great cook!
④ I downloaded the recipe from the Internet.
⑤ Hurry up, or you'll be late for the appointment.

12 대화를 듣고, 여자의 마지막 말에 대한 남자의 응답으로 가장 적절한 것을 고르시오.

① I'm sorry I can't. I have too much work to do.
② I'd better go see a doctor before it gets worse.
③ I'm happy to do it. I could make some extra cash.
④ I admire you. I also want to do something good.
⑤ Then I'm all right. Let's work the night shift tonight.

13 대화를 듣고, 남자의 마지막 말에 대한 여자의 응답으로 가장 적절한 것을 고르시오.

▶ Woman : ____________________

① If I were you, I wouldn't buy that bag.
② Really? I believe you were overcharged.
③ Wow! I think you made a good purchase.
④ Absolutely. This is our rock-bottom price.
⑤ It is too high. Please give me a better price.

14 대화를 듣고, 여자의 마지막 말에 대한 남자의 응답으로 가장 적절한 것을 고르시오. [3점]

▶ Man : ____________________

① Don't play jokes like that in the future.
② Did you also visit the beaches in Hawaii?
③ I really envy you. I really want to go there, too.
④ It sounds like a great dream. I hope it comes true.
⑤ I think you got overexcited. Please calm down a bit.

15 다음 상황 설명을 듣고, Kimberly가 Howard 부인에게 할 말로 가장 적절한 것을 고르시오. [3점]

▶ Kimberly : Mrs. Howard, ____________________

① good idea! Do you want me to keep it a secret?
② how many people did you invite to the party?
③ congratulations! Can I help you with anything?
④ if so, should I wear something formal to the party?
⑤ would you let me know if you can come as soon as possible?

[16~17] 다음을 듣고, 물음에 답하시오.

16 여자가 하는 말의 주제로 가장 적절한 것은?

① an effective plan for a diet
② how to lose weight effectively
③ several causes of being overweight
④ ways of burning calories with exercise
⑤ harmful effects of being overweight on health

17 언급된 운동이 아닌 것은?

① 수영
② 조깅
③ 요가
④ 자전거 타기
⑤ 에어로빅

01

M: Look at this photo! This was me 3 months ago. And now look at me. Don't I look fantastic? I've been going to the Ace Fitness Club, a fitness center that ______________________________ ______________________. I lost 15 pounds during the first month I was enrolled! Do you want to try too? Just call 1-800-232-2112 and tell them when you want to start. The membership fee is just $30 a month. Once you join, ______________ ______________________________________ from a qualified doctor who puts you on a low-fat diet and an exercise program. Join now! ____________ ______________________.

02

W: Kevin, do you have a minute?

M: Sure, is it about the article that I wrote for the school magazine?

W: Yes. ______________________________________ about the article.

M: Of course. I would love your feedback.

W: I asked you to write the article with 1,000 words or fewer, but it looks like you wrote over 1,500 words. It's just too long.

M: I'm sorry, but I had so many things to say.

W: I'm afraid your lengthy article won't fit into the magazine.

M: Alright. ______________________________.

W: And please remember that you must think of your readers when you write. It's important that they clearly understand your writing at all times.

M: I understand. It looks like ______________________ ____________________. Thank you for your advice.

03

W: Hello, this is Brianna Wood.

M: Brianna, it's Dylan at Rooftop Entertainment.

W: Oh, hello, Dylan. You're busy preparing to move your office.

M: Yeah, I'm pretty busy. I have good news. Do you remember the movie for which you auditioned to play a troubled twenty-something?

W: Yes, ______________________________. You told me that.

M: Yeah, but I just received a call from the director. ____ in his movie.

W: Really? I can't believe it. I really want to work with him. What kind of character is it?

M: It's not the leading role, but it's an important supporting role. I think ______________________ ______________________.

W: Yeah! I'll take any role in his movie. I'd love to do it.

M: Okay. Can you visit the office this Friday? ______ ____.

04

M: Sandra, ______________________________________!

W: Oh, James. I didn't know you liked to ski.

M: I'm all about snowboarding these days. _______ ______________________________?

W: I brought my kid here so he can get some skiing lessons. He loves skiing.

M: Where is your kid? Oh, he's the one holding a ring, right? The coach ______________________ ____________________.

W: No, that's not him. Do you see the big yellow arch ______________________________________? James is standing right in front of the arch.

M: Oh, he's so big now. By the way, it seems the kids' ski school is like a playground. There's a big snowman with a cone hat.

W: Isn't it cute? Look at the big bird behind the snowman.

M: I understand why your son loves the school.

05

W: Hello, Ben. Glad to see you. Are you waiting for a bus?

M: Yeah. Where are you going, Alison?

W: I'm going home. My grandmother will visit my home tonight, so ______________________.

M: Oh, that's nice. I'm going downtown to buy something for my friend's birthday.

W: Are you waiting for the number 65? It passes through downtown.

M: Right. It's ______________________.

W: But, if I remember right, it doesn't come often.

M: You're right. ______________________ for more than 10 minutes.

W: Why don't you check when the bus will arrive with your smartphone?

M: I would, but the battery is dead.

W: Then I'll do it for you. Wait a second.

M: Alright. Thanks for your help.

06

M: Good morning. I'm planning a trip to Alaska this summer and ______________________ ____________ some information on the airfare.

W: Sure. When do you want to travel?

M: On July 18th, returning on August 1st. How much is a round-trip ticket to Alaska?

W: Well, American Airlines is offering 550 dollars per person for a round-trip ticket. ____________ ________________.

M: Does that include taxes?

W: No, it doesn't include taxes. The total will be 620 dollars including taxes.

M: That's pretty expensive. ______________________ ______________?

W: That's the cheapest. Weekend flights are usually more expensive.

M: Then I can change the date. How about leaving on July 15th and returning on the 29th?

W: Then it'll be 510 dollars, and taxes will be 60 dollars.

M: That sounds better. I'd like to reserve two tickets.

07

W: Have you been over to Riley's house recently?

M: No, I haven't. Is everything okay with her?

W: Actually, no. ______________________ since her dog died.

M: Oh, no, that's awful. Have you talked to her?

W: I called her and tried to invite her to the mall the other day, but she said ______________________ ________________.

M: I expect she's having a really hard time, so that makes sense.

W: Well, I'd thought that maybe she might ________ ______________________________, but it seems like she just wants to stay in.

M: Why don't you go to her house and hang out with her there? I expect she's lonely.

W: That's a good idea.

M: You could watch a movie together and do something fun, like baking a cake.

W: Okay, I'll give her a call.

08

M: Hello, nice to meet you. My name is Anthony. I spoke with you on the phone yesterday.

W: Hi, I'm Jenny.

M: ______________________. I was so impressed by your last performance. I couldn't believe you knocked down your opponent in one shot.

W: Thank you. So what can I do for you?

M: I want to promote a match between you and Sara Peterson.

W: Sara Peterson ______________________ in the world? She is very strong. So what kind of contract are we looking at?

M: I'm thinking of giving you $350,000 before the match. I'll also pay for ______________________ ______________________. And the match will be sponsored by Smith Sportswear.

W: Hmm.... When and where will the match be?

M: I'm planning to hold the match in LA on January 28th.

W: Hmm.... Not a bad deal. I'll think about it and let you know in three days.

09

W: Attention all students of Kamo High School. We will begin our very own school film festival ______________________________. The film festival will feature short and long films from talented students at our school. All students can participate by submitting a short or long film ______________________________. Short films must not be longer than 5 minutes, and long films must be longer than 15 minutes. If you're interested in this event, submit your application by September 5th. ______________________________, a list of their names will be posted on October 5th. ______________________________ for viewing in the school's concert hall all throughout October. Start filming today!

10

W: Hi, how can I help you?

M: I'd like to rent a car for 4 days.

W: What kind of car do you have in mind?

M: I'm traveling with 5 people and have a lot of luggage, so I probably need an SUV.

W: I see. ______________________________ the rental?

M: I'd like to spend no more than $60 a day, which would include insurance.

W: If that's the case, you have 3 options. Would you like GPS navigation?

M: Yes, most definitely. I'm traveling in this area, so I don't know my way around.

W: Got it. It looks like you'll have these two choices.

M: ______________________________ the car at this location? I'd like to drop the car off at the San Francisco airport.

W: Yes, I have a car in mind. This car ______________________________ at a different location.

M: Great. I'll take that car then.

11

M: It smells good. What are you making?

W: It's a dish I learned to make. ______________________________.

M: Smells great. Can I get a little taste right now? ______________________________.

12

W: I have to work tonight at Marcia's restaurant, but ______________________________. I was wondering if you could work my shift.

M: Sure, I'm free. But are you sure it will be alright with your manager?

W: Yes, ______________________________. You have to work from five to nine.

13

W: Is that the new bag you bought recently? It looks fancy.

M: Do you really think so? I was a little unsure about the color.

W: It's very cool. ______________________________. It's very flattering on you.

M: ______________________________.

W: Is brown a trendy color these days?

M: No, not really. Brown just happens to be my favorite color.

W: It seems very strong. What material is that?

M: It's made of the best sheepskin.

W: Well, it looks pretty expensive. It's definitely a designer bag.

M: Yeah, ______________________________ because of the price, but when I found out it was 40% off, I snapped it up.

14

M: Boy, it looks like you're really happy today.

W: Happy? I'm beyond happy. ____________________ ____________________.

M: Did you win the lottery or something?

W: No, but it feels like I did.

M: So hurry and tell me what happened.

W: I was listening to the radio, and the radio station ____________________ ____________________ to Hawaii.

M: Oh my gosh. Did you get some tickets?

W: I called ten times, and ____________________ ____________________ and got two free tickets! Can you believe it?

M: That's amazing. You've always wanted to visit Hawaii. So who's the lucky person you're taking to Hawaii?

W: I'm thinking of taking my mother.

15

M: Kimberly ____________________ for her mother. It will be her mother's 48th birthday next month. Kimberly plans to invite several of her mother's friends to the party. Kimberly decides to call one of her mother's friends, Mrs. Howard. Kimberly tells Mrs. Howard about her plans and also invites her to the party. However, Mrs. Howard already has previous plans. She doesn't know ____________________. But Kimberly needs to know how many people will be attending the party ____________________ ____________________. In this situation, what would Kimberly most likely say to Mrs. Howard?

16-17

W: It seems like everyone these days ____________________ ____________________. From low-calorie options at the restaurant to workout plans, everyone has their own plan for having a skinny body. However, it's really simple to lose that fat without spending a lot of money on specially-prepared foods and personal workout trainers. ____________________, you don't need to do anything fancy. Just follow these steps. First, cut out junk food and fast food entirely. No more hamburgers and hot dogs, no more sodas, and no more potato chips and candy. Second, eat less carbs, like pasta and bread, and add more vegetables and fruits to your daily intake. Finally, eat as much food as you want in your first helping, but ____________________ only that, and ____________________ for another meal. Exercise is also important for burning calories and fat. Whether it's swimming or jogging, do something that makes you move and ____________________ ____________________. To build your muscles, try some basic yoga exercises or biking. Yoga is easy to do in your own home, and there are free videos on the Internet.

01 다음을 듣고, 남자가 하는 말의 목적으로 가장 적절한 것을 고르시오.

① 응급조치 요령을 가르쳐 주려고
② 진료 시간 변경에 대해 알려 주려고
③ 현재 진료 가능한 다른 병원을 알려 주려고
④ 병원으로 전화한 사람들에게 안내해 주려고
⑤ 인터넷으로 진료 예약하는 방법을 안내하려고

02 대화를 듣고, 여자의 의견으로 가장 적절한 것을 고르시오.

① 아침 식사를 거르지 말아야 한다.
② 식사 사이에 간식을 챙겨 먹는 것이 좋다.
③ 체중 감량 시 식이요법과 운동을 병행해야 한다.
④ 건강을 위해 적당한 수면 시간을 유지해야 한다.
⑤ 과식을 방지하려면 공복을 느끼기 전에 먹어야 한다.

03 대화를 듣고, 두 사람의 관계를 가장 잘 나타낸 것을 고르시오.

① 컴퓨터 강사 – 수강생
② 로봇 공학 교수 – 지도 학생
③ 서점 직원 – 손님
④ 신문 기자 – 로봇 공학자
⑤ 도서관 직원 – 도서관 이용자

04 대화를 듣고, 그림에서 대화의 내용과 일치하지 않는 것을 고르시오.

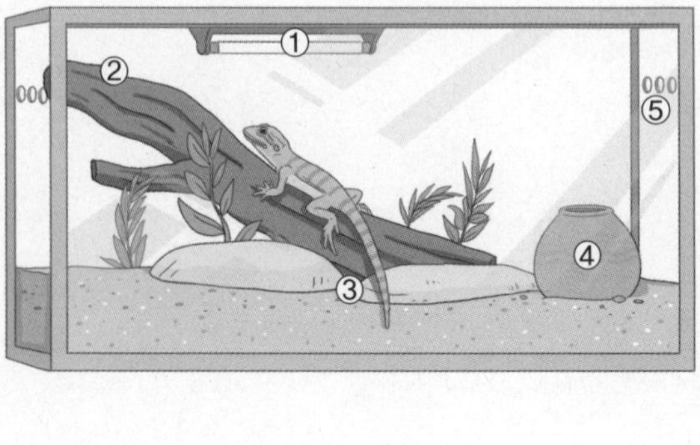

05 대화를 듣고, 여자가 대화 후에 바로 할 일로 가장 적절한 것을 고르시오.

① 산책하러 가기
② 남편에게 전화하기
③ 준호의 집 방문하기
④ 아들의 학교에 찾아가기
⑤ 준호에게 무언가를 사 주기

06 대화를 듣고, 여자가 지불할 금액을 고르시오. [3점]

① $144 ② $176 ③ $180
④ $206 ⑤ $210

07 대화를 듣고, 남자가 잠이 들지 못하는 이유를 고르시오.

① 낮잠을 오래 자서
② 걱정거리가 있어서
③ 바깥의 소음이 심해서
④ 시험공부를 해야 해서
⑤ 커피를 너무 많이 마셔서

08 대화를 듣고, 고전 독서가 주는 이점에 관해 언급되지 않은 것을 고르시오.

① 상상력 발달 ② 교훈 습득
③ 어휘력 발달 ④ 정서 함양
⑤ 역사 소개

09 Unity-For-All 인턴직에 관한 다음 내용을 듣고, 일치하지 않는 것을 고르시오.

① 뉴욕 본부에서 일하게 된다.
② 7월 1일에 시작하며 6주 과정이다.
③ 18세가 넘으면 누구나 신청할 수 있다.
④ 지원 마감일은 2026년 4월 30일이다.
⑤ 지원서는 웹사이트에서 내려받을 수 있다.

10 다음 표를 보면서 대화를 듣고, 두 사람이 볼 영화를 고르시오.

Roger Robertson's Movie Guide!				
	Movie Title	Genre	Reviewer's Comments	Stars
①	About Melissa	Romantic Comedy	Daniel Lee is miscast Great actor, but wrong role	★★
②	AvaAva World	Science Fiction	Computer generated graphics look real	★★★★★
③	Shot'em up!	Action	Typical action movie, but good acting	★★★
④	The Line Up	Thriller	Great story	★★★
⑤	Robot Rulers	Science Fiction	Great story	★★

11 대화를 듣고, 남자의 마지막 말에 대한 여자의 응답으로 가장 적절한 것을 고르시오.

① They don't fit my body.
② This jacket looks great!
③ The large size is too tight.
④ No problem. That'll be $75.
⑤ Sure. Just wait for a moment.

12 대화를 듣고, 여자의 마지막 말에 대한 남자의 응답으로 가장 적절한 것을 고르시오.

① Two of us are enough.
② I'll start by writing a script.
③ I have a few people in mind.
④ My parents will come to see it.
⑤ Not every school play is interesting.

13 대화를 듣고, 남자의 마지막 말에 대한 여자의 응답으로 가장 적절한 것을 고르시오.

▶ Woman : ______________________

① My sister is having a baby soon.
② I think so, too. We should get married.
③ I will talk to her if you would like me to.
④ I wish I had a brother instead of just a sister.
⑤ Your girlfriend is really beautiful and smart.

14 대화를 듣고, 여자의 마지막 말에 대한 남자의 응답으로 가장 적절한 것을 고르시오. [3점]

▶ Man : ______________________

① That's a really strange thing to do.
② I'll let her use my cell phone next time.
③ Don't use your cell phone in the car, dear.
④ I can't understand why she's so irresponsible.
⑤ Maybe she's more responsible than you think.

15 다음 상황 설명을 듣고 Mr. Collins가 Sue에게 할 말로 가장 적절한 것을 고르시오. [3점]

▶ Mr. Collins : ______________________

① Why don't you request maternity leave, then?
② The project has finally been completed thanks to you.
③ Congratulations! I'm sure you'll be a good mother.
④ Working mothers badly need help from their husbands.
⑤ Extra manpower will lessen your team members' workload.

[16~17] 대화를 듣고, 물음에 답하시오.

16 남자가 하는 말의 주제로 가장 적절한 것은?

① disadvantages of living in a small room
② how to make a small space more livable
③ the necessity of cleaning a house regularly
④ ways of arranging furniture for a small room
⑤ effects of exposure to natural light in a room

17 언급된 물품이 아닌 것은?

① table ② sofa ③ mirror
④ curtain ⑤ bookshelf

09 Sense Up 듣기 모의고사 DICTATION

01

M: Thank you for calling the Collingwood Clinic. ______________________ right now. Our regular hours of operation are from 8 a.m. to 5 p.m. Monday through Friday. We are also open on Saturday from 10 a.m. to 3 p.m. If you are calling to make an appointment, please ______________________, and we will call you back during business hours to confirm it. If this is an emergency, please call 911 or the doctor hotline at 1-800-555-4321. A doctor ______________________ and advise you what to do in an emergency.

02

M: Hey, Kate, do you want to get something to eat?

W: I think I'll wait to have lunch. It's still early.

M: I guess so. I didn't have breakfast so I'm really hungry.

W: Why didn't you have breakfast?

M: I was tired this morning, so I ______________________.

W: I never do that. It only takes a few minutes to have some cereal, and that gives me the energy I need for the morning.

M: Well, I'm ______________________, also.

W: Then you might be surprised to learn that those who skip breakfast ______________________ than those who don't.

M: I didn't know that. Maybe I should start eating breakfast again.

03

W: Good morning. It's raining a lot. There's an umbrella stand next to the door.

M: Great. I didn't want to ______________________. Thank you.

W: Sure. How can I help you?

M: I'm doing a research paper on robotics.

W: Is there a particular book you're looking for?

M: Not really. I just need all the information I can get.

W: ______________________ our research database? You can look for specific topics by logging into our online database.

M: That's convenient. ______________________ the material? Actually, I'm not a student at this university.

W: Of course. You can create an account here. Fill out this form, please.

M: Thanks. I'd also like to check out some reference books.

W: I'm afraid you're ______________________. You can only make copies. We have some printers connected to the computers.

M: Oh, I see.

04

W: Chris, this must be the cage of the lizard you're raising.

M: Yes, I arranged everything in his house, too.

W: That's amazing. ______________________ of his house.

M: It's an ultraviolet lamp. They need this kind of lighting to be healthy.

W: It looks like you placed a big tree branch inside. Is there a particular reason why?

M: Lizards like ______________________. Look, the lizard is moving now.

W: Oh, I see. You put two flat rocks under the branch.

M: Yes, I put rocks and leaves so it looks like his natural environment.

W: Good. Is the large dish of water for the lizard to drink?

M: That's right. Can you see those holes on the side walls? They're for ventilation.

W: Wow, ______________________ on it!

05

M: Mom... I know why you're angry, but please understand.

W: Your teacher called and then Junho's mom called. She ________________________________ her house and talk. Tell me exactly what happened.
M: Junho and his friend ______________________ ______________, calling me names like 'pig boy.'
W: You should ______________________________ __________________!
M: I couldn't.
W: I should phone your father. Then you'd really ______________________.
M: I know.
W: You know I have to go to school tomorrow to talk to the teacher.
M: I'm sorry.
W: Well, stay here while I talk to Junho's mom.

06

M: How can I help you?
W: How much is this carry-on bag?
M: It's $190. It weighs just 4 pounds, which is light.
W: Well, it's ________________________________. Do you have a cheaper one?
M: Hmm, how about this rolling backpack? It's $30 cheaper than the carry-on. You can roll it or wear it on your back.
W: That looks convenient. I'll take it.
M: ________________________________; black, charcoal, and berry. Which one do you want?
M: I'd like berry. Do you have a travel pillow?
M: Sure. How about this one? It's a neck pillow and __________________ the bus or plane.
W: Let me see. The price tag says 20 dollars.
M: ________________________________. It's 20 percent off. What do you say?
W: Great. I'll take it. Here's my card.

07

M: Hi, Mom.
W: Daniel, why are you still awake? It's 3 a.m.
M: I couldn't get to sleep.
W: What's the reason? I thought you went to bed around 11.
M: I did. I got into bed, closed my eyes, and ________ __________________, but I couldn't.
W: Hmm.... Normally, you don't have any difficulty sleeping. Did you take a nap today?
M: I wished I could, but ______________________ ______________ for tomorrow's test all afternoon.
W: You should be tired then. Are you worried about something?
M: No, but I guess I did drink a lot of coffee today.
W: Well, that's probably the reason! Too much caffeine disrupts sleep.
M: I know, but I needed ______________________ ________________ without feeling sleepy.
W: Even so, you shouldn't drink caffeine late in the day. Now you'll be even more tired tomorrow.
M: You're right. I'll be careful.

08

W: Hi, Vance!
M: Vanessa? I didn't know you shopped at this bookstore.
W: Actually, I'm here to pick up a book for my son, Tom.
M: *Greek and Roman Mythology*? That's fairly advanced for an elementary schooler.
W: This book contains easier versions of the classics. It's ________________________________ __________________.
M: I see. So, do you think young children understand the lessons the classics teach?
W: Even if they don't completely understand, they definitely learn that ______________________ ______________________.
M: But isn't the vocabulary too difficult for a young reader?
W: There are some challenging words, but that helps the child learn.
M: I still don't see ______________________ ________________ for children than other books.
W: Well, classical literature has one more benefit. It introduces history to children. It's very educational.
M: You have a point. I think I'll buy a copy for my daughter as well.

09

W: Unity-For-All is a non-profit organization providing ______________________________ all over the world. We are now hiring students for the summer 2026 internship program at our New York headquarters. The internship program will start on July 1st and will last for six weeks. Those who are applying for the internship position ______________________________ in a university and must be over 18 years of age. Interns ______________________________ full-time employees in their day-to-day activities. The deadline to apply for the summer 2026 internship position is April 30, 2026. Please note that ______________________________ after the deadline. You may download the application by visiting our website at www.unityforall.org.

10

M: Let's go see the movie that's Roger Robertson's top pick.

W: He's the movie critic for the Sun Times, right?

M: Yeah, I usually love his top picks. Let's go and see *AvaAva World* this weekend. He gave it five stars.

W: John, I ______________________________. I don't want to see a science fiction flick!

M: OK. No science fiction.

W: Hey, *About Melissa* is playing. Sandra said it was great. You like Daniel Lee, don't you?

M: I don't mind him. But Roger only gave the movie two stars. I'm not seeing a two star movie. I trust Roger!

W: Hmm.... It's a tough choice then.

M: You choose. But you know I like action movies.

W: I know. But ______________________________ something that has a great story?

M: OK. ______________________________. I'll check the show times.

11

M: Excuse me. Do you have this jacket in a larger size?

W: Yes, I'll bring you one. ______________________________?

M: Either a large or an extra large. ______________________________?

12

W: I'm not sure what to do for the talent show. Do you have any ideas?

M: We should ______________________________, but we'll need more people.

W: Great idea. Can you think of anyone else ______________________________?

13

W: What's wrong, Brian?

M: My girlfriend ______________________________.

W: Why? What happened?

M: Well, she doesn't like the fact that you and I are such good friends.

W: Oh, she's ______________________________?

M: Yes, which is strange because you are like a sister to me.

W: And I think of you as a brother. Did you explain that to her?

M: I tried to. I told her that we have been friends since we were babies.

W: What did she say?

M: She said that we sounded like a match made in heaven! ______________________________ that she has the wrong idea about us?

14

W: Hi, everyone, I'm home.

M: Hi, honey.

W: Where's Jennifer?

M: She ______________________. I thought you knew where she is.

W: No, I don't.

M: Well, it's only 8:30.

W: She ______________________ without telling us. She doesn't have a cell phone anymore.

M: Just buy her a new one.

W: She's too careless. Her last cell phone was only one week old and she lost it.

M: Maybe she's with Julie. Phone Julie's mom.

W: Oh! I ______________________ ______________. It's from Jennifer. She sent a message with Julie's cell phone.

M: Where is she?

W: Studying at Julie's house. And she also tried to call when I was driving.

15

W: Sue is an employee at a large company, and she is expecting a baby in five months. After going to human resources ______________________ ______________, she returns to her desk. As the day passes, she begins to worry about what will happen to her project because it is important to the company. Because she is the director, she worries that ______________ ______________________ to her teammates. On a break, she discusses this anxiety with Mr. Collins, her immediate supervisor. Mr. Collins listens carefully because he understands that Sue ______________________________ her teammates. He wants to reassure Sue and relieve her worries. In this situation, what would Mr. Collins most likely say to Sue?

16-17

M: Small rooms are a reality for a lot of people. But just because you live in a small space it doesn't mean you have to feel uncomfortable. With a little organization and proper decorating, you can escape some of your frustration. First, make sure everything actually stays in its place. Keep small items like remote controls in storage baskets, and don't allow things like newspapers and books ______________ ______________. Also, just because your space is small, don't shy away from big furniture. ________ ______________________ in the middle of the room and keep the rest of the room simple. A lot of small furniture can make a room feel cluttered. Use a single color for the wall and use other colors for accents. Another important element is the mirror. Mirrors are ______________________ and creating the illusion of more space. Placing a large mirror near or across from a window is always effective. The natural light will make the room feel bigger and brighter. Hang curtains outside the window frame ______________________. By following these guidelines, living in small spaces doesn't have to be so uncomfortable.

01 다음을 듣고, 여자가 하는 말의 목적으로 가장 적절한 것을 고르시오.

① 개교 30주년 행사 참여를 부탁하려고
② 학교를 위한 기부금 모금을 독려하려고
③ 학부모 회의에 참석한 것에 감사하려고
④ 개교 30주년 기념 전시회를 안내하려고
⑤ 축제 준비를 위한 학부모 회의를 소집하려고

02 대화를 듣고, 남자의 의견으로 가장 적절한 것을 고르시오.

① 지구 온난화를 막는 방법을 실천해야 한다.
② 포장 재료를 재활용하는 것이 환경에 좋다.
③ 환경을 위해 과도한 상품 포장을 피해야 한다.
④ 고급 포장일수록 소비자의 눈길을 사로잡는다.
⑤ 쓰레기 매립지를 확보하는 것이 점점 어려워진다.

03 대화를 듣고, 두 사람의 관계를 가장 잘 나타낸 것을 고르시오.

① 패션 디자이너 – 모델
② 사진작가 – 배우
③ 의사 – 환자
④ 메이크업 아티스트 – 예비 신부
⑤ 신랑 – 신부

04 대화를 듣고, 그림에서 대화의 내용과 일치하지 않는 것을 고르시오.

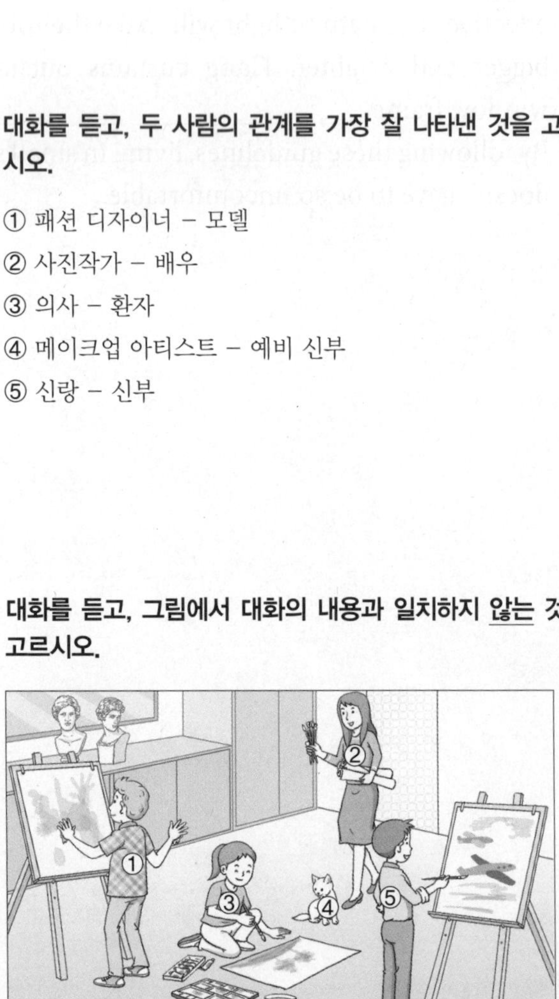

05 대화를 듣고, 여자가 할 일로 가장 적절한 것을 고르시오.

① 아이들 돌보기
② 피자 주문하기
③ 외출 준비하기
④ 결혼 선물 사기
⑤ 저녁 식사 준비하기

06 대화를 듣고, 남자가 지불할 금액을 고르시오. [3점]

① $264 ② $320 ③ $344
④ $480 ⑤ $504

07 대화를 듣고, 여자가 서울을 좋아하는 이유를 고르시오.

① 쇼핑하기 좋아서
② 치안이 안전해서
③ 야경이 훌륭해서
④ 대중교통이 편리해서
⑤ 아름다운 고궁이 있어서

08 대화를 듣고, 대학 선택의 기준에 관해 언급되지 않은 것을 고르시오.

① 전공 ② 전공 학과의 학교 순위
③ 수업료 ④ 위치
⑤ 장학금

09 The Royal Palace에 관한 다음 내용을 듣고, 일치하지 않는 것을 고르시오.

① 월요일에는 문을 열지 않는다.
② 오전 10시부터 오후 3시까지 문을 연다.
③ 7세 미만 아동은 입장료를 받지 않는다.
④ 안내원 해설을 원하면 미리 예약해야 한다.
⑤ 궁 안에 선물 가게가 있다.

정답 및 해설 p.38

10 다음 표를 보면서 대화를 듣고, 남자가 수강할 강의를 고르시오.

Edmund College Summer Courses				
Course	Department	Unit	Time	Semester
① A	psychology	3	Tue. & Fri.	1st semester
② B	business	4	Mon. & Wed.	2nd semester
③ C	fine arts	4	Tue. & Thurs.	1st semester
④ D	sociology	3	Tue. & Thurs.	2nd semester
⑤ E	arts	3	Mon. & Fri.	1st semester

11 대화를 듣고, 남자의 마지막 말에 대한 여자의 응답으로 가장 적절한 것을 고르시오.

① Don't try to take shortcuts. Just study hard.
② The bookstore is just next to the coffee shop.
③ Sure. Just let me know their titles and authors.
④ I'm anxious about the result of the examination.
⑤ That's right. You should develop a habit of reading.

12 대화를 듣고, 여자의 마지막 말에 대한 남자의 응답으로 가장 적절한 것을 고르시오.

① You should open a restaurant.
② The beef is so tender and juicy.
③ This was my mother's secret recipe.
④ This is the best grilled beef steak ever.
⑤ I'd love some but I'm really full, thanks.

13 대화를 듣고, 남자의 마지막 말에 대한 여자의 응답으로 가장 적절한 것을 고르시오.

▶ Woman : ______________________

① That's okay. I don't want to interrupt you.
② No, that is not the question I'm asking you.
③ I don't want to bother you. I can take care of it.
④ Oh, please! I can't concentrate on the movie at all.
⑤ I'm not angry with you. I'm just angry with myself.

14 대화를 듣고, 여자의 마지막 말에 대한 남자의 응답으로 가장 적절한 것을 고르시오. [3점]

▶ Man : ______________________

① Don't worry. I'll screen your calls.
② OK. I'll help you prepare for the report.
③ Sorry. He's just gone out for a moment.
④ All right. I'll call again in the afternoon.
⑤ Hold on. Let me see whether he has arrived.

15 다음 상황 설명을 듣고, Jonathan이 Madison에게 할 말로 가장 적절한 것을 고르시오. [3점]

▶ Jonathan : Madison, ______________________

① I'm sorry my cats caused you so much trouble.
② I understand your situation, but I can't help you.
③ your cats are adorable. What are neighbors for?
④ then why don't you look into an animal shelter?
⑤ I can't find anyone to look after my cats. What should I do?

[16~17] 다음을 듣고, 물음에 답하시오.

16 남자가 하는 말의 주제로 가장 적절한 것은?

① educational uses of movies
② how to classify movie genres
③ various benefits of watching movies
④ movies as a source of entertainment
⑤ the growing popularity of documentaries

17 언급된 영화 장르가 아닌 것은?

① 공상과학 영화　② 모험 영화
③ 다큐멘터리　④ 판타지 영화
⑤ 역사 영화

10 Sense Up 듣기 모의고사 DICTATION

01

W: First of all, thank you so much for joining us today. We know it's not easy for parents ______________ ______________________________________ during the school week. As some of you may already know, Virgil High School will be celebrating its 30th anniversary ______________________________ through a variety of events and activities. We'll be holding a sports event that will have teachers and students competing with each other. Also, our school will set up a bazaar ______________ ____________________________ next month. All used items you donate to us will be part of our school yard sale. ______________________ ________________ of the parents to make our events a success!

02

W: Look at what I got from my sister! It's a box of premium brand cookies.

M: It's very impressive, but why do the cookies all need to be individually wrapped?

W: I think it's artistically done and pleasing to the eye.

M: That's true, but ________________________ the excessive packaging.

W: What do you mean?

M: It's terrible for our environment. In fact, ________ ________________________________ packing materials.

W: Oh, my. I had no idea it was so much.

M: Producing packaging uses up natural resources, energy, and water. And __________________________ ________________.

W: Oh, then we need to help manufacturers change their packaging habits.

M: Right! We can start by complaining and boycotting their products. Packaging is destroying our environment every day. It's a serious problem.

03

M: Now tilt your head backwards.

W: Sure.

M: I need to put on some more powder. Close your eyes. I don't want the powder ____________________ ________________.

W: Okay.

M: When does your wedding photo shoot start?

W: ______________________________ at two o'clock.

M: We need to hurry then. You still need to put on your wedding dress, so we don't have much time. Now, close your eyes.

W: Sure.

M: I'm going to put on a heavy eyeliner since you need to take photos.

W: Are you going to put on false eyelashes?

M: Yes. Just a moment. I need to add some touches to your eyes. Alright, you're all set. __________ ____________________________. What do you think?

W: I love it. It doesn't look like me.

04

W: Oh, Jack! I didn't expect to see you here. Are you here to participate in the art event?

M: Oh, hi, Miranda. My son has art lessons here, and ____________________________.

W: I see. My daughter has a lesson here once a week.

M: We can look at the kids through this big window here. Oh, look at my Daniel!

W: Oh, is he the boy __________________ ______________________ with his hands? He seems very creative.

M: He's quite naughty as you can see. I don't know why the teacher is letting him do that. She is just standing ________________________.

W: I'm sure it's because she wants to make a creative environment for the kids. My daughter, Anna, is painting on the floor over there.

M: Oh, there's a cat sitting on the floor watching her paint.

W: Look at the boy on the right. He's drawing an airplane. He draws very well.
M: He looks very artistic.

05

W: George! Back so soon! ____________________ the kids to the beach?
M: Yeah, they loved it.
W: Where are they now?
M: They're in the car. We're going to have pizza for dinner.
W: We're going out for pizza?
M: Not you. You're going to get dressed up and go out with Cathy and the girls.
W: But I can't! I ______________________________ ________________ the kids.
M: I'll take care of the kids. You go to dinner with Cathy tonight. Come on, her wedding is next week. She's your best friend. It's important.
W: Okay... if you insist....
M: I do! Now __________________________ before I change my mind!

06

M: We'd like to rent a car. How much is it for a day?
W: We have a sedan for only 60 dollars a day.
M: Wow, that's expensive! ____________________ ____________________?
W: A compact car is 30 dollars a day, and a standard-sized car is 40 dollars. We also have hybrid cars. As you know, hybrid cars have excellent gas mileage.
M: I'm not interested in hybrid cars. I think a compact will be too small because ____________________ ______________________________. I want a standard-sized.
W: Okay. How many days will you need the car for?
M: We'd like to rent it for 8 days. Do we need to buy insurance, too?
W: ____ ______________, but you can purchase extra coverage as well, if you'd like.
M: I want to purchase extra coverage.
W: It will cost you an extra 3 dollars per day. Can I see your driver's license?
M: Sure. Here you are.

07

M: It seems like ______________________________ ______________.
W: Not really. But I'd like to travel more.
M: So, how do you like Seoul?
W: I completely love it! I've only been here for two weeks, but I don't want to leave.
M: What do you like best? Do you like __________ ____________________________?
W: Well, no. But I was surprised lots of people shop on the streets till late at night. In American big cities, getting around at night can be scary sometimes.
M: What do you mean?
W: ____________________________, and there are a lot of scary people and violence.
M: Oh, that's right.
W: But here in Seoul, I don't feel any of that! I feel completely safe here, and not at all nervous! That's why I like Seoul.
M: That's wonderful to hear. I'm so glad that you're happy here. Seoul also has beautiful ancient palaces.
W: Yes, I know.

08

M: I need your advice regarding some colleges, Ms. Johnson.
W: How can I help?
M: ______________________________, and I can't decide where I want to go.
W: First, you should think about ______________ ______________ and see which schools have the strongest department in that field. You wanted to major in math, right?
M: Initially, I did. But now I'd like to study economics.
W: Then let's see ______________________________ in that major. Also, consider the tuition.
M: I cannot attend a school whose tuition is over $10,000.
W: And the location? Do you have to be close to home?
M: ______________________, but I can't be too far. Since most of my family is in Virginia, I don't want to go to the west coast like LA or San Francisco.
W: Let's see. Well, it looks like you have your answer.
M: Thank you so much for your help.

09

M: We welcome you to The Royal Palace in Bangkok. The Royal Palace is open to the public from 10:00 a.m. to 3:00 p.m., Wednesday to Sunday. ______________ ______________________________ that are not open to the public. The entrance fee for adults is $12, and it's $7 for children over 7 years old. All children under the age of 7 ______________ ______________. We have guides for various languages including English, Chinese, and Korean. If you'd like a guide during your visit, please contact us in advance and make a reservation. ______________ ______________________. Make sure to stop by our gift shop. You can find it easily just outside the palace. There are souvenirs, postcards, and plenty of books on the palace.

10

M: I'm planning to register for a summer course.
W: What kind of course? Will it be a course for your business major?
M: No. I want to take something else. But I haven't decided what to take yet.
W: How many units ______________________________?
M: I'd like something that's 3 units. I need to work this summer, so ______________________.
W: When will you be working?
M: Monday and Wednesday, from 9 a.m. to 3 p.m.
W: It looks like you'll be very busy. ______________ ______________________________. Which one will you take?
M: What are the dates for the two semesters?
W: The first semester begins on May 19 and ends June 26. The second semester begins on June 29 and ends August 7.
M: I'm planning to travel in July, so ______________ ______________________.
W: I guess this course is the one for you.
M: You're right. It seems like I don't have a choice.

11

M: Mom, I have a final exam next week. I'm very busy.
W: But ______________________________. You look tired. Your dad and I are going shopping. Is there anything you need?
M: Yes, ______________________________ on Elm Street? I need some books for my sociology class.

12

W: ______________________________ the grilled beef steak with garlic herb butter?
M: It was absolutely delicious. I didn't know ______________ ______________________.
W: I'm glad you like it. Would you like a second helping?

13

M: Amber, sorry for interrupting, but do you know why the man is being chased?

W: It's because ______________________.

M: Really? I didn't know that. Who did he murder and why?

W: Actually, he didn't. Didn't you see that?

M: No, I didn't. It's not easy to understand. Uh... what's the short man's role? Is he a spy?

W: What are you talking about? There isn't a spy in this movie.

M: Oh, I mean the short man ______________ ______________.

W: He is just an extra. Nobody! Please stop asking questions.

M: Okay. I thought ______________________ ______________ in this movie. I have one more question. Why did that man's brother get angry?

14

M: Good morning, Linda! How was your weekend?

W: Not bad. How about you?

M: Great. I went hiking near White Mountain.

W: Sounds great. By the way, are you busy right now?

M: Yeah. ______________________ from our customers. And I should copy all these papers, too.

W: ______________________, doesn't it?

M: It sure does. Oh, Mr. Reed of MT Company just called and wanted you to call him back.

W: All right. I'll call him later. Seth, I need to finish up this report by 11. And I have to prepare a presentation. ______________________ ______________.

M: I see. You're terribly busy, too.

W: No kidding. ______________________ ______________, please. If someone calls, tell him or her I stepped out of the office. OK?

15

W: Madison is planning to visit France and Italy for a month this summer. But she doesn't know what to do about her two cats. She obviously can't take them on her trip. So, she calls her friends ______ ______________________ who will look after her cats, but to no avail. Some of her friends ______________________, and some are taking off for vacations at the same time too. Then she runs into her neighbor, Jonathan, and tells him about her situation. Jonathan volunteers to look after her cats for a month. Madison ____________ ______________________ for this kind offer. Afterward, what would Jonathan most likely say to Madison in return?

16-17

M: Movies are enjoyed and loved by all, and they have the ability to influence our lives. While movies offer great entertainment, they are also very useful for enhancing an individual's mental health. They ______________________________ and momentarily forget about their daily concerns and problems. Through watching a science-fiction movie or an adventure film, a person __________ ______________________________ by becoming absorbed in the characters in the movie. Movies are also highly informative, especially the ones that ______________________ ______________. When you watch another person's life in a movie, you get more information concerning the current world we are living in. Documentaries also ______________________ ______________, and they are generally very interesting to watch. Historical films offer vital data about how life was in the past. Watching historical movies can help you get more data concerning historical events, like the Civil War or World War 1 or 2. Through watching educational movies, individuals can also expand their vocabulary and further enhance their knowledge.

11 Sense Up 듣기 모의고사

01 **다음을 듣고, 남자가 하는 말의 목적으로 가장 적절한 것을 고르시오.**

① 환경단체 가입을 권유하려고
② 친환경 제품의 사용을 권장하려고
③ 회사 비품의 재활용을 독려하려고
④ 건전지 사용을 줄일 것을 당부하려고
⑤ 폐건전지 처리 방법에 대해 공지하려고

02 **대화를 듣고, 여자의 의견으로 가장 적절한 것을 고르시오.**

① 대중가요의 소재가 더욱 다양해져야 한다.
② 대중가요는 아이들이 듣기에 적절하지 않다.
③ 어린이를 위한 동요가 많이 만들어져야 한다.
④ TV 광고 음악은 신중하게 고를 필요가 있다.
⑤ 노래 가사에 비속어를 쓰지 못하도록 해야 한다.

03 **대화를 듣고, 두 사람의 관계를 가장 잘 나타낸 것을 고르시오.**

① 반려견 주인 - 동물 조련사
② 떠돌이 개 보호자 - 수의사
③ 자원 봉사자 - 동물 보호소 직원
④ 동물 프로그램 제작자 - 출연자
⑤ 떠돌이 개 구조자 - 경찰관

04 **대화를 듣고, 그림에서 대화의 내용과 일치하지 <u>않는</u> 것을 고르시오.**

05 **대화를 듣고, 남자가 여자를 위해 할 일로 가장 적절한 것을 고르시오.**

① 귀걸이 새로 사 주기
② 함께 수업에 참여하기
③ 여자에게 빚진 것 갚기
④ 게시판에 분실물 올리기
⑤ 잃어버린 귀걸이 찾아 주기

06 **대화를 듣고, 남자가 지불할 금액을 고르시오. [3점]**

① $20　② $36　③ $46
④ $56　⑤ $76

07 **대화를 듣고, 여자가 저녁 식사 초대를 거절한 이유를 고르시오.**

① 몸이 좋지 않아서
② 이미 저녁을 먹어서
③ 체중 감량 중이어서
④ 어머니와 함께 병원에 가야 해서
⑤ 건강검진을 앞두고 금식해야 해서

08 **다음을 듣고, 허블 망원경(Hubble Space Telescope)에 관해 언급되지 않은 것을 고르시오.**

① 발사 연도　② 크기
③ 무게　④ 제작 기간
⑤ 폐기 계획

09 **마야의 피라미드에 관한 다음 내용을 듣고, 일치하지 <u>않는</u> 것을 고르시오.**

① 가장 오래된 것은 거의 3천 년 전에 지어졌다.
② 최고 높이가 60미터이다.
③ 계단이 가파르고 꼭대기가 평평하다.
④ 일부는 종교의식에 사용되었다.
⑤ 신에게 경의를 표하기 위해 지어지기도 했다.

10 다음 표를 보면서 대화를 듣고, 여자가 구입할 반죽기를 고르시오.

Hillcrest Electric Mixers				
Model	Price	Cordless	Color	Warranty (in years)
① A	$78	○	Black	2
② B	$65	○	White	1
③ C	$62	○	Silver	2
④ D	$59	○	Black	1
⑤ E	$57	×	Silver	2

11 대화를 듣고, 여자의 마지막 말에 대한 남자의 응답으로 가장 적절한 것을 고르시오.

① That's a beautiful shirt.
② It won't cost too much.
③ They can't remove the stain.
④ There's one behind the supermarket.
⑤ You should have been more careful.

12 대화를 듣고, 남자의 마지막 말에 대한 여자의 응답으로 가장 적절한 것을 고르시오.

① I'm more than happy to help you out.
② Call me when you're ready to pick it up.
③ I'll be gone before the end of the month.
④ My new apartment won't be far from here.
⑤ The washing machine is only two years old.

13 대화를 듣고, 여자의 마지막 말에 대한 남자의 응답으로 가장 적절한 것을 고르시오. [3점]

▶ Man : ______________________

① Maybe you should switch to the piano.
② Learning on your own is the best way.
③ I can sign you up for beginner's lessons.
④ Sorry, I don't know how to play the guitar.
⑤ You should practice more to get a good grade.

14 대화를 듣고, 남자의 마지막 말에 대한 여자의 응답으로 가장 적절한 것을 고르시오.

▶ Woman : ______________________

① See, you shouldn't jump to conclusions.
② He must ask before he borrows things.
③ I'm really sorry for accusing you.
④ Jacob shouldn't have put it there.
⑤ Where have you found it?

15 다음 상황 설명을 듣고, Simon이 옆 테이블에 앉은 부부에게 할 말로 가장 적절한 것을 고르시오. [3점]

▶ Simon : ______________________

① Let me help my son finish his meal first.
② Please tell your kids to behave themselves.
③ Please stop your children from asking questions.
④ I may need to interrupt. What was your question?
⑤ Have your kids be seated. The show is going to start.

[16~17] 다음을 듣고, 물음에 답하시오.

16 남자가 하는 말의 주제로 가장 적절한 것은?

① tips for selecting proper sports activities
② how to prevent possible training injuries
③ understanding the advantages of exercise
④ age limits for participating in sports activities
⑤ the importance of warming up before playing sports

17 언급된 스포츠가 <u>아닌</u> 것은?

① 장거리 달리기
② 테니스
③ 골프
④ 야구
⑤ 볼링

11 Sense Up 듣기 모의고사 DICTATION

01

M: Unfortunately, many of the devices at this company ______________________ that eventually end up in landfills. Experts say that discarding used batteries in this way may have potentially harmful effects on the environment. This is because batteries contain heavy metals and various toxic chemicals ______________, underground water supplies, and the sea. For this reason, we will begin collecting our used batteries for recycling. A box for used batteries will be set up in the supply room. When you have batteries ______________________, simply place them in the box. When the box is full, ______ ______________________ a recycling center. Please remember to do this for the environment.

02

W: Hi, John. What's up?

M: Hi, Marie, I'm trying to find some songs Amy would like.

W: Ah, your brother's daughter. That's nice. How old is she now?

M: She's turning 7 next week. ______________ ________ her birthday party. Good idea, right?

W: Hmm.... I don't think so. Many pop songs have adult themes.

M: Marie, I wouldn't pick anything advocating violence, ______________________.

W: Of course, but love songs are also aimed at a mature audience.

M: That's true. How about Chris Black's new song? The one in the cola advertisement.

W: ______________________, but I remember there's a lot of slang in that song. She could pick up some bad speaking habits.

M: Good point. Then children's songs are my only choice.

W: That's an idea.

03

M: Hello, I called you an hour ago. I'm Steve Dale.

W: Hi, Mr. Dale. ______________________ the examining table? What happened? He's limping.

M: Yes, he can't walk and he's hardly eating.

W: Is he your dog or a stray dog?

M: He's a stray dog ______________________.

W: He looks much thinner than dogs should be at his age.

M: Yes, I'm really worried about it.

W: Do you know ______________________?

M: No, but I saw a hole in the yard this morning. He might have gotten his leg caught in that.

W: Hmm, I should take an X-ray. Could you bring him this way?

M: Sure. Do you think he'll be okay?

W: Well, just ______________________, I think he needs a cast.

M: Oh, no! That's too bad.

W: Can you hold his leg here?

M: Okay.

04

W: What do you think, Grandpa?

M: You decorated the living room for Christmas! It looks nice!

W: Yes, finally. Do you like the banner that says "Merry Christmas" on the wall?

M: It's great! Where did you get that candle ________ ______________________?

W: Actually, I got that from one of the old boxes in storage.

M: Oh, look at those cute socks hanging from the fireplace. They're wonderful!

W: I made the flower-patterned one in the middle, and Mom made the other two.

M: Wow! You did excellent work. And what are those on the floor?

W: Those are presents for you, Grandpa! They're a secret. You're ______________________ until Christmas Eve.

M: I know. Don't worry. I won't. By the way, did you

use the big star I gave to you the other day?

W: Of course. I ______________________ the Christmas tree on the right side of the fireplace.

M: Oh, I found it. I think it's a perfect match with the tree!

05

M: Why are you ______________________ when you should be in class, Mary?

W: One of my earrings fell out and is lost in this thick carpet.

M: That's terrible. Is it expensive?

W: It has a diamond in it and ______________________.

M: She'll be really upset if you lose it.

W: Yes, especially since I didn't ask her permission to wear them.

M: Well, you ______________________ if you miss class too. I'll look for it while you are in class.

W: That would be really great. I ______________________.

M: Anything to keep you from getting grounded twice!

06

M: I found these rolls of film in a desk drawer and I want to ______________________.

W: We don't develop film here anymore. We will ______________________.

M: That's fine. I'm not really in a hurry. I'm just curious to know ______________________.

W: It will take about 5 days and there is a processing fee plus a fee per photo.

M: And how much is that?

W: For each roll, it is $10 for processing plus $1 for each picture.

M: Well, there are 12 pictures on this roll and 24 on the other.

W: Yes, that will be $36 ______________________. And then you have to add the processing fee.

M: Wow, for two rolls... that's expensive.

07

M: Nadia, did you hear that ______________________ dinner together to celebrate the end of the semester?

W: What a great idea! Where are you going?

M: We're meeting tonight at O'Sullivan's. You should come!

W: I'm afraid I can't, but thanks for inviting me.

M: This isn't because of your diet, is it?

W: Of course not! It's just that I have to go to the hospital tonight.

M: Oh? ______________________ your recent medical checkup?

W: No. My mother isn't feeling well, and she ______________________ her to the hospital tonight. I already promised.

M: That is important. I hope she feels better soon.

W: Thanks, and maybe we can have dinner together soon.

M: ______________________.

08

W: The Hubble Space Telescope is surely the most successful space telescope of all time. Launched in 1990 from the space shuttle Discovery, the telescope ______________________ of a doubledecker bus — 13 m long, 4 m across, and weighing 11,000 kg. It has a 2.4-meter-wide mirror, several cameras, and electronic detectors ______________________. Hubble's power lies in the fact that it is ______________________ — so its photographs are not distorted. Now that the telescope is getting old, its fate is uncertain. ______________________ for the last time, and NASA will soon end its program. At this time, NASA may crash it safely into the ocean or recover it for future study.

09

M: The ancient Mayan pyramids of Mexico and Central America ______________________ each year. The oldest of these structures was completed nearly 3,000 years ago. Without modern tools, the Mayans ______________________ pyramids that are over 60 meters tall. All of the pyramids have steep steps and a flat top. Some were used for religious ceremonies, and priests would stand on top where everyone could see them. Others ______________________ gods, and their steps were not to be used. Because they look so similar, even experts ______________________ ______________________ what a particular Mayan pyramid was used for.

10

W: Jack, I'm looking for an electric mixer. I need to get one for my baking class.

M: You have a catalog. There are ______________________ ____________.

W: I know! I think the Hillcrest mixers are pretty reputable. But they have so many models.

M: First of all, how much are you willing to spend?

W: No more than 70 dollars. I think I can find ______________________.

M: I think you're right. You can buy something mid-range for that price. Would you like a cordless one?

W: I think that would come in very handy.

M: Well, that ______________________ a bit. Is there a particular color you'd like?

W: I don't want anything that's dark, so a brighter option is better.

M: Okay. You'll pay a little more but I think it'll ______ ______________________. Well, it looks like you have two choices left.

W: I need more than a one-year warranty so I'll go for this one.

M: Good. That mixer fulfills all of your requirements.

11

W: Do you see this stain? I spilled grape juice all over this shirt!

M: Oh, isn't that your favorite shirt? ____________ ______________________ to a laundry.

W: I think I have to. Do you know ______________ ______________________________?

12

M: The house that I'm moving into doesn't have a washing machine.

W: Instead of buying one, ______________________ ______________________? I won't need it after I move out.

M: ______________________________. When are you moving out?

13

W: I bought a guitar last week, but I still can't play it.

M: Well, ______________________________ really good at an instrument.

W: I don't have years! I'm entering the talent show at my school in two months!

M: It sounds like you need some intensive lessons and a lot of practice.

W: When I asked my friend what was ____________ ______________________________, he said the guitar!

M: For some people, it is easy. For me, it was very hard, but ______________________________.

W: If I practice very hard, how good can I get in two months?

M: Well, the more you practice, ______________ ______________________.

W: I'll practice really hard if you let me take lessons from you.

14

M: Cathy, have you seen my new red pen?

W: No, I haven't seen it.

M: I'm sure I left it on my desk. Jacob ________ ____________________.

W: Huh? Why do you say that?

M: He was telling me how much he liked it. But he shouldn't take it ____________________.

W: Hold on. You don't know he took it.

M: Look, it was on my desk and it's not there now. And he ____________________________ today.

W: You're not ________________. Have you looked carefully for it?

M: Yeah. But, hmm, let me see. Oh, here it is.

W: Where was it?

M: __________________________________ and into my bag.

15

W: Simon ______________________ at a restaurant with his son James. At the next table a couple have just finished dinner and are having a serious conversation. When Simon starts eating, two boys start running around the restaurant and making noises. Other people in the restaurant ________________________________. One of the boys calls "Mom." The woman at the next table answers, but does nothing to stop the kids from interrupting others who are still eating. Simon believes ______________________________ ______________ in public places, and he doesn't want his son to follow the other boys' example. He ____ to the couple at the next table. In this situation, what would Simon most likely say to the couple?

16-17

M: Thinking of starting a new physical activity program? If so, you ______________________ of a training injury. Training injury can happen ______________________________ too much physical activity too quickly. So before starting a new physical activity, find out what can cause injury and how to safely increase your activity level. First, a training injury typically ________ ____________________________. For example, among the most common factors causing injury in long distance runners and tennis players are training errors. Going too fast, exercising for too long, or simply doing ____________________ ____________________________ can lead to a training injury. Wrong technique can also damage your body. If you use poor form as you do training exercises, for example, swinging a golf club or throwing a baseball, it can cause a training injury. Although a training injury can happen to anyone, you ________________________________ if you have certain medical conditions. Training injuries are also more likely to occur as you get older. For these reasons, it's a good idea to talk to your doctor before starting a new activity. Your doctor may offer tips to ______________ ______________________________ for you.

01 다음을 듣고, 여자가 하는 말의 목적으로 가장 적절한 것을 고르시오.

① 약물 남용에 대해서 경고하려고
② 공부를 잘하는 방법을 소개하려고
③ 긍정적 사고방식을 갖도록 격려하려고
④ 질병을 이기는 현명한 방법을 알리려고
⑤ 인간의 심리에 대한 연구 기금을 모금하려고

02 대화를 듣고, 두 사람이 하는 말의 주제로 가장 적절한 것을 고르시오.

① 자취 생활의 장단점
② 룸메이트와 잘 지내는 요령
③ 중고 물품 거래 시 유의사항
④ 대학교 기숙사 확충의 필요성
⑤ 대학생의 자취 생활비를 줄이는 방법

03 대화를 듣고, 두 사람의 관계를 가장 잘 나타낸 것을 고르시오.

① 지원자 – 지원자
② 면접관 – 지원자
③ 입학 사정관 – 학생
④ 관리자 – 종업원
⑤ 교수 – 학생

04 대화를 듣고, 그림에서 대화의 내용과 일치하지 않는 것을 고르시오.

05 대화를 듣고, 여자가 남자에게 부탁한 일로 가장 적절한 것을 고르시오.

① 여자를 괴롭히지 않기
② 모기 방지 크림 구해 주기
③ 여자에게 친구 소개해 주기
④ 여자의 방에서 모기 없애 주기
⑤ 여자를 대신해 친구에게 부탁하기

06 대화를 듣고, 남자가 지불할 금액을 고르시오. [3점]

① $52 ② $55 ③ $62
④ $67 ⑤ $70

07 대화를 듣고, 여자가 영화 시사회에 참석할 수 없는 이유를 고르시오.

① 출장을 가야 해서
② 표를 구하지 못해서
③ 영화에 출연해야 해서
④ 시사회 장소가 너무 멀어서
⑤ 다른 시사회에 가기로 해서

08 대화를 듣고, 면접에서 유의해야 할 사항으로 언급되지 않은 것을 고르시오.

① 표정 ② 시선 처리 ③ 목소리
④ 복장 ⑤ 시간 엄수

09 아이스크림 막대기로 만든 배에 관한 다음 내용을 듣고, 일치하지 않는 것을 고르시오.

① 만든 사람의 직업은 스턴트맨이다.
② 전체 길이는 15미터에 달한다.
③ 배의 첫 출발지는 영국이다.
④ 항해 중 아이슬란드를 방문할 것이다.
⑤ 어린이들이 배 제작에 참여했다.

정답 및 해설 p.46

10 다음 표를 보면서 대화를 듣고, 여자가 선택한 자원봉사 프로그램을 고르시오.

Hope Project Abroad

Country	Required Language	Duration of Project	Type of Work	Date of Departure
① Senegal	French	3 months	well digging	June 3
② Bolivia	Spanish	2 months	child education	July 1
③ Ecuador	Spanish	1 month	child education	June 17
④ Paraguay	Spanish	3 months	building homes	June 12
⑤ Peru	Spanish	1 month	building homes	July 19

11 대화를 듣고, 남자의 마지막 말에 대한 여자의 응답으로 가장 적절한 것을 고르시오.

① It's not far. Let's walk.
② I had a really small lunch.
③ I'm too tired to eat out tonight.
④ I could eat sandwiches every day.
⑤ Your roast-beef sandwiches are the best.

12 대화를 듣고, 여자의 마지막 말에 대한 남자의 응답으로 가장 적절한 것을 고르시오.

① I did, but nothing's changed.
② His friends really bother me.
③ It's definitely against the rules.
④ I enjoy having all-night parties.
⑤ He hasn't said anything about it.

13 대화를 듣고, 남자의 마지막 말에 대한 여자의 응답으로 가장 적절한 것을 고르시오. [3점]

▶ Woman : ______________________

① Comic books are really good holiday reading.
② You should have everything packed by now.
③ I have to choose my books first.
④ Let's find the ones I suggested, OK?
⑤ Think about it. I have to go pay for these.

14 대화를 듣고, 여자의 마지막 말에 대한 남자의 응답으로 가장 적절한 것을 고르시오. [3점]

▶ Man : ______________________

① No problem. Your role is not really important.
② You did a great job in *West Side Story*.
③ Time flies when you're having fun.
④ You can't go back on your word.
⑤ I'm sure he won't mind at all.

15 다음 상황 설명을 듣고, Diane이 Owen에게 할 말로 가장 적절한 것을 고르시오.

▶ Diane : ______________________

① Watch out, or you'll slip and fall.
② Sorry, it completely slipped my mind.
③ Of course. How can I be of assistance?
④ Please be more careful with my camera.
⑤ Good bye. I hope you have a great vacation.

[16~17] 다음을 듣고, 물음에 답하시오.

16 남자가 하는 말의 주제로 가장 적절한 것은?

① how to get closer to kids
② toys that can be dangerous
③ creative gifts for young children
④ how to select appropriate gifts for kids
⑤ the harmful substances in baby products

17 언급된 제품이 아닌 것은?

① 고무풍선 ② 금속 장신구
③ 면제품 ④ 털이 많은 인형
⑤ 나무 블록

12 Sense Up 듣기 모의고사 DICTATION

01

W: People who think they will be successful are successful. Those who think they will fail do fail! ____________________ by lots of new research. Researchers have shown that positive thoughts ____________________ ____________________ diseases. In drug tests, positive thinkers who are given a worthless sugar pill often become as healthy as those actually taking medicine. Their positive thoughts help heal them. In life, you must think positively to be successful. If you think you can't understand advanced math, for example, you'll never be able to do it. And if you think speaking English is too hard, ____________________ ____________________. The first step to success is saying "I can do it."

02

M: Jennifer, ____________________ my budget for attending university?

W: Wow, that's a lot! Can you afford to spend that much?

M: No, but what can I do? It's only the essentials.

W: Well, ____________________ ____________________ if you had a roommate.

M: I guess that would save a lot of money.

W: Also, ____________________ for eating out. Why don't you try cooking at home?

M: I don't know how to cook, and I don't have any pots or pans.

W: It would be cheaper to buy some kitchenware and a cookbook than to eat out every day.

M: I guess you're right. Can you suggest anything else?

W: You should consider buying used furniture and textbooks. It will ____________________ ____________________.

03

M: Ms. Evans, please come in and ____________________ ____________________.

W: Thank you. Oh... Mr. Jenner, is that you?

M: Sarah!

W: Yes, you remember. You changed companies?

M: Yes, last year.

W: I didn't know you had left KS Media.

M: A good opportunity came up here. But ____________________ ____________________ interviewing you. What happened after your internship at KS ended?

W: ____________________ for the last two years.

M: When do you graduate?

W: This summer. I hope to work in the global business department here at Big Top Corporation.

M: Well, when I was your supervisor at KS Media, I was really happy with your work. But working here in the global business department would be very different.

W: I know that. But ____________________.

M: OK.

04

W: What are you drawing?

M: I just finished drawing my invitation for our club's Halloween party.

W: It's so impressive! ____________________ a spider and its web at the top!

M: Thank you! I also thought the big full moon in the center would be nice.

W: Good. The moon really makes the words, Halloween Party, stand out. You even drew ____________________ ____________________.

M: Bats are symbolic of Halloween. Do you like the flying broom near the bats?

W: Of course. ____________________ you just drew a broom without a witch.

M: I wanted to draw a witch at first, but I changed my mind. Do you think I should draw one?

W: No, I like it. I think this is more suggestive.

M: I also drew three carved pumpkins on the bottom.

정답 및 해설 p.46

W: They're called jack-o-lanterns, right? You have everything that represents Halloween in this picture.

M: Thanks. I'm so ______________________________ ______________. I should show this to the other club members now.

05

W: Seho, look at ______________________________!

M: Ouch! The mosquitoes bit you all night long.

W: They sure did. ______________________________?

M: Not a bit.

W: What's your secret?

M: I usually use a special cream before I go to bed.

W: But I don't like the sticky feeling.

M: Then you should get a mosquito net. They're perfect ______________________________.

W: Where can I get one?

M: Actually, the other night, my friend Haesu said she had an extra one in her closet.

W: That's great. Will you ask Haesu if she can ______ ______________________________?

M: No problem.

06

W: Excuse me, sir. Are these books yours?

M: Yes, these three are mine.

W: OK. ______________________________ for you now — $15, $35, and $20. Is that everything?

M: Yes. But I'd like a paper bag, please.

W: OK, it's ______________________________, so the total is $70. How will you be paying?

M: Cash. But, oh, wait a minute. I have some gift certificates. Can I use them here?

W: Let me see.... Yes, you can. You have three $5 certificates. I'll ______________________________ ______________.

M: Oh, and here's my Readers' Book Club card. I want the points for this purchase.

W: No problem. Let me put it through the machine. Oh, it says you have 3,000 points before this purchase. ______________ $3. Do you want to apply those points to this purchase?

M: Yes, please.

07

M: Hi, Aunt Sharon! Here is a ticket to my movie premiere. I hope you can come.

W: I'd love to. I can't believe you are in a movie!

M: I didn't ______________________________. Don't expect too much, okay?

W: Still, I'm impressed. So, the place is the Twin Oaks Theater, right?

M: Yes, ______________________________ your home.

W: And it's on Saturday at 7 p.m.? I think I have something on that day.... Let's see....

M: You don't have to work on the weekend, do you?

W: No. But I'll be away on a business trip. I'm so sorry.

M: ______________________________. That's okay.

W: I heard that tickets for this movie premiere are very hard to get. It's a shame to lose this chance.

M: ______________________________ in several theaters soon. You can see it later.

W: Okay. I promise I'll come to your next premiere.

08

M: Hi, Cindy. How are you?

W: Hi, Jim. ______________________________, I'm nervous about my job interview.

M: That's understandable. I felt the same way before my first few interviews.

W: Really? Did you do well?

M: Actually, no. But I learned a few things. For instance, you should ______________________________.

W: Okay. What else?

M: Even though you are nervous, be sure to speak loudly and clearly.

W: I'll try to give a good impression with my voice. And I should dress formally, right?

M: Yes, it's important to look your best. Make sure your hair and clothes are neat.

W: It's in the morning, so ______________________ ______________________ to give myself plenty of time.

M: Definitely. You don't want to be late. Interviewers look down on that.

W: Well, thanks. I feel ______________________ ______________________.

M: No problem. Good luck.

09

M: What do you do with that ice-cream stick after eating an ice-cream bar? You ______________ ______________, right? Well, Robert McDonald, a Hollywood stunt man, built a 15-meter long Viking ship from ice-cream sticks. ______________ ______________ from the Netherlands to England and then from England to North America. On the way to America he will visit Iceland and Greenland as the Vikings also did long ago! The ship ______________ 15 million ice-cream sticks and McDonald got the help of more than 5,000 children to build it. He said he wanted ______________ that anything is possible. So what could you build from 15 million ice-cream sticks?

10

W: I want to sign up for some volunteer work this summer.

M: Wow, great. Where do you want to go?

W: Well, I ______________________ ______________, so I'd like to go to a country that requires Spanish.

M: Then, you should probably head down to South America. How long do you plan to do this?

W: For about one month or two months. I think that would ______________________ ______________ the people and culture there.

M: That's a great idea. What kind of work do you want to do?

W: My major is computer science, so I'd like to teach kids computer skills. Would you like to come with me?

M: If I decide to go, I should participate in a home building project since I'm studying architecture. But I already signed up for summer school.

W: Oh, I see.

M: ______________________?

W: I'll be busy in June, so I'll probably leave in July. So this program is my best option.

M: I really hope you have a wonderful experience.

11

M: I'm hungry. Do you ______________ ______________?

W: Sure. Let's go to the sandwich shop on the corner.

M: We had sandwiches yesterday. ______________ ______________ them?

12

W: ______________________ your new roommate?

M: Not well. He always invites his friends over late at night.

W: ______________________ him that it bothers you?

13

W: Danny? There you are! Are you ready to go? I'm tired.

M: Hang on a second, will you? ______________ ______________ to take on our holiday.

W: But we've been in the bookstore for ages. And I gave you ______________________ ______________________.

M: Sorry, I started reading comic books and forgot all your suggestions.

W: Comic books are too simple. Well, hurry up! I've already paid for my books.

M: What did you get?

W: *Gossip Girl* and *Sisterhood of the Traveling Pants*. You wouldn't like them.

M: Yeah, I don't think I'll enjoy those. ______________________________?

14

W: Hi, Bob.

M: Hi, Jessica. ______________________________? You don't look so good.

W: It's the school play. It's too much work.

M: But you're the leading actress.

W: I know and I promised Mr. Hampton I'd do a great job.

M: Yes, you promised. He'll be angry if you don't ______________________________. He didn't want to give you the leading role at first.

W: Yes, I know. I ______________________________ when we were doing *West Side Story*, the previous play.

M: Betty also wanted the leading role?

W: Yes, but I am so busy with my classes. And I'm busy applying to universities, too.

M: I understand. You've got to try to use your time wisely.

W: I'll try, but honestly ______________________________.

15

W: Owen is Diane's good friend and co-worker. They have many good memories of each other. Owen needs to ask Diane for a favor. Diane has two digital cameras. She bought one and ______________________________. This Saturday, Owen is going away and he wants to borrow one of Diane's cameras because last month he slipped and dropped her camera. ______________________________. On Monday, Owen asked Diane ______________________________ him one of her cameras. Diane said it was not a problem. All week Owen kept expecting Diane to bring the camera to work. But Diane never did. She ______________________________. On Friday, Owen asks Diane about the camera. In this situation, what is Diane most likely to say to Owen?

16-17

M: Giving is ______________________________ to show you care, but it can be difficult to choose a gift for someone else's child. Children develop at different rates, and their interests can change from year to year. Fortunately, there are a few guidelines ______________________________. Most importantly, check with the parents first whenever possible. This will give you important clues about the child's likes and dislikes. Then check the gift-buying guides of your favorite online toy stores. But ______________________________, safety is most important. To begin with, avoid anything that a young child could choke on. Rubber balloons, for example, are especially dangerous. Also, be aware that metal jewelry may contain toxic materials. Similarly, be careful when selecting cotton products, since most cotton ______________________________ pesticides at one point. Even wooden blocks may contain poisonous chemicals from the factory. ______________________________ when you see the smiling face of the child who receives your gift.

01 다음을 듣고, 남자가 하는 말의 목적으로 가장 적절한 것을 고르시오.

① 항공기 지연을 알리려고
② 수하물 찾는 곳을 안내하려고
③ 항공사 홈페이지를 홍보하려고
④ 수하물 분실 시 신고 방법을 알려주려고
⑤ 고객 불만 신고서 작성법을 설명하려고

02 대화를 듣고, 여자의 의견으로 가장 적절한 것을 고르시오.

① 가공식품 제조 과정이 공개되어야 한다.
② 가공식품 섭취 시 유통기한에 주의해야 한다.
③ 다양한 자연식품을 적극적으로 개발해야 한다.
④ 가공식품보다 자연식품을 섭취하는 것이 좋다.
⑤ 식품 구매 시 영양 성분을 확인할 필요가 있다.

03 대화를 듣고, 두 사람의 관계를 가장 잘 나타낸 것을 고르시오.

① 출판사 직원 - 공상과학 소설가
② 카메라 감독 - 인공지능 과학자
③ 광고주 - 카피라이터
④ 다큐멘터리 감독 - 작가
⑤ 방송 프로그램 제작자 - 홍보 담당자

04 대화를 듣고, 그림에서 대화의 내용과 일치하지 <u>않는</u> 것을 고르시오.

05 대화를 듣고, 여자가 할 일로 가장 적절한 것을 고르시오.

① 간식 사오기
② DVD 빌리기
③ 여행 취소하기
④ 음식 요리하기
⑤ 엄마에게 허락받기

06 대화를 듣고, 남자가 지불할 금액을 고르시오. [3점]

① $2.50 ② $3.00 ③ $3.50
④ $4.50 ⑤ $5.00

07 대화를 듣고, 여자가 바지를 반품하지 <u>못한</u> 이유를 고르시오.

① 해야 할 일이 많아서
② 영수증을 잃어버려서
③ 할인 판매 상품이라서
④ 반품 가능한 날짜가 지나서
⑤ 반품 대신 교환만 가능해서

08 다음을 듣고, 해외여행을 저렴하게 하는 방법으로 언급되지 <u>않은</u> 것을 고르시오.

① 기내 수화물만 가져가기
② 친구들과 같이 가기
③ 여행자용 숙소 이용하기
④ 현지 현금 인출기 이용하기
⑤ 국제 학생증 소지하기

09 투표에 관한 다음 내용을 듣고, 일치하지 <u>않는</u> 것을 고르시오.

① 등록된 투표자는 선거 전에 등록 카드를 받는다.
② 등록 카드에는 투표 장소와 시간이 적혀 있다.
③ 등록 카드를 지참해야 투표가 가능하다.
④ 우편으로 투표가 가능한 경우도 있다.
⑤ 투표용지를 사용 못할 경우 특별한 투표 장치가 있다.

10 다음 표를 보면서 대화를 듣고, 두 사람이 선택할 호텔을 고르시오.

Hotels in Los Angeles

Hotel Name	Cost (per night)	Swimming Pool	Free Internet	Airport Shuttle
① Apple Inn	$220	×	×	○
② The Belfast	$250	○	○	×
③ Oasis 7	$300	○	○	○
④ Travel Lodge	$220	○	×	×
⑤ Family Stay	$250	○	○	○

11 대화를 듣고, 여자의 마지막 말에 대한 남자의 응답으로 가장 적절한 것을 고르시오.

① Of course. I'll recommend a good laptop.
② I wonder what else you got for your birthday.
③ Sorry, but I don't know much about computers.
④ I'm waiting to install a newly updated program.
⑤ You should limit the time you spend on the Internet.

12 대화를 듣고, 남자의 마지막 말에 대한 여자의 응답으로 가장 적절한 것을 고르시오.

① No, I prefer to take a rest.
② Honestly, my job is very tiring.
③ Yes, I'll visit so many tourist spots.
④ Overseas experience can be valuable.
⑤ Yeah, I've already applied for several.

13 대화를 듣고, 여자의 마지막 말에 대한 남자의 응답으로 가장 적절한 것을 고르시오.

▶ Man : ______________________

① I will do the best I can. Don't worry.
② The café closes at midnight, so we should go soon.
③ I'm not getting paid enough to do this anymore.
④ We should switch to singing instead of dancing.
⑤ We should've learned a different dance sequence.

14 대화를 듣고, 남자의 마지막 말에 대한 여자의 응답으로 가장 적절한 것을 고르시오. [3점]

▶ Woman : ______________________

① Neither do I. But I'm trying.
② It's not always against the law.
③ Either one of us must stop first.
④ I have no problem with downloading.
⑤ I think we have to buy an MP3 player.

15 다음 상황 설명을 듣고, Foster 선생님이 Angus에게 할 말로 가장 적절한 것을 고르시오. [3점]

▶ Ms. Foster : ______________________

① That's not fast enough, Angus! Try harder!
② I think we'd better have your leg checked first.
③ You deserved to win all those medals. Good job!
④ These hurdles are too high. I'll get the lower ones.
⑤ Did you get some rest yesterday? Finally it's the day.

[16~17] 다음을 듣고, 물음에 답하시오.

16 남자가 하는 말의 주제로 가장 적절한 것은?

① tips for selecting pets
② ways to get rid of stress
③ advantages of having pets
④ efforts to take care of pets
⑤ comparison of various pets

17 언급된 반려동물이 <u>아닌</u> 것은?

① dog ② cat ③ goldfish
④ hamster ⑤ lizard

01

M: May I have your attention, please? This is an announcement for passengers of Interconnect Airlines. Making sure that ____________________ ____________________ is extremely important to us. In the unfortunate event of lost property, however, you must fill out a Passenger Baggage Loss Claim form. A copy of this form may be obtained from an Interconnect Airlines employee, or you can download it from our website at www.ica.com. Please note that missing property ____. We strongly advise our passengers to do this ____________________. Once we receive your form, we will do our best to return your luggage to you as soon as possible. Thank you very much.

02

M: Are you hungry? I have an extra energy bar that you can have.

W: Thanks, but I brought some snacks of my own. Plus, I try to avoid processed foods.

M: Oh, really? ____________________?

W: Unlike natural foods, I ____________________ how the ingredients will affect my body.

M: I know what you are saying, but these energy bars have been developed for athletes. Surely they are good for us.

W: I understand your point, but doctors are constantly updating their views on ____________________ ____________________. I prefer to trust Mother Nature instead.

M: Well, don't hesitate to ask me later, if you change your mind.

03

M: Rachel, can I speak to you for a minute?

W: Sure. Is something wrong?

M: I feel that we should make some changes to the story.

W: Why do you think so?

M: I'm afraid our audience ____________________ if the narration continues this long.

W: I'm sorry you feel that way. Do you have any good ideas?

M: Why don't we put a few more interviews with scientists in the film?

W: Okay. There is a list of AI scientists I met while writing the script. ____________________ some of them to interview?

M: All right. Let's have a meeting tomorrow at 11 a.m. and talk about it. I hope my decision ____________________ too much.

W: No problem. It's an honor for me to be a part of your documentary film.

M: You've had a lot of experience with AI, so it's very helpful for my directing. And I'll call the camera director, Philip, to the meeting, too.

W: Okay.

04

M: Hey, look at this photo of our family. It's pretty old. Maybe more than 10 years.

W: ____________________! Is that really your dad wearing the striped shirt on the left side of the picture? He looks so young!

M: Yes, it's him. And the shirt was a birthday gift from Mom.

W: It's cool. Hey, look at the dog ____________________ ____________________.

M: Yeah, he was our dog, Spike. He really loved that ball!

W: I see. ____________________? Is it Susan, or Julie?

M: It's Susan. Julie was on a girl scout trip at that time.

W: Oh, yeah? But why does Susan look upset in this picture?
M: It was probably because she lost her rabbit-shaped balloon.
W: She must have loved that balloon. Why is your mom pointing at the watermelon on the table?
M: That's because it was so sweet!

05

W: Hi, Mark. What's up?
M: I've just rented some DVDs.
W: Yeah. I can see that. You've rented a bunch of Harry Potter movies.
M: Yeah. I've rented the first four movies. I'm having a Harry Potter DVD party at my house today. ____________________?
W: Oh, that's right.
M: I invited you last week, but you said your family would be traveling this weekend.
W: Oh, ______________________________.
M: Join us then. We're starting at three in the afternoon. My mom is cooking a lot of food. Lisa is bringing some drinks and Justin is bringing some snacks.
W: Can I bring some snacks, too?
M: ____________________. We'll have plenty of food.
W: OK. I'll phone my mom right now and ________ ____________________.

06

M: How much is the bus fare?
W: It depends. The basic fare is $2.50. Then you add 50 cents more for ____________________ ______________.
M: Is there a map of the different zones at the bus stop?
W: Yes, there is. Look, there are four zones in the city. The downtown area is zone A, then zone B circles zone A.
M: Each zone ______________________________.
W: Yes. And we are here in zone C, the Eastside village.
M: And we want to go to the Art Museum downtown.
W: So you ______________________________, $2.50, plus the additional fare for two zones.
M: What about you?
W: Oh, I have a monthly three-zone transit card. It's cheaper.

07

W: Hi, honey. What are you doing?
M: Oh, nothing. By the way, whose pants are in this bag?
W: Did you forget? Those are the ones I wanted to return because I ____________________ ____________________.
M: Oh, right. You were going to do that yesterday, weren't you?
W: That was my plan, but I failed.
M: I guess you were ____________________.
W: No, I took them to the store, but they wouldn't accept them.
M: I don't understand. You kept the receipt, didn't you?
W: I did. The problem was that they were on sale at the time of purchase.
M: Now I get it. Sometimes, sale items ____________ ____________________.
W: Right. So, I'll just give them away to someone.
M: That's a good idea. At least they won't go to waste.

08

W: Few things are more valuable than the experience of traveling abroad, but it can be expensive! Luckily, it's not impossible with the right planning. To begin with, you ____________________. Baggage fees are the worst. Bring only a carry-on to avoid baggage fees. Next, bring friends. ____________________ means splitting expenses, from your hotel room, to cabs, to food. Plus, you'll feel significantly safer. Also, traveler's checks and credit cards ____________________. Using local ATMs is a safer and cheaper option. Finally, your student status ____________________ on flights, hotels, transportation, and other attractions. If you're staying in your home country, your college ID should work. But for travel overseas, consider an International Student ID Card.

09

M: If you're a registered voter, ____________________ before the election date. It will indicate where your polling place is and when you can vote. Your polling place will probably be a nearby school or community hall. It will be open between 6 a.m. and 6 p.m. You can bring your registration card with you but ____________________. If you have difficulty in getting to the polling place, contact the election commission to apply to vote by mail. And if you have a disability that makes it impossible to vote on ballot papers, ____________________. Or ask for assistance from the election official.

10

M: Julie, do you have any idea ____________________ Los Angeles?

W: Sure. I found these hotels online. What do you think?

M: The Oasis 7 looks the best, but I'm a little ____________________.

W: Me too. 300 dollars a night is a bit much. It would be nice to have a pool though.

M: I agree. ____________________ the swimming pool last time.

W: Right. You also need Internet access for work, don't you?

M: Yes, I do. I really need the Internet.

W: Okay, so there are two left to choose from. Do we need a shuttle to the airport?

M: That would ____________________ to the airport in the morning. I think we want a shuttle service.

W: There's only one choice then.

11

W: Guess what? I got a new laptop computer as a birthday present.

M: Wow! ____________________.

W: But ____________________ the Internet. Could you help me with that?

12

M: I'm going to Europe during the summer to travel. ____________________?

W: I think I'll stay here and ____________________.

M: Does that mean you are going to have a part-time job?

13

W: Let's ____________________. The talent contest is in a month.

M: Exactly! A month. So let's relax and go see a movie or get a coffee.

W: How can we relax ____________________?

M: Easy. We put our coats on and walk down to the café!

W: You aren't committed to this show like I am.

M: I'm committed, but I'm exhausted. Nobody can learn a dance sequence when they are this tired.

W: Just one more time and then I promise, we'll take a break.

M: All right. But you have to ____________________ ____________________ for the next few weeks.

W: I promise. But you have to promise to work extra hard when we do practice.

14

M: I download a lot of MP3 files these days.

W: So do I.

M: It's ______________________________. 99 cents a song and I download 30 or 40 files a month.

W: So you don't download the files of others for free?

M: No. _______________, but I stopped.

W: Me too. I always download from pay sites.

M: There's so much __________________________. Movies, textbooks, computer programs.... It just doesn't feel right.

W: I know, but my friends are always offering me DVDs of new movies ______________________ ______________________.

M: I don't think it's easy to stop playing or listening to illegally copied works.

15

W: Angus has been training hard for the inter-school sports next week. He ______________________ ____________ in several track and field events, including high jump, long jump, and the 200 meter hurdles. The school's P.E. teacher, Ms. Foster, is very proud of Angus and thinks he has an excellent chance of winning several medals at the inter-school sports. However, she has noticed that he is limping now, __________________________ _______________. Ms. Foster knows that Angus will ignore a slight injury and she ___________ ______________________. She thinks that if he's sore, he must rest. Angus approaches Ms. Foster and says he's ready to practice his long jumps. In this situation, what is Ms. Foster most likely to say to Angus?

16-17

M: Have you heard about guide dogs for the blind? These animals ______________________________ ______________. However, the average pet also has much to offer. Dogs and cats in particular are __________________________. Even the most stressful day is no match for a happy puppy with a wagging tail. Dogs can also provide security for the home against robbers. Goldfish are another popular choice. By raising goldfish, children learn responsibility as they maintain the aquarium and keep up with feeding. Maintaining the goldfish tank can be an event ______________ ______________________________________. Hamsters are another alternative to the traditional cat or dog. They are cute little pets that _________ __________________________. And it's fun to watch them climb through a series of tubes or run on an exercise wheel. There are many benefits to owning a pet rabbit, too. They're lovely, funny, quiet, and clean. But one thing many people may not realize is that rabbits are ecologically-friendly. They eat greens, which you can find in your own backyard. You can _________________________ ________________ and feed your bunnies your unwanted weeds. So, why not bring a pet into your life?

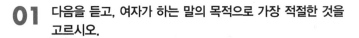

01 다음을 듣고, 여자가 하는 말의 목적으로 가장 적절한 것을 고르시오.

① 디지털 사진의 보관법을 설명하려고
② 새로 오픈한 사진관을 소개하려고
③ 디자인 강좌 개설을 안내하려고
④ 사진 앨범 제작업체를 광고하려고
⑤ 디지털 사진술의 변천사를 설명하려고

02 대화를 듣고, 남자의 의견으로 가장 적절한 것을 고르시오.

① 유년 시절 자원봉사를 하는 것은 가치가 있다.
② 자원봉사 단체에 대한 재정적 지원이 필요하다.
③ 아이가 조부모와 유대 관계를 갖는 것은 중요하다.
④ 다양한 유소년 자원봉사 프로그램을 만들어야 한다.
⑤ 독거노인을 위한 복지제도 강화 방안을 마련해야 한다.

03 대화를 듣고, 두 사람의 관계를 가장 잘 나타낸 것을 고르시오.

① 건설회사 직원 – 건설회사 사장
② 환경 운동가 – 환경 운동가
③ 목재상 – 목수
④ 인테리어 디자이너 – 고객
⑤ 미술관 관장 – 화가

04 대화를 듣고, 그림에서 대화의 내용과 일치하지 않는 것을 고르시오.

05 대화를 듣고, 남자가 여자를 위해 할 일로 가장 적절한 것을 고르시오.

① 생신 파티 준비하기
② 생신 선물 추천하기
③ 대신 선물 사러 가기
④ 뷔페 레스토랑 예약하기
⑤ 쇼핑몰까지 태워다 주기

06 대화를 듣고, 여자가 지불할 금액을 고르시오. [3점]

① $20 ② $30 ③ $40
④ $46 ⑤ $50

07 대화를 듣고, 남자가 파티에 참석하지 못한 이유를 고르시오.

① 이사를 도와야 해서
② 출장을 떠나야 해서
③ 병문안을 가야 해서
④ 아이들을 돌봐야 해서
⑤ 늦게까지 일해야 해서

08 대화를 듣고, 독감 증상을 완화하는 방법으로 언급되지 않은 것을 고르시오.

① 휴식 취하기 ② 차 마시기
③ 소금물로 입 헹구기 ④ 가습기 사용하기
⑤ 약 복용하기

09 미래 도시 전람회에 관한 다음 내용을 듣고, 일치하지 않는 것을 고르시오.

① 유명한 기술자와 건축가가 참여했다.
② 피라미드 형태의 미래 도시도 선보인다.
③ 지하에 건설된 터널 도시도 전시한다.
④ 투어는 두 가지 언어로 제공된다.
⑤ 등록은 로비에서 해야 한다.

10 다음 자료를 보면서 대화를 듣고, 여자가 선택할 일정을 고르시오.

	Seoul to New York with 1 stop		
	Flight 1		**Flight 2**
	Departure-Arrival	Time between connecting flights	Departure-Arrival
①	Seoul – Paris 09:00 – 20:00	36 hrs	Paris – New York 08:00 – 15:00
②	Seoul – Seattle 10:00 – 20:00	3 hrs	Seattle – New York 23:00 – 05:15
③	Seoul – Dubai 08:00 – 19:00	18 hrs	Dubai – New York 13:00 – 05:00
④	Seoul – Tokyo 10:00 – 12:30	34 hrs	Tokyo – New York 22:30 – 23:35
⑤	Seoul – LA 23:30 – 11:30	7 hrs	LA – New York 16:30 – 22:40

11 대화를 듣고, 여자의 마지막 말에 대한 남자의 응답으로 가장 적절한 것을 고르시오.

① After a 15-minute break.
② Andrew will go on stage soon.
③ It's about employee welfare benefits.
④ Your presentation was just wonderful.
⑤ There was heavy traffic due to a car accident.

12 대화를 듣고, 남자의 마지막 말에 대한 여자의 응답으로 가장 적절한 것을 고르시오.

① Please get some coffee, too.
② The supermarket is very large.
③ There are several cafés nearby.
④ There's one just past the gas station.
⑤ I work part-time at the convenience store.

13 대화를 듣고, 여자의 마지막 말에 대한 남자의 응답으로 가장 적절한 것을 고르시오. [3점]

▶ Man : ______________________________

① I will buy some cookies for me.
② I am sure you'll get a good grade.
③ There are various kinds of cookies here.
④ I can tell you if they taste delicious or not.
⑤ They tasted very good. Can I have another?

14 대화를 듣고, 남자의 마지막 말에 대한 여자의 응답으로 가장 적절한 것을 고르시오.

▶ Woman : ______________________________

① No, she doesn't look at all like me.
② Yes, I look a lot older than my age.
③ I agree. I have to take better care of her.
④ Right, she doesn't need any financial help.
⑤ Yeah, she looks much younger than her age.

15 다음 상황 설명을 듣고, Nathan이 Shawn에게 할 말로 가장 적절한 것을 고르시오. [3점]

▶ Nathan : ______________________________

① Is it my turn to take out the garbage?
② Let me know before you invite someone.
③ We have to clean the room every Sunday.
④ Did you have a party without inviting me?
⑤ I'd appreciate it if you'd clean up after yourself.

[16~17] 다음을 듣고, 물음에 답하시오.

16 남자가 하는 말의 주제로 가장 적절한 것은?

① the importance of eye contact
② common reasons that people lie
③ common evidence of telling a lie
④ how to communicate effectively at work
⑤ conversation manners with acquaintances

17 언급된 단서가 <u>아닌</u> 것은?

① 말의 높낮이
② 놀란 표정
③ 억지 미소
④ 초조한 눈빛
⑤ 시선 회피

01

W: Attention, photographers! The last few years have seen an amazing change in digital photography. But do you ever feel that something is missing? ______________________ a real photo album? Well, we're here to help. The Photo Den, located on the corner of Oak Street and Fourth Avenue, specializes in the creation of high-quality photo albums. There are ______________________. You can even choose the type of paper and size of the album. Just upload your photos and choose your style. We'll do the rest. Check out our prices online at photoden.com, or ______________ at 777-8383. Experience the joy of a quality photo album!

02

M: Honey, how about taking Kate to our volunteer club this weekend?

W: Isn't she ______________________? I'm a little worried.

M: This time we're planning to help some elderly people who live alone. I'm sure she can do it if she ______________________.

W: Yeah, that might be a good experience to have during childhood.

M: Right. I think more children need to learn the importance of volunteer work. It can be a valuable experience for them.

W: I agree. They can learn that volunteering is ______________________.

M: Besides, children can do a lot for others even though they're young.

W: You're right. I hope Kate learns a lot from volunteering.

03

W: So, Mr. Ross, are you happy with the overall concept?

M: Yes. I'm especially pleased about using environmentally friendly materials.

W: You do understand, however, the cost of those materials is ______________________.

M: Yes, but I will save hundreds of dollars on my home heating bills after this remodeling.

W: The recycled wood you've chosen for the flooring brings costs down too.

M: OK, what's the next stage?

W: Now, I ______________________ throughout your house.

M: And then when can I expect to see the first drawings?

W: The creative process can take several weeks, but I should ______________________ by September 1st.

M: OK, I got it.

04

M: Mom, I took a picture of the stage for our school play. I'd love to show you.

W: Okay. Wow, did you make everything by yourselves? I can't believe it!

M: Thanks, Mom. That big pumpkin on the left ______________________.

W: Oh? How is that possible?

M: It's simple. We already placed the carriage behind the pumpkin. When the fairy touches the pumpkin, smoke will come out. Then ______________________.

W: What a clever idea!

M: How do you like the square-shaped well?

W: It's a perfect match for the play.

M: Do you see the rock behind the well? That's where I'll pop out during the play.

W: Great. The rock really looks real. And... where's the clock? You know it's important in this play.

M: I know. It's right there on the castle on the far right of the stage.

W: Yes, I see that ______________________.

05

W: It's Mom's 55th birthday next Friday.

M: Oh, that's right. Are we going to have a dinner party somewhere?

W: Yes, we're all going to a buffet restaurant. Do you have any idea ______________________________?

M: I don't know. I always leave that to you.

W: Well, I wish you'd come up with some ideas sometimes.

M: I don't know what she likes. You know I'm not good at buying gifts.

W: I guess ______________________________. I think I should go shopping today. I have a busy week coming up.

M: Well, I can ______________________________ by car right now. I'm going to work out at the gym and it's on the way.

W: Good idea. Give me five minutes to get ready.

M: OK. I need five minutes to pack my gym bag, too.

06

W: I need some business cards for the new vice president and a new salesperson.

M: You'll want the premium package for the new vice president. Premium cards have color, any illustration of your choice, and coating. They're 30 dollars for 1,000 cards.

W: And for the new salesperson?

M: The basic package. Black print on uncoated white cards ______________________________ ____________________. 10 dollars for 1,000 cards.

W: OK. 1,000 cards for the vice president and 2,000 cards for the salesperson.

M: What color and illustration do you want for the vice president?

W: ______________________________. I'll order hers tomorrow.

M: And the basic package?

W: I'll get it today. I have the salesperson's phone numbers here.

M: Good.

W: Do I ______________________________?

M: Sure. 20% off.

W: Thanks.

07

W: Michael, you didn't come to the party last night. I missed you.

M: ______________________________. Did you have fun at the party?

W: Brandon was late. We waited an hour for him since it was his farewell party. He's leaving for New York next week.

M: He ______________________________.

W: He said he had to help his sister move yesterday. Since there was a lot to pack, it took much longer than he thought.

M: Then the party must have finished later.

W: Yes, but we had a wonderful time. By the way, why didn't you come? Were you busy at work?

M: No, I had to take care of my kids at home because my wife went to Chicago.

W: For a business trip?

M: No. Her mother is in the hospital for heart problems, so she's taking care of her.

W: I'm sorry to hear that.

M: ______________________________ ____________________ now.

08

W: Hello?

M: Hi, Mom. I'm really sorry, but I don't think ______________________.

W: What's wrong, Steven? You sound sick.

M: I caught the flu. My entire body hurts.

W: Then you'd better get plenty of rest. That's the best way to recover.

M: Of course. I'll be staying home tonight. But I doubt if I'll get much sleep with this sore throat.

W: Try gargling with salt water. That always works when my throat is raw.

M: Thanks, Mom. I will ______________________.

W: Oh, and please use the humidifier I bought for you. This dry winter air will only ______________________.

M: Good idea. I'd completely forgotten to turn it on. I also bought some aspirin for my fever.

W: Good. Get some rest, and I'll come check on you tomorrow.

09

M: Welcome to the City of the Future Exhibition. Here you will see famous engineers' and architects' visions of the modern city. Room 1 features a model of Pyramid City. ______________________ like a 1 km-tall pyramid. This city will house up to 750,000 people. Room 2 features Tunnel City. It's an underground utopia for a future time when the sun and air ______________________. And finally, Room 3 shows Greenhouse City, which recreates a healthy Earth atmosphere completely under glass. Tours will be available in English, Korean and Chinese. In order to allow the most people to enjoy this great exhibit, ______________________.

10

W: My travel agent emailed this flight schedule to New York. I need to decide which flight to take.

M: Weren't there any non-stop schedules available?

W: No, it's high season, ______________________.

M: What is the most important thing for you?

W: I don't want a flight that leaves Seoul in the afternoon.

M: You ______________________.

W: Yes. And I want to visit one of the stopover cities on the way there.

M: Then, you need more than 15 hours between connecting flights.

W: Right, but I'd love ______________________.

M: You don't want to arrive in New York too early in the morning or late at night, though.

W: You're right, I don't. ______________________!

11

W: I'm so sorry. I'm late because ______________________.

M: Don't worry, Jackie. The conference was postponed a little.

W: ______________________. Who's going to give the first presentation?

12

M: I'm going to the convenience store. Do you want anything?

W: Some snacks, please. But you should go to the supermarket instead. It's ______________________.

M: I know, but the nearest one is closed now. ______________________?

13

M: Mom, what are you cooking?

W: Actually, I'm baking some cookies.

M: Great! ________________________.

W: They aren't for you. It's kind of a test for me.

M: A test?

W: You know I'm taking that baking class at a cooking institute downtown.

M: Yes, I know that.

W: Well, I ____________________________________ ______________________ and bring them to class tomorrow. The teacher is going to taste them and give me a grade.

M: You mean if the cookies taste great, you'll get a good grade?

W: That's right.

M: Then you really need my help.

W: Huh? ____________________________?

14

M: Your apartment is nice, Susie. Can I look at those photographs over there?

W: Yes, of course. Look at this one. Everyone in my family is here. It was taken at my brother's wedding three years ago.

M: Hmm... three years ago, so you are 12 in the photograph. You ___________________________.

W: Of course! I'm not a child anymore.

M: Hmm... your grandmother ___________________ __________________________________.

W: She really takes care of herself. She walks in the park and eats healthy food.

M: Is she in her mid-50s?

W: No, she is 63 in that photograph. Look at this photograph of the two of us taken a few weeks ago.

M: Wow, ____ "she really takes care of herself."

15

W: Shawn and Nathan share a dorm room at the university. Nathan is very careful ______________ _____________________ that may bother Shawn or look bad when he has friends over. Nathan recently took a trip home for the weekend. He cleaned up the room and took out the trash before he left for home on Friday. When he returns on Sunday night, ______________________________ ________________. The garbage is overflowing, ____, and there are empty pizza boxes and soda bottles everywhere. This isn't the first time Shawn has left a mess in the room. Nathan thinks Shawn needs to be more careful to stay together, and it is a good chance to tell him what he thinks. In this situation, what would Nathan most likely say to Shawn?

16-17

M: Welcome back. We've spent a lot of time talking about the concept of truth, but what about the opposite? We believe someone who has an "honest face," and don't believe someone who has "nervous eyes," but why? In fact, a liar's body and voice do give clues that he or she is not telling the truth. When people are lying, they tend to ____________ ___________________________________. And they tend to close their eyes or blink rapidly. This is considered to be a form of behavior that ________ ___________________________________ of closing their eyes so it cannot be seen that they're lying. Even though it's a very childlike behavior, a lot of us still do it in adulthood. Liars also __________ ________________________________, saying "uh" and "er" a lot. People make forced smiles, if they smile at all, and they often avoid showing their hands. And yes, nervous eyes can indicate that a person is lying. Also, people telling a lie tend to _______________________________________ they are speaking to.

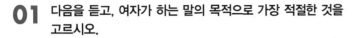

01 다음을 듣고, 여자가 하는 말의 목적으로 가장 적절한 것을 고르시오.

① 화재 대피요령을 설명하려고
② 항공편 운항 일정을 확인시키려고
③ 공항 시설의 일시적 폐쇄를 알리려고
④ 출국 승객의 보안 검색 재개를 알리려고
⑤ 공항 내의 소지품 분실 사고를 알리려고

02 대화를 듣고, 남자의 의견으로 가장 적절한 것을 고르시오.

① 안구 건조증을 수술로 치료할 수 있다.
② 유년기에 시력 관리를 하는 것이 중요하다.
③ 눈 건강을 위해 안과 정기 검진이 필요하다.
④ 시력 교정술은 신중히 생각해야 할 문제이다.
⑤ 눈의 피로를 덜기 위해 안구 운동을 해야 한다.

03 대화를 듣고, 두 사람의 관계를 가장 잘 나타낸 것을 고르시오.

① 환자 – 의사
② 간호사 – 접수 담당자
③ 종업원 – 관리자
④ 관객 – 마술사
⑤ 고객 – 점술가

04 대화를 듣고, 그림에서 대화의 내용과 일치하지 <u>않는</u> 것을 고르시오.

05 대화를 듣고, 여자가 남자에게 부탁한 일로 가장 적절한 것을 고르시오.

① 편지 분류하기
② 편지 더미 치우기
③ 답장 대신 써 주기
④ 스팸 메일 차단하기
⑤ TV 프로그램에 출연하기

06 대화를 듣고, 남자가 상점에 지불해야 하는 금액을 고르시오. [3점]

① \$20 ② \$30 ③ \$50
④ \$55 ⑤ \$60

07 대화를 듣고, 사진 촬영이 연기된 이유를 고르시오.

① 악천후가 예보되어서
② 여자 모델이 다리를 다쳐서
③ 촬영 장소를 구하지 못해서
④ 사진작가의 귀국이 늦어져서
⑤ 먼저 촬영해야 하는 광고가 생겨서

08 대화를 듣고, UC Berkeley에 관해 언급되지 <u>않은</u> 것을 고르시오.

① 재학생 수 ② 개설 학과
③ 노벨상 수상자 수 ④ 설립 연도
⑤ 연례 축구전

09 공장 견학에 관한 다음 내용을 듣고, 일치하지 <u>않는</u> 것을 고르시오.

① 방문증을 휴대해야 한다.
② 기계를 직접 작동해 볼 수 있다.
③ 황색 선을 따라 이동해야 한다.
④ 견학은 주차장에서 끝난다.
⑤ 단축 코스를 이용할 수 있다.

10 다음 표를 보면서 대화를 듣고, 여자가 선택할 강의를 고르시오.

Winter Language Courses				
Course	Language	Dates	Focus	Days
① A	Chinese	1/7 – 2/4	speaking & writing	Monday, Wednesday, Friday
② B	Chinese	1/7 – 1/31	speaking	Tuesday & Thursday
③ C	Japanese	1/7 – 2/4	speaking & writing	Monday, Wednesday, Friday
④ D	French	1/14 – 2/4	speaking	Monday, Wednesday, Friday
⑤ E	French	1/14 – 1/31	grammar	Tuesday & Thursday

11 대화를 듣고, 남자의 마지막 말에 대한 여자의 응답으로 가장 적절한 것을 고르시오.

① The last bus already left.
② There is one every ten minutes.
③ It depends where you are going.
④ Bus services are poor in this area.
⑤ It's between 6 a.m. and 11:30 p.m.

12 대화를 듣고, 여자의 마지막 말에 대한 남자의 응답으로 가장 적절한 것을 고르시오.

① I'll choose Vietnam instead.
② You should go and check yourself.
③ I've been to four different countries.
④ Cultural differences don't mean much.
⑤ I would plan ahead so as not to waste time.

13 대화를 듣고, 남자의 마지막 말에 대한 여자의 응답으로 가장 적절한 것을 고르시오.

▶ Woman : ____________________

① I will go and ask him right now.
② Would you like me to describe him?
③ I will call my sister and ask her now.
④ I'll take the puppy food for poodles, please.
⑤ The dog is brown with a white spot on its nose.

14 대화를 듣고, 여자의 마지막 말에 대한 남자의 응답으로 가장 적절한 것을 고르시오. [3점]

▶ Man : ____________________

① I don't like surfing. It's too scary.
② Let's just wait here for your father.
③ It's too hot to do anything. Let's watch TV.
④ Great! Do you remember which park it was?
⑤ Then let's go to the beach that you mentioned.

15 다음 상황 설명을 듣고, Robbie가 Sean에게 할 말로 가장 적절한 것을 고르시오. [3점]

▶ Robbie : ____________________

① It's no big deal. The new guy isn't very good.
② You are good enough to play goalkeeper this time.
③ In order to make the playoffs, we need a new team leader.
④ To my regret, the coach is changing goal-keepers next game.
⑤ Have you ever thought about becoming a professional player?

[16~17] 다음을 듣고, 물음에 답하시오.

16 남자가 하는 말의 주제로 가장 적절한 것은?

① some ways to make a staycation enjoyable
② necessity of vacations in our everyday life
③ things to consider when planning a vacation
④ advantages and disadvantages of a staycation
⑤ differences between a staycation and a real vacation

17 언급된 장소가 아닌 것은?

① amusement park
② art gallery
③ historical site
④ local museum
⑤ theater

01

W: Attention passengers. There has been a security violation in the International Terminal. Mysterious packages have been left in Terminal B. We are sorry for the inconvenience, but we need to evacuate the airport immediately ________________________ ________________________. So we'll temporarily close the facilities and cease airport operations. All flights currently on the runways __________ ________________________________, but arriving passengers will not be allowed to leave their planes. We expect the delay ________________________ ____________________ while we are investigating. Please proceed to the nearest exit with all of your possessions. Walk, do not run. We will do our best to speed everyone through security when normal operations begin again. Thank you.

02

M: Hi, Megan. Where are you going?

W: Hi, Neal. I'm going to the eye clinic for a regular eye checkup.

M: Oh, are you having problems ________________ ________________?

W: No, I just want to check if my eyes are fine.

M: You've been wearing glasses since you were very young, right?

W: Yes, it's pretty uncomfortable. So, I'm considering laser eye surgery.

M: But I heard about ________________________ ________________________, and I don't think it's a good idea.

W: Really? I also know about some problems that I might experience after the surgery, like dry eyes.

M: Some people have blurry vision afterward, so I think ____ to think about it.

W: Okay, I see. Thanks!

03

M: So what do you want me to tell you?

W: For me your date of birth is important.

M: ________________________________ my hands or anything?

W: No, but ________________________________ __________ the exact date and time of your birth on this paper.

M: OK. Now what?

W: Now I need to check this chart. Hmm... I see.

M: What is it?

W: Well, according to my chart you have a very lucky period coming up.

M: Really? ________________________________ a new job overseas!

W: Yes, I see. I believe your luck will be in New York. I have a strong feeling about this.

M: A feeling?

W: Yes, of course. I don't just rely on my chart for this. I have a special gift.

04

W: That's a great picture, Tom.

M: You think so? It was taken at my uncle Sam's apple farm last weekend. I went there with my family.

W: It looks like a good time. Is that your mother ________________________________?

M: Yes, she was setting out food for a picnic. We ate after taking this picture.

W: It looks like ________________________________ ________________________ beside her.

M: That's my younger sister, Susan. She was so hungry! It was really funny.

W: Is that your family's dog running around?

M: No, that's Max. He's my uncle's dog, but he looks just like ours.

W: They do look similar. And I'll guess that's your uncle ________________________?

M: Right. He is using that long stick to reach high into the trees. You can only see three trees behind him, but it's a huge farm.

W: It must be a lot of work!

05

W: Wow. Ever since I was on that TV show, I have been getting so much fan mail.

M: There must be 500 letters here!

W: Yes, and that is only this week. I have another pile from last week, too.

M: Are you going to answer every letter?

W: Well, most of them. Some are from men ________ ________________________________!

M: Even without those letters, it's still going to take weeks to answer the rest.

W: Not if you ________________________________.

M: OK. Tell me ____________________________.

W: First, make three piles. One is for letters from children, the next is from adults, and the third is for guys who want to marry me.

M: I think I know ______________________________ ____________________________!

06

W: Let's see... the total is $55.

M: Isn't this hat $20 and this T-shirt $30?

W: They are.

M: Then ______________________________________?

W: You have to pay a 10% sales tax.

M: Really?

W: But I see that you're a tourist, so I am sure you can get a sales tax rebate.

M: Rebate? You mean __________________________ ________________ the sales tax, the 10% extra?

W: Yes.

M: Great. I'm from Singapore. Here's my passport.

W: I don't need your passport. You must pay the tax now, but you can ______________________. You apply at the airport __________________________.

M: OK.

07

M: Hello?

W: Mr. Smith, this is Jumi from Jamia Advertising. Do you have a few minutes to talk?

M: Yes, the photographer gave me a break before the next shoot.

W: Okay. It's about this weekend's photo shoot on Jeju Island.

M: Oh, I heard that ____________________________ ________________ on Jeju Island this weekend. Was the location changed?

W: No, but the woman ________________________ ______________________ has a problem.

M: Lana Jacobs? Did something happen?

W: She hurt her leg on the runway while rehearsing for an upcoming fashion show.

M: I hope she will recover soon. What will happen to the shoot?

W: ____________________________. We'll contact you after speaking with Ms. Jacobs' agency.

M: Okay. I understand.

08

W: Danny, do you want to do something with me this weekend?

M: I'd love to, but I'm afraid my family already has plans to visit my sister this weekend.

W: Oh, she's a student at UC Berkeley, isn't she?

M: That's right. It's a large school, ________________ ______________________________.

W: They've also had many famous professors over the years, including 70 Nobel Prize winners.

M: I didn't know that. I guess you have an interest in Berkeley then?

W: My father attended Berkeley and ______________ ____________________________. I know all about its history, from its foundation in 1868 to the current day.

M: Then I guess you know that the annual football game versus Stanford will take place this weekend?

W: Of course. That's a famous rivalry that ________ ______________________________. I wish I could go with you.

M: At least I can tell you all about it when I get back.

09

M: Welcome to a tour of Green Factory. I'm James, your tour guide today. Everyone must sign out and carry a visitor badge. This badge ______________________________ a locator device that can be activated in the event of an emergency. The machinery is actively producing cereal during your visit. It has many moving parts that could cause bodily injury. For your safety, please ______________________________. The entire tour ______________________________, and it will end at the parking lot. For a shorter version, use any of the three shortcuts. People with any type of heart trouble should consider using the shortcuts at difficult points of the tour.

10

M: Hi, Clara. What are you looking at?

W: It's a schedule of winter language courses. ______________________________, so I'm checking the course schedule.

M: I know you've been studying Japanese. So, ______________________________?

W: I'd like to try something different.

M: So, what about the dates? Can you start on the 7th?

W: Oh, I almost forgot ______________________ that week. I can start on the 14th.

M: That leaves two. ______________________, I'd take speaking. That's always more fun.

W: I agree, but I'm afraid I have music lessons on Wednesdays and Fridays.

M: Sounds like the decision has been made then.

W: I guess so. I'll sign up today. Thanks for your help.

11

M: Excuse me, but has the number 31 bus passed by here?

W: Yes, ______________________________. There will be another one soon.

M: ______________________________?

12

W: Richard, you spent a summer in Europe, didn't you?

M: I did, but it wasn't a very satisfying trip. ______________________________.

W: Really? If you could go again, ______________________ differently?

13

M: May I help you find anything?

W: Yes, I am taking care of my sister's dog while she is ______________________, and I need some food for it.

M: OK. Do you know what kind of dog it is?

W: It is a large brown dog. I don't know what kind of dog it is.

M: Do you know how old it is? If it's a puppy, we have special food for them.

W: He is just under one year old.

M: Hmm... ______________________________ being a puppy and an adult. It would really help to know the breed.

W: I said that it is big. Doesn't that help?

M: "Big" isn't ______________________________. Is there any way you can find out?

14

M: Hey, Tara! Thanks for inviting me to your house again.

W: Hi, Justin. ______________________________ ______________ today?

M: It was so nice last week when your dad _________ _________________.

W: Sorry, we can't go surfing today. Dad's playing golf all day.

M: Oh, my. I brought my swimsuit with me. I really wanted to swim or surf today.

W: Well, then, let's go to a water amusement park! I'll find one on the Internet.

M: Hmm, I don't really like crowds, especially at those big water parks.

W: It's not so hot today, so they _________________ ____________________. And I heard one of them has big surfing waves.

15

W: Robbie is the captain of the soccer team. His best friend, Sean, plays goalkeeper on the team. But a new player ______________________________ _______________ and is even better than Sean at the goalpost, so the coach has decided to _______ ______________________________. Sean has been the goalkeeper for two seasons now and ______________________________________ __________. The coach thinks Robbie should tell Sean about the change in the lineup for the next game. Robbie doesn't want to do it, but the coach insists that ______________________________ as a team leader. In this situation, what is Robbie most likely to say to Sean?

16-17

M: Many people dream of a wonderful vacation, but they can't have a vacation __________________ ____________. A staycation is the best option for people in such circumstances. A staycation is a kind of vacation ________________________ ____________, take a whole day trip and get back to your place at night. In order to have a proper staycation, you need to plan things to do. First, turn off your alarm. A good vacation _________ ___________________. Also, find new and fun activities. You can visit an amusement park or an art gallery. You can also explore places such as historical sites or local museums around you. Turn off your phone. Pretend that you're half a world away ______________________________. Go to bed when you'd like and wake up when you'd like. The best part of vacationing is taking the time to truly relax with an afternoon snooze. Pull the shades down, put on some soothing music and spend your afternoon basking in ____________ ____________________. You can enjoy all these things without flying off to a Caribbean island. In a sense, a staycation is actually better than a real vacation. Plan your staycation today!

01 다음을 듣고, 남자가 하는 말의 목적으로 가장 적절한 것을 고르시오.

① 성적 평가 방식을 안내하려고
② 신입생에게 환영 인사를 하려고
③ 개인정보 보호 강화를 요청하려고
④ 학생증을 발급받는 방법을 알려주려고
⑤ 강의 자료 다운로드 받는 방법을 설명하려고

02 대화를 듣고, 여자의 의견으로 가장 적절한 것을 고르시오.

① 쓰레기 무단 투기를 강력히 규제해야 한다.
② 등산로에는 쓰레기통이 없는 편이 더 낫다.
③ 우천 시 등산객의 등산로 출입 제한이 필요하다.
④ 등산은 주말에 하기 좋은 여가 활동 중 하나이다.
⑤ 안전 수칙을 제대로 지킨다면 안전한 등산이 가능하다.

03 대화를 듣고, 두 사람의 관계를 가장 잘 나타낸 것을 고르시오.

① 방송국 직원 – 시청자
② 방송 진행자 – 기부 희망자
③ 장애 어린이 부모 – 자원봉사자
④ 자선 재단 직원 – 후원 신청자
⑤ 자원봉사센터 직원 – 지원 학생

04 대화를 듣고, 그림에서 대화의 내용과 일치하지 않는 것을 고르시오.

05 대화를 듣고, 남자가 할 일로 가장 적절한 것을 고르시오.

① 펜과 종이 가져오기
② 학생회의에 참여하기
③ 포스터 디자인 고르기
④ 포스터에 그림 그리기
⑤ 학생회장 후보로 등록하기

06 대화를 듣고, 여자가 지불할 금액을 고르시오. [3점]

① $180 ② $225 ③ $250
④ $315 ⑤ $350

07 대화를 듣고, 남자가 한국어 수업에 등록한 이유를 고르시오.

① 자기계발을 위해서
② 업무상 한국어가 필요해서
③ 한국 문화에 관심이 있어서
④ 한국으로 여행갈 계획이어서
⑤ 아내의 가족들과 가까워지고 싶어서

08 대화를 듣고, Heller 경력 개발 센터에 관해 언급되지 않은 것을 고르시오.

① 구직 정보 사이트 ② 면접 교육
③ 평균 임금 정보 ④ 이력서 작성 지원
⑤ 온라인 적성검사

09 도서 축제에 관한 다음 내용을 듣고, 일치하지 않는 것을 고르시오.

① 어린이용 도서가 전시되는 축제이다.
② 89개국의 책이 전시된다.
③ 작가들이 직접 책을 읽어 주는 시간이 있다.
④ 일부 유명 동화는 무대에서 상연된다.
⑤ 전시된 책 중 구입이 가능한 것도 있다.

10 다음 표를 보면서 대화를 듣고, 남자가 구매할 활동량 추적기를 고르시오.

Activity Tracker

Model	Color	Waterproof	GPS	Price
① A	Gray	×	×	$30
② B	Black	×	×	$40
③ C	Green	×	○	$50
④ D	Red	○	○	$80
⑤ E	White	×	○	$70

11 대화를 듣고, 남자의 마지막 말에 대한 여자의 응답으로 가장 적절한 것을 고르시오.

① I had no idea. Let's go.
② This campus is really large.
③ I'm sure it's not too far from here.
④ If you're late, you might miss something.
⑤ I'm having trouble with my history class.

12 대화를 듣고, 여자의 마지막 말에 대한 남자의 응답으로 가장 적절한 것을 고르시오.

① Thanks for making lunch.
② Sure. I'll boil the noodles.
③ I'll order some drinks, too.
④ I can take you to the store.
⑤ Don't forget to buy vegetables.

13 대화를 듣고, 남자의 마지막 말에 대한 여자의 응답으로 가장 적절한 것을 고르시오. [3점]

▶ Woman : ____________________

① You need to pay a large tax to import animals.
② I'm afraid animals are not allowed in our hotel.
③ It's OK. I will notify the security guards of that.
④ That's possible. But you must bring it in a carrier.
⑤ I'll put your puppies in this basket for you to carry home.

14 대화를 듣고, 여자의 마지막 말에 대한 남자의 응답으로 가장 적절한 것을 고르시오.

▶ Man : ____________________

① Sorry, I cannot help you this time.
② That's why I want you to come with me.
③ Neither do I. So let's look around more.
④ Yes, those are really fashionable clothes.
⑤ No, I don't think you need a lot of money.

15 다음 상황 설명을 듣고, Janice가 Bob에게 할 말로 가장 적절한 것을 고르시오. [3점]

▶ Janice : ____________________

① Do you think we'll reach the peak soon?
② Can you stick with me? I'd appreciate it.
③ I can't believe they're getting a separation.
④ What does everyone usually do after hiking?
⑤ What made you become a member of the club?

[16~17] 다음을 듣고, 물음에 답하시오.

16 여자가 하는 말의 주제로 가장 적절한 것은?

① how to pack a travel suitcase
② how to prepare for a long plane ride
③ negative aspects of a long plane trip
④ taking advantage of free services of airlines
⑤ the importance of preparing well for a trip

17 언급된 물건이 아닌 것은?

① 담요 ② 안대 ③ 귀마개
④ 양말 ⑤ 치약과 칫솔

01

M: Welcome, freshmen! I'm Professor Nate Brunswick and I'll be teaching "Intro to Economics" this semester. For each lecture, there will be ________ ________________________. Let me explain a bit more about this. First, you ________________ ________________________ the school's homepage to see the files. Your ID is your school ID number and the password is your date of birth. Once you are on the homepage, you should find the "reference" section. Type our lecture's name into the search box to get the materials. Additionally, I strongly recommend that you change your initial password into something unique. I hope you will ____ soon.

02

M: Wow! This view is incredible!

W: It is. This trail is popular because it's easy and safe.

M: It's great. Thanks for inviting me. If you hadn't, I ____ all weekend without seeing this.

W: I'm glad you're enjoying the hike. But we should head down because it'll be dark soon.

M: Alright, but I want to find a trash can first.

W: There aren't any. We ________________________ ________________________.

M: Really? Why hasn't the local government installed trash cans?

W: Because someone would have to hike up here to empty them.

M: But now people leave their trash on the ground.

W: Even if there were trash cans, the cans would quickly fill up and spill over. The result might be even worse.

M: You may be right. It's ________________________ ______________ our garbage.

03

W: Warm Heart Foundation. This is Katelyn Hudson.

M: Hello, my name is Joshua Miller and I watched the program about your foundation's Wheelchairs for Kids project on TV last night.

W: Oh, thank you for calling us. You watched the program that was aired yesterday.

M: Yes. ________________________________ your dedication to children in need.

W: I'm glad to hear it. We're hoping that more people take an interest in this project.

M: I hope so, too. I'm calling today because I wanted to know ________________________ I could do to help them.

W: Of course, there are many ways you can help. You can donate money or donate a wheelchair ______ ________________________.

M: I see. I don't have any wheelchairs so I can help out financially.

W: That would be wonderful, too. You can make a donation through our foundation's website.

M: Okay. I will donate just twenty dollars since I'm a student. Is that okay?

W: Absolutely. Every little bit of help counts.

04

W: What a nice view!

M: Yeah, it really is! Do you see the palm trees ____?

W: Oh, that looks so exotic!

M: We're lucky we could get this room. I can see the entire resort from here.

W: I know. Do you see the round swimming pool? ____.

M: I'd prefer to lie down on one of the pool chairs on the right and read a book.

W: Good idea! I like the polka-dot patterned beach umbrellas next to the chairs. I think it's fitting.

M: ________________________________.

W: Wait a minute. What's that sitting by the edge of the swimming pool? Is it some kind of animal?

M: I think it's a frog-shaped water fountain.

W: Oh, yeah. Now I can see water ______________ ________________________. How cute!

M: I think this vacation is just what we wanted.

05

W: Noah, I'm nervous about my campaign for student council president.

M: Why do you say that? You're definitely the best student for the job.

W: Thanks for saying so, but I don't think many students ________________________________.

M: So, what are you going to do? Do you have an idea?

W: I suppose a few more campaign posters could help. I've got some paper here. Could you help me?

M: Of course. Do you need pens or decorations?

W: ________________________. I just need someone to draw a few eye-catching pictures.

M: I can do that for you. I love to draw.

W: Great! Thank you so much.

M: I'm happy to help. __________________________ ______________?

W: I haven't. So, I'll choose a design first.

06

M: Can I help you find anything?

W: Yes. I'm looking for a nice floor lamp for my new apartment.

M: We have several that you might be interested in. ________________________________ for $120.

W: I like the simple design, but ________________ ________________. What about this silver one?

M: That is actually part of a two-lamp set that sells for $350.

W: Could I buy one __________________________?

M: I'm afraid not. However, we do have this similar lamp. It's currently $200.

W: I like it. I'll take it, and I'll use this 10% discount offer that I received in the mail.

M: I'm afraid ______________________ if your total is over $250.

W: Oh. In that case, I'll take the set with two silver lamps.

M: Great choice.

07

W: Hi, I'm Lucy.

M: Nice to meet you. My name's Parker. So, why did you ____________________________?

W: My company is planning to send me to Seoul in a few months. I'll need to speak Korean to deal with clients. What about you?

M: My wife is Korean. I'm trying to learn the language so I can ______________________________.

W: Oh, really? How did you meet her?

M: We met in university. We were both history majors.

W: That's interesting. Does your wife's family live here, in Chicago?

M: No, but they visit occasionally. We actually had the wedding in Busan. It was my first trip to Korea, and I really enjoyed it.

W: In that case, maybe ______________________ ________________ about Korean culture.

M: I'd be happy to share what I know, but ________ __________________________.

08

M: Heller's Career Development Center, Rich speaking. How may I help you?

W: Hi. I recently graduated from university, and I'm having some trouble with my job search.

M: Then ______________________________. We maintain a career-related website that is full of currently available positions.

W: That might help, but to be honest, ______________ ______________________ interviews.

M: Well, we also offer one-on-one interview training sessions.

W: Oh, and my friend mentioned that you help with résumé creation as well.

M: Right. And you can ____________________ ____________________. That will help you find the most suitable job.

W: Great. Then I'll call back later and make an appointment.

M: Why don't I send you an email with some further information?

W: Okay. That could be really helpful. Thanks.

09

W: Welcome to the Children's Book Festival at the New York Exhibition Center. There are 89 publishers of children's books from 15 different countries ______________________________________. Your children are sure to have fun reading the books on display. Authors will also read their books for children. Some famous stories ________ ____________________. The festival is also for writers. There will be writing workshops for writers of children's stories. Many of the books on display ____________________. Please ask if you are interested in purchasing a book. Enjoy the festival!

10

W: Honey, what are you looking at?

M: I'm shopping for an activity tracker online. I thought ______________________________ ______________ for my father.

W: That's a good idea. Which color do you want to buy?

M: I thought about the gray one first, but he doesn't like that color.

W: Does your father need one that's waterproof? ____ ____________________________ water sports.

M: I guess you're right. We don't need one that's waterproof.

W: But he definitely needs one with GPS.

M: Of course. With GPS, he can keep track of where he hikes and bikes.

W: Then, ______________________________. What do you think?

M: Hmm... I don't want to spend more than $60.

W: You're right. ______________________________ ______________________.

M: Okay. I'll order it now.

11

M: We'd better leave now for history class. I don't want to be late.

W: We still have ten minutes. ________________ __________________?

M: ____________________ that it's been moved to the other side of campus?

12

W: Honey, I'm back from the store. What are you doing?

M: Nothing special. ______________________ ______________________?

W: I'm thinking pasta. ______________________ ______________________ while I'm preparing salad?

13

W: Would you like to upgrade to a first class ticket?

M: Maybe. How much will that cost?

W: You can either use some of your air miles or you can pay $600 extra.

M: I think I will use my air miles. Will I still have sufficient miles to upgrade ____________________ ____________?

W: Let me check. Hmm... it looks like ____________ ____________________________ for an upgrade both ways.

M: I think ________________________. And can I request a special meal?

W: Sure. We offer vegetarian, Muslim and low-fat.

M: I would like the vegetarian meal please.

W: All right. And is there anything else I can do for you today?

M: Yes, I was wondering ______________________ ______________________.

14

M: My parents have given me some money to buy some new clothes.

W: Good. I think you need some new clothes.

M: You mean my clothes look old and unfashionable?

W: Well, I don't want to criticize, but ___________ ______________________.

M: So I am going clothes shopping this afternoon. Would you like to join me?

W: Hmm... but I don't have any money. And I'm sure my parents ____________________________.

M: Why is that?

W: They gave me money for new clothes a few weeks ago.

M: Oh? But ________________________________?

W: Hmm....

M: Actually, I need you to come to help me pick out clothes.

W: OK. You don't really know ________________ ________________.

15

M: Janice hates exercising. But since she _________ ____________________________, she decides to start exercising. She'd like to do something outside, so she joins the hiking club at her office. The first hike she goes on is not an easy one. The trail is steep, rising quickly and sharply. But _________ __________________. She doesn't give up. Finally, she reaches the top. On the way down, however, the members of the hiking club form small groups. Each group ______________________________. Janice is worried as the two hikers in front of her ______________________. She stops and turns around. She sees Bob. He is the only member of her club she can see. In this situation, what would Janice most likely say to Bob?

16-17

W: Good preparation is the key to enjoying a comfortable flight. ________________________ ________________________, the better! First, bringing your own soft blanket and pillow can really ______________________________. Though airlines usually offer them, it's wise to use your own. Having an eye mask will help you sleep and rest your eyes. Though the lights in a plane will be turned off on an overnight flight, you may still want ________________________________. Similarly, ear plugs can help you block unwanted noise. You may get stuck near two people who talk constantly, so you want to protect yourself just in case. Again, some planes may offer ear plugs, but ______________________________. If you're the kind of person who needs to brush his or her teeth after every meal, then it might be a good idea to bring a small toothbrush and toothpaste on the flight. Though it won't be super easy to brush your teeth in the tiny airplane bathroom, it's better than having bad breath.

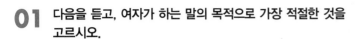

01 다음을 듣고, 여자가 하는 말의 목적으로 가장 적절한 것을 고르시오.

① 쓰레기 분리배출 방법을 안내하려고
② 쓰레기 배출 장소의 변경을 공지하려고
③ 쓰레기를 지정된 날에 배출할 것을 당부하려고
④ 쓰레기 분리배출을 해야 하는 이유를 알려주려고
⑤ 쓰레기 분리배출 미실시로 인한 문제점을 고발하려고

02 대화를 듣고, 남자의 의견으로 가장 적절한 것을 고르시오.

① 유기동물 보호소를 늘려야 한다.
② 반려동물 사육법을 지도해야 한다.
③ 유기동물의 입양을 장려해야 한다.
④ 반려동물 등록제를 시행해야 한다.
⑤ 반려동물 유기를 법으로 처벌해야 한다.

03 대화를 듣고, 두 사람의 관계를 가장 잘 나타낸 것을 고르시오.

① 교장 선생님 – 신임 교사
② 해양학자 – 사회자
③ 담임 교사 – 학부모
④ 동물원 사육사 – 관람객
⑤ 소아과 의사 – 보호자

04 대화를 듣고, 그림에서 대화의 내용과 일치하지 않는 것을 고르시오.

05 대화를 듣고, 남자가 할 일로 가장 적절한 것을 고르시오.

① 강아지의 주인을 찾아보기
② 응급치료법을 듣고 시행하기
③ 강아지를 병원에 데리고 가기
④ 다친 강아지와 함께 있어 주기
⑤ 강아지가 있는 장소 알려 주기

06 대화를 듣고, 여자가 지불할 금액을 고르시오. [3점]

① $200 ② $230 ③ $260
④ $290 ⑤ $320

07 대화를 듣고, 남자가 오전 회의에 가지 못하는 이유를 고르시오.

① 프린터가 고장 나서
② 회의 시간을 착각해서
③ 컴퓨터 수리를 해야 해서
④ 발표 자료 파일을 분실해서
⑤ 테스트 결과가 나오지 않아서

08 대화를 듣고, 제품 판매 방안에 관해 언급되지 않은 것을 고르시오.

① TV 광고 제작 ② 판매 사원 교육
③ 광고 책자 제작 ④ 제품 시연회
⑤ 할인 판매 행사

09 인턴십 프로그램에 관한 다음 내용을 듣고, 일치하지 않는 것을 고르시오.

① 매년 여름 시행하는 프로그램이다.
② 전공에 관계없이 지원할 수 있다.
③ 재학생은 특정 학년만 지원 가능하다.
④ 이력서는 4월 26일까지 제출해야 한다.
⑤ 결과는 지원 마감 다음 주에 개별 통보된다.

10 다음 표를 보면서 대화를 듣고, 남자가 선택할 곡을 고르시오.

List of Songs for Mother's Birthday

Song	Genre	Artist	Date of release
① The Baby	country	Sam Jones (male)	2021
② Dear Mama	hip hop / R&B	Mike Green (male)	1995
③ Superwoman	soul, R&B	Ava Stoll (female)	2020
④ Mama	pop, dance	The Zebras (females)	1996
⑤ Hey Mama	hip hop	Ben Waters (male)	2022

11 대화를 듣고, 남자의 마지막 말에 대한 여자의 응답으로 가장 적절한 것을 고르시오.

① I'll send your paper when I send mine.
② Really? Let's find out why that happened.
③ Mr. Holstein is always very slow in replying.
④ You must have forgotten to send it back to me.
⑤ It's probably because I changed my e-mail address.

12 대화를 듣고, 여자의 마지막 말에 대한 남자의 응답으로 가장 적절한 것을 고르시오.

① Being an actor is very hard.
② He died at the end of the movie.
③ Horror movies really don't appeal to me.
④ I don't know his name, but he's cool.
⑤ My brother used to be a child actor.

13 대화를 듣고, 남자의 마지막 말에 대한 여자의 응답으로 가장 적절한 것을 고르시오.

▶ Woman : ____________________

① Well, I just can't get used to it.
② Where would you like me to sit?
③ I think you have to practice more.
④ Me too. I've always sat on the floor.
⑤ I used them a lot when I was a child.

14 대화를 듣고, 여자의 마지막 말에 대한 남자의 응답으로 가장 적절한 것을 고르시오. [3점]

▶ Man : ____________________

① Excuse me, I can't hear you very well.
② No, as long as I remember, that's correct.
③ That's OK. I really studied hard last year.
④ Don't worry. I promise I won't let you down.
⑤ That's too bad. I hope grandma feels better soon.

15 다음 상황 설명을 듣고, Kevin이 Stacy에게 할 말로 가장 적절한 것을 고르시오. [3점]

▶ Kevin : ____________________

① I think we ordered too much food.
② We shouldn't cook so much next time.
③ This was a great choice for our anniversary.
④ Let's ask the server to wrap up the food.
⑤ I will probably be hungry again later.

[16~17] 다음을 듣고, 물음에 답하시오.

16 남자가 하는 말의 주제로 가장 적절한 것은?

① how to deal with snoring
② things that disturb sound sleep
③ how and why some people snore
④ the functions of the human nose
⑤ the influence of snoring on one's health

17 언급된 요인이 아닌 것은?

① 높은 베개
② 알레르기
③ 비만
④ 식습관
⑤ 짧은 목

01

W: Dear residents: As you well know, every Monday morning the garbage truck comes and collects the garbage ______________________________. This means no garbage should be left out for collection on any other day of the week. Garbage that you put out on the wrong day causes many problems. Waste paper, including newspaper and milk cartons, ______________________________. When it's windy, for example, it gets blown all over town and has to be picked up from lawns and parking lots. That's why we limit the time you can place garbage outside for collection from Sunday afternoon to early Monday morning! ______________________________ in our efforts to make our neighborhood a better place to live!

02

W: Honey, where did you get this cute little kitten?

M: I saw her wandering around the neighborhood and felt bad, so I decided to bring her home.

W: Oh, she ______________________________! How could someone do that?

M: People often don't realize that pets are a huge responsibility. ______________________________, they abandon the animal.

W: But it's so sad. I wish people would learn to treat animals with respect.

M: Personally, I think it's a social issue and strict measures could discourage people from abandoning pets.

W: Well, I don't think that's a long-term solution. Instead, people need to ______________________________.

M: That would be the best, but ______________________________ would lead to real change.

W: You have a point.

03

W: Thank you for coming, Mr. Brown. Did you have any trouble finding the classroom?

M: Not at all, Ms. Grey. I'm glad to meet you, and ______________________________ Tommy's school life.

W: He is adjusting well to school. You should be very proud.

M: That's good to hear. He says your lessons are quite enjoyable.

W: ______________________________ a variety of activities. Young students have a lot of energy and like to try new things.

M: I see. By the way, what are those posters on the wall?

W: That's from a group project the students did on ocean life. I had them research sea animals.

M: So that's why Tommy ______________________________ whales. He sure learned a lot.

W: I'm glad to hear that. He is an active learner. I'm ______________________________ his participation.

M: That's wonderful. Do you have any of his work I could see?

W: Yes, I have some of Tommy's assignments right here. Let's look at a few together.

M: Great.

04

W: Brandon, your desk is messy. Why don't you clean up?

M: Sorry, Mom, but I like it the way it is.

W: But ______________________________ and all the books are piled up on your desk. If you put them back on the bookshelves, you would have more space.

M: I know, but I ______________________________.

W: All right. What about those cups on the right corner of the desk? I think I have seen them there for three straight days.

M: I forgot. I'll take them to the kitchen in a minute.

W: And the picture on the wall looks like ______________________________.

M: Oh, no. I didn't know that. I'll fix it later.

W: Hmm... I'm glad to see that your model planes hanging from the ceiling ________________ ________________________.

M: That's because they're my favorite.

W: Really? OK, great. I'll buy two cards then.

M: All right, to confirm: 21st and 22nd of March, $200 package plus the Super Saver cards for two adults.

W: Yes, that's right.

05

W: Hello, Parkview Animal Hospital. How may I help you?

M: I have an emergency. I was driving down Main Street and ________________________________ lying on the street.

W: Is the dog conscious?

M: Yes, he is breathing very heavily and moaning a bit.

W: ________________________________?

M: I'm afraid not. This neighborhood is very quiet at this time of day.

W: Then you're going to have to bring the dog in yourself.

M: I don't think I can. I am very allergic to dogs and if I touch him, I ________________________________ _______________. And then we will both need a doctor.

W: OK. Please stay with the dog and we will send someone to pick him up.

06

M: Hepburn Springs Hotel.

W: Hi, I'd like to book a room for two adults and three children for March 21st and 22nd please.

M: We have a special weekend family package then; $200 for two days.

W: I see. ____?

M: Passes to the zoo and the children's museum, worth $90.

W: Sounds good.

M: We also sell a Super Saver card. With this card you can use local restaurants and the hot spring spas ___________________________.

W: How much is that?

M: $15 per adult. It's ________________________________ ____________________.

07

M: Hello.

W: Hi, Dan. What's up? Did something happen?

M: Yes, it did. ________________________________ at 10 this morning, right?

W: Yes, exactly. No specific changes have been made to the schedule yet. Is there something wrong with the test results?

M: I don't have them yet. My computer crashed last night and ________________________________ to retrieve the file.

W: Oh, no. Please don't tell me that you've lost the entire file.

M: Well, not exactly. I did back it up.

W: Oh, ____________________________. You really scared me!

M: I took my computer to the shop first thing this morning. They say it will be ready by noon so I'm afraid I can't get to the meeting in time.

W: Well, _________________________ that you didn't lose the file.

M: I will print it out as soon as I get my hands on it.

W: Thank you. I'll put off the meeting until later this afternoon.

08

M: Nicole, do you have a minute?
W: Sure, Darren. What's up?
M: Well, the boss ______________________ ______________________ to market our company's new line of printers.
W: TV commercials have been successful in the past. ______________________?
M: That was my first idea, too. But we don't have the money right now.
W: How about providing more training to our sales staff?
M: That could help. I'd also like to make some new brochures.
W: Good idea! The old brochures ______________ ______________ the features of our new printers.
M: Right. And I think a sale would attract some new customers.
W: I'll talk to Dave about that. He'll know ________ ______________________.
M: Thanks. I think we have a good plan.

09

M: The Sun Broadcasting Company is calling aspiring journalists. We offer a summer internship program every year, and it starts this July. For students who are thinking about a career in journalism, this internship is ______________________ ______________________ in the broadcasting industry. But there are some things you should be aware of ______________________ ______________. First, applicants should be majoring in a related field of journalism. Second, the internship is available to college graduates as well as current college students, but when it comes to college students, only seniors can apply. Lastly, interested applicants should submit a résumé and a cover letter by April 26th. You ______________ ______________________ during the following week.

10

M: Paige, you enjoy listening to music, don't you?
W: Of course. I love music.
M: Can you help me then?
W: Sure. What is it?
M: I made a video for my mom's birthday, and I was wondering if you could help me choose the background music for the video.
W: Oh, that's so sweet of you. I'd love to __________ ______________________. Wait a minute. Choose a song from the list of five songs here. They're all good.
M: Thanks. My mom isn't fond of hip hop, so we'll skip those two.
W: ______________________? Is there a particular artist that your mom likes?
M: She prefers listening to female artists.
W: Then you'll have to choose from these two.
M: I think ______________________. She might not know some of the new songs. I really appreciate your help.
W: It's my pleasure. I'm sure your mom is going to be thrilled.

11

M: Bell, did you submit your term paper to Professor Holstein?
W: Yes, I ______________________. Did you?
M: Actually, I just sent an e-mail, but ______________ ______________.

12

W: Jay, *Vampire Horror* ______________________ ______________. Do you want to watch it?
M: I saw it before, but I'd love to watch it again.
W: Okay. By the way, do you know ______________ ______________________?

13

M: You use chopsticks really well, Wendy.

W: Well, I ________________________ before I came to Korea.

M: Oh? How did you learn to use them?

W: Well, when I was living in Canada, I used to go to many Asian restaurants. And in those restaurants I ____________________________________.

M: I see. But I'm sorry to say that you don't look too comfortable sitting on the floor.

W: Actually, I'm not. I never sat on the floor until I came here.

M: Really?

W: Yeah. And I've been here for six months, but when I sit on the floor, I ________________________ ______________.

M: Oh, that's too bad. I grew up sitting on the floor. It's natural for me.

14

M: Good morning, Mom. When did you come home?

W: Around 2 a.m. You were sleeping then. Did you study last night?

M: Yes, I did. Don't worry.

W: I visited Grandma and Grandpa. They __________ ____________________________.

M: I know. How is Grandma's back?

W: Not good. But there is ____________________ ________________. Is your school bag ready?

M: I just have to put the homework I was doing last night in it.

W: I'm glad to see you're working harder. Remember you promised __________________________.

M: I know. I didn't study much last year. But I'm doing my best now.

W: Well, that's good to hear. I ________________ ________________.

15

W: Today is Kevin and Stacy's third anniversary. To celebrate, the couple ________________ ____________________________ at a fancy restaurant. There, they ate, drank, and talked about their life together. They both had a wonderful time and greatly enjoyed the delicious food. Kevin ordered a steak and lobster dish, and Stacy had the baked salmon. ____________________ by the size of the meals. Now as the evening ____________________, there is still a lot of food remaining. Stacy mentions that it's a shame to waste such delicious food. Kevin agrees and thinks it would be a good idea to ________________ ________________________. In this situation, what would Kevin most likely say to Stacy?

16-17

M: Snoring is instantly recognizable. It's the loud sound that ______________________________ ________________. In the worst cases, the animal-like sounds of a person snoring can awaken even the heaviest sleeper in a nearby bed. But your noisy, dreaming roommate isn't trying to wake you on purpose. When we fall asleep, our muscles begin to relax. This causes our throats to contract. And a smaller throat has ____________________ ________________________. In some people, this narrowing of the throat is extreme. When air is forced through such a tight throat, the back of the throat vibrates. The vibration is what produces ____________________________________. Some common causes of snoring include sleeping with your head up too high on pillows, illnesses and allergies that cause excess fluid in the throat, and obesity. Physical factors, such as an extraordinarily small jaw or short neck, ________ ____________________. Of course, some of these factors cannot be controlled, but others can, meaning there is some hope for the snorer's family.

01 다음을 듣고, 여자가 하는 말의 목적으로 가장 적절한 것을 고르시오.

① 미술전 관람을 독려하려고
② 학교 봄 축제를 홍보하려고
③ 축제 자원봉사자를 모집하려고
④ 신학기 적응 방법을 조언하려고
⑤ 전시 부스의 운영 요령을 설명하려고

02 대화를 듣고, 남자의 의견으로 가장 적절한 것을 고르시오.

① 시(市)는 지하철 노선을 확장해야 한다.
② 시(市)에서 새로운 공원을 건설해야 한다.
③ 공원 내 여러 체력 단련 기구를 배치해야 한다.
④ 시민들을 위한 다양한 공연 프로그램이 필요하다.
⑤ 규칙적인 운동은 건강에 긍정적인 영향을 미친다.

03 대화를 듣고, 두 사람의 관계를 가장 잘 나타낸 것을 고르시오.

① 음악 선생님 – 학생
② 작곡가 – 가수
③ 악기 판매원 – 고객
④ 피아노 조율사 – 피아노 주인
⑤ 바이올린 연주자 – 지휘자

04 대화를 듣고, 그림에서 대화의 내용과 일치하지 않는 것을 고르시오.

05 대화를 듣고, 여자가 남자에게 부탁한 일로 가장 적절한 것을 고르시오.

① 여자에게 돈 맡기기
② 대표로 선물 고르기
③ 같이 쇼핑하러 가기
④ 선물 살 돈 모아 오기
⑤ 생일 파티 일정 알리기

06 대화를 듣고, 남자가 지불할 금액을 고르시오. [3점]

① $60 ② $65 ③ $75 ④ $80 ⑤ $90

07 대화를 듣고, 여자가 걱정하는 이유를 고르시오.

① 연주회에 늦어서
② 꽃다발이 망가져서
③ 사촌과 언쟁을 해서
④ 장난감을 사지 못해서
⑤ 꽃이 배달되지 않아서

08 대화를 듣고, 라플레시아(Rafflesia)에 관해 언급되지 <u>않은</u> 것을 고르시오.

① 크기 ② 생존 방식 ③ 개화 시기 ④ 냄새 ⑤ 번식 방법

09 Wellbeing Fitness에 관한 다음 내용을 듣고, 일치하지 <u>않는</u> 것을 고르시오.

① 최근에 개업한 헬스클럽이다.
② 에어로빅과 필라테스 강습을 제공한다.
③ 개인 트레이너들이 맞춤형 프로그램을 짜준다.
④ 회원들은 모든 시설을 이용할 수 있다.
⑤ 이번 달에 등록하면 3일 무료 체험을 할 수 있다.

10 다음 표를 보면서 대화를 듣고, 두 사람이 선택할 버스 투어를 고르시오.

Evergreen City 1-Day Bus Tour Schedule				
Tour	Time of Departure & Arrival	Lunch	Price	Location of Departure
①	9 a.m. – 4 p.m.	○	$98	in front of City Hall
②	9 a.m. – 4 p.m.	○	$78	in front of City Hall
③	9 a.m. – 5 p.m.	×	$58	in front of Grand Station
④	1 p.m. – 6 p.m.	×	$48	in front of Grand Station
⑤	9 a.m. – 5 p.m.	○	$68	in front of Grand Station

11 대화를 듣고, 여자의 마지막 말에 대한 남자의 응답으로 가장 적절한 것을 고르시오.

① You can have mine if you want.
② I'll ask Mom to help you with that.
③ Thank you for making breakfast today.
④ Let's make some more muffins.
⑤ It's the one with blue spots.

12 대화를 듣고, 남자의 마지막 말에 대한 여자의 응답으로 가장 적절한 것을 고르시오.

① It's on every Friday night at 9 p.m.
② Let's watch it together and find out.
③ The best dancer doesn't always win.
④ The judges are the same every week.
⑤ There's a romantic comedy with my favorite actor.

13 대화를 듣고, 여자의 마지막 말에 대한 남자의 응답으로 가장 적절한 것을 고르시오. [3점]

▶ Man : ______________________

① Don't worry. I can fix your faucet for you.
② Thanks, but I already have it written down.
③ How did you know I have to clean my room?
④ All right, I will be calling the security right away.
⑤ Don't take a long time. A repairman is arriving soon.

14 대화를 듣고, 남자의 마지막 말에 대한 여자의 응답으로 가장 적절한 것을 고르시오. [3점]

▶ Woman : ______________________

① OK. I'll take care of it. Don't worry.
② I told him you were performing surgery.
③ I'll suggest the patient come in to visit you.
④ Should I tell him to wait five more minutes?
⑤ Do you want me to cancel the rest of your appointments?

15 다음 상황 설명을 듣고, John이 점장에게 할 말로 가장 적절한 것을 고르시오.

▶ John : ______________________

① I'm afraid the game is almost over.
② How much longer is it going to be?
③ I ordered pepperoni pizzas, not cheese.
④ Maybe we should just eat the cheese pizzas.
⑤ I've been waiting more than 50 minutes already!

[16~17] 다음을 듣고, 물음에 답하시오.

16 남자가 하는 말의 주제로 가장 적절한 것은?

① how to take pictures of landscape
② tips for taking good pictures of people
③ camera settings for landscape photography
④ how to become a professional photographer
⑤ differences between portrait and landscape photography

17 고려할 요소로 언급되지 않은 것은?

① angle
② eye contact
③ distance
④ background
⑤ focus

01

W: Good afternoon, students. I hope you are ________ ____. Following tradition, the spring school festival will begin next week. ____________________________ ________________________. There will be a play, music performances, and much more to enjoy. In past years, the most popular event has been the art show. It will be held from 9 a.m. to 5 p.m. with many works of art and festival pictures ________________________. Those who wish to set up an art booth should sign up now. Art booths will be located next to the gym, but space is limited. You are welcome to display any paintings, sculptures, drawings, or other artwork at your booth. We hope everyone enjoys the festival, and ____________________________ your friends and family!

02

M: Hi, Hazel. I'm surprised to see you here.

W: Yes, well, I come here to play badminton when I can.

M: It's ____________________________________, right?

W: It takes about 25 minutes on the subway, but there aren't any parks in my neighborhood.

M: I guess this is ____________________________ ____________ on this side of the city.

W: Right. The city was planning to build another park in my neighborhood, but the plans were cancelled.

M: I remember that. A new concert hall was built on that location instead.

W: Right. It's a shame because the concert hall is rarely used and the residents of my neighborhood have ____.

M: I agree. I hope the city reconsiders building some new parks.

03

W: Excuse me, is there anything I can help you with?

M: Well, I'm actually shopping for my daughter. She's in a band.

W: You're a good father. What instrument does she play?

M: ____________________________________ for years, and she also plays the guitar. She's so talented.

W: That's impressive. Maybe I should show you our selection of acoustic guitars.

M: Actually, she's been talking about learning the violin. That's why I'm here.

W: I see. Well, the violins you see here are all good quality.

M: ______________________________ as a gift for her?

W: Hmm, the size can make a big difference. I could recommend one based on her age, but __________ ______________________________ your daughter to the store.

M: Oh, I hadn't thought of that. You've saved me from a big mistake. I'll return on a later date.

W: No problem. Come back anytime. We're open every day until eight.

04

W: Come this way, Tyler. I guess this store is having a sale.

M: Oh, you're right. It says, "SALE 50% off," right up there.

W: Wow! ________________________! We can buy ski equipment at a reasonable price here.

M: That's right. I'm thinking about buying a helmet for skiing. I think the one the mannequin's wearing ____.

W: I think so too. Oh, look at the mittens. I love them. That style with buckles is in fashion nowadays.

M: You mean the ones on the left?

W: Yes. ______________________________ with my ski jacket.

M: Great. That would be cool.

W: Oh. Didn't you say you needed ski boots? How about the ones next to the box? They look very comfortable.

M: Yes. Those look perfect. I should check if they have the right size for me.

W: I hope they do. Also, I need to check those snowboards ______________________.

M: Okay, let's go inside the store to take a closer look.

05

W: Do you know that it's Wendy's birthday on Friday?

M: Oh, I forgot. How old will she be?

W: Fifteen, ______________________.

M: I'll have to go and buy her a present.

W: I thought we could collect some money from everyone and then buy her one nice present.

M: Good idea. How much would you like everyone to give? Five dollars?

W: Yes, ______________________.

M: OK. Here's my money.

W: Actually, I was wondering ______________ ______________ and collect the money from everyone.

M: Oh? OK.

W: If you do that, I'll be the one who'll go and buy the gift.

M: I don't have a problem with that.

06

M: Hello.

W: Hello, Peter? This is Kelly. ______________ ______________ that I advertised on the gym's noticeboard for $50, right?

M: That's right. Is there a problem? You said you could deliver them tomorrow.

W: Yes, but, I just checked on the map and your house ______________________. I wonder if you could also pay me $10 for gas.

M: I beg your pardon, but we already agreed on a total price.

W: Yes, you're right. But ______________ ______________. Okay forget it, same price.

M: Good. Umm.... Kelly, do you still have the weight training DVDs for $30?

W: Yes, I do. If you like, you can ______________ ______________.

M: Great. I'll buy them too. And you'll deliver both the weights and DVDs tomorrow?

W: Yes, I'll be there at 10.

07

M: Jessica, is everything okay? You look stressed.

W: I am a little stressed. My cousin has a piano recital this evening.

M: That's amazing! ______________ ______________? What's stressing you out?

W: Of course I am happy. So, I ordered a bouquet of flowers for her.

M: There's no flower shop around here, so ______________ ______________.

W: Right, the bouquet was delivered by the florist this morning, and I put it in the refrigerator to keep it cool ______________________ for the recital.

M: What happened?

W: My little son found it and took it to his room and ruined it.

M: Oh, ______________________.

W: Yeah. The recital is in two hours, and I don't know what to do.

M: Your cousin will understand. Hmm.... Maybe there is a flower shop near the recital hall.

08

W: Take a look at this picture, David.
M: That's the biggest flower I've ever seen. What is it?
W: It's a Rafflesia flower, and it's about 90 cm in diameter. I think we can use it for the topic of our report.
M: Good idea. So, what's the rest of the plant look like?
W: The flower is the whole plant. It can't ______________________.
M: Then it's a parasite living on other plants?
W: Right. Another unusual thing is its smell. It smells like rotting meat!
M: That's disgusting. I'm glad there aren't any growing around here. So, ______________________?
W: When it dies, it becomes a sticky pool of seeds and liquid. The seeds stick to the feet of animals and ______________________.
M: What an unusual plant!

09

M: Summer is coming, and that means it's time to lose some weight, get in shape, and look your best. So, ______________________ fitting into that favorite swimsuit, why not join Wellbeing Fitness? Wellbeing Fitness is a newly-opened fitness center for improving your health. We provide various classes such as aerobics and Pilates. We have ______________________ who can develop a customized program to help you meet your goals. The use of all facilities, including the shower room and the lockers, ______________________. Until the end of this month, we are offering special discounts to those who register for a 3-month membership. Don't miss out on this incredible opportunity ______________________!

10

M: Let's take the 1-Day bus tour tomorrow. ______________________ the city.
W: Sounds good. I heard there are several city bus tours, so let's check the Internet.
M: Oh, here we go. There are ______________________. Let's first decide on the time.
W: We have dinner plans with the Johnson family, so we have to be back here no later than 5 p.m.
M: Then let's take a tour that leaves early in the morning.
W: I agree. How about lunch?
M: Since it's our first time, let's get ______________________. But I don't want to spend more than $80 per person.
W: Got it. One tour leaves from Grand Station and the other from City Hall.
M: I heard Grand Station is far from here. ______________________.
W: Then it looks like we have only one choice. It only takes 10 minutes to City Hall.
M: Okay. I think this is our best option.

11

W: I'm hungry. Can I have ______________________?
M: Sure. Just don't take the blueberry one. Mom is saving it for her breakfast.
W: I can't tell which one that is. ______________________?

12

M: ______________________ the channel? I want to watch a movie.
W: Actually, I was hoping to watch *Dancing with the Stars*. It starts in five minutes.
M: I like that show, too. ______________________?

13

M: Hi! I'm Jake. I live downstairs from you.

W: Nice to meet you, Jake. I'm Allison. ____________ ____________________________?

M: I noticed some water dripping from my bathroom ceiling and wondered if you could check where it's coming from.

W: Really? Let me run and check.

M: Yes, please hurry.

W: Uh oh. I ____ while I was cooking and forgot about it. I turned the faucet off now.

M: I'm quite sure my ceiling is damaged. It might be expensive to fix.

W: I'm really sorry. I'll pay for the repair.

M: Well, I need to call the maintenance man first.

W: Do you have his number? ____________________ ____________________.

14

W: Good morning, Doctor Silver.

M: Good morning, Judy. __________________________ _____________ this morning?

W: Mrs. Jenkins is coming in for what she described as flu-like symptoms.

M: OK. And then who?

W: And then you have the Russell twins. Their mother said they are both coughing a lot.

M: Anyone else?

W: Oh, and your friend, Mr. Hill, called. He wants you to call him back ______________________________.

M: Oh boy. If he calls back, please tell him I'm busy. He ____.

W: He was very insistent that you call him.

M: Well, please make up some kind of excuse. I really don't want to be disturbed by him today.

15

W: John has invited some of his friends to his house to watch a football game. After the first half, his team is winning and everyone ________________ ______________. John decides to order pizza for everyone. He calls the pizza shop and orders two large pepperoni pizzas. The manager tells John ____. After 30 minutes, the delivery man arrives with three cheese pizzas. John explains that the order is incorrect, and the delivery man returns to the shop. Another 20 minutes passes as everyone grows hungry. John calls to ask about his order. The manager explains that __________________ ___________________ and asks John to wait for 30 minutes. In this situation, what would John most likely say to the manager?

16-17

M: On Monday, we discussed many ways of taking remarkable pictures of landscapes while traveling. Today, we're going to ______________________ ____________________________. When you use people as a focal point, it's important for you to create a certain wow factor. For example, instead of using the common method of placing a person in the center, try experimenting with different angles and perspectives. Some good methods are to get up high and shoot down on a person, or to get close to the ground and shoot up. ____________ ________________________ is eye contact. You can have the person look directly at the lens, or ______________________________. The distance between you and your subject also has a huge impact on the feel of the picture. Don't be afraid to experiment with extreme close-ups. These have the power to capture the full force of an emotion. Also, ______________________________ a bit. Sometimes, the perfect way to highlight one subject is to blur out all the others. Hopefully, these strategies will help you ______________________ ______________________________.

01 다음을 듣고, 남자가 하는 말의 목적으로 가장 적절한 것을 고르시오.

① 자사 제품을 홍보하려고
② 실험 참가자들을 모집하려고
③ 제품 홈페이지를 소개하려고
④ 환경보호 방법을 안내하려고
⑤ 화학 물질의 위험성을 경고하려고

02 대화를 듣고, 여자의 의견으로 가장 적절한 것을 고르시오.

① 대면 강의는 비대면 강의보다 효과적이다.
② 일대일 피드백은 학습에 긍정적인 영향을 미친다.
③ 새 학기를 위한 효과적인 학습 계획을 세워야 한다.
④ 수업 정원이 많으면 제대로 된 교육을 받을 수 없다.
⑤ 적극적인 수업 참여는 학업 성취도 향상으로 이어진다.

03 대화를 듣고, 두 사람의 관계를 가장 잘 나타낸 것을 고르시오.

① 사회자 – 운동선수
② 행사 진행자 – 초청 강사
③ 기자 – 농구 감독
④ 아나운서 – 경기
⑤ 의사 – 환자

04 대화를 듣고, 그림에서 대화의 내용과 일치하지 <u>않는</u> 것을 고르시오.

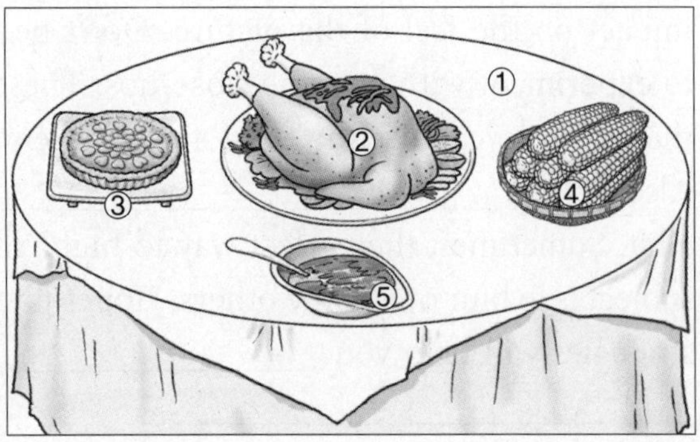

05 대화를 듣고, 남자가 여자를 위해 할 일로 가장 적절한 것을 고르시오.

① 쓰레기 내놓기
② 저녁 식사 준비하기
③ 어머니와 시장에 가기
④ 욕조에 뜨거운 물 받기
⑤ 어머니께 마사지해 드리기

06 대화를 듣고, 여자가 지불할 금액을 고르시오. [3점]

① $120　② $140　③ $180
④ $220　⑤ $240

07 대화를 듣고, 남자가 자동차 구입을 망설이는 이유를 고르시오.

① 차가 오래된 것이라서
② 자동차 크기가 너무 작아서
③ 사고가 한 번 났던 자동차라서
④ 나중에 유지 수리비가 더 들 것 같아서
⑤ 정기적으로 자동차 정비 검사를 받지 않아서

08 대화를 듣고, 모금 행사에 관해 언급되지 <u>않은</u> 것을 고르시오.

① 장소　② 행사 시간
③ 추첨 행사　④ 초청 인사
⑤ 입장료

09 Elephant grass에 관한 다음 내용을 듣고, 일치하지 <u>않는</u> 것을 고르시오.

① 생존에 물과 영양분이 거의 필요하지 않다.
② 오래전부터 가축의 먹이로 사용되어 왔다.
③ 주요 작물의 해충 피해를 막아준다.
④ 발전소에 연료를 공급하는 데 쓰일 수 있다.
⑤ 현재 아프리카의 주된 에너지원 중 하나이다.

10 다음 표를 보면서 대화를 듣고, 두 사람이 선택할 캠핑장을 고르시오.

Camping Grounds in Ventura County

	Toilets & Showers	Children's playground	Swimming pool	Pets	1-night fee
①	○	○	○	allowed	$120
②	○	×	○	not allowed	$120
③	○	○	○	not allowed	$100
④	○	○	○	allowed	$100
⑤	×	×	×	not allowed	$70

11 대화를 듣고, 남자의 마지막 말에 대한 여자의 응답으로 가장 적절한 것을 고르시오.

① I don't think you can help me.
② I'll help you choose the perfect song.
③ It's great that you filmed the entire trip.
④ It's not difficult at all. Let me show you.
⑤ I'm really looking forward to the field trip tomorrow.

12 대화를 듣고, 여자의 마지막 말에 대한 남자의 응답으로 가장 적절한 것을 고르시오.

① My plan was a success thanks to your help.
② If you're free, find other clubs for us to join.
③ Of course. Table tennis is good for staying in shape.
④ Sure. Could you give me a hand making club posters?
⑤ I'm afraid that we already have enough members.

13 대화를 듣고, 남자의 마지막 말에 대한 여자의 응답으로 가장 적절한 것을 고르시오.

▶ Woman : ______

① I'm good at making important decisions.
② I'm not picky. Really, it doesn't matter.
③ Steak please. I'd like it well-done.
④ I'll treat you to dinner tonight.
⑤ May I take your order?

14 대화를 듣고, 여자의 마지막 말에 대한 남자의 응답으로 가장 적절한 것을 고르시오. [3점]

▶ Man : ______

① Still, you should tell them. It's your life.
② I'm afraid they will be disappointed with you.
③ Then change your major to medical science.
④ Yes, it would be disrespectful to think for yourself.
⑤ It's OK. They know architects require some training.

15 다음 상황 설명을 듣고, Mary가 Jane의 어머니에게 할 말로 가장 적절한 것을 고르시오. [3점]

▶ Mary : ______

① Jane can have some more time to prepare.
② I'll have tomorrow's lesson prepared shortly.
③ I'm glad you shared Jane's concerns with me.
④ I'll talk with her about that tomorrow after class.
⑤ I hope Jane feels well enough to come to school soon.

[16~17] 다음을 듣고, 물음에 답하시오.

16 여자가 하는 말의 주제로 가장 적절한 것은?

① upcoming expansion work on the parking lot
② introduction of the designated parking system
③ apologies over the recent construction noise
④ guidance on safety precautions for the elevator
⑤ notification of the apartment maintenance schedule

17 언급된 장소가 아닌 것은?

① 주차장
② 엘리베이터
③ 쓰레기 수거장
④ 정원
⑤ 놀이터

19 Sense Up 듣기 모의고사 DICTATION

01

M: Most modern household cleaning products contain unnecessary chemicals. ______________________________________ and skin disorders in children and illnesses in adults, but they are also destroying our environment. Orange Magic company uses oil from 100 percent organically grown oranges to manufacture our unique cleaning products. Our laboratories conduct careful tests ______________________________________. Our website, orangemagic.com, contains page after page of positive reviews from hundreds of customers. Leave your address when you visit the website and we'll send a free sample set of our bestselling cleaners, so you can ______________________________________. Satisfaction guaranteed.

02

M: Well, the first day of school is over. How were your classes?

W: They seem alright, but I'm worried about the number of students.

M: My classes were fairly crowded also, but I still ______________________.

W: It's not just a matter of getting a seat. For instance, almost everyone in my philosophy class wanted to speak, but ______________________.

M: I suppose it would be nice if classes were smaller.

W: Of course. We need opportunities to talk directly with our professors and get feedback from them.

M: So you think that we aren't getting ______________________?

W: With as many students in a class as we have, I don't see how we possibly could be.

03

W: Now let's welcome today's guest, Steven Adams. Thank you for coming, Steven.

M: It's my pleasure, Sharon.

W: First off, congratulations on ______________________. You must be pleased.

M: Winning is a team effort, but yes, I've practiced hard, and I'm scoring points.

W: Now, I've heard a rumor ______________________. Is that true?

M: Unfortunately, it is. It happened during practice when I was running for the ball.

W: Does that mean we won't see you on the court for a while? The fans will be disappointed.

M: Doctors say I can play again in a few weeks. Until then, I'll work on my 3-point shooting.

W: With over 22 points per game, ______________________ you have much room for improvement.

M: I appreciate you saying so, but I want to give my best for the fans every time.

W: We hope you recover soon. Thanks for coming, Steven.

M: Thank you, Sharon.

04

M: Rebecca, it's about time. Are you done with the Thanksgiving dinner yet?

W: Almost done. Would you ______________________?

M: Okay. Oh, everything looks perfect. And what's this? I've never seen this oval table before.

W: I borrowed it from next door.

M: It will be perfect for 6 people.

W: Honey, I think the turkey in the middle will taste delicious. I cooked it ______________________.

M: It smells good. And what's on the square plate to the left of the turkey?

W: It's a pumpkin pie. The kids will like it.

M: That's my favorite, too. Is ______________________ from uncle Bill's farm

last week?
W: Yes, it's still very fresh.
M: I see. And what's in the bowl with a spoon in it?
W: Do you mean, the bowl behind the turkey? That's cranberry sauce. ________________________ turkey.

05

W: Jimmy, would you ________________________?
M: I think that's what Dad does every night.
W: There's a big bucket ________________________ here that he didn't take last night.
M: Actually, Dad said he would take it out tonight.
W: OK, then, I'm going to take a rest.
M: Mom, you look tired.
W: It's my back again. I carried heavy shopping bags home from the market today.
M: You should have a nice hot bath. ______________ the bathtub for you?
W: No, you need to eat your dinner. It's nearly ready.
M: Come sit down for just a few minutes, Mom. Let me rub your back and neck.
W: All right, Jimmy. But ________________________ ________________!
M: Don't worry, it won't get cold.

06

W: Excuse me, I like these two pairs of shoes, but I can't figure out ________________________ ________________________. The sign in front of the store says, "Up to 50% off everything."
M: Hmm.... Can I see that pair?
W: The sticker on these high heels says $200. Are they 50% off?
M: No, I'm sorry. ________________________ and the items there are only 30% off the sticker price.
W: ________________________. I'll take them. I love the color and the brand. Now what about these casual shoes?
M: Oh, those are 50% off.
W: But they don't have a price sticker on them, so how much are they?
M: $40, ma'am.
W: You mean the sale price or the regular price?
M: The sale price, ma'am.
W: OK, I'll take them.

07

M: Hello, I'm here to buy a car. Can you show me the car you have for sale?
W: Yes, here it is. It's a Fiat 500L. What do you think of it?
M: How much mileage does the car have?
W: It has 14,582 miles. It's a 2015 model.
M: Well... It's ________________________, isn't it?
W: It may be a little small, but I can assure you that ________________________.
M: Has the car ever been involved in an accident?
W: No, I have an eight-year accident-free driving history.
M: Sounds good. What about its paint job? It's not very clean and shiny. ________________________ ________________?
W: I do maintenance checkups on it regularly. It runs very smooth!
M: What would be the final price of the car?
W: It's 12,500 dollars.
M: Well, ________________________ later for repairs and new paint, so I'm not sure it's reasonable. Thanks, anyway.

08

W: Hello. How may I help you?

M: Hi, I'm calling for information about Sunshine Hospital's 15th annual fundraiser.

W: Great. The fundraiser is a fun event that welcomes the entire community.

M: I see. And ______________________________?

W: No. The fundraiser will be at Memorial Park, located off exit 10 on Highway 95.

M: I'm hoping to bring my family in the afternoon. When does it finish?

W: It's open from 9 a.m. to 10 p.m., and the prize lottery begins at 2 p.m.

M: Is a lottery ticket ______________________________ ______________________?

W: No. Entrance is $15, and lottery tickets are sold for $5 each.

M: Oh, I see. That's a little expensive.

W: ______________________________. We're giving away TVs, digital cameras, and much more.

M: Well, thank you for your help.

09

W: Elephant grass is a tall grass that is native to the savannahs of Africa. It requires little water or nutrients for its survival, and therefore ________ ______________________________. Traditionally, it has been used primarily for feeding domestic animals; however, it is now being used for pest management. Fields of elephant grass are planted ______________________________ from important crops like corn. This technique is especially effective against moths because moths are strongly attracted to it. This grass can also be used to fuel power stations and replace traditional sources of energy, such as coal. Furthermore, it can be processed into bio-oil or bio-gas. Although ______________________________, it has the potential to provide energy to African communities.

10

W: How about going camping this weekend?

M: That's a great idea. Let's rent a camping van this time.

W: That'll be so much fun! The kids will love it.

M: Let's first make a reservation.

W: We need a place that has a restroom and a shower facility.

M: Right. The camping van ______________________ ______________________ inside the car.

W: The kids will be rolling in the dirt and having fun, so we definitely need them to take a shower. A playground and swimming pool ______________ ____________________.

M: Of course.

W: Oh, we also need to think about our dog, Freya. Since we won't be at a hotel, I'd like to __________ ______________________.

M: Yes, we should. I'm sure the kids will like playing with Freya at the campground.

W: How much will everything cost? We can't spend more than $100 per night.

M: Don't worry. There's a campground that's perfect for us. I'll reserve a spot now.

11

M: Hey, Kate! Can you ______________________?

W: Sure. Are these videos from the field trip last week?

M: Yes, but I don't know ______________________ ____________ into the video clip.

12

W: Congratulations on becoming the new president of our table tennis club!

M: Thank you. ______________________ will be to recruit new club members.

W: ______________________. Would you like me to help you?

13

M: Where will your company transfer you?
W: Los Angeles or New York. I can choose.
M: Which city do you prefer?
W: I ______________________________.
M: Really? I think Los Angeles would be better because it's warmer.
W: I like cold weather, so it's OK. Hmm. You know ______________________________. But we've been talking a long time. Let's go to a restaurant to eat.
M: Sounds good. How about Chinese food?
W: Sure.
M: Oh, there is a good Italian place near here.
W: ______________________________. I like everything.
M: But tell me what you would like to have.

14

M: So have you decided ______________________________ at university next year?
W: Well, my mother and father want me to study law, so I guess that's it.
M: What? You can't let them decide what you will do for the rest of your life!
W: They are my parents. I have to obey their wishes.
M: But what about your wishes?
W: It ______________________________.
M: Have you even thought about what you want?
W: Yes, I want to study architecture. I would like to design skyscrapers.
M: Did you tell your parents that?
W: No. I couldn't possibly tell them I don't want to become a lawyer.
M: Why not?
W: ______________________________?

15

M: Mary is a teacher at a public elementary school. After the day's classes, she is about to leave her classroom, when she receives a phone call from a mother. The mother ______________________________, Jane, is very upset. Jane told her mother that she's scared about failing a class project. Jane says she ______________________________ because she was sick and missed some classes. Suddenly, Mary realizes that she ______________________________ to Jane. So, Mary tells the mother that she will give Jane extra time to prepare for the project. The mother sounds relieved but still wonders what her daughter should do to prepare. In this situation, what would Mary most likely say to the mother?

16-17

W: Good morning, residents. This is the security office for Health Village apartments. We ______________________________ and promise to keep this message brief. Today, we want to remind you about the schedule for ______________________________ this week. On Monday and Tuesday, the underground parking area will be cleaned and repainted. Cleaning starts at 9 a.m. No cars may be parked in the parking areas during these times. Cars may return at 6 p.m. on the same day. On Wednesday and Thursday, ______________________________. Please use the stairs instead during these times. On Friday, the garbage collection and recycling areas will be cleaned. So ______________________________ that will be placed nearby. On Saturday, pesticide will be sprayed on all plants surrounding the apartments and throughout the gardens. Make sure to close your windows on this day and ______________________________. Again, we apologize for the inconvenience. With your help, this work will go smoothly and we can all enjoy the benefits. Thank you for your cooperation.

01 다음을 듣고, 남자가 하는 말의 목적으로 가장 적절한 것을 고르시오.

① 허리케인이 끝났음을 알리려고
② 주민들에게 대피령을 내리려고
③ 허리케인에 대비하는 방법을 알리려고
④ 폭풍으로 인한 피해 주민들을 위로하려고
⑤ 기상 주의보가 발효되는 과정을 설명하려고

02 대화를 듣고, 두 사람이 하는 말의 주제로 가장 적절한 것을 고르시오.

① 다양한 학습 과제 유형
② 온라인 기반 학습의 장점
③ 수업 선택 시 고려해야 할 요소
④ 개개인에게 맞는 학습법의 중요성
⑤ 강의식 수업과 토론식 수업의 차이점

03 대화를 듣고, 두 사람의 관계를 가장 잘 나타낸 것을 고르시오.

① 정비소 직원 – 손님
② 경찰관 – 보행자
③ 면접관 – 구직자
④ 전자제품 판매원 – 고객
⑤ 설문 조사원 – 행인

04 대화를 듣고, 그림에서 대화의 내용과 일치하지 않는 것을 고르시오.

05 대화를 듣고, 여자가 할 일로 가장 적절한 것을 고르시오.

① 가스 밸브 열기
② 수리기사 부르기
③ 엄마에게 전화하기
④ 집주인에게 말하기
⑤ 버스 터미널에 전화하기

06 대화를 듣고, 남자가 지불할 금액을 고르시오.

① $70 ② $80 ③ $90
④ $100 ⑤ $110

07 대화를 듣고, 여자가 친구에게 화가 난 이유를 고르시오.

① 약속 시간에 항상 늦어서
② 자신의 외모에 대해 놀려서
③ 블로그에 자신의 험담을 써서
④ 자신의 사진을 마음대로 게시해서
⑤ 자신이 아끼는 사진을 지워버려서

08 대화를 듣고, Yellowstone 국립공원에 관해 언급되지 않은 것을 고르시오.

① 위치 ② 기온 ③ 크기
④ 화산 활동 ⑤ 서식 동물

09 I Tower에 관한 다음 내용을 듣고, 일치하지 않는 것을 고르시오.

① 높이는 250미터이다.
② 1975년에 세워졌다.
③ 200미터 지점부터 전망대가 있다.
④ 전망 2, 3층은 전망 1층에서 걸어갈 수 있다.
⑤ 전망 3층에는 회전 레스토랑이 있다.

10 다음 표를 보면서 대화를 듣고, 남자가 찾아갈 의사를 고르시오.

Physicians in Evergreen City

Physician	Location	Specialty	Years of experience	Gender
① Dr. Roberts	Highland Ave.	internal medicine	23 yrs.	male
② Dr. Phillips	Main St.	allergies	9 yrs.	female
③ Dr. Brown	Pine St.	internal medicine	19 yrs.	male
④ Dr. Jones	Maple Ave.	allergies	2 yrs.	female
⑤ Dr. Reed	Fifth Ave.	allergies	7 yrs.	male

11 대화를 듣고, 여자의 마지막 말에 대한 남자의 응답으로 가장 적절한 것을 고르시오.

① It's in a wedding hall downtown.
② I think they should have jobs first.
③ Marriage is a basic social institution.
④ It's better to get married in the spring.
⑤ Most older people are already married.

12 대화를 듣고, 남자의 마지막 말에 대한 여자의 응답으로 가장 적절한 것을 고르시오.

① Don't worry. Our report is perfect.
② I sent you an email with my answer.
③ It feels great to finally be on vacation.
④ Here, I'll give you my cell phone number.
⑤ There will be a question and answer session.

13 대화를 듣고, 여자의 마지막 말에 대한 남자의 응답으로 가장 적절한 것을 고르시오. [3점]

▶ Man : ______________________

① Not really. You don't take care of house chores.
② I've been a manager for five years.
③ Yes, he loves *Winnie the Pooh*.
④ I can, but it is a really tough job.
⑤ I was really happy when you were not here.

14 대화를 듣고, 남자의 마지막 말에 대한 여자의 응답으로 가장 적절한 것을 고르시오. [3점]

▶ Woman : ______________________

① Don't give in this time, please.
② Yes, we should have just one more.
③ You're right. It doesn't do any harm.
④ I wish my dad could quit smoking too.
⑤ I'm sorry but you can't smoke in here.

15 다음 상황 설명을 듣고, Fredricks 선생님이 수민에게 할 말로 가장 적절한 것을 고르시오. [3점]

▶ Mr. Fredricks : ______________________

① Thank you for holding the door open.
② Can you make copies for everyone?
③ Do you have any questions?
④ Can you give a handout to every student?
⑤ How much exercise do you get every week?

[16~17] 다음을 듣고, 물음에 답하시오.

16 여자가 하는 말의 주제로 가장 적절한 것은?

① the best study methods
② tips for better test-taking
③ ways to improve memory
④ how to manage a busy schedule
⑤ how to remain calm under pressure

17 언급된 긴장 해소 방법이 아닌 것은?

① 눈 감기　② 근육 이완하기
③ 생각 비우기　④ 심호흡하기
⑤ 조용한 음악 감상하기

01

M: Now that the hurricane season is over, we should examine what we did wrong this year. In April, Hurricane Sally did little damage, but if she had been stronger, she ______________________ a lot more damage as residents were not ready. When a hurricane watch is issued, you must do several things to prepare for the coming hurricane. You must put tape on your house's windows. Then you must ______________________________. It's also important to bring outdoor furniture inside. If you can't bring it inside, you must tie it down. Then, you must ______________________________: food, water, and a battery-powered radio.

02

W: Hi, Kevin. Are you going to be in Ms. Jackson's writing class?

M: No, I decided to take an online writing class instead.

W: I didn't know we had that option. Anyway, ______________________ to take the class in person?

M: That's ______________________, but once I saw all the things that are available online, I changed my mind.

W: I guess it will be nice to be able to pause the lectures anytime you want.

M: Of course. Plus, I can listen to them on my own schedule.

W: What are the assignments like?

M: There are mini-quizzes and assignments just like in any class, but everything is graded immediately. There are even chat rooms ______________________ the lectures and get help.

W: Wow, maybe I'll try that next time.

03

W: Good afternoon. May I ask you a few questions?

M: How long will it take? I'm on my way to the bank.

W: Not long. And I can ______________________________.

M: What is it?

W: A toiletry set for traveling: shampoo and conditioner, soap, and a toothbrush.

M: OK. I guess I have a few minutes.

W: I'd like to ask your opinion about electronics such as televisions, DVD players, and digital cameras.

M: OK.

W: ______________________________ the best reputation for quality?

M: KDT does! When I want to buy electronics, I always buy KDT stuff.

W: Why is that?

M: I know they are well made. ______________________________.

W: OK. And I have a few more questions.

M: Go ahead.

04

M: Alice, did you finish designing the new cinema discount coupons?

W: Sure, Bob. Take a look, and ______________________________.

M: Oh, I like the font you chose for "Discount Coupon" in the top left!

W: That's good to hear. I was worried it might be too big.

M: Not at all. ______________________ the star under it advertising 30% off.

W: I hope it's not too small. I wanted to keep this image of a huge bucket of popcorn in the center.

M: I like what you've done. After all, the bucket in the center and the sodas all around it are the main attraction.

W: ______________________________.

M: And there was still plenty of room for the cinema's information in the bottom right corner.

W: Right. I included both the website and the address.

M: It looks like you thought of everything. Let's _____ ___________________________.

W: Great.

05

M: Hello?

W: Dad, it's Jenny. There's a problem. The boiler is broken. It's freezing and I haven't had hot water for two days.

M: Are you sure the gas valve is turned on?

W: Dad, I'm not that stupid.

M: Sorry, dear. Then, the pipe ___________________ ___________________. Did you tell the landlady about it?

W: I did. But she said that if it froze and burst I should fix it by myself.

M: You should call the repair technician right now.

W: I already did. But, it's Friday night. He __________ ______________________ until Monday morning. Dad, I need a hot shower. I'm coming home for the weekend.

M: If you do, we'll be happy. But I'm not sure _______ ______________________. It's already the weekend.

W: Yes, you're right. I should call the bus station first. Could you come and pick me up if there aren't any tickets left? I can't stay here for the whole weekend.

M: OK, I will. I'll tell your mother you're coming.

W: Thanks, Dad!

06

W: How can I help you?

M: I want to buy my nephew something as a graduation gift. Could you recommend one? He's going to ______________________________.

W: If that's the case, how about a nice wallet?

M: Good idea. How much are they?

W: This brown leather wallet is $90 and this fabric one is $40.

M: I think ___________________________________. I'll take that black leather wallet. Is it also $90?

W: It was originally $100 but it's 20 dollars off now.

M: Sounds great.

W: If you want, we can put your nephew's name on it since it's a personalized wallet.

M: Really? How much does it cost and ______________ ______________________________?

W: You just pay an additional $10 and it'll take about 30 minutes.

M: Okay. ____________________. I hope my nephew will love it.

W: I'm sure it'll be a very special gift for him.

07

M: ____, Kelly?

W: I'm just in a bad mood. Don't worry about it.

M: I'm your friend, and I'm always happy to listen.

W: Thanks, but it's just something Lydia did that really upset me.

M: Was she late for an appointment again? That really ________________________________.

W: I know what you mean, but no. She took some pictures of me that look ridiculous.

M: Well, that's not so bad. Just some funny faces, right?

W: Yes, but I look really bad in the photos, and she put them on her blog!

M: Oh, now I get it. That would make me mad too.

W: She ____ before uploading the pictures.

M: Why don't you ask her to delete the photos?

W: I will. Hopefully, she'll understand my point of view.

08

M: Rebecca, are these pictures from your trip to the United States?

W: They are. The one you are looking at right now was taken in Yellowstone National Park.

M: It looks beautiful. It's somewhere ____________ ____________________________, right?

W: It's mainly in the state of Wyoming, but parts of it are in Montana and Idaho.

M: I didn't know that. It ______________________ ______________.

W: It covers nearly 9,000 square kilometers, and much of it is volcanic.

M: Do you have any pictures of the volcanoes? I'd like to see them.

W: No. There aren't any active volcanoes in Yellowstone at the moment, but the entire park ___________ ___________________.

M: That's a scary thought. Oh, what about this picture? Is this a bear?

W: Yes, Yellowstone is home to many black bears, bison, mountain goats, and deer, but I was really lucky to get that picture.

09

W: Welcome to I Tower. ____________________ for the elevator, I'll tell you about I Tower. I Tower, which is 250 meters tall, was originally built in 1975 as a communications tower. Even now it sends and receives radio and TV signals. But these days, I Tower ____________________ ________________ its scenic views. There are three observatory floors beginning at the 200-meter mark. You get off the main elevator at Observation Floor 1. Then you must take another elevator to go to either the café and bakery on Observation Floor 2 or the romantic Sky View restaurant on Observation Floor 3. The Sky View restaurant spins, ____________________________ ____________________________. Thank you. Please enjoy the view.

10

M: Hi, Julia. The school nurse told me ____________ ______________________________. But I don't know what to do since I'm an exchange student.

W: Do you have a doctor in mind?

M: She recommended five doctors in this area.

W: Let's take a look. The doctor on Highland Avenue is too far away from the school. It probably takes about an hour and a half to get there from here.

M: Well, since I don't have a car, I guess __________ ________________. Which doctor is the closest?

W: All the other doctors are about 30 minutes away. Is your cough due to a cold or an allergy?

M: I don't have a cold. It's due to an allergy.

W: Then you should see a doctor ________________ ______________.

M: You're right. And I'd like someone who's been in practice for at least 5 years.

W: Then you'll have to choose from these two doctors.

M: Hmm... I think I'll be more comfortable with a male doctor.

W: It looks like this doctor is the one for you.

M: Thanks. I'll call and ______________________ now.

11

W: Robert and Sara ________________________ ______________________ next month.

M: Wow, aren't they really young for that?

W: Maybe. ____________________________ people should get married?

12

M: Thanks for finishing this report. I'll ask you tomorrow if I have questions.

W: Actually, I'll ______________________ tomorrow. But I can still answer questions if you have any.

M: Okay, great. How can I ________________ ______________?

13

W: Hi, honey. I'm home.

M: Oh, hi. I'm happy to see you.

W: Happy? Why? Is anything wrong?

M: No, ______________________________. It's just nice that you're home. How was the manager's meeting?

W: OK. How was Ethan?

M: Everything was fine. I picked him up from daycare. And we played in the park for a while.

W: In the sandbox?

M: Yes, he loves that. Don't worry. I washed his hands when we came home.

W: ______________________________?

M: Spaghetti. And we had some salad, too.

W: He ate a lot?

M: Yes, don't worry. Next we watched one of his DVDs. It was *Winnie the Pooh*. And then he went to bed.

W: Well done. ______________________ without me.

14

M: Guess what, Sunny! I've quit smoking.

W: Congratulations, Uncle Bob! ______________ ______________, and bad for your health. When did you quit?

M: Almost three weeks ago. It's hard. I still have a strong desire to smoke.

W: Have you tried nicotine patches? Dad used them when he quit smoking.

M: Um, I should try them. I'll do anything to be successful this time.

W: So, you ________________________?

M: Four or five times. I started smoking a long time ago.

W: What happened when you tried to quit before?

M: I ______________________________ because I told myself "Go on, just one little cigarette won't hurt."

15

M: As Mr. Fredricks comes into the classroom, the class stands up. Mr. Fredricks is carrying a lot of papers, so Sumin walks over and ____________ ____________________. He says he doesn't. After putting all the papers down on the teacher's desk, Mr. Fredricks ______________ ______________. He says that today's English grammar class will be about the present perfect tense. He has made copies of some exercises he typed up yesterday. While he writes an explanation on the board, he ____________________ ____________ the exercises. He decides to ask Sumin to do this. In this situation, what would he most likely say to Sumin?

16-17

W: Let's say it's the middle of the school year and you are really busy. You have assignments, projects, and afterschool activities. Now a test is coming up and you have to do well on it. How should you study to get the best results? First, most people do better ______________________________ instead of large blocks. This should be obvious because it's easier to remember small amounts of information than large amounts. So, try to study a little every day. This can include many simple things like reading a little of your textbook, reviewing the day's notes, or researching online. ______________________________, it's just a matter of staying calm during the test. If you are so nervous that you blank out, you might need a mini-break. Keep your eyes closed for a while and relax all of your muscles. Try to ____________ ____________________, take a few deep breaths, or imagine yourself in a relaxing location. Finally, if you can, it's a good idea to spend some time in the testing location before the test. ______________________________ when the big day arrives.

01 다음을 듣고, 여자가 하는 말의 목적으로 가장 적절한 것을 고르시오.

① 충분한 물 섭취의 중요성을 알리려고
② 안전하고 편리한 정수기를 광고하려고
③ 건강을 위해 생수 마시기를 권유하려고
④ 수돗물 정수 시스템의 안전성을 홍보하려고
⑤ 새로 들여온 정수기의 사용법을 설명하려고

02 대화를 듣고, 여자의 의견으로 가장 적절한 것을 고르시오.

① 아이에게 적정한 금액의 용돈을 줘야 한다.
② 계획을 세워서 신중하게 돈을 관리해야 한다.
③ 지나친 소비는 가계에 부정적 영향을 미친다.
④ 세부적으로 가계부를 작성하는 것이 중요하다.
⑤ 선물 구매 시에는 가격을 1순위로 고려해야 한다.

03 대화를 듣고, 두 사람의 관계를 가장 잘 나타낸 것을 고르시오.

① 방송국 PD – 시청자
② 청소 대행업체 직원 – 고객
③ 환경 단체 직원 – 후원 신청자
④ 지역 관공서 직원 – 자원봉사자
⑤ 자선 모금 방송 진행자 – 모금 후원자

04 대화를 듣고, 그림에서 대화의 내용과 일치하지 않는 것을 고르시오.

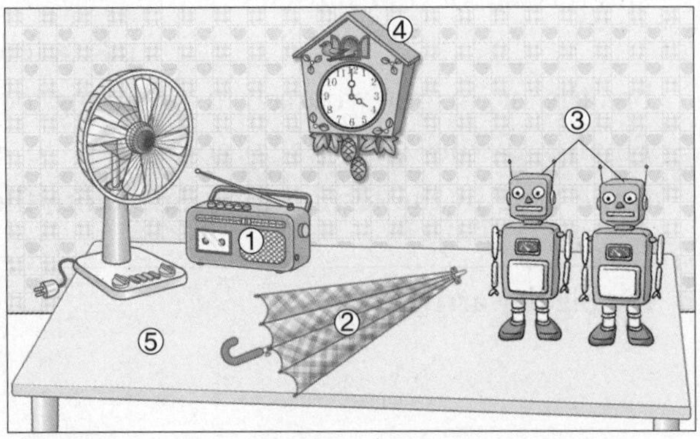

05 대화를 듣고, 남자가 여자에게 부탁한 일로 가장 적절한 것을 고르시오.

① 여자의 집 위치 안내하기
② 변경된 집 주소 불러주기
③ 어머니께 메시지 남겨주기
④ 소포가 도착할 때까지 기다리기
⑤ 어머니께서 오실 때까지 기다리기

06 대화를 듣고, 남자가 지불할 금액을 고르시오. [3점]

① $12 ② $15 ③ $16
④ $18 ⑤ $19

07 대화를 듣고, 남자가 Ina의 전화번호가 필요한 이유를 고르시오.

① 저녁 식사에 초대하려고
② 빌려준 책을 돌려받으려고
③ 과제의 제출기한을 물어보려고
④ 만나기로 한 약속을 연기하려고
⑤ 과제를 함께할 것을 제안하려고

08 대화를 듣고, Aruba에 관해 언급되지 않은 것을 고르시오.

① 위치 ② 활동 가능 스포츠
③ 평균 기온 ④ 공용어
⑤ 교통편

09 Intelligent Waistcoat에 관한 다음 내용을 듣고, 일치하지 않는 것을 고르시오.

① 언어 장애가 있는 아이들을 위한 제품이다.
② 옷에 장착된 기계를 통해 의사소통이 가능하다.
③ 전기를 송수신할 수 있는 천으로 만들어졌다.
④ 컴퓨터 칩이 접촉 횟수를 파악하여 음성을 만들어낸다.
⑤ 저렴한 가격으로 대량 생산할 수 있다.

10 다음 표를 보면서 대화를 듣고, 두 사람이 주문할 낚시 의자를 고르시오.

Fishing Chairs

Model	Foldable	Number of Cup Holders	Price	Color
① A	○	1	$49	Green
② B	○	2	$64	Blue
③ C	○	2	$58	Red
④ D	○	3	$99	Blue
⑤ E	×	3	$62	Red

11 대화를 듣고, 남자의 마지막 말에 대한 여자의 응답으로 가장 적절한 것을 고르시오.

① My eyesight isn't as good as it used to be.
② The monitor you're using is not a brand-new one.
③ I'll show you how to adjust the monitor's settings.
④ I don't think that eating carrots improves eyesight.
⑤ Rest your eyes frequently when working on a monitor.

12 대화를 듣고, 여자의 마지막 말에 대한 남자의 응답으로 가장 적절한 것을 고르시오.

① I prefer casual styles.
② A large is much too big for you.
③ I don't think brown is my color.
④ I think a medium might be perfect.
⑤ I'm afraid we don't have anything bigger.

13 대화를 듣고, 남자의 마지막 말에 대한 여자의 응답으로 가장 적절한 것을 고르시오. [3점]

▶ Woman : ______________________

① Can I be your campaign manager?
② You're right. She is far more qualified.
③ Don't be ridiculous. You deserve better.
④ She wouldn't be satisfied with the position.
⑤ That kind of campaign won't win my vote.

14 대화를 듣고, 여자의 마지막 말에 대한 남자의 응답으로 가장 적절한 것을 고르시오.

▶ Man : ______________________

① I think he doesn't want to have dinner today.
② How about if we all have dinner together?
③ I should have called him before he did.
④ Tell him he is always welcome here.
⑤ Can we go out some other time?

15 다음 상황 설명을 듣고, Sara가 Jake에게 할 말로 가장 적절한 것을 고르시오. [3점]

▶ Sara : ______________________

① You should see your doctor before it gets worse.
② It's important to get enough rest to fully recover.
③ I don't think you can play soccer again this month.
④ I couldn't have played with a broken leg like you did.
⑤ You should have followed your doctor's instructions.

[16~17] 다음을 듣고, 물음에 답하시오.

16 남자가 하는 말의 주제로 가장 적절한 것은?

① animals that blend with their environment
② differences between land and sea animals
③ how competition drives evolution
④ animals that survive in harsh climates
⑤ how to find and identify various animals

17 언급된 동물이 아닌 것은?

① seahorse ② butterfly ③ cheetah
④ rabbit ⑤ frog

21 Sense Up 듣기 모의고사 DICTATION

01

W: As you know, about 60 percent of your body is water, and you ______________________________ ____________. The standard recommendation is to drink at least eight 8-ounce glasses a day. But while you're doing all this drinking, ____________ ____ to your body. That's why I'm going to introduce the Pureit water purifier to you. It not only helps in purifying the water __________________________ _____________ and protects you from waterborne diseases. Plus, you can get hot and cold water anytime you want. This energy saving water purifier comes with a warranty of one year and is easily available at a small price. With Pureit, stay healthy and fit.

02

W: Corey, we should buy a birthday present for Grandmother. Do you think you can __________ ________________?

M: Gee, I'm afraid I can't. I've already used a lot of money this month for a new computer, a new phone, and some new clothes and shoes.

W: I'm afraid you spent too much money at once. Maybe you need to use your money more carefully.

M: You're right. But I don't know _______________ ________________________.

W: It's not difficult. You can record your income and expenses in a personal accounts book.

M: I guess it would ____________________________ ____________________.

W: That's what I mean. You should always have some extra money in case of emergency.

M: OK. Thank you for your concern.

03

W: Greener World. This is Joan Stuart.

M: Hello, my name is Alan Kyle and I'm calling about a program that I watched on TV last night.

W: Oh, hello. That must be ______________________ __________________ that was aired on TWBS.

M: Yes, I was very touched by the stories of your effort and dedication to preserve the Ronda River.

W: I'm happy to hear it. We're hoping that more people take an interest in the preservation of the Ronda River.

M: I hope so, too. I'm calling today because I wanted to help your organization.

W: There are many ways you can help the environment here at Greener World. You can _______________ _________________ the Ronda River.

M: Oh, unfortunately I live far away so I can't do that. But I can help out financially.

W: That would be wonderful, too. You can make a donation through our website. You can help us with a $50 or more donation.

M: ______________________________ your website?

W: Type "Greener World" in the search box. We really appreciate all your support.

04

W: James, ______________________________ in here?

M: That's my hobby. I collect old things.

W: Interesting! Oh, look at the radio next to a fan. I've seen radios with antennas, just like that one, in old movies.

M: Yes, my parents said that was a very popular model at one time.

W: I see. So, where did you get that umbrella lying across the table? It looks very old.

M: My grandfather gave it to me. I like ___________ ______________________________.

W: It's great. Hey, I think I've seen these robots that are facing each other somewhere.

M: They are characters from a famous, animated TV show.

W: That's right! By the way, the clock ___________ ________________ looks very old too. Does it still work?
M: Yes, it does. Every hour, the cuckoo comes out and announces the time.
W: That's unique. ___________________________?
M: This square table. It is also more than 50 years old.

05

W: Hello?
M: Hi, is Mrs. Green there?
W: Not at the moment. ______________________?
M: No. But I talked to her an hour ago and she said she'd be home all afternoon. ________________ __________________________.
W: My mom told me to stay at home until you came.
M: Oh, OK. I had promised your mom I'd be there by now, but I am way behind schedule in my deliveries.
W: When will you drop off the package?
M: About 5:30. Could you be sure you're there at that time?
W: Yes, but please hurry. ____________________ ______________?
M: Well, I know the area around Ace Apartments very well.
W: OK.
M: I'll visit you around 5:30.

06

W: Can I help you with anything?
M: I'm not sure. I'm taking care of a friend's dog __________________________, and I need to buy some dog food.
W: First of all, I'd like to recommend this brand. It has all natural ingredients __________________ __________________.
M: The price tag says $45! I do want to get something healthy, but that's a lot.
W: That's the price for the largest size. A small bag is only $12.
M: Oh, that's only $3 more than this Happy Chow. ___________________________. I'll get that.
W: We are also offering two package deals. For an extra $7, you can get this chew toy, or for an additional $6, you can get these samples of canned food.
M: The toy ________________________ but the canned food couldn't hurt. I'll take it.
W: Great. I'll ring you up at the counter.

07

M: Kim, do you know Ina's phone number?
W: I think ___________________ in my phone. Why?
M: I let her borrow a book from me, but now I realize that I need it for an assignment.
W: Well, I'm going to meet her for dinner soon. Want to join us?
M: Thanks, but I'm in a hurry. I have to finish this assignment by tomorrow morning, but _______ ______________________.
W: Are you talking about the group project for history class? Because I think that was postponed.
M: You're right. It was. This is something for Mr. Gerson's class.
W: Oh. I've heard ______________________. Is that true?
M: It is. He won't accept anything that is even a minute late.
W: Well, in that case, here's the number. Good luck.
M: Thanks. Have a nice dinner.

08

W: Honey, have you given any thought to our vacation?
M: I have, and I think Aruba sounds perfect.
W: Aruba? That's an island in the Caribbean Sea, right?
M: Yes, it's 30 km north of Venezuela and about the size of Dokdo.
W: That's tiny! ______________________________?
M: Well, it's famous for water sports. We can try surfing, scuba diving, and even fishing.
W: Oh, that sounds fun! ________________________?
M: I heard that the average temperature is about 27 degrees year-round. ________________________ ______________.
W: Then we should start to prepare. I'd like to learn at least a few phrases in the local language.
M: Good idea. Dutch is the official language, but English and Spanish are also spoken.
W: Oh, this is going to be so much fun!

09

M: My invention, the "Intelligent Waistcoat," will give the power of speech to disabled children who have, until now, never been able to talk. It's made of a touch-sensitive cloth attached to an electronic speech machine, so that children wearing it can communicate simply ________________________ ________________ of their waistcoat. The cloth is unique in that it can send and receive electricity. When the cloth is touched, a computer chip ______________________________________ and translates the touch into speech through the voice machine. Most importantly, the waistcoat can be produced in large quantities at a low cost and washed normally. These characteristics of the "Intelligent Waistcoat" will help disabled children to ____ through sound.

10

M: Jennifer, we have to buy a fishing chair for our family trip next week. I'd like to order one online.
W: Good. ____________________________________ ________________.
M: Of course. Foldable chairs are easy to store and transport.
W: And we need a chair with cup holders.
M: I think so. Cup holders are ________________ ________________ drinks, snacks, and phones.
W: Let's buy one with at least two cup holders.
M: Got it. What about the price?
W: I don't want to ____________________________ $70 on a fishing chair.
M: Okay. Now we should choose one of these two. Would you like to buy a cheaper one?
W: Well, since we already have a red fishing chair, I want ________________________________ this time even if it's more expensive.
M: It's settled. Let's order it right away.

11

M: I can't see the letters on the monitor clearly.
W: Oh, your eyes ______________________ from working so much.
M: ____________________. Is there anything I can do for my eyes?

12

W: ______________________________ the brown jacket?
M: I don't think ____________________. It's only a small.
W: I'll ask the clerk for a larger size. What do you wear?

13

M: I hope ____________________ as class president.
W: I didn't know you were running. Good luck.
M: Does that mean you're going to vote for me?
W: My best friend Susan is ____________________ ______________ too.
M: I thought I was your best friend.
W: You are my best guy friend. Susan is my best girl friend.
M: Anyway, ____________________________ to be president than her.
W: Based on what?
M: Based on the fact that I'm more popular than her.

14

M: Hello, Jane. What time do you want to meet?
W: Hi. Well, I have to wait for a phone call, so I'm not sure.
M: Can't you just ____________________________ on your cell phone?
W: Yes, but if I get this phone call, I will have to go somewhere else.
M: You mean, you have another appointment? We have been planning this date for a week!
W: __________________. One of my clients is in town. I may have to have dinner with him.
M: But our date is also important.
W: I know. Then what should I tell him _________ _____________?
M: I've got an idea.
W: What's that?

15

W: Sara and Jake are good friends. Jake plays soccer for a small local team, and Sara often comes to the games. A few months ago, however, __________ ________________________________. He broke his leg and was unable to play for two months. On the third month, Jake __________________ ________________. His doctor told Jake to rest for another two months. Jake didn't listen though. He was anxious to play and couldn't wait. But just ten minutes into his first game, Jake fell in pain. His injury __________________________. Now Jake is on the phone with Sara. He's complaining that he can't play soccer for another two months. Sara is annoyed by this. She thinks it's Jake's fault _________________________________. In this situation, what would Sara most likely say to Jake?

16-17

M: Last time, we talked about how animals in nature are ________________________________ _______________. And we learned that this has caused animals to evolve some truly amazing abilities. These abilities help them survive in harsh climates, escape predators, and find food. One particularly fascinating adaptation is the ability to blend with the environment. This can be seen everywhere in the oceans. For example, the pigmy seahorse attaches itself to the coral it lives with and ________________________________. On land, hiding oneself is just as popular. Most owls, for instance, are a shade of grey __________ ____________________ against the grey trunks of trees. In the grasslands of Africa, a cheetah's brown coat hides it well in the dry plants of its surroundings. High in the mountains, a white rabbit disappears into the snow. And in tropical jungles, a green frog is almost impossible to spot. ________________________________ to think of how your favorite animal has adapted to its surroundings.

01 다음을 듣고, 여자가 하는 말의 목적으로 가장 적절한 것을 고르시오.

① 회사의 신상품을 홍보하려고
② 독립영화 제작을 제안하려고
③ 신입사원의 입사를 축하하려고
④ 새로운 사업 구상안을 발표하려고
⑤ 과제를 수행하는 방법을 안내하려고

02 대화를 듣고, 두 사람이 하는 말의 주제로 가장 적절한 것을 고르시오.

① 다양한 문화 체험의 중요성
② 지역별 문화 격차 해소 방안
③ 지역 문화 시설 확충의 필요성
④ 지역 시민을 위한 문화 축제 종류
⑤ 저소득 계층을 위한 문화생활 지원비 확대

03 대화를 듣고, 두 사람의 관계를 가장 잘 나타낸 것을 고르시오.

① 미용사 – 고객
② 치과 의사 – 환자
③ 간호사 – 접수원
④ 가구점 직원 – 손님
⑤ 외과 의사 – 환자 보호자

04 대화를 듣고, 그림에서 대화의 내용과 일치하지 않는 것을 고르시오.

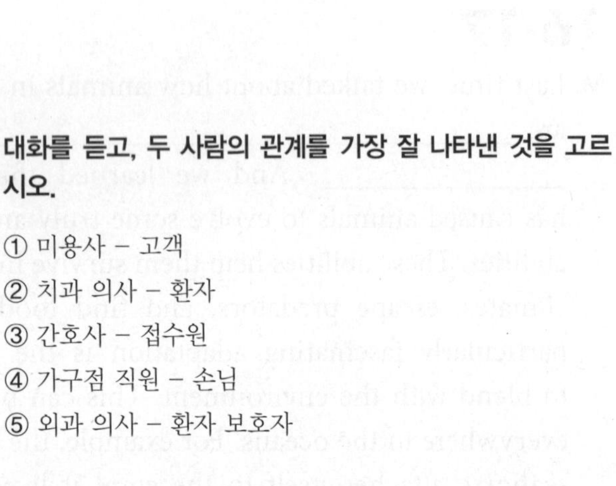

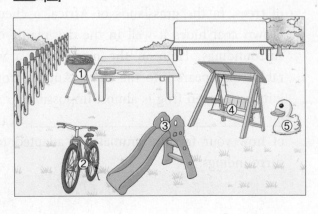

05 대화를 듣고, 남자가 할 일로 가장 적절한 것을 고르시오.

① 담요 가져오기
② 리포트 작성하기
③ 스웨터 준비하기
④ 친구에게 전화하기
⑤ 인터넷에서 사진 찾기

06 대화를 듣고, 여자가 지불할 금액을 고르시오. [3점]

① $80 ② $160 ③ $200
④ $240 ⑤ $340

07 대화를 듣고, 여자가 짧은 머리를 하기로 한 이유를 고르시오.

① 기분 전환을 위해서
② 이번 시즌 유행이라서
③ 머리카락이 심하게 손상되어서
④ 긴 머리는 관리하기 어렵다고 느껴서
⑤ 새 영화에서 맡은 배역에 맞추기 위해서

08 다음을 듣고, Ice Hotel에 관해 언급되지 않은 것을 고르시오.

① 규모 ② 객실 수
③ 실내 온도 ④ 부대시설
⑤ 숙박료

09 Stonehenge에 관한 다음 내용을 듣고, 일치하지 않는 것을 고르시오.

① 묘지였다는 추측이 있다.
② 푸른색의 암석이 사용되었다.
③ 이곳의 암석으로 다리와 홍수 방벽을 만들었다.
④ 1970년대 후반부터 관광객의 접근이 금지되고 있다.
⑤ 오늘날 예전 모습의 4분의 1이 소실되었다.

10 다음 표를 보면서 대화를 듣고, 남자가 예약할 항공편을 고르시오.

Flight	Stopover	Departure date	Length of stay
① UA7293	Nonstop	12. 12.	7 days
② OZ2468	Tokyo, Japan	12. 12.	14 days
③ AA8426	Nonstop	12. 20.	7 days
④ UA7421	Tokyo, Japan	12. 20.	14 days
⑤ KE5673	Nonstop	12. 20.	14 days

11 대화를 듣고, 여자의 마지막 말에 대한 남자의 응답으로 가장 적절한 것을 고르시오.

① The report is due in two days.
② I think he lent you the wrong CD.
③ You should change your password.
④ Right. James is great with computers.
⑤ I can lend you my laptop if you'd like.

12 대화를 듣고, 남자의 마지막 말에 대한 여자의 응답으로 가장 적절한 것을 고르시오.

① I don't want to hurt Mr. Kim's feelings.
② I'd rather deal with it on my own.
③ He's such a boring instructor!
④ You should do your part to help.
⑤ I'm tired of doing all the work myself.

13 대화를 듣고, 여자의 마지막 말에 대한 남자의 응답으로 가장 적절한 것을 고르시오. [3점]

▶ Man : ____________________

① Just ask her who that guy was.
② Why don't you ask him out for a date?
③ I think it's time to give her another chance.
④ Go and apologize. This is a good opportunity.
⑤ Me, neither. Chuck would never have done that.

14 대화를 듣고, 남자의 마지막 말에 대한 여자의 응답으로 가장 적절한 것을 고르시오. [3점]

▶ Woman : ____________________

① Let's go and buy you a new soccer uniform.
② Good idea. Otherwise, he wouldn't call me.
③ I did, but he can't come until tomorrow.
④ Just hang it to dry. It's sunny outside.
⑤ Don't worry. I've already had it fixed.

15 다음 상황 설명을 듣고, Kate의 아버지가 Kate에게 할 말로 가장 적절한 것을 고르시오.

▶ Kate's father : ____________________

① It might be time to rethink your goals.
② I'll help you prepare for your next audition.
③ I'm worried that you've been working too hard.
④ I'm sure all your struggles will pay off someday.
⑤ Maybe you need to spend more time practicing.

[16~17] 다음을 듣고, 물음에 답하시오.

16 여자가 하는 말의 주제로 가장 적절한 것은?

① an advertisement for a new English dictionary
② guide on how to use an online English dictionary
③ history of the compilation of English dictionaries
④ efficient ways to memorize and pronounce words
⑤ a sale of an English dictionary for young children

17 사전에 등재된 것으로 언급되지 않은 것은?

① 인터넷 속어 ② 발음 ③ 어원
④ 삽화 ⑤ 색인

01

W: Good morning, everyone. Congratulations to all of you for ______________________________ of the training program. Today, you're going to work in teams to make a UCC video to promote our shoes. Your team ____________________ six members. Each team can choose any one of our products and then ask for a sample of the product from our design team. You may cast anyone in the video, but the main character must be one of your team members. You should make two versions of the film — a one-minute video and a thirty-second video. Please upload your video file to our company's website by 12 p.m., ____________________________________ tomorrow. Enjoy the project.

02

W: Hi, Jack. How was your trip?

M: It was great! I had such a good time. I visited public art galleries, live performances in the parks, weekend street fairs, and so on.

W: ____________________________________ here, too.

M: You know, there is a proposal to increase funding for cultural facilities in our town. I really _______ _______________.

W: That's pleasing to hear. We really need facilities such as museums, stadiums, and public concert halls.

M: That's right. We ____________________ next month.

W: I'd be very happy if the proposal is passed.

M: Of course.

03

W: I'll recline your chair. Can you move a little upward?

M: I see. Is that okay?

W: All right. ______________________________?

M: Ah, yes, it does.

W: Look at this monitor. There is some inflammation of the gums. You also have __________________ ___________.

M: That's not good news.

W: I'll move your chair up again. Don't worry. There are just two and they are superficial.

M: Then I won't need surgery?

W: No, I'll just get these two fillings drilled and taken care of.

M: Oh, okay. Can you do it now?

W: No, you'll need to ______________________ ____________ the receptionist on the way out. You should get it done as soon as possible.

M: Yes, I'll do that.

04

M: ______________________. Why don't we clear out some of the junk in the backyard and plant some trees?

W: That's a great idea. We need some shade anyway.

M: Since we don't use that barbecue grill next to the fence, let's remove it.

W: But that spot doesn't get much sunshine. I don't think it's good for trees.

M: Good point. Oh, look at __________________ ______________. Whose is it?

W: That's mine. I don't have any other place to keep it.

M: Okay, then. How about the slide next to the bicycle? The kids are grown up. I don't think they use it anymore.

W: We ______________________________. They have two kids.

M: That would be nice. What else? The swing in front of the bench looks very old.

W: Yeah, but I like to sit on it and drink coffee.

M: Okay. We'll leave the swing. But I think the duck beside the swing isn't necessary.

W: You're right. Let's move it and plant some trees.

05

W: I don't like our homework topic. Scientific terms like "static electricity" are difficult.

M: Don't worry, Jisu. We just need to find some websites about it.

W: But the teacher said we need pictures and a visual to show ____________________.

M: Then why don't we start by searching for pictures?

W: I suppose pictures showing static electricity _____ ____________________________ online.

M: Right. And for the visual, we need a sweater and a small blanket.

W: I'll bring the sweater tomorrow, but I'm afraid I don't have a blanket.

M: No problem. ____________________. Now, what else is there to do for this assignment?

W: That just leaves the writing. I'll call you later _____ ____________________________.

M: Sounds good. Don't forget to bring everything tomorrow.

W: Okay. See you later.

06

W: Were you able to ___________________________?

M: Yes. It seems the leak is coming from some old pipes connected to your upstairs bathroom.

W: All right. ___________________________________?

M: The parts will cost $80. That doesn't include labor.

W: How much do you think the labor will be?

M: It will probably take around 4 hours to complete the job. That's $160.

W: So $240 in total? ___________________________. Maybe I should check with someone else.

M: I guarantee that any plumber in this city will charge at least $200.

W: Still, ____________________________________.

M: Suit yourself, but if you don't take care of that leak soon, you're going to find yourself with an additional $100 in floor damage.

W: Okay. Then I'll take care of it now.

07

M: What can I do for you today?

W: I haven't made up my mind, but I think I might want to ____________________________.

M: That is the style this season, and many actresses are choosing short hair.

W: True, but I've never been one to follow trends.

M: Yes, I know. Anyway, your hair looks very healthy. You must ____________________________.

W: That's the thing. It's so difficult to maintain. I'm so tired of washing it and waiting for it to dry.

M: I can imagine. Well, you do have the perfect face for short hair.

W: ________________________________ in the past, so I guess there is no reason not to trust you.

M: Alright. Then I'll get started.

08

M: You've probably never heard of the Swedish village of Jukkasjarvi because it's really only famous for one thing: its Ice Hotel. The Ice Hotel is _______ _______________________ — it's a hotel made entirely of ice and snow! The hotel is huge, measuring around 5,000 square meters, and it contains more than 30,000 cubic meters of snow and 3,000 tons of ice. _____________________ _________________ with beds made of ice. As you might expect, the hotel isn't very warm. The indoor temperature is kept between −5 and −8 degrees Celsius. Luckily, guests have plenty to distract them from the cold. The Ice Hotel features an ice restaurant, an ice bar, and a wide variety of winter activities. If you're feeling adventurous, ________________________________?

09

W: Stonehenge is a circular arrangement of huge stones in southern England, and it was built between 3,500 and 5,000 years ago. No one knows exactly why Stonehenge was built, but ____ being a place of worship or a sacred burial ground. It consists of two types of stone: sandstone and a bluish stone called "bluestone." Over the years, many of this monument's stones ______________________________ and used to make bridges, dams, or flood walls. And some of the smaller stones have been damaged by visitor contact. So, visitors have been prohibited from approaching the monument since 1978. Thus, what we see today are only the ruins of Stonehenge, about one-fourth of ______________________________.

10

W: Honey, were you able to find any flights for our trip to New York?

M: Well, ____, but I did find these five.

W: Oh, let me take a look at that.

M: I don't know about you, but I'd really prefer a nonstop flight.

W: Of course. Let's avoid a stopover if we can. But don't forget that I have to work until the 14th.

M: Right. ____________________. So, how many days would you like to spend in New York?

W: It's a big city with many famous attractions, but I think 7 days should be enough.

M: You might be right, but we probably ____ to the U.S. soon.

W: On second thought, I agree. Longer is better.

M: Then we've decided. I'll make the reservations.

11

W: James lent me this CD for my report, but ______________________________________.

M: Didn't you get the password from him?

W: No, he said ______________________________ after I insert it.

12

M: I'm looking forward to Mr. Kim's lab class. It's always so much fun.

W: ______________________________. My lab partner is so lazy!

M: That's too bad. ______________________________ Mr. Kim about it?

13

W: Oh, no! There she is!

M: Who? Mia?

W: Yes. She ______________________________.

M: Why? What did you do?

W: I saw her last weekend at the movies with some guy. I assumed it was her brother because she has been dating Chuck for so long.

M: Oh, no! You asked her about Chuck?

W: Yes, I asked her ______________________________ and if this was her brother or cousin.

M: That wasn't very tactful. What did she say?

W: Nothing. She started crying and left the theater immediately.

M: You didn't know what happened to her and Chuck, did you?

W: I had no idea at that time. But only today I found out she doesn't see Chuck anymore.

M: That's too bad.

W: I don't know ______________________________.

14

M: Mom, where is my soccer uniform?

W: It's in the laundry basket. I ________________ ________________.

M: But I need it for the game tomorrow morning.

W: Can you wash it by hand, please? I have to go to work now.

M: OK. But ________________ the washing machine?

W: It broke this morning. The water ________________ ________________.

M: Will my uniform be dry in time for the game?

W: Yes, of course. Use the automatic clothes dryer.

M: OK. And how about calling a repair technician?

15

M: Kate works at a coffee shop part time, but her real passion is acting. She takes acting classes at a nearby college, ________________ ________________, and practices night and day. Whenever there are auditions for a professional movie or play, Kate goes. Unfortunately, Kate has been unsuccessful for almost a year, and today was no different. After failing an afternoon audition, she comes home to find her father in the kitchen. ________________, and her father is worried. He has seen how hard she works, and he's worried that too many experiences of failure ________________. He wants to say something to encourage her. In this situation, what would Kate's father most likely say to Kate?

16-17

W: Language lovers can rejoice because Oxford's ________________. And it's been updated to include Internet slang, such as "onliner." Since the first dictionary was published over 250 years ago, new words not only have been added over time, but the pronunciation of words has also changed. In fact, only a few hundred years ago, "mice" was pronounced "mace." ________________ ________________ and for fascinating reasons. Oxford has done a wonderful job of following these changes while providing current pronunciation information. The origins of words have also been included in the most interesting cases. For example, did you know that "jumbo," meaning "very large," was originally an African word for "elephant"? Plus, there are now even more full-color illustrations ________________ ________________. These are combined with notes on common usage to aid your learning, ________________ for any student. With this well-respected dictionary, you can feel the amazing evolution of the English language. Free 7-day online trials will be offered for the next three days. Don't miss this chance!

01 다음을 듣고, 여자가 하는 말의 목적으로 가장 적절한 것을 고르시오.

① 카탈로그의 테마에 관해 설명하려고
② 컬러 프린터의 추가 구매를 요청하려고
③ 직원들에게 프로젝트 마감일을 알려주려고
④ 직원들이 프로젝트를 완수하도록 동기를 부여하려고
⑤ 직원들에게 특정 프린터를 사용해달라고 요청하려고

02 대화를 듣고, 남자의 의견으로 가장 적절한 것을 고르시오.

① 보행 시 휴대전화를 사용해서는 안 된다.
② 무단횡단을 방지하기 위한 교육이 필요하다.
③ 보행자를 배려하는 운전 습관을 들여야 한다.
④ 장시간의 휴대전화 사용은 건강에 좋지 않다.
⑤ 운전 시 휴대전화 사용은 법으로 금지해야 한다.

03 대화를 듣고, 두 사람의 관계를 가장 잘 나타낸 것을 고르시오.

① 디자이너 – 모델
② 기자 – 영화감독
③ 관객 – 영화배우
④ 스턴트우먼 – 보안 요원
⑤ 영화 평론가 – 시나리오 작가

04 대화를 듣고, 그림에서 대화의 내용과 일치하지 <u>않는</u> 것을 고르시오.

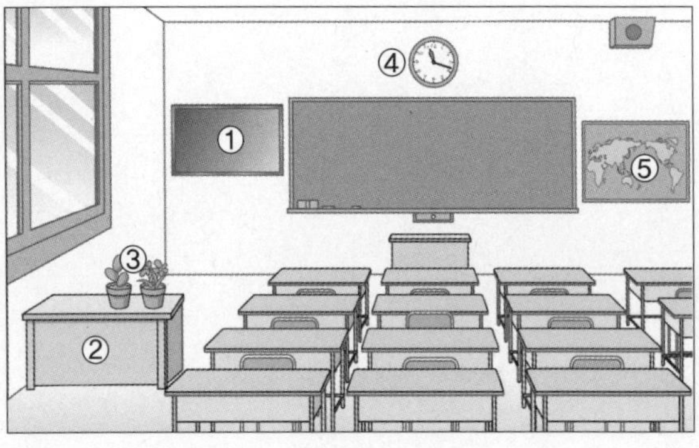

05 대화를 듣고, 여자가 남자에게 부탁한 일로 가장 적절한 것을 고르시오.

① 발코니석 구해주기
② 오케스트라 오디션 잡아주기
③ 공연장의 전화번호 알려주기
④ 대기자 명단에 이름 올려주기
⑤ 공연 초대장을 우편으로 부쳐주기

06 대화를 듣고, 남자가 지불할 금액을 고르시오. [3점]

① $400 ② $440 ③ $459 ④ $510 ⑤ $540

07 대화를 듣고, 여자가 영화표를 취소한 이유를 고르시오.

① 상영 시간이 길어서
② 수영 수업을 들어야 해서
③ 양로원에 자원봉사하러 가려고
④ 영화가 지루하다는 평을 들어서
⑤ 다음 주에 친구와 함께 영화를 보려고

08 대화를 듣고, Mensa에 관해 언급되지 <u>않은</u> 것을 고르시오.

① 창설 연도 ② 회원 자격
③ 회원 수 ④ 운영 목표
⑤ 아동 가입 가능 여부

09 Aloe vera에 관한 다음 내용을 듣고, 일치하지 <u>않는</u> 것을 고르시오.

① 100센티미터까지 자랄 수 있다.
② 여름에 꽃이 핀다.
③ 의료 목적으로 이용되기도 한다.
④ 해충에 취약한 편이다.
⑤ 여러 나라에서 대규모로 생산된다.

10 다음 표를 보면서 대화를 듣고, 두 사람이 등록할 강좌를 고르시오.

Winter School Programs			
Program	Fee	Period	Tutor
① Ski	$150	January 15 – 17	Scott
② Chinese	$50	January 11 – 31	Wang
③ Yoga	$30	January 15 – 26	Rose
④ Guitar	$40	January 2 – 15	Adam
⑤ Swimming	$40	January 2 – 15	David

11 대화를 듣고, 여자의 마지막 말에 대한 남자의 응답으로 가장 적절한 것을 고르시오.

① You really shouldn't skip class.
② Okay. I'll see you at the next lecture.
③ I don't know, but he asked to see me.
④ I want to talk to you about the lectures.
⑤ The professor will be angry if you're not there.

12 대화를 듣고, 남자의 마지막 말에 대한 여자의 응답으로 가장 적절한 것을 고르시오.

① I think your sister's band is amazing.
② I don't want to miss her performance.
③ I'm really impressed with her drumming.
④ I should talk to her about that right away.
⑤ Thanks for letting me audition for your band.

13 대화를 듣고, 여자의 마지막 말에 대한 남자의 응답으로 가장 적절한 것을 고르시오.

▶ Man : ______________________

① Then I'll reschedule the staff basketball match.
② Sarah should stop working so many shifts.
③ I couldn't find anyone to replace her.
④ That spot is always open for everybody.
⑤ Can I introduce a friend who's available?

14 대화를 듣고, 남자의 마지막 말에 대한 여자의 응답으로 가장 적절한 것을 고르시오. [3점]

▶ Woman : ______________________

① You can eat this food. Peanuts are not harmful.
② I shouldn't have ordered so many dishes! I'm full!
③ Then, why don't we swap? Here, you have mine.
④ We'd better tell them to hurry and bring my meal.
⑤ I warned the chef not to serve you any peanuts.

15 다음 상황 설명을 듣고, Peter가 Chris에게 할 말로 가장 적절한 것을 고르시오. [3점]

▶ Peter : ______________________

① I'm sorry, I've had a long day.
② I'm really glad to meet all of you.
③ Could you please speak a little slower?
④ I want to tell you everything about Germany.
⑤ Let me know if you don't understand something.

[16~17] 다음을 듣고, 물음에 답하시오.

16 남자가 하는 말의 주제로 가장 적절한 것은?

① the purpose of CCTVs
② how to set up a CCTV at home
③ advantages and disadvantages of CCTVs
④ how to improve the quality of CCTV footage
⑤ the relation between CCTVs and a crime rate

17 CCTV가 설치되는 장소로 언급되지 않은 것은?

① 주차장
② 상점
③ 경찰서
④ 엘리베이터
⑤ 거리

23 Sense Up 듣기 모의고사 DICTATION

01

W: Good afternoon, everyone. I know it's been a long meeting, but I have one final thing to add. As many of you know, my team is ____________________ ____________________ with our current project. All this week, we're going to be printing samples for the fall fashion catalog. Because fall colors are important to the theme, we're relying on the office's sole color printer for our samples. Last week, this led to a major problem when ____________________. To avoid this and ensure everything runs as smoothly as possible, please use one of the two black-and-white printers for other business. With any luck, the catalog will be completed soon and ____________________ ____________________. Thanks for your time, everyone.

02

M: I just saw an accident right outside our building.

W: Really? What happened?

M: A car ____________________ to avoid hitting a woman who was crossing the street, but there wasn't enough space so it hit another car.

W: Wow, was anyone injured?

M: Fortunately, no one was hurt. The woman was extremely lucky. She was playing with her phone and not paying attention at all.

W: I think that is becoming more common these days. Usually, people simply ____________________ ____________ on the street while paying attention to their phones, but serious accidents do happen.

M: After seeing what I just saw, I don't think people should use their phones while walking anymore for everyone's safety.

W: You're right. ____________________ __________.

03

W: I'd like to ask about working with Tom.

M: Well, Tom is a great guy, ____________________ ____________________.

W: He's my favorite star, but it was reported in the newspaper that he was really demanding during the filming.

M: Don't believe ____________________ ____________________. He never demanded this or that on the set. And he did all of his own stunts: even that amazing one where he jumped from the helicopter to the train.

W: So you'd work with him again.

M: Yes, I hope to direct him in my next film. Because of the positive reaction from audiences and people like yourself, the studio has already asked me about continuing the story.

W: Really? My viewers will be excited to hear that.

M: It's true.

W: Then I can't wait to go and see your next film.

M: Well, wait for ____________________.

W: It'll be hard, but I'll try.

04

W: Hello, Principal Dawson.

M: Hi, Christine. I stopped by to ask ____________________ ____________________.

W: It's going well. I'm setting up my classroom. I just finished attaching the TV to the wall to the left of the blackboard.

M: You put it on the wall? It used to be on the table below the window, right?

W: Right. But the TV was too low, so students in the back couldn't see it.

M: Good job. Then where's the table?

W: The table is still there, but I put ____________________ ____________________.

M: They'll get plenty of sunshine there. Great idea!

W: And I left the national flag above the blackboard.

M: Yes, ____________________.

W: But I moved the map of the world to the right side of the blackboard.

M: Oh, and you took down the picture that was there before. Good, it was old anyway.

05

M: Thank you for calling Ticket Box. How may I help you?

W: I need to buy two tickets to a show for Saturday.

M: What show ________________________________ ________________?

W: Do you have any tickets left for *Cats* or *42nd Street*? I want great seats.

M: OK. I can tell you right now that *Cats* and *42nd Street* are both sold out.

W: How about *Rent*?

M: There are only balcony seats left.

W: Can you ________________________________ for orchestra seats then?

M: Yes, we can. Sometimes people do cancel. Which show?

W: I would like to see the Saturday night show of any of the three we discussed.

M: All right. We will call you ____________________ ________________________.

06

W: Can I help you find anything?

M: Well, I'm interested in these two cameras. Could you ________________________________?

W: I'd be happy to. The one on the left has twice the memory and comes with an extreme wide-angle lens.

M: So that's why it costs an extra $250. I think that is more camera than I need.

W: I see. Then, how about the camera on the right? It is a great value at $400.

M: ________________________________, I would like an extra memory card.

W: Good idea. Each memory card costs $40. However, we are offering a package deal that includes a tripod.

M: A package deal?

W: Yes. It includes the camera, one additional memory card, and a $70 tripod, ______________ ______________________________.

M: I already have a tripod that I love, so I'll just get the camera and the memory card.

W: Great choice.

07

W: Hi, Will.

M: Hi, Clair.

W: What are you going to do this weekend?

M: I'm going to ______________________________ ____________________, like I usually do. You're planning to see a movie, right?

W: I was going to see *Hidden Dragon*, but I cancelled the tickets.

M: Oh, really? Then I guess you have time to come with me to the senior center.

W: I'm afraid not. I __________________________ ______________________. It's every Saturday and Sunday at 5 p.m.

M: That sounds like a lot of fun. Besides, I've heard that *Hidden Dragon* is really long and boring anyway.

W: Really? I know it's ______________________ ________________, but I've read some good reviews.

M: Not me. I'll probably avoid it. Anyway, have a good weekend.

08

W: Honey, do you have any other puzzle books? Lisa finished the one you gave her.

M: She finished the whole book in two hours?

W: Yes, and now she's bored again. Every parent thinks ________________________________, but we really might be.

M: Maybe she should join Mensa. It's the high-IQ society ________________________________ ________________ in 1946.

W: Well, she'd have to take an IQ test and score in the top 2% to join.

M: I think she'd pass. And Mensa could do a lot to foster her intelligence. That's the purpose of the society, after all.

W: By the way, can children join? What would she do there?

M: Of course. They provide activities and games ________________________________.

W: Then, let's talk to her about membership tonight.

M: All right.

09

M: Aloe vera is a stemless or nearly stemless plant ____________________________. It can grow to a height of 100 cm, and it produces flowers in the summer. Its natural range is unclear, as the species has been widely cultivated throughout the world for its medical uses. Furthermore, it's commonly grown as a decorative plant in many households. The aloe vera is relatively __________ ______________________________ but requires well-drained sandy potting soil and bright sunny conditions. However, these plants can burn under too much sun or die ________________________ ____________________. Large-scale agricultural production of aloe vera is undertaken in many countries to supply the cosmetics industry with aloe vera gel.

10

W: Do you have any plans for the winter holiday?

M: No. I hope it's not too boring. What about you?

W: I'm thinking about ________________________ ________________________________. Why don't you join me?

M: That could be fun. Hey, let's try skiing!

W: Look at the price. I can't afford $150.

M: I didn't see that. Well, you're always saying that ____. Guitar lessons?

W: I'm sorry, but I'm going to stay with my grandparents at the beginning of January. I'll be back on the 10th.

M: Then I guess David's class is not an option either.

W: Right. We could study Chinese, but __________ ________________________________.

M: I completely agree with you. I also need to exercise.

W: Great. I'll sign us up.

11

W: Should I ________________________ in the lecture hall?

M: Sorry, I have to meet with my professor, so I ________________________.

W: Really? What's so important?

12

M: Hi, Cindy. ________________________ for a rock band?

W: Yes, I've always wanted to play the drums.

M: Really? My sister is the leader of a band and ________________________________.

13

M: Bye, Mrs. Reade. See you next Saturday!

W: Oh, Corey, before you leave, ______________ ____________________?

M: Sure, Mrs. Reade. What is it?

W: I need you to take on Sarah's Wednesday shift. She starts college next month.

M: Yes, she does. ______________________________?

W: 6 p.m. to around 10:30 p.m., depending on how busy we are.

M: I'm sorry, but I can't. I have basketball on Wednesdays at 8.

W: But you're my best worker here at Ollie's Fried Chicken.

M: I like working for you, too, but I can't quit my basketball team.

W: Will you think about it, please? ____________ ______________________________.

14

M: It took quite a long time to get here, sorry. Thanks for inviting me to lunch, anyway.

W: Well, you said you wanted to try Malaysian food.

M: It smells so good in here! __________________ ______________________?

W: The coconut rice meal. I'm having spicy shrimp soup with noodles.

M: And here it is! Uh-oh. Mary, are these peanuts in my food?

W: Yes, why?

M: I'm sorry, but I can't eat this dish. ____________ ____________________________.

W: But there aren't many. Can't you take them out?

M: No, even the tiniest trace of a peanut will nearly kill me.

W: Really? I had no idea! ______________________ ________________ for you.

M: We don't have time. I only have 30 minutes left for my lunch break.

15

W: Peter is an exchange student from Germany. Today, he arrives in Canada, where __________________ ___________________________. Although Peter has studied English for several years, this is only the second time he has spoken with native English speakers. He has also just gotten off a long flight, and he's a bit tired and nervous. Meanwhile, his host family is very excited to meet Peter. The boy, Chris, is especially ______________________ _____________ Peter. He's asking many questions, one after another, and he seems disappointed in Peter's answers. Peter is doing his best but can't understand ______________________________ __________________. He thinks he just needs a bit more time to process the conversation. In this situation, what would Peter most likely say to Chris?

16-17

M: These days, CCTVs can be seen almost everywhere. They ____ and protect businesses. They're also a cheap alternative to a full-time security guard. They work especially well in low-traffic areas. For example, many parking garages rely on CCTVs to protect the cars and their owners. Shops place them in hard-to-see locations to prevent theft. And they're in many elevators ______________________ ______________. They're also useful on busy and dangerous streets. By recording license-plate numbers from cars, they allow police to identify reckless drivers and issue fines. Still, there are drawbacks that must be considered. Their low-quality cameras offer terrible image quality. Even when criminals are filmed, the videos capturing their actions often ______________________ ______________. Then there is the price. Someone must be paid to watch the cameras or some form of video storage must be purchased. Over thousands of hours, this really adds up. Finally, there is the cost we all pay through loss of privacy. After all, it isn't only the criminals ____________________ ______________.

01 다음을 듣고, 남자가 하는 말의 목적으로 가장 적절한 것을 고르시오.

① 유가 상승에 대해 경고하려고
② 유류세 인하 정책을 알리려고
③ 대중교통 이용을 권장하려고
④ 연료 절약 운전법을 소개하려고
⑤ 물가 상승의 부작용을 설명하려고

02 대화를 듣고, 여자의 의견으로 가장 적절한 것을 고르시오.

① 유권자는 투표권을 반드시 행사해야 한다.
② 학생회장 선거는 공정하게 이루어져야 한다.
③ 후보자의 인지도가 높을수록 당선 확률이 높다.
④ 투표 전에는 후보자 선거 공약을 확인해야 한다.
⑤ 학생회는 임원별 주요 활동 내역을 공개해야 한다.

03 대화를 듣고, 두 사람의 관계를 가장 잘 나타낸 것을 고르시오.

① 버스 기사 – 경찰
② 운전자 – 정비공
③ 보행자 – 보행자
④ 택시 기사 – 승객
⑤ 승객 – 승객

04 대화를 듣고, 그림에서 대화의 내용과 일치하지 <u>않는</u> 것을 고르시오.

05 대화를 듣고, 여자가 할 일로 가장 적절한 것을 고르시오.

① 컴퓨터 수리하기
② 남자와 벼룩시장에 가기
③ 판매자가 협회에 전화 걸기
④ 인터넷으로 판매자 등록하기
⑤ 남자에게 인형 만드는 법 가르쳐주기

06 대화를 듣고, 남자가 지불할 금액을 고르시오. [3점]

① $35 ② $39 ③ $45
④ $46 ⑤ $49

07 대화를 듣고, 남자가 Kensington 대학을 선택한 이유를 고르시오.

① 집에서 더 가까워서
② 등록금이 더 저렴해서
③ 장학금 제도가 더 좋아서
④ 교수 당 학생 수가 더 적어서
⑤ 전공 커리큘럼이 더 유명해서

08 대화를 듣고, Henri Matisse에 관해 언급되지 <u>않은</u> 것을 고르시오.

① 출생 국가 ② 화풍(畵風)
③ 작품의 주요 소재 ④ 스승
⑤ 작품명

09 다음 안내 방송을 듣고, 일치하지 <u>않는</u> 것을 고르시오.

① 도서관 이용 시간이 끝나가고 있다.
② 대출 카운터 이외의 대출 시스템을 갖추고 있다.
③ 추가 인원이 대출 업무를 돕고 있다.
④ 대출 카운터는 모두 1층에 있다.
⑤ 도서관 카드는 신분증으로 대체 가능하다.

10 다음 표를 보면서 대화를 듣고, 두 사람이 등록할 강좌를 고르시오.

The Rinx – Ice Skating School				
Class	Target Age	Day & Time	Instructor Experience	Fee
① A	4-6	Tuesday 1 p.m. – 3 p.m.	10 years	$62
② B	5-10	Tuesday 3 p.m. – 5 p.m.	8 years	$58
③ C	5-12	Wednesday 1 p.m. – 3 p.m.	6 years	$42
④ D	6-12	Monday 1 p.m. – 3 p.m.	6 years	$44
⑤ E	7-12	Wednesday 3 p.m. – 5 p.m.	4 years	$36

11 대화를 듣고, 여자의 마지막 말에 대한 남자의 응답으로 가장 적절한 것을 고르시오.

① Sounds good to me.
② Let's meet in the middle.
③ I'm going to change lockers.
④ Please help me open my lock.
⑤ This locker is already occupied.

12 대화를 듣고, 남자의 마지막 말에 대한 여자의 응답으로 가장 적절한 것을 고르시오.

① You'd better cancel the picnic.
② But I don't work on weekends.
③ Thanks, but it's too far to walk.
④ In that case, I'd love to join you.
⑤ Only if my car has enough room.

13 대화를 듣고, 여자의 마지막 말에 대한 남자의 응답으로 가장 적절한 것을 고르시오. [3점]

▶ Man : ______________________

① My child is also sick from eating a toy.
② I will watch to see if he gets any worse.
③ I don't buy plastic toys for my children.
④ Please throw the puppy something to fetch.
⑤ The emergency room at the hospital is too crowded.

14 대화를 듣고, 남자의 마지막 말에 대한 여자의 응답으로 가장 적절한 것을 고르시오.

▶ Woman : ______________________

① You can apply for a store credit card.
② How much is the discount for him?
③ Have I met your brother before?
④ Does he take the same size as you?
⑤ Do you want it medium or well-done?

15 다음 상황 설명을 듣고, Cole이 Todd에게 할 말로 가장 적절한 것을 고르시오. [3점]

▶ Cole : ______________________

① I don't want to embarrass you anymore.
② You could be blamed for what you didn't do.
③ Please don't litter. It makes us both look bad.
④ My parents told me not to eat ice cream any more.
⑤ You should report this littering to the school principal.

[16~17] 다음을 듣고, 물음에 답하시오.

16 남자가 하는 말의 주제로 가장 적절한 것은?

① advantages of multivitamins
② the dangers of poor nutrition
③ illnesses related to bad eating habits
④ types and effects of health supplements
⑤ side effects from the misuse of health supplements

17 언급된 영양제(nutritional supplements)의 효능이 아닌 것은?

① 근육 강화　　② 체중 감량
③ 탈모 방지　　④ 뼈의 건강 유지
⑤ 피부 건강 유지

01

M: Almost every day, the price of oil ____________ ________________________. So the government has announced plans to reduce the gasoline tax for the summer months. The purpose of this tax break is ________________________________ to drive their vehicles and use their car air conditioners during the hottest time of the year. The gasoline tax will reduce the cost of gas by an average of $6 for each tank full of gasoline. An average driver will save up to $120 for the three-month period. Since working families are the backbone of the economy, the government ________________________________ them in this time of difficulty.

02

M: Hi, Susan. ______________________________?

W: I'm going to vote for student council president.

M: Oh, that's right. Today is the last day. I'll certainly be glad when Tony is no longer our president.

W: Yeah, ______________________________ ______________. So I guess you already voted?

M: Not this semester. I don't need to vote, because Tony is too unpopular to ever get re-elected.

W: Jim! That's exactly how he got elected the first time. Everyone assumed that he couldn't win, so very few people actually voted against him.

M: That could never happen again. Besides, I'm really busy.

W: You should vote. I'm not going to spend next semester ____________________ about the student council if you don't even vote.

M: Okay, I'll come with you.

03

W: What's going on, sir?

M: An officer ____________________.

W: What for?

M: I guess because the driver didn't stop at the sign back there.

W: Maybe you're right. It's hard to see that stop sign, with the tree branches hanging over it.

M: I'm already late for a meeting. I wish __________ __________________________ for so long.

W: Oh, the driver is getting off.

M: Isn't the officer going to give him a ticket?

W: I think something is wrong with the bus.

M: Yes, the officer is looking into the engine compartment.

W: Oh no. Can you see the smoke coming out of it?

M: The driver is ________________________.

W: People are starting to get off.

M: I need to find a taxi. Today is not my day.

04

W: What are you looking at?

M: This is a photo from our family camping trip last weekend. Take a look.

W: Oh, it's you sitting on the dock of the pond and fishing. It must have been taken at ____________ ______________________ a fish! Your fishing rod is bent.

M: Yes, that's right. I was so happy to catch a big fish.

W: Good. The woman stirring the pot over the fire is your mother, right?

M: Yes, she is preparing lunch. My father __________ ______________.

W: You mean the man who is holding a bunch of firewood?

M: Right. He got it all for the fire.

W: He seems like a camping expert. I see a camping car near your father. Is it yours?

M: We rented it. Usually ____________________ in my father's truck and sleep in a tent, but this time we rented a camping car. It was fantastic!

W: Sounds great! I also like the two chairs on the right. They look very comfortable.

M: Exactly. We rented them at the same camping gear shop.

W: It looks like you had a wonderful time. __________ ________________________ with my family, too.

정답 및 해설 p.94

05

M: You made these puppets yourself? They're really cool.

W: Thanks. My son loves these animal characters.

M: You're very artistic.

W: I can ______________________________.

M: Well, I'm not very good with my hands. But I think these are so good that people will buy them.

W: Buy them?

M: Sure. Try selling them at the flea market in your area. You can go there next Saturday. ________ ________________ is register with the sellers' association.

W: Could you tell me how to register?

M: You can register online.

W: But my computer isn't working. It has a virus.

M: You can register by phone then.

W: Oh, I can use Larry's laptop. I'll get it right now.

M: And __________________ a lot more before the weekend.

06

M: I am returning my cell phone. I'd like to ________ __________________. My name is Howard Wright.

W: Just a minute, Mr. Wright.

M: The daily rental rate is $7, but a weekly rate is $45, right?

W: Yes, you're right. Here's your bill.

M: I don't see any charges for the calls I made.

W: Well, you signed up for the global roaming service. All your call charges __________________ ______________ in America.

M: Oh? Hmm... but my bill shouldn't be $52.

W: Oh, really?

M: I had the phone for a week, seven days, not eight days. And when I rented this cell phone, I paid a $10 refundable deposit.

W: Hmm... let me check. Yes, you're right. You rented the phone for only one week, and your deposit ____________________. I'll change the bill.

07

W: Jack, did you __________________________ ______________?

M: I did, Ms. Flint. I chose Kensington University over my other option.

W: What was it that finally made up your mind?

M: Well, I started by comparing some basic points, like the distance from my home.

W: They are both relatively close.

M: Yes, that __________________________ ________________. So I looked at tuition.

W: Kensington is the more expensive of the two, I think.

M: Right, and then I looked at scholarships, but I was still confused.

W: Did you give any thought to the majors offered by each school?

M: Actually, that's what finally made a difference. Kensington's biology program is renowned.

W: They also have fewer students per teacher.

M: I __________________________ that.

W: Anyway, you made a great decision.

08

M: Heather, have you thought of anyone to write our report about?

W: I think we should write about Henri Matisse because I've always loved his paintings.

M: That sounds good. To start with, I know that he was born in 1869 in France, and ______________________________ Picasso's.

W: Picasso and Matisse were actually very close. They met in 1906 and remained lifelong friends.

M: I know that they were both Impressionists. Did Matisse learn his technique from Picasso?

W: No. Picasso ______________________________ Matisse. Matisse learned to paint primarily from Gustave Moreau at an academy in Paris.

M: It looks like we already have several good details for our report. By the way, what's your favorite Matisse?

W: I think *The Plum Blossoms*, which he painted in 1948 and is now kept in New York's Museum of Modern Art, is my favorite because of its deep reds.

M: I ______________________________.

09

W: Attention library patrons. We ______________________________. Please make all of your selections and take them to one of the checkout counters or the self-checkout scanners just to the right of the main counters. For your convenience, we ______________________________ to allow you to avoid long lines. Checkout counters are located on the first floor near the main entrance and on the basement level near the parking garage entrance. Remember, if you do not have your library card with you, your driver's license or passport ______________________________. Thank you for using the Parkview Public Library and have a pleasant evening.

10

W: Honey, look at this flyer. The Rinx is open for the winter season.

M: Good news! They offer great ice skating lessons for children. Olivia wants to ______________________________.

W: Here's a chart of what they offer.

M: Since Olivia is 8 years old, she shouldn't take this class.

W: Yeah. And she has to attend a dance class on Monday afternoon, so ______________________________.

M: Now we have three options. I think we should think about the instructor's amount of experience.

W: I agree with you. ______________________________, the better.

M: Then I think we'll go with this class.

W: Wait a minute! We should consider the fees. I don't want to spend more than $50.

M: Then let's choose the second most experienced instructor.

W: Okay. Let's sign up right now.

11

W: Oh, I can't reach my locker, because it's too high.

M: Yeah? Well, mine is on the bottom. It's so ______________________________.

W: I have an idea. ______________________________?

12

M: ______________________________ by the river tomorrow. You should come.

W: Unfortunately, I work tomorrow morning, and my office is far from the river.

M: Your office isn't far from my house. ______________________________ and pick you up?

13

W: This is the Willow Creek Pet Hospital, how may I help you?

M: My dog is sick. I'm really worried about him.

W: That's too bad. What are your dog's symptoms?

M: He started vomiting last night, and he ________ ________________________ anything today.

W: OK. It sounds like he may have eaten something bad, like a piece of plastic or metal.

M: Well, he is still very young and curious.

W: Take a look around your home and tell me if there is ____________________________________.

M: OK. Wait a minute. Yes, I found something. Part of a plastic toy that belongs to my child. ________ ______________________________.

W: Well, if he gets worse, I think you should contact us or bring him in.

14

M: Excuse me, ______________________________ in this sweater?

W: This one? Sure. It's a lovely sweater.

M: Yes, I like the color and the pattern.

W: Well, it's funny, but I ______________________ a medium. I'll check in the back.

M: Please hurry, I'm late for lunch.

W: OK. Here it is. I finally found a medium.

M: It's $45, right?

W: Yes, but with a store credit card you can get a 10% discount. It's our Wild Wednesday sale. Everything is 10% off.

M: Well, I'll buy another one for my brother then. Maybe he'll ______________________________ for lunch.

15

W: Todd and Cole walk home from school together each day. Todd often buys an ice cream from the corner store ______________________ and eats it. When he is done, Todd throws the wrapper on the ground ________________________. Sometimes, there may be a trash can nearby, but he won't bother to put it in the can. Cole ______ __________________________ that littering is bad and that litterers look ignorant. Sometimes people shake their heads when they see Todd litter. This embarrasses Cole. In this situation, what would Cole most likely say to Todd?

16-17

M: It's hard for our bodies to get ______________ ________________________ from regular food. For this reason, many people take special pills called health supplements. Because health supplements affect the body, it's important to talk to your doctor before starting a new supplement. __________________________, let's talk a bit about them. First, there is one supplement that almost everyone should be taking, and this is a basic multivitamin. Multivitamins ____________ _____________________ us the extra nutrients that our bodies need. Then there are mineral supplements. Among them, calcium is the most important for maintaining healthy bones. Nutritional supplements form a third category of supplements. In fact, they are really specialty supplements ____ such as making your muscles stronger, losing weight, preventing hair loss, maintaining healthy skin, and a number of other reasons.

25 Sense Up 듣기 모의고사

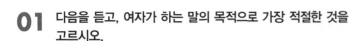

01 다음을 듣고, 여자가 하는 말의 목적으로 가장 적절한 것을 고르시오.

① 적십자 후원 회원 가입을 촉구하려고
② 응급 처치 교육의 필요성을 강조하려고
③ 응급 처치 교육 프로그램을 홍보하려고
④ 교내 응급 구조 안전 요원 배치를 요청하려고
⑤ 안전교육 강화 교사 연수 프로그램을 공지하려고

02 대화를 듣고, 여자의 의견으로 가장 적절한 것을 고르시오.

① 부모님께 예의를 갖추는 것은 당연하다.
② 대화를 할 때에는 서로 눈을 마주쳐야 한다.
③ 가족 간의 소통을 위해서는 대화가 필요하다.
④ 문자 메시지보다 실제로 만나서 대화해야 한다.
⑤ 집중을 위해 한 번에 한 가지 일만 하는 것이 좋다.

03 대화를 듣고, 두 사람의 관계를 가장 잘 나타낸 것을 고르시오.

① 대사관 직원 – 방문객
② 여행사 직원 – 고객
③ 호텔 직원 – 호텔 투숙객
④ 지하철 승무원 – 지하철 승객
⑤ 택시 콜센터 직원 – 서비스 이용 고객

04 대화를 듣고, 그림에서 대화의 내용과 일치하지 않는 것을 고르시오.

05 대화를 듣고, 남자가 지금 할 일로 가장 적절한 것을 고르시오.

① 학교에 가기
② 역사 시험 공부하기
③ Carol의 집에 가기
④ Carol에게 전화하기
⑤ Olivia의 수학 공부 도와주기

06 대화를 듣고, 두 사람이 지불할 금액을 고르시오. [3점]

① $1,380 ② $1,520 ③ $1,620
④ $1,720 ⑤ $1,960

07 대화를 듣고, 남자가 장학금을 신청할 수 없는 이유를 고르시오.

① 1학년 학생이라서
② 2년간 거주하지 않아서
③ 자원봉사 경력이 없어서
④ 교수 추천을 받지 못해서
⑤ 지난 학기 성적이 안 좋아서

08 대화를 듣고, 중고 물품 판매에 관해 언급되지 않은 것을 고르시오.

① 상품 판매 시기 ② 판매 상품 선정 기준
③ 판매 광고 방법 ④ 상품 진열 방법
⑤ 가격 결정 방법

09 솔로몬제도(Solomon Islands)에 관한 다음 내용을 듣고, 일치하지 않는 것을 고르시오.

① 유럽인은 1568년에 처음 방문했다.
② 제 2차 세계대전 당시 격전지였다.
③ 인구의 4분의 1이 농어업에 종사한다.
④ 관광객들에게 스쿠버 다이빙이 인기 있다.
⑤ 2007년과 2013년에 큰 지진을 겪었다.

정답 및 해설 p.98

10 다음 표를 보면서 대화를 듣고, 두 사람이 관람할 영화를 고르시오.

THE JASPER CINEMA Christmas Special			
Title	Genre	Starting Time	Running Time
① Love and Hate	Romance	11:00 a.m.	135 mins
② Space Shuttle	Science Fiction	2:30 p.m.	162 mins
③ The Last Adventures	Animation	5:30 p.m.	93 mins
④ Broken	Action	9:10 p.m.	119 mins
⑤ Night and Darkness	Horror	10:00 p.m.	97 mins

11 대화를 듣고, 남자의 마지막 말에 대한 여자의 응답으로 가장 적절한 것을 고르시오.

① The forecast says it will be warm tomorrow.
② It wasn't cold when I left my house.
③ This spicy soup will warm you up.
④ I think we should eat at home tonight.
⑤ Thanks, I can't believe I forgot my sweater.

12 대화를 듣고, 여자의 마지막 말에 대한 남자의 응답으로 가장 적절한 것을 고르시오.

① Yes, they should help me sleep well.
② I'll take them as soon as I get home.
③ I'm sure you'll feel better tomorrow.
④ It's important to listen to your doctor.
⑤ It says I shouldn't take more than two at once.

13 대화를 듣고, 남자의 마지막 말에 대한 여자의 응답으로 가장 적절한 것을 고르시오. [3점]

▶ Woman : ______

① Let's go buy some vegetables for the garden.
② I'll help you. Let me change my clothes.
③ I think you should plant the trees first.
④ When everything's ready, I'll call you back.
⑤ If I'm not back in two days, start without me.

14 대화를 듣고, 여자의 마지막 말에 대한 남자의 응답으로 가장 적절한 것을 고르시오.

▶ Man : ______

① I'm sorry, I have too many clients to see.
② Really? In that case, this haircut is free!
③ That's an impressive line-up of guests.
④ It's too late to change your hairstyle now.
⑤ I'm so sorry, I shouldn't have talked you into it.

15 다음 상황 설명을 듣고, Luke의 누나가 Luke에게 할 말로 가장 적절한 것을 고르시오. [3점]

▶ Luke's sister : ______

① It was careless of you to lose your phone.
② I'm glad you've created a sensible budget.
③ You can come to me whenever you need help.
④ You shouldn't spend all your money on a phone.
⑤ You'd better get in the habit of saving for emergencies.

[16~17] 다음을 듣고, 물음에 답하시오.

16 남자가 하는 말의 주제로 가장 적절한 것은?

① the influence music has had on society
② effective ways to draw public attention
③ how to become a successful musician
④ ways to help the poor people of the world
⑤ the importance of listening to a variety of music

17 언급된 국가가 아닌 것은?

① France ② Vietnam
③ Somalia ④ Ethiopia
⑤ United States

01

W: First aid is an essential life skill that equips young people with the confidence, ______________________________ in a first aid emergency. Children as young as six can learn basic first aid, including how to recognize an emergency and call for help. It could help thousands of people a year. For example, I heard of a 12-year-old who ______________________________ during lunchtime. Yet first aid isn't usually part of the curriculum. The Red Cross has tirelessly campaigned for years that all schools should teach first aid. It makes perfect sense to ______________________________. All students should be taught what to do in an emergency. It would help keep them safer.

02

W: Chris, you need to listen to me. I'm trying to tell you something important.

M: I am listening, Mom.

W: Maybe you are, but ______________________________. Just put down your phone for a few minutes.

M: I'm just checking my messages. I can ______________________________.

W: I'm sure you can, dear. But it's impolite not to look at someone who is talking to you.

M: Okay, I'm sorry. I guess ______________________________.

W: Maybe your friends don't mind, but there are plenty of people who agree with me.

M: You're right. I'm paying attention now.

03

W: Good evening.

M: Hello. I need to be at the Korean Embassy at 9 a.m. tomorrow. Can you book a taxi for me, please?

W: I'm sorry sir, but traffic in the morning is very bad. A taxi to the embassy ______________________________.

M: Oh. Then what should I do?

W: Take the Sky Train. It's very convenient and fast.

M: Great. ______________________________?

W: Exit the hotel lobby, turn right, and you'll see City Hall Station. Catch a train from there to Embassy Station.

M: Excellent. ______________________________ in the morning?

W: Well, the train trip takes about 15 minutes. Therefore, 8:30 will be fine. Would you like a wake-up call?

M: No, but thank you!

04

W: Hi, Eric. It's me, Jessica.

M: Hi, Jessica. Are you there yet?

W: Not yet. I'm passing by a music store ______________________________.

M: Then you're almost there. Do you see the sign that says "Dr. Cho's Dental Clinic" on the 2nd floor?

W: Just a minute. Oh, right there. I think I found it.

M: It's on the 1st floor of the same building.

W: You mean the one with ______________________________?

M: That's right.

W: Okay. Now I'm here. How long will it take for you to get here?

M: Actually, ______________________________. But I'll be there in 15 minutes.

W: Take your time. I'll sit on the bench in front of the restaurant. There's a menu board standing beside the entrance. Why don't I select the menu to save time?

M: That's a good idea. Dinner is on me.

05

W: Hello.

M: Hi, Olivia. This is Jerry. Are you studying math?

W: I was. I studied for two hours.

M: Well, I've just started. And ________________ ________________________.

W: Jerry, it's too late. I can't help you. And I'm going out now.

M: Where are you going?

W: To Carol's house. She and I made a plan to study for the history test together.

M: That's what I studied first. ________________ ____________________.

W: I'll help you tomorrow morning. Get to school as early as you can.

M: ________________________ to Carol's too?

W: You must phone and ask her first.

M: OK. I'll do that.

W: Good. Let me know what she said after that.

06

M: Honey, do you have a minute?

W: Of course. What's up?

M: I'm looking at plane tickets for our trip to Canada, and I'd like your opinion.

W: Okay. ____________________________?

M: Well, the cheapest option is $690 per ticket, but we would have to transfer twice.

W: That sounds inconvenient. How much for a direct flight?

M: For weekend flights, each ticket is $980. We could save a little bit ________________________ ______________.

W: That would be fine with me. It looks like there are two options. What's the difference?

M: The $760 ticket is for economy class. For $810 we can sit in economy plus, ________________ ______________.

W: I'm willing to pay an extra $50 for that.

M: Great. Then it's settled.

07

M: Excuse me. I'm here to apply for the Moore scholarship this semester.

W: Are you aware of all the requirements?

M: I'm not quite sure.

W: The Moore scholarship is not available to first-year students. Students starting from the second year ________________________________.

M: I'm a sophomore.

W: You must have maintained a B average or better for the past two semesters.

M: My grades are ________________________. I received mostly As in all my classes.

W: You also need a recommendation from one of your professors, and you need some experience in volunteer work.

M: I see. I think ________________________.

W: One more thing, since it's for Virginia residents, you and your parents must have lived in Virginia continuously for 2 years.

M: Really? I moved from New Hampshire last year.

W: Well, I'm sorry, but you can't apply for this scholarship then.

08

W: Honey, don't you think ________________ ______________?

M: I couldn't agree more. I guess we could have a garage sale.

W: Great idea! My family would have them when I was young, so I know a few tips.

M: Oh, really? Like what?

W: To begin, we want to attract the most customers. So, a non-holiday weekend is perfect.

M: Makes sense. I suppose we also want to ________ ________________________.

W: It's even better to advertise in a newspaper.

M: Okay. And I guess we want to put our nicest items out by the street to grab attention.

W: Of course. Now, ____________________. Usually, around 25% of the item's original cost is best.

M: Great. I think this will be a fun way to make some money.

09

M: Located northeast of Australia and east of Papua New Guinea, the Solomon Islands are a group of nearly 1,000 islands in the Pacific Ocean. Humans have lived on the islands for over 30,000 years, but the first visit by a European was in 1568. During the Second World War, the Solomon Islands were ______________________________, but afterward, the islands were relatively peaceful until a civil war broke out in 1998. Today, around three-quarters of its population ______________________________. Tourism is also an important source of income for the islands, and scuba diving is especially popular with visitors. The islands have suffered two major earthquakes in 2007 and 2013. Each resulted in a 5 to 10 meter tsunami that ______________________________.

10

W: Oh, look! The Jasper Cinema is having a Christmas special.
M: That's nice. Why don't we watch a movie later?
W: I was thinking the same thing. *Love and Hate* is romantic. What do you think?
M: Don't forget that we promised to have lunch with your parents at 12 today.
W: Oh, right. Well, I know you like *Space Shuttle*, but 162 minutes is just too long.
M: I agree. And ______________________________. But a horror film just doesn't seem appropriate for Christmas.
W: ______________________________. I say we go to the earlier one. Then we can have dinner afterward.
M: Are you sure? I've never seen *Broken* before.
W: Yes, I do not want to get back home too late.
M: Okay, then. ______________________________.

11

M: I'm hungry. Let's go outside and get something to eat.
W: Okay, but it's really cold. Do you ______________________________?
M: I probably do, but ______________________________?

12

W: Are you still sick? Maybe you should go home and rest.
M: ______________________________. I'll just take some of these pills that I bought.
W: Those can make you sleepy. ______________________________?

13

W: Where did all those potted vegetable plants come from?
M: I went to the garden center and bought them.
W: What do you plan to do with them?
M: I thought we could plant a garden with some vegetables.
W: That sounds like a good idea.
M: First I'm going to draw up ______________________________.
W: I forgot you have a degree in landscape architecture.
M: ______________________________ since I was very little.
W: Really? Anything you want me to do for you?
M: Yes. Maybe you could ______________________________ for me with a shovel.

14

M: OK, Julia, here's a mirror for you, so you can see the back.

W: Wow, it looks great! You are a genius hair stylist!

M: A shorter haircut really suits you, don't you think?

W: Yes, I'm glad ______________________.

M: Always a pleasure, Julia, and not just because you're a big star!

W: Thank you, Adrian! I have to run! I'm on stage at the Concert Hall at 8!

M: I wish ______________________________.

W: Well, why don't you? Do you have to work late?

M: No, you're my last client today, but your show tonight is sold out.

W: But that's no problem! I'll ______________________________!

15

W: Luke just started his first job two months ago. After his first paycheck, Luke ______________________. The budget divided all of his money among rent, food, entertainment, clothing, and transportation. He was proud of this budget and ______________. Unfortunately, one week before his second paycheck, Luke lost his phone and needed to buy another. ______________________________, Luke went to his older sister. Luke's sister was happy to help and gave him some money. But she worried that Luke wasn't planning for emergencies. She felt he could be smarter about ______________________, and she wanted to offer some advice. In this situation, what would Luke's sister most likely say to Luke?

16-17

M: Are you a music lover who is only interested in your favorite musician's music? I think that is unlikely, but if you are, I hope you will take a minute to think about all the social issues that music has brought to public attention and helped with. In the 1960s, musicians from Europe and North America sang songs ______________________________ the Vietnam War. And these protests greatly helped to end the war. In the 1980s, famine in Somalia was raised as a global issue, and rock musicians held concerts ______________________________. Similar efforts brought food to thousands of hungry people suffering in Ethiopia. Millions of people watched, donated money, and learned about the famine, and results followed. Country stars like Willie Nelson have also gotten involved. In 1985, Nelson and others launched Farm Aid, a concert ______________________ in the United States. Worldwide, musicians and their music are ______________________________. They are bringing awareness to real issues and providing hope.

01 다음을 듣고, 남자가 하는 말의 목적으로 가장 적절한 것을 고르시오.

① 졸업생들을 격려하려고
② 신입생들을 환영하려고
③ 학교 연례행사를 안내하려고
④ 평생 교육의 중요성을 강조하려고
⑤ 학문적 성공을 이루는 방법을 설명하려고

02 대화를 듣고, 남자의 의견으로 가장 적절한 것을 고르시오.

① 건강한 아침 식단 구성이 중요하다.
② 적정 체중을 유지해야 건강할 수 있다.
③ 오전 시간을 효율적으로 사용해야 한다.
④ 규칙적으로 아침 식사를 하는 것이 좋다.
⑤ 아침 운동을 하면 수업 집중력이 높아진다.

03 대화를 듣고, 두 사람의 관계를 가장 잘 나타낸 것을 고르시오.

① 토크쇼 프로듀서 – 토크쇼 사회자
② 고객 – 백화점 점원
③ 잡지 편집장 – 기자
④ 패션 디자이너 – 미용 전문가
⑤ 사진작가 – 모델

04 대화를 듣고, 그림에서 대화의 내용과 일치하지 않는 것을 고르시오.

05 대화를 듣고, 여자가 지금 할 일로 가장 적절한 것을 고르시오.

① 잡초 뽑기 ② 설거지하기
③ 영화 보러 가기 ④ 진공청소기 돌리기
⑤ 정원에 꽃 심기

06 대화를 듣고, 여자가 지불할 금액을 고르시오. [3점]

① $68 ② $72 ③ $74
④ $80 ⑤ $88

07 대화를 듣고, 여자가 눈물을 흘린 이유를 고르시오.

① 슬픈 이야기를 들어서
② 눈에 이물질이 들어가서
③ 남자가 짓궂은 장난을 쳐서
④ 가족과 떨어져 살게 되어서
⑤ 돌아가신 할머니 생각이 나서

08 대화를 듣고, 아파트에 관해 언급되지 않은 것을 고르시오.

① 침실 개수 ② 난방 방식 ③ 월 임대료
④ 공공요금 ⑤ 보안

09 Borders Book Club에 관한 다음 내용을 듣고, 일치하지 않는 것을 고르시오.

① 이번 달 모임은 5월 10일 오후 5시에 열린다.
② 모임에 참석하기 전에 이달의 책을 읽어야 한다.
③ 15세 이상이면 클럽에 가입할 수 있다.
④ 아이들을 데려오는 경우 아이들에게 책을 읽어 준다.
⑤ 회원 가입 신청 시 등록비는 무료이다.

10 다음 표를 보면서 대화를 듣고, 여자가 사기로 한 카메라를 고르시오.

Point and Shoot Digital Cameras

Product Description	Price	Optical Zoom	Color	LCD Screen
① Nice 380	$216.05	34X(22-765mm)	black	2.5 inches
② Bullet SX	$299.00	50X(24-1200mm)	white	2.5 inches
③ Phoenix XG	$229.00	52X(24-1248mm)	white	3.5 inches
④ Lumini FZ	$347.99	24X(24-576mm)	black	3.5 inches
⑤ DMC-LX	$243.15	3.8X(24-90mm)	white	3.5 inches

11 대화를 듣고, 여자의 마지막 말에 대한 남자의 응답으로 가장 적절한 것을 고르시오.

① Then you can use my cell phone. Here you are.
② I don't know what to do. We're outside the city.
③ Be careful. The next time your car will be towed.
④ Right. It's good to charge the battery frequently.
⑤ Yes, because this is a situation of great emergency!

12 대화를 듣고, 남자의 마지막 말에 대한 여자의 응답으로 가장 적절한 것을 고르시오.

① You won't. I can tell you really hate animals.
② I'm going to open a clinic for sick animals later.
③ That's right. It's my job to take the dog for walks.
④ It seems like you love animals. You're welcome to join!
⑤ I'm sorry. We don't have room for more members.

13 대화를 듣고, 여자의 마지막 말에 대한 남자의 응답으로 가장 적절한 것을 고르시오.

▶ Man : ______________________

① That was a great party. Thanks for inviting me.
② I really can't. I wish you would have called earlier.
③ It sounds like you had a great weekend. I'm jealous.
④ I can't wait to see you guys. I'll see you tomorrow!
⑤ I'm disappointed in you! This is the third time you cancelled on me!

14 대화를 듣고, 남자의 마지막 말에 대한 여자의 응답으로 가장 적절한 것을 고르시오. [3점]

▶ Woman : ______________________

① I understand, and I know how you feel.
② No. It's on my way, so don't worry about it.
③ You're right. Walking is good for your health.
④ I'll repeat it again. Make sure you write it down.
⑤ I'm sorry to cause you any trouble, but it's urgent.

15 다음 상황 설명을 듣고, Nicole이 Austin에게 할 말로 가장 적절한 것을 고르시오. [3점]

▶ Nicole : ______________________

① Why don't we pull over and ask for directions?
② I don't like being outside after dark. Let's go home.
③ Thank you for fixing the GPS. Now we won't get lost.
④ Don't be so upset. Let's go to a different restaurant.
⑤ I think you're so stubborn. You made us late for dinner.

[16~17] 다음을 듣고, 물음에 답하시오.

16 여자가 하는 말의 주제로 가장 적절한 것은?

① tips for getting started volunteering
② how to find the right volunteer opportunity
③ volunteering as a method to improve social skills
④ the advantages and disadvantages of volunteering
⑤ volunteering as an opportunity for career development

17 언급된 곳이 <u>아닌</u> 것은?

① 병원 ② 요양원 ③ 환경단체
④ 유적지 ⑤ 박물관

01

M: All of you are probably eager to start a new chapter in your life. Many of you will soon encounter many opportunities. Some of you may be ____________ ______________________________. Once you enter the real world, you will meet people from all walks of life and have a variety of experiences. You may feel that ________________________ ______________ is not relevant to your future needs. But you'll realize later that everything you've learned will be useful and important. Do not be afraid of your future, but be ready to take on the upcoming challenges and opportunities after this graduation. We are very proud of all of you and ____________________________________.

02

M: Hi, Kelly. Where are you going? ____________ ______________________.

W: Hey, Chuck. I'm going to the cafeteria. I'm so hungry!

M: You're going now? Didn't you have breakfast?

W: No. I never wake up early enough.

M: That's why you're always hungry in the morning. I think you ____________________________ __________________ and have breakfast.

W: You're right, but it's hard to get out of bed in the morning.

M: Yes it is, but eating breakfast will increase your ability to concentrate. It might improve your grades.

W: That's true. I've also read that eating breakfast regularly can ________________________ a healthy weight.

M: Then, you know what you have to do from tomorrow.

W: Okay. You win. I'll start tomorrow.

03

M: Kayla, I think we need to talk about the show now.

W: Sure. Did you finish the final runway outfits?

M: ______________________________.

W: Can I see them?

M: Sure. These are photos of them. The main colors of this season are deep turquoise and navy blue.

W: Wow, great! Your designs are always stunning! You said the theme of this show is "water," didn't you?

M: Yes, I really ______________________________.

W: Then I think I'll have to put something bright, like gold or green eyeshadow, on their eyelids. Is that okay with you?

M: That sounds beautiful. How about their hair?

W: I guess long soft wavy hair ______________ ______________________.

M: I trust your judgment. You'll do wonderfully!

04

M: What's this photo?

W: It's a picture of Loy, a dog that won Best in Show in last year's dog show.

M: Who's the person holding Loy? The long-haired woman who has a white strap around her arm __________________________.

W: That's my sister. She's a trainer. The number on her arm is the participant number.

M: Oh, I see. Your sister looks really cool. Is the man who's holding the encased ribbon your father?

W: No, he's the head of the dog-show committee. And the woman ______________________________ is also a committee member.

M: You're talking about the woman who's wearing a long dress, right?

W: Yes.

M: Then who's the lady on the other side who has short hair and is holding a bouquet of flowers?

W: She's also a committee member. All of the things they were holding were given to Loy.

M: There's ______________________________ Loy. I guess he got that, too.

W: Yeah. As far as I remember, my sister was even interviewed by the local newspaper after this picture was taken.

05

W: Dad, ________________________ my allowance? I seem to go over my budget every month.

M: I think you're getting enough money.

W: Come on, Dad. Don't I deserve more now that I'm older?

M: Then how about this? I won't increase your allowance, but you can earn money ____________ ________________________________.

W: Is there any work I can do today? I need to go see a movie tonight, but I'm $10 short.

M: Well, the house needs to be vacuumed and cleaned and there are dirty dishes piled up in the sink, but I guess ________________________________ in the garden.

W: Are we going to plant flowers?

M: Yes, but we need to get rid of the weeds first. I'll pay you $10 an hour.

W: $10 an hour? Okay.

06

W: Just a minute. Is this the right street?

M: Didn't you say you wanted to go to Sandy Elementary School?

W: Yes, but this area ________________________ ____________________. I've been here before, but I don't remember this area.

M: Don't worry. ____________________________. Do you see the school over there?

W: Oh, I see. Wow, that was really fast. You really know your way around here.

M: I've been a taxi driver in this area for the past 19 years. Okay, here we are.

W: I see that the fare is exactly $60.

M: But we're ________________________________, so there is an extra 20% charge to the total fare.

W: Oh, I totally forgot about that. I don't have any cash with me, so is it okay to pay by credit card?

M: Of course.

W: Please add another $8 for your tip.

M: Thank you so much, ma'am. Hold on. Here's your card.

07

M: Excuse me, I believe this is my seat.

W: Oh, sorry about my bag. Let me move it. I was a little preoccupied.

M: No worries. You ________________________. Hi, my name is Mr. Doolittle.

W: I'm sorry? Is that really your name?

M: Haha. No, I was just ________________________. My real name is Matthew Ruben.

W: Hi, I'm Kate.

M: I hope you found that funny because you seemed so very sad.

W: Is it that obvious? How embarrassing.

M: There's nothing to be embarrassed about. We all get sad from time to time.

W: Actually, I am on my way home from my grandmother's funeral. The thought of not seeing her anymore ________________________. She meant a lot to my family.

M: I'm really sorry to hear that. Losing someone is always heartbreaking. But I hope you get over your sorrow soon.

W: Thanks.

08

W: Come this way. This is the living room.

M: It's very nice and spacious.

W: Yes, as you already know, there are two big bedrooms in this apartment.

M: How about heating? Is it central heating?

W: No, you can ________________________ ________________________.

M: I see. Does the rent include utility bills?

W: It includes water and gas but not electricity. Of course, you're responsible for telephone and Internet service.

M: Does the apartment building offer security?

W: Yes, it has 24-hour security ________________ ____________________________.

M: Good. I like it.

W: I guarantee ________________________________ ____________________ in this part of town.

09

W: To all customers of Borders Bookstore: we'd like to remind you of our popular Borders Book Club. This month's book club meeting will be at 5 p.m., Sunday, May 10th. Please pick up this month's book, *The History of Food* by Anthony Boyl and ______________________________ regarding the book. Due to the popularity of our book club, the club ______________________________. If you're interested, sign up today to join one of our groups. The sign-up sheet is located at the information desk on the first floor. Anyone aged 15 or older may join the club. In case you want to bring your children along, we also offer a book reading for them. So make this a family affair. There is a one-time registration fee of $5 that ______________________________. For further information, please check out our website at www.bordersbooks.com.

10

W: Matthew, I'd like to get a compact digital camera for my summer trip. I was wondering if you could help me choose the right one.

M: I'd love to help. First, I need to know ______________________________ on the camera.

W: I was thinking of spending around $200-$300. No more than that.

M: Got it. How about a zoom lens?

W: Sure. ______________________________.

M: Then more than 24X optical zoom would be enough.

W: All right. And I like bright colors.

M: So you ______________________________. And I'm sure you want a large LCD screen, right?

W: Oh, yes, I want something larger than 3 inches because I'd like something easy to see.

M: Okay. I think this is the one you want.

W: Yes, I think so. Thanks for helping me.

11

W: Excuse me. ______________________________? My car won't start. I don't know why.

M: Oh, I'm sorry to hear that. Why don't you call an auto repair service?

W: The problem is that ______________________________.

12

M: I heard you started a new club for people ______________________________.

W: Yes, we've got seven members so far, but we're always looking for more!

M: ______________________________? I've got a dog at home, and I want to be a vet.

13

W: Hello, Joseph. This is Olivia.

M: Oh, Olivia. Long time, no see. How have you been?

W: Good. I'm enjoying school life these days. How about you?

M: ______________________________. I'm usually in the lecture hall, research lab, or in the library. I recently started a new project with one of my professors.

W: I knew it. Do you have some time tomorrow?

M: Tomorrow? It's Friday, right? What time?

W: Seven in the evening. ______________________________ and I want you to come.

M: Oh, I can't. I have other plans. Professor Morgan invited me over for dinner.

W: You have to come! Tyler, Alex, Victoria, and Harry are all coming. I told them that you would be coming.

M: I'm sorry, but I can't. I already promised the professor that I would be coming.

W: Can't you ______________________________? How often do we get together like this?

14

W: Hi, Minsu. What are you doing here?

M: Oh, Megan, hi. I didn't expect to meet you here. What are you doing here?

W: I live around here. I'm ____________________ the gym. I thought you lived in the school dormitory.

M: I do. I'm just looking for the Moore Career Center. I heard that they offer free classes for foreigners.

W: Oh, Moore Career Center is __________________ ____________________________.

M: Really? I guess I got off at the wrong stop. Can you tell me how to get there?

W: Sure. You go straight down this street and make a right at the next traffic light. And....

M: Please wait. I want to write it down or else I'll forget.

W: ____________________________________? I'll give you a ride. It'll only take us ten minutes.

M: That'd be great. I hope ______________________ _________________.

15

M: Nicole and Austin want to have dinner at a nice restaurant outside the city, and they reserve a table for 7 p.m. While driving to the restaurant, the GPS in his car stops working and they get lost. Since it's getting dark, they're ________________ ____________________________________. They try to ask someone for directions, but there is nothing outside. After half an hour, they find someone, and the person gives very nice directions. But they arrive late at the restaurant and _______________ ______________________. Austin isn't very happy about it and blames himself for not checking the GPS beforehand. But Nicole ________________ ______________________. In this situation, what would Nicole most likely say to Austin?

16-17

W: With busy lives, it can be hard to find time to volunteer. However, volunteering is ____________ ____________________________________. If you're considering a new career, volunteering can help you get experience in your area of interest. Even if you're not planning on changing careers, volunteering gives you the opportunity to practice ____ ___________, such as teamwork, communication, problem solving, project planning, task management, and organization. In some fields, you can volunteer directly at an organization that does ______________________________________. For example, if you're interested in nursing, you could volunteer at a hospital or a nursing home. Just because volunteer work is unpaid does not mean the skills you learn are basic. Many volunteering opportunities provide extensive training. For example, you could become an experienced environmental activist while volunteering for an environmental organization or a knowledgeable art historian while donating your time as a museum guide. Volunteering can also help you ____ and use them to benefit the greater community. Now can you set aside the time for volunteering?

01 다음을 듣고, 여자가 하는 말의 목적으로 가장 적절한 것을 고르시오.

① 인터넷상의 불법 파일 공유를 금지시키려고
② 컴퓨터 바이러스 감염 예방법을 알리려고
③ 바이러스 감염 시 대처법을 설명하려고
④ 안전한 파일 공유 방법을 설명하려고
⑤ 새로운 바이러스 백신을 홍보하려고

02 대화를 듣고, 두 사람이 하는 말의 주제로 가장 적절한 것을 고르시오.

① 적성 파악의 중요성
② 미래 유망 직업의 종류
③ 성공하는 사람들의 특징
④ 성격별 적합한 직업 유형
⑤ 직업 결정 시 고려할 사항

03 대화를 듣고, 두 사람의 관계를 가장 잘 나타낸 것을 고르시오.

① 쇼핑객 – 상점 직원
② 주택 판매자 – 부동산 중개인
③ 집 주인 – 세입자
④ 경매업자 – 경매 참여자
⑤ 신문 기자 – 제보자

04 대화를 듣고, 그림에서 대화의 내용과 일치하지 않는 것을 고르시오.

05 대화를 듣고, 남자가 할 일로 가장 적절한 것을 고르시오.

① 침대 옮기기
② 카펫 청소하기
③ 우유병 소독하기
④ 아기 우유 먹이기
⑤ 오렌지주스 만들기

06 대화를 듣고, 남자가 지불할 금액을 고르시오. [3점]

① $15 ② $16 ③ $21
④ $24 ⑤ $29

07 대화를 듣고, 여자가 Dolby Industries에 입사하려는 이유를 고르시오.

① 출퇴근이 편리해서
② 높은 급여를 제공해서
③ 안정적인 노후를 보장해서
④ 근무시간 조절이 가능해서
⑤ 업무가 자신의 성격에 잘 맞아서

08 대화를 듣고, Vatican City에 관해 언급되지 않은 것을 고르시오.

① 위치 ② 인구
③ 화폐 ④ 주 수입원
⑤ 주요 명소

09 다음 여행 인솔자의 설명을 듣고, 일치하지 않는 것을 고르시오.

① 여행객들은 지금 처음 모였다.
② 시장에는 다양한 상품들이 있다.
③ 시장에서는 구매할 때 흥정을 해야 한다.
④ 여행객들은 앞으로 두 시간 정도 쇼핑을 하게 된다.
⑤ 중앙 광장은 내일 다시 방문할 예정이다.

10 다음 표를 보면서 대화를 듣고, 여자가 구매할 세트를 고르시오.

Necklace-making Kits					
Set	Silver beads	Gold beads	Shell beads	Wire (meters)	Price
① Beginner set	10	0	50	2	$10
② Intermediate set	10	8	100	4	$17
③ Advanced set	24	10	100	6	$25
④ Deluxe set	40	20	100	10	$40
⑤ Ultra set	50	50	200	15	$80

11 대화를 듣고, 여자의 마지막 말에 대한 남자의 응답으로 가장 적절한 것을 고르시오.

① I'll try them next time.
② Four or five will be fine.
③ Its shelf life is 10 months.
④ The pizzas are already spicy.
⑤ We only ordered four pizzas.

12 대화를 듣고, 남자의 마지막 말에 대한 여자의 응답으로 가장 적절한 것을 고르시오.

① I'll introduce you to her.
② I like cleaning up for her.
③ My new roommate is great.
④ She left wet towels everywhere.
⑤ I think that's one of her advantages.

13 대화를 듣고, 여자의 마지막 말에 대한 남자의 응답으로 가장 적절한 것을 고르시오. [3점]

▶ Man : ____________________

① Fire engines are on the way now.
② Children shouldn't play with fire.
③ Try to put out the fire with your family.
④ I'm sorry that you got fired from your job.
⑤ Global warming is an emergency of nature.

14 대화를 듣고, 남자의 마지막 말에 대한 여자의 응답으로 가장 적절한 것을 고르시오.

▶ Woman : ____________________

① That's my favorite book too.
② Try an informative TV show.
③ You shouldn't watch so many soaps.
④ But everybody needs to have a little fun.
⑤ I don't think so. That book is easy to read.

15 다음 상황 설명을 듣고, Paul이 Ted에게 할 말로 가장 적절한 것을 고르시오. [3점]

▶ Paul : ____________________

① I don't want to bother you.
② When is your next job interview?
③ Please don't ask me how it went.
④ Sorry, I'm very disappointed in you.
⑤ Can I ask you a personal question?

[16~17] 다음을 듣고, 물음에 답하시오.

16 여자가 하는 말의 주제로 가장 적절한 것은?

① reducing the amount of water consumption
② tips on how to save energy in your household
③ economic benefits of buying used appliances
④ the need to develop energy efficient technology
⑤ maintaining the appropriate indoor temperature

17 에너지를 절약하는 방법으로 언급되지 않은 것은?

① 온수 대신 냉수 사용하기
② LED 전구로 교체하기
③ 사용하지 않을 때는 컴퓨터 끄기
④ 세탁물을 꽉 채워서 세탁기 사용하기
⑤ 실내 온도를 20도로 유지하기

01

W: Hi, this is Karen James with *Today's Technology Report* on KWSC radio. Well, there is a new virus ______________________________ ____________________. One million computers have been infected in the last week alone. Once downloaded, the virus allows thousands of advertisements to pop up. Today, I want to ______________________________. First of all, update your anti-virus software. If it's not scanning your computer automatically, then turn on this feature. Secondly, avoid peer-to-peer networks. The recent virus ____________________ ____________________. So you should not download movies or songs from these networks. They could be hiding viruses.

02

M: Did you finish the homework of searching for your future job?

W: Not yet. I need more time to think. There are so many jobs in the world.

M: Would you like some tips ____________________ ____________________?

W: Sure, what are they?

M: Start ______________________________ ____________________. If you are social, it is a good idea to find a job interacting with people.

W: Like a consultant or a marketer?

M: Right.

W: So, we should know our talents. For example, if someone is gifted in art, they might want to be an art teacher or a painter. What else?

M: Well, the most important thing is to find a job you enjoy.

W: ______________________________. I hope these tips help me find the right career.

M: I think they will.

03

W: How's the housing market nowadays?

M: Prices are really low right now.

W: Yes, it's really too bad. I wish we had a choice but we don't.

M: Everyone says prices will go up next year.

W: I know, but my husband's company is transferring him to Chicago.

M: Have you found a new house in Chicago?

W: Yes, we have. But we can't buy it ____________________ ____________________.

M: OK. I understand. If we set a low price for your house, it will sell quickly.

W: How much ______________________________?

M: I will do some research and phone you tomorrow.

W: Thank you. You can show buyers the house ____________________.

M: OK. I'll put ads in the paper tomorrow.

04

M: What photo is this? It looks like a make-up room.

W: You're right. It's a picture of me in the make-up room ____________________ in the school theater last year.

M: The mirror in front of you with all the light bulbs around the edge is really cool.

W: It's because we need a lot of lighting when applying make-up.

M: ____________________ of a witch? There's a broom and pointed hat on the shelf on top of the mirror.

W: No. There was a witch in the play, but I played the princess. Do you see the dress with all the lace in the closet on the right? That was ____________________ ____________________.

M: Wow, how beautiful! Did you wear the crown on top of the closet?

W: Yeah. I had to wear the crown.

M: What was inside the two large pieces of luggage next to the mirror?

W: Some costumes and accessories for the play. We borrowed them from a professional theater company.
M: Sounds like fun. It's too bad I missed the play.
W: We're doing another play this year, so I'll let you know in advance.

05

M: Caroline, what are you doing? You said you have a headache.
W: I'm boiling Harper's bottles.
M: I'll do that. You don't look yourself. ____________ ________________ for a while?
W: I'm all right. And it's almost done. I just need to place the bottles to dry upside-down on a drying rack.
M: Is it necessary to boil baby bottles?
W: Absolutely. ______________________________ ___________________, viruses and bacteria can gather on them.
M: I see. Are you really okay? I bought a bag of oranges on the way home. I'll make some fresh-squeezed orange juice for you.
W: No, thanks. I'm really okay, and I have a ton of things to do. The carpet in our room needs to be cleaned.
M: Oh, Caroline. I vacuumed the carpet last Saturday.
W: But ____________________________________ tomorrow, so I'd like to do it again before the bed arrives.
M: Okay. I'll do that now. You need a rest.

06

M: Excuse me, how much are these T-shirts right here?
W: The colored ones or the plain white ones?
M: The colored ones.
W: They are $8 each.
M: Are the plain white ones less expensive?
W: Yes, they are. They are $5 each. But ____________ ____________________________ right now. If you buy two T-shirts, you _________________ ____________________.
M: On both types?
W: Yes. The offer applies to both colored and plain white T-shirts.
M: Great. I'll take a red one, a blue one and, hmm... a black one.
W: OK, three colored T-shirts. Do you want any plain white T-shirts, too?
M: Well, I don't really need any right now, but I will take one.

07

M: You look happy! What's up?
W: I just got a call from Dolby Industries. They offered me a job!
M: That's great! You ________________________ ____________ for that company.
W: You think so? I know the commute won't be easy, but I'm really excited to start.
M: Then ___________________________________ ______________ with Jeoffrey Laboratories? You mentioned they were offering a high salary.
W: I will cancel that interview. The position at Dolby will let me choose my own hours, and it has the potential to become a career for me.
M: That sounds like a wise decision. _____________ ____________________ for dinner to celebrate?
W: I'd love that. You're the best friend!

08

M: Amy, I'm ______________________! How was Italy?

W: It was great. I stayed with my grandmother in Rome and visited my cousin who works inside Vatican City.

M: That's a separate Italian-speaking country inside the city of Rome, right?

W: Right. It's incredibly small. There are only around 500 permanent residents.

M: Then I guess your cousin doesn't live inside the Vatican?

W: The Vatican ______________________ the Pope, and only Catholic officials can become citizens. My cousin works there, but she lives in Rome.

M: Most of the countries in that part of Europe use the Euro as their currency. Is the Vatican the same?

W: Yes. It's so small that ______________________ ______________________ tourism and church fundraising.

M: That's really interesting. I'd like to visit there sometime.

09

M: Well, everyone ______________________. Thank you for getting back on the bus right on time. Now we'll be going to Shindong Market, which is famous for ______________________ ______________________. You can buy anything from a pet dog to a sofa or a new suit. You should remember to bargain hard at the market. You can ______________________ in the market. On the way there we'll pass the city's central plaza with its famous water fountain. You don't have to worry about taking pictures now. We'll return to look around the plaza tomorrow. I hope you enjoy the second half of the day's tour.

10

W: I'm finally going to order the necklace kit my mom ______________________.

M: That sounds neat.

W: I need to choose from these kits on the list.

M: But it really ______________________.

W: I'll make you something "manly" that you can wear.

M: Like a shell necklace that surfers wear?

W: For a shell necklace I'll need more shells ______________________ ______________________.

M: And you should make something nice for your mom to thank her.

W: I was thinking of something with a lot of silver.

M: Like the one with 50 silver beads?

W: No, that's too expensive. It should be under $50. But more than 20 silver beads, definitely.

M: And you could make birthday presents!

W: So I'll need a set with as much wire as possible.

M: Then you should get this one.

11

W: Okay, here are the five large pizzas you ordered. Enjoy.

M: Thanks so much. Oh, ______________________ ______________________ of hot sauce?

W: That's no problem. ______________________ ______________________?

12

M: Anna, why did you ______________________ ______________________?

W: I changed because my last roommate was too dirty.

M: I don't understand. ______________________ ______________________?

13

M: Hello, you have reached the fire department. What is ____?

W: The house next door to mine is on fire.

M: Can you give me the address, please?

W: Yes, it's 1001 Maple Street.

M: Do you know if anyone is home? Are there any children or elderly people living there?

W: A young couple lives there with their grandmother and their small baby.

M: Can you see the flames from your house?

W: No. So far, ________________________ thick, black smoke.

M: If you think it is safe, please ________________ ____________________ to see if anyone answers.

W: OK. I'll do that now. When can you get here?

14

M: What's that magazine you're reading?

W: It's a TV guide. Do you know what the most popular TV show here is?

M: Umm, is it the BBC news?

W: No, it's *Neighbours*. It says here that *Neighbours* ____ in the U.K. since 1986. And it has ______________ ________________________ of 11 million people!

M: Wow. That's billions of hours wasted on a TV soap opera. I don't believe it.

W: I love *Neighbours*. It's great. I watch it every day.

M: That's terrible. If you need a break, do some exercise, or read a good book.

15

M: Paul is graduating and looking for a job. He has had a few job interviews but ____________________ ________________________________. He has been disappointed a few times because he thought the interview had gone well. But today Paul had a terrible interview. He was asked questions ____________________________________, so he answered poorly. On the bus going home, Paul meets a friend, Ted. He asks Paul ____________ ________________________________. Paul says he had a job interview. Paul knows Ted will ask him about the interview. But he is disappointed and ____________________________________ right now. In this situation, what is Paul most likely to say to Ted?

16-17

W: If you do the following things you can save up to $1,500 per year, and you'll be saving the environment. Less oil will be burnt and the carbon footprint ________________________________ will be smaller. To begin with, go around your house and replace 100 watt light bulbs with energy efficient 60 watt bulbs, substituting longer-lasting LED bulbs wherever possible. It's also time to change a few of your bad habits: turn off the computer ______________________________; use the washing machine only when you have a full load; and turn down the heat in your house. It is recommended that you keep indoor temperatures around 20℃, not 24℃ or 25℃. If you feel cold, wear a sweater, and ________________________ ________________ in rooms your family is not using. Lastly, think about replacing old, inefficient appliances. New ones are expensive, but _______ __________________________________.

01 다음을 듣고, 남자가 하는 말의 목적으로 가장 적절한 것을 고르시오.

① 국제 학생 클럽 가입을 독려하려고
② 국제 학생 클럽 창단을 제안하려고
③ 국제 학생 교류의 밤 행사를 홍보하려고
④ 국제 문화 교류의 중요성을 강조하려고
⑤ 국제 학생 클럽이 주최하는 자선 행사를 안내하려고

02 대화를 듣고, 여자의 의견으로 가장 적절한 것을 고르시오.

① 운전 시 전방주시가 가장 중요하다.
② 운전자는 교통 법규를 준수해야 한다.
③ 졸음 운전은 음주 운전만큼이나 나쁘다.
④ 장거리 운전일수록 사고 위험이 높아진다.
⑤ 교통사고 방지를 위한 정부 대책이 필요하다.

03 대화를 듣고, 두 사람의 관계를 가장 잘 나타낸 것을 고르시오.

① 전기 기술자 - 수리 의뢰인
② 상점 주인 - 고객
③ 의사 - 제약회사 직원
④ 교사 - 학생
⑤ 치과 의사 - 환자

04 대화를 듣고, 그림에서 대화의 내용과 일치하지 않는 것을 고르시오.

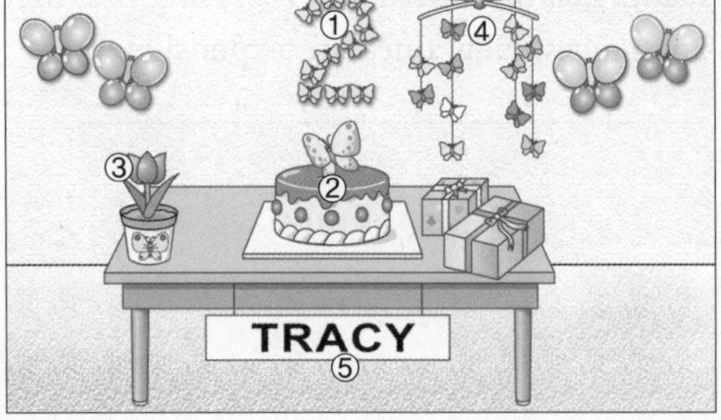

05 대화를 듣고, 남자가 할 일로 가장 적절한 것을 고르시오.

① 욕실 청소하기
② 손님들 모셔오기
③ 부엌에서 도와주기
④ 아이스크림 만들기
⑤ 식료품점에 다녀오기

06 대화를 듣고, 여자가 지불할 금액을 고르시오. [3점]

① $490 ② $570 ③ $650
④ $1,570 ⑤ $1,650

07 대화를 듣고, 남자가 옷차림에 신경 쓰는 이유를 고르시오.

① 데이트가 있어서
② 새 옷을 구입해서
③ 연주회에 참석해서
④ 고교 동창을 만나서
⑤ 파티에 가기로 해서

08 대화를 듣고, 주차장 이용에 관해 언급되지 않은 것을 고르시오.

① 주차 대행 여부 ② 주차장 이용 시간
③ 주차 요금 ④ 주차비 할인 혜택
⑤ 세차 서비스

09 Venice 고등학교 음악회에 관한 다음 내용을 듣고, 일치하지 않는 것을 고르시오.

① 학교 강당에서 목요일 저녁에 개최된다.
② 크리스마스 뮤지컬과 록 밴드의 공연도 있다.
③ 12세 미만 어린이의 입장료는 성인 입장료의 반값이다.
④ Venice 고교 학생은 무료로 입장할 수 있다.
⑤ 수익금은 Venice 고등학교 장학기금으로 쓰인다.

정답 및 해설 p.110

10 다음 표를 보면서 대화를 듣고, 여자가 선택할 커피 추출기를 고르시오.

Coffee Machines

Coffee Machine	Capacity	Price	Heater	Built-in grinder
① A	12 cups	$117.99	○	○
② B	10 cups	$150.00	○	○
③ C	8 cups	$84.00	×	×
④ D	12 cups	$99.95	○	×
⑤ E	10 cups	$146.41	○	○

11 대화를 듣고, 여자의 마지막 말에 대한 남자의 응답으로 가장 적절한 것을 고르시오.

① Cheer up. Have confidence in yourself.
② She's right. That cut looks perfect on you.
③ Oh, dear! You shouldn't have cut your hair.
④ You've really changed. I didn't recognize you!
⑤ You say you do, but you don't care about me.

12 대화를 듣고, 남자의 마지막 말에 대한 여자의 응답으로 가장 적절한 것을 고르시오.

① Sure. I'll move to another seat.
② Okay. I'll save your seat for you.
③ Yes, your seats are in the fifth row.
④ No, all the seats are currently taken.
⑤ I'm sorry, but you can't take that chair.

13 대화를 듣고, 여자의 마지막 말에 대한 남자의 응답으로 가장 적절한 것을 고르시오. [3점]

▶ Man : ________________

① I just came to your office a moment ago.
② They are in the file cabinet near the desk.
③ You should try to figure out what all this is for.
④ We were talking about the information you needed.
⑤ I wonder if you could help me solve this problem.

14 대화를 듣고, 남자의 마지막 말에 대한 여자의 응답으로 가장 적절한 것을 고르시오.

▶ Woman : ________________

① You make a good point. I'll try your advice.
② Well, I don't think so. He is a true gentleman.
③ I understand. I'm sure he'll respect you as well.
④ Right. I'll ask my teacher if I can change my partner.
⑤ Yes. That's a common problem with most team projects.

15 다음 상황 설명을 듣고, Lauren이 행상인에게 할 말로 가장 적절한 것을 고르시오. [3점]

▶ Lauren : ________________

① How long have you had it? How old is it?
② I like its color and design. How much is it?
③ Here's thirty-five pounds. Can you gift-wrap this?
④ It's a bit expensive. Can you come down a little?
⑤ Can you tell me where the nearest shopping mall is?

[16~17] 다음을 듣고, 물음에 답하시오.

16 여자가 하는 말의 주제로 가장 적절한 것은?

① the effects of plastic on marine life
② why marine resources need to be developed
③ methods to deal with pollution in the oceans
④ why ocean pollution is linked to human health
⑤ a warning about the seriousness of marine pollution

17 오염을 유발하는 것으로 언급되지 않은 것은?

① 병　② 스티로폼 조각
③ 플라스틱 낚시 장비　④ 기름
⑤ 공장 폐수

01

M: The International Student Club of Maple University is an organization consisting of all the international students at the university. ____ to learn more about the lifestyle and culture of the United States as well as other countries. The International Student Club also hosts the annual International Night. It is a magical event ____, excellent food, and entertainment. This year it will be held at the Maple Theater at 6 p.m. on May the 13th. Doors open at 5:30 p.m. and ____. Tickets will cost $5 for adults and $3 for children under the age of 12.

02

W: Watch out! ____!

M: I'm sorry. I think I just dozed off for a second there.

W: Oh, dear. It's because you've been driving for five hours straight.

M: It's fine. I think I'll be okay.

W: Do you know ____ when you're sleepy? I'll take over.

M: Let me roll down the window and play some loud music. That'll help.

W: Yes, but be careful. A sleepy driver is ____ who's drunk.

M: It's really not so bad. Just keep talking to me and I'll be all right.

W: I think you should either pull over and get some rest or let me drive.

M: Okay. How about getting some rest at the next rest stop area?

W: Great idea. A ten-minute nap can do wonders.

M: Okay, I'll take your advice.

03

W: How long have you had this problem?

M: Well, it's been quite a while. And recently it started to really bother me.

W: I wish ________________________________. It looks pretty serious.

M: I've been so busy with work.

W: I won't be able to treat it in one visit. I'll have to work on it for several weeks. Is that okay with you?

M: I guess I have no choice. I'm in so much pain right now. I can't eat anything ____. If I bite something, it sends a painful shockwave down one side of my head.

W: Your cavity has gotten so bad that we'll have to pull out your roots.

M: Really? Doesn't that hurt?

W: Yes, it will be a painful treatment, but it ____.

M: I see. When should I make the appointment?

W: You can check with the receptionist.

04

W: John! Come and have a look!

M: Wow! Did you decorate all this for Tracy? It's absolutely lovely.

W: The concept for the party is butterflies. ________________________________ at the number 2 on the wall, it's all made with butterflies.

M: It's amazing. Did you make those paper butterflies by yourself?

W: I sure did. And look at those balloon butterflies, two on each side. ________________________?

M: I'll say. The cake in the middle is also decorated with a butterfly.

W: You know that Tracy loves butterflies.

M: I see that you decorated the little flower pots next to the cake with butterflies, too.

W: Since Tracy is turning two, I placed two pots.

M: Great. You also have butterfly mobiles ____. What a great idea!

W: Take a look at the front of the decorated table.

M: Oh, you hung a banner with Tracy's name on it. You really are the best mom.

05

M: Do you have everything you need?
W: Almost. ______________________________ ____________ for dessert. But we have plenty of homemade ice cream in the refrigerator.
M: I'm sure they'll like your ice cream. But I could go to the grocery store if you'd like.
W: No, thank you. Oh, did you clean the living-room bathroom for the guests?
M: Sure. I did that in the morning.
W: You're the best. I hope your colleagues like my cooking. Frankly, I'm a little nervous.
M: Don't worry about a thing. You're the best cook around.
W: If it's okay with you, ______________________ ______________________ in the kitchen.
M: What can I do?
W: It'd be a great help if you could chop some vegetables for me.
M: No problem! ____________________________.

06

W: What's going on? What is that horrible sound?
M: It's from the car's brakes. __________________ ____________. That's the sound of metal rubbing on metal.
W: That's incredibly dangerous!
M: Yes, it's dangerous. A brake job costs $450.
W: That's very expensive. But _________________ _________________. I think I need to have an inspection to make sure everything else is okay.
M: Okay. It costs $40. And we'll give you an oil change free of charge.
W: Great. Anything else?
M: Hmm.... You need to change the two back tires. Tires cost $80 each.
W: I see. Well, ____________________________ if I install a new stereo system?
M: It's around $1,000.
W: Really? Oh, forget about it. Just the brakes, an inspection, and tires.
M: Okay.

07

W: Arnold, are you still standing in front of the mirror? Isn't it time for you to leave?
M: I'll be done in a few minutes. Does my jacket go well with my pants?
W: Are you going to a fancy party? ____________ ____________________________ with the way you look?
M: No, there's no party.
W: Oh, you're attending the orchestra concert? Is it today?
M: The concert ____________________________. Mom, I want your honest opinion.
W: The jacket looks great on you. Oh, you're going out on a date? I didn't know you had a girlfriend.
M: Mom, you know that I don't have a girlfriend. I'm getting together with some friends from high school tonight.
W: Oh, so you want to look good in front of them.
M: I ____________________________________.
W: Don't worry, you look very handsome. Have fun!

08

W: Excuse me, I'd like to park here. What should I do?

M: You can ______________________________ over there.

W: I just learned how to drive, and I'm not sure if I can park in that small space. Do you think you could park my car for me?

M: Sure, I can do that for you.

W: Thank you so much. Should I leave my keys in the car?

M: Yes, please. For how long will you park your car? We're open from 6 a.m. to 10 p.m.

W: ______________________________ two hours. How much is the parking fee?

M: It's $15 for the first hour and $5 for every 30 minutes thereafter.

W: Wow, that's expensive. Are there ______________ ______________________?

M: If you'd like, we offer a quick car wash. Of course, we charge for that service.

W: I'm all right then. Thank you for parking my car.

M: Here's your stub. Please don't lose it.

09

W: Attention please. I'd like to ______________ ______________________ the upcoming winter concert at Venice High School. We will be holding the concert on Thursday, December 21 at 6:30 p.m. in the school auditorium. ______________ ______________________ a Christmas musical by our award-winning choral group. Also, our very own rock band, Metal, will showcase some of their own songs for us. So don't miss this event. Tickets are $6 for adults and $2 for children under the age of 12. All students of Venice High School ______________________________. All money will go to the Venice High Scholarship fund, so please come and support our school.

10

W: I'm looking for a coffee machine.

M: What kind do you prefer, an espresso machine or a drip coffee maker?

W: I'd like a drip coffee maker. I like drip coffee and the machines ______________________________ espresso machines.

M: All right. How many cups do you need to make at once?

W: I have to make at least 10 cups at once because I have a big family.

M: ______________________________?

W: I can pay up to 120 dollars. But the cheaper the better.

M: Well, the cheapest coffee maker doesn't have a heater.

W: No, I want a coffee maker ______________ ______________________. And I also want a machine with a built-in grinder.

M: Okay. Then this is exactly what you want, I think. It does a nice job keeping coffee hot for at least three hours and has a grinder which has 5 grind settings.

W: That would be great. I'll take it.

11

W: What do you think of my hair, Clark?

M: ______________________________. It looks really cute. You look great.

W: My stylist said my face ______________ ______________ with this cut.

12

M: Excuse me. ______________________________ ______________?

W: No, you can take it. I'll move my bag.

M: Thanks. Also, ______________________________ ______________ one seat so my son and I can sit together?

13

M: ________________________ from the survey.

W: All right, Chris. This is what I want.

M: I'm glad you like it.

W: So, can you get more information for me?

M: No problem. I can get more information for you. This...

W: Excuse me. Hello? Oh, yes! I'm sorry. I'm ______ ____. Can I call you back later? Thank you.

M: ________________________?

W: Not at all. I'm very ________________________.

M: That's all right.

W: Now, where were we?

14

M: What's wrong, Chloe? You look worried.

W: It's because of the project for Mr. Nelson's class.

M: Did something happen?

W: I ________________________________, Jason. We don't get along very well. I really want a new partner.

M: What's the problem?

W: ________________________________. He refuses to listen to anything I have to say.

M: Well, did you listen to any of Jason's ideas?

W: They're not that great. I think ______________ ______________________________.

M: Chloe, I'm sure Jason feels the same way about his ideas. You need to put yourself in his shoes.

W: Oh! I didn't think about that.

M: Why don't you show respect for his opinion first? That way you can do the best job possible.

15

M: Lauren has decided to visit her best friend in London during the summer vacation. This is her first visit to England, so she's anxious to fill her days ____. She likes antiques, so she decides to check out the biggest flea market in London. Vendors ______ ____________________________________. She quickly takes notice of some antique plates at a stand. She asks the vendor ________________ ____________________________. They're thirty-five pounds, which she thinks is too expensive. She doesn't want to spend that much money for plates. But she __________________________________ without asking for a possible discount. In this situation, what would Lauren most likely ask the vendor?

16-17

W: Did you know that there is a man-made island in the middle of the Pacific Ocean? That island ____________________________________ that people have thrown into the sea. All of the currents meet in this place, and __________________ ______________ all of our litter and trash, such as bottles and styrofoam pieces. It's disgusting, isn't it? Every day, we drive ships and boats over the surface of the sea, polluting the seas with litter. According to the National Academy of Sciences, fishermen lose or throw away an estimated 150,000 tons of plastic fishing gear each year. This plastic trash ________________________________. And then there are oil spills, some of the most dangerous events of all. When a large-scale oil spill happens in the ocean, hundreds of thousands of animals are killed or injured. Our oceans are one of the world's most precious resources, but _______ ______________________________. We have to do something to protect the oceans, or we will lose them forever.

29 Sense Up 듣기 모의고사

01 **다음을 듣고, 남자가 하는 말의 목적으로 가장 적절한 것을 고르시오.**

① 연료 효율이 높은 신형 자동차를 홍보하려고
② 교통난 해소를 위해 대중교통 이용을 권장하려고
③ 연료 절감을 위해 자동차 함께 타기를 권유하려고
④ 자동차 배기가스를 줄이기 위한 방안에 대해 조언하려고
⑤ 자동차 사고 시 위급 상황에 대처하는 방법을 설명하려고

02 **대화를 듣고, 여자의 의견으로 가장 적절한 것을 고르시오.**

① 효율적인 학업 계획이 성적을 좌우한다.
② 수면 시간은 학습 성과와 상관관계가 있다.
③ 학생 때부터 절제하는 소비 습관이 필요하다.
④ 학생은 책임감을 갖고 자제할 줄 알아야 한다.
⑤ 규칙적인 생활 습관을 갖는 것이 성공의 지름길이다.

03 **대화를 듣고, 두 사람의 관계를 가장 잘 나타낸 것을 고르시오.**

① 주차장 손님 - 주차장 직원
② 가게 손님 - 그릇 가게 주인
③ 가구 구입자 - 가구점 직원
④ 식당 손님 - 식당 직원
⑤ 호텔 투숙객 - 호텔 직원

04 **대화를 듣고, 그림에서 대화의 내용과 일치하지 않는 것을 고르시오.**

05 **대화를 듣고, 여자가 남자를 위해 할 일로 가장 적절한 것을 고르시오.**

① 저녁 식사 준비하기
② 축하 파티 열어주기
③ 대학 지원서 작성 도와주기
④ 부동산 중개 웹사이트 추천해주기
⑤ 부동산 중개인의 전화번호 알려주기

06 **대화를 듣고, 여자가 지불할 금액을 고르시오. [3점]**

① $32 ② $45 ③ $55
④ $58 ⑤ $87

07 **대화를 듣고, 여자가 직장을 그만두려는 이유를 고르시오.**

① 봉급이 적어서
② 상사가 힘들게 해서
③ 승진을 하지 못해서
④ 꿈을 이루기 위해서
⑤ 근무시간이 길어서

08 **대화를 듣고, 책을 고르는 방법에 관해 언급되지 않은 것을 고르시오.**

① 친구의 추천 받기
② 서평(書評) 읽어보기
③ 도서 판매 순위 참고하기
④ 좋아하는 작가의 다른 작품 찾아보기
⑤ 책의 앞부분과 중반부 훑어보기

09 **Green Acre Club 장학생 선발에 관한 다음 내용을 듣고, 일치하지 않는 것을 고르시오.**

① 3명의 고등학생에게 수여한다.
② 경제적 형편과 성적에 의해 선발한다.
③ 신청서는 클럽 사무실에 제출해야 한다.
④ 학교 성적표가 신청서에 첨부되어야 한다.
⑤ 신청 마감 후 1개월 후에 수령자를 발표한다.

정답 및 해설 p.114

10 다음 표를 보면서 대화를 듣고, 두 사람이 선택할 유모차를 고르시오.

Albee Baby Shop - Strollers

Stroller	Handles	Wheels	Weight (pounds)	Storage Basket	Price
① A	umbrella type	4	11	×	$280
② B	adjustable bar	3	23	×	$480
③ C	adjustable bar	4	16	○	$685
④ D	adjustable bar	4	18	○	$425
⑤ E	adjustable bar	6	32	○	$600

11 대화를 듣고, 여자의 마지막 말에 대한 남자의 응답으로 가장 적절한 것을 고르시오.

① Wow! It's great! You did a good job.
② That's okay. I wouldn't be concerned.
③ Not really. It doesn't mean much at all.
④ Why not? Let's go out. Dinner is on me.
⑤ Don't mention it. It was the least I could do.

12 대화를 듣고, 남자의 마지막 말에 대한 여자의 응답으로 가장 적절한 것을 고르시오.

① Well, not now. I'll give it a try next time.
② Yes, that's why people like bungee jumping.
③ Don't worry about it. I'm sure you can make it.
④ Just try it. I'm sure you'll have a lot of fun with it.
⑤ Come on. It's free to join, so there's nothing to lose.

13 대화를 듣고, 여자의 마지막 말에 대한 남자의 응답으로 가장 적절한 것을 고르시오. [3점]

▶ Man : ______________________

① All right. I'll be waiting for your call then. Bye.
② Sounds great. I don't think I'll be busy tomorrow.
③ Sure. I hope someday we'll see each other again.
④ That's right. I support you one hundred percent.
⑤ OK. I'll leave the arrangement of time and place to you.

14 대화를 듣고, 남자의 마지막 말에 대한 여자의 응답으로 가장 적절한 것을 고르시오.

▶ Woman : ______________________

① That's right. Just let it go and stop fighting it.
② Yes. It's much better to be here than at my place.
③ No, I think you are the one who's making all the noise.
④ Absolutely! The view from the upper terrace is fantastic!
⑤ There's too much noise. Please keep your volume down.

15 다음 상황 설명을 듣고, Ashley가 Logan에게 할 말로 가장 적절한 것을 고르시오. [3점]

▶ Ashley : ______________________

① Don't worry about me. I'll be at the station on time.
② I'm sorry I'm late. I hope we didn't miss the train.
③ This is the third time you've been late this week.
④ Just a moment! I'll get it for you right away.
⑤ Thanks for everything. I'll really miss you.

[16~17] 다음을 듣고, 물음에 답하시오.

16 여자가 하는 말의 주제로 가장 적절한 것은?

① types of outdoor leisure activities
② reasons for the popularity of camping
③ how to get rid of stress from daily life
④ considerations when choosing camping gear
⑤ the necessity for campers to learn survival skills

17 언급된 사고가 <u>아닌</u> 것은?

① 벌레 물림 ② 화상 ③ 열병
④ 감염 ⑤ 낙석

01

M: Your car is responsible for emitting as much carbon dioxide a year as your entire house is. These emissions ______________________ ______________________, and cause smog. One of the easiest ways to reduce emissions is simply to change our mindset about driving. ______________________ rather than private automobiles. Most forms of public transportation have lower pollutant emissions per passenger than private vehicles. If you must drive, consider carpooling. ______________________ as that will minimize emissions. Drive at a steady speed and avoid rapid acceleration, which increases fuel consumption and pollutant emissions. Avoid idling for long periods. If purchasing a new car, choose a fuel-efficient model.

02

W: Hello?

M: Hello.

W: Andy, are you still in bed? Do you have any idea what time it is?

M: Hey, Mom. What's wrong? Why are you calling me so early in the morning?

W: Early in the morning? It's noon right now!

M: Noon? It can't be! I have a paper ______________________, and I haven't finished yet!

W: Oh, Andy, why did you ______________________ until the last minute?

M: I didn't have time to work on it this past week.

W: You're a college student and you need to be more responsible from now on.

M: I understand. I'm doing my best.

W: Your school work should be a top priority. You need to be able to ______________________.

M: I know. I'll try harder next time.

03

M: Can I park in front here?

W: No, you can't. If you give us your key, we'll park your car for you.

M: Okay. Do you ______________________?

W: Do you have a reservation?

M: No, I don't. ______________________?

W: Yes. Since it's a weekday, you're lucky.

M: Great. Would you happen to have a table by the window?

W: I'm sorry, but all those tables are reserved.

M: Oh, okay. I have another question. Do you have dishes for a vegetarian?

W: Absolutely. We ______________________ our special vegetarian dishes. Wait here for a second.

M: Sure.

04

W: Dave, are you at home?

M: Yes, Grandma! Is something wrong?

W: I just arrived at the community center and realized that I left my reading glasses at home. Do you think ______________________?

M: Of course. Where did you put them?

W: They should be in my bedroom. First look at the nightstand on the left side of my bed.

M: You mean the table ______________________? They're not there.

W: Then look on top of the dresser that's right next to the bed.

M: No, there's just a teddy bear on it. They're ______________________ at the foot of the bed.

W: Where did I put them? Oh, why don't you look on top of the drawers by the window with the TV on top?

M: No, they're not there.

W: Wait. They're in my bag!

M: Oh, that's great!

05

W: Hello?

M: Hi, Aunt Jane. It's Paul. Guess what!

W: ______________________________?

M: Yes! I just got a call from the University of Washington. I've been accepted!

W: Congratulations! I'm so proud of you. What are you going to do before school starts?

M: Well, I need to find a place to stay ____________ ______________________.

W: Why don't you stay with me? My place is only fifty minutes from the university.

M: I appreciate the offer, but I want to live closer. I'll do some research online.

W: If you say so. You know, I have a friend who is a real estate agent. ______________________ a good deal.

M: That would be incredible. Could you give me her number?

W: Of course. I'll send it via text message.

M: Thanks, Aunt Jane.

06

W: Wow, it's really fantastic!

M: It really is. I heard this is ______________ ______________________ for Halloween.

W: Yeah, but it's very expensive. I'd like to buy an Elsa costume from the movie *Frozen*, but it's $87. I can't afford it.

M: They have some sale items. Come this way. Look! It's a Wonder Woman costume. It was originally 80 dollars, but it's 60% off now.

W: But ______________________. I want something new.

M: Then how about this Black Widow costume? It's also on sale.

W: Well, I like this Cat Woman costume. This cat hood and black eye mask ____________________ ________ the black jump suit.

M: Let's see. It was originally 90 dollars, and it's 50% off now.

W: Great. And I'd like to buy these long black gloves, too. They're 10 dollars.

M: They're not on sale.

W: That's okay. What are you going to get?

M: I'm going to get the Spider-Man costume. It's 58 dollars altogether.

W: It looks great.

07

M: I just heard from Brian that you're leaving us. Is that really true?

W: I'm afraid so. I ______________________ a few days ago.

M: Is it because you didn't get a promotion last quarter?

W: Honestly, I was disappointed, but that's not the reason.

M: I know our boss gives you a hard time sometimes. But ______________________.

W: I didn't like him at first, but I do have great respect for him now.

M: Well, then it must be the salary. You're not happy with your salary.

W: Actually, I'm fine with what I receive.

M: Then I don't understand ______________ __________.

W: It's no one's fault. It's just that this 9-to-5 job doesn't suit me very well. I've always wanted to be a chef, so I've ____________________ ______________.

M: Wow, I'm impressed. It takes a lot of courage to make such a big change. I wish you the best of luck.

08

W: Mr. Martin, could you help me find some books to read over the summer?

M: Of course. I'm happy to help you.

W: I've asked some friends, and they gave me ______ ____________________________.

M: That's a great way. Another thing you can do is to try book reviews. You can read them in newspapers and also online.

W: Right. Book reviews are definitely helpful, but sometimes there are so many different opinions that it's hard to choose.

M: I can understand. If you have a favorite author, check out ______________________________.

W: I didn't think of that.

M: Another thing you could do is to pick up a book and get a rough idea about it by reading a page or two in the beginning. Then, read a page in the middle of the book.

W: Oh, what a great idea. Thank you so much for ______________________________, Mr. Martin.

M: My pleasure, and happy reading!

09

W: We have an exciting announcement to make. The generous people of the Green Acre Club are giving away a $4,000 scholarship to 3 high-school students. Students who have a financial need along with exceptional grades will be qualified for the scholarship. If you meet these requirements, pick up an application form from the Green Acre's main office right now. Please note that ______________________________ to the Green Acre Club office by October 15, 2024. The application ______________________________ from your high school. You will be contacted for an interview a few weeks after ______________________________. A second interview will be held for finalists. Award notifications will be sent out at the end of the year. Check out their website at www.greenacre.com for more information.

10

W: We need to buy a stroller for our baby.

M: Look at this one. It has curved handles like an umbrella. It's lightweight, compact, and easy to fold.

W: But it's not comfortable for the baby. I want a standard stroller ______________________________.

M: Okay. How about a three-wheel stroller? Its wheels are bigger and look stronger.

W: That's a jogging stroller. We can ______________________________ when we run. But doctors recommend not using it until the baby is about 6 months old.

M: Then we can't buy it, because our baby is a newborn.

W: Right. And we should think about the weight. I think we need one that weighs less than 20 pounds.

M: Good point.

W: I also want ______________________________ beneath the seat.

M: You're right. That's ideal for holding diaper bags and purses. Let's get the lighter one.

W: I'd like to stay under $500. ______________________________.

M: Okay. Then I think this is what we want. Let's get it.

11

W: Ethan, ______________________________? Oh, you're smiling.

M: Yes! I got the job. I'll start work next week.

W: Congratulations! I knew it. ______________________________!

12

M: I'm going to go to the Tana River and try bungee jumping. How about going together?

W: I've never been bungee jumping. It looks dangerous because ______________________________.

M: As far as I know, the rope has never broken. ______________________________!

13

W: William, you're finally back! We've missed you! You've been away for too long.

M: Is everything alright here?

W: Everything is just fine. How was your honeymoon in Spain?

M: It was incredible! My wife and I bought you a little souvenir. Here you go. It's a traditional hand-painted plate.

W: You didn't have to! It's absolutely lovely. ________________________________.

M: Do you and Evan have any plans for this Saturday evening?

W: Saturday? I'll have to check with Evan, but I'm pretty sure we have nothing special planned. ________________________________?

M: You and Evan did so much for us at the wedding, so we'd like to ________________________________ this Saturday.

W: Oh, how sweet! Let me check with Evan, and I'll give you a ring tonight and let you know.

14

M: Allison! You're still here in the library? Do you have an exam tomorrow?

W: No, I'm just reading a novel. I just don't want to go home early.

M: Why is that? Did you argue with your family?

W: No, it's not that. Did I say ________________________________?

M: Yes, you said it's a newly-renovated, spacious apartment.

W: But the problem is that ________________________________ and extremely noisy.

M: Really? That's annoying and stressful.

W: ________________________________. The windows and walls are not properly soundproofed, so I can hear car engines, buses, and garbage trucks.

M: Oh, that's terrible.

W: I can't concentrate on anything at home.

M: So ________________________________.

15

M: Logan and Ashley are friends. They plan to go on a picnic tomorrow. They plan to go to Bear Mountain, a mountain located outside the city. Because they don't have a car, they booked train tickets to Bear Mountain. It will ________________________________. The train runs only twice a day, once in the morning and once in the evening. If they miss the 7:30 train in the morning, they can't go to the picnic. Logan is concerned because Ashley is ________________________________. He tells Ashley that their plans will be ruined if she's late. Logan reminds Ashley again that ________________________________. In this situation, what would Ashley most likely say to Logan?

16-17

W: More and more people are releasing stress and finding peace of mind in nature, even if it's only for the weekend. People enjoy back-packing, simply walking, or even cycling along back-country roads. Similarly, the popularity of camping has increased greatly in the last few years. People head to stores to purchase camping gear so they can ________________________________. New equipment has ________________________________ with little difficulty. In fact, people have become so dependent on the gear that they have forgotten the importance of learning basic survival skills in case of an emergency. A simple accident could be life-threatening if not handled carefully. So, campers need to learn some basic skills. If you're going on a short hike in the mountains, you need to learn how to handle insect bites or possible burns. And, if you decide to visit a more isolated area, you ________________________________ fevers, infections, or minor injuries, such as a sprained ankle, on your own. By preparing yourself, you can ________________________________ life-threatening scenarios.

01 다음을 듣고, 여자가 하는 말의 목적으로 가장 적절한 것을 고르시오.

① 경기를 관람하러 온 방청객을 맞이하려고
② 경기 관람 시 유의사항을 설명하려고
③ 경기 참가자를 새롭게 모집하려고
④ 결승전 경기 진행 방식을 숙지시키려고
⑤ 결승전에 올라온 참가자들을 소개하려고

02 대화를 듣고, 남자의 의견으로 가장 적절한 것을 고르시오.

① 합창을 할 때는 서로 화합해야 한다.
② 성악가는 목을 관리하는 데 주의해야 한다.
③ 문화예술에 대한 재정 지원을 확대해야 한다.
④ 라이벌은 실력 상승에 필수 불가결한 요소이다.
⑤ 성공에는 재능보다 후천적인 노력이 더 중요하다.

03 대화를 듣고, 두 사람의 관계를 가장 잘 나타낸 것을 고르시오.

① 고객 – 가구점 직원
② 식당 종업원 – 손님
③ 집주인 – 인테리어 디자이너
④ 모델 – 의상 디자이너
⑤ 연극배우 – 무대감독

04 대화를 듣고, 그림에서 대화의 내용과 일치하지 않는 것을 고르시오.

05 대화를 듣고, 남자가 여자에게 부탁한 일로 가장 적절한 것을 고르시오.

① 전자사전 구입하기
② 프랑스어 가르쳐주기
③ 방과 후 수업 알아보기
④ 무료 온라인 강의 찾아보기
⑤ 프랑스어 수업 시간 조정하기

06 대화를 듣고, 여자가 지불할 금액을 고르시오.

① \$11 ② \$15 ③ \$22
④ \$26 ⑤ \$30

07 대화를 듣고, 남자가 시험 성적이 나쁠 것으로 예상하는 이유를 고르시오.

① 부정행위를 해서
② 시험 시간에 졸아서
③ 시험 시간에 지각을 해서
④ 시험 범위를 잘못 알아서
⑤ 공부를 열심히 하지 않아서

08 대화를 듣고, 혼자 여행하는 것의 장점으로 언급되지 않은 것을 고르시오.

① 이동의 자유 ② 숨은 명소 방문
③ 현지 음식 향유 ④ 독립심 향상
⑤ 저렴한 경비

09 Singapura에 관한 다음 내용을 듣고, 일치하지 않는 것을 고르시오.

① 싱가포르의 국보로 지정되었다.
② 뒷다리가 앞다리보다 약간 길다.
③ 익힌 음식은 잘 먹지 않는다.
④ 몸이 아주 따뜻하다.
⑤ 호기심이 많고 사람과 잘 어울린다.

10 다음 표를 보면서 대화를 듣고, 여자가 주문할 베드트레이를 고르시오.

Bed Trays

Model	Material	Foldable Legs	Handles	Color
① A	wood	○	×	Dark Brown
② B	plastic	×	○	White
③ C	wood	○	○	Black
④ D	wood	○	○	Brown
⑤ E	wood	×	×	Gray

11 대화를 듣고, 여자의 마지막 말에 대한 남자의 응답으로 가장 적절한 것을 고르시오.

① It's $7 for both.
② I'll find our seats.
③ Here's some money.
④ Just the popcorn will be fine.
⑤ The movies are getting expensive.

12 대화를 듣고, 남자의 마지막 말에 대한 여자의 응답으로 가장 적절한 것을 고르시오.

① It will only take a few minutes.
② I'll be studying there all day long.
③ I'm sure we have time after the concert.
④ The library is open until 9 p.m. on weekdays.
⑤ That was the longest concert I've ever been to.

13 대화를 듣고, 여자의 마지막 말에 대한 남자의 응답으로 가장 적절한 것을 고르시오. [3점]

▶ Man : ______

① Then we should give it a miss this time.
② How about 7 a.m. tomorrow morning?
③ Luckily, you're experienced.
④ How far is it to the next shelter?
⑤ Did you check on the weather for the weekend?

14 대화를 듣고, 남자의 마지막 말에 대한 여자의 응답으로 가장 적절한 것을 고르시오. [3점]

▶ Woman : ______

① Thanks a lot. I really appreciate you helping me out.
② How about if I use yours tonight for the last time?
③ That's great. Thanks a lot for finding them for me.
④ Mom will really yell at you when she finds out.
⑤ I don't think you can afford new earphones.

15 다음 상황 설명을 듣고, David가 Lisa에게 할 말로 가장 적절한 것을 고르시오. [3점]

▶ David : ______

① Are you sure we have Jack's correct phone number?
② How many times have you volunteered for the homeless?
③ We should go over to Jack's house and give him a ride.
④ Can you tell me what made you join the volunteer club?
⑤ Why don't you go to the soup kitchen while I check up on Jack?

[16~17] 다음을 듣고, 물음에 답하시오.

16 남자가 하는 말의 주제로 가장 적절한 것은?

① a promotion of a unique book club
② tips for organizing your personal library
③ the benefits of sharing books with neighbors
④ why people should donate books to a charity
⑤ recruitment of new members to a travel club

17 BookCrossing에 관해 언급되지 않은 것은?

① 회원 수
② 공유 도서 수
③ 이용 비용
④ 이용 방법
⑤ 설립 연도

30 Sense Up 듣기 모의고사 DICTATION

01

W: Thank you all for coming down here. I'm really excited about today's results. Now, all contestants, please listen carefully. You will soon find out that at the finals the game will be played differently ______________________. You don't need to press your buzzers when answering a question anymore. I'll ______________________ ______________________ individually. And the game will consist of three rounds instead of two. The most significant difference is the third round. The winner will be the first player to answer correctly in a set of questions. __________ ______________________?

02

M: Which singer is your sister?

W: That's her on the left. She just finished singing her solo.

M: Wow, I'm really impressed. She's as good as a professional singer.

W: She would be very happy to hear that. She practices her singing every day in hopes of becoming a famous singer.

M: Practice is the key. ______________________ ______________________ if you have enough determination.

W: Actually, I don't think she needs to practice that much.

M: Really? What makes you say that?

W: She has always had a good voice. Some people ______________________ amazing talents.

M: Yeah, they may fulfill their dreams more easily, but I think ______________________ ______________________ to succeed.

03

W: Thanks for coming over. Would you like something to drink?

M: Just a glass of water, please.

W: No problem.

M: So, I looked at the living room pictures you sent via e-mail and brought some matching fabric samples.

W: They look beautiful. ______________________ ______________________?

M: Yes. Is there anything you like?

W: I really like the blue one.

M: Great choice! The blue ______________________ __________ your white sofa and other furniture.

W: I also need help in picking paint colors for the wall. Would you recommend one?

M: Sure, but first, let me measure the windows for the curtain.

W: Oh, ______________________. With your help, this place is going to look fabulous!

04

M: Hi, honey. What's this? Are these the decorations for Jim's graduation party?

W: That's right. What do you think?

M: Everything looks great! I especially like the photos ______________________.

W: They're all pictures from his school life. He looks so happy, doesn't he?

M: He does. Did you ______________________ __________ the arch-shaped banner that says "Happy Graduation!"?

W: No, I just stood up on a chair. The balloons above the banner were ______________________ __________.

M: You did a good job. I like that there are round ones and heart-shaped ones.

W: Thanks. I also brought in the rectangular table from the kitchen to set things on.

M: Good idea. The cake smells delicious, too.

W: And it looks nice between his present and graduation cap. Oh, I think he'll be excited when he sees this.

M: Me too, honey. Let's get lots of pictures.
W: Of course!

05

M: How is Karen doing with her French class?
W: ______________________________. I think we should do something to help.
M: Does she need a dictionary? I could look for an electronic one at the store.
W: No, she already has one.
M: Maybe we could enroll her in an after-school program.
W: That's a good idea, but is there ______________________________?
M: I'm not sure. We should get details from her school.
W: I think we can get information about it on the school website.
M: Right. Could you check today?
W: Sure. I'll do that. And ______________________________ for Karen if we can't find a good program.
M: Sounds good.

06

W: My son and I ______________________________.
M: Well, we're offering a special discount today to encourage more people to exercise.
W: Great. How much?
M: Mountain bikes ______________________________ for $15 for the day, and we will give you a free water bottle for each bike.
W: Is that it?
M: We have 10-speed bikes for $11 for the day instead of the usual $20 rental fee.
W: ______________________________ only for a couple of hours?
M: For less than 4 hours you'll need to pay half of the full-day rate.
W: Then we'll take two mountain bikes. We'll ______________________________ only for a couple of hours.
M: OK.

07

W: Hi, Ben!
M: Oh, hi.
W: What happened? You look very upset.
M: I met Mr. Brown, my biology teacher. I will ______________________________.
W: Why? Didn't you study hard for the exam?
M: Yes, I did. I studied for several days for that exam. I even practiced with all of the old exams from the previous semester.
W: Then why are you worried about it? I know ______________________________. Oh, did you study the wrong chapter for the test?
M: No, my alarm clock broke and I was late for the exam. ______________________________ of the test.
W: Really? I think you should talk to the teacher.
M: I did. I just met with him, but he said it's my fault. Actually, he's right.
W: Oh, boy!
M: I don't know what to do.

08

M: Hi, Jenna. What are you doing?
W: I'm searching for a packaged tour to the Philippines.
M: You speak English fluently. So, why do you want a packaged tour?
W: Well, it's convenient. Plus, it's ______________________________.
M: I suppose so, but you can go anywhere you want when you travel alone.
W: That's true, but how would I find the best restaurants and attractions?
M: There's plenty of information on the Internet, and actually, traveling alone is a great chance to find hidden attractions and authentic local cuisine.
W: Hmm.... It would be nice to avoid some of the tourist traps.
M: Exactly. Also, ______________________________ than a packaged tour.
W: Then I could use the extra money for souvenirs. You know, I might do that.
M: Trust me. ______________________________.

09

M: The Singapura is ______________________ in the world, with large eyes, a black-tipped tail, and brown or gray coloring. In 1990, the Singapore Government adopted it as their national mascot and later declared it to be a National Treasure. The Singapura is small but muscular, and its back legs are slightly longer than its front legs. Singapuras typically weigh between 5 and 8 pounds, and ______________________ between males and females. Their diet is typical, but they especially enjoy treats of cooked chicken or ham. Despite their size, Singapuras are surprisingly warm and can feel very pleasant on the lap; just one of many reasons Singapuras ______________________. They are lively and extremely curious, and they are not afraid of humans.

10

M: What are you doing, Rose?

W: I'm looking at bed trays online. My mother ______________________, so she has to remain in bed for a few weeks.

M: I'm sorry to hear that. A bed tray would be really useful for her. Let me help you choose.

W: Sure. Do you already have a bed tray?

M: Yeah, I have a plastic bed tray, but it's not good. I ______________________.

W: Got it. I think a tray with legs is more convenient.

M: Exactly. Why don't you choose a tray with foldable legs? You can ______________________.

W: Good idea. What about side handles?

M: They are very useful! A tray with side handles is ______________________.

W: Okay! I'll get one of these two. Hmm, My mother doesn't like black.

M: Then it's settled. This is what you want.

W: All right. Thanks for helping me.

11

W: Before we enter the theater, ______________________.

M: I spent all my money on the tickets. ______________________?

W: Of course. Do you want some soda, too?

12

M: I'm ready to go to the concert. How about you?

W: Almost. I just ______________________, and then I'll be ready.

M: You're going to the library? ______________________?

13

W: Kurt, come on. ______________________ this dorm room. It's Friday night! Time for some fun!

M: Just let me shut my computer down.

W: So, ______________________?

M: I'm going hiking tomorrow.

W: I've never been hiking.

M: Really? Come with me!

W: Tomorrow? I'd love to! What time and where?

M: I'm planning to do the Tara Trail.

W: What is that?

M: It's an easy 8 km walk. Is 7 a.m. ______________________?

W: Hang on. Isn't the weather supposed to be bad this weekend?

M: Is it? I hadn't bothered to check. It's been so good lately.

W: I'm pretty sure they said heavy rain was expected all weekend.

14

M: What's wrong, Jenny?

W: I can't seem to find my earphones for my cell phone. I've looked everywhere, but I can't find them.

M: ______________________________.

W: I can't afford a new pair.

M: They can't be that expensive.

W: I went to a shop two weeks ago. They're 20,000 won.

M: You could save some of the money you get from Mom and Dad each week.

W: That's not easy to do. I need to spend that money on other stuff.

M: Then ask Mom and Dad for more money so that you can buy a new pair.

W: Mom will just yell and tell me ____________ ____________________.

M: Yeah. I know.

W: And you rarely use yours. I really need them tonight.

M: But lately ________________________, you've got them.

15

W: It is Saturday morning, and David is with his friend Lisa. ________________________ for an hour for Jack, another good friend of theirs, to arrive. The three of them had gotten acquainted with each other at the school volunteer club and had planned to go to a local soup kitchen to serve meals to the homeless. David and Lisa ________ ____________________ Jack several times, but he is not picking up the phone. It is unlike Jack to be so late without calling, and Lisa is worried that something might have happened to him. Since David knows where Jack lives, he thinks that Lisa should ________________________ __________ while he goes to Jack's house to see if everything's okay. In this situation, what would David most likely say to Lisa?

16-17

M: On your shelves you probably have __________ ________________________. Why not share them with others? Select one of your favorite books that nobody is reading at the moment. Then register it on the BookCrossing website, and ______________________________. BookCrossing is a global book club for book-lovers that crosses time and space. It has 300,000 members, sharing 1.5 million books, all over the world. And ____________________. A BookCrossing member leaves a book somewhere ______________________________, and registers this book on the BookCrossing website. The person who finds the book reads it and passes it on again. This continues until it gets lost or someone doesn't pass it on. Each reader can also put their comments about the book on the BookCrossing website. This way, __________ ______________________________ can keep track of its journey.

Let's
Check.

Sense Up Study Diary

계획적인 학습을 위한 다이어리

Start date . . .

Finish date . . .

I wish ...

이어지는 Study Diary에 나의 학습을 기록해보세요. **Continued »**

1st ~ 3rd week

일주일에 5회씩 / 꼼꼼히 학습하기 / 6주 완성

PLAN		DO		SEE - 어휘 표현 정리
DAY 1 MON	01회	□ 문제 풀이 □ 받아쓰기와 표현 암기	score □ / 17	
DAY 2 TUE	02회	□ 문제 풀이 □ 받아쓰기와 표현 암기	score □ / 17	
DAY 3 WED	03회	□ 문제 풀이 □ 받아쓰기와 표현 암기	score □ / 17	
DAY 4 THU	04회	□ 문제 풀이 □ 받아쓰기와 표현 암기	score □ / 17	
DAY 5 FRI	05회	□ 문제 풀이 □ 받아쓰기와 표현 암기	score □ / 17	
DAY 1 MON	06회	□ 문제 풀이 □ 받아쓰기와 표현 암기	score □ / 17	
DAY 2 TUE	07회	□ 문제 풀이 □ 받아쓰기와 표현 암기	score □ / 17	
DAY 3 WED	08회	□ 문제 풀이 □ 받아쓰기와 표현 암기	score □ / 17	
DAY 4 THU	09회	□ 문제 풀이 □ 받아쓰기와 표현 암기	score □ / 17	
DAY 5 FRI	10회	□ 문제 풀이 □ 받아쓰기와 표현 암기	score □ / 17	
DAY 1 MON	11회	□ 문제 풀이 □ 받아쓰기와 표현 암기	score □ / 17	
DAY 2 TUE	12회	□ 문제 풀이 □ 받아쓰기와 표현 암기	score □ / 17	
DAY 3 WED	13회	□ 문제 풀이 □ 받아쓰기와 표현 암기	score □ / 17	
DAY 4 THU	14회	□ 문제 풀이 □ 받아쓰기와 표현 암기	score □ / 17	
DAY 5 FRI	15회	□ 문제 풀이 □ 받아쓰기와 표현 암기	score □ / 17	

week 4th ~ 6th

일주일에 5회씩 / 꼼꼼히 학습하기 / 6주 완성

PLAN		DO		SEE - 어휘 표현 정리
DAY 1 MON	16회	☐ 문제 풀이 ☐ 받아쓰기와 표현 암기	score ☐ / 17	
DAY 2 TUE	17회	☐ 문제 풀이 ☐ 받아쓰기와 표현 암기	score ☐ / 17	
DAY 3 WED	18회	☐ 문제 풀이 ☐ 받아쓰기와 표현 암기	score ☐ / 17	
DAY 4 THU	19회	☐ 문제 풀이 ☐ 받아쓰기와 표현 암기	score ☐ / 17	
DAY 5 FRI	20회	☐ 문제 풀이 ☐ 받아쓰기와 표현 암기	score ☐ / 17	
DAY 1 MON	21회	☐ 문제 풀이 ☐ 받아쓰기와 표현 암기	score ☐ / 17	
DAY 2 TUE	22회	☐ 문제 풀이 ☐ 받아쓰기와 표현 암기	score ☐ / 17	
DAY 3 WED	23회	☐ 문제 풀이 ☐ 받아쓰기와 표현 암기	score ☐ / 17	
DAY 4 THU	24회	☐ 문제 풀이 ☐ 받아쓰기와 표현 암기	score ☐ / 17	
DAY 5 FRI	25회	☐ 문제 풀이 ☐ 받아쓰기와 표현 암기	score ☐ / 17	
DAY 1 MON	26회	☐ 문제 풀이 ☐ 받아쓰기와 표현 암기	score ☐ / 17	
DAY 2 TUE	27회	☐ 문제 풀이 ☐ 받아쓰기와 표현 암기	score ☐ / 17	
DAY 3 WED	28회	☐ 문제 풀이 ☐ 받아쓰기와 표현 암기	score ☐ / 17	
DAY 4 THU	29회	☐ 문제 풀이 ☐ 받아쓰기와 표현 암기	score ☐ / 17	
DAY 5 FRI	30회	☐ 문제 풀이 ☐ 받아쓰기와 표현 암기	score ☐ / 17	

ANSWER

정답 모음

01회 모의고사

01. ④ 02. ③ 03. ① 04. ② 05. ②
06. ② 07. ⑤ 08. ⑤ 09. ③ 10. ①
11. ① 12. ① 13. ⑤ 14. ① 15. ④
16. ① 17. ④

02회 모의고사

01. ④ 02. ⑤ 03. ④ 04. ② 05. ④
06. ③ 07. ⑤ 08. ② 09. ④ 10. ②
11. ② 12. ④ 13. ④ 14. ① 15. ②
16. ⑤ 17. ⑤

03회 모의고사

01. ③ 02. ③ 03. ④ 04. ③ 05. ③
06. ③ 07. ② 08. ④ 09. ④ 10. ③
11. ⑤ 12. ③ 13. ① 14. ② 15. ⑤
16. ③ 17. ④

04회 모의고사

01. ② 02. ① 03. ② 04. ③ 05. ④
06. ② 07. ③ 08. ④ 09. ④ 10. ④
11. ① 12. ③ 13. ③ 14. ⑤ 15. ④
16. ② 17. ①

05회 모의고사

01. ② 02. ④ 03. ⑤ 04. ④ 05. ①
06. ③ 07. ④ 08. ④ 09. ⑤ 10. ③
11. ④ 12. ② 13. ⑤ 14. ② 15. ①
16. ⑤ 17. ②

06회 모의고사

01. ④ 02. ③ 03. ④ 04. ② 05. ⑤
06. ③ 07. ④ 08. ② 09. ② 10. ③
11. ③ 12. ③ 13. ② 14. ② 15. ④
16. ② 17. ⑤

07회 모의고사

01. ④ 02. ② 03. ④ 04. ④ 05. ③
06. ② 07. ⑤ 08. ⑤ 09. ② 10. ②
11. ② 12. ② 13. ⑤ 14. ③ 15. ⑤
16. ④ 17. ④

08회 모의고사

01. ② 02. ③ 03. ③ 04. ② 05. ⑤
06. ④ 07. ⑤ 08. ② 09. ③ 10. ③
11. ② 12. ③ 13. ③ 14. ③ 15. ⑤
16. ② 17. ⑤

09회 모의고사

01. ④ 02. ① 03. ⑤ 04. ④ 05. ③
06. ② 07. ⑤ 08. ④ 09. ③ 10. ④
11. ⑤ 12. ③ 13. ③ 14. ⑤ 15. ⑤
16. ② 17. ⑤

10회 모의고사

01. ① 02. ③ 03. ④ 04. ② 05. ③
06. ③ 07. ② 08. ⑤ 09. ⑤ 10. ①
11. ③ 12. ⑤ 13. ④ 14. ① 15. ③
16. ③ 17. ④

11회 모의고사

01. ⑤ 02. ② 03. ② 04. ⑤ 05. ⑤
06. ④ 07. ④ 08. ④ 09. ② 10. ③
11. ④ 12. ③ 13. ③ 14. ① 15. ②
16. ② 17. ⑤

12회 모의고사

01. ③ 02. ⑤ 03. ② 04. ④ 05. ⑤
06. ① 07. ① 08. ② 09. ③ 10. ②
11. ④ 12. ① 13. ④ 14. ④ 15. ②
16. ④ 17. ④

13회 모의고사

01. ④ 02. ④ 03. ④ 04. ③ 05. ⑤
06. ③ 07. ③ 08. ③ 09. ③ 10. ⑤
11. ③ 12. ⑤ 13. ① 14. ① 15. ②
16. ③ 17. ⑤

14회 모의고사

01. ④ 02. ① 03. ④ 04. ⑤ 05. ⑤
06. ③ 07. ④ 08. ② 09. ④ 10. ①
11. ② 12. ④ 13. ④ 14. ⑤ 15. ⑤
16. ③ 17. ②

15회 모의고사

01. ③ 02. ④ 03. ⑤ 04. ④ 05. ①
06. ④ 07. ② 08. ② 09. ② 10. ⑤
11. ② 12. ⑤ 13. ③ 14. ④ 15. ④
16. ① 17. ⑤

16회 모의고사

01. ⑤ 02. ② 03. ④ 04. ① 05. ④
06. ④ 07. ⑤ 08. ③ 09. ② 10. ③
11. ① 12. ② 13. ④ 14. ② 15. ②
16. ② 17. ④

17회 모의고사

01. ③ 02. ⑤ 03. ③ 04. ④ 05. ④
06. ② 07. ③ 08. ④ 09. ② 10. ④
11. ② 12. ④ 13. ① 14. ④ 15. ④
16. ③ 17. ④

18회 모의고사

01. ② 02. ② 03. ③ 04. ⑤ 05. ④
06. ② 07. ② 08. ③ 09. ⑤ 10. ②
11. ⑤ 12. ② 13. ② 14. ① 15. ⑤
16. ② 17. ④

19회 모의고사

01. ① 02. ④ 03. ① 04. ⑤ 05. ⑤
06. ③ 07. ④ 08. ④ 09. ⑤ 10. ④
11. ④ 12. ④ 13. ② 14. ① 15. ④
16. ⑤ 17. ⑤

20회 모의고사

01. ③ 02. ② 03. ⑤ 04. ④ 05. ⑤
06. ③ 07. ④ 08. ② 09. ④ 10. ⑤
11. ② 12. ④ 13. ④ 14. ① 15. ④
16. ② 17. ⑤

ANSWER

정답 모음

21회 모의고사

01. ②	02. ②	03. ③	04. ③	05. ④
06. ④	07. ②	08. ⑤	09. ④	10. ②
11. ⑤	12. ④	13. ⑤	14. ②	15. ⑤
16. ①	17. ②			

22회 모의고사

01. ⑤	02. ③	03. ②	04. ②	05. ①
06. ④	07. ④	08. ⑤	09. ⑤	10. ⑤
11. ②	12. ②	13. ④	14. ③	15. ④
16. ①	17. ⑤			

23회 모의고사

01. ⑤	02. ①	03. ②	04. ④	05. ④
06. ②	07. ②	08. ③	09. ④	10. ③
11. ③	12. ④	13. ⑤	14. ③	15. ③
16. ③	17. ③			

24회 모의고사

01. ②	02. ①	03. ⑤	04. ④	05. ④
06. ①	07. ⑤	08. ③	09. ④	10. ③
11. ①	12. ④	13. ②	14. ④	15. ③
16. ④	17. ④			

25회 모의고사

01. ②	02. ②	03. ③	04. ①	05. ④
06. ③	07. ②	08. ②	09. ③	10. ③
11. ②	12. ⑤	13. ②	14. ②	15. ⑤
16. ①	17. ①			

26회 모의고사

01. ①	02. ④	03. ④	04. ⑤	05. ①
06. ④	07. ⑤	08. ③	09. ⑤	10. ③
11. ①	12. ④	13. ②	14. ②	15. ④
16. ⑤	17. ④			

27회 모의고사

01. ②	02. ⑤	03. ②	04. ④	05. ②
06. ③	07. ④	08. ⑤	09. ①	10. ④
11. ②	12. ④	13. ①	14. ④	15. ③
16. ②	17. ①			

28회 모의고사

01. ③	02. ③	03. ⑤	04. ③	05. ③
06. ③	07. ④	08. ④	09. ③	10. ①
11. ②	12. ①	13. ④	14. ①	15. ④
16. ⑤	17. ⑤			

29회 모의고사

01. ④	02. ④	03. ④	04. ③	05. ⑤
06. ③	07. ④	08. ③	09. ⑤	10. ④
11. ④	12. ①	13. ①	14. ②	15. ①
16. ⑤	17. ⑤			

30회 모의고사

01. ④	02. ⑤	03. ③	04. ⑤	05. ③
06. ②	07. ③	08. ④	09. ③	10. ④
11. ④	12. ①	13. ①	14. ②	15. ⑤
16. ①	17. ⑤			

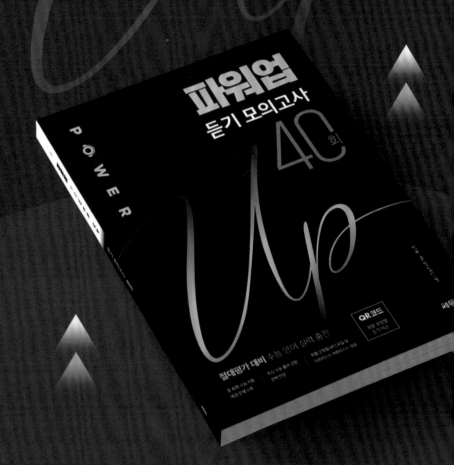

쎄듀런

1 구문

판매 1위 '천일문' 콘텐츠를 활용하여 정확하고 다양한 구문 학습

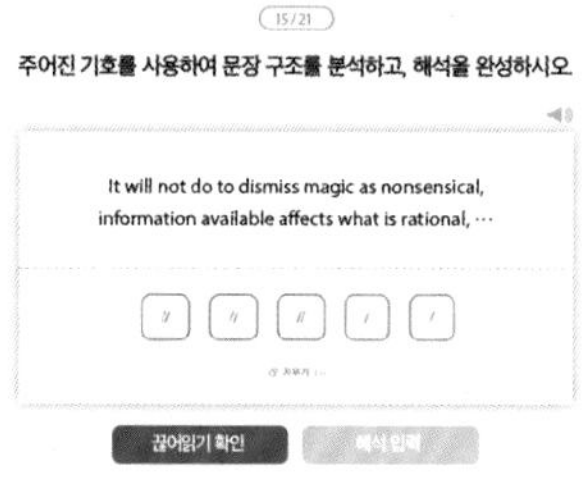
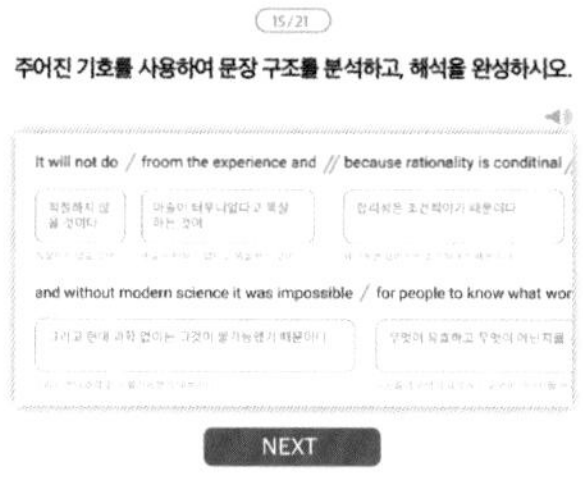

끊어읽기 | 해석하기 | 문장 구조 분석 | 해설·해석 제공 | 단어 스크램블링 | 영작하기

2 문법·서술형

쎄듀의 모든 문법 문항을 활용하여 내신까지 해결하는 정교한 문법 유형 제공

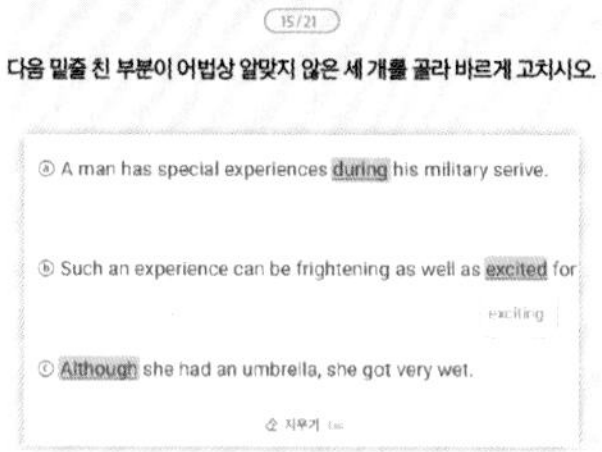
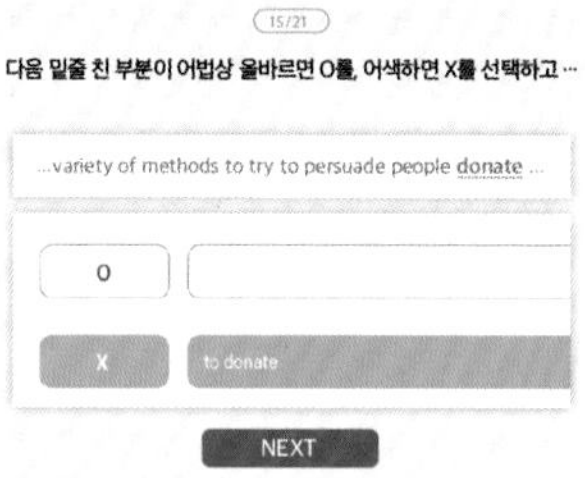

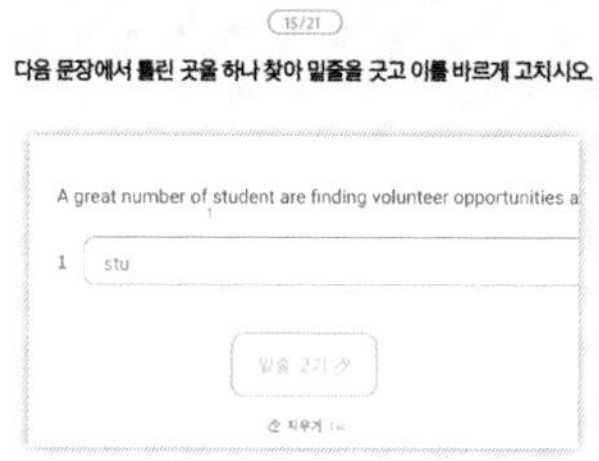

객관식과 주관식의 결합 | 문법 포인트별 학습 | 보기를 활용한 집합 문항 | 내신대비 서술형 | 어법+서술형 문제

3 어휘

초·중·고·공무원까지 방대한 어휘량을 제공하며 오프라인 TEST 인쇄도 가능

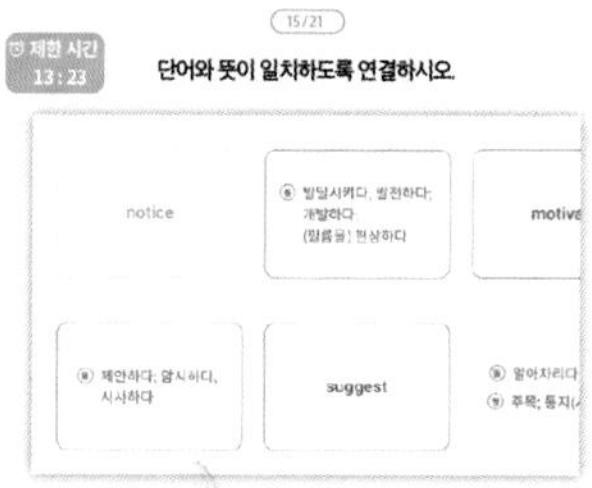

영단어 카드 학습 | 단어 ↔ 뜻 유형 | 예문 활용 유형 | 단어 매칭 게임

4 선생님 보유 문항 이용

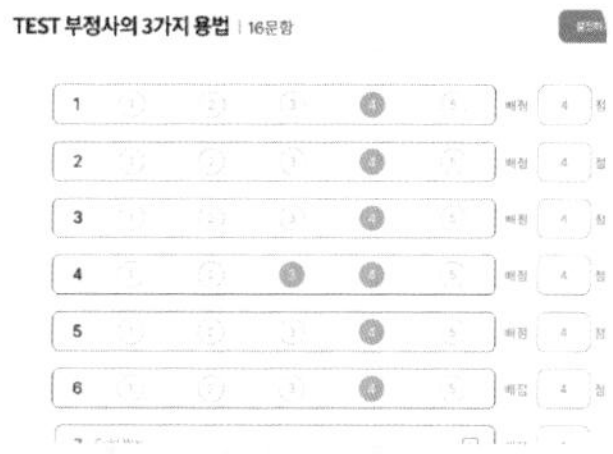

Online Test | OMR Test

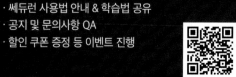

cafe.naver.com/cedulearnteacher

쎄듀런 학습 정보가 궁금하다면?

쎄듀런 Cafe

· 쎄듀런 사용법 안내 & 학습법 공유
· 공지 및 문의사항 QA
· 할인 쿠폰 증정 등 이벤트 진행

쎈쓰업

듣기 모의고사 30회

정답 및 해설

SENSE

쎄듀

쎈쓰업

듣기 모의고사

30회

정답 및 해설

01 Sense Up 듣기 모의고사 ANSWERS & COMPREHENSION

본문 p.8

01. ④	02. ③	03. ①	04. ②	05. ②	06. ②	07. ⑤	08. ⑤	09. ③	10. ①
11. ①	12. ①	13. ⑤	14. ①	15. ④	16. ①	17. ④			

01 화자가 하는 말의 목적 | ④

▶ 텃밭 가꾸기의 여러 장점을 나열한 뒤 텃밭 가꾸기를 시작하기에 좋은 안내서를 소개하고 있다. 마지막에 지금 안내서를 구매하면 에코백을 무료로 얻을 수 있다고 홍보하고 있다.

M: Parents know **how challenging it can be** to get kids to eat enough vegetables, but gardening may help. Research shows that when kids help grow vegetables, they are more likely to eat more produce and try different kinds, too. The benefits of gardening don't end there. It also is a great way to get the entire family outside for fresh air and physical activity. If you want to try **vegetable gardening with your kids**, Rena Brown's *Vegetable Gardens* will be a good guide to start. This delightful, newly published guide will get families excited about growing their own vegetables. In *Vegetable Gardens*, you'll get all the inspiration and knowledge you need to get out there and start planting. Order now, and you'll get an eco bag for free.

남: 부모님들은 아이들에게 충분한 채소를 먹이는 것이 얼마나 도전적일 수 있는지 알고 있습니다만 텃밭 가꾸기가 도움이 될 것입니다. 연구는 아이들이 채소를 키우는 것을 도울 때 더 많은 농작물을 먹고 다른 종류 또한 시도할 가능성이 더 크다는 것을 보여줍니다. 텃밭 가꾸기의 장점은 거기에서 끝나지 않습니다. 그것은 또한 온 가족이 신선한 공기와 신체적 활동을 위해 밖으로 나가도록 하는 훌륭한 방법입니다. 여러분이 자녀들과 야채 텃밭 가꾸기를 시도하고 싶다면, Rena Brown의 〈Vegetable Gardens〉가 시작하기에 좋은 안내서가 될 것입니다. 이 몹시 유쾌한, 새로 출판된 안내서는 가족들이 자기가 먹을 야채를 재배하는 것에 대해 흥미를 느끼게 할 것입니다. 〈Vegetable Gardens〉에서, 여러분은 그곳에 나가 가꾸기 시작하는 데 필요한 모든 영감과 지식을 얻게 될 것입니다. 지금 주문하시면 에코백을 무료로 얻게 되실 겁니다.

어휘 **challenging** 도전적인 / **gardening** 텃밭[정원] 가꾸기; 원예 / **produce** 농산[생산]물; 생산하다 / **entire** 전부[전체]의; 온전한 / **inspiration** 영감; 영감[자극]을 주는 것[사람]

02 의견 | ③

▶ 여자는 소음 공해가 심각한 문제임에도 사람들이 지금까지 별다른 관심을 기울이지 않았다고 말하며, 이러한 사실이 변해야 정부도 관여하게 될 거라고 했다.

W: Minsu, you don't look good. What's up?

M: I **haven't been sleeping well**. The street noise bothers me at night. There are people laughing and shouting, honking horns, and loud music.

W: I can imagine **how stressful it is** to live near a busy street.

M: It is. A recent news story reported that many people, especially in cities, suffer from hearing loss and sleep disorders.

W: I saw that, too.

M: If only the government would take responsibility.

W: The news also said that many countries are now taking steps to reduce noise pollution.

M: Isn't the problem equally serious in our own country?

W: I think so, but so far we **haven't paid much attention to** the issue.

M: You're right.

W: The government **won't become involved** unless that changes.

여: 민수야, 기분이 안 좋아 보여. 무슨 일이야?

남: 잠을 잘 못 자고 있어. 밤에 거리의 소음이 날 성가시게 해. 웃고 소리 지르는 사람들, 빵빵대는 경적 소리, 시끄러운 음악이 있지.

여: 번화가 근처에 사는 게 얼마나 스트레스가 많은지 짐작이 가.

남: 정말 스트레스야. 최근 신문 기사에서 특히 도시에 사는 사람 다수가 청력 손실과 수면 장애를 겪고 있다고 보도했어.

여: 나도 그 기사를 봤어.

남: 정부가 책임을 져준다면 좋을 텐데.

여: 기사에서는 소음 공해를 줄이기 위해 현재 조치를 취하고 있는 나라가 많다고도 했어.

남: 그 문제는 우리나라에서도 똑같이 심각하지 않아?

여: 나도 그렇게 생각하지만, 우리는 지금까지 그 문제에 많은 관심을 기울이지 않았어.

남: 네 말이 맞아.

여: 그게(사람들이 관심을 기울이지 않는다는 사실이) 변하지 않는 한 우리 정부도 관여하려 들지 않을 거야.

어휘 **honk** (자동차 경적이) 울리다; 빵빵((자동차 경적 소리)) / **horn** (차량의) 경적; (양 · 소 등의) 뿔 / **disorder** (신체 기능의) 장애[이상]; 엉망, 어수선함 / **noise pollution** 소음 공해

03 관계 | ①

▶ 남자는 기사 내용에 대해 평가를 하고 인쇄 시기를 조정하는 일을 하는 편집장이고, 여자는 사건을 조사해서 독자에게 알리는 일을 하는 기자이다.

M: Hey, Allison. **What are you working on** at the moment?

W: I'm working on the case I told you about. But I only need a couple of days.

M: You know I **had to delay printing** because of your story?

W: It will be worth it! I promise.

M: Have you found something interesting?

W: According to my sources, a high-ranking government official accepted inappropriate donations!

M: Wow, that's big.

W: And his wife owns some land in Amherst. But only yesterday the local government announced a plan to build a new town in that region. They'll make a fortune.

M: You're right! This is **worth waiting for**. It will be an interesting article.

W: Well, it's my job to get the facts and tell the readers.

남: Allison 씨, 지금 무슨 일을 하고 있나요?

여: 말씀드렸던 사건을 조사하고 있어요. 하지만 며칠만 더 주세요.

남: 당신 기사 때문에 내가 인쇄를 미뤄야 했던 걸 알고 있죠?

여: 그럴 만한 가치가 있는 사건이에요! 약속드릴게요.

남: 흥미 있는 사건을 발견했어요?

여: 제 소식통에 따르면 한 고위 공무원이 부적절한 기부금을 받았어요!

남: 와, 큰 사건이군요.

여: 그리고 그의 부인이 Amherst 지역에 땅을 소유하고 있어요. 그런데 바로 어제 지방 정부가 그 지역에 뉴타운을 건설한다는 계획을 발표했어요. 그들은 큰돈을 벌겠죠.

남: 그렇군요! 이건 기다릴 만한 가치가 있네요. 재미있는 기사가 되겠군요.

여: 음, 진실을 찾아서 독자들에게 알리는 것이 제 일이죠.

어휘 **case** 사건 / **source** 소식통 / **donation** 기부(금), 기증(품) / **fortune** 거금; 운

04 그림 불일치 | ②

▶ 남자는 열쇠를 하트 모양 쿠션 옆에 두었다고 했다.

W: Honey, **isn't it time for** our favorite comedy show? Let's watch!

M: Great idea! I love it because it's so funny. I'll just turn on the TV. Wait a minute, have you seen the remote control?

W: I think I saw it on the table next to the stairs.

M: I don't see it there. I thought I left it next to the heart-shaped cushion on the sofa. But it's gone.

W: Hmmm.... Have you checked next to the flower pot in front of the window?

M: I searched there already, but I didn't see it.

W: I remember I **saw you reading a newspaper** on the carpet.

M: Yeah, I was. But there's nothing on the carpet **except the newspaper**.

W: That's strange.

M: Oh, I found it! It was under the newspaper. That's why I couldn't see it.

W: Honey, please leave the remote control in the tray next to the TV. **That's where it belongs**.

M: All right. I will next time.

여: 여보, 우리가 좋아하는 코미디 쇼 할 시간 아니에요? 같이 봐요!

남: 좋은 생각이에요! 그 프로그램 정말 웃겨서 좋아요. 내가 TV를 켤게요. 잠깐만요, 리모컨 봤어요?

여: 계단 옆 테이블 위에서 본 것 같은데요.
남: 거기엔 안 보여요. 소파 위 하트 모양 쿠션 위에 둔 것 같은데 없어졌어요.
여: 흠…. 창문 앞에 있는 화분 옆도 찾아봤어요?
남: 거기도 이미 찾아봤는데 안 보여요.
여: 당신이 카펫 위에서 신문 읽고 있는 걸 본 기억이 나는데요.
남: 그래요. 그랬죠. 근데 카펫 위에는 신문 말고는 없어요.
여: 이상하네요.
남: 아, 찾았어요! 신문 밑에 있었어요. 그래서 안 보였던 거예요.
여: 여보, 리모컨은 TV 옆에 있는 쟁반에다 좀 두세요. 거기가 제자리예요.
남: 다음부턴 그렇게 할게요.

어휘 **flower pot** 화분 / **tray** 쟁반

05 추후 행동 | ②

▶ 남자가 학교 축제에 자원봉사를 같이하자고 권유하자 여자가 흔쾌히 동의하였고, 지원 마감 시간이 내일이라는 말에 당장 지원하겠다고 하였다.

M: Joyce, have you heard about our school festival?
W: Yes, I heard it'll begin next Friday. I'm looking forward to it.
M: It'll be great fun. By the way, **I'm supposed to volunteer** at the festival.
W: Did you apply for it? What are you going to do there?
M: We'll help out with tasks such as guiding visitors, assisting with parking and picking up garbage.
W: Sounds great.
M: How about joining us? **More than 300 people will be participating** in the festival, so we need more volunteers for such a large number of visitors.
W: All right. I'll do that. Please tell me how I can sign up.
M: You can do it at our school's website using your smartphone. The deadline is tomorrow.
W: Tomorrow? Then I'll do it right now.
M: I'm sure **it'll be a great experience**. And there'll be a volunteer meeting at the student's union on Tuesday.

남: Joyce, 우리 학교 축제에 대해 들었니?
여: 응, 다음 주 금요일에 시작할 거라고 들었어. 기대하고 있어.
남: 정말 재미있을 거야. 그건 그렇고, 난 축제에 자원봉사하기로 했어.
여: 거기 지원했어? 거기서 뭐를 할 거니?
남: 손님들을 안내하거나 주차를 돕거나 쓰레기 줍는 것 같은 일을 도울 거야.
여: 훌륭한데.
남: 함께 하는 건 어때? 축제에 300명 넘는 사람들이 참여할 거라서 그렇게 많은 수의 방문객을 위해 더 많은 자원봉사자가 필요해.
여: 좋아. 할게. 어떻게 참가하는지 알려줘.
남: 네 스마트폰을 이용해서 우리 학교 웹사이트에서 그걸 할 수 있어. 마감 시간은 내일이야.
여: 내일이라고? 그러면 지금 당장 할게.
남: 아주 좋은 경험이 될 거라고 확신해. 그리고 화요일에 학생회관에서 자원봉사자 모임이 있을 거야.

어휘 **be supposed to-v** v하기로 되어 있다 / **guide** 안내하다 / **assist** 돕다 / **garbage** (음식) 쓰레기 / **participate** 참가하다 / **sign up** 참가하다, 등록하다 / **deadline** 마감 시간 / **student's union** (대학 구내의) 학생회관

06 금액 | ②

▶ 남자(여자의 아빠)는 두 강좌가 포함된 패키지 강좌를 등록할 것이므로 총 200달러를 지불해야 한다.

W: What are you looking at, Dad?
M: I'm looking at the summer course schedule of a language institute for you. I remember you said **you would like to go** to China during winter vacation.
W: That's right. Can I see?
M: Sure.
W: It says they have two lower-level courses. Chinese Grammar starts in July, and Chinese Speaking begins in August.
M: I see that. **How much do they cost**?
W: Each course is $120. But if you sign up for a package that includes both of them, the price is $200.
M: OK, I'll register you for the package. We can save $40! And I heard that I can get a 10 percent discount **by using a credit card**.
W: But look, we can see that packaged lectures are excluded from the discount, so we can't benefit from it.
M: I didn't see that, but you're right. Anyway, I'll register you for the package.
W: Thanks, Dad.

여: 뭘 보고 계세요, 아빠?
남: 어학원에서 네가 들을 만한 여름 강좌 일정표를 보고 있단다. 네가 겨울방학 동안에 중국에 가고 싶다고 말했던 게 생각나서.
여: 맞아요. 저도 봐도 돼요?
남: 물론이지.
여: 초급 강좌가 두 개 있네요. 중국어 문법은 7월에 시작하고, 중국어 회화는 8월에 시작하는군요.
남: 그렇구나. 수강료는 얼마니?
여: 강좌당 120달러예요. 그런데 두 강좌를 포함하는 패키지 강좌를 신청하면 200달러고요.
남: 그렇구나. 그럼 패키지 강좌로 등록해야겠다. 40달러를 절약할 수 있잖니! 그리고 신용카드를 사용하면 10퍼센트 할인을 받을 수 있다고 들었어.
여: 하지만 보세요, 패키지 강좌는 (신용카드) 할인에서 제외라고 되어 있어요. 그러니 카드 할인은 못 받겠어요.
남: 그 설명은 못 봤는데, 네 말이 맞아. 어쨌든 패키지 강좌에 등록해줄게.
여: 고마워요, 아빠.

어휘 **language institute** 어학원 / **exclude A from B** B에서 A를 제외하다, 배제하다

07 이유 | ⑤

▶ 남자는 여자가 늦은 이유가 교통 체증 때문이라고 짐작하였지만, 여자는 사실 휴대 전화를 집에 놓고 와서 되돌아가야 했다고 설명했다.

W: Hi, Jack. I'm terribly sorry I'm late again.
M: That's okay. I know **how bad traffic can be** at rush hour.
W: Right. That's why I took the subway. I thought I could avoid any traffic jams.
M: Oh, then why are you late? You **didn't go the wrong way**, did you?
W: No. I even left my house on time.
M: Let me guess. You forgot your bag at home.
W: Almost. Actually, I forgot my phone at home. I had to go all the way back from the station to get it.
M: Anyway, you're here now. Let's get set up for the meeting.
W: Of course. I have the files in my bag. I prepared everything last night.
M: Great. We still **have plenty of time**.

여: 안녕하세요, Jack. 또 늦어서 정말 미안해요.
남: 괜찮아요. 혼잡 시간대에 얼마나 교통이 안 좋을 수 있는지 알고 있거든요.
여: 맞아요. 그래서 전 지하철을 탔죠. 교통 체증을 피할 수 있을 거라고 생각했거든요.
남: 아, 그렇다면 왜 늦은 건가요? 길을 잘못 들지는 않았죠, 그렇죠?
여: 그럼요. 심지어 집에서도 제시간에 나왔어요.
남: 제가 추측해볼게요. 당신은 집에 가방을 두고 나왔어요.
여: 거의 맞아요. 사실, 집에 휴대 전화를 두고 왔어요. 저는 그것을 가지러 역에서 되돌아가야 했죠.
남: 어쨌든, 당신은 지금 여기 왔잖아요. 이제 회의를 준비합시다.
여: 그럼요. 제 가방에 파일들이 있어요. 지난밤에 모두 준비했죠.
남: 좋아요. 우리는 아직 시간이 충분해요.

어휘 **terribly** 정말로, 너무, 몹시 / **rush hour** (출퇴근) 혼잡 시간대 / **traffic jam** 교통 체증 / **on time** 제시간에, 시간을 어기지 않고 / **set up** 준비하다; 설치하다

08 언급하지 않은 것 | ⑤

▶ 해석 참조

M: What are you watching, Amy?
W: It's a nature documentary about desert cottontails. Aren't they cute?
M: Sure! I love rabbits. So, **where was this filmed**?
W: It was filmed in the animal's natural habitat, the deserts, grasslands, and woodlands of western North America.
M: I thought they would **live in groups**, but this one is all alone.
W: Actually, they're mostly solitary animals. They live alone **whenever possible**.
M: Interesting! It sure looks hot there!
W: That's why they search for food in the early morning or evening, when the sun is down.

M: Makes sense. It must be **difficult to raise a family**, as well.
W: The show said they breed in the spring and the young leave the nest after only two weeks.
M: Wow, I never knew!

남: Amy, 뭘 보고 있니?
여: 사막솜꼬리토끼에 대한 자연 다큐멘터리야. 귀엽지 않니?
남: 물론이지! 나는 토끼를 좋아해. 그런데 이건 어디에서 촬영된 거니?
여: 사막솜꼬리토끼가 사는 자연 서식지에서 촬영되었어. 북아메리카 서쪽 지역의 사막, 초원, 삼림 지대 같은 곳(① 서식지) 말이야.
남: 난 그것들이 무리 지어 살 것이라 생각했는데, 이 토끼는 혼자 있네.
여: 사실, 사막솜꼬리토끼는 대체로 혼자 있기를 좋아해. 그것들은 가능하면 혼자 살거든(② 단독 생활).
남: 흥미롭네! 저긴 정말로 더워 보여!
여: 그래서 그것들은 해가 없는 이른 아침이나 저녁에 먹이를 찾아다녀(③ 먹이 찾는 시간).
남: 이해가 돼. 가족을 꾸리는 것도 힘들 거야.
여: 이 다큐멘터리에 의하면 그것들은 봄에 번식하고(④ 번식 시기) 새끼들이 고작 2주 후에 보금자리를 떠난다고 하네.
남: 와, 전혀 몰랐어!

어휘 **grassland** 초원 / **woodland** 삼림 지대 / **solitary** 혼자 있기를 좋아하는; 혼자의 / **breed** 번식하다, 새끼를 낳다; (동식물의) 품종

09 내용 불일치 | ③

▶ 밖에서는 후각이 뛰어난 사냥개이지만 집에서는 좋은 친구라고 했다.

W: Do you want to get a dog? Then, here is a breed that you might want. The Vizsla is **a breed that originated** in Hungary. The Vizsla is a medium-sized dog with a deep golden rust color and can be shorthaired or wire-haired. He is a natural hunter with an excellent nose in the field, and he is **a good companion at home**. The Vizsla is generally shy, and may be startled by sudden noises. He loves to please his owner and is very easy to train. Sadly, this unique breed **almost became extinct** in Hungary during the years between the two World Wars. Luckily, the dogs survived and now are quite popular in the United States.

여: 개를 한 마리 기르고 싶으신가요? 그렇다면 여러분이 원할지도 모르는 품종이 하나 있습니다. Vizsla는 헝가리에서 생겨난 품종입니다. Vizsla는 짙은 황금색 녹빛으로 중형견이며 털이 짧거나 빳빳할 수 있습니다. 그 개는 들판에서는 탁월한 후각을 지닌 타고난 사냥개이고 집에서는 좋은 친구입니다. Vizsla는 보통 겁이 많아 갑작스러운 소음에 깜짝 놀랄 수 있습니다. 그 개는 주인을 기쁘게 하기를 좋아하여 길들이기가 매우 쉽습니다. 유감스럽게도 이 독특한 품종은 두 번의 세계 대전 기간 동안에 헝가리에서 거의 멸종될 뻔했습니다. 다행히도 그 개는 살아남아 지금은 미국에서 상당히 인기가 있습니다.

어휘 **originate** 비롯되다, 유래하다 / **rust** 녹빛; (금속의) 녹 / **shorthaired** (동물이) 털이 짧은 / **wire-haired** 털이 빳빳한 / **companion** 친구, 동반자 / **startle** 깜짝 놀라게 하다 / **extinct** 멸종된

10 도표 이해 | ①

▶ 문이 두 개인 차는 고려 대상이 안 되며 수동 기어는 필수 조건이다. 그리고 가족 5명이 함께 탑승 가능하며 전기로만 운행이 가능하면 연비는 큰 문제가 되지 않는다.

W: What are you looking at?
M: It's a catalogue of the latest hybrid cars.
W: You're buying a hybrid? I thought you loved your SUV.
M: Well, **it's not very practical**. I never took it into the mountains anyway.
W: What is the main thing you are looking for?
M: Well, two doors is definitely out. My mom is **too old to crawl into the backseat** like that.
W: Don't you prefer to drive a manual transmission?
M: Yes, **it's a must**. And I need room for my wife, son, and my parents. Together there are 5 of us.
W: I guess it comes down to mileage and whether you want to drive purely on electricity.
M: I want a car that has full-electric capability. **If it has this**, mileage isn't that important.

여: 무엇을 보고 있어요?
남: 최신 하이브리드 자동차 카탈로그예요.
여: 하이브리드 차를 구입하게요? 당신이 지금 타고 있는 SUV를 좋아한다고 생각했어요.
남: 음, 그 차는 그렇게 실용적이지 않아요. 그걸 타고 산에 가본 적이 한 번도 없어요.
여: 찾고 있는 주요 사항이 무엇이에요?
남: 음, 문이 두 개 달린 자동차는 확실히 안 돼요. 그처럼 뒷자리로 몸을 굽혀 들어가기엔 어머니께서 너무 연세 드셨어요.
여: 수동 변속기 차량을 선호하지 않으세요?
남: 네, 그건 필수사항이에요. 아내와 아들 그리고 부모님까지 앉을 공간도 필요하고요. 모두 5명이에요.
여: 그럼 연비와 순전히 전기만으로 운행이 가능한지 여부에 달렸군요.
남: 전기만으로 운행 가능한 차를 원해요. 이 기능을 가지고 있다면, 연비는 그렇게 중요하지 않아요.

어휘 **hybrid** 하이브리드(전기, 휘발유 병용)의 / **SUV** (sport utility vehicle의 약자) 스포츠용 차량 / **practical** 실용적인 / **manual** 수동식의 / **transmission** 변속기 / **come down to A** 결국 A로 귀결되다 / **mileage** 연비, 주행 거리 / **capability** 성능; 능력

11 짧은 대화에 이어질 응답 | ①

▶ 등산이 예정된 내일 날씨가 나쁠 거라는 일기예보에 남자는 어떻게 하면 좋을지를 묻고 있다. 이에 가장 적절한 응답을 찾는다.

① 우리의 계획을 연기해야 할 것 같아.
② 대신 버스를 타고 가면 어떨까?
③ 우리는 비옷을 가져왔어야 했는데.
④ 오늘 일기예보가 틀렸어.
⑤ 등산하면 기운이 날 거야.

M: Helen, **are you ready for** tomorrow's climb to the top of Mt. Seorak?
W: Not really. **The weather forecast predicted** heavy rain and strong winds. I was going to call you.
M: No way! What should we do?
W: ______________________________

남: Helen, 내일 설악산 정상에 등반할 준비 됐어?
여: 아니, 일기예보에서 폭우와 강풍을 예보했잖아. 너한테 전화할 참이었는데.
남: 말도 안 돼! 우리 어떻게 해야 하지?
여: ______________________________

12 짧은 대화에 이어질 응답 | ①

▶ 이전에도 같은 문제가 발생했는지 묻는 여자의 말에 적절한 남자의 응답을 찾는다.

① 아니, 하지만 차가 이제 10년 되었거든.
② 내 생각에 새 차를 사야 할지도 몰라.
③ 내가 더 나은 정비소를 추천해줄 수 있을 것 같아.
④ 응, 더 나은 장소에서 발생할 수도 있었어.
⑤ 정비소에서는 흔한 문제라고 그러시더라.

W: It's lucky that you were near a repair shop **when your car broke down**.
M: I know, but I'm worried that it might become a regular problem.
W: Are you saying **this has happened** before?
M: ______________________________

여: 네 차가 고장 났을 때 정비소 근처에 있었던 건 정말 행운이야.
남: 알아, 하지만 난 이런 일이 자주 일어날까 봐 걱정이야.
여: 이런 일이 전에도 일어났다는 말이니?
남: ______________________________

어휘 **regular** 잦은, 주기적인

13 긴 대화에 이어질 응답 | ⑤

▶ 동생을 위한 선물 구입에 제한 없이 돈을 쓰겠다는 남자의 말에 대한 적절한 답변을 찾는다.

① 다음에 오실 때 할인해 달라고 말씀하세요.
② 죄송합니다만, 제가 동생분의 병을 알아야겠습니다.
③ 이 계좌에 잔고가 얼마나 있습니까?
④ 유통기한이 지난 소시지는 반품하실 수 없습니다.
⑤ 동생분께 정말 친절하시군요. 좋은 것들로 넣어 드리겠습니다.

M: Do you sell imported cheese and sausages here?
W: Yes, **we have a large selection**.
M: Great. I'm looking for a mixed selection to give as a gift.
W: We can choose a variety of sausages and some nice cheese for you.

M: Can you also **wrap it nicely in a basket**?
W: I think we can arrange that for you. What's the occasion?
M: My brother is in the hospital **with a broken leg**.
W: I'm so sorry to hear that. I hope he gets well soon.
M: I'm sure he would appreciate that you said that.
W: How much would you like to spend?
M: I'm not worried about the cost when it involves my brother.
W: ______________________________

남: 수입 치즈와 소시지를 여기서 판매합니까?
여: 네, 제품이 많이 있습니다.
남: 잘됐네요. 선물을 하려고 여러 상품이 섞여 있는 제품을 찾고 있는데요.
여: 다양한 소시지와 질 좋은 치즈를 선택해 드릴 수 있습니다.
남: 바구니에 보기 좋게 포장해 주실 수 있나요?
여: 저희가 그렇게 해 드릴 수 있을 거예요. 어떤 일로 선물하시나요?
남: 동생이 다리가 부러져서 입원해 있어요.
여: 안됐네요. 동생분께서 빨리 회복하시길 바랍니다.
남: 그 애도 그렇게 말씀해 주신 것을 감사하게 여길 겁니다.
여: 손님께서는 얼마를 지출하실 생각이신지요?
남: 동생을 위해서라면 비용은 걱정하지 않아요.
여: ______________________________

어휘 **import** 수입하다 / **arrange** 준비하다, 마련하다 / **occasion** 특별한 일, 행사
| 선택지 어휘 | **account** 계좌 / **expiration date** 유통기한; 만료일

14 긴 대화에 이어질 응답 | ①

▶ 기름진 중국 요리가 아닌 한식이 건강에 좋고 영양이 풍부하니 같이 먹으러 가자는 여자의 설득에 적절한 대답을 고른다.

① 좋아요. 제 허리둘레를 위해서 한번 먹어볼게요.
② 좋아요. 오늘 밤에는 매운 음식이 좋겠어요.
③ 제가 어느 정도 살을 빼야 한다고 생각하세요?
④ 한국말을 하시는 줄은 몰랐네요.
⑤ 물론, 중식보다는 한식을 더 좋아해요.

W: What kind of restaurant do you want to go to tonight?
M: Let's go to the new French restaurant. It'll be romantic.
W: Hmm... I was thinking of Korean food.
M: Korean food? **I've never tried it**.
W: **You ought to**. It's healthy and delicious.
M: Actually, I am trying to lose weight and eat healthy food.
W: Then Korean food **would be perfect for you**.
M: But if it's going to be Asian cuisine, you know I love Chinese food.
W: I know you do. But many of the dishes we love are really oily, like deep-fried noodles.
M: But Korean food is spicy.
W: Some things are, but others aren't so spicy. Remember it's really healthy, nutritious food.
M: ______________________________

여: 오늘 밤에는 어떤 식당에 가고 싶으세요?
남: 새로 생긴 프랑스 식당으로 가요. 낭만적일 거예요.
여: 음… 전 한식을 먹을까 생각 중이었어요.
남: 한식이요? 한 번도 먹어 본 일이 없어요.
여: 먹어 보셔야 해요. 건강에도 좋고 맛도 좋아요.
남: 사실, 전 살을 빼고 건강식을 먹으려고 노력 중이에요.
여: 그럼 한식이 당신에게 가장 적합할 거예요.
남: 하지만 아시아 요리를 먹는다면, 제가 중식을 좋아하는 걸 알잖아요.
여: 알아요. 하지만 우리가 좋아하는 요리 대부분이 튀김 국수 같은 정말 기름진 요리예요.
남: 하지만 한식은 맵잖아요.
여: 일부는 그렇지만 다른 것들은 그렇게 맵지 않아요. 한식은 정말 건강에 좋고 영양가가 높다는 사실을 기억하세요.
남: ______________________________

어휘 **cuisine** 요리 / **oily** 기름진 / **spicy** 매운, 양념이 많은 / **nutritious** 영양분이 풍부한
| 선택지 어휘 | **waistline** 허리둘레

15 상황에 적절한 말 | ④

▶ Heather는 룸메이트들과 잘 지내고 있지만, 언제나 자신이 청소를 하게 되는 것이 불만이다. 그래서 청소를 교대로 하고 누가 했는지 기억하자고 말하고 싶다. 그러므로 계획을 세워서 청소를 나누어서 하자고 말하는 것이 가장 적절하다.

① 오늘은 네가 저녁을 준비할 차례야.
② 이 더러운 방에서 사는 게 지겨워.
③ 새로운 기숙사로 이사할 계획이야.
④ 일정을 짜서 청소를 나누어 하자.
⑤ 이번 주 토요일에 어디로 쇼핑하러 가고 싶니?

M: Heather lives in a dormitory with two other roommates. She's been living with the same roommates for two years now, and they've all become good friends. On the weekends, they **frequently go out to shop** or eat together. All three of them usually get along with hardly any disagreements. Heather's very happy with the current situation **except for one thing**. It seems like she's always the one stuck with the cleaning. She rarely sees her roommates clean, so she wants to suggest that they somehow **rotate and keep track of** who cleaned the room. In this situation, what would Heather most likely say to her roommates?

남: Heather는 기숙사에서 다른 두 명의 룸메이트와 함께 산다. 그녀는 지금 2년 동안 같은 룸메이트들과 함께 살고 있고, 그들은 모두 친한 친구가 되었다. 주말마다 그들은 종종 함께 쇼핑하거나 밥을 먹으러 나간다. 그들 세 명 모두 거의 다투지 않고 대개 잘 지낸다. Heather는 한 가지를 제외하고는 현재 상황에 아주 만족하는데, 꼼짝없이 청소를 해야 하는 사람이 언제나 그녀인 것 같다는 점이다. 그녀는 룸메이트들이 청소하는 것을 좀처럼 보지 못해서, 어떻게든 일을 교대로 하고 누가 방을 청소했는지 계속 알고 있어야 한다고 제안하고 싶다. 이러한 상황에서 Heather가 룸메이트들에게 할 말로 가장 적절한 것은 무엇인가?

어휘 **frequently** 종종, 자주 / **be[get] stuck with** 싫은 일을 강요당하다 / **rotate** (일을) 교대로 하다; 회전하다 / **keep track of** ~에 대해 계속 파악하고 있다

16~17 세트 문항 | 16. ① 17. ④

▶ 16. 안전 운전을 위하여 지켜야 할 사항들을 나열하고 있다.

① 안전 운전 방법
② 교통량 감소법
③ 차량 운전법
④ 운전하면서 깨어 있는(졸지 않는) 방법
⑤ 운전 자신감 향상법

▶ 17. 해석 참조

W: Common sense and calm thinking are essential for smart drivers. For example, common sense says it's **not smart to drive extra fast** when you are running late. Why? Because doing this in city traffic saves you **no more than a few seconds**, and greatly increases the risk of accidents. Next, it's absolutely important to keep a space of three seconds between your car and the vehicle ahead. This space gives you life-saving time to **take action before a crash**. Most important of all, though, is to give your full attention to the job and never smoke or eat at the wheel. It's not illegal, but if it leads to careless driving it could land you in trouble with the law. **Talking on an ordinary cell phone** while driving is illegal. Of course, some special systems allow you to talk without holding your phone. Similar to eating, drinking soft beverages at the wheel is not illegal, but it can carry the same careless-driving penalty. A study found that those who took a sip of a drink at the wheel were 22% **slower than those who didn't**.

여: 상식과 차분한 사고는 똑똑한 운전자에게 필수적입니다. 예를 들어, 상식에 의하면 늦고 있을 때 필요 이상으로 빠르게 운전하는 것(① 고속 주행)은 똑똑하지 못합니다. 이유는 무엇일까요? 도심 교통에서 그렇게 하는 것은 겨우 몇 초를 절약해줄 뿐이고 사고 위험은 매우 높이기 때문입니다. 다음으로, 앞선 차량과 당신의 차를 3초 간격으로 유지하는 것은 절대적으로 중요합니다. 이 공간은 당신이 사고 전에 행동을 취할, 생명을 구할 시간을 주기 때문입니다. 그러나 무엇보다 가장 중요한 것은 운전에 완전히 집중하는 것이며 운전하면서 절대 흡연(② 흡연)이나 취식(③ 식사)을 하지 않는 것입니다. 그것이 불법은 아니지만 부주의한 운전으로 이끈다면 법적으로 문제가 될 수 있습니다. 운전하면서 일반 핸드폰으로 통화하는 것은 불법(⑤ 핸드폰 통화)입니다. 물론 특별한 시스템을 갖춘 것이면 손에 전화기를 들지 않고도 말할 수 있습니다. 취식과 유사하게, 운전하면서 청량음료를 마시는 것은 불법이 아니지만 똑같이 부주의 운전으로 처벌받을 수 있습니다. 한 연구에 의하면 운전하면서 음료수를 마시는 사람들은 그렇지 않은 사람들보다 (위험에 대한 반응 속도가) 22퍼센트 더 느렸습니다.

어휘 **common sense** 상식, 양식 / **no more than** 단지 ~에 지나지 않다 (= only) / **absolutely** 절대적으로 / **crash** (자동차 충돌 · 항공기 추락) 사고 / **at the wheel** 운전 중에 / **land A in trouble** A를 곤경에 빠뜨리다 / **penalty** 처벌; 벌칙 / **sip** (음료를) 조금씩 마시다, 홀짝이다

02 Sense Up 듣기 모의고사
ANSWERS & COMPREHENSION

본문 p.14

01. ④ 02. ⑤ 03. ④ 04. ② 05. ④ 06. ③ 07. ⑤ 08. ② 09. ④ 10. ②
11. ② 12. ④ 13. ④ 14. ① 15. ② 16. ⑤ 17. ⑤

01 화자가 하는 말의 목적 | ④

▶ 여자는 마지막에 '지갑과 마음을 열어 최대한 베풀어 달라'는 말로 기부금 모금을 직접적으로 요청하고 있다.

W: My message to you is a very simple one. Our hospital helps the poorest children of Afghanistan. **Our goal is to stay open**, to continue our work in caring for the sick and injured children of this country. To this end, your support **is absolutely vital**. Our hospital urgently needs more beds and new medical equipment. A donation of as little as $20 will **provide the supplies we need** to save at least 50 babies from death. Without your help, many of these children will have no hope. Open your wallets and your hearts. Give **as much as you can**. Every single cent will be immediately put to use.

여: 제가 여러분께 드리고 싶은 말씀은 아주 간단합니다. 저희 병원은 아프가니스탄의 극빈층 어린이들을 돕습니다. 저희의 목표는 병원 운영을 계속하여 이 나라의 병들고 다친 어린이들을 돌보는 일을 계속하는 것입니다. 이 목표를 이루기 위해서는 여러분의 지원이 절대적으로 필요합니다. 저희 병원은 더 많은 병상과 새로운 의료장비가 시급히 필요합니다. 단돈 20달러의 기부로 적어도 아이 50명의 목숨을 살리는 데 필요한 보급품을 마련할 수 있습니다. 여러분의 도움이 없다면, 이들 중 많은 어린이들에게는 아무런 희망이 없을 것입니다. 여러분의 지갑과 마음을 열어주십시오. 할 수 있는 만큼 베풀어 주십시오. 단돈 1센트도 곧바로 요긴하게 쓰일 것입니다.

어휘 **to this end** 이 목적을 이루기 위해서는, 이 목적으로 / **vital** 필수적인 / **urgently** 긴급히 / **put A to use** A를 잘 이용하다

02 의견 | ⑤

▶ 남자는 책상에서 낮잠을 자면 허리가 아프고 불편하며, 적당한 낮잠은 학습 성과를 증가시킬 수 있다는 전문가의 이야기를 근거로 교내에 낮잠을 잘 수 있는 공간을 마련해야 한다고 말하고 있다.

W: You look tired. Are you okay?
M: I haven't been getting enough sleep because I've been watching the Olympics.
W: I see. Sometimes I **feel tired in class** because I don't sleep well at night. When that happens, I nap during a break.
M: But it's uncomfortable and it hurts my back **if I nap on a desk**.
W: You're right. It's impossible to sleep soundly.
M: I wish we had another place to sleep.
W: It sounds like you want a room for napping.
M: Why not? In fact, just a few beds in the break room would be enough.
W: That would **help to relieve stress**, but shouldn't we spend our time in more productive ways?
M: Well, experts say that napping for 10 to 30 minutes **can increase study performance**.
W: I didn't know that.

여: 피곤해 보이는구나. 괜찮아?
남: 올림픽을 보느라 잠을 충분히 못 자고 있어.
여: 그렇구나. 난 밤에 제대로 못 자서 수업 중에 가끔 피곤할 때가 있어. 그럴 때는, 쉬는 시간 동안 낮잠을 자.
남: 하지만 책상에서 낮잠을 자면 불편하고 허리가 아파.
여: 네 말이 맞아. 깊이 자는 건 불가능하지.
남: 잠을 잘 수 있는 다른 곳이 있으면 좋겠어.
여: 낮잠을 자기 위한 공간을 바라는 것 같구나.
남: 왜 아니겠어? 사실, 휴게실에 침대 몇 개면 충분할 거야.
여: 그건 스트레스를 푸는 데 도움이 되겠지만, 시간을 더 생산적으로 써야 하지 않을까?
남: 음, 전문가들이 말하기를 10분에서 30분 동안의 낮잠은 학습 성과를 증가시킬 수 있대.
여: 그건 몰랐어.

어휘 **soundly** (잠이 든 모양이) 깊이[곤히]; 견실하게, 확실하게 / **productive** 생산적인

03 관계 | ④

▶ 미술 선생님이 제자의 작품을 보고 칭찬하는 내용의 대화이다.

W: That is really good! Your work **has come a long way**.
M: Well, I owe it all to you. I never worked with clay before this class.
W: I **can't take any credit**. I think your true talent is coming out.
M: Well, I was inspired by your piece that was in the big show last year.
W: Ah, the one that you said looked like the moon **with a bite out of it**?
M: Yes. Sorry I said that. That was before I understood art.
W: That's OK. I always tell the class that art is subjective.
M: So it's OK if I still think it looks like the moon?
W: I'll **let you in on a little secret**: I think it looks like the moon, too!

여: 저 작품은 정말 좋구나! 네 작품은 크게 발전하고 있어.
남: 음, 모두 선생님 덕분이에요. 이 수업을 듣기 전에는 점토로 작업해 본 적이 없어요.
여: 내 덕분이라니. 너의 진정한 재능이 나타나고 있는 것이라고 생각한다.
남: 음, 작년에 큰 전시회에 출품하셨던 선생님의 작품에 영감을 받았어요.
여: 아, 네가 한 입 베어 먹은 달처럼 생겼다고 한 작품 말이니?
남: 네, 그렇게 말해서 죄송해요. 그땐 제가 예술을 이해하기 전이었어요.
여: 괜찮아. 난 예술은 주관적인 것이라고 아이들에게 항상 말한단다.
남: 그럼, 그 작품이 여전히 달처럼 생겼다고 생각해도 괜찮으세요?
여: 내가 작은 비밀을 하나 일러 주마. 나도 그 작품이 달처럼 생겼다고 생각한단다!

어휘 **come a long way** 크게 발전[진보]하다 / **clay** 점토, 찰흙 / **take credit** 공적을 차지하다 / **inspired** 영감을 받은 / **subjective** 주관적인 / **let in on** (비밀을) 일러 주다, 알리다

04 그림 불일치 | ②

▶ 여자는 수건을 걸어두는 건 옛날 규정이고 지금은 카운터 위에 접어 둔다고 했다.

W: Now, I'll show you **how to prepare the bathroom**.
M: Okay, I'm ready.
W: First, check the mirror above the sink. If there's any dirt, you should get rid of it completely.
M: All right. I'll **keep that in mind**.
W: Next, two towels should be prepared.
M: Would you like me to hang them on the rack?
W: No. That used to be the policy, but now we **leave them folded** on the counter.
M: Okay. Where does the soap go, then?
W: It goes on the left side of the sink. Right in front of the tissue with the pyramid logo on it.
M: I see. What about the bathrobe?
W: The bathrobe should be on a hanger, and you **should hang it on the wall**. Now, that's all. Can you remember everything I told you?
M: No problem. I think I've got it.

여: 자, 이제 욕실 준비하는 법을 보여줄게요.
남: 네, 준비됐습니다.
여: 먼저, 세면대 위에 있는 거울을 점검하세요. 먼지가 있으면 말끔히 제거해야 해요.
남: 잘 알겠습니다. 명심할게요.
여: 다음으로, 수건 두 개가 준비되어야 합니다.
남: (수건) 걸이에 걸어야 하나요?
여: 아뇨, 예전엔 그게 규정이었는데 지금은 카운터 위에 접어둡니다.
남: 알겠습니다. 그럼 비누는 어디에 놓아야 하죠?
여: 세면대 왼쪽에 두세요. 피라미드 로고가 있는 티슈 바로 앞에요.
남: 알겠어요. 목욕 가운은요?
여: 목욕 가운은 옷걸이에 걸어서 벽에 걸어야 해요. 자, 이제 다 됐네요. 제가 한 얘기 다 기억할 수 있겠어요?
남: 문제없어요. 이해한 것 같아요.

어휘 **sink** (욕실) 세면대; (주방) 싱크대 / **rack** 걸이, 선반, 받침대 / **policy** 규정 / **fold** 접다.

개다 / **logo** 상표 / **bathrobe** 목욕 가운 / **hanger** 옷걸이

05 추후 행동 | ④

▶ 남자는 생일 파티가 시작한 지 20분이 지났기 때문에 가기에 늦었다고 생각했지만, 여자의 조언을 받아들여 결국 가기로 했다.

W: Hey Andrew! How's the research paper going?
M: I just need to write the last paragraph. It will be done tomorrow.
W: Good for you! Maybe you can help me with mine next.
M: **What's the topic of your paper**?
W: I'm writing about the effects of dams on the environment.
M: I'd love to help, but I don't know anything about that subject.
W: Well, that's okay. There are many reference books in the school library. Oh, by the way, aren't you supposed to go to Jack's birthday party today?
M: Yeah... but **it's a little late to go** now. The party started twenty minutes ago.
W: Well, you know how the saying goes, "**better late than never**."
M: Umm.... I guess you're right. I'd better head out.
W: Hey, don't forget your bag.

여: 이봐 Andrew! 연구 보고서 어떻게 되어가고 있어?
남: 마지막 단락만 작성하면 돼. 내일 끝날 거야.
여: 잘됐네! 어쩌면 그다음엔 내 보고서를 도와줄 수 있겠다.
남: 보고서 주제가 뭔데?
여: 댐이 환경에 미치는 영향에 대해 쓰고 있어.
남: 나도 도와주고 싶은데, 그 주제에 대해 아무것도 몰라.
여: 음, 괜찮아. 학교 도서관에 참고 도서가 많이 있거든. 아, 그런데 오늘 Jack의 생일 파티에 가기로 하지 않았니?
남: 응… 그런데 지금 가기에는 좀 늦었어. 파티가 20분 전에 시작됐거든.
여: 글쎄, '늦더라도 하지 않는 것보다는 낫다'라는 속담이 있잖아.
남: 음…. 네 말이 맞는 것 같아. 가는 게 좋겠어.
여: 이봐, 가방 잊지 마.

어휘 **reference book** 참고 도서 / **be supposed to-v** v하기로 되어 있다 / **head out** (구어) 향하다, 출발하다

06 금액 | ③

▶ 전체 수리 비용이 500달러이므로, 10퍼센트 할인을 받으면 450달러를 내야 하고 30달러를 할인받으면 470달러를 내야 한다. 따라서 할인 폭이 큰 10퍼센트 할인으로 할 것이다.

W: I need to pay for the work **being done on my car**.
M: OK. Do you have a membership card for our business?
W: Yes, I do. Here you are.
M: Great, that will **get you 10 percent off** right away.
W: Excellent. What is the total?
M: Well, before the discount it is $500.
W: Do you accept this coupon? I **received it a few days ago** from my card company.
M: Let me see. Oh yes, you can use this coupon. With this, any customer gets a $30 discount from the total service fee.
W: That means I only need to pay $420?
M: I'm sorry, no. We can offer only one kind of discount at a time. To get $30 off, you have to give up the 10 percent discount.
W: Then I'll definitely choose **the bigger discount**.

여: 차를 수리한 비용을 내려고요.
남: 알겠습니다. 저희 가게의 회원 카드를 가지고 계시는지요?
여: 네, 그렇습니다. 여기요.
남: 좋습니다. 10퍼센트를 바로 할인해 드리겠습니다.
여: 잘됐네요. 총 얼마인가요?
남: 음, 할인 전 가격이 500달러입니다.
여: 이 쿠폰을 받나요? 카드 회사에서 며칠 전에 받은 거예요.
남: 어디 볼까요. 아 네, 이 쿠폰을 사용하실 수 있습니다. 이 쿠폰으로 총 서비스 요금에서 30달러를 할인받으실 수 있습니다.
여: 제가 420달러만 내면 된다는 말씀인가요?
남: 죄송합니다만, 그렇지 않습니다. 저희는 한 번에 한 가지의 할인 혜택만 제공해드릴 수 있습니다. 30달러를 할인받으시려면 10퍼센트 할인은 포기하셔야 합니다.
여: 그럼 당연히 더 크게 할인이 되는 쪽을 선택할게요.

어휘 **definitely** 물론, 분명히

07 이유 | ⑤

▶ 여자의 마지막 말에서 남자의 딸이 피아노 교습에 참여할 수 없는 이유가 나온다. 이전에 피아노 교습을 받지 않은 아이들을 대상으로 하는 것인데 남자의 딸은 1년간 피아노 교습을 받았으므로 해당되지 않는다.

W: How can I help you?
M: I heard your Piano Laboratory is looking for children to receive free piano lessons. I'd like to **sign up my daughter for it**.
W: Do you know this is part of student teacher training?
M: Yes, I read it in this brochure.
W: Keyboard majors in our university will teach the children. How old is your child?
M: She's 8 years old. **This class is for** children ages 7-9, right?
W: Yes. It's a three-month program beginning September 9.
M: Okay. My daughter **is really interested in playing** the piano. She took piano lessons for a year.
W: Really? I'm sorry, but she can't participate in this program. This is for children with no previous piano lessons.
M: Oh, I didn't know that. **She'll be disappointed**.

여: 뭘 도와드릴까요?
남: 여기 피아노 연구소가 무료 피아노 교습을 받을 학생들을 찾고 있다고 들었어요. 거기 제 딸을 등록시키고 싶습니다.
여: 이게 교생 훈련의 일부인 걸 알고 계시죠?
남: 예, 이 팸플릿에서 읽었습니다.
여: 우리 대학의 건반악기 전공자들이 아이들을 가르칠 겁니다. 아이가 몇 살이죠?
남: 여덟 살입니다. 이 강좌가 7세에서 9세까지 연령의 아이들을 위한 거죠, 맞죠?
여: 예. 9월 9일 시작하는 3개월짜리 프로그램입니다.
남: 알겠어요. 제 딸이 피아노를 연주하는 데 정말 관심이 많아요. 1년간 피아노 교습을 받았답니다.
여: 정말이요? 죄송하지만 따님은 이 프로그램에 참여할 수 없어요. 이건 이전에 피아노 교습을 받지 않은 아이들을 대상으로 하거든요.
남: 아, 그걸 몰랐군요. 제 아이가 실망하겠는데요.

어휘 **laboratory** 연구소, 실험실 / **student teacher** 교생, 교육 실습생 / **brochure** 팸플릿, 소책자 / **participate** 참가하다 / **previous** 이전의, 앞의

08 언급하지 않은 것 | ②

▶ 해석 참조

M: **Among the great figures of recent history** is Nelson Mandela. Born in Transkei, South Africa in 1918, he was the son of the chief advisor of the Tembu tribe. As a young man, he moved to Johannesburg to study law. Later, he would join the African National Congress (ANC) party and **become involved in active resistance** against the ruling party's racist agenda. In 1961, he helped establish the ANC's military, partly in response to the Sharpeville Massacre a year earlier. In 1964, he **was sent to prison for life**, and he remained there until 1990. After being released from prison, Mandela became a symbol for peace. He won the Nobel Peace Prize in 1993 and became president of South Africa in 1994. After stepping down in 1999, **he focused on combating poverty** and HIV/AIDS through the Nelson Mandela Foundation. Today, he is deeply respected in South Africa, where he is remembered as "the father of the nation."

남: 최근 역사상 위대한 인물 중 하나로 손꼽히는 이는 넬슨 만델라(Nelson Mandela)입니다. 1918년, 남아프리카공화국의 Transkei(① 출생지)에서 태어난 그는 Tembu족 족장의 아들이었습니다. 젊었을 때 그는 법을 공부하기 위해 요하네스버그로 건너갔습니다. 이후 그는 아프리카민족회의(ANC)에 가입하여 집권당의 인종 차별적 지침에 저항하는 운동에 적극적으로 가담했습니다. 1961년에 넬슨 만델라는 일 년 전에 발생한 Sharpeville 학살에 어느 정도 대응하여 ANC의 군사조직 설립에 일조했습니다. 1964년에는 종신형을 선고받아 1990년까지 투옥되었습니다(③ 투옥 기간). 감옥에서 석방된 후, 만델라는 평화의 상징이 되었습니다. 1993년에 노벨 평화상을 수상(④ 수상 내역)하고 나서 1994년에는 남아프리카공화국의 대통령이 되었습니다. 1999년에 퇴임한 후에 그는 넬슨 만델라 재단을 통해

가난과 에이즈 퇴치 운동에 전력을 쏟았습니다(⑤ 퇴임 후 활동). 오늘날, 넬슨 만델라는 남아프리카공화국에서 진심으로 존경받고 있는데, 그곳에서 그는 '남아프리카공화국의 아버지'로 기억되고 있습니다.

어휘 **chief** 우두머리; 족장; 최고의; 주요한 / **advisor** 고문, 조언자 / **involved** 관련된; 몰두하는 / **resistance** 저항 / **ruling party** 집권당, 여당 / **racist** 인종 차별의; 인종차별주의자 / **agenda** 행동 강령[지침]; 의제 / **step down** 물러나다 / **combat** 싸우다, 투쟁하다; 전투 / **foundation** 재단; 설립

09 내용 불일치 | ④

▶ 16세기 영국에서 엘리자베스 여왕 1세가 립스틱을 인기 있게 만들었다.

W: Lipstick can be seen nearly everywhere, but do you know its history? Lipstick dates back at least 5,000 years to the ancient city of Ur, near Babylon. At that time, colorful stones **were crushed and then applied** to the lips for color. The ancient Egyptians also had a form of lipstick. Unfortunately, the chemicals it contained were poisonous and led to several deaths. Meanwhile, Cleopatra's lipstick was made from crushed insects such as beetles. During the 16th century, Queen Elizabeth I made lipstick popular among rich people in England. She introduced the trend of white faces **contrasted with blood red lipstick**. In 1884, the first commercial lipstick was invented by perfumers in Paris, and by the end of the 19th century a French cosmetic company **had begun manufacturing it**.

여: 립스틱은 거의 어디에서나 볼 수 있지만, 그 역사에 대해서 알고 계신가요? 립스틱의 역사는 적어도 5,000년 전 바빌론 부근의 우르라는 고대 도시로 거슬러 올라갑니다. 그 당시에는 입술에 색을 내기 위해 형형색색의 돌을 으깨 발랐습니다. 고대 이집트인들도 일종의 립스틱이 있었습니다. 불행히도, 거기 포함된 화학물질은 독성이 있어 몇몇 사람을 죽음에 이르게 했습니다. 한편, 클레오파트라의 립스틱은 딱정벌레와 같은 곤충을 으깬 것으로 만들어졌습니다. 16세기 영국에서는 엘리자베스 여왕 1세 때문에 부유한 사람들 사이에서 립스틱이 인기를 얻게 되었습니다. 그녀는 핏빛같이 붉은 립스틱과 하얀 얼굴이 대조되는 트렌드를 선보였습니다. 1884년, 최초의 판매용 립스틱이 파리에서 향수 제조업자들에 의해 발명되었고, 19세기 말 무렵에는 프랑스의 화장품 회사가 그것을 대량 생산하기 시작했습니다.

어휘 **date back** (**to**) 역사가 (~까지) 거슬러 올라가다 / **crush** 눌러 부수다, 뭉개다 / **apply** (크림 등을) 바르다; 신청하다; 적용하다 / **beetle** 딱정벌레 / **contrast A with B** A를 B와 대조하다, 대비시키다 / **cosmetic** 화장품 / **manufacture** (대규모로) 생산하다

10 도표 이해 | ②

▶ 여자는 시내에 있고 침실이 두 개이며 현재 살고 있는 아파트의 집세(700달러)와 기름값(400달러)을 합한 것과 같은 집세의 아파트를 선택할 것이다.

W: Bill, I need some advice. I'm apartment hunting.
M: Show me your list of apartments.
W: Here.... I live in the suburbs now and I want to live downtown. But downtown apartments are too expensive and too small.
M: Really? You live in a suburban two-bedroom apartment, right?
W: Yes, **it's cheap and spacious.**
M: I don't think it's cheap. It might be only $700 in rent but how much do you spend on gas driving downtown to work?
W: Over $400 a month.
M: And that's only gas. There are repairs and.... So, these downtown apartments aren't **as expensive as you think**.
W: But they are smaller.
M: Well, there's one downtown apartment **with the same number of rooms**. It's no more expensive than living in suburbia if you include the gas.
W: You're right. I guess I should move downtown.
M: I think so.

여: Bill, 조언이 좀 필요해. 나는 아파트를 구하고 있어.
남: 네 아파트 목록을 보여줘.
여: 여기 있어…. 지금은 교외에 살고 있는데 시내 중심가에서 살고 싶어. 그렇지만 시내에 있는 아파트는 너무 비싸고 너무 작아.
남: 정말? 너는 교외에 있는 침실 두 개짜리 아파트에 살고 있잖아, 맞지?
여: 응, 그 아파트는 싸고 넓어.
남: 나는 싸다고 생각하지 않아. 집세가 700달러밖에 들지 않을지 모르지만, 시내로 출근하는 데 기름값으로 얼마를 쓰니?
여: 한 달에 400달러 넘게.
남: 그것은 기름값일 뿐이고, 수리비도 있고…. 그러니까, 이 시내 아파트들은 네가 생각하는 것만큼 비싸지 않아.
여: 그렇지만 그것들은 더 좁아.
남: 음, 방 개수가 같은 시내 아파트가 하나 있어. 기름값을 포함한다면 교외에서 사는 것만큼 저렴해.
여: 네 말이 맞아. 시내로 이사해야 할 것 같아.
남: 나도 그렇게 생각해.

어휘 **suburb** 교외 *cf.* **suburban** 교외의, 교외에 사는 *cf.* **suburbia** 교외 (거주자); 교외풍의 생활 방식 / **spacious** (방 등이) 넓은

11 짧은 대화에 이어질 응답 | ②

▶ 어느 것을 사야 할지 모르겠다는 여자에게 남자는 생각해볼 시간을 줄지 물었다. 이에 대한 가장 적절한 응답을 찾는다.

① 제 생각엔 그렇게 오래 걸리지 않을 것 같아요.
② 그게 가장 좋겠네요. 고마워요.
③ 고맙습니다만, 그냥 구경만 하는 거예요.
④ 저는 둘 중에서 더 저렴한 것을 추천합니다.
⑤ 어떤 특별한 기능을 찾고 계시나요?

M: These two TVs are the most popular on the market today.
W: Each is good **in its own way**. I don't know which to choose.
M: Why don't I give you **some time to think it over**?
W: ________________

남: 이 두 대의 TV가 요즘 매장에서 가장 인기가 좋습니다.
여: 각자 나름대로 좋네요. 어느 것을 골라야 할지 모르겠어요.
남: 고객님께 생각할 시간을 드릴까요?
여: ________________

12 짧은 대화에 이어질 응답 | ④

▶ 피자 배달이 오지 않는다는 남자의 말에 여자가 문의 전화는 해보았는지 물었다. 이에 적절한 응답을 찾는다.

① 응, 그 가게는 보통 제시간에 배달해 줘.
② 아니, 누가 나한테 전화했는지 모르겠어.
③ 음, 나중에 네게 전화할게.
④ 몇 번이나 해 봤지만 통화 중이었어.
⑤ 우리가 그 가게에서 주문한 건 이번이 처음이야.

W: Is there something wrong, Robert?
M: Yes, I ordered a pizza an hour ago but **it still hasn't been delivered**.
W: Did you call to find out **why it's so late**?
M: ________________

여: 무슨 일 있니, Robert?
남: 응, 한 시간 전에 피자를 주문했는데 아직도 배달이 안 됐어.
여: 왜 그렇게 늦는지 전화해 봤어?
남: ________________

13 긴 대화에 이어질 응답 | ④

▶ 남자는 원하는 맛의 아이스크림이 없어서 현재 가게에서 먹을 수 있는 것 중 한 가지를 선택했다. 이때 종업원인 여자의 적절한 반응을 찾는다.

① 손님께서 원하시는 어떤 맛이든 선택하세요.
② 대단히 죄송하지만, 그것은 지금 다 떨어졌습니다.
③ 딸기 맛을 달라고 하셨죠, 그렇죠?
④ 제가 정말 좋아하는 맛이에요. 선택하신 것을 후회하지 않으실 거예요.
⑤ 손님께서 왜 바닐라 아이스크림을 좋아하시지 않는지 모르겠군요.

M: I'd like to get a scoop of strawberry ice cream, please.
W: Yes, sir. Just one minute. *[pause]* I'm sorry, we're **all out of strawberry**.
M: Then how about a scoop of raspberry instead?
W: Sorry, sir. We are out of raspberry as well.
M: This isn't my lucky day. You **don't have any of my favorites**.
W: We've just had a large group of teenage customers. That's why. I'm sure we can find something that you like.
M: Tell me **what other flavors you can offer**.

W: We have Banana Coconut, Vanilla, Walnut, Apple Mint, and Chocolate Chip available.
M: OK. I'll try something new today!
W: Thank you for understanding.
M: I'll try the first one. Give me one scoop of it, please.
W: ______________________________

남: 딸기 아이스크림 하나 주세요.
여: 네 손님. 잠시만 기다리세요. *[잠시 후]* 죄송합니다. 딸기 맛이 떨어졌습니다.
남: 그럼 대신 라즈베리는 있나요?
여: 죄송합니다, 손님. 라즈베리도 다 떨어졌습니다.
남: 오늘은 운이 없네요. 제가 좋아하는 것은 아무것도 없군요.
여: 방금 십 대 손님들 큰 그룹이 와서 그렇게 되었습니다. 손님께서 좋아하시는 맛을 저희가 찾아 드릴 수 있을 거예요.
남: 팔 수 있는 어떤 다른 맛이 있는지 알려 주세요.
여: 저희는 바나나 코코넛, 바닐라, 호두, 애플민트, 그리고 초콜릿 칩이 있습니다.
남: 알겠습니다. 오늘은 새로운 것을 먹어 볼게요!
여: 이해해 주셔서 감사합니다.
남: 첫 번째 것으로 할게요. 하나 주세요.
여: ______________________________

어휘 **scoop** 국자 / **be out of** (필요한 물건이) 떨어지다, 동이 나다

14 긴 대화에 이어질 응답 | ①

▶ 음식이 잘못 나왔는데도 불편한 상황을 만들고 싶지 않아서 웨이터를 부르지 않으려는 여자에게 남자가 할 수 있는 제안을 유추해 본다.

① 걱정하지 말아요. 내가 다 이야기할게요.
② 매달 당신을 이곳에 데리고 올게요.
③ 여유를 가지고 편히 있어요. 나아질 거예요.
④ 식당이 곧 문을 닫으니까, 음식을 마저 먹어요.
⑤ 웨이터가 가져온 것이 무엇이든 그냥 먹는 게 어때요?

W: Oh no! The waiter brought the wrong food. I ordered a burger with cheese and bacon.
M: We'll just call him back over and **have him fix it**.
W: No. I don't want to start trouble.
M: Don't be silly. It's his job to make sure we get what we ordered.
W: **Let's not cause a scene**.
M: But if you aren't going to enjoy your meal, you **should get it fixed**.
W: I don't want to make him mad.
M: Like I said before, it's his job. He will feel worse if we don't say anything and he realizes it later.
W: I'm not sure. I **feel a little uncomfortable** about this.
M: ______________________________

여: 아, 이럴 수가! 웨이터가 음식을 잘못 가져다줬어요. 전 치즈와 베이컨이 들어간 햄버거를 시켰는데요.
남: 웨이터를 불러서 바꿔오도록 하죠.
여: 아니요. 문제를 만들고 싶지 않아요.
남: 바보같이 굴지 말아요. 우리가 주문한 것을 제대로 받게 해주는 것이 그 사람의 일이에요.
여: 소란을 피우지 말자고요.
남: 하지만 음식을 맛있게 먹지 못할 거면, 그것을 바로잡아야 해요.
여: 그 사람을 언짢게 만들고 싶지는 않아요.
남: 내가 전에도 말했듯이, 그게 그 사람의 일이에요. 우리가 아무 말도 하지 않고 그 사람이 그것을 나중에 알게 되면 더 언짢을 거예요.
여: 잘 모르겠어요. 이런 상황은 좀 불편해요.
남: ______________________________

어휘 **scene** 소동, 야단법석 | 선택지 어휘 | **finish off** (음식 등을) 다 먹어 치우다

15 상황에 적절한 말 | ②

▶ Susan의 동네가 생소한 Blair가 목적지까지 빨리 가기 위해 할 수 있는 말을 유추한다.

① 내일 영화가 몇 시에 시작하죠?
② 그곳으로 가는 지름길을 아세요?
③ 말하지 않아서 정말 미안해요.
④ 당신의 집으로 가는 방향을 알려 주시겠어요?
⑤ 어떤 종류의 영화를 보는 것을 선호하세요?

W: Blair's friend, Mitchell, thought Blair would get along with Susan. So Mitchell arranged for Blair and Susan to go to a movie together. Susan lives in a neighborhood which Blair **is unfamiliar with**. Before driving there, he looks at a map and takes the easiest route possible **so as not to get lost**. Not having driven there before means, however, that **he has misjudged the time**. He arrives at Susan's house 20 minutes late. Susan is not angry, as Blair phoned her from his car. Blair introduces himself and apologizes. Blair says they **had better go right away**. So they get in the car. Blair knows they are behind schedule and need to get to the theater quickly. In this situation, what would Blair most likely say to Susan?

여: Blair의 친구인 Mitchell은 Blair가 Susan과 잘 어울릴 것이라고 생각했다. 그래서 Mitchell은 Blair와 Susan이 같이 영화를 보러 가도록 주선했다. Susan은 Blair에게는 생소한 동네에 살고 있다. 그곳으로 운전해 가기 전에, 그는 약도를 보고 길을 잃지 않기 위해 가능한 가장 쉬운 길을 택한다. 그러나 그곳으로 운전해서 간 적이 없어서 그는 시간을 잘못 계산했다. 그는 Susan의 집에 20분 늦게 도착한다. Blair가 차에서 전화했기 때문에 Susan은 화나지 않았다. Blair는 자신을 소개하고 사과를 한다. Blair는 바로 출발하는 것이 좋겠다고 말한다. 그래서 그들은 차를 탄다. Blair는 예정보다 늦어서 극장에 빨리 가야 한다는 사실을 안다. 이러한 상황에서 Blair가 Susan에게 할 말로 가장 적절한 것은 무엇인가?

어휘 **arrange** 준비하다, 예정을 세우다 / **unfamiliar** 익숙지 않은 / **route** 길, 노정 / **misjudge** 잘못 판단을 내리다 / **behind schedule** 예정보다 늦게

16~17 세트 문항 | 16. ⑤ 17. ⑤

▶ 16. 상대적으로 높은 지위에 있는 사람들은 낮은 지위의 사람들에 비해 사생활이 더 보호되는 사적 공간을 제공받고 있다는 것을 예를 들어 설명하고 있다.

① 직장에서 개인적 자유에 대한 가이드
② 부당한 노동 관행에 대처하는 방법
③ 개인 공간을 유지하는 것의 중요성
④ 건강한 직장 내 위계에 대한 정의
⑤ 사회적 지위와 개인 공간 사이의 관계

▶ 17. 해석 참조

M: I want you to imagine your dream job. Do you **have it in mind**? Without any clues about your personal goals, I'm willing to bet that for many of you the dream includes money, respect, and a large office. These are the common indicators of success across a variety of cultures. We don't find it surprising that people with higher status are generally given more space and privacy. For instance, we knock before entering our **boss's office**, but we walk into **the office work area** without hesitating. And we'd probably be quite surprised to find the head of our company working in a tiny office or somewhere open to distractions. Likewise, in many schools, teachers have offices, dining rooms, and even toilets that are private, but students do not have such special places. In the world of show business, stars receive **their own dressing rooms or private trailers**. These are places where they can prepare in peace for their big performances. Even in the military, this relation can be easily seen — new recruits practically sleep on top of each other, while **generals typically receive private housing**.

남: 여러분이 꿈꾸는 직업을 상상해보시기 바랍니다. 생각이 나셨나요? 여러분의 개인적인 목표에 대해 아무런 단서가 없어도, 제가 기꺼이 장담하건대 여러분 중 많은 분의 경우 그 꿈에 돈, 존경심, 넓은 사무실이 포함되어 있습니다. 이런 것들은 다양한 문화에서 성공의 흔한 척도이지요. 우리는 더 높은 지위를 가진 사람들에게 일반적으로 더 넓은 공간과 개인적 자유가 주어지는 것이 놀랍다고 생각하지 않습니다. 예를 들어 ① 상사의 사무실에 들어가기 전에는 문을 두드리지만, 사무실 구역은 주저하지 않고 걸어 들어갑니다. 그리고 우리는 아마도 회사의 사장이 조그만 사무실에서 일을 한다거나 주의가 산만해지는 어딘가에서 일하는 것을 알게 되면 상당히 놀라게 될 것입니다. 이와 마찬가지로, 많은 학교에서 ② 교사들은 개인용 사무실, 식당, 심지어 화장실까지 있지만, 학생들은 그러한 특별 장소들이 없습니다. ③ 연예계에서 스타들은 개인 분장실이나 개인 트레일러를 제공받습니다. 이러한 곳들은 그들의 큰 공연을 위해 편안히 준비할 수 있는 곳들입니다. 군대에서도 이런 관련성을 쉽게 찾아볼 수 있는데, 신병들은 사실상 서로 엉겨 붙어 자지만, ④ 장군들은 보통 개인 주택을 제공받습니다.

어휘 **bet** 틀림없다; 돈을 걸다 / **indicator** 지표 / **status** 지위, 신분 / **privacy** 사적 자유; 사생활 / **distraction** (주의) 집중을 방해하는 것 / **show business** 연예계 / **dressing room** 분장실, 탈의실 / **recruit** 신병; 신입 사원 / **practically** 사실상, 거의; 실용적으로 / **general** (군대의) 대장, 장군 / **housing** 주택 | 선택지 어휘 | **hierarchy** 위계, 계층[계급]

01. ③ 02. ③ 03. ④ 04. ③ 05. ③ 06. ③ 07. ② 08. ④ 09. ④ 10. ③
11. ⑤ 12. ③ 13. ① 14. ② 15. ⑤ 16. ③ 17. ④

01 화자가 하는 말의 목적 | ③

▶ 독립기념일에 공식적인 불꽃놀이를 즐기는 게 가장 좋지만 가정에서 하려면 허가받은 상점에서 합법적인 제품을 구입하고, 점화 시 보안경을 쓰고, 아이들에게 주지 말라고 하는 등의 안전 수칙들을 나열하고 있다.

W: The Fourth of July is coming. It's common for families and friends to **get together to celebrate** the day. You can watch fireworks in your backyard on this day. There will be a public firework display near your home and it's the best way to enjoy the fireworks. Why? Every year, hundreds of fires are caused by home fireworks on the Fourth of July. If you want to **create your own fireworks** in your backyard, make sure you select legal "consumer" fireworks from a licensed store. It's also important to wear safety glasses when igniting fireworks. Never give fireworks to young children even if they are only sparklers and if an adult is nearby. **Keep your family safe** and make it a memorable Fourth of July this year.

여: 독립기념일이 다가오고 있습니다. 그날을 축하하기 위해 가족과 친구들이 흔히들 함께 모입니다. 여러분은 이날에 뒷마당에서 불꽃놀이를 볼 수 있습니다. 여러분의 집 근처에서 보이는 공식적인 불꽃놀이가 있을 것이고 그것이 불꽃놀이를 즐기는 가장 좋은 방법입니다. 왜냐고요? 매년 수백 건의 화재가 독립기념일에 가정 불꽃놀이에서 발생합니다. 여러분이 여러분의 뒷마당에서 자신만의 불꽃놀이를 해보려고 한다면 반드시 허가받은 상점에서 합법적인 '소비자용' 폭죽을 선택해야 합니다. 또한 폭죽을 점화할 때 보호 안경을 쓰는 것이 중요합니다. 단지 작은 폭죽이고 어른이 근처에 있다고 해도 어린아이들에게 절대 폭죽을 주지 마십시오. 가족을 안전하게 지켜 올해 독립기념일을 추억하게 하십시오.

어휘 **Fourth of July** 7월 4일 (미국 독립 선언 기념일), 독립기념일 / **firework** 불꽃놀이, 폭죽 / **firework display** 불꽃놀이 / **legal** 합법의 / **consumer** 소비자 / **licensed** 허가를 받은 / **safety glasses** 보안경 / **ignite** 점화하다, 불을 붙이다 / **sparkler** (손에 들고 터뜨리는 작은) 폭죽 / **memorable** 기억할 만한, 인상적인

02 의견 | ③

▶ 남자는 아이에게 충분한 금액의 용돈을 주고 그것을 스스로 관리하게 하는 것이 아이의 금전 개념을 길러주어 장기적으로 좋을 것이라고 생각한다.

W: Oliver, does your son receive an allowance?
M: Of course. Why?
W: Actually, I'm wondering about **how much money would be appropriate** as an allowance for my daughter.
M: Well, in my case, I give my son $20 every Monday.
W: Don't you think $20 a week is too much for a teenage boy?
M: **It might seem like a lot**, but he usually takes care of all his needs with that money.
W: So, you never give him extra when he asks?
M: Right. I want my son to learn the value of money **as he gets older**.
W: I see. That does seem like a good way for him to learn to manage money.
M: Hopefully, it will be better for him in the long run.
W: That's reasonable. Thanks for the advice.

여: Oliver, 당신 아들은 용돈을 받나요?
남: 물론이죠. 왜요?
여: 실은 딸아이에게 줄 용돈으로 얼마가 적당한지 궁금해서요.
남: 글쎄요, 제 경우에는 매주 월요일에 아들에게 20달러를 줘요.
여: 십 대 남자아이에게 한 주에 20달러는 너무 많다고 생각하지 않으세요?
남: 많아 보일 수도 있지만 제 아들은 그 돈으로 자기에게 필요한 모든 걸 다 해결한답니다.
여: 그러면 아들이 더 달라고 요청해도 절대로 주지 않나요?
남: 네. 저는 아들이 자라면서 돈의 가치를 터득했으면 하거든요.
여: 그렇군요. 그 아이가 돈 관리하는 법을 배우기에 정말 좋은 방법인 것 같아요.
남: 바라건대, 결국에는 아들에게 더 좋을 거예요.
여: 일리 있는 얘기예요. 조언 고마워요.

어휘 **allowance** 용돈; 허용량 / **appropriate** 적절한 / **hopefully** 바라건대; 희망을 갖고 / **in the long run** 결국에는 / **reasonable** 타당한, 합리적인

03 관계 | ④

▶ 여자는 저택에 관해 설명을 하고 다음 일정을 안내하고 있으며, 남자는 여자에게 저택 관련 질문들을 하고 있다. 이로 미루어 보아 여행 안내인과 여행객의 대화임을 알 수 있다.

W: Could everyone please follow me?
M: Excuse me, I didn't hear. When was this residence built?
W: It was built in 1847.
M: And you said it was built for some of the King's family to live in.
W: That's right.
M: It's very beautiful. Can **I go look at that end of the building**?
W: No, I'm sorry. This palace **does not allow people to walk around freely**.
M: OK, I understand.
W: Thank you. We're going to walk to the Palace's Secret Garden now. After the Secret Garden **our last stop will be** a small museum detailing the history of the palace.
M: Oh? So I can learn more about the palace in the museum.
W: Yes, and you can even buy a book detailing the palace's history.
M: Good.

여: 모두 저를 따라오시겠어요?
남: 죄송하지만 못 들었어요. 이 저택이 언제 지어졌다고요?
여: 1847년에 세워졌어요.
남: 그리고 왕실 가족이 살기 위해서 지었다고 하셨죠?
여: 맞습니다.
남: 아주 아름답네요. 건물의 저 끝쪽에 가서 봐도 되나요?
여: 죄송하지만 안 됩니다. 이 궁전은 방문객들이 마음대로 돌아다닐 수 없습니다.
남: 알겠습니다. 이해해요.
여: 감사합니다. 이제 궁전의 비원으로 걸어갈 거예요. 비원을 돌아본 뒤 우리가 마지막으로 둘러볼 곳은 궁전의 역사를 상세히 보여주는 작은 박물관이 될 것입니다.
남: 아? 그럼 박물관에서 궁전에 대해 더 많이 알 수 있겠네요.
여: 네, 그리고 궁전의 역사를 상세히 설명하는 책을 구매하실 수도 있습니다.
남: 좋아요.

어휘 **residence** 저택, 주택 / **palace** 궁전; 왕실; 대저택 / **detail** 상술하다; 세부사항

04 그림 불일치 | ③

▶ 남자는 오른쪽 원 안에 새가 있다고 했다.

M: Amy, do you have time now? I'd like to show you **the first draft of the book design**.
W: Sure, I'm free. *[pause]* Oh, you put the title "Changing Seasons" on the top. That's nice.
M: Yes, **I set it in** Gothic type to make it simple and powerful.
W: Good idea. I also like the two round circles in the middle.
M: I wanted to show what this book is about, so I put an important object in each circle.
W: That's an excellent idea. **The tree in the left circle** reminds me of the apple tree in the story.
M: That's right. And the bird in the right circle is the one that escapes from the cage.
W: I see. And you put the author's picture **on the bottom left with his name beside it**. That's a good way to highlight such a famous author.
M: Thanks.

남: Amy, 지금 시간 있어요? 북디자인 초안을 보여주려고요.
여: 네, 시간 돼요. *[잠시 후]* 오, 제목 'Changing Seasons'를 맨 위에 넣었네요. 좋아요.
남: 네, 심플하고 강한 느낌을 주려고 고딕체를 썼어요.
여: 좋은 생각이에요. 중간에 있는 두 개의 둥근 원도 좋네요.
남: 이 책이 무엇에 관한 것인지 보여주고 싶어서 각 원에 중요한 사물을 넣었죠.
여: 훌륭해요. 왼쪽 원에 있는 나무는 이야기 속에 나오는 사과나무를 연상하게 하네요.

남: 맞아요. 그리고 오른쪽 원에 있는 새는 새장을 탈출한 그 새에요.
여: 그렇군요. 왼쪽 밑에 저자의 사진을 넣고 그 옆에 이름을 넣었네요. 그렇게 유명한 작가를 강조할 수 있는 좋은 방법이에요.
남: 고마워요.

어휘 **draft** 초안 / **remind A of B** A에게 B를 생각나게 하다 / **cage** 새장 / **highlight** 강조하다

05 추후 행동 | ③

▶ 남자는 교과서를 잃어버린 여자를 위해, 교과서를 가지고 있지만 더 이상 필요하지 않은 친구에게 빌려줄 수 있는지 전화를 걸어 물어봐 주겠다고 했다.

[Phone rings.]
W: This is Linda speaking.
M: Hey, Linda. It's Jason. **Have you started studying** for your philosophy exam?
W: No, not yet.
M: But the exam is in two days!
W: I know, but **I've misplaced my textbook**. I've looked everywhere for it. I even went to the bookstore to purchase a new one, but they're all sold out.
M: Oh no. Do you at least want **to make copies from mine**?
W: It would be great if I could.
M: Actually, I have a better idea. A friend of mine has the textbook. He might be able to lend it to you.
W: **Are you sure** he doesn't need it?
M: Yes, he took the class last semester. I'll let you know immediately after I call and ask him.
W: Thanks a million. You're a lifesaver.

[전화벨이 울린다.]
여: Linda입니다.
남: 저기, Linda. 나 Jason이야. 철학 시험 공부 시작했니?
여: 아니, 아직 안 했어.
남: 하지만 시험이 이틀 후야!
여: 알아, 그렇지만 교과서를 잘못 두어 잃어버렸거든. 다 찾아봤어. 새것을 사려고 서점에 가기까지 했는데, 교과서가 다 팔려버렸어.
남: 오, 저런. 내 교과서라도 복사해 줄까?
여: 그럴 수 있다면 좋겠어.
남: 사실 내게 더 좋은 생각이 있어. 내 친구 한 명이 그 교과서를 가지고 있는데, 그 애가 네게 교과서를 빌려줄 수 있을지도 몰라.
여: 그 애가 교과서가 필요 없는 게 확실해?
남: 응, 그 애는 지난 학기에 그 수업을 들었거든. 내가 친구에게 전화해서 물어보고 바로 네게 알려줄게.
여: 정말 고마워. 넌 생명의 은인이야.

어휘 **misplace** ~을 잘못 두어 잃어버리다 / **sold out** 다 팔린, 품절의 / **lifesaver** 목숨을 구해주는 것, 곤경에서 구해주는 것[사람]

06 금액 | ③

▶ 극장표가 성인은 한 장에 12달러, 어린이는 8달러인데, 각각 2장씩 필요하므로 합계는 40달러이다. 여자의 신용카드로 10퍼센트 할인을 받을 수 있으므로 지불할 금액은 36달러이다.

W: Let's take the kids and go see *Koala 2* this Saturday afternoon.
M: There is a sequel to *Koala*?
W: Yes, you and the kids loved the first one. **Let's book the tickets** on the Internet now.
M: *[pause]* OK. **So we need two adult tickets**. Click there. It shows the price, $12 per ticket.
W: And three tickets for the children.
M: No, only Linda and Lisa can come. Derek is busy on Saturday afternoon. He is going to a birthday party for a friend.
W: OK. **Let me click here**. Tickets for the children are $8 each. Wow! That's still expensive for children.
M: Yes, it's only a 30 percent discount from the adult price. But, honey, don't forget you'll get a 10 percent discount with your credit card.
W: Good!

여: 이번 주 토요일 오후에 아이들을 데리고 〈코알라 2〉를 보러 갑시다.
남: 〈코알라〉의 속편이 있나요?
여: 네, 당신과 아이들이 첫 번째 편을 아주 좋아했잖아요. 지금 인터넷으로 표를 예매합시다.
남: *[잠시 후]* 자, 그럼 성인 표 2장이 필요하죠. 저기를 클릭해요. 가격을 보여주네요. 한 장에 12달러예요.
여: 그리고 아이들 표 3장이요.
남: 아뇨, Linda와 Lisa만 갈 수 있어요. Derek은 토요일 오후에 바빠요. 친구 생일 파티에 갈 예정이거든요.
여: 알겠어요. 여기를 클릭할게요. 어린이 표는 각각 8달러예요. 와! 어린이용인데도 비싸군요.
남: 네, 성인 가격에서 겨우 30퍼센트 할인되네요. 그렇지만 여보, 당신 신용카드로 10퍼센트 할인받을 거라는 것을 잊지 마요.
여: 잘됐어요!

어휘 **sequel** (책, 영화의) 속편, 후편 / **discount** 할인; 할인하다

07 이유 | ②

▶ 여자가 남자에게 오늘 저녁 식사를 대접하겠다고 하고 예약을 하려고 했지만 당일 예약을 받지 않아 못 가게 되었다.

W: Do you have any plans this evening, Bob?
M: No, I don't have anything planned. Why?
W: I want to **take you out to dinner**. You always treat me so it's time for me to treat you for once.
M: You really don't have to.
W: I insist. There's a restaurant that recently got great reviews. I heard it's amazing. It's called Bluehill.
M: Oh, I've heard about that place. I've been wanting to go, too. But I hope their prices are not too high.
W: Don't worry about it! Remember, I'm paying tonight.
M: Thank you so much, Laura! Do you know **where the exact location is**?
W: Let me check my phone to find their exact location. It's not very far. I'll make a reservation. Oh, dear!
M: What's wrong?
W: The website says same-day reservations **are not accepted**. I should have made the reservation yesterday.
M: Well, it's totally fine. We can go another time.

여: 오늘 저녁에 무슨 계획 있나요, Bob?
남: 아니오, 어떤 계획도 없어요. 왜요?
여: 저녁 식사에 모시고 싶어서요. 항상 사주셔서 이번에는 제가 대접해드릴 때예요.
남: 정말 그럴 필요 없어요.
여: 그렇게 해요. 요즘 평이 좋은 식당이 있어요. 굉장하다고 들었어요. Bluehill이라고 해요.
남: 아, 그곳에 대해 들었어요. 나도 가고 싶었어요. 하지만 가격이 너무 비싸지 않기를 바라요.
여: 그건 걱정 말아요! 오늘 밤은 내가 낼 거라는 걸 기억하세요.
남: 정말 고마워요, Laura! 정확한 장소가 어딘지 알아요?
여: 정확한 장소를 찾기 위해 휴대폰으로 확인해볼게요. 그렇게 멀지 않아요. 내가 예약을 할게요. 아, 이런!
남: 뭐가 잘못되었나요?
여: 당일 예약은 안 받는다고 웹사이트에 나와 있네요. 어제 예약을 했어야 했는데.
남: 음, 정말 괜찮아요. 다른 때 가죠.

어휘 **treat** 대접하다 / **for once** 이번에는 / **insist** 강력히 요구하다[주장하다] / **review** 평가, 비평 / **exact** 정확한 / **reservation** 예약 / **accept** 받아들이다

08 언급하지 않은 것 | ④

▶ 해석 참조

W: Please have a seat, Jim.
M: Okay. Is there a problem?
W: Not at all. In fact, I've decided to make you a team leader.
M: That's great! I can already think of several talented individuals I'd like to work with.
W: The skills of the team members are **the first consideration as a team leader**. But a successful team must also work together.
M: I see. So, they should have a common goal and personalities **that work well together**?
W: Exactly. A team also needs the right resources to be successful.
M: I'll do my best to provide them with everything they need.
W: **I trust that you will**. Finally, it's important for a team to feel effective.
M: Then, I should give them some freedom and power to make their own decisions?

W: I think you've got it. You're going to be great.

여: Jim, 앉으세요.
남: 네. 문제가 있나요?
여: 전혀요. 실은 당신을 팀 리더로 결정했어요.
남: 굉장한 소식이네요! 저는 벌써 제가 같이 일하고 싶은 재능 있는 사람들 몇 명을 생각해낼 수 있어요.
여: 팀 리더로서 팀원들의 기술은 첫 번째 고려 사항이죠. 하지만 성공적인 팀은 또 함께 일을 해야만 합니다.
남: 알겠습니다. 그래서 공동의 목표를 가지고(① 공동의 목표) 함께 일을 잘하는 성격(② 팀원 간의 화합력)을 가지고 있어야 하는 거죠?
여: 정확합니다. 팀은 또한 성공하기 위해 적절한 자원이 필요하죠(③ 적절한 자원).
남: 팀원들이 필요한 모든 것을 제공하기 위해 최선을 다하겠습니다.
여: 당신은 그럴 거라고 믿어요. 마지막으로, 팀이 유능하다고 느끼게 하는 것이 중요합니다.
남: 그렇다면 팀원들에게 스스로 결정할 수 있는 자유와 권한(⑤ 팀원의 의사 결정 권한)을 주어야겠네요?
여: 잘 이해하신 것 같네요. 당신은 훌륭히 해내겠는데요.

어휘 **talented** (타고난) 재능이 있는 / **consideration** 고려 (사항) / **resource** 자원

09 내용 불일치 | ④

▶ 보관할 때는 최대한 공기가 거의 없는 채로 비닐봉지에 넣으라고 했다.

M: Kale, a vegetable with green or purple leaves, is a memory-enhancing food, **along with salmon**, tuna, and spinach. It is a relative of the wild cabbage and comes in several varieties, **all of which differ in taste**, texture, and appearance. Originally from Asia Minor, it was brought to Europe around 600 B.C. Kale is available throughout the year, although it is most widely available during its peak, from the middle of winter through the beginning of spring. **When buying kale**, it's wise to choose ones with smaller-sized leaves since these tend to have a milder flavor. To store kale, place it in a plastic bag **with as little air as possible**. It will keep for up to 5 days but will grow increasingly bitter as the days pass.

남: 케일은 녹색 또는 자주색 잎이 있는 채소인데, 연어, 참치 그리고 시금치와 함께 기억력을 높이는 음식입니다. 이것은 양배추와 동류이며 여러 품종으로 나오는데, 이 모든 종류가 맛, 질감, 외양이 다릅니다. 원래 소아시아에서 왔는데, 기원전 600년경에 유럽으로 전해졌습니다. 케일은 제철인 한겨울부터 초봄까지 가장 많이 먹을 수 있긴 하지만, 일 년 내내 먹을 수 있습니다. 케일을 살 때는, 잎이 더 작은 것을 고르는 것이 현명한데, 맛이 더 부드러운 경향이 있기 때문입니다. 케일을 보관하기 위해서는, 가능한 한 공기가 거의 없는 채로 비닐봉지에 넣으십시오. 이렇게 하는 것은 5일까지 보관이 되겠지만, 날이 지날수록 쓴 맛이 점점 더 강해질 것입니다.

어휘 **enhance** 높이다, 향상하다 / **relative** 동류; 친척; 비교상의 / **variety** (식물 등의) 품종; 다양성 / **texture** 질감; (직물의) 감촉 / **bitter** (맛이) 쓴; 격렬한; 쓰라린

10 도표 이해 | ③

▶ 코트 걸이는 현관에 놓기 위해 180cm 이하여야 하고, 무료 배송을 받기 위해 8kg 미만의 무게여야 한다. 소재 중에서 강하지 않고 긁힘에 취약한 나무는 제외하고 남은 두 항목 중 조금 더 비싼 것으로 선택한다고 하였다.

W: Honey, do you remember talking about getting a coat rack for the hallway?
M: Sure, I remember. Why? **Did you find one you like**?
W: There are a few in this catalog. Why don't you take a look?
M: Let me see.... The largest one looks nice. But would it fit in our hall?
W: No, I measured this morning, and 180 cm is the largest we can get.
M: That's too bad. Oh, it says we can get free shipping on orders under 8 kg. **Let's take advantage of that**.
W: Okay. What about the material? Wood looks nice, don't you think?
M: Of course, but it's not very strong, and it's susceptible to scratches.
W: That leaves two, and I'm afraid **the cheaper one would break easily**.
M: That's a good point. Let's get the more expensive one of the two.
W: Great. I'll place the order this afternoon.

여: 여보, 현관에 놓을 코트 걸이를 사는 것에 대해 얘기했던 것 기억나요?
남: 그럼요, 기억나요. 왜요? 맘에 드는 것 찾았어요?
여: 이 카탈로그에 몇 개가 있어요. 한번 보는 게 어때요?
남: 봅시다…. 가장 큰 것이 멋져 보이네요. 하지만 이게 현관에 맞을까요?
여: 아뇨, 아침에 (높이를) 쟀는데, 180cm가 우리가 살 수 있는 가장 큰 것이에요.
남: 안타깝네요. 아, 8kg 미만의 주문에 대해서는 배송료가 무료라고 하네요. 그것을 이용합시다.
여: 그래요. 소재는 어떤가요? 나무가 괜찮아 보이는데, 그렇지 않나요?
남: 물론이죠. 하지만 나무는 그다지 강하지 않고 긁힘에 취약해요.
여: 그러면 두 개가 남는데, 더 저렴한 것은 쉽게 부러질 것 같아요.
남: 좋은 지적이에요. 둘 중 더 비싼 것으로 구매합시다.
여: 그래요. 오후에 주문할게요.

어휘 **coat rack** 코트 걸이 / **hallway** 현관; 복도(= hall) / **fit in** ~에 맞다 / **measure** 재다, 측정하다 / **shipping** 배송; 해상 운송; 선박 / **take advantage of** ~을 이용하다[기회로 활용하다] / **material** 소재, 재료; 자료; 물질적인 / **be susceptible to A** A에 취약하다[민감하다] / **leave** 남기다; 떠나다; 그만두다 / **place an order** 주문하다

11 짧은 대화에 이어질 응답 | ⑤

▶ Jessica와 함께하기로 한 것이 무엇인지를 묻는 것이므로 이에 가장 적절한 응답을 고른다. ⑤는 구체적인 계획을 응답한 것은 아니지만 귀가 시간에 따라 계획이 달라진다는 것으로서 자연스런 대화 상황에서 얼마든지 나올 수 있는 내용이다. ④는 Jessica만의 계획이므로 적절치 않다.

① Jessica는 이미 미술관에 있어.
② 난 새로운 전시품들을 정말 보고 싶어.
③ 우리 셋이 함께 갈 수 있다고 생각해.
④ 그녀는 오늘 밤에 그림을 완성하기를 바라고 있어.
⑤ 그건 그녀가 언제 집에 가야 하는지에 달려 있어.

M: I'm going to an art museum after school. **Want to join me**?
W: I would, but I **am going to do something** with Jessica.
M: That's no problem. By the way, what are you going to do?
W: ______________________________

남: 나는 방과 후에 미술관에 갈 거야. 나와 같이 가고 싶니?
여: 그러고 싶지만, Jessica와 뭔가를 할 거라서.
남: 괜찮아. 그런데, 너희 뭘 하려고 하니?
여: ______________________________

어휘 **by the way** 그런데 《대화에서 화제를 바꿀 때 씀》

12 짧은 대화에 이어질 응답 | ③

▶ 영화를 보기 전에 대화하는 상황이다. 영화에서 주연 배우가 훌륭한 연기를 했고 원작 소설에 대한 관심까지 불러일으켰다는 이야기를 듣고 남자가 할 수 있는 가장 적절한 응답을 고른다. ④는 영화를 이미 본 뒤에 할 수 있는 말이다.

① 나도 연기에 관심 있어.
② 맞아. 네 글은 믿어지지 않을 정도야.
③ 아, 이제 훨씬 더 기대되는걸.
④ 좋아. 한 번 더 보자.
⑤ 넌 늘 내 기대를 충족시키는구나.

W: You are **expecting a lot** from this movie, aren't you?
M: Yes. I heard the main actor did an excellent job.
W: Right. What's more, the movie **has sparked interest** in the original novel.
M: ______________________________

여: 이 영화를 많이 기대하고 있구나, 그렇지?
남: 응. 주연 배우가 연기를 굉장히 잘했다고 들었어.
여: 맞아. 게다가, 이 영화는 원작 소설에 대한 관심을 불러일으켰어.
남: ______________________________

어휘 **spark** 촉발시키다; 불꽃을 일으키다 | 선택지 어휘 | **incredible** 믿을 수 없는, (너무 좋거나 커서) 믿어지지 않을 정도인 / **meet A's expectations** A의 기대에 부응하다; A의 예상대로 되다

13 긴 대화에 이어질 응답 | ①

▶ 미국에서는 월(月)부터 써야 하므로 여자는 자신의 지원서를 고쳐서 6(월)을 10(일)보다 앞에 쓸 것이다.

① 그럼 바꿔서 6자를 먼저 쓸게요.
② 여기에 제 생년월일을 적나요?
③ 그럼 이 양식 작성을 마쳤어요.
④ 저와 함께 문제를 해결하실래요?
⑤ 문제는 제가 미국에서 태어나지 않았다는 거예요.

M: **Have you finished filling out** the application?
W: Actually, I have a question.
M: Yes?
W: Here it says, "Date of birth." I'm not sure **I filled it out correctly**. I wrote down the day, the month, and then the year.
M: No, write down the month, the day, and then the year.
W: Oh? On this form I wrote down 10/6/1992 because I was born on the 10th of June in 1992.
M: In America we always put the month first.
W: Really? In my country **we always put the day first**.
M: Not here. People here will think you were born in October.
W: ______________________________

남: 지원서를 다 작성하셨습니까?
여: 사실, 질문이 있어요.
남: 네?
여: 여기에 '생년월일'이라고 적혀 있는데요. 제대로 작성했는지 모르겠어요. 저는 일, 월, 그리고 연도의 순으로 썼어요.
남: 안 됩니다. 월, 일, 연도의 순으로 쓰셔야 해요.
여: 네? 제가 1992년 6월 10일에 태어나서 이 신청 용지에 10/6/1992라고 적었어요.
남: 미국에서는 월(月)을 항상 먼저 적어요.
여: 그래요? 우리나라에서는 일(日)을 항상 먼저 쓰거든요.
남: 여기는 그렇지 않아요. 이곳 사람들은 당신이 10월에 태어났다고 생각할 거예요.
여: ______________________________

어휘 **fill out** 용지에 기입하다 / **application** 지원(서); 적용 / **form** 문서 양식, 신청 용지

14 긴 대화에 이어질 응답 | ②

▶ 여자가 James의 전화번호를 몰라서 전화를 걸 수 없는 상황이므로 남자는 James의 번호를 가르쳐 주려고 할 것이다.

① 제 전화번호는 3486-9274입니다.
② 전화기 옆에 있는 메모지에 적혀 있어요.
③ 아, 그러실 필요 없어요. 과자는 충분하거든요.
④ 그의 주소는 Ocean시 Coastal Highway 57번지입니다.
⑤ 감사합니다. 마실 것은 저기 냉장고 안에 있어요.

[Knock, knock, knock.] [Door opens.]
W: Hi, Larry.
M: Hi, Cecilia. Come on in. You're a little late. The game **is about to start**.
W: Sorry. Thanks for inviting me to watch the soccer game at your house. Your house is nice.
M: Thank you. We usually all relax and watch TV there in the living room.
W: **Is that where we are going to watch** the game?
M: Yes. By the way, do you know when James will be here?
W: **He said he'd come** as quickly as he could. Oh.... I've bought potato chips and other snacks for everyone.
M: Thanks. I'll go into the kitchen and get some drinks. Let me take your jacket. And please have a seat.
W: **Let me help you with the drinks**.
M: It's OK. Would you call and tell James to hurry up?
W: But I don't have my cell phone, so I don't know his number.
M: ______________________________

[똑, 똑, 똑.] [문이 열린다.]
여: 안녕하세요, Larry.
남: 안녕하세요, Cecilia. 들어오세요. 좀 늦으셨네요. 경기가 막 시작하려고 해요.
여: 죄송해요. 축구를 보자고 집으로 초대해 주셔서 감사해요. 집이 좋네요.
남: 고마워요. 우리는 주로 모두 거실에서 쉬면서 TV를 본답니다.
여: 우리가 거기에서 경기를 볼 건가요?
남: 네. 그런데 James는 언제 올지 아세요?
여: 가능한 한 빨리 오겠다고 했어요. 아…. 함께 먹으려고 감자칩과 과자를 사 왔어요.
남: 고마워요. 부엌에 가서 마실 것을 내올게요. 재킷을 저에게 주시고 앉으세요.
여: 음료 내오는 것을 도울게요.
남: 괜찮아요. James에게 빨리 오라고 전화해 주실래요?
여: 하지만 저는 휴대폰이 없어서 그의 전화번호를 몰라요.
남: ______________________________

어휘 **be about to-v** 막 v하려고 하다 | 선택지 어휘 | **fridge** 냉장고

15 상황에 적절한 말 | ⑤

▶ 최근 너무 바쁜 Mike가 도서관 책을 반납할 시간이 없어 Nick이 도와주고 싶어 하는 상황이다.

① 책 가져가는 것을 잊지 마.
② 빵집에서 네가 하는 일을 도와주고 싶어.
③ 너는 한꺼번에 너무 많은 일을 하려고 하는 것 같아.
④ 걱정하지 마. 내가 네 도서관 벌금을 내줄게.
⑤ 내가 도서관에 이 책들을 반납해 주길 바라니?

W: Nick is a college student. He shares an apartment with two other students. One of the students, Mike, **has been very stressed out lately**. Mike has several reports to finish this week. He also has two final exams to take. **On top of that**, he works part time at a small bakery. Today, Nick notices some of Mike's library books in the living room. **He sees that the books are due** today. Nick mentions this to Mike, but Mike says he's far too busy. He says that he only has a few minutes **before his shift starts** at the bakery. Nick understands Mike's situation and he wants to help Mike avoid any library fines. In this situation, what would Nick most likely say to Mike?

여: Nick은 대학생이다. 그는 두 명의 다른 학생들과 아파트를 같이 쓴다. 학생들 중 한 명인 Mike는 최근 매우 스트레스를 받고 있다. Mike는 이번 주에 끝내야 할 몇 개의 리포트가 있다. 그는 또한 치러야 할 기말 시험이 두 개 있다. 게다가, 그는 자그마한 빵집에서 아르바이트를 하고 있다. 오늘, Nick은 Mike가 도서관에서 빌린 책 몇 권이 거실에 있는 것을 발견한다. 그는 그 책이 오늘이 반납 만기일임을 알고 있다. Nick은 이를 Mike에게 말하지만, Mike는 자신이 정말 너무 바쁘다고 한다. Mike는 빵집의 교대 시간 시작이 몇 분 밖에 남지 않았다고 말한다. Nick은 Mike의 상황을 이해하고 그가 도서관 벌금을 피하도록 돕고 싶다. 이러한 상황에서 Nick이 Mike에게 할 말로 가장 적절한 것은 무엇인가?

어휘 **stress out** 스트레스를 주다 / **on top of that** 게다가; 그 위에 / **due** 지불[반납] 기일이 된; 예정된 / **shift** 교대근무; 변화; 이동하다

16~17 세트 문항 | 16. ③ 17. ④

▶ 16. 바나나, 쌀, 허브차 등을 열거하면서 배탈을 완화시키는 데 좋은 음식을 소개하고 있다.

① 배탈의 주요 원인
② 바나나와 쌀의 영양적 가치
③ 배탈을 완화할 수 있는 여러 가지 음식들
④ 아플 때 먹는 최고의 음식과 최악의 음식
⑤ 식중독이 즉시 치료되어야 하는 이유

▶ 17. 해석 참조

M: Do you have an upset stomach? Sadly, your doctor may say that the best treatment is simply to wait until the symptoms disappear. However, choosing the right foods may **make that waiting period a bit easier**. For example, bananas have been used for generations to soothe upset stomachs. They contain kalium, which you may need if you lost too much water from vomiting. Their sugars will also provide much needed calories at a time when you're probably not eating enough. Rice is another soothing food **that helps to ease digestion**. In fact, potatoes or oats are also good. **These foods don't sit in the stomach** for a long time and they don't push your body to produce more acid. If you can't eat anything solid, herbal teas without caffeine can also help a troubled stomach. Chamomile is a favorite, but any herbal tea **is a great way to get liquid** into your body. With the right choices and plenty of rest, you'll be feeling better in no time at all.

남: 배탈이 나셨나요? 안타깝게도 의사들은 단순히 증상이 사라질 때까지 기다리는 것이 가장 좋은 치료법이라고 할 겁니다. 그러나 올바른 음식을 선택하면 기다리는 시간을 다소 쉽게 만들 수도 있죠. 예를 들어, ① 바나나는 여러 세대를 걸쳐 아픈 위를 가라앉히는 데 이용되어 왔습니다. 그것들(바나나들)에는 칼륨이 들어있는데, 구토로 탈수 증상을 보일 때 필요한 것이지요. 바나나의 당은 또한 제대로 먹지 못할 때 필요한 칼로리를 공급해 줄 것입니다. ② 쌀은 소화가 잘되도록 해주는 또 다른 진정 효과가 있는 음식이고요. 실제로, ③ 감자나 귀리도 좋습니다. 이 음식들은 위장에 오래 머물지 않아서 인체가 위산을 더 만들어내도록 압박하지 않죠. 딱딱한 것을 먹을 수 없다면 카페인이 들어가지 않은 ⑤ 허브차가 탈이 난 위장에 도움을 줄 수도 있습니다. 캐모마일 차가 제일 좋지만 어떤 허브차라도 몸에 수분을 주는 좋은 방법이지요. 올바른 음식들과 충분한 휴식이면 여러분은 금방 좋아지실 거예요.

어휘 **upset stomach** 배탈 / **treatment** 치료(법) / **symptom** 증상 / **soothe** 누그러뜨리다, 완화시키다 / **kalium** 칼륨 / **vomiting** 구토 / **digestion** 소화 / **oat** 귀리 / **acid** 산 / **solid** 딱딱한, 단단한 / **herbal** 허브의, 허브로 만든 / **chamomile** 캐모마일(허브의 일종) / **in no time (at all)** 당장, 지체 없이

01. ②	02. ①	03. ②	04. ③	05. ④	06. ②	07. ③	08. ④	09. ④	10. ④
11. ①	12. ③	13. ③	14. ⑤	15. ④	16. ②	17. ①			

01 화자가 하는 말의 목적 | ②

▶ 스마트폰에 생산적이고 유익한 앱이 많이 있다고 한 뒤, 교육용 앱인 Khan Academy의 특징과 장점을 나열하며 홍보하고 있다.

M: Often parents worry that their children **never stop using their smartphones**. They are concerned that their children play too many games. However, there are **a lot of more productive and beneficial** apps for students on smartphones. One of the best of them is Khan Academy. For kids, Khan Academy teaches simple math, reading, and languages in a fun way using cute animal characters. For high school students, there are more than 10,000 videos and explanations of math, science, economics, history, and so on. Additionally, they can ask teachers questions on the app. The most amazing thing is that it's all free. Download it today! Make your smartphone even smarter with this app. Khan Academy **is available in five languages**.

남: 흔히 부모님들은 자녀들이 스마트폰 사용을 결코 멈추지 않는 것을 걱정합니다. 그들은 자녀들이 너무 많은 게임을 한다고 염려합니다. 그러나 스마트폰에는 학생들을 위한 더 생산적이고 유익한 앱들이 많이 있습니다. 그것들 중 가장 좋은 것 가운데 하나는 Khan Academy입니다. 아이들을 위해 Khan Academy는 간단한 수학과 독해, 그리고 언어를 귀여운 동물 캐릭터를 사용하여 재미있게 가르칩니다. 고등학생을 위해 수학, 과학, 경제, 역사 등의 10,000개가 넘는 동영상과 설명이 있습니다. 게다가 그들은 앱에서 선생님들에게 질문을 할 수 있습니다. 가장 놀라운 것은 이 모든 것이 무료라는 겁니다. 오늘 그것을 내려받으세요! 이 앱으로 여러분의 스마트폰을 훨씬 영리하게 하세요. Khan Academy는 5개의 언어로 이용 가능합니다.

어휘 **productive** 생산적인 / **beneficial** 유익한 / **explanation** 설명(서); 이유

02 의견 | ①

▶ 여자는 에너지 드링크에 해로운 성분이 들어있고, 자주 마시면 위험한 행동과 그릇된 결정을 야기한다고 하였다. 즉, 에너지 드링크의 유해성에 관해 이야기하고 있다.

W: Did you **manage to finish your paper** in time?
M: Barely. I had to stay up all night working on it. I must have had at least four energy drinks.
W: Whoa, you **should stay away from energy drinks** if you can.
M: Why? They have less caffeine than a cup of coffee.
W: That's true for most of them, but they also contain many other harmful ingredients. I heard that some students **have gotten very sick** from them and have even had to go to the hospital.
M: Really? I didn't know that.
W: The news said that kids who regularly consume energy drinks are more likely to engage in risky behavior and make poor life decisions.
M: I only drink them to stay awake, but maybe I should stop.

여: 너 보고서 어떻게든 제시간에 끝냈니?
남: 간신히. 그거 하느라 밤을 새야 했어. 분명 에너지 드링크를 적어도 네 캔은 마셨을 거야.
여: 워, 가능하면 에너지 드링크를 멀리해야 해.
남: 왜? 그건 커피 한 잔보다 카페인이 더 적게 들어있어.
여: 그건 대부분 사실이지만, 거기에는 다른 해로운 성분도 많이 들어있어. 몇몇 학생이 그걸 마시고 많이 아파서 병원까지 가야 했던 적이 있다고 들었어.
남: 정말? 그건 몰랐어.
여: 뉴스에서 에너지 드링크를 자주 마시는 아이들이 위험한 행동에 가담하고 인생 문제에 관해 그릇된 결정을 내릴 가능성이 더 높다고 했어.
남: 난 깨어 있으려고 마실 뿐이지만, 그만 마셔야 할까 봐.

어휘 **barely** 간신히, 겨우 / **ingredient** 성분, 재료 / **regularly** 자주; 규칙적으로 / **consume** 마시다, 먹다; 소모하다 / **engage in A** A에 관여[참여]하다 / **risky** 위험한

03 관계 | ②

▶ 병원에서 밤샘 근무를 하며 환자의 호출에 응답하는 사람(남자)은 간호사이고, 아파서 잠을 못 잤다며 자신의 상태를 설명하는 사람(여자)은 입원 환자이다.

M: Good morning, Miss James, how are you feeling this morning?
W: Not so good. I **found it very difficult to sleep** last night.
M: Sorry to hear that! What was bothering you? We do have a bit of trouble with noise from the ambulances coming and going.
W: No, it wasn't noisy. Perhaps it was **the meal I was served** last night.
M: What did you have?
W: Nothing special; pumpkin soup, steamed rice, some fruit, that's all.
M: Did you have pain in your stomach?
W: Yes, quite a lot actually.
M: Well, that's to be expected after your operation. You know one of us **is on duty all night**; whenever you're in pain you should press the button next to your bed.
W: I don't want to cause you any trouble.
M: Miss James! **That's what we're here for**!

남: 좋은 아침이에요, James 양. 오늘 아침에는 몸이 좀 어때요?
여: 별로예요. 어젯밤에 잠자기가 아주 힘들었어요.
남: 잠을 못 잤다니 유감이에요! 뭐가 불편하셨어요? 오가는 구급차 소리 때문에 문제가 좀 있긴 해요.
여: 아니에요, 그건 시끄럽지 않았어요. 아마 어젯밤에 제공된 식사가 문제인 것 같았어요.
남: 무엇을 드셨죠?
여: 특별한 건 없었어요. 호박죽, 밥, 과일 조금이 전부예요.
남: 복통이 있었나요?
여: 네, 실은 아주 많이 아팠어요.
남: 음, 그것은 수술 후에 있을 수 있는 증상이에요. 아시다시피 저희 중 한 명은 밤새도록 근무를 하니, 아플 때는 언제나 침대 옆에 있는 버튼을 누르세요.
여: 어떤 불편도 끼치고 싶지 않아서요.
남: James 양! 그것이 저희가 여기에 있는 이유예요!

어휘 **on duty** 근무 중인

04 그림 불일치 | ③

▶ 남자는 스웨터를 배낭 안에 두었다고 말했다.

W: Have you finished packing for the trip yet, Mike?
M: I'm working on it now, Mom.
W: I washed the sneakers you asked for and **put them beside the bed**.
M: Yes, I saw them. Thanks, Mom.
W: No problem. Will you bring a backpack or a suitcase?
M: We might go hiking on the second day, so it will be **better to bring a backpack**. It's on the bed.
W: Okay. You know, the weather forecast said it'll be freezing. Why don't you bring **a couple of sweaters**?
M: I already put them in my backpack.
W: Okay. Please make sure to bring your baseball cap, also.
M: I **put it on the table** so that I'll remember to wear it tomorrow.
W: Well done. By the way, have you seen the dog? I haven't seen him all day.
M: He's right here, under the table. I think he wants to follow me.

여: 여행 짐 다 쌌니, Mike?
남: 지금 하고 있어요, 엄마.
여: 네가 부탁한 운동화 빨아서 침대 옆에 뒀다.
남: 네, 봤어요. 고마워요, 엄마.
여: 아니야. 배낭 가져갈 거니, 아님 여행 가방 가져갈 거니?
남: 두 번째 날 하이킹 갈지 모르니까 배낭 가져가는 게 나을 거 같아요. 침대 위에 있어요.
여: 그래, 저기, 일기예보에 많이 추울 거라던데. 스웨터 두 벌 정도 가져가지 그러니?
남: 배낭 안에 이미 넣어뒀어요.
여: 그래. 야구 모자도 꼭 가져가야지.
남: 내일 그거 쓰고 가는 거 잊지 않으려고 탁자 위에 두었어요.
여: 잘했구나. 근데, 개 못 봤니? 하루 종일 보이질 않네.
남: 바로 여기 있어요. 탁자 밑에요. 나를 따라가고 싶어 하는 거 같아요.

어휘 **pack** (짐을) 꾸리다; 묶음[꾸러미] / **work on** ~에 노력을 들이다 / **freezing** 너무나 추운

05 추후 행동 | ④

▶ 딸아이가 아픈 상황에서 부모가 각자 할 일을 나누고 있다. 여자는 식사 준비와 병원 예약을 하고 남자는 약국에서 약을 사 오겠다고 했다.

W: I'm concerned about our daughter, honey. She looks really sick.
M: You're right. She already took some cold medicine, but **she's still getting worse**.
W: I think it's more serious than just a cold. I'd better make a doctor's appointment.
M: Good thinking. Do you want me to do it?
W: That's okay. I'll do it before I prepare her breakfast.
M: Is she feeling well enough to eat? Last night, she went straight to bed after her bath.
W: She needs to eat something, even if it's just a little soup. Also, **could you bring her medicine** from the living room?
M: I don't think there's any left. I'll get some more from the pharmacy.
W: Thank you. I'll **make an appointment** and then make her breakfast while you go to the pharmacy.
M: Sounds good. And don't worry too much. She'll be okay.
W: I hope **she gets better soon**.

여: 우리 딸이 걱정돼요, 여보. 애가 정말 아파 보여요.
남: 맞아요. 아이가 이미 감기약을 먹었지만, 계속 나빠지고 있어요.
여: 그냥 감기보다 더 심각한 것 같아요. 병원에 예약하는 게 낫겠어요.
남: 좋은 생각이에요. 내가 예약할까요?
여: 괜찮아요. 아이가 먹을 아침 식사를 준비하기 전에 내가 할게요.
남: 먹을 수 있을 정도로 괜찮아졌나요? 어젯밤, 목욕 후에 바로 잠자리에 들더군요.
여: 뭐라도 먹어야 해요, 수프 약간이라도요. 그리고 거실에서 아이 약 좀 가져와 줄래요?
남: 약이 남아있는 것 같지 않아요. 내가 약국에서 약을 더 사 올게요.
여: 고마워요. 당신이 약국에 다녀올 동안 나는 (병원을) 예약하고 나서 아침 식사를 준비하고 있을게요.
남: 좋아요. 그리고 너무 걱정하지 말아요. 아이는 괜찮을 거예요.
여: 우리 딸이 곧 호전되길 바라요.

어휘 **concerned** 걱정[염려]하는 / **get worse** (병, 상황 따위가) 나빠지다, 악화되다 (↔ get better (병, 상황 따위가) 호전되다, 좋아지다) / **make an appointment** (진료, 상담 등을) 예약하다 / **straight** 바로, 곧장; 일직선의 / **pharmacy** 약국

06 금액 | ②

▶ 어린이 열 명 단체 티켓 두 장($60×2)과 성인 티켓 네 장($15×4)을 구매했고 10% 추가 할인이 적용되므로 여자가 지불할 금액은 162달러이다.

[Phone rings.]
M: Wonderland Dream Park, Nathan speaking. How may I help you?
W: I'm a kindergarten teacher, and I'd like to bring my class to your amusement park. **How much will it cost**?
M: Tickets for children under 12 are $9 each. Older children and adults can enter for $15.
W: There will be a total of 4 adults and 20 children under the age of 12. Do you **offer group discounts**?
M: We do. You can purchase a pack of 10 child tickets for $60. Likewise, a pack of 10 adult tickets costs $100.
W: In that case, I'll need two 10-packs of children's tickets and **four individual adult tickets**.
M: Great. How would you like to pay?
W: I'll pay by credit card, and I'll use my Smart Shopping card for an additional 10% off.
M: Okay. Great. Is there anything else I can do for you?
W: No, that's all. Thanks.

[전화벨이 울린다.]
남: Wonderland Dream Park의 Nathan입니다. 무엇을 도와드릴까요?
여: 저는 유치원 선생님인데요, 놀이동산에 저희 반 아이들을 데리고 가고 싶습니다. 요금이 얼마나 들까요?
남: 12세 미만 어린이용 티켓은 9달러입니다. 12세 이상 어린이와 성인은 15달러에 입장하실 수 있습니다.
여: 총 네 명의 어른과 12세 미만의 어린이 20명이 있는데요. 단체 할인을 해주시나요?
남: 그렇습니다. 어린이 열 명 단체 티켓을 60달러에 구매하실 수 있습니다. 마찬가지로, 성인 열 명 단체 티켓은 100달러입니다.
여: 그렇다면, 저는 어린이 열 명 단체 티켓 두 장과 성인용 개별 티켓 네 장이 필요하겠네요.
남: 좋습니다. 요금은 어떻게 지불하시겠습니까?
여: 신용카드로 지불할게요. 그리고 Smart Shopping 카드를 사용해서 10% 추가 할인을 받겠습니다.
남: 알겠습니다. 좋습니다. 제가 도와드릴 것이 더 있나요?
여: 아뇨, 그게 다예요. 감사합니다.

어휘 **additional** 추가의

07 이유 | ③

▶ 여자는 기숙사 등록 기간이 아직 남았고 방 크기도 상관하지 않으며 이전 룸메이트도 좋았다고 했다. 다만 기숙사에서 일부 사람들이 시끄러워서 거기서 더 이상 살 수가 없다고 했다.

M: Hi, Madison! **What are you checking out** on the bulletin board?
W: I was looking for an apartment, but the rent is pretty high.
M: Why don't you stay in the dorm, then? **Is the registration closed** already?
W: No, it's due next week.
M: Oh, let me guess. The dorm room is a bit small. Do you want a more spacious room?
W: It's not that. I don't mind the size of the room.
M: You had some trouble with your roommate last semester, right?
W: No, my ex-roommate was a great person. But the people in the dorm make a lot of noise.
M: **I can't deny that**. There are some people having parties and making noise even at midnight.
W: Yeah! They don't mind all the warnings and complaints. I'm a little sensitive to the noise, so I can't live there anymore.
M: I understand.

남: 안녕, Madison! 게시판에서 뭘 살펴보고 있는 거니?
여: 아파트를 찾고 있었는데 임대료가 꽤 비싸네.
남: 그러면 기숙사에서 지내지 그래? 등록이 벌써 끝났니?
여: 아니야, 그건 다음 주까지야.
남: 아, 내가 맞춰볼게. 기숙사 방이 좀 작지. 넌 더 넓은 방을 원하는 거니?
여: 그건 아니야. 난 방 크기는 상관하지 않아.
남: 지난 학기 네 룸메이트하고 문제가 좀 있었구나, 맞지?
여: 아니야, 내 이전 룸메이트는 아주 좋은 사람이었어. 하지만 기숙사에 있는 사람들이 많이 시끄러워.
남: 아니라고 할 수가 없지. 자정에도 파티하면서 시끄러운 사람들이 좀 있지.
여: 그래! 그들은 모든 경고와 항의에도 신경 쓰지 않아. 난 소음에 좀 예민해서 거기서 더 이상 살 수가 없어.
남: 이해해.

어휘 **check out** 살펴보다, 확인하다 / **bulletin board** 게시판 / **dorm**(= dormitory) 기숙사 / **registration** 등록 / **spacious** 넓은 / **deny** 부정하다 / **warning** 경고 / **complaint** 항의, 불평 / **sensitive** 민감한, 예민한

08 언급하지 않은 것 | ④

▶ 해석 참조

M: Hi, Yuna. How's your college search going?
W: Hi, Will. *[pause]* Umm... **I'm pretty confused**, I guess.
M: Yeah, me too. I spent last night reading about the Ivy League schools.
W: Ah, those are eight universities: Brown, Columbia, Cornell, Dartmouth, Harvard, Pennsylvania, Princeton, and Yale.
M: Right. They're located in the northeastern United States. My dad really **wants me to go to** Brown.
W: It's a good school. By the way, do you know why it's called the "Ivy League"?
M: I read that those eight schools form a football league, meaning they play games against one another.
W: Oh, **that makes sense**. And the name of "Ivy" is probably because the buildings are old and covered in ivy.
M: Right, but **the name wasn't officially accepted** until 1954. It's rather recent.

W: Interesting.

남: 안녕, Yuna야. 대학교 알아보는 건 어떻게 돼 가니?
여: 안녕, Will. *[잠시 후]* 음... 난 좀 혼란스러워.
남: 아, 나도 그래. 나는 어젯밤에 Ivy League 학교들에 관한 글을 읽었어.
여: 아, 브라운, 컬럼비아, 코넬, 다트머스, 하버드, 펜실베이니아, 프린스턴, 예일(① 소속 대학) 이 여덟 개 대학이잖아.
남: 맞아. 그 학교들은 미국 북동부(② 위치)에 위치해 있어. 우리 아빠는 내가 브라운대학교에 가길 정말 바라셔.
여: 괜찮은 학교잖아. 그런데, 너는 왜 'Ivy League'라고 불리는지 아니?
남: 난 그 여덟 개 학교가 서로 경기를 치른다는 의미의 축구 리그를 만들었다고 읽었어.
여: 아, 일리가 있네. 그리고 'Ivy'란 이름은 아마 그 학교 건물들이 오래돼서 담쟁이덩굴로 뒤덮여 있기 때문일 거야(③ 이름의 유래).
남: 맞아. 근데 그 이름은 1954년(⑤ 공식 창립연도)이 돼서야 공식적으로 인정되었어. 꽤 최근 일이지.
여: 흥미롭네.

어휘 **ivy** 담쟁이덩굴 / **league** (스포츠 경기의) 리그; 연합, 연맹 / **officially** 공식적으로

09 내용 불일치 | ④

▶ 웹사이트에서 서식을 작성하여 신청할 수 있다.

W: Best Tour, your first choice for traveling Europe, is currently offering a unique "Experience Spain" package. This is a one-week trip to Spain. It visits Madrid and Barcelona, and **has an optional stop** in Toledo. There are several other options as well, so prices vary, but round-trip airfare and hotel accommodations are included. Each city has a choice of two hotels. And if you love to swim, hotels with indoor pools are **available for an additional charge**. To sign up, simply visit our website at www.besttour.com, fill out the form, and then call to confirm with us afterward. Please keep in mind that this package is likely to be extremely popular, so make sure to **sign up at least two weeks in advance** of your trip.

여: 유럽 여행을 위한 최고의 선택인 베스트 투어는 현재 특별한 '스페인 체험' 패키지를 제공하고 있습니다. 이 투어는 일주일 동안의 스페인 여행입니다. 마드리드와 바르셀로나를 방문하고, 톨레도에서 머무는 것을 선택할 수 있습니다. 여러 가지 다른 선택 사항도 있어서 가격이 다양하지만, 왕복 항공료와 호텔 숙박이 포함되어 있습니다. 각 도시에서 두 호텔 중 하나를 선택하실 수 있습니다. 수영하는 것을 좋아하신다면, 실내 수영장이 있는 호텔을 추가 요금을 내고 이용하실 수 있습니다. 신청하시려면, 그저 저희 웹사이트인 www.besttour.com을 방문하셔서 서식을 작성하신 후 저희에게 확인 전화를 해주십시오. 이 패키지가 굉장히 인기 있을 것 같다는 것을 명심하셔서, 여행을 가시기 최소한 2주 전에는 꼭 신청해 주십시오.

어휘 **optional** 선택적인 ***cf.* option** 선택(권) / **round-trip** 왕복 여행의 / **airfare** 항공 요금 / **accommodation** 숙소, 숙박 시설 / **sign up** 참가하다, 가입하다; 등록하다 / **confirm** 사실임을 보여주다[확인해 주다]

10 도표 이해 | ④

▶ 12월에 지원을 마감하고 실내에서 일하며 장학금 혜택이 있는 일자리를 선택할 것이다.

M: Hey, are you still looking for a job?
W: Yeah, but I haven't found anything interesting. Why do you ask?
M: Capilano Suspension Bridge Park is looking for people. Check out this ad.
W: *[pause]* Oh, learning to make repairs would be interesting. But **the deadline has passed**.
M: The others don't close until December. How about sanitation work?
W: Frankly, **I'd rather do indoor work**.
M: I guess you're not willing to clean the grounds then. What are you interested in?
W: Helping a chef sounds a lot better to me.
M: I always enjoy your cooking, but I'm sure the job will be **harder than you think**.
W: Yeah, you're right. So I guess **it's down to two**. Free admission for family members would be nice.
M: True, but a scholarship opportunity might be more valuable.
W: Hmm... I think you're right. I will apply for that one.
M: Good choice.

남: 저기, 너 여전히 일자리를 구하고 있니?
여: 응, 그런데 괜찮은 것을 아직 찾지 못했어. 왜 묻는 거야?
남: Capilano Suspension Bridge 공원에서 사람을 구하고 있거든. 이 광고를 봐.
여: *[잠시 후]* 아, 수리하는 걸 배우면 재밌겠다. 그런데 기한이 지났는걸.
남: 다른 일자리들은 12월에 마감해. 환경 미화 일은 어때?
여: 솔직히, 나는 실내에서 일하고 싶어.
남: 그럼 넌 거리를 청소하고 싶지 않겠구나. 어떤 것에 관심이 있니?
여: 주방 보조가 나에게 훨씬 잘 맞을 거야.
남: 난 늘 네가 만든 요리를 좋아하지만, 그 일은 분명 네가 생각하는 것보다 더 힘들 거야.
여: 그래, 네 말이 맞아. 그럼 두 개로 좁혀지는 것 같아. 가족 무료입장이 좋을 것 같은데?
남: 맞아. 하지만 장학금 혜택이 더 쓸모 있을 것 같아.
여: 음··· 네 말이 맞는 것 같아. 그것을 지원할래.
남: 좋은 선택이야.

어휘 **sanitation** 공중 위생; 위생 시설 / **accountant** 회계사 ***cf.* account** 《주로 복수형》 회계(會計) / **admission** (승인을 받고) 들어감, 입장, 입학; 시인[인정]

11 짧은 대화에 이어질 응답 | ①

▶ 만나기로 한 장소인 과학 실험실이 4층에 있는지 물어보는 남자의 말에 가장 적절한 응답을 고른다.

① 사실, 그건 바로 그 위에 5층에 있어.
② 나를 만나는 데 시간을 내줘서 고마워.
③ 내가 실험을 끝내자마자 얘기할 수 있을 거야.
④ 나는 발표 때문에 매일 밤 그곳에 있어.
⑤ 네가 전에 과학 실험실에 가본 일이 없다니 놀랍다.

M: I think we need to meet and discuss our presentation.
W: Well, I'll be in the science lab tonight. **Why don't you meet me there**?
M: I think **I know where that is**. It's on the fourth floor, right?
W: ______________________________

남: 내 생각에 우린 만나서 발표에 관해 의논해야 할 것 같은데.
여: 음, 난 오늘 밤에 과학 실험실에 있을 거야. 거기서 만나는 게 어때?
남: 난 그게 어디 있는지 알 거 같아. 4층에 있지, 그렇지?
여: ______________________________

12 짧은 대화에 이어질 응답 | ③

▶ 파티에 가지고 올 것이 없는지 묻는 여자의 질문에 가장 적절한 응답을 찾는다.

① 모두 다 맛있어 보인다.
② 네가 원하는 사람은 누구나 데리고 와도 돼.
③ 마실 거라면 좋겠어.
④ 도와줘서 정말 고마워.
⑤ 네가 가져온 것을 저쪽에 놓아두렴.

W: Do you need any help **setting up for tonight's party**?
M: I don't think so. Everything is almost ready.
W: All right. Then is there **anything that I should bring**?
M: ______________________________

여: 오늘 밤에 있을 파티를 준비하는 거 도와줄까?
남: 아니야 괜찮아. 거의 다 준비됐어.
여: 좋아. 그럼 내가 가져올 건 없니?
남: ______________________________

13 긴 대화에 이어질 응답 | ③

▶ 여자는 남자의 부상이 심각하다고 생각하므로 남자가 병원에 가서 진료를 받을 것을 권할 것이다.

① 그 다리로 계속 걸으면 좋아질 거야.
② 다리 위에 얼음을 좀 올려놓는 게 어떠니?
③ 나중에 후회하는 것보다 미리 조심하는 게 좋아.
④ 농구 코트는 실내 체육관에 있단다.
⑤ Tom이 네 치료비를 내야 한다고 생각해.

W: Why are you limping?
M: I fell playing basketball and Tom **landed on my ankle**.
W: That sounds like a rough game.
M: It was just an accident. We were both going for a rebound.
W: Let me see your ankle. Ouch! It's as big as the basketball you were

playing with!
M: Do you think it's broken?
W: I'm not sure. How does it feel **when you stand on it**?
M: Really bad.
W: If you don't get to the doctor soon, you may not play basketball for a long, long time.
M: Do you think I need the doctor? Maybe I could just **put some ice on it**.
W: ______________________________

여: 왜 절뚝거리고 있니?
남: 농구 경기를 하다가 넘어졌는데 Tom이 제 발목 위로 떨어졌어요.
여: 격렬한 경기였던 것 같구나.
남: 그냥 사고였어요. 우리 둘 다 리바운드를 하려고 했거든요.
여: 발목을 보자. 아이코! 네가 가지고 농구하는 농구공만큼 크게 부었구나!
남: 부러진 것 같나요?
여: 확실치는 않아. 그 발로 서면 느낌이 어떠니?
남: 정말 아파요.
여: 빨리 병원에 가지 않으면 아주 오랫동안 농구를 못할지도 몰라.
남: 병원에 가야 한다고 생각하세요? 그 발목에 얼음을 좀 올려놓으면 될지 몰라요.
여: ______________________________

어휘 **limp** 절뚝거리다 / **land** 떨어지다 | 선택지 어휘 | **gymnasium** (실내) 체육관, 경기장

14 긴 대화에 이어질 응답 | ⑤

▶ 건강하지 않은 방식으로 빨리 살을 빼고자 하는 딸에게 아버지가 할 수 있는 대답을 고른다.

① 너는 건강식에 대해 잘못된 생각을 가지고 있어.
② 아니, 네가 매일 아침 식사를 걸러야 한다고 생각해.
③ 이런 시기에는 우리 모두 도움을 청할 수 있을 거야.
④ 네 친구들도 저녁 먹는 데 함께 데려가는 게 어떠니?
⑤ 있잖니, 살을 빼려면 시간이 걸리고 노력이 필요하단다.

M: When are you going to come down and eat dinner? We are waiting for you.
W: I'm trying to lose weight, so **I'm skipping dinner**.
M: That's not healthy, and it's not the best way to lose weight.
W: Well, that's what my friends told me I should do.
M: Sorry to say this, but your friends are wrong. Remember, **I used to be very overweight**.
W: Just let me try it my way, and **we'll see if it works**.
M: I can't let you do that. I'm your father, and I care about your well-being.
W: I hate being so fat!
M: Honey, you just need to exercise more and eat healthier foods.
W: I don't have time for exercise. And **it's the fastest way to lose weight**.
M: ______________________________

남: 언제 내려와서 저녁 먹을 거니? 모두 기다리고 있단다.
여: 살을 빼려고 해서 저녁을 거르려고요.
남: 그건 건강상 좋지 않아. 그리고 살을 빼는 가장 좋은 방법도 아니고.
여: 음, 친구들이 그렇게 해야 한다고 했어요.
남: 이런 말을 해서 미안하지만, 네 친구들이 틀렸단다. 나도 몹시 과체중이었다는 것을 기억해라.
여: 제 방식대로 하게 해주세요. 그리고 효과가 있는지 우리 지켜봐요.
남: 그렇게 하게 둘 수는 없지. 나는 네 아버지고 너의 건강이 염려된단다.
여: 저는 뚱뚱한 게 싫단 말예요!
남: 얘야, 넌 단지 운동을 더 많이 하고 건강에 좋은 음식을 먹어야 해.
여: 운동할 시간이 없어요. 그리고 이게 살을 빼는 가장 빠른 방법이에요.
남: ______________________________

어휘 **overweight** 과체중의 / **well-being** 건강, 안녕(安寧), 행복 | 선택지 어휘 | **slim down** 살을 빼다

15 상황에 적절한 말 | ④

▶ 피아노 레슨을 받느라 더 이상 스터디 모임에 참여할 수 없는 상황에서 할 수 있는 말을 고른다.

① 나는 스터디 모임에 참여하는 게 훨씬 더 중요하다고 생각해.
② 피아노 레슨을 받을 시간이 없을까 봐 걱정 돼.
③ 너를 주말에 대신 만나야 할 것 같아.
④ 미안하지만 더 이상 스터디 모임에 참여할 수가 없을 것 같아.
⑤ 이 스터디 모임은 화학 공부하는 데 정말 도움이 됐어.

M: Alice is a junior in high school. This semester, she is taking a particularly difficult chemistry class. **To help with the assignments and tests**, she and a few other students formed a study group. The group meets twice a week, on Mondays and Thursdays, and **it's been really helpful** for Alice. Unfortunately, Alice's mom insists that Alice take piano lessons. Just yesterday, **her mom signed her up** for lessons that are the same time as her study group. Alice is not happy about giving up her study group, but she **has no choice but to attend** the piano lessons. Now, Alice receives a call from Janice, one of the study-group members. Janice asks if Alice is ready for tonight's meeting. In this situation, what would Alice most likely say to Janice?

남: Alice는 고등학교 2학년생이다. 이번 학기에 그녀는 유독 어려운 화학 수업을 듣고 있다. 과제와 시험공부를 돕기 위해, 그녀는 몇몇 학생들과 스터디 모임을 만들었다. 그 모임은 일주일에 두 번, 월요일과 목요일에 만나며 Alice에게 정말 도움이 되었다. 안타깝게도, Alice의 엄마는 그녀가 피아노 레슨을 받아야 한다고 고집하신다. 바로 어제, 엄마는 Alice를 피아노 레슨에 등록하셨고 스터디 모임과 일정이 겹치게 되었다. Alice는 스터디 모임을 그만둬야 하는 게 속상하지만 어쩔 수 없이 피아노 레슨을 받아야 한다. 지금 Alice는 스터디 모임의 멤버 중 한 명인 Janice로부터 온 전화를 받는다. Janice는 Alice에게 오늘 밤 모임에 올 수 있는지 묻는다. 이러한 상황에서 Alice가 Janice에게 할 말로 가장 적절한 것은 무엇인가?

어휘 **junior** (고교의) 2학년의; 손아래의; 후배의 / **chemistry** 화학 / **have no choice but to-v** v할 수밖에 없다

16~17 세트 문항 | 16. ② 17. ①

▶ 16. 친구를 사귀는 방법으로, 경청할 것과 음악, 영화, 스포츠, 수집 등의 취미를 공유할 것을 제안하고 있다.

① 남의 말을 더 잘 경청하는 사람이 되는 방법
② 친구를 사귀는 다양한 방법들
③ 친구가 되는 것의 의미
④ 다른 사람들과 즐길 수 있는 취미들
⑤ 오래 지속되는 우정의 가치

▶ 17. 해석 참조

W: Let's talk a little bit about friendship. It means different things to different people, and every friendship is unique. Everybody has his or her own way to make friends, but there are a couple of things that you can do to become successful at it. First, **the most important thing is to listen**. Whether you're having dinner together or just hanging out, always be ready to listen. Secondly, **share your interests or hobbies**, and do things together. Any hobby can work, but some seem to be better for making friends than others. For example, many people love music, so you can make many friends by developing an active interest in it. Similarly, **keeping up on the latest films** will give you plenty to talk about with most people. Likewise, playing a popular sport, such as soccer, will help you connect with others. But special hobbies, like collecting comic books, are also good. They often lead to more meaningful friendships, and they **reach out to different types of people**. As you can see, there are many ways. What has worked for you?

여: 우정에 대해 얘기 좀 해봅시다. 우정은 사람마다 각각 다른 의미를 지니고 우정은 모두 특별합니다. 사람들마다 친구를 사귀는 자신만의 방법을 가지고 있습니다만 여러분이 그것에 (친구를 사귀는 데) 성공하기 위해 할 수 있는 몇 가지 방법이 있습니다. 첫째, 가장 중요한 것은 들어주는 것입니다. 같이 저녁을 하거나 단지 같이 어울릴 때, 항상 들을 준비가 되어 있어야 합니다. 둘째, 관심사나 취미를 공유하고 그것을 같이 하십시오. 어떤 취미도 좋습니다만 어떤 취미는 다른 취미보다 친구를 사귀는 데 더 좋을 수도 있습니다. 예를 들어, 많은 사람들은 ② 음악을 좋아하기 때문에 그것에 적극적인 관심을 기울여 친구를 사귈 수 있습니다. 비슷하게는, 최신 ③ 영화에 대해 알고 있으면 대부분의 사람들과 이야기할 거리를 많이 갖게 됩니다. 마찬가지로 축구처럼 대중적인 ④ 스포츠를 해도 다른 사람들과 연결되는 데 도움이 되죠. 그러나 만화책 ⑤ 수집과 같은 특수한 취미도 좋습니다. 이것들은 종종 좀 더 의미 있는 우정으로 이어지기도 하고 다른 유형의 사람들과 연결되게도 해줍니다. 보시다시피 여러 가지 방법이 있죠. 여러분에겐 어떤 방법이 효과가 있었나요?

어휘 **hang out** 어울리다, 함께 시간을 보내다 / **keep up** (뉴스 · 유행 등에 대해) 알게 되다[알다]

01. ② **02.** ④ **03.** ⑤ **04.** ④ **05.** ① **06.** ③ **07.** ④ **08.** ④ **09.** ⑤ **10.** ③
11. ④ **12.** ② **13.** ⑤ **14.** ② **15.** ① **16.** ⑤ **17.** ②

01 화자가 하는 말의 목적 | ②

▶ 선거에 참여해서 유능한 사람을 시장으로 선출하라는 내용이므로 시장 선거 참여를 독려하는 것이 목적이다.

W: Hello, my name is Julie Christen, president of the election committee. June 12th is the day **we will be electing a mayor** for Jay Valley. I hope all of you will take part in this election and vote for a person **who is competent** to be mayor of Jay Valley. It is everyone's right and duty to vote in this election. Unfortunately, the voting rate has been decreasing over the past twenty years. As a citizen, please **show your interest and concern** for this community by voting. We hope to see you at the election booths on June 12th, between 9 a.m. and 6 p.m. Thank you.

여: 안녕하십니까. 저는 선거위원회 위원장인 Julie Christen입니다. 6월 12일은 Jay Valley의 시장을 선출하는 날입니다. 저는 여러분 모두가 이번 선거에 참여하셔서 Jay Valley의 시장이 되기에 유능한 분께 투표하실 수 있기를 바랍니다. 이번 선거에 투표하는 것은 우리 모두의 권리이자 의무입니다. 유감스럽게도, 지난 20년간 투표율이 감소해오고 있습니다. 한 명의 시민으로서, 투표에 참여하셔서 지역사회에 대한 여러분의 관심을 보여주십시오. 저희는 6월 12일 오전 9시부터 오후 6시 사이에 투표소에서 여러분을 뵙기를 희망합니다. 감사합니다.

어휘 **committee** 위원회 / **competent** 유능한, 능력[자격]이 있는 / **voting rate** 투표율 / **community** 지역사회; 공동체 / **booth** (칸막이를 한) 작은 공간, 부스

02 의견 | ④

▶ 남자는 매운 음식이 우리의 식욕을 자극하고 암세포를 죽일 수 있으며 체내 콜레스테롤이 쌓이는 것을 막아줄 수 있다고 이야기하고 있다.

M: Tracy, do you like Mexican food?
W: Yes, I love enchiladas. **Have you ever tried** enchiladas?
M: No, I heard they're very hot and spicy.
W: Yeah, I feel like I'm riding a roller coaster when I eat them.
M: I understand. Hot, spicy food **stimulates our appetite**.
W: Yeah, and it's good for weight loss. I heard an ingredient in hot, spicy food can **cause the body to burn** bonus calories.
M: That ingredient is capsaicin. I heard capsaicin also has the ability to kill some cancer cells.
W: Yes, I read that in the newspaper!
M: And it can protect against the buildup of cholesterol in the blood.
W: That's why I like enchiladas. Are you sure you don't want to try them?
M: I'm sure. My eyes **start tearing up** when I eat spicy food, and I can't control it.

남: Tracy, 멕시코 음식을 좋아하니?
여: 응, 난 엔칠라다를 좋아해. 엔칠라다를 먹어본 적이 있니?
남: 아니, 엔칠라다는 매우 맵다고 들었어.
여: 그래 맞아. 그걸 먹을 때면 마치 롤러코스터를 타고 있는 것 같은 기분이 들어.
남: 이해해. 매운 음식은 우리의 식욕을 자극하잖아.
여: 맞아. 게다가 체중 감량에도 효과가 있어. 매운 음식에 들어있는 한 성분이 신체가 여분의 칼로리를 소모시키게 할 수 있다고 들었거든.
남: 그건 캡사이신이라는 성분이야. 나는 캡사이신이 암세포를 죽일 수 있는 효능도 가지고 있다고 들었어.
여: 맞아, 나도 신문에서 읽었어!
남: 그리고 그건 혈액 내에 콜레스테롤이 쌓이지 않도록 막아주기도 해.
여: 그래서 내가 엔칠라다를 좋아한다니까. 너 정말 안 먹어보고 싶어?
남: 응. 매운 음식을 먹으면 눈에서 눈물이 쏟아지기 시작하는데 그게 조절이 안 돼.

어휘 **enchilada** 엔칠라다(옥수수 빵(tortilla)에 고기를 넣고 매운 소스를 뿌린 멕시코 음식) / **stimulate** 자극하다, 활발하게 하다 / **appetite** 식욕 / **ingredient** 성분, 재료 / **capsaicin** 캡사이신(고추의 매운 성분) / **buildup** 축적, 비축; 증강, 강화

03 관계 | ⑤

▶ 남자가 이틀 동안 출장을 간 사이에 남자의 개가 밤새 짖고 뛰어서 아래층에 살고 있는 여자가 잠을 한숨도 자지 못했다며 불평하는 것으로 보아 아래층 거주자가 위층 거주자와 나누는 대화임을 알 수 있다.

W: Hello, Mr. Clarke. I want to speak to you about something.
M: Oh, Ms. Scot. Come on in. **Would you care for** some coffee or tea?
W: I'm fine, thank you. I brought some homemade cookies for you.
M: They look delicious. Thank you.
W: I came here to talk about your dog. He **won't stop barking** when you're not home.
M: Really? My dog's very quiet and well-behaved when I'm home with him.
W: That may be true when someone is at home, but the minute you leave, he becomes a very different dog.
M: Oh, I can't believe it.
W: **While you were on your business trip** for two days, he jumped up and down and barked all night.
M: Oh, that's awful.
W: I couldn't get any sleep for those two nights, since I live downstairs.
M: I'm terribly sorry about that. I will speak to a dog trainer and **see what I should do**.

여: Clarke 씨, 안녕하세요. 당신과 이야기를 좀 나누고 싶습니다.
남: 아, Scot 씨. 들어오세요. 커피나 차를 드릴까요?
여: 전 괜찮습니다, 고마워요. 당신에게 드리려고 집에서 구운 쿠키를 가져왔어요.
남: 맛있어 보이는군요. 감사합니다.
여: 당신의 개에 대해 이야기하러 왔어요. 그 개가 당신이 집에 안 계실 때 계속 짖어대서요.
남: 정말인가요? 집에 함께 있을 때 제 개는 매우 조용하고 얌전하거든요.
여: 누군가가 집에 있을 때는 그럴 수도 있겠지만, 당신이 없으면 바로 전혀 다른 개가 된답니다.
남: 이런, 믿을 수가 없군요.
여: 당신이 이틀간 출장으로 집을 비운 사이에 그 개는 밤새 펄쩍펄쩍 뛰면서 짖어댔어요.
남: 아, 말도 안 돼요.
여: 제가 아래층에 살기 때문에 그 이틀 동안 잠을 한숨도 못 잤어요.
남: 그 점에 대해 정말로 죄송하게 생각합니다. 개 조련사와 이야기해 보고 제가 무엇을 해야 하는지 알아보겠습니다.

어휘 **Would you care for ...?** …하시겠어요? / **well-behaved** 얌전한, 예의 바른

04 그림 불일치 | ④

▶ 여자아이는 게를 쫓고 있다고 했으므로 ④가 일치하지 않는다.

M: Honey, take a look at this picture.
W: Oh, is that from your trip to the beach with your brother's family?
M: Yeah, we had a great time. Look at my nephew!
W: He's **the one surfing**, right? I'm impressed!
M: I was too. And on the left, you can see my brother's wife. She's **putting on some sunscreen** under a parasol.
W: She's smart to avoid the sun. Hey, who are the two boys playing with a ball on the sand?
M: I'm not sure, actually. They were there with another family.
W: Well, I certainly recognize your niece. She's **the one chasing a crab**!
M: Haha, right! She almost caught it, but then she fell in love with that giant sand sculpture on the right.
W: Oh, it looks like such a good time! **I wish I could've been there**.

남: 여보, 이 사진을 봐요.
여: 아, 이건 형님네 가족과 함께 해변으로 여행 가서 찍은 사진이죠?
남: 맞아요. 무척 즐거운 시간을 보냈죠. 내 조카 좀 봐요!
여: 그 애가 파도타기를 하고 있는 아이죠? 놀라운데요!
남: 나도 놀랐어요. 그리고 왼쪽에서 내 형수님이 보일 거예요. 형수님은 파라솔 아래에서 자외선 차단제를 바르고 계세요.
여: 해를 피하고 계시니 현명하시네요. 아, 모래 위에서 공을 가지고 노는 두 소년은 누구인가요?
남: 실은, 나도 잘 모르겠어요. 그 애들은 다른 가족과 함께 온 것 같아요.
여: 음, 당신의 여자 조카는 분명히 알아보겠어요. 그 애는 게를 쫓고 있군요!
남: 하하, 맞아요! 그 애는 게를 거의 잡을 뻔했지만, 오른쪽에 있는 거대한 모래 조각상에 마음을 빼겨버렸어요.
여: 아, 정말 즐거운 한때인 것 같아요! 나도 거기에 있었다면 좋았을 텐데요.

어휘 **impressed** 인상 깊게 생각하는 / **sunscreen** 자외선 차단제

05 부탁한 일 | ①

▶ 밴드를 결성한 여자는 키보드 연주자와 보컬을 담당할 사람이 필요하다고 말하면서 남자에게 밴드에 합류해 줄 것을 요청하고 있다.

[Cell phone rings.]
M: Hello.
W: Hi, Travis. It's me, Mary.
M: Oh, hey, Mary. I **haven't heard from you in weeks**. What's up?
W: I just got back from a vacation and have started something new and exciting.
M: What's going on? Tell me.
W: Well, a few of my friends and I decided to start a band.
M: A band? You mean a music band? That sounds really cool!
W: It's a rock band, and we're calling ourselves, "Supersonic."
M: I really like the name. **This reminds me of when** we used to play together. Remember when you played guitar and I sang?
W: I'll never forget those days. Actually, we need a keyboard player and someone who can do the vocals, too. I was hoping **you could join our band**.
M: Oh, wow. That's a great offer, but I'm really busy these days.
W: Travis, we desperately need you. A club has already booked us for a performance, and **we can't do it without you**.
M: Well, I need to think it over.

[휴대전화 벨이 울린다.]
남: 여보세요.
여: 안녕, Travis. 나 Mary야.
남: 아, 안녕, Mary. 몇 주 동안 너에게서 소식을 듣지 못했는데. 무슨 일이니?
여: 이제 막 휴가를 마치고 돌아와서 새롭고 신나는 일을 시작했지.
남: 무슨 일인데? 말해봐.
여: 음, 내 친구 몇 명과 함께 밴드를 결성하기로 했거든.
남: 밴드? 음악하는 밴드 말하는 거니? 정말 멋진데!
여: 록 밴드야. 그리고 자칭 'Supersonic'이라고 불러.
남: 이름이 참 마음에 든다. 우리가 함께 연주하던 때를 생각나게 해. 넌 기타를 연주하고 내가 노래를 불렀던 때가 기억나니?
여: 난 그날들을 결코 잊지 못할 거야. 실은, 우린 키보드 연주자와 보컬을 맡아줄 사람도 필요해. 네가 우리 밴드에 합류하기를 바랐어.
남: 이런, 와. 굉장한 제안이지만, 요즘 정말 바빠서 말이야.
여: Travis, 우린 네가 절실히 필요해. 클럽에서 이미 우릴 공연에 예약해 놓았는데 네가 없이는 공연할 수가 없어.
남: 그럼, 생각 좀 해봐야겠네.

어휘 **remind A of B** A에게 B를 생각나게 하다 / **desperately** 필사적으로; 절망적으로

06 금액 | ③

▶ 남자는 2달러짜리 크림 트뤼플 4개, 3달러짜리 견과류 트뤼플 3개, 그리고 2달러짜리 초콜릿 막대 사탕을 6개 샀으므로 남자가 지불할 금액은 29달러이다.

W: Welcome to The Chocolate Factory. How can I help you?
M: I'd like to buy a box of chocolates for my wife.
W: How sweet! **I'd be happy to help**. What kind of chocolate does she like?
M: Well, truffles are her favorite.
W: We're **having a special sale** this weekend.
M: Sounds great. How much are they?
W: The truffles with a cream filling are $2 each, and the ones with nuts are $3.
M: In that case, I'll take four with the cream filling and three with nuts.
W: Okay. Four cream filling and three nuts. Is there **anything else you'd like**?
M: How much are these chocolate lollipops?
W: They're $2 each.
M: I'll take six.
W: All right. Shall I **start boxing everything for you**?
M: Yes, please.

여: Chocolate Factory에 오신 것을 환영합니다. 무엇을 도와드릴까요?
남: 제 아내에게 줄 초콜릿 한 상자를 구매하고 싶어요.
여: 자상하셔라! 기꺼이 도와드리겠습니다. 아내분은 무슨 초콜릿을 좋아하시나요?
남: 음, 트뤼플이 제 아내가 가장 좋아하는 겁니다.
여: 저희가 이번 주말에는 특별 할인 행사를 진행하고 있습니다.
남: 좋습니다. 얼마죠?
여: 크림이 채워진 트뤼플은 개당 2달러이고 견과류가 들어간 것은 3달러입니다.
남: 그렇다면, 저는 크림 필링 트뤼플 4개와 견과류 트뤼플 3개로 하겠습니다.
여: 알겠습니다. 크림 필링 트뤼플 4개와 견과류 트뤼플 3개입니다. 또 원하시는 것 있나요?
남: 이 초콜릿 막대 사탕은 얼마인가요?
여: 개당 2달러입니다.
남: 6개 사겠습니다.
여: 알겠습니다. 전부 상자에 담아드릴까요?
남: 네, 부탁합니다.

어휘 **truffle** 트뤼플 (동그란 모양의 초콜릿 과자) / **lollipop** 막대 사탕 / **box** 상자에 넣다

07 이유 | ④

▶ 여자의 집주인이 아파트 건물을 팔아서 모든 세입자가 다음 달 말까지 이사를 가야 한다고 말했다.

M: Hey, Crystal. Why are you checking out the classified ads?
W: I'm looking for **a place to move into**.
M: A new apartment? I thought you were happy with your roommate.
W: Debby and I **get along really well**. We actually live in a nice two-bedroom apartment right now.
M: I thought so. Your place is near Riverside Park, right? I heard that's a great area. So what's the problem? **Are you having trouble with** your neighbors?
W: No, not at all. They're nice.
M: Then what is it?
W: Well, my landlord has recently sold the apartment building, and all the tenants **need to move out** by the end of next month.
M: Oh, that's too bad. Have you ever thought about living on campus? You could save a lot of time and money.
W: Hmm.... It's definitely something to think about.

남: 저기, Crystal. 왜 신문 광고란을 확인하는 거야?
여: 난 새로 이사 갈 곳을 찾고 있거든.
남: 새 아파트 말이니? 난 네가 룸메이트를 마음에 들어 한다고 생각했는데.
여: 나랑 Debby는 정말 잘 지내. 사실 우린 지금 방이 두 개인 멋진 아파트에 살고 있어.
남: 그렇다고 생각했어. 너희 집은 Riverside 공원 근처에 있지? 좋은 지역이라고 들었어. 그런데 뭐가 문제야? 이웃들과 문제라도 있는 거야?
여: 아니, 전혀. 이웃들은 친절해.
남: 그럼 문제가 뭔데?
여: 글쎄, 집주인이 최근에 아파트 건물을 팔아버려서 모든 세입자가 다음 달 말까지 이사를 가야 해.
남: 이런, 그것참 안됐다. 교내에서 사는 건 생각해본 적 있니? 시간과 돈을 많이 아낄 수 있어.
여: 음…. 그것도 꼭 고려해봐야겠다.

어휘 **classified ad** (신문의) 안내 광고 / **get along well** 잘 지내다 / **landlord** 주인, 임대주 / **tenant** 세입자 / **campus** (대학) 교정 / **definitely** 분명히[틀림없이]; 절대(로)

08 언급하지 않은 것 | ④

▶ 해석 참조

[Phone rings.]
M: Hello, you've reached Copymax. This is Allan Goldberg speaking. **How may I assist you**?
W: Hello, I'm calling from Mannington Company. **One of our copiers is** out of order.
M: Could you give me the model number for the copier?
W: It's QM 4829.
M: **What seems to be the problem**?
W: All our copies are coming out with black dots and marks. And the paper often gets jammed.
M: May I ask when you purchased the machine?
W: I'm not sure, but it's definitely over five years old.
M: Your warranty is no longer valid, so you'll have to pay for the parts that are replaced. Will that be all right with you?
W: Sure.
M: I'll **send the technician over** tomorrow morning.
W: Great. Thanks for your help.

[전화벨이 울린다.]
남: 안녕하세요. Copymax입니다. 저는 Allan Goldberg입니다. 어떻게 도와드릴까요?
여: 여보세요. Mannington 회사에서 전화드립니다. 저희 복사기 중 한 대가 고장 나서요.
남: 복사기의 제품 번호를 말씀해주시겠습니까?
여: QM 4829(① 제품 번호)입니다.
남: 무엇이 문제인 것 같나요?
여: 복사물에 전부 검은 점과 자국이 묻어 나와요. 용지도 자주 복사기에 걸리고요(② 문제점).
남: 언제 복사기를 구매하셨는지 여쭤봐도 될까요?
여: 확실하지는 않지만, 분명 5년은 넘었어요(③ 구입 시기).
남: 품질 보증서의 유효기간이 지나서, 교체되는 부품에 대한 비용을 내셔야 합니다. 괜찮으시겠습니까?
여: 물론이죠.
남: 내일 오전(⑤ 수리 기사 방문일)에 기사를 보내드리겠습니다.
여: 좋습니다. 도와주셔서 감사합니다.

어휘 **assist** 돕다 / **out of order** 고장 난 / **get jammed** (기계 등에) 걸리다, 끼이다 / **warranty** (제품의) 품질 보증서; 보증 / **valid** 유효한; 타당한 / **replace** 교체하다; 대신하다 / **send over** 파견하다 / **technician** 기사, 기술자

09 내용 불일치 | ⑤

▶ 공원은 연중무휴로 개방된다고 했으므로 야영도 연중 내내 가능하다.

M: Welcome to Red Valley National Park. While here, there are a few things you should keep in mind. We ask that you only **use the designated hiking trails** within the park. For those of you who are here to camp, you can do so only in the campsites. You are **prohibited from setting up your tents** or eating outside the campsites as it can be dangerous. There are also a few precautions you must take within the campsites. Please **make sure you clean** the grill after a barbecue. Also, never store food inside your tent. All food should be stored in the steel containers located at each site. This is to prevent wildlife from entering the sites for food. Red Valley National Park **is open year round**. Peak season in the park is from July to September.

남: Red Valley 국립공원에 오신 여러분을 환영합니다. 여기에 계시는 동안, 명심하셔야 할 몇 가지 사항이 있습니다. 여러분들께서는 오직 공원 내 지정된 등산로만 이용해 주시기를 부탁드립니다. 야영하러 오신 분들은 야영장에서만 야영하실 수 있습니다. 위험할 수도 있으므로, 야영장 밖에서 텐트를 설치하시거나 식사하시는 것은 금지됩니다. 또한, 야영장 내에서 반드시 지켜주셔야 할 몇 가지 주의사항이 있습니다. 바비큐를 드시고 난 뒤에는 반드시 그릴을 닦아 주시기 바랍니다. 그리고 절대로 텐트 안에 음식을 보관하지 마십시오. 모든 음식은 각 야영장에 위치한 철제 용기에 보관되어야 하는데, 이는 야생동물들이 먹이를 구하러 야영장 안으로 들어오지 못하게 하기 위함입니다. Red Valley 국립공원은 연중무휴입니다. 이 공원의 성수기는 7월부터 9월까지입니다.

어휘 **designated** 지정된 / **trail** 오솔길; 루트[코스]; 자국 / **precaution** 예방 조치; 조심, 경계 / **store** 비축하다; 저장하다 / **container** 그릇, 용기 / **peak season** 성수기

10 도표 이해 | ③

▶ 여자는 털 알레르기가 있는 남편 때문에 털이 덜 빠지면서도 중간 크기이며, 딸아이와 함께 달려줄 활동적인 개를 원했지만 집을 지켜줄 개는 원하지 않았다.

M: Hi. Are you here **to adopt a dog today**?
W: Yes, I'd really like a companion for my daughter. She is 15 years old now.
M: What should I take into account **when matching you with a dog**?
W: My husband has a mild allergy to animal fur, so I need something that won't shed everywhere and that's easy to clean up after.
M: There are dogs that shed less, so I'd recommend **taking one of those home**. What size dog are you looking for?
W: I'd like a medium size dog.
M: How much daily exercise will you give your dog? I mean, some energetic dogs need a lot of exercise.
W: Oh, I see. I'm hoping the dog will be a jogging companion for my daughter. So I want an active dog.
M: Okay. Do you want a dog that will protect your house? Do you want a dog **that barks loudly at strangers**?
W: No, I don't want a "Beware of Dog" dog. I just want a playful dog for my daughter.
M: Then, I know exactly which dog is good for you.

남: 안녕하세요. 오늘 개를 입양하러 오셨나요?
여: 네. 저는 딸아이에게 친구가 되어 줄 개를 원합니다. 딸아이는 지금 열다섯 살이에요.
남: 어울릴 만한 개를 고를 때, 제가 무엇을 고려해야 할까요?
여: 제 남편은 동물 털에 약한 알레르기가 있어요. 그래서 사방에 털을 날리지 않으면서 뒤처리가 쉬운 것을 원합니다.
남: 털이 적게 빠지는 개들이 있는데, 그중 한 마리를 집에 데려가실 것을 권해드리고 싶군요. 어떤 크기의 개를 찾고 계시나요?
여: 중간 크기의 개를 원합니다.
남: 개를 하루에 얼마나 운동을 시키실 건가요? 그러니까, 기운 넘치는 일부 개들은 많은 운동량이 필요해서요.
여: 아, 알겠습니다. 저는 개가 조깅할 때 제 딸아이와 함께 달려줄 친구가 되어주길 바랍니다. 그래서 전 활동적인 개를 원해요.
남: 네. 집을 지켜줄 개를 원하시나요? 낯선 사람에게 크게 짖어대는 개를 원하시나요?
여: 아니요. 저는 '맹견 주의'류 개는 원하지 않아요. 단지 제 딸아이를 위해 장난기 많은 개를 원합니다.
남: 그렇다면, 정확히 어느 개가 당신에게 좋을지 알겠네요.

어휘 **adopt** 입양하다; 채택하다 / **companion** 친구; 동반자 / **take A into account** A를 고려하다 / **shed** (동물이) 털갈이를 하다; 떨어뜨리다 / **energetic** 활기에 찬 / **beware of A** A를 조심하다 / **playful** 장난기 많은

11 짧은 대화에 이어질 응답 | ④

▶ 지금 청소를 할 수 없는 이유를 묻는 여자의 말에 가장 적절한 응답은 생일 파티에 가봐야 한다고 말한 ④이다.

① 이번엔 '미안해'란 말로는 부족해요.
② 빨리 청소를 시작하는 게 좋을걸요.
③ 저도 제가 자주 약속을 지키지 않는다는 걸 알고 있어요.
④ 오늘 Tim이 저를 생일 파티에 초대했단 말이에요.
⑤ 집에 돌아왔을 때, 전 숙제를 끝내야 했어요.

W: Michael, look at all this mess! Clean your room.
M: I'm sorry, Mom. I promise **I'll clean it up** tomorrow.
W: I want you to clean it up today. **Why can't you do it** now?
M: ____________________

여: Michael, 이 어질러 놓은 것들 좀 봐! 방 청소 좀 하렴.
남: 죄송해요, 엄마. 내일 청소하겠다고 약속할게요.
여: 엄마는 네가 오늘 방을 청소하면 좋겠어. 왜 지금 청소할 수 없다는 거니?
남: ____________________

12 짧은 대화에 이어질 응답 | ②

▶ 여자가 남자를 제자로 오해하자 남자가 자신을 소개하였으므로 이에 사과하는 응답이 적절하다.

① 글쎄요, 사람을 잘못 보신 것 같군요.
② 아! 기억하지 못해서 미안하구나.
③ 이것 참 우연이구나! 그게 내가 여기 온 이유야.
④ 훌륭하구나! 네 어머니는 널 분명 자랑스러워하실 거야.
⑤ 맞아, 반 친구들이랑 아직 연락하고 지내니?

M: Good afternoon, Professor Sherman. I'm not sure **if you can remember me**. I'm Jim Bradley.
W: Oh, Jim. You were a student of my History class last year, weren't you?
M: No, you **must have confused me** with someone else. I'm the son of your friend, Joyce Bradley.
W: ____________________

남: 안녕하세요, Sherman 교수님. 저를 기억하실지 모르겠어요. 저는 Jim Bradley예요.
여: 오, Jim이구나. 넌 작년에 내 역사 수업을 들었던 학생이지?
남: 아니요, 저를 다른 사람과 혼동하신 것 같아요. 저는 교수님의 친구분이신 Joyce Bradley 씨의 아들입니다.
여: ____________________

어휘 **confuse A with B** A와 B를 혼동하다 | 선택지 어휘 | **coincidence** 우연의 일치 / **be in touch with A** A와 연락하고 지내다

13 긴 대화에 이어질 응답 | ⑤

▶ 축구 경기에서 또다시 패배해서 운동을 그만두어야 할지 고민하는 여자에게 남자는 격려의 말을 할 것이다.

① 괜찮아. 내가 네 팀원들에게 이야기할게.
② 응, 너는 운동을 더 일찍 시작했어야 했어.
③ 미안하지만, 나는 시간이 충분하지 않아.
④ 정말 잘했어. 네가 매우 자랑스러워.

⑤ 속상해하지 마. 다음엔 잘할 수 있을 거야.

M: How was your weekend, Sydney?
W: Don't ask. It was terrible **because we lost again**.
M: Oh, did you have a woman's soccer match at school?
W: Yeah, we trained so hard this time, and we **couldn't even score a point**.
M: Oh, I'm sorry to hear that.
W: I had a few chances to score a goal but missed. Everyone **was counting on me**, and I let them down.
M: What was the score?
W: It was four to zero.
M: How disappointing for everyone on the team!
W: I don't know if I should continue playing. I **might have to quit the team**.
M: ______________________

남: Sydney, 주말은 어땠니?
여: 묻지 말아줘. 우리가 또 패배해서 끔찍했어.
남: 아, 학교에서 여자 축구 경기했니?
여: 응, 우린 이번에 엄청 열심히 훈련했는데, 한 점도 못 냈어.
남: 이런, 그 말을 들으니 유감이야.
여: 내가 득점할 기회가 몇 번 있었는데 놓쳤어. 모두가 나에게 기대했는데, 내가 그들을 실망시켰어.
남: 점수는 어땠는데?
여: 4대 0이야.
남: 팀원 모두가 얼마나 실망했을까!
여: 내가 운동을 계속해야 할지 모르겠어. 팀을 그만두어야 할까 봐.
남: ______________________

어휘 **count on A** A를 기대하다[믿다]; A를 확신하다 / **let A down** A를 실망시키다

14 긴 대화에 이어질 응답 | ②

▶ 그리스 출신 아내의 생일에 요리를 해주기 위해 그리스 요리책을 보고 있다는 남자의 말을 듣고 여자는 남자를 칭찬하는 말을 할 것이다.

① 많이 먹어. 네가 그리스 요리를 좋아하면 좋겠어.
② 넌 정말 훌륭한 남편이야. 네 아내는 정말 운이 좋은걸.
③ 이거 맛있네! 저녁 식사에 초대해 줘서 고마워.
④ 네 아내가 널 이해해 줄 거라고 확신해. 스트레스받지 마.
⑤ 너무 많이 걱정하지 마. 네 아내가 곧 괜찮아지길 바라.

W: Hey, Ethan. What are you reading **that's so interesting**?
M: Oh, Julia. I didn't know you were standing there.
W: Is it an interior decor magazine? Everything looks so colorful.
M: It's actually a Greek cookbook.
W: Why is a graphic designer reading a cookbook? I guess you want to get some visual ideas from the magazine. It has a really nice layout.
M: Actually, **it's not for work**.
W: It isn't? Is this a secret hobby **that I didn't know about**? I had no idea you were a cook.
M: My wife is Greek and it's her birthday next week. I **want to cook something special** for my wife.
W: ______________________

여: 이봐, Ethan. 뭘 그렇게 재미있게 읽고 있어?
남: 아, Julia. 네가 거기에 서 있는 줄 몰랐어.
여: 실내 장식에 관한 잡지인가? 모든 게 매우 화려해 보여.
남: 사실은 그리스 요리책이야.
여: 왜 그래픽 디자이너가 요리책을 읽고 있니? 그 잡지에서 시각적인 발상을 좀 얻고 싶은 거지? 정말로 배치가 잘 되어 있어.
남: 실은, 일 때문이 아니야.
여: 아니라고? 이건 내가 몰랐던 비밀스러운 취미인가? 네가 요리사인지 몰랐는데.
남: 내 아내가 그리스 사람인데 다음 주가 생일이거든. 아내를 위해서 특별한 것을 요리하고 싶어.
여: ______________________

어휘 **decor** (건물의 실내) 장식 / **visual** 시각의 / **layout** 배치 | 선택지 어휘 | **Help yourself.** 많이 드세요.

15 상황에 적절한 말 | ①

▶ 회의에 늦을 것 같아 걱정하는 남자는 천천히 운전 중인 택시 기사에게 서둘러 달라는 말을 할 것이다.

① 죄송합니다. 회의에 늦을까 봐 그러는데, 서둘러 주세요.
② 실컷 웃었네요. 이야기 즐거웠습니다.
③ 무슨 일이 있나요? 왜 차가 이렇게 밀리나요?
④ 서두르지 않으시면, 제 비행기를 놓칠 거예요.
⑤ 안전하게 운전해주셔서 정말 안심이에요.

W: Robert just arrived at the Dallas International Airport for a business trip. He **is scheduled for several meetings** in the afternoon after his arrival. He **hops into a taxi** and asks the driver to go downtown where his company's headquarters is located. Fortunately, it isn't rush hour, so **there isn't too much traffic**. His taxi driver seems friendly and quite talkative. Robert also notices that he is a cautious driver. In fact, he seems to drive a little too safely because he is driving very slowly. When Robert looks at his watch, he **starts to get a little nervous** because he feels he might not make it to the meeting on time. In this situation, what would Robert most likely say to the taxi driver?

여: Robert는 출장을 가기 위해 방금 댈러스 국제공항에 도착했다. 도착 후 그는 오후에 몇몇 회의에 참석할 예정이다. 그는 급히 택시를 타고 기사에게 회사의 본사가 있는 시내로 가 줄 것을 요청한다. 다행히도 혼잡한 시간대가 아니라서 차가 너무 많지 않다. 그가 탄 택시의 기사는 친절하고 매우 말이 많은 사람 같다. Robert는 그가 안전하게 운전하는 기사라는 것도 알아차린다. 사실, 그가 좀 지나치게 안전하게 운전하는 것 같은데, 이는 그가 매우 천천히 운전하고 있기 때문이다. Robert는 시계를 보고, 제시간에 회의에 참석할 수 없을 것 같다는 느낌이 들어 조금씩 초조해지기 시작한다. 이러한 상황에서 Robert가 택시 기사에게 할 말로 가장 적절한 것은 무엇인가?

어휘 **hop into** ~에 뛰어 올라타다 / **headquarters** 본사[본부] / **cautious** 조심스러운, 신중한 / **make it** 제시간에 도착하다; 성공하다

16~17 세트 문항 | 16. ⑤ 17. ②

▶ 16. 가족과 함께 집에서 요리한 음식을 먹는 것이 가족 관계에 좋다는 내용이다.

① 가정 요리의 인기
② 가족 내 갈등의 원인
③ 나쁜 식습관이 건강에 미치는 영향
④ 가족 관계를 개선하는 방법
⑤ 좋은 가족 관계를 위한 가정 요리

▶ 17. 해석 참조

M: There is a saying that a family that eats together, stays together. With a busy lifestyle, people **are increasingly eating out** and not cooking at home. But this can break up the healthy dynamics of a family unit. So, it's important for a family to spend time cooking and eating together. Cooking at home can **help repair strained relationships** among family members. It brings the family together and opens up communication. It allows the family to share problems or issues in their everyday lives. In addition, cooking for your loved ones is an expression of love. A mother who bakes an apple pie or makes pancakes is sending the message that **she has taken precious time** to make something delicious and wholesome for her family. A homemade pudding is filled with a parent's love and care, **unlike a store-bought pudding**. Also, the aroma of delicious food at home such as ribs, pasta, or baked chicken will certainly please anyone in the house and help everyone feel the true comforts of home. Clearly, home cooking is not only more delicious **but it also dramatically affects** the relationships in a family.

남: '함께 모여 식사하는 가족은 흩어지지 않는다'는 말이 있습니다. 바쁜 삶의 방식 탓에, 사람들은 점점 더 외식을 하고 집에서 요리를 하지 않고 있습니다. 그러나 이것은 가족 공동체를 지탱하는 건전한 원동력을 무너뜨릴 수 있습니다. 그러므로 가족이 함께 요리해서 먹는 데 시간을 쓰는 것은 중요합니다. 집에서 요리를 하면 가족 구성원 간의 불편한 관계를 개선하는 데 도움이 될 수 있습니다. 그것은 가족을 한데 모으게 하고 의사소통이 이루어지게 합니다. 그것은 가족이 각자의 삶에서 갖고 있는 문제점들을 함께 나눌 수 있도록 합니다. 게다가, 사랑하는 사람을 위해서 요리를 하는 것은 사랑을 표현하는 것입니다. ① 사과 파이를 굽거나 ③ 팬케이크를 만드는 어머니는 자신의 가족을 위해 맛있고 몸에 좋은 것을 만드는 데 소중한 시간을 썼다는 메시지를 전달하고 있는 것입니다. 집에서 만드는 ④ 푸딩은 가게에서 파는 푸딩과는 달리, 부모의 사랑과 정성이 가득 담겨 있습니다. 또한 갈비, 파스타, ⑤ 구운 닭고기처럼 집에서 만드는 맛있는 음식의 향기는 분명 집안 모든 이들을 즐겁게 할 것이며 모두가 가정의 진정한 안락함을 느끼도록 해줄 것입니다. 분명히, 집에서 요리하면 더 맛있을 뿐만 아니라 가족 간의 관계에도 극적인 영향을 미칩니다.

어휘 **increasingly** 점점 더 / **break up** 부수다, 분해하다 / **dynamics** 원동력; 힘, 활력 / **unit** 구성단위 / **strained** 불편한; 긴장한 / **wholesome** 건강에 좋은 / **aroma** 향기 / **comfort** 안락, 편안; 위안하다 / **dramatically** 극적으로 / **affect** 영향을 미치다

01. ④	02. ③	03. ④	04. ②	05. ⑤
06. ③	07. ④	08. ②	09. ②	10. ③
11. ③	12. ③	13. ②	14. ②	15. ④
16. ②	17. ⑤			

01 화자가 하는 말의 목적 | ④

▶ 화재가 보고되었고 이는 훈련이 아니라고 하면서 대피 방법을 알려주고 있다.

W: May I have your attention, please. This is your emergency operator. A fire has been reported. Please **leave the building immediately** through the nearest exit. This is not a drill. I repeat, this is not a drill. All persons shall **proceed to the stairs**, walk down to the lobby and exit the building. DO NOT USE THE ELEVATORS! After you leave the building, please move away from the exits. Disabled persons should be taken to the closest smoke-free stairwell to await evacuation by the Fire Department. You will be notified when it is safe to re-enter the building. We will **keep you informed of the situation**.

여: 주목해 주십시오. 저는 비상사태 운영자입니다. 화재가 보고되었습니다. 가장 가까운 출구를 통해 즉시 건물을 떠나십시오. 이것은 훈련이 아닙니다. 반복합니다. 이것은 훈련이 아닙니다. 모든 사람들은 계단으로 향하시고 로비로 걸어 내려가서 건물에서 나가십시오. 엘리베이터를 이용하지 마십시오! 건물을 떠난 뒤에는 출구로부터 멀리 이동하십시오. 장애가 있는 분들은 연기가 없는 가장 가까운 계단통으로 옮겨져서 소방서가 대피시켜줄 것을 기다려야 합니다. 건물에 다시 들어오는 것이 안전하면 공지드리겠습니다. 상황을 계속 알려드리겠습니다.

어휘 **emergency** 비상사태 / **operator** 운영자 / **exit** 출구; 나가다, 떠나다 / **drill** 훈련 / **proceed to** ~로 나아가다 / **disabled** 장애를 가진 / **stairwell** 계단통(건물 내부에 계단이 나 있는 공간) / **evacuation** 대피, 피난 / **notify** 공지하다

02 의견 | ③

▶ 여행자 보험이 필요하냐는 여자의 질문에 남자는 갑자기 입원해야 하거나 중요한 물건을 잃어버렸을 때를 대비해 여행자 보험이 필요하다고 설명하고 있다.

M: Mia, how is the packing going?
W: **I'm almost done**, Dad. I just need to pack my first-aid kit.
M: Okay. You're bringing sunscreen and a hat also, right?
W: Of course.
M: Hmm.... I see your passport here. By the way, did you get travel insurance?
W: I didn't. Why? Do you think it's necessary?
M: Yes, I do. Anything could happen in a foreign country. You **should be prepared**.
W: What's the benefit of having insurance?
M: It will cover you if you suddenly need to be hospitalized.
W: I guess **it's better to be safe than sorry**.
M: Right. Plus, insurance covers the loss of important items, like your passport.
W: That could be useful. **I'd better buy an insurance policy** at the airport.
M: I'd rather we look online first.
W: Okay. Let's do that.

남: Mia, 짐 꾸리는 건 어떻게 돼가니?
여: 거의 다 됐어요, 아빠. 제 구급상자만 챙기면 돼요.
남: 그래. 자외선 차단제와 모자도 가지고 가지?
여: 물론이죠.
남: 음…. 여권은 여기 있구나. 그런데 여행자 보험은 들었니?
여: 아뇨. 왜요? 아빠는 그게 필요하다고 생각하세요?
남: 그럼. 외국에선 어떤 일이 일어날지 몰라. 대비해 놓아야 한단다.
여: 보험에 들면 좋은 점이 뭐예요?
남: 네가 갑자기 입원해야 한다면 보험이 (그 비용을) 보장해 줄 거야.
여: 제 생각에도 나중에 후회하는 것보다 미리 조심하는 편이 낫겠어요.
남: 맞아. 그리고 (여행자) 보험은 여권처럼 중요한 물건을 잃어버려도 (그에 대한 비용을) 보장해 준단다.
여: 유용하겠는 걸요. 공항에서 보험 하나 들어야겠어요.
남: 우선 인터넷으로 함께 검색해보는 게 좋겠구나.
여: 좋아요. 그렇게 해요.

어휘 **first-aid kit** 구급상자 / **insurance** 보험 / **cover** (보험으로) ~을 보장하다 / **hospitalize** 입원시키다

03 관계 | ④

▶ 자신이 근무하는 회사에서 어떤 직원을 채용하고 싶은지를 설명하는 것으로 보아 여자는 회사의 인사 업무를 담당하는 사람이며, 알맞은 사람을 찾아주겠다고 말하는 것으로 보아 남자는 구직자와 회사를 연결해 주는 직업소개소 직원으로 추론할 수 있다.

[Phone rings.]
M: Hello?
W: Hi! This is Judy Brown at Business Systems Incorporated.
M: Yes, Ms. Brown. How can I help you?
W: We're looking for an administrative assistant, someone who can use a computer, do some filing... **that sort of thing**.
M: Oh, I'm sure we can find someone who's qualified. **Why don't you tell me** a little bit more about the job responsibilities?
W: We need someone to answer the phone and take messages. They must have a good telephone voice.
M: Uh-huh.
W: And someone who's willing to work evenings once in a while, when things get busy.
M: Weekends, too?
W: No, probably not.
M: Well, let me look through our files and find someone **whose qualifications are just right**. I'll call you tomorrow afternoon. Is that okay?
W: Okay. I'll be waiting for your call. Thanks.

[전화벨이 울린다.]
남: 여보세요?
여: 안녕하세요! 저는 Business Systems 사(社)의 Judy Brown이라고 합니다.
남: 네, Brown 씨. 무엇을 도와드릴까요?
여: 저희는 컴퓨터를 사용할 줄 알고, 서류 정리 같은 일을 할 수 있는 행정사무 보조원을 구하고 있습니다.
남: 오, 저희가 적임자를 찾아 드릴 수 있을 거라 확신합니다. 담당 업무에 대해 좀 더 말씀해 주시겠습니까?
여: 전화를 받고 메시지를 받아 줄 사람이 필요합니다. 전화 목소리가 좋아야 하고요.
남: 그렇군요.
여: 그리고 일이 바빠지면 가끔 기꺼이 야근을 해 줄 사람으로요.
남: 주말에도 말입니까?
여: 아뇨, 아마 그렇지 않을 겁니다.
남: 음, 서류들을 살펴보고 자격이 딱 맞는 사람을 찾아 드리겠습니다. 내일 오후에 전화 드리죠. 괜찮겠습니까?
여: 좋아요. 전화 기다리고 있겠습니다. 감사합니다.

어휘 **incorporated** 법인 조직의, (주식) 회사의 / **administrative** 행정[관리]상의 / **qualified** 적임의, 자격이 있는 ***cf.*** **qualification** 자격; 면허 / **be willing to-v** 기꺼이 v하다

04 그림 불일치 | ②

▶ 여자가 천장에 매달린 새 다섯 마리 중 두 마리를 남자의 아들인 Sean이 색칠했다고 했다. 그러므로 천장에 매달린 새는 다섯 마리여야 하는데 그림에서는 천장에 매달린 새가 두 마리이므로 대화의 내용과 일치하지 않는다.

M: Hi, I'm Sean's father.
W: Come on in, Mr. Nelson. Thank you for coming to the teacher/parent conference.
M: My pleasure. Wow! Did the children draw the trees and dinosaurs on the wall?
W: Yes, they did. Do you **see the five birds hanging** from the ceiling? Sean colored two of them.
M: Sean really loves birds. Are these photos of the students on the bulletin board on the right?
W: Yes, they're photos of children **participating in various activities** here at the kindergarten. There's a picture of Sean there, too. See if you can find him.
M: The children all look so happy. Thank you for taking such good care

of them.

W: It's my pleasure. Let me find your name tag on the table. The ribbon on the tag was made by the kids. Oh, here it is.

M: They're so cute!

W: The conference **will be held** on the second floor. Go past the balloon arch and up the stairs.

M: Wow, I really feel like I'm in a fairy tale.

남: 안녕하세요. 저는 Sean의 아버지입니다.
여: 들어오세요. Nelson 씨. 교사 학부모 회의에 와주셔서 감사합니다.
남: 천만에요. 와! 벽의 나무와 공룡을 아이들이 그렸나요?
여: 예. 아이들이 했어요. 천장에 매달려 있는 새 다섯 마리 보이세요? Sean이 그중 두 마리를 색칠했답니다.
남: Sean은 정말 새를 좋아하죠. 오른쪽 게시판에 있는 이것들은 학생들 사진인가요?
여: 예. 여기 유치원에서 다양한 활동에 참여하는 아이들의 사진입니다. 저기 Sean의 사진도 있답니다. 그 애를 찾을 수 있는지 보세요.
남: 아이들 모두가 무척 행복해 보이네요. 아이들을 이렇게 잘 돌보아주시니 감사합니다.
여: 제가 좋아서 하는 건데요. 탁자 위에서 이름표를 찾아드릴게요. 이름표의 리본은 아이들이 만들었답니다. 아, 여기 있군요.
남: 정말 귀엽네요!
여: 회의는 2층에서 열릴 것입니다. 풍선 아치를 통과해서 계단으로 올라가세요.
남: 와, 정말로 제가 동화 속에 있는 기분이에요.

어휘 **conference** 회의 / **dinosaur** 공룡 / **ceiling** 천장 / **bulletin board** 게시판 / **participate** 참가하다 / **kindergarten** 유치원 / **name tag** 명찰, 이름표 / **tag** 표 / **arch** 아치; 아치형 구조물 / **fairy tale** 동화

05 추후 행동 | ⑤

▶ 남자는 〈Let's Talk〉의 URL 주소를 알려 주려고 했지만, 여자가 라디오 소리에 잠이 깨고 싶다고 하자 라디오 주파수를 문자 메시지로 보내 주겠다고 했다.

M: Hey, Kara. Did you do this morning's English quiz?

W: The one in the newspaper?

M: No, the one on the *Let's Talk* radio program.

W: Oh, I've heard that's an excellent show.

M: It is. The quiz is really hard, but **I got all the answers right** today!

W: Wow, I should listen to the show too. Where do I find it?

M: I subscribe to the Internet radio podcast and listen on my computer. I'll give you the URL address.

W: But I've got a clock radio. I'd like **to wake up to the radio**.

M: In that case, I'll send you the radio frequency number by text message.

W: Okay. What time is *Let's Talk* on?

M: Eight a.m., Monday through Friday.

W: Thanks, Ben.

남: 이봐, Kara. 오늘 아침의 영어 퀴즈 풀었니?
여: 신문에 있던 퀴즈?
남: 아니, 〈Let's Talk〉 라디오 프로그램에서 나온 거.
여: 아, 그 프로그램이 아주 훌륭하다고 들었어.
남: 그래. 퀴즈가 정말 어렵지만, 나는 오늘 답을 다 맞혔어!
여: 와, 나도 그 프로그램을 들어야겠다. 어디서 그걸 찾을 수 있지?
남: 나는 인터넷 라디오 팟캐스트로 구독해서 (라디오 프로그램을) 컴퓨터로 들어. 내가 URL 주소를 줄게.
여: 하지만 나는 시계가 달린 라디오가 있어. 라디오 소리에 잠이 깨고 싶어.
남: 그렇다면 라디오 주파수를 문자 메시지로 보내 줄게.
여: 알겠어. 〈Let's Talk〉는 몇 시에 해?
남: 월요일에서 금요일까지 아침 8시야.
여: 고마워, Ben.

어휘 **subscribe** (신문, 잡지 등을) 구독하다 / **clock radio** 시계[타이머]가 달린 라디오 / **frequency** 주파수; 빈도

06 금액 | ③

▶ 여자는 오후 스키 이용권(40달러)을, 남자는 종일 스키 이용권(75달러)을 구매할 것이므로 두 사람이 지불할 금액은 115달러이다. 리프트 무료 이용권이 있어 리프트 비용은 지불할 필요가 없다.

W: What time is it?

M: It's 10:30. **It took us a long time to get here**.

W: Traffic was bad.

M: Now, should we get full-day ski passes?

W: Maybe not. Let's see, the full-day ski passes are $75, and the lift fee is $20.

M: Oh, I have two free lift coupons, so **we don't need to pay for the lift**.

W: That's nice.

M: What about the afternoon passes?

W: They're $40. But what will we do until 12:30?

M: I don't know.

W: Hmm, I guess we could shop for ski stuff.

M: Well, you know I **haven't skied in a long time**. I really want to ski a lot. Let's get full-day passes.

W: You start without me then. You know I usually get tired after a few runs anyway. I'll buy an afternoon pass.

M: OK. I'll meet you at the top of the mountain at 1.

여: 몇 시예요?
남: 10시 30분이요. 여기 오는 데 오래 걸렸네요.
여: 교통상황이 안 좋았어요.
남: 그럼, 스키 종일 이용권을 살까요?
여: 글쎄요. 어디 보자. 스키 종일 이용권이 75달러이고 리프트 이용료가 20달러네요.
남: 아, 무료 리프트 쿠폰이 2장 있으니 리프트 이용료는 지불할 필요가 없어요.
여: 잘됐네요.
남: 오후 이용권은 어때요?
여: 40달러네요. 하지만 12시 30분까지 뭘 하고 있죠?
남: 모르겠어요.
여: 음, 스키 용품을 쇼핑할 수 있겠네요.
남: 글쎄요, 알다시피 난 오랫동안 스키를 타지 않았잖아요. 난 정말 스키를 많이 타고 싶어요. 종일 이용권으로 사요.
여: 그럼 나 빼고 먼저 타요. 난 몇 번만 타면 쉽게 피로해지는 거 알잖아요. 난 오후 이용권을 살게요.
남: 알겠어요. 1시에 산 정상에서 만나기로 해요.

어휘 **pass** 정기권, 무료 승차권 / **run** (스키의) 활강

07 이유 | ④

▶ 제품 시연 장소인 회의실이 다른 행사를 위해 예약되어서 내일로 연기되었다고 말했다.

W: Hi, William. What are you working on?

M: I'm preparing the handouts for this afternoon's product demonstration. **How do they look**?

W: Great, except for one thing. Didn't you see the email announcing the delay of the demonstration?

M: Oh, no! I guess the research-and-development team **failed to meet their deadline**.

W: Actually, it is just because the conference room **was accidentally booked for another event**. The demonstration will be tomorrow instead.

M: I'm a little embarrassed, but I suppose I can use the extra time to gather some more data.

W: Good thinking. Anyway, I have to hurry to a meeting with my team leader. He just returned from his business trip to London.

M: Okay. Good luck with that! Talk to you later.

여: 안녕, William. 뭐 하고 있니?
남: 오늘 오후에 있을 제품 시연을 위한 유인물을 준비하는 중이야. 어때 보여?
여: 한 가지만 제외하면 훌륭해. 그 시연이 연기된다는 것을 고지하는 이메일을 못 봤니?
남: 안 돼! 연구개발팀이 마감 기한에 맞추는 것을 실패했나 보네.
여: 사실, 단지 회의실이 실수로 다른 행사를 위해 예약되었기 때문이야. 대신 그 시연은 내일 열릴 거야.
남: 좀 당황스럽지만, 자료를 좀 더 모을 수 있는 여분의 시간을 사용할 수 있겠네.
여: 좋은 생각이야. 어쨌든, 난 우리 팀장과의 회의에 서둘러 가야 해. 그분이 런던 출장에서 막 돌아오셨거든.
남: 알겠어. 행운을 빌게! 나중에 얘기하자.

어휘 **handout** 유인물, 인쇄물 / **demonstration** 실연(實演), 시범 설명; 입증 / **announce** 고지[통지]하다, 알리다 / **deadline** 마감 시간, 최종 기한 / **accidentally** 잘못하여; 우연히 / **book** 예약하다 / **suppose** 가정하다; 추측하다

08 언급하지 않은 것 | ②

▶ 해석 참조

W: The leopard cat is a small wildcat native to South and East Asia. **Its name is derived from** its leopard-like spots, but its relation to the leopard is distant. Leopard cats are similar in size to house cats, but more slender with longer legs. Their feet are poorly-suited to walking on snow and they consequently avoid areas where snow depths exceed 10 cm. They eat meat, **feeding on a variety of small prey** including lizards, birds, and insects. They give birth to between two and four kittens at a time, and the kittens remain in the cave until they are about one month old. In the wild, leopard cats have an average lifespan of approximately 4 years, but **they have been known to live** up to 20 years if raised by humans.

여: 삵은 남아시아와 동아시아가 원산지인 작은 야생고양이입니다. 그것의 이름은 표범과 같은 반점에서 비롯되었으나, 표범과의 관련은 멉니다. 삵은 집고양이와 크기가 비슷하지만, 더 긴 다리를 가지고 있고 더 날씬합니다(① 생김새). 그것들의 발은 눈 위를 걷는 것에 적합하지 않고, 그 결과 적설량이 10센티미터가 넘는 지역은 피합니다. 그것들은 육식을 하는데, 도마뱀, 새 그리고 곤충을 포함한 여러 가지 작은 먹이를 먹고 삽니다(③ 먹이 습성). 한 번에 두 마리에서 네 마리 사이의 새끼를 낳으며(④ 번식력), 새끼들은 생후 약 한 달이 될 때까지 동굴에서 지냅니다. 야생에서는, 삶의 평균 수명이 약 4년이지만, 사람이 기르는 경우에는 20년까지 산다고 알려졌습니다(⑤ 평균 수명).

어휘 **derive (from)** (~에서) 비롯되다; 유래하다 / **distant** 먼; 동떨어진 / **slender** 날씬한, 호리호리한 / **suited** 적당한, 적합한, 어울리는 / **consequently** 그 결과, 따라서 / **exceed** 넘다, 초과하다 / **feed on** (동물이) ~을 먹고살다[먹다] / **lifespan** 수명

09 내용 불일치 | ②

▶ 경기는 매년 열린다고 했다.

M: Welcome competitors, spectators, and viewers at home! This is the seventh Global Cyber Games. Even though it is our seventh year, few people outside the gaming world **seem to know about the competition**. So let me tell you about the Global Cyber Games. The Global Cyber Games **have been modeled after** the Olympics. Every year a different city hosts the competition. And while at the games, the competitors all live together in one village. Moreover, all the competitors here have passed the qualifying round in their home country. This year we have over 770 competitors from 70 nations competing. I want to **wish them all good luck**!

남: 선수들과 관중들 그리고 가정의 시청자 여러분, 환영합니다! 제7회 글로벌 사이버 게임입니다. 일곱 번째 해가 되었지만, 게임 세계 밖에 계신 분들은 이 대회에 대해 거의 모르시는 것 같습니다. 그래서 제가 글로벌 사이버 게임에 대해서 설명해 드리겠습니다. 글로벌 사이버 게임은 올림픽을 본떠서 만들어졌습니다. 매년 다른 도시가 대회를 개최합니다. 그리고 대회에 참가하는 동안, 선수들은 모두 한 마을에서 합숙합니다. 게다가 이곳의 모든 선수는 자국에서 열린 예선 경기를 통과했습니다. 올해는 70개국에서 온 770명이 넘는 선수들이 경쟁합니다. 모든 선수에게 행운이 따르기를 빕니다!

어휘 **competitor** (시합) 참가자; 경쟁자 ***cf.* competition** 대회, 시합; 경쟁 **compete** 경쟁하다 / **spectator** 관중 / **model A after[on] B** B를 본떠서 A를 만들다 / **host** 개최하다; 주최자, 개최지 / **qualifying round** 예선 경기

10 도표 이해 | ③

▶ 어린이용 메뉴가 있고 점심시간에 영업을 하며, 예약을 받는 식당 중에 집에서 더 가까운 곳을 선택하였다.

M: **Have you figured out** where to go for Mom's birthday?
W: Well, I did some research online and found five restaurants that have very good reviews.
M: Okay. Let's take a look.... We need a restaurant that has a children's menu, so this one's out.
W: How about this restaurant?
M: Well, **it's closest to our house**, but they're not open for lunch.
W: You're right, and I guess that's a problem since we're planning to have lunch.
M: What about this one? They're open for lunch.
W: Yeah, but we also need to go somewhere **where they take reservations**.
M: Right, almost all restaurants will be crowded at lunchtime. We're left with only two choices then. Why don't you pick?
W: Hmm.... Let's go to the one closer to home.
M: Sounds good to me!

남: 엄마 생신 때 어디로 갈지 알아봤어?
여: 음, 내가 인터넷으로 조사를 좀 해서 평가가 아주 좋은 식당 다섯 곳을 찾아냈어.
남: 알았어. 한번 보자…. 우리는 어린이용 메뉴가 있는 식당이 필요하니까, 이건 제외야.
여: 이 식당은 어때?
남: 글쎄, 우리 집에서 가장 가깝지만 점심시간에 열지 않네.
여: 네 말이 맞아. 그리고 우리는 점심을 먹을 계획이니까 그건 문제인 것 같아.
남: 이건 어때? 여기는 점심시간에 영업해.
여: 응, 하지만 우리는 또한 예약을 받는 곳에 가야 해.
남: 맞아, 거의 모든 식당이 점심시간에 붐빌 거야. 그럼 두 가지 선택권만이 남네. 네가 고르는 게 어때?
여: 음…. 집에서 더 가까운 곳으로 가자.
남: 난 좋아!

어휘 **figure out** 알아내다, 이해하다

11 짧은 대화에 이어질 응답 | ③

▶ 영수증을 챙겨두지 않았는지 묻는 남자의 말에 가장 적절한 응답을 찾는다.

① 가지고 있어요, 그걸 가져오는 것을 잊어버렸네요.
② 가지고 있어요, 이 바지는 엉망이 되었네요.
③ 안 가지고 있어요, 어쩌다가 버렸어요.
④ 안 가지고 있어요, 집에 있는 서랍장 안에 있어요.
⑤ 그럼요, 거기 가격이 저렴해요.

M: These pants are too small. **Could you return them** for me?
W: I don't know if the store will accept them.
M: I think they will. **Didn't you keep the receipt**?
W: ______________________________

남: 이 바지는 너무 작아요. 나 대신 환불해 줄 수 있어요?
여: 가게에서 받아줄지 모르겠네요.
남: 받아줄 것 같아요. 당신 영수증 챙겨두지 않았어요?
여: ______________________________

어휘 **receipt** 영수증 | 선택지 어휘 | **ruin** 엉망으로 만들다, 망치다 / **by accident** 우연히; 실수로 / **competitive** (가격이) 저렴한, 경쟁력 있는

12 짧은 대화에 이어질 응답 | ③

▶ 새집을 찾아야 하는 상황에서 부동산에 가보겠다는 여자의 말에 휴가라서 함께 갈 수 있다는 응답이 가장 적절하다.

① 난 이 부동산 중개소를 못 믿겠어.
② 다행히도, 우리는 이곳을 빨리 찾았어.
③ 내가 쉬는 날이라서 우리 같이 갈 수 있어.
④ 내가 오늘 늦게 이삿짐센터에 전화할게.
⑤ 그 사람들이 새집 찾는 걸 우리가 도와줄 수 있어.

W: Wow, I didn't realize **we have to move out so soon**, did you?
M: No. We really need to hurry up and find a new place.
W: Exactly! **Do you want me to visit** a real estate agency?
M: ______________________________

여: 와, 난 우리가 이렇게 빨리 이사 나가야 할 줄은 미처 몰랐어. 너는 알았니?
남: 아니. 우리 정말 서둘러서 새집을 찾아야 해.
여: 맞아! 내가 부동산 중개소에 들러볼까?
남: ______________________________

어휘 **real estate agency** 부동산 중개소 | 선택지 어휘 | **day off** 쉬는 날, 휴가

13 긴 대화에 이어질 응답 | ②

▶ 여자는 Carla가 약속 시간을 지키지 않고 빌려 간 물건도 돌려주지 않아 불만이다.

① 알았어. 지금 바로 그 애에게 전화할게.
② 그러게, 난 그 애의 태도에 질렸어.
③ 그 애가 너에 대해서 어떻게 생각하든 관심 없어.
④ 책을 돌려줘서 고마워, Carla.
⑤ 그 애는 점심을 먼저 먹지 말았어야 했는데.

M: Hi, Jenna. Is something wrong?
W: Not really. I am just waiting for Carla. We're supposed to go and eat lunch together.
M: What time **is she supposed to meet you**?
W: Fifteen minutes ago!
M: Oh?
W: I wish she were reliable like you.
M: Me?
W: When we make an appointment, you **show up on time**. And when

you borrow something, you always give it back before I ask you.

M: Let me guess — she borrowed something and didn't give it back.

W: That's right. It was a book, and I needed it for a test yesterday.

M: Well, if she's late right now, why don't you phone her?

W: She should phone me. She's **the one who is late**.

M: I agree. It's like she doesn't care.

W: ____

남: 안녕, Jenna야. 무슨 일 있니?
여: 아니. Carla를 기다리고 있었던 것뿐이야. 점심 식사를 같이하기로 했거든.
남: 너랑 몇 시에 만나기로 했는데?
여: 15분 전에!
남: 그래?
여: 난 그 애가 너만큼 믿을 수 있는 사람이면 좋겠다.
남: 나?
여: 약속을 하면 너는 제시간에 나오잖아. 그리고 뭔가를 빌려 가면 항상 내가 말하기 전에 그것을 돌려주고.
남: 그러니까 그 애가 뭔가를 빌려 가서는 돌려주지 않았다는 거지.
여: 맞아. 책이었는데 시험 때문에 어제 내가 필요했거든.
남: 그럼, 그 애가 지금 늦는다면 전화를 해보지 그러니?
여: 그 애가 나에게 전화를 해야지. 늦은 건 바로 그 애니까.
남: 동의해. 그 애는 신경을 쓰지 않는 것 같구나.
여: ____

어휘 **reliable** 믿을 수 있는, 신뢰할 수 있는 / **make an appointment** 약속을 하다 / **show up** 나오다, 나타나다 / **on time** 제시간에 | 선택지 어휘 | **be fed up with** ~에 진저리가 나다[싫증 나다] / **attitude** 태도

14 긴 대화에 이어질 응답 | ②

▶ 여자는 셔츠를 찾으러 이곳을 다시 방문해야 하는지 궁금해하고 있다. 이에 대한 적절한 응답을 찾는다.

① 걱정 마세요. 비싸지 않습니다.
② 걱정하지 마세요. 제가 그것을 집으로 보내 드리겠습니다.
③ 지금 당장 셔츠를 가져가시는 것이 어떻겠습니까?
④ 새 옷을 만들 수 있는지 물어보겠습니다.
⑤ 죄송합니다. 셔츠값은 받지 않도록 하겠습니다.

W: Hi. I'm here to pick up the shirts **I dropped off to have cleaned** yesterday.

M: OK. Do you have your ticket?

W: No, but my last name is Stark.

M: Let me see... it looks like your shirts aren't going to be ready until 5 p.m.

W: But I was told they would be ready in 24 hours. That means 2 p.m.

M: I'm sorry, ma'am. That really means **by the end of business** the next day.

W: I'm leaving for the airport at 5 p.m. And I don't have anything to wear for the meeting in London. **What am I supposed to do**?

M: We have some spare shirts in your size that we can loan you.

W: OK, then. I should borrow some. Anyway, do I need to come here to pick up my shirts again?

M: ____

여: 안녕하세요. 어제 세탁을 맡긴 셔츠를 찾으러 왔습니다.
남: 알겠습니다. 티켓을 가지고 계신가요?
여: 아니요. 제 성은 Stark입니다.
남: 어디 보자… 손님의 셔츠는 오후 5시가 되어야 준비될 것 같습니다.
여: 하지만 24시간이면 준비된다고 들었는데요. 그게 오후 2시고요.
남: 죄송합니다, 손님. 그건 다음날 영업시간이 끝날 때까지란 뜻입니다.
여: 저는 오후 5시에 공항으로 떠나는데 런던에서 회의에 참석할 때 입을 옷이 하나도 없어요. 어떻게 해요?
남: 저희에게 손님 사이즈에 맞는 여분의 셔츠가 몇 벌 있는데 빌려드릴 수 있습니다.
여: 좋습니다. 그럼 몇 벌 정도 빌려야겠군요. 그런데 제 셔츠를 찾으러 여기 다시 와야 하나요?
남: ____

어휘 **drop off** (사람, 물건을) 내려놓다 / **spare** 여분의, 예비의 / **loan** 빌려주다 | 선택지 어휘 | **charge** (요금, 값을) 청구하다

15 상황에 적절한 말 | ④

▶ Susan은 강아지를 좋아하지만, 부모님의 허락을 받지 못해 강아지를 키울 수 없다. Carol이 여행 가는 동안 강아지를 돌봐달라고 Susan에게 부탁한 상황인데, 그 기간 동안 Susan의 아버지는 출장을 가신다. 그러므로 Susan은 어머니께 허락을 받아야 한다고 말하는 것이 가장 적절하다.

① 우리 엄마가 개를 키워도 된다고 하셨어.
② 다음 주에 떠나서 돌봐줄 수 없어.
③ 즐거운 여행하고 Roger에게 내 안부를 전해줘.
④ 그러고 싶지만, 먼저 엄마의 허락을 받아야 해.
⑤ 네가 원한다면 내가 Roger를 매일 산책시킬 수 있어.

W: Susan loves dogs, but when Susan asked her mom last year about having a dog, her mom said that a dog **would make the apartment too dirty**. She also said Susan's father wouldn't agree to it. So, Susan doesn't have a dog. Next week Carol, a friend of Susan's, is going on a five-day trip for summer vacation with her family. Carol needs someone to take care of her pet puppy, Roger, so she asks Susan what she is doing next week. Susan says her dad is **on a long business trip**, so she and her mom are just staying home. Carol asks Susan **if she can look after** Roger. In this situation, what would Susan most likely say to Carol?

여: Susan은 강아지를 매우 좋아하지만, 지난해 Susan이 어머니께 강아지를 키우자고 했을 때, 어머니는 강아지 때문에 아파트가 너무 지저분해질 거라고 말씀하셨다. 어머니는 또한 Susan의 아버지가 그것에 동의하시지 않을 거라고 하셨다. 그래서 Susan은 강아지가 없다. 다음 주에 Susan의 친구인 Carol은 가족과 함께 5일간 여름휴가를 떠날 예정이다. Carol은 반려견 Roger를 돌봐줄 누군가가 필요해서 Susan에게 다음 주에 무엇을 하는지 물어본다. Susan은 아버지가 장기 출장을 가셔서 자신과 어머니는 집에 그냥 있을 거라고 한다. Carol은 Susan에게 Roger를 돌봐줄 수 있는지 물어본다. 이러한 상황에서 Susan이 Carol에게 할 말로 가장 적절한 것은 무엇인가?

어휘 **business trip** 출장 | 선택지 어휘 | **take A for a walk** A를 산책시키다 / **permission** 허락, 허가

16~17 세트 문항 | 16. ② 17. ⑤

▶ 16. 다양한 분야에서 게임을 교육적으로 활용하는 예에 관해 설명하고 있다.

① 게임이 학습에 미치는 부정적인 영향
② 교육적 용도로서의 게임 활용법
③ 대학 교육 개혁의 방안
④ 우주 관광 산업에 대한 긍정적 전망
⑤ 다양한 성인 학습 도구 개발의 필요성

▶ 17. 해석 참조

M: Adults **who grew up playing** video games will do more good than harm. That's because they recognize the power of video games as educational tools. Gaming **can be used to develop skills** that help adults handle some of the world's most serious problems, and it's already being used in several important areas. For instance, firefighters **are using it to prepare for** biochemical disasters. University administrators are using it to reinvent higher education. Military services are using it to prepare for battle. And even space agencies worldwide are using it to explore mission types. When the pressures are high and the choices fast-paced and complex, using games to explore the options can provide substantial advantages. But institutions like schools, universities, and governments **will start to utilize its full potential** only when regular adults get comfortable with the tools of gaming.

남: 비디오 게임을 하며 자란 성인들은 해를 끼치기보다는 도움이 되는 일을 더 할 것입니다. 이는 그들이 교육적 도구로서 비디오 게임이 지니는 영향력을 잘 인지하고 있기 때문입니다. 게임은 성인들이 세상의 가장 심각한 문제 중 일부를 해결하는 데 도움이 되는 기술을 개발하기 위해 쓰일 수 있고, 몇몇 중요한 영역에서는 이미 사용 중이기도 합니다. 예컨대, 소방관은 생화학적 재난 상황에 대비하기 위해 게임을 사용하고 있습니다(① 소방서). 대학 관리자는 대학 교육을 개혁하는 데 게임을 사용하고 있습니다(② 대학). 군대는 전투를 대비하는 데 게임을 사용하고 있습니다(③ 군대). 심지어 전 세계의 항공 우주국은 수행할 임무의 유형을 탐색하는 데에도 게임을 사용하고 있습니다(④ 항공 우주국). (결정에 대한) 압박이 심하고 선택이 복잡한데 신속하게 결정되어야 할 때, 선택 사항을 탐색하려는 목적으로 게임을 활용하는 것은 상당한 이점을 줄 수 있습니다. 하지만 오직 일반 성인들이 게임이라는 도구를 사용하는 것에 익숙해질 때, 비로소 학교, 대학, 정부와 같은 기관이 게임이 지니고 있는 잠재력을 최대로 활용하기 시작할 것입니다.

어휘 **do good[harm]** 도움이[해가] 되다 / **biochemical** 생화학의 / **administrator** 관리자, 행정인 / **reinvent** 개혁하다; 재발명[고안]하다 / **fast-paced** 빨리 진행되는 / **substantial** 상당한 / **utilize** 활용하다 | 선택지 어휘 | **outlook** 전망; 관점 / **necessity** 필요(성); 필수품

01. ④	02. ②	03. ④	04. ④	05. ③	06. ②	07. ⑤	08. ⑤	09. ②	10. ②
11. ②	12. ②	13. ⑤	14. ③	15. ⑤	16. ④	17. ④			

01 화자가 하는 말의 목적 | ④

▶ ~ water will be cut off from 10 a.m. to 5 p.m. on September 12th에 여자가 하는 말의 목적이 드러나 있다. 즉, 수도관 공사로 인한 단수를 안내하려는 것이 목적이다.

W: The Blue Bell Canyon County Water Company **would like to make an announcement** to all Northville residents. We have good news for Northville residents **who have complained about the dirty water** that flows through rusty water pipes. In order to provide you with cleaner water, we will undergo construction of new water pipes. Due to this major construction, water will be cut off from 10 a.m. to 5 p.m. on September 12th. We apologize for the inconvenience but **ask for your cooperation** as we will provide you with cleaner water. We ask that you prepare a personal reservoir of water before the construction. For further information, please call 915-1121, or visit our website www.bluecanwater.com.

여: Blue Bell Canyon County 수도 회사는 모든 Northville 주민 여러분께 안내 말씀 드립니다. 녹슨 수도관에서 흘러나오는 더러운 물 때문에 불편을 호소하셨던 Northville 주민들께 희소식입니다. 여러분께 더 깨끗한 물을 공급하기 위해서 새 수도관 공사를 하고자 합니다. 이 큰 공사로 인해, 9월 12일 오전 10시부터 오후 5시까지 단수될 것입니다. 불편을 끼쳐 죄송합니다만, 더 깨끗한 물을 공급해드릴 것이므로 협조 부탁드립니다. 공사 전 개별 저수통을 준비하시기를 부탁드립니다. 더 많은 정보를 원하시면, 915-1121로 전화를 주시거나 저희 웹사이트인 www.bluecanwater.com을 방문해주십시오.

어휘 **make an announcement** 발표하다, 공표하다 / **resident** 주민, 거주자 / **rusty** 녹슨 / **undergo** 치르다, 겪다; 견디다 / **inconvenience** 불편 / **cooperation** 협력; 협조 / **reservoir** 저수지, 저수통; 비축, 저장

02 의견 | ②

▶ 동물 보호소에서 봉사활동을 하는 남자가 유기견의 실태에 대해 사람들이 관심을 가져야 한다고 말하고 있다.

W: Scott, do you want to see a movie this Saturday?
M: Sounds fun, but I can't. I'll be at the animal shelter.
W: Oh, that's right. I forgot that you volunteer there. How is that going?
M: Well, it's alright. I love the dogs, and the other volunteers are great, but sometimes **it's heartbreaking**.
W: The animal shelter is doing great work. Is it really that bad?
M: Yes. There are so many dogs **that are abandoned every week**. People are so careless sometimes.
W: That is sad. At least there are people like you **who try to help**.
M: Thanks, but the number of abandoned dogs isn't going to decrease unless a lot more people get involved.

여: Scott, 이번 주 토요일에 영화 보러 갈래?
남: 재미있겠다, 그런데 안 돼. 동물 보호소에 있을 거거든.
여: 아, 맞다. 네가 거기서 자원봉사하는 걸 깜빡했어. 어떻게 되어가고 있니?
남: 음, 괜찮아. 난 개를 사랑하고 다른 자원봉사자들도 아주 좋아. 하지만 때때로 가슴이 찢어질 듯이 아파.
여: 동물 보호소에서는 훌륭한 일을 하고 있잖아. 상황이 정말 그렇게 나쁘니?
남: 응. 매주 버려지는 개들이 아주 많아. 사람들은 때때로 아주 경솔해.
여: 애석한 일이야. 적어도 너처럼 도와주려는 사람들이 있잖아.
남: 고마워, 하지만 훨씬 더 많은 사람이 관여하지 않으면 유기견 수는 줄어들지 않을 거야.

어휘 **shelter** 보호소, 쉼터 / **heartbreaking** 가슴이 찢어질 듯한, 가슴 아프게 하는 / **abandon** 버리다 ***cf.*** **abandoned dog** 유기견

03 관계 | ④

▶ 벽으로 알았던 구조물이 전시회의 작품임을 알리며 사진 촬영을 제지하고 엽서 파는 곳을 알려주는 것으로 보아 남자는 미술관 직원이고 여자는 관람객임을 알 수 있다.

M: Excuse me, ma'am. You **aren't allowed to lean there**.
W: Why? My legs are killing me, so I just need to rest on this wall for a minute. I must have walked miles today. Do I have to ask permission first?
M: No, but I'm afraid it's not a wall.
W: What are you talking about?
M: That is **a piece from an exhibition**. The title is right over there. It says, "2050 Fifth Avenue."
W: Oh, really? I'm so sorry. I just thought it was a decorative wall in the corner.
M: No, it's a sculpture from an up-and-coming young artist named James Spacy.
W: Really? Now I'd like to take a photo of it.
M: Hold on. You **shouldn't take photos here**.
W: Oh, I'm sorry. I just want to have a photo of this piece as a souvenir.
M: You can purchase post cards at the shop near the entrance.
W: Okay. Thanks.

남: 저, 실례합니다. 거기에 기대시면 안 됩니다.
여: 왜요? 다리가 너무 아파서 이 벽에 잠시만 기대야겠어요. 오늘 수 마일은 걸은 것 같아요. 먼저 허락을 구해야 하나요?
남: 아니요, 하지만 그건 벽이 아닙니다.
여: 무슨 말씀 하시는 거예요?
남: 그건 전시회의 작품입니다. 제목이 바로 거기 있습니다. '2050 Fifth Avenue'라고 되어 있군요.
여: 오, 그래요? 정말 죄송합니다. 전 단지 코너에 장식해놓은 벽이라고 생각했어요.
남: 아니요, James Spacy라는 전도유망한 젊은 작가의 조각품입니다.
여: 정말요? 그렇다면 그 사진을 찍고 싶군요.
남: 잠시만요, 여기에서 사진을 찍으실 수 없습니다.
여: 아, 죄송해요. 전 단지 기념으로 이 작품의 사진을 갖고 싶어요.
남: 입구 근처의 가게에서 엽서를 구매하실 수 있습니다.
여: 알겠어요. 감사합니다.

어휘 **lean** 기대다; 기울이다 / **rest** (어떤 것에) 기대다; 쉬다 / **permission** 허락, 허가 / **decorative** 장식이 된, 장식용의 / **up-and-coming** 전도유망한, 떠오르는 / **souvenir** 기념(품) / **purchase** 구매하다; 구매

04 그림 불일치 | ④

▶ 여자가 가져온 사진에서처럼 탁자에 깃발이 꽂힌 화병을 두겠다고 했는데 그림에는 술병과 컵이 놓여 있으므로 일치하지 않는다.

W: I found a picture of a porch that I really like. Here it is.
M: Let's take a look. There are plants **on both sides of the front steps** that lead to the door.
W: Yes, and look at the bird-shaped postbox.
M: You mean the postbox **hanging on the wall** next to the door? It looks so cute.
W: The porch also has two rocking chairs. You and I can sit on the chairs for a relaxing evening.
M: There's also a side table between the chairs. We can put drinks, like beer and wine, on it.
W: No way. I want to put a vase with flags on the table like **they did in the picture**.
M: Okay. When we **rock back and forth** on the rocking chairs, we will be able to see the hanging potted plants on the ceiling.
W: All the greenery will **help us relax even more**.
M: Sounds good.

여: 내가 정말 마음에 든 현관 사진을 찾았어. 자, 여기 있어.
남: 한번 보자. 문으로 이어지는 앞 계단 양쪽에 화초가 있네.
여: 응, 그리고 새 모양으로 생긴 우편함을 봐.
남: 문 옆의 벽에 걸린 우편함을 말하는 거야? 아주 귀여워 보이네.
여: 현관에는 흔들의자 2개도 있어. 너랑 내가 그 의자에 앉아서 편안한 저녁을 보낼 수 있어.
남: 의자 사이에 작은 탁자도 있어. 우린 그 위에 맥주와 와인 같은 마실 것을 놓을 수 있어.
여: 안 돼. 난 사진에서처럼 탁자 위에 깃발을 꽂은 꽃병을 두고 싶어.
남: 그래. 우리가 흔들의자에 앉아 앞뒤로 흔들거리면, 천장에서 대롱거리는 화분에 든 화초를 볼

수 있을 거야.
여: 녹색 화초들은 모두 우리가 더 편히 쉬는 데 도움이 될 거야.
남: 좋아.

어휘 **porch** 현관 / **rocking chair** 흔들의자 ***cf.*** **rock** 흔들다 / **greenery** 푸른 화초[나뭇잎]

05 추후 행동 | ③

▶ 남자는 여자에게 보고서의 모든 수치를 다시 확인해 오류를 바로잡아 달라고 했다.

M: Can I talk to you for a minute?
W: Of course, Mr. Johnson.
M: **I was looking over** your financial report for last quarter and the figures must be inaccurate.
W: Are you sure? I was very careful.
M: Based on our yearly budget, **we can't have spent this much money** in the last quarter alone.
W: Let me take a look. *[pause]* Oh, it looks like I entered the wrong numbers into this column here. I'm so sorry.
M: That's alright. But **I should give it to** Ms. Thomson at the meeting tomorrow.
W: Right, that's at 10 a.m.
M: So, I just want you to check all the figures again and correct the errors. Can you do that?
W: Sure. No problem. I'll take care of it.

남: 잠시 이야기 나눌 수 있을까요?
여: 물론입니다. Johnson 씨.
남: 당신이 작성한 지난 분기 재무보고서를 살펴보고 있었는데 수치에 분명 오류가 있는 것 같아요.
여: 정말요? 신경 써서 작성했는데요.
남: 연간 예산으로 미뤄볼 때, 지난 한 분기 동안에만 이렇게 많은 돈을 지출했을 리가 없어요.
여: 한번 볼게요. *[잠시 후]* 아, 여기 이 열에 제가 수치를 잘못 기입한 것 같군요. 정말 죄송합니다.
남: 괜찮아요. 그런데 내일 회의에서 Thomson 씨에게 그걸 제출해야 해요.
여: 네, 회의는 오전 10시에 있고요.
남: 그래서 말인데, 당신이 (보고서의) 모든 수치를 다시 확인해 오류를 바로잡아 줬으면 해요. 할 수 있겠어요?
여: 물론이죠. 문제없습니다. 제가 처리할게요.

어휘 **quarter** 사분기(1년의 4분의 1) / **inaccurate** 부정확한, 오류가 있는(↔ accurate 정확한) / **column** 열, 세로줄; (원형) 기둥; (신문 · 잡지의) 칼럼

06 금액 | ②

▶ 남자는 가장 싼 표인 80달러짜리 표 3장을 샀고 12달러짜리 프로그램 책자를 샀으므로 지불할 총액은 252달러이다.

W: Good evening. How can I help you?
M: Hi, I'd like to buy some tickets for the musical, *Mamma Mia*. Do you **have three seats open tonight**?
W: Yes. Where would you like to sit?
M: Where are the best seats **that you have left**?
W: Well, the best seats are in the orchestra section, in the center.
M: How much does it cost to be in the orchestra?
W: It costs 250 dollars per seat.
M: That's too expensive for us. What's the next best seating?
W: Up in the middle section of the theater, the seats are $180, but **they've all been sold**. We only have 120-dollar tickets and 80-dollar tickets.
M: Oh, then I'd like **the cheaper ones**. Three, please.
W: All right. Would you like to buy a program book? It's 12 dollars.
M: Yes, please. I'd like one.

여: 안녕하세요. 어떻게 도와드릴까요?
남: 안녕하세요. 뮤지컬 〈Mamma Mia〉의 표를 사고 싶은데요. 오늘 저녁 세 자리가 가능한가요?
여: 네. 어디에 앉고 싶으신가요?
남: 남은 좌석 중 가장 좋은 자리가 어디인가요?
여: 음, 가장 좋은 자리는 1층 앞쪽 중앙 좌석입니다.
남: 그 자리는 얼마인가요?
여: 한 좌석당 250달러입니다.
남: 저희가 지불하기에 너무 비싸군요. 그다음으로 좋은 자리는 어디죠?
여: (그보다) 뒤쪽 극장 가운데 부분으로, 180달러입니다만, 그 자리는 모두 매진입니다. 120달러짜리 표와 80달러짜리 표만 남았습니다.
남: 오, 그러면 더 저렴한 것들로 할게요. 세 장 부탁합니다.
여: 알겠습니다. 프로그램 책자를 구매하시겠어요? 12달러입니다.
남: 네. 하나 주세요.

어휘 **orchestra section** 1층 앞쪽 좌석

07 이유 | ⑤

▶ 여자의 여동생이 휴대전화를 두고 온 상점이 다음 정류장 근처에 있다고 했으므로 휴대전화를 찾기 위해 내리는 것이다.

W: Alright, I'll talk to you later. *[Beep: sound of a cell phone being hung up]* Arnie, **something just came up**, and I can't go to the bookstore with you. I have to **get off at the next stop**.
M: Is something wrong? The next stop is the Cineplex. Are you going to see a movie?
W: It's not that. I just got off the phone with my sister and she said she lost her phone.
M: Oh, that's too bad. Does she know where it is?
W: Yeah, she said she left it at a store while she was shopping.
M: Did she tell you which store it was?
W: It happens that the store is next to the Cineplex, so **that's why I have to get off**.
M: Oh, I see. Where is she?
W: She's already at home, so she **asked me to pick up her phone**.
M: Well, why don't we get off together? I'll go to the bookstore tomorrow.
W: That's a great idea. There's also a place that has delicious cookies, so let's stop by there, too.
M: It's time to get off. Let's go.

여: 알겠어, 나중에 얘기해. *[휴대전화 끊는 소리]* Arnie, 방금 일이 생겨서, 너랑 서점에 갈 수 없어. 난 다음 정류장에서 내려야 해.
남: 안 좋은 일이야? 다음 정류장은 Cineplex야. 너 영화 볼 거니?
여: 그런 게 아니야. 방금 여동생과 전화를 끊었는데, 휴대전화를 잃어버렸대.
남: 오, 안됐구나. 휴대전화가 어디 있는지 그 애가 알고 있니?
여: 응, 물건을 사던 중에 가게에 놓고 왔대.
남: 어느 가게인지 말해줬어?
여: 마침 그 가게가 Cineplex 옆이라서 내가 내려야 하는 거야.
남: 아, 알겠어. 동생은 어디 있어?
여: 이미 집에 가서, 나에게 휴대전화를 찾아와 달라고 부탁했어.
남: 음, 우리 같이 내리는 게 어때? 서점은 내일 갈게.
여: 좋은 생각이야. 맛있는 쿠키를 파는 곳도 있으니까, 거기도 들르자.
남: 이제 내려야 해. 가자.

어휘 **get off** (버스, 기차 등에서) 내리다; (전화를) 끊다

08 언급하지 않은 것 | ⑤

▶ 해석 참조

[Phone rings.]
M: Royal Globe. Is there anything I can help you with today?
W: Yes. I found **some problems with a globe** that I bought the other day from your website.
M: I'm sorry to hear that. May I ask what the problem is?
W: The description said it was a desktop globe, but it's too small.
M: Oh, but **its size is specified online**.
W: And it has a problem with the batteries. You said it has a glow-in-the-dark feature, but **it doesn't glow**.
M: I'm sorry to hear that.
W: Also, the color of the sea should be blue, but it looks gray. And the worst problem is that the names of two countries are reversed.
M: Really?
W: Yeah! "Canada" is at the bottom and "United States" is on top. It should be **the other way around**.
M: Oh, no! That's a terrible mistake. I'm so sorry. I'd be happy to give you your money back.

[전화벨이 울린다.]
남: Royal Globe입니다. 오늘 제가 도와드릴 일이 있을까요?
여: 네. 며칠 전에 홈페이지에서 구매한 지구본에 문제가 있어서요.

남: 그렇다니 죄송합니다. 무엇이 문제인지 여쭤봐도 될까요?
여: 설명에는 탁상 지구본이라고 되어 있었는데, 너무 작군요(① 작은 크기).
남: 오, 하지만 크기는 홈페이지에 명시되어 있습니다.
여: 그리고 건전지에 문제가 있어요(② 건전지 불량). 야광 기능이 있다고 했는데, 빛나지 않아요.
남: 죄송합니다.
여: 또, 바다 색깔은 파란색이어야 하는데, 회색으로 보이고요(③ 흐린 색깔). 그리고 가장 심한 문제는 두 나라의 이름이 바뀌어 있다(④ 국가명 표기 오류)는 거예요.
남: 정말요?
여: 네! 'Canada'가 아래에 있고 'United States'가 위에 있어요. 반대로 되어야 하지요.
남: 오, 이런! 그건 심각한 실수군요. 정말 죄송합니다. 기꺼이 환불해 드리겠습니다.

어휘 **the other day** 며칠 전에, 일전에 / **description** (제품의) 설명서, 해설; 서술, 묘사 / **specify** (구체적으로) 명시하다 / **glow-in-the-dark** 야광의 / **reverse** (위치를) 서로 바꾸다, 뒤바꾸다 / **the other way around** 반대로, 거꾸로

09 내용 불일치 | ②

▶ No prior acting experience is required.라는 말로 보아 연기 경험이 있는 어린이를 대상으로 강습하는 것은 아니다.

M: Do you have a child **that's a natural performer**? Hudson Talent Agency is looking for up-and-coming child actors. We are currently offering classes to help talented children become professional musical actors. No prior acting experience is required. Our classes are held every Saturday from 10 a.m. to noon, from May 5th to July 5th. All children who are enrolled in our program will have **a chance to audition for a role** in the hit Broadway musical, *Annie*. Students will practice a number of songs and dance routines to prepare for the musical audition. Applications will be taken on a first come, **first served basis**. If you'd like more information regarding the program, contact our program director, Terry Theissen. Our number is 313-545-1500. Call us today.

남: 타고난 연기자인 아이를 두고 계십니까? Hudson Talent Agency는 전도유망한 아역 배우를 모집하고 있습니다. 저희는 현재 재능 있는 아이들을 전문 뮤지컬 배우로 양성하는 수업을 제공하고 있습니다. 이전의 연기 경험은 필요하지 않습니다. 수업은 5월 5일부터 7월 5일까지 매주 토요일 오전 10시부터 정오까지 열립니다. 저희 프로그램에 등록하는 모든 아이들은 인기 브로드웨이 뮤지컬 〈Annie〉에서의 역할을 위한 오디션 기회가 주어집니다. 학생들은 뮤지컬 오디션을 준비하기 위해 많은 노래와 춤 동작을 연습할 것입니다. 신청은 선착순으로 받을 것입니다. 프로그램에 관해 더 많은 정보를 원하시면, 프로그램 책임자인 Terry Theissen에게 연락해 주십시오. 번호는 313-545-1500입니다. 오늘 전화해 주세요.

어휘 **performer** 연기자, 연주자 / **enroll** 등록하다 / **routine** 정해진 춤 동작; 일과 / **application** 신청, 지원; 적용 / **on a first come, first served basis** 선착순으로

10 도표 이해 | ②

▶ 여자는 저녁 시간에 하고 50달러 미만의 수강료를 내는 중간 강도의 수업을 원했다. 강사의 성별은 둘 다 좋다고 했다.

W: Hello, I'd like to sign up for a fitness class, please.
M: Is this your first time taking a class at the YMCA, ma'am?
W: Yes, I just joined the gym last week, and now I'm **trying to explore my options**!
M: Here's a schedule containing all of our classes. You'll need to take into account what time you want your class to be, first.
W: I work from 9 a.m. to 5 p.m., so I can't do anything in the morning or afternoon. What sorts of things do you offer in the evening?
M: How difficult would you like your class to be?
W: I want at least **a little bit of a challenge**! I'm here to lose weight, after all.
M: Understood. A medium-level class might suit you just right, then. Which do you prefer, a male or female trainer?
W: I'm fine with either.
M: The last thing to consider would be the price of the classes. You'll want to **take your budget into account** when choosing a class.
W: I'm looking for something under $50. What do you **have in that range**?
M: I think I know exactly what class will be perfect for you.

여: 안녕하세요. 운동 수업을 신청하고 싶은데요.
남: YMCA에서 수업을 들으시는 건 이번이 처음이신가요, 부인?
여: 네, 지난주에 막 체육관에 등록했고, 이제 선택사항을 알아보려고 해요!
남: 여기 모든 수업이 제시된 편성표가 있습니다. 먼저 수업은 언제가 좋으신지 고려해보셔야 해요.
여: 제가 오전 9시부터 오후 5시까지 일하기 때문에 아침이나 오후에는 아무것도 할 수 없어요. 저녁에는 어떤 것들이 있죠?
남: 수업 강도는 어떤 걸 원하세요?
여: 적어도 약간은 힘든 것이 좋겠어요! 결국, 살을 빼려고 온 거니까요.
남: 알겠습니다. 그럼 중간 강도의 수업이 딱 맞겠네요. 남자 강사나 여자 강사 중 어느 분을 선호하세요?
여: 둘 다 괜찮아요.
남: 마지막으로 생각하실 것은 수강료겠네요. 수업을 고르실 때 예산을 고려하고 싶으시겠지요.
여: 50달러 미만의 것을 찾고 있어요. 그 범위에 어떤 것이 있나요?
남: 정확히 어떤 수업이 부인께 딱 맞을지 알 것 같군요.

어휘 **sign up for** ~을 신청하다 / **take A into account** A를 고려하다 | 선택지 어휘 | **meditation** 명상, 묵상 / **moderately** 알맞게, 적당히

11 짧은 대화에 이어질 응답 | ②

▶ 역사 시험 범위가 너무 넓어서 밤새워 공부했다는 남자의 이야기를 듣고 시험 범위가 줄어든 것을 듣지 못했느냐는 여자의 말에 가장 적절한 응답을 찾는다.

① 좋아, 넌 역사를 매우 잘했어.
② 정말이야? 그럼 괜히 헛수고만 한 거네!
③ 응, 한편으론 이해가 돼.
④ 걱정하지 마. 그게 네 잘못이 아니란 걸 우리 모두 알아.
⑤ 음, 그게 그의 진심이었는지 아닌지는 모르겠어.

W: What did you do last night?
M: **I studied all night** for today's history test. There were too many chapters to study!
W: Oh, no! Didn't you hear that several chapters **won't be on the test**?
M: ______________________________

여: 어젯밤에 뭐 했니?
남: 오늘 있을 역사 시험을 위해 밤새워 공부했어. 공부할 챕터가 너무 많았어!
여: 아, 이런! 챕터 몇 개는 시험에 안 나올 거란 걸 듣지 못한 거니?
남: ______________________________

어휘 | 선택지 어휘 | **for nothing** 헛되이; 공짜로

12 짧은 대화에 이어질 응답 | ②

▶ 식탁이 비싸다고 하며 자신의 예산을 벗어났다는 말에 그만한 값어치가 있다고 응답할 수 있을 것이다.

① 제게는 중요하지 않아요.
② 하지만 그 가격만한 가치가 있어요.
③ 지금 저는 거의 파산이에요.
④ 그게 바로 제가 원하는 거예요.
⑤ 훨씬 더 비싼 것들도 있어요.

M: This table **looks solid and stylish**. How much is it?
W: It's 853 dollars plus tax.
M: Well, it's a bit expensive. It's out of my budget.
W: ______________________________

남: 이 탁자는 튼튼하고 스타일이 좋아 보이는군요. 얼마인가요?
여: 853달러에 세금이 붙습니다.
남 음, 좀 비싸네요. 제 예산을 벗어나요.
여: ______________________________

어휘 **solid** 튼튼한; 단단한, 고체의 | 선택지 어휘 | **bankrupt** 파산한; 결여된

13 긴 대화에 이어질 응답 | ⑤

▶ 함께 연주회에 가게 되어 좋아하던 여자가 아이들을 돌봐주러 8시까지 가야 한다며 난감해하고 있으므로 이에 대한 응답은 그 전에 끝나니 걱정하지 말라는 말이 가장 적절하다.

① 다른 아이들과 노는 것은 언제나 재밌어.
② 그분의 아이들을 연주회에 데려오면 안 돼.
③ 넌 미리 저녁을 먹었어야 했는데.
④ 난 왜 네가 자립해서 살고 싶어 했는지 이해해.
⑤ 걱정하지 마, 연주회는 그 전에 끝날 거야.

W: Hi! How are you, Alexis?
M: Pretty well. **I'm kind of bored**, though. What do you feel like doing?
W: Well, we could go to the lake and do some kayaking.
M: We did that last week. How about going to a concert? Do you like classical music?

W: Yes, I love it! You know I play the violin!
M: I read in the newspaper that the Blue County Philharmonic is playing at the new symphony hall tonight.
W: Sounds terrific. **When should we meet**?
M: The concert starts at 4:30 p.m. How about meeting at 4?
W: I'd love to. *[pause]* Oh, no. I'm afraid I can't. **I'll be in trouble** if the concert goes late.
M: Why? Do you have another plan tonight?
W: Yes, I need to be at Mr. Albert's house by 8:00 p.m. **I have to babysit his kids** until 10:30.
M: ______________________________

여: 안녕! 어떻게 지냈니, Alexis?
남: 잘 지내. 하지만 약간 지루해. 뭐 하고 싶니?
여: 음, 우린 호수에 가서 카약을 탈 수 있어.
남: 그건 지난주에 했잖아. 연주회에 가는 게 어때? 너 클래식 음악 좋아하니?
여: 응, 정말 좋아해! 나 바이올린 연주하는 거 알잖아!
남: Blue County 교향악단이 오늘 저녁 새로 지은 심포니 홀에서 공연한다고 신문에서 읽었어.
여: 멋진데. 우리 언제 만날까?
남: 연주회가 오후 4시 30분에 시작해. 4시에 만나는 게 어때?
여: 좋아. *[잠시 후]* 오, 이런. 나 못 갈 거 같아. 연주회가 길어지면 문제가 생길 거야.
남: 왜? 오늘 저녁에 다른 계획이 있니?
여: 응, 오후 8시까지 Albert 씨 집에 가야 해. 10시 30분까지 그 집 아이들을 봐줘야 하거든.
남: ______________________________

어휘 **philharmonic** 교향악단 | 선택지 어휘 | **beforehand** 미리, 사전에 / **earn one's way** 자립해서 살다

14 긴 대화에 이어질 응답 | ③

▶ 파티에서 만났던 사람을 고향으로 가는 비행기에서 우연히 만나 이야기하다가 서로 초등학교 동창임을 알게 된 상황에서 할 수 있는 말은 ③이다.

① 와! 지난 2년 동안 너 많이 변했구나!
② Stephanie는 내 가장 좋은 친구이고 내 롤모델이야.
③ 여기서 너를 만나다니 정말 우연의 일치네! 세상 좁구나!
④ 죄송하지만, 다른 사람과 저를 혼동한 것 같아요.
⑤ 부모님께 안부 전해줘. 즐거운 휴일 보내!

M: Excuse me. Will you **kindly allow me to pass**? My seat is 3C.
W: Sure. Go ahead.
M: Thanks. Oh, **have we met before**?
W: Well, I'm not sure.
M: Weren't you at Stephanie's party last Saturday?
W: Yes, I was. Were you there, too?
M: Yeah. Now I remember. You're her friend, right? I'm her colleague, Joseph Whittier.
W: Nice to see you again. I'm Emily Nicholas. Are you going home for the Christmas holiday?
M: Yes, I'm from Denver, and my parents still live there.
W: Oh, really? I'm also from Denver. Joseph Whittier... Oh, **didn't you happen to graduate from** Lincoln Elementary School?
M: Yes, I did. Yeah! Now I remember your name. You're Emily!
W: ______________________________

남: 실례합니다. 제가 좀 지나가게 해주시겠어요? 제 자리는 3C예요.
여: 그럼요. 어서 가세요.
남: 감사합니다. 오, 전에 우리 만난 일이 있던가요?
여: 음, 잘 모르겠는데요.
남: 지난 토요일 Stephanie의 파티에 있지 않았어요?
여: 네, 있었어요. 당신도 거기 있었어요?
남: 네, 이제 기억나네요. 그녀의 친구죠? 저는 그녀의 동료인 Joseph Whittier예요.
여: 다시 만나서 반가워요. 전 Emily Nicholas예요. 크리스마스 휴가로 고향에 가는 중이신가요?
남: 네, 전 Denver 출신이고, 부모님이 여전히 거기 살고 계세요.
여: 오, 정말요? 저도 Denver 출신이에요. Joseph Whittier라··· 오, 혹시 Lincoln 초등학교 졸업하지 않았어요?
남: 네, 맞아요. 그래! 이제 네 이름이 기억났어. 너 Emily구나!
여: ______________________________

어휘 **colleague** 동료 | 선택지 어휘 | **coincidence** 우연의 일치 / **give one's regards to A** A에게 안부를 전하다

15 상황에 적절한 말 | ⑤

▶ 친구의 생일 파티에 갑자기 못 가게 되었을 때 할 말을 고른다.

① 내 친구들은 모두 이미 거기에 있어.
② 다음 달에 널 만나겠다고 약속할게.
③ 30분 뒤에 너희 집에 갈게.
④ 24시간 대기 중인 의사가 있어.
⑤ 미안하지만, 오늘 밤에 갈 수 없을 것 같아.

W: Grace and Megan are best friends. Megan's **birthday is coming up**, and naturally she invited Grace to her birthday party. It is going to be a sleepover, and Megan invites several of her closest friends. Grace told Megan that **she would definitely come**, but this evening, on the night of the party, Grace's mother is very sick. Her mother has got a bad cold, so Grace **must look after her mother**. Her father is **on a business trip**, and her brother is in New York to study. Now Grace picks up the phone and dials Megan's number. In this situation, what would Grace most likely say to Megan over the phone?

여: Grace와 Megan은 가장 친한 친구이다. Megan의 생일이 다가오고 있고, 당연히 그녀는 Grace를 생일 파티에 초대했다. 밤샘 파티가 될 예정이고, Megan은 가장 친한 친구 몇몇을 초대한다. Grace는 Megan에게 꼭 가겠다고 말했지만, 파티가 있는 오늘 저녁, Grace의 어머니는 매우 편찮으시다. 그녀의 어머니는 독감에 걸리셔서 Grace는 어머니를 돌봐야 한다. 그녀의 아버지는 출장 중이시고, 그녀의 오빠는 New York에서 공부 중이다. 이제 Grace는 전화기를 들어 Megan의 번호를 누른다. 이러한 상황에서 Grace가 Megan에게 전화로 할 말로 가장 적절한 것은 무엇인가?

어휘 **sleepover** 밤샘 파티, 함께 자며 놀기 | 선택지 어휘 | **on call** 대기 중인

16~17 세트 문항 | 16. ④ 17. ④

▶ 16. 컴퓨터 게임을 통한 학습을 언급하면서 교육용 컴퓨터 게임의 출시를 광고하고 있다.

① 컴퓨터 게임의 해로운 영향
② 창의력을 증진시킬 수 있는 최고의 컴퓨터 게임
③ 가르치는 데 유용한 다양한 교실 게임들
④ 새로운 교육용 컴퓨터 게임의 출시
⑤ 어린 나이에 게임하는 것에 대한 논란들

▶ 17. 해석 참조

M: Are you overwhelmed with the increasing amount of schoolwork and discouraged about your poor performance at school? Do you **get so absorbed in** playing your favorite computer game that you forget what time it is? We have good news for you. We've come up with a variety of games to help you study **a wide range of subjects** you learn at school. For instance, a game called *The Unknown World* makes history come alive for you as you experience historical events through digital, real-time travel. With *Exciting Numbers*, you can learn math in a fun way while playing number games. Another, called *Wonderful Odyssey*, **allows you to explore** countries, cities, rivers, mountains, and lakes through a ride on a helicopter and learn a lot about geography **in an imaginative way**. *A Brilliant Storyteller* helps you learn a work of literature through quiz games **categorized by grade levels**. Please visit our website now and buy one of these new and exciting games. You'll see results almost immediately!

남: 더 늘어나는 학업량에 압도되고 학교에서의 낮은 성적에 낙심하시나요? 시간을 잊을 정도로 좋아하는 컴퓨터 게임을 하는 데 몰두하나요? 그런 여러분께 희소식이 있습니다. 저희는 학교에서 배우는 광범위한 과목을 공부하는 데 도움을 줄 다양한 게임을 내놓아 왔습니다. 예를 들어, 〈The Unknown World〉라는 게임은 여러분이 역사적 사건들을 디지털 방식의 실시간 여행을 통해 경험하면서 ① 역사를 생생하게 느끼게 해줍니다. 〈Exciting Numbers〉로는, 숫자 게임을 하면서 재미있게 ② 수학을 배울 수 있습니다. 〈Wonderful Odyssey〉라는 또 다른 게임은 헬리콥터를 타고 국가, 도시, 강, 산, 호수를 탐험하며 창의적인 방법으로 ③ 지리에 관해 많은 것을 배우게 해줍니다. 〈A Brilliant Storyteller〉는 학년별로 분류된 퀴즈 게임을 통해 ⑤ 문학 작품을 배우도록 도와줍니다. 지금 저희 홈페이지를 방문하셔서 이 새롭고 신나는 게임 중 하나를 구매해 보십시오. 거의 즉각적으로 효과를 보실 것입니다!

어휘 **overwhelmed** 압도된 / **discouraged** 낙심한 / **absorbed** 몰두한, 빠져 있는 / **come up with** ~을 내놓다; ~을 생각해내다 / **a wide range of** 광범위한 / **come alive** 생생하게 보이다, 활기를 띠다 / **real-time** 실시간의 / **imaginative** 창의적인, 상상력이 풍부한 / **categorize** (범주로) 분류하다 | 선택지 어휘 | **release** 출시, 개봉; 방출; 발매[개봉]하다; 방출하다 / **controversy** 논란

01. ② 02. ③ 03. ③ 04. ② 05. ⑤ 06. ④ 07. ⑤ 08. ② 09. ③ 10. ③
11. ② 12. ③ 13. ③ 14. ③ 15. ⑤ 16. ② 17. ⑤

01 화자가 하는 말의 목적 | ②

▶ 헬스클럽의 전화번호와 수강료 등을 이야기하고 지금 가입하라고 권하는 내용으로 보아 헬스클럽을 광고하고 있음을 알 수 있다.

M: Look at this photo! This was me 3 months ago. And now look at me. Don't I look fantastic? I've been going to the Ace Fitness Club, a fitness center that **offers a guaranteed weight-loss program**. I lost 15 pounds during the first month I was enrolled! Do you want to try too? Just call 1-800-232-2112 and tell them when you want to start. The membership fee is just $30 a month. Once you join, **you are entitled to a free consultation** from a qualified doctor who puts you on a low-fat diet and an exercise program. Join now! **You won't regret it**.

남: 이 사진을 좀 보세요! 이건 저의 3개월 전 모습입니다. 그리고 지금의 저를 보세요. 제가 정말 멋져 보이지 않나요? 저는 Ace 헬스클럽에 다니고 있는데, 보장된 체중 감량 프로그램을 제공하는 곳입니다. 저는 제가 등록한 첫 달에 15파운드를 감량했어요! 여러분도 시도해보고 싶으신가요? 1-800-232-2112로 전화하셔서 시작하고 싶은 시간을 말씀해 주시기만 하면 됩니다. 회비는 한 달에 30달러밖에 되지 않습니다. 일단 가입하시면, 여러분에게 저지방 식단과 운동 프로그램을 알려드릴 전문의로부터 무료 상담을 받으실 수 있습니다. 지금 가입하세요! 후회하시지 않을 겁니다.

어휘 **guaranteed** 보장된, 확실한 / **enroll** 등록하다 / **entitle** 자격[권리]을 주다 / **consultation** 상담; 자문 / **qualified** 자격(증)이 있는

02 의견 | ③

▶ 여자는 기사를 작성할 때 기사의 분량을 지켜야 하고 독자를 생각해야 한다고 말하고 있다.

W: Kevin, do you have a minute?
M: Sure, is it about the article that I wrote for the school magazine?
W: Yes. **I want to discuss a few details** about the article.
M: Of course. I would love your feedback.
W: I asked you to write the article with 1,000 words or fewer, but it looks like you wrote over 1,500 words. It's just too long.
M: I'm sorry, but I had so many things to say.
W: I'm afraid your lengthy article won't fit into the magazine.
M: Alright. **I'll make sure to shorten it**.
W: And please remember that you must think of your readers when you write. It's important that they clearly understand your writing at all times.
M: I understand. It looks like **I have a lot to work on**. Thank you for your advice.

여: Kevin, 시간 좀 있니?
남: 물론이야. 내가 학교 잡지에 쓴 기사에 관한 거니?
여: 응. 그 기사에 관해 몇 가지 사항을 의논하고 싶어.
남: 물론이야. 네 의견을 듣고 싶어.
여: 나는 1,000단어 또는 그보다 적게 기사를 써 달라고 했는데, 네가 1,500단어를 넘게 쓴 것 같아. 너무 길어.
남: 미안해, 하지만 말하고 싶은 게 정말 많았어.
여: 네 긴 기사는 잡지에 적합하지 않을 것 같아.
남: 알겠어. 확실히 줄여볼게.
여: 그리고 네가 글을 쓸 때 독자들을 생각해야 한다는 것을 기억해줘. 언제나 독자들이 너의 글을 분명하게 이해하는 것이 중요해.
남: 알겠어. 내가 노력할 게 많아 보이는구나. 조언 고마워.

어휘 **lengthy** 너무 긴, 장황한 / **fit into** ~에 적합하다, 꼭 들어맞다; 어울리다

03 관계 | ③

▶ 남자는 여자가 오디션을 봤던 영화에서 조연을 맡게 된 것을 알리고 계약을 위해 사무실로 오라고 했다. 이로 미루어 보아 배우의 에이전트와 배우 사이의 대화임을 알 수 있다.

[Phone rings.]
W: Hello, this is Brianna Wood.
M: Brianna, it's Dylan at Rooftop Entertainment.
W: Oh, hello, Dylan. You're busy preparing to move your office.
M: Yeah, I'm pretty busy. I have good news. Do you remember the movie for which you auditioned to play a troubled twenty-something?
W: Yes, **but I wasn't selected**. You told me that.
M: Yeah, but I just received a call from the director. **He'd like to give you a different role** in his movie.
W: Really? I can't believe it. I really want to work with him. What kind of character is it?
M: It's not the leading role, but it's an important supporting role. I think **it's a good opportunity for you**.
W: Yeah! I'll take any role in his movie. I'd love to do it.
M: Okay. Can you visit the office this Friday? **We need to draw up a contract**.

[전화벨이 울린다.]
여: 여보세요. Brianna Wood입니다.
남: Brianna, 저는 Rooftop 엔터테인먼트의 Dylan입니다.
여: 아, 안녕하세요, Dylan. 사무실 이전을 준비하느라 바쁘시죠.
남: 네, 정말 바빠요. 좋은 소식이 있어요. 괴로워하는 20대 역할을 오디션 봤던 영화 기억나요?
여: 네, 그렇지만 뽑히진 못했죠. 당신이 말해줬잖아요.
남: 네, 그런데 방금 그 감독으로부터 전화를 받았어요. 그의 영화에서 당신에게 다른 역할을 주고 싶대요.
여: 정말요? 믿을 수가 없어요. 그 감독님과 정말로 함께 일해보고 싶었거든요. 어떤 역할인가요?
남: 주연은 아니지만, 중요한 조연 역할이에요. 당신에게 좋은 기회인 것 같아요.
여: 그럼요! 그 감독님 영화에서 어떤 역할이든 맡을 거예요. 정말로 하고 싶어요.
남: 알겠어요. 이번 주 금요일에 사무실에 방문할 수 있어요? 우리 계약서를 작성해야 해요.

어휘 **troubled** 괴로운, 힘든 / **leading role** 주연 *cf.* **supporting role** 조연 / **draw up a contract** 계약서를 작성하다

04 그림 불일치 | ②

▶ 대화에서는 코치가 막대기를 들고 남자아이의 뒤에 서 있다고 했지만 그림에서는 링을 들고 있으므로 서로 일치하지 않는다.

M: Sandra, **what a lovely surprise**!
W: Oh, James. I didn't know you liked to ski.
M: I'm all about snowboarding these days. **So what brings you here**?
W: I brought my kid here so he can get some skiing lessons. He loves skiing.
M: Where is your kid? Oh, he's the one holding a ring, right? The coach **is holding a stick behind him**.
W: No, that's not him. Do you see the big yellow arch **over there on the right**? James is standing right in front of the arch.
M: Oh, he's so big now. By the way, it seems the kids' ski school is like a playground. There's a big snowman with a cone hat.
W: Isn't it cute? Look at the big bird behind the snowman.
M: I understand why your son loves the school.

남: Sandra, 정말 뜻밖에 반갑네요!
여: 아, James. 당신이 스키를 좋아하는지 몰랐어요.
남: 요즘 스노보드에 푹 빠져 있거든요. 그런데 여기에 어쩐 일이세요?
여: 스키 수업을 받을 수 있도록 아이를 데려왔어요. 스키를 좋아하거든요.
남: 아이가 어디 있나요? 아, 링을 들고 있는 아이 맞죠? 코치가 뒤에서 막대기를 들고 있고요.
여: 아니에요. 오른편 저쪽에 크고 노란 아치형 구조물 보이시죠? James는 그 아치 바로 앞에 서 있어요.
남: 아, 정말 많이 컸네요. 그런데 아이들 스키 학교는 마치 놀이터 같아요. 고깔모자를 쓴 큰 눈사람이 있어요.
여: 귀엽지 않나요? 눈사람 뒤에 있는 큰 새 좀 보세요.
남: 당신의 아이가 왜 (스키) 학교를 좋아하는지 알겠네요.

어휘 **arch** 아치형 구조물 / **cone hat** 고깔모자

05 추후 행동 | ⑤

▶ 남자의 스마트폰 배터리가 다돼서 버스 도착 시각을 확인할 수 없자, 여자는 자신이 알아보겠다고 했다.

W: Hello, Ben. Glad to see you. Are you waiting for a bus?
M: Yeah. Where are you going, Alison?
W: I'm going home. My grandmother will visit my home tonight, so **I have to prepare dinner**.
M: Oh, that's nice. I'm going downtown to buy something for my friend's birthday.
W: Are you waiting for the number 65? It passes through downtown.
M: Right. It's **the fastest way to get there**.
W: But, if I remember right, it doesn't come often.
M: You're right. **I've been waiting here** for more than 10 minutes.
W: Why don't you check when the bus will arrive with your smartphone?
M: I would, but the battery is dead.
W: Then I'll do it for you. Wait a second.
M: Alright. Thanks for your help.

여: 안녕, Ben. 널 보니 반갑다. 버스 기다리고 있니?
남: 응. Alison, 넌 어디 가니?
여: 집에 가. 할머니께서 오늘 밤에 우리 집에 오실 거라서 저녁을 준비해야 해.
남: 아, 좋은 일이구나. 난 친구 생일을 위해 뭔가 사러 시내에 가는 길이야.
여: 65번 버스를 기다리는 거야? 그게 시내를 지나가잖아.
남: 맞아. 그곳에 가는 가장 빠른 방법이지.
여: 그런데 내 기억이 맞는다면, 그 버스는 자주 오지 않는데.
남: 네 말이 맞아. 난 여기서 십 분도 넘게 기다리고 있어.
여: 버스가 언제 도착할지 네 스마트폰으로 확인해보는 게 어때?
남: 그러고 싶지만, 배터리가 다됐어.
여: 그러면 내가 해줄게. 잠시만 기다려.
남: 알았어. 도와줘서 고마워.

어휘 **pass through** (어떤 도시 등을) 지나[거쳐]가다

06 금액 | ④

▶ 남자는 510달러에 세금 60달러가 합해진 합계 570달러짜리 티켓 2장을 구입하기로 했다. 그러므로 지불 총액은 1,140달러이다.

M: Good morning. I'm planning a trip to Alaska this summer and **was wondering if you could give me** some information on the airfare.
W: Sure. When do you want to travel?
M: On July 18th, returning on August 1st. How much is a round-trip ticket to Alaska?
W: Well, American Airlines is offering 550 dollars per person for a round-trip ticket. **It's a direct flight**.
M: Does that include taxes?
W: No, it doesn't include taxes. The total will be 620 dollars including taxes.
M: That's pretty expensive. **Do you have any lower rates**?
W: That's the cheapest. Weekend flights are usually more expensive.
M: Then I can change the date. How about leaving on July 15th and returning on the 29th?
W: Then it'll be 510 dollars, and taxes will be 60 dollars.
M: That sounds better. I'd like to reserve two tickets.

남: 안녕하세요. 이번 여름에 알래스카 여행을 계획 중인데, 항공 요금에 대해 정보를 좀 얻을 수 있을까 해서요.
여: 물론이에요. 언제 여행가길 원하세요?
남: 7월 18일에 가서 8월 1일에 돌아오는 것으로요. 알래스카 왕복 티켓은 가격이 얼마인가요?
여: 음, 아메리칸 항공에서는 왕복 티켓을 1인당 550달러에 제공하고 있어요. 직항편이고요.
남: 세금 포함 가격인가요?
여: 아니요, 세금을 포함하지 않습니다. 세금을 포함하면 총 620달러예요.
남: 꽤 비싸네요. 좀 더 저렴한 요금이 있나요?
여: 그게 가장 싼 거예요. 주말 항공편은 보통 더 비싸거든요.
남: 그럼 제가 날짜를 바꿀 수 있어요. 7월 15일에 떠나서 29일에 돌아오는 건 어떤가요?
여: 그러면 510달러이고, 세금은 60달러예요.
남: 그게 더 낫네요. 2장 예약하고 싶어요.

어휘 **airfare** 항공 요금 / **rate** 요금; 비율; 속도

07 이유 | ⑤

▶ 친구가 개를 잃은 슬픔으로 외출을 꺼리는 상황이라고 하자 남자는 여자에게 친구 집에 가서 함께 시간을 보낼 것을 권유했다. 여자는 이에 동의하며 친구에게 전화하겠다고 했으므로 답은 ⑤이다.

W: Have you been over to Riley's house recently?
M: No, I haven't. Is everything okay with her?
W: Actually, no. **She's been so miserable** since her dog died.
M: Oh, no, that's awful. Have you talked to her?
W: I called her and tried to invite her to the mall the other day, but she said **she didn't feel like going out**.
M: I expect she's having a really hard time, so that makes sense.
W: Well, I'd thought that maybe she might **want to be distracted from the situation**, but it seems like she just wants to stay in.
M: Why don't you go to her house and hang out with her there? I expect she's lonely.
W: That's a good idea.
M: You could watch a movie together and do something fun, like baking a cake.
W: Okay, I'll give her a call.

여: 최근에 Riley 집에 간 일 있니?
남: 아니. 그 애는 잘 지내고 있는 거지?
여: 사실, 아니야. 개가 죽은 뒤로 정말 괴로워하고 있어.
남: 아, 이런, 말도 안 돼. 그 애랑 얘기해봤어?
여: 지난번에 전화해서 쇼핑몰로 나오게 하려고 해봤는데, 외출하고 싶은 기분이 아니라고 말했어.
남: 내 생각엔 그 애가 정말로 힘든 시간을 보내고 있는 것 같아. 그래서 그러는 것도 이해가 돼.
여: 음, 나는 그 애가 그 상황에서 주의를 다른 곳으로 돌리고 싶을지도 모른다고 생각했는데, 그냥 집에 있고 싶어 하는 것 같아.
남: 그 애 집에 가서 함께 시간을 보내는 게 어때? 그 애는 외로울 거야.
여: 좋은 생각이야.
남: 영화를 같이 보거나 케이크 굽기처럼 재밌는 일을 할 수 있을 거야.
여: 알겠어. 그 애에게 전화해볼게.

어휘 **distract** (주의를) 딴 데로 돌리다 / **hang out with** ~와 시간을 보내다

08 언급하지 않은 것 | ②

▶ 해석 참조

M: Hello, nice to meet you. My name is Anthony. I spoke with you on the phone yesterday.
W: Hi, I'm Jenny.
M: **I'm a big fan of yours**. I was so impressed by your last performance. I couldn't believe you knocked down your opponent in one shot.
W: Thank you. So what can I do for you?
M: I want to promote a match between you and Sara Peterson.
W: Sara Peterson **who is currently ranked third** in the world? She is very strong. So what kind of contract are we looking at?
M: I'm thinking of giving you $350,000 before the match. I'll also pay for **all the expenses including training and airfare**. And the match will be sponsored by Smith Sportswear.
W: Hmm.... When and where will the match be?
M: I'm planning to hold the match in LA on January 28th.
W: Hmm.... Not a bad deal. I'll think about it and let you know in three days.

남: 안녕하세요, 만나서 반갑습니다. 제 이름은 Anthony입니다. 어제 전화로 이야기 나누었죠.
여: 안녕하세요. Jenny입니다.
남: 저는 당신의 열렬한 팬입니다. 지난번 당신의 경기에 정말 감명받았어요. 한방에 상대를 때려눕혔다는 게 믿기지 않아요.
여: 감사합니다. 그럼 제가 뭘 해드리면 될까요?
남: 저는 당신과 Sara Peterson(① 대결 선수)과의 시합을 주최하고 싶습니다.
여: 현재 세계 랭킹 3위인 Sara Peterson이요? 그녀는 정말 강해요. 그럼 우리는 어떤 계약을

검토하는 거죠?
남: 저는 당신에게 시합 전에 35만 달러를 주는 것을 생각하고 있습니다. 훈련과 항공 요금을 포함한 모든 비용 또한 지불할 거고요. 그리고 시합은 Smith 스포츠웨어(③ 후원사)에서 후원할 겁니다.
여: 음…. 시합은 언제 그리고 어디서 열리나요?
남: LA(④ 시합 장소)에서 1월 28일(⑤ 시합일)에 시합을 개최할 계획입니다.
여: 음…. 나쁘지 않은 거래군요. 생각해보고 3일 후에 알려드리죠.

어휘 **knock down** 때려눕히다 / **opponent** 상대; 반대자 / **look at** ~을 검토하다, 살피다; ~을 보다

09 내용 불일치 | ③

▶ 단편 영화는 5분을 넘지 않고 장편 영화는 15분보다 길어야 한다.

W: Attention all students of Kamo High School. We will begin our very own school film festival **in the first week of October**. The film festival will feature short and long films from talented students at our school. All students can participate by submitting a short or long film **individually or as a group**. Short films must not be longer than 5 minutes, and long films must be longer than 15 minutes. If you're interested in this event, submit your application by September 5th. **Once the winners are chosen**, a list of their names will be posted on October 5th. **The winning films will be available** for viewing in the school's concert hall all throughout October. Start filming today!

여: Kamo 고등학교의 모든 학생은 주목하십시오. 우리만의 학교 영화제를 10월 첫 주에 시작할 것입니다. 영화제는 우리 학교에서 재능 있는 학생들의 단편 영화와 장편 영화를 특집으로 할 것입니다. 모든 학생은 개인 또는 그룹으로 단편 또는 장편 영화를 제출함으로써 참여할 수 있습니다. 단편 영화는 5분을 넘지 않아야 하고, 장편 영화는 15분보다 길어야 합니다. 이 행사에 관심이 있다면, 9월 5일까지 신청서를 제출해 주십시오. 수상자가 결정되면, 10월 5일 수상자들의 이름이 공고될 것입니다. 수상작들은 10월 내내 학교 콘서트홀에서 보실 수 있습니다. 오늘 촬영을 시작하십시오!

어휘 **feature** 특집으로 하다; 특징, 특색

10 도표 이해 | ③

▶ 남자는 우선 SUV를 원했고 렌트비는 보험료 포함해서 하루에 60달러를 넘지 않는 차를 렌트하고 싶어 했다. 또 GPS 내비게이션을 원했고 차를 빌리는 장소가 아닌 다른 장소(공항)에서 반환하기를 원했다. 이 모든 조건을 충족시키는 것은 ③이다.

W: Hi, how can I help you?
M: I'd like to rent a car for 4 days.
W: What kind of car do you have in mind?
M: I'm traveling with 5 people and have a lot of luggage, so I probably need an SUV.
W: I see. **Do you have a budget for** the rental?
M: I'd like to spend no more than $60 a day, which would include insurance.
W: If that's the case, you have 3 options. Would you like GPS navigation?
M: Yes, most definitely. I'm traveling in this area, so I don't know my way around.
W: Got it. It looks like you'll have these two choices.
M: **Do I have to return** the car at this location? I'd like to drop the car off at the San Francisco airport.
W: Yes, I have a car in mind. This car **can be dropped off** at a different location.
M: Great. I'll take that car then.

여: 안녕하세요, 뭘 도와드릴까요?
남: 4일간 자동차 한 대를 빌리고 싶습니다.
여: 어떤 종류의 차를 생각하고 계신가요?
남: 다섯 사람과 여행하고 짐도 많아서 SUV가 필요할 것 같아요.
여: 알겠습니다. 렌트비에 대한 예산이 있는지요?
남: 보험을 포함해서 하루에 60달러 넘게 쓰고 싶지 않아요.
여: 그러면 3가지 선택권이 있습니다. GPS 내비게이션을 원하시나요?
남: 예, 확실히 그렇습니다. 제가 이 지역을 여행하는 거라서 지리에 밝지 않아요.
여: 알겠습니다. 이 두 가지 선택이 있으신 것 같군요.
남: 제가 이 장소로 차를 반납해야 하나요? San Francisco 공항에서 차를 반납하고 싶은데요.
여: 예, 생각하는 차가 하나 있습니다. 이 차는 다른 장소에서 반납하실 수 있습니다.
남: 아주 좋군요. 그러면 그 차로 하겠습니다.

어휘 **have in mind** 생각하다, 염두에 두다 / **luggage** (여행용) 짐 / **SUV** 스포츠실용차(sport utility vehicle) / **budget** 예산 / **insurance** 보험 / **option** 선택(권) / **GPS** 위성 위치 확인 시스템(global positioning system) / **navigation** 내비게이션, 항법 / **know one's way around** ~의 지리에 밝다 / **drop off at** ~에 갖다 놓다, 내려 주다

11 짧은 대화에 이어질 응답 | ②

▶ 식사를 준비 중인 여자에게 남자가 지금 맛을 좀 볼 수 있는지 물었으므로 좀 더 기다리라고 응답한 ②가 가장 적절하다.

① 오늘 밤 여기 와 주셔서 감사합니다.
② 아니요, 아직 다 되지 않았어요. 조금만 참아요.
③ 맛있어요. 당신은 정말로 훌륭한 요리사예요!
④ 인터넷에서 조리법을 다운로드받았어요.
⑤ 서두르지 않으면 당신은 약속에 늦을 거예요.

M: It smells good. What are you making?
W: It's a dish I learned to make. **I'm sure you'll like it**.
M: Smells great. Can I get a little taste right now? **I can't wait any longer**.
W: ______________________________

남: 냄새가 좋네요. 뭘 만드는 중이에요?
여: 이건 내가 만드는 법을 배운 요리예요. 당신은 분명히 이 요리를 좋아할 거예요.
남: 냄새가 정말 좋아요. 지금 맛을 조금만 볼 수 있을까요? 더는 못 기다리겠어요.
여: ______________________________

12 짧은 대화에 이어질 응답 | ③

▶ 자기 대신 식당에서 저녁 교대 근무를 해줄 수 있는지 묻고 있는 여자에게 남자가 할 응답으로는 ③이 적절하다. 남자가 I'm free라고 한 것으로 보아 ①은 정답이 될 수 없다.

① 미안하지만 안 될 것 같아. 할 일이 너무 많아.
② 나는 더 심해지기 전에 병원에 가보는 게 좋겠어.
③ 기꺼이 할게. 여분의 돈도 벌 수 있으니까.
④ 너를 존경해. 나도 뭔가 좋은 일을 하고 싶어.
⑤ 그렇다면 난 괜찮아. 오늘 밤에 야간 근무를 하자.

W: I have to work tonight at Marcia's restaurant, but **I don't feel well**. I was wondering if you could work my shift.
M: Sure, I'm free. But are you sure it will be alright with your manager?
W: Yes, **as long as it's okay with you**. You have to work from five to nine.
M: ______________________________

여: 나는 오늘 밤 Marcia의 식당에서 일해야 하는데, 몸이 좀 안 좋아. 네가 내 교대 근무를 해줄 수 있는지 궁금해.
남: 물론이야. 나는 시간 괜찮아. 그런데 너의 관리자도 괜찮다고 할지 확실한 거야?
여: 응, 네가 괜찮다고 하기만 하면. 5시부터 9시까지 일하면 돼.
남: ______________________________

13 긴 대화에 이어질 응답 | ③

▶ 남자가 산 가방을 여자가 좋아 보인다고 하면서 관심을 보이고 있다. 비싸 보이는 유명 디자이너 상품인데 40% 할인해 샀다고 말했으므로 적절한 응답은 ③일 것이다.

① 내가 너라면 저 가방을 사지 않을 텐데.
② 정말? 너 바가지 쓴 것 같은데.
③ 와! 너 싸게 잘 산 것 같아.
④ 물론입니다. 이것은 최저가입니다.
⑤ 그건 너무 비싸요. 더 싼 가격에 주세요.

W: Is that the new bag you bought recently? It looks fancy.
M: Do you really think so? I was a little unsure about the color.
W: It's very cool. **It fits you perfectly**. It's very flattering on you.
M: **Thanks for the compliment**.
W: Is brown a trendy color these days?
M: No, not really. Brown just happens to be my favorite color.
W: It seems very strong. What material is that?
M: It's made of the best sheepskin.
W: Well, it looks pretty expensive. It's definitely a designer bag.

M: Yeah, **I was reluctant to get it at first** because of the price, but when I found out it was 40% off, I snapped it up.
W: ___________________________

여: 그거 네가 최근에 새로 산 가방이니? 고급스러워 보인다.
남: 정말로 그렇게 생각해? 색에 대해서 약간 확신이 없었거든.
여: 정말 멋있어. 너에게 완벽하게 어울려. 너를 정말 돋보이게 해.
남: 칭찬 고마워.
여: 요즘 갈색이 유행하는 색이니?
남: 아니, 그렇진 않아. 단지 갈색이 내가 가장 좋아하는 색이라서.
여: 가방이 정말 튼튼해 보여. 소재가 뭐야?
남: 최고급 양가죽으로 만들어진 거야.
여: 음, 매우 비싸 보여. 분명 유명 디자이너 가방이야.
남: 맞아. 처음엔 가격 때문에 사는 걸 망설였는데, 40% 할인한다는 걸 알고 바로 샀지.
여: ___________________________

어휘 **fancy** 고급의, 값비싼; 화려한 / **flattering** 돋보이게 하는; 아첨하는 / **designer** 유명 디자이너가 만든, 유명 브랜드의; 디자이너 / **reluctant to-v** v하길 주저하는, 마지못해 v하는 / **snap up** 덥석 사다 | 선택지 어휘 | **overcharge** 바가지를 씌우다, (금액을 너무) 많이 청구하다 / **make a good purchase** 싸게 구입하다 / **rock-bottom** 최저의, 최하의

14 긴 대화에 이어질 응답 | ③

▶ 라디오 방송국에서 하와이 왕복 티켓을 무료로 받아 기뻐하는 여자에게 남자가 할 말은 부러워하는 내용이 적절하다.

① 앞으로 그런 장난은 치지 마.
② 하와이에 있는 해변들도 방문했니?
③ 정말 부럽다. 나도 그곳에 정말로 가보고 싶어.
④ 위대한 꿈인 것 같아. 이뤄지길 바랄게.
⑤ 너 너무 흥분한 것 같아. 좀 진정해 봐.

M: Boy, it looks like you're really happy today.
W: Happy? I'm beyond happy. **You'll never guess what happened to me**.
M: Did you win the lottery or something?
W: No, but it feels like I did.
M: So hurry and tell me what happened.
W: I was listening to the radio, and the radio station **was giving away some free round-trip tickets** to Hawaii.
M: Oh my gosh. Did you get some tickets?
W: I called ten times, and **I finally got through** and got two free tickets! Can you believe it?
M: That's amazing. You've always wanted to visit Hawaii. So who's the lucky person you're taking to Hawaii?
W: I'm thinking of taking my mother.
M: ___________________________

남: 이야, 너 오늘 정말로 행복해 보이는데.
여: 행복? 행복 그 이상이야. 내게 무슨 일이 있었는지 넌 결코 짐작도 못할 거야.
남: 복권 같은 거라도 당첨된 거야?
여: 아니, 하지만 그런 기분이야.
남: 그러니 얼른 무슨 일이 있었는지 말해 봐.
여: 라디오를 듣고 있었는데, 라디오 방송국에서 무료 하와이 왕복 티켓을 나눠주는 거야.
남: 세상에. 네가 그 티켓을 받은 거야?
여: 내가 열 번 전화했는데, 결국 통화가 돼서 공짜 티켓을 두 장 받았어! 믿어지니?
남: 정말 놀랍다. 넌 언제나 하와이에 가보고 싶어 했잖아. 그래서 네가 하와이에 데려갈 행운아는 누구니?
여: 어머니를 모시고 갈까 생각하고 있어.
남: ___________________________

어휘 **boy** (놀람 · 감탄 등을 나타내어) 아이고, 어머나 / **win a lottery** 복권에 당첨되다

15 상황에 적절한 말 | ⑤

▶ 엄마를 위한 파티를 준비하면서 엄마의 친구분들을 파티에 초청하는 상황이다. 참석 여부를 확실히 알지 못하는 사람에게 할 말로는 ⑤가 적절하다.

① 좋은 생각이에요! 제가 비밀로 해주길 원하세요?
② 파티에 사람들을 몇 명 초대하셨나요?
③ 축하해요! 제가 뭐 도와 드릴 일이 있을까요?
④ 그렇다면, 파티에 정장 같은 것을 입고 가야 할까요?
⑤ 오실 수 있는지를 가능한 한 빨리 알려주시겠어요?

M: Kimberly **is preparing a surprise party** for her mother. It will be her mother's 48th birthday next month. Kimberly plans to invite several of her mother's friends to the party. Kimberly decides to call one of her mother's friends, Mrs. Howard. Kimberly tells Mrs. Howard about her plans and also invites her to the party. However, Mrs. Howard already has previous plans. She doesn't know **if she can attend the party or not**. But Kimberly needs to know how many people will be attending the party **as soon as possible**. In this situation, what would Kimberly most likely say to Mrs. Howard?

남: Kimberly는 어머니를 위해 깜짝 파티를 준비 중이다. 다음 달이 어머니의 48번째 생신이다. Kimberly는 파티에 어머니의 몇몇 친구분들을 초대하려고 계획한다. Kimberly는 어머니의 친구 중 한 분인 Howard 부인에게 전화하기로 한다. Kimberly는 Howard 부인에게 자신의 계획에 관해 이야기하고 파티에도 초대한다. 하지만 Howard 부인은 이미 선약이 있다. 그녀는 파티에 참석할 수 있는지 없는지를 알 수 없다. 그러나 Kimberly는 파티에 얼마나 많은 사람이 참석할지 가능한 한 빨리 알아야 한다. 이러한 상황에서 Kimberly가 Howard 부인에게 할 말로 가장 적절한 것은 무엇인가?

어휘 **previous** 이전의, 앞의

16~17 세트 문항 | 16. ② 17. ⑤

▶ 16. it's really simple to lose that fat without ~ foods and personal workout trainers라는 말이 나온 후 구체적인 방법들이 나열되고 있으므로 ②가 주제로 가장 적절하다.

① 식이요법을 위한 효과적인 계획
② 효과적으로 체중을 줄이는 방법
③ 과체중의 몇 가지 원인
④ 운동으로 열량을 소모하는 방법
⑤ 과체중이 건강에 미치는 해로운 영향

▶ 17. 해석 참조

W: It seems like everyone these days **is obsessed with losing weight**. From low-calorie options at the restaurant to workout plans, everyone has their own plan for having a skinny body. However, it's really simple to lose that fat without spending a lot of money on specially-prepared foods and personal workout trainers. **When it comes to the diet**, you don't need to do anything fancy. Just follow these steps. First, cut out junk food and fast food entirely. No more hamburgers and hot dogs, no more sodas, and no more potato chips and candy. Second, eat less carbs, like pasta and bread, and add more vegetables and fruits to your daily intake. Finally, eat as much food as you want in your first helping, but **resolve to eat** only that, and **save the rest** for another meal. Exercise is also important for burning calories and fat. Whether it's swimming or jogging, do something that makes you move and **gets your heart rate going**. To build your muscles, try some basic yoga exercises or biking. Yoga is easy to do in your own home, and there are free videos on the Internet.

여: 요즘 모든 사람이 체중을 감량하는 것에 사로잡혀 있는 것처럼 보입니다. 식당의 저열량 선택 사항부터 운동 계획까지, 모든 사람이 깡마른 몸을 갖기 위한 자신만의 계획을 가지고 있습니다. 그러나 특별히 준비된 음식과 개인 운동 트레이너에 많은 돈을 쓰지 않고도 지방을 줄이는 것은 매우 간단합니다. 식이요법에 관해서라면, 값비싼 어느 것도 할 필요가 없습니다. 이 단계들만 따라 해 보세요. 첫 번째, 정크푸드와 패스트푸드를 전부 끊으세요. 더 이상의 햄버거와 핫도그, 탄산음료, 감자튀김과 사탕은 안 됩니다. 두 번째, 파스타와 빵 같은 탄수화물 식품을 덜 먹고, 하루 섭취량에 더 많은 채소와 과일을 추가하세요. 마지막으로, 처음 한 그릇을 먹을 때 원하는 만큼의 음식을 드세요. 하지만 그것만 먹기로 다짐하고 나머지는 다른 식사를 위해 남겨 두세요. 운동 또한 열량과 지방을 소모하는 데 중요합니다. ① 수영이든 ② 조깅이든, 여러분을 움직이게 하고 심박수가 뛰게 하는 무언가를 하세요. 근육을 만들기 위해, 기초적인 ③ 요가 운동이나 ④ 자전거 타기를 시도해 보세요. 요가는 집에서 하기 쉽고, 인터넷에 무료 영상들도 있습니다.

어휘 **be obsessed with** ~에 사로잡혀 있다 / **workout** 운동 / **when it comes to** ~에 관해서라면 / **cut out** 그만두다; 삭제하다 / **carb** 탄수화물 식품 / **intake** 섭취(량) / **helping** (음식의) 양, 그릇; 조력, 원조 / **resolve** 다짐[결심]하다; 해결하다

01. ④ 02. ① 03. ⑤ 04. ④ 05. ③ 06. ② 07. ⑤ 08. ④ 09. ③ 10. ④
11. ⑤ 12. ③ 13. ③ 14. ⑤ 15. ⑤ 16. ② 17. ⑤

01 화자가 하는 말의 목적 | ④

▶ 병원 진료 시간 이전이나 이후에 전화를 건 사람들을 대상으로 하는 자동 응답 안내멘트이다.

M: Thank you for calling the Collingwood Clinic. **Nobody is available to take your call** right now. Our regular hours of operation are from 8 a.m. to 5 p.m. Monday through Friday. We are also open on Saturday from 10 a.m. to 3 p.m. If you are calling to make an appointment, please **leave a message after the tone**, and we will call you back during business hours to confirm it. If this is an emergency, please call 911 or the doctor hotline at 1-800-555-4321. A doctor **will be able to assist you** and advise you what to do in an emergency.

남: Collingwood 병원에 전화해 주셔서 감사합니다. 지금은 전화를 받을 수 없습니다. 저희 병원의 진료 시간은 월요일에서 금요일까지 오전 8시부터 오후 5시까지입니다. 저희는 토요일에도 오전 10시부터 오후 3시까지 진료를 합니다. 예약을 하고자 전화하신 분들은 삐 소리 후 메시지를 남겨 주시기 바랍니다. 예약 확인을 위해 진료 시간에 다시 전화를 드리겠습니다. 응급 상황이라면 911이나 의료진 직통 전화 1-800-555-4321로 전화 걸어 주십시오. 의료진이 도와 드릴 수 있을 것이며 응급 상황에서 어떻게 해야 할지 상담을 해 드릴 것입니다.

어휘 **available** (일에 응할 수 있는) 시간이 있는; 이용할 수 있는 / **appointment** 예약, 약속 / **business hours** 영업시간 / **confirm** 확인하다 / **emergency** 응급, 비상사태 / **hotline** 직통 전화 / **assist** 돕다

02 의견 | ①

▶ 여자는 아침 식사의 이점과 아침 식사를 하지 않을 때의 단점을 근거로 들어 아침 식사를 거르지 말아야 한다고 말하고 있다.

M: Hey, Kate, do you want to get something to eat?
W: I think I'll wait to have lunch. It's still early.
M: I guess so. I didn't have breakfast so I'm really hungry.
W: Why didn't you have breakfast?
M: I was tired this morning, so I **decided to sleep a bit longer**.
W: I never do that. It only takes a few minutes to have some cereal, and that gives me the energy I need for the morning.
M: Well, I'm **trying to lose a little weight**, also.
W: Then you might be surprised to learn that those who skip breakfast **are more likely to be overweight** than those who don't.
M: I didn't know that. Maybe I should start eating breakfast again.

남: 얘, Kate, 뭐 좀 먹을래?
여: 난 점심 먹는 걸 기다릴까 해. 아직 이른 시간이잖아.
남: 맞아. 난 아침을 먹지 않아서 정말 배고파.
여: 왜 아침을 먹지 않았니?
남: 오늘 아침에 피곤해서 좀 더 오래 자기로 했거든.
여: 난 절대 안 그래. 시리얼을 먹는 데는 몇 분밖에 안 걸리고, 그건 내게 오전에 필요한 에너지를 주거든.
남: 음, 난 살을 좀 빼려고 노력하는 중이기도 해.
여: 그렇다면 아침을 거르는 사람들이 거르지 않는 사람들보다 과체중이 될 가능성이 더 높다는 것을 알면 놀랄지도 몰라.
남: 그건 몰랐어. 어쩌면 아침을 다시 먹기 시작해야 할 것 같아.

03 관계 | ⑤

▶ 연구 논문을 작성하기 위한 자료를 찾는 남자에게 여자가 온라인 데이터베이스에 관해 설명한다. 또 참고 도서를 대출하고자 하는 남자에게 여자는 복사만 가능하다고 말하고 있으므로 두 사람은 도서관 직원과 도서관 이용자임을 알 수 있다.

W: Good morning. It's raining a lot. There's an umbrella stand next to the door.
M: Great. I didn't want to **carry my umbrella with me**. Thank you.
W: Sure. How can I help you?
M: I'm doing a research paper on robotics.
W: Is there a particular book you're looking for?
M: Not really. I just need all the information I can get.
W: **Have you checked** our research database? You can look for specific topics by logging into our online database.
M: That's convenient. **Can I make copies of** the material? Actually, I'm not a student at this university.
W: Of course. You can create an account here. Fill out this form, please.
M: Thanks. I'd also like to check out some reference books.
W: I'm afraid you're **not allowed to check them out**. You can only make copies. We have some printers connected to the computers.
M: Oh, I see.

여: 안녕하세요. 비가 많이 오네요. 문 옆에 우산꽂이가 있습니다.
남: 아주 좋네요. 우산을 가지고 들어가고 싶지 않았어요. 감사합니다.
여: 물론이죠. 무엇을 도와드릴까요?
남: 저는 로봇 공학에 관한 연구 논문을 작성하고 있어요.
여: 찾고 있는 특정한 책이 있나요?
남: 아뇨. 저는 단지 제가 얻을 수 있는 모든 정보가 필요해요.
여: 저희 연구 데이터베이스를 확인해 보셨나요? 저희 온라인 데이터베이스에 접속하시면 특정한 주제들을 찾으실 수 있습니다.
남: 그거 편리하네요. 제가 그 자료를 복사할 수 있나요? 사실 전 이 대학의 학생이 아니에요.
여: 그럼요. 여기에서 계정을 만드실 수 있습니다. 이 양식을 작성해 주세요.
남: 감사합니다. 저는 참고 도서 몇 권도 대출하고 싶습니다.
여: 유감스럽게도 그것들을 대출하실 수 없습니다. 복사만 하실 수 있어요. 저희는 컴퓨터에 연결된 프린터 몇 대가 있습니다.
남: 아, 알겠습니다.

어휘 **paper** 논문; 과제 / **robotics** 로봇 공학 / **database** 데이터베이스(데이터를 집적해 놓고 이용할 수 있도록 한 시스템) / **log into** ~에 접속하다 / **make a copy** 복사하다, 사본을 만들다 / **material** 자료; 재료 / **account** (정보 서비스) 이용 계정; 계좌 / **fill out** ~을 작성하다 / **check out** 대출하다; 내보내다 / **reference book** 참고 도서

04 그림 불일치 | ④

▶ 대화에서는 도마뱀이 마실 물이 담긴 접시가 있다고 했는데 그림에는 항아리가 있으므로 일치하지 않는다.

W: Chris, this must be the cage of the lizard you're raising.
M: Yes, I arranged everything in his house, too.
W: That's amazing. **There's a lamp on the ceiling** of his house.
M: It's an ultraviolet lamp. They need this kind of lighting to be healthy.
W: It looks like you placed a big tree branch inside. Is there a particular reason why?
M: Lizards like **to climb on things**. Look, the lizard is moving now.
W: Oh, I see. You put two flat rocks under the branch.
M: Yes, I put rocks and leaves so it looks like his natural environment.
W: Good. Is the large dish of water for the lizard to drink?
M: That's right. Can you see those holes on the side walls? They're for ventilation.
W: Wow, **you did a fantastic job** on it!

여: Chris, 이게 네가 기르는 도마뱀 우리구나.
남: 응, 도마뱀 집에 있는 모든 것도 내가 준비했어.
여: 굉장하다. 집 천장에 램프가 있네.
남: 자외선램프야. 도마뱀들이 건강하려면 이런 종류의 조명이 필요하거든.
여: 우리 안에 커다란 나뭇가지를 둔 것 같은데. 특별한 이유가 있는 거니?
남: 도마뱀들은 기어오르는 걸 좋아하거든. 봐, 도마뱀이 지금 움직이고 있어.
여: 아, 알겠어. 나뭇가지 밑에 평평한 돌을 두 개 두었구나.
남: 응, 자연환경같이 보이게 하려고 돌하고 나뭇잎을 놓았어.
여: 좋구나. 물이 담긴 커다란 접시는 도마뱀이 마시기 위한 거니?
남: 맞아. 옆쪽의 벽에 난 구멍들이 보이니? 그것들은 통풍을 위한 거야.
여: 와, 너 아주 잘해놓았구나!

어휘 **cage** 우리, 새장 / **lizard** 도마뱀 / **arrange** 준비하다, 배열하다 / **ceiling** 천장 / **ultraviolet** 자외선의 / **ventilation** 통풍, 환기

05 추후 행동 | ③

▶ She wants me to come over to her house and talk.와 마지막 말인 stay here while I talk to Junho's mom으로 보아 여자는 대화 후에 준호네 집을 방문할 것이다.

M: Mom... I know why you're angry, but please understand.
W: Your teacher called and then Junho's mom called. She **wants me to come over to** her house and talk. Tell me exactly what happened.
M: Junho and his friend **started picking on me**, calling me names like 'pig boy.'
W: You should **turn your head and walk away**!
M: I couldn't.
W: I should phone your father. Then you'd really **be in trouble**.
M: I know.
W: You know I have to go to school tomorrow to talk to the teacher.
M: I'm sorry.
W: Well, stay here while I talk to Junho's mom.

남: 엄마… 왜 그렇게 화가 나셨는지 알겠어요. 하지만 이해해주세요.
여: 네 선생님이 전화하셨고 그런 다음 준호 엄마한테서도 전화가 왔어. 내가 준호네 집에 와서 이야기 좀 하기를 원하시더구나. 어떤 일이 있었는지 정확히 말해보렴.
남: 준호와 그 애의 친구들이 먼저 괴롭히기 시작했어요. 저를 '돼지'라고 험담하면서요.
여: 너는 그냥 고개를 돌려서 가버리면 돼!
남: 그렇게 할 수가 없었어요.
여: 네 아버지에게 전화해야겠다. 그러면 너는 정말 혼날 거야.
남: 알아요.
여: 내가 내일 학교에 가서 선생님과 면담해야 하는 것을 알고 있지?
남: 죄송해요.
여: 그럼, 준호 어머니와 이야기할 동안 너는 여기 있어라.

어휘 **come over** 오다; (지나가는 길에) 들르다 / **pick on** 괴롭히다, 못살게 굴다 / **call A names** A를 욕하다

06 금액 | ②

▶ 여자는 190달러보다 30달러 더 싼 기내 가방을 샀으므로 160달러짜리 가방을 샀고 20달러짜리 목베개를 20% 할인받아 샀으므로 16달러를 합하면 총액은 176달러이다.

M: How can I help you?
W: How much is this carry-on bag?
M: It's $190. It weighs just 4 pounds, which is light.
W: Well, it's **beyond my budget**. Do you have a cheaper one?
M: Hmm, how about this rolling backpack? It's $30 cheaper than the carry-on. You can roll it or wear it on your back.
W: That looks convenient. I'll take it.
M: **It's available in three colors**; black, charcoal, and berry. Which one do you want?
M: I'd like berry. Do you have a travel pillow?
M: Sure. How about this one? It's a neck pillow and **works great on** the bus or plane.
W: Let me see. The price tag says 20 dollars.
M: **That one just went on sale**. It's 20 percent off. What do you say?
W: Great. I'll take it. Here's my card.

남: 뭘 도와드릴까요?
여: 이 기내용 가방은 얼마인가요?
남: 190달러입니다. 단지 4파운드 무게라서 가볍습니다.
여: 음, 제 예산을 초과하는군요. 더 싼 것 있나요?
남: 음, 이 (바퀴) 굴리는 배낭은 어떠신가요? 기내용 가방보다 30달러 더 쌉니다. 그걸 굴리거나 등에 멜 수 있습니다.
여: 편리해 보이는군요. 그걸 살게요.
남: 검정색, 짙은 회색, 딸기색의 세 가지 색깔이 가능합니다. 어떤 것을 원하세요?
여: 딸기색이 좋겠어요. 여행용 베개 있나요?
남: 그럼요. 이건 어떠세요? 목베개이고 버스나 비행기에서 효과가 좋습니다.
여: 볼게요. 가격표에 20달러라고 쓰여 있군요.
남: 막 할인 판매에 들어가서 20퍼센트 할인됩니다. 어떠세요?
여: 잘됐네요. 그걸 살게요. 여기 제 카드가 있습니다.

어휘 **carry-on** 기내 휴대의; 기내 휴대 수하물 / **weigh** 무게가 ~이다 / **budget** 예산 / **roll** 굴리다 / **convenient** 편리한 / **charcoal** 짙은 회색 / **pillow** 베개

07 이유 | ⑤

▶ 잠들기 어렵게 하는 이유들을 여자가 남자에게 질문하는 과정에서 남자는 커피를 많이 마셔서 그런 것 같다고 하였다.

M: Hi, Mom.
W: Daniel, why are you still awake? It's 3 a.m.
M: I couldn't get to sleep.
W: What's the reason? I thought you went to bed around 11.
M: I did. I got into bed, closed my eyes, and **tried to fall asleep**, but I couldn't.
W: Hmm.... Normally, you don't have any difficulty sleeping. Did you take a nap today?
M: I wished I could, but **I was busy studying** for tomorrow's test all afternoon.
W: You should be tired then. Are you worried about something?
M: No, but I guess I did drink a lot of coffee today.
W: Well, that's probably the reason! Too much caffeine disrupts sleep.
M: I know, but I needed **something to help me study** without feeling sleepy.
W: Even so, you shouldn't drink caffeine late in the day. Now you'll be even more tired tomorrow.
M: You're right. I'll be careful.

남: 안녕하세요, 엄마.
여: Daniel, 왜 아직도 깨어 있니? 새벽 세 시란다.
남: 잠들 수 없었어요.
여: 이유가 뭐니? 네가 11시쯤 자러 간다고 생각했는데.
남: 그랬죠. 침대로 가서 눈을 감고 자려고 노력했지만 잘 수 없었어요.
여: 음…. 보통 잠드는 데 문제가 전혀 없었잖아. 오늘 낮잠 잤니?
남: 그러길 바랐지만, 오후 내내 내일 시험을 위해 공부하느라 바빴어요.
여: 그렇다면 분명 피곤하겠구나. 혹시 걱정거리가 있니?
남: 아뇨, 하지만 제 생각에 오늘 확실히 커피를 많이 마신 것 같아요.
여: 음, 그게 아마 이유겠구나! 카페인이 너무 많으면 수면을 방해하지.
남: 저도 알아요. 하지만 졸리지 않고 공부하도록 도와주는 무언가가 필요했어요.
여: 그렇더라도, 저녁 시간에 카페인을 마시면 안 된단다. 이제 너는 내일 훨씬 더 피곤해할 거야.
남: 엄마 말씀이 맞아요. 제가 조심할게요.

어휘 **fall asleep** 잠들다 / **take a nap** 낮잠을 자다 / **probably** 아마 / **caffeine** 카페인 / **disrupt** 방해하다, 지장을 주다; 붕괴하다

08 언급하지 않은 것 | ④

▶ 해석 참조

W: Hi, Vance!
M: Vanessa? I didn't know you shopped at this bookstore.
W: Actually, I'm here to pick up a book for my son, Tom.
M: *Greek and Roman Mythology*? That's fairly advanced for an elementary schooler.
W: This book contains easier versions of the classics. It's **good for developing a child's imagination**.
M: I see. So, do you think young children understand the lessons the classics teach?
W: Even if they don't completely understand, they definitely learn that **good is rewarded and evil is punished**.
M: But isn't the vocabulary too difficult for a young reader?
W: There are some challenging words, but that helps the child learn.
M: I still don't see **why it would be more appropriate** for children than other books.
W: Well, classical literature has one more benefit. It introduces history to children. It's very educational.
M: You have a point. I think I'll buy a copy for my daughter as well.

여: 안녕하세요, Vance 씨!
남: Vanessa 씨? 당신이 이 서점에서 책을 사시는 줄 몰랐어요.
여: 사실은 아들 Tom에게 책을 한 권 사주려고 왔어요.
남: 〈그리스 로마 신화〉요? 초등학생에겐 꽤 고급 수준이잖아요.
여: 이 책은 고전을 더 쉬운 버전으로 담고 있어요. 아이의 상상력을 키우는 데 좋은 책이에요(① 상상력 발달).
남: 그렇군요. 그러면 당신은 고전이 주는 교훈을 어린아이들이 이해한다고 생각하시는군요?
여: 완전히 이해하지는 못하더라도 권선징악에 대해서는 확실히 배우죠(② 교훈 습득).

남: 하지만 나이 어린 독자들이 읽기에는 어휘가 너무 어렵지 않나요?
여: 어려운 단어들이 좀 있지만, 아이가 학습하는 데 도움이 될 거예요(③ 어휘력 발달).
남: 그래도 저는 왜 이 책이 다른 책들보다 아이들에게 더 적합한지는 모르겠어요.
여: 음, 고전문학은 이점이 하나 더 있어요. 아이들이 역사를 접하게 해주거든요(⑤ 역사 소개). 그건 매우 교육적이에요.
남: 맞는 말씀이신 것 같네요. 제 딸에게도 한 권 사줘야겠어요.

어휘 **mythology** 신화 / **advanced** 고급[상급]의; 진보한 / **appropriate** 적절한, 알맞은

09 내용 불일치 | ③

▶ 중반부에 지원자들은 18세가 넘는 대학생이어야 한다는 내용이 나온다.

W: Unity-For-All is a non-profit organization providing **aid to people living in poverty** all over the world. We are now hiring students for the summer 2026 internship program at our New York headquarters. The internship program will start on July 1st and will last for six weeks. Those who are applying for the internship position **must be enrolled as a student** in a university and must be over 18 years of age. Interns **will be expected to assist** full-time employees in their day-to-day activities. The deadline to apply for the summer 2026 internship position is April 30, 2026. Please note that **no application will be accepted** after the deadline. You may download the application by visiting our website at www.unityforall.org.

여: '모두를 위한 단합(Unity-For-All)'은 전 세계에 가난하게 사는 사람들에게 원조를 제공하는 비영리 단체입니다. 현재 뉴욕 본부에서 2026 여름 인턴십 프로그램에 참가할 학생들을 채용하고 있습니다. 인턴십 프로그램은 7월 1일에 시작해 6주 동안 계속될 것입니다. 인턴직에 지원하는 분들은 대학생으로 등록되어 있어야 하며 18세가 넘어야 합니다. 인턴사원은 정규직 직원의 일일 활동을 도울 것으로 예상됩니다. 2026 여름 인턴직 지원 마감일은 2026년 4월 30일입니다. 마감일 이후에는 지원서가 접수되지 않음을 유의해 주십시오. 지원서는 웹사이트 www.unityforall.org에 방문하셔서 내려받으시면 됩니다.

어휘 **non-profit** 비영리적인 / **internship** 인턴직, 직업 연수[훈련] ***cf.* intern** 인턴(사원); (의학) 수련의 / **enroll** 등록[입학]하다, (이름을) 명부에 올리다

10 도표 이해 | ④

▶ 여자가 안 보겠다고 한 공상과학 영화와 남자가 안 보겠다고 한 별 두 개짜리 영화를 제외한다. 마지막에 여자가 제의한 스토리가 괜찮은 영화를 보는 것에 남자가 동의했으므로 이에 해당하는 것은 ④이다.

M: Let's go see the movie that's Roger Robertson's top pick.
W: He's the movie critic for the Sun Times, right?
M: Yeah, I usually love his top picks. Let's go and see *AvaAva World* this weekend. He gave it five stars.
W: John, I **hate that sort of movie**. I don't want to see a science fiction flick!
M: OK. No science fiction.
W: Hey, *About Melissa* is playing. Sandra said it was great. You like Daniel Lee, don't you?
M: I don't mind him. But Roger only gave the movie two stars. I'm not seeing a two star movie. I trust Roger!
W: Hmm.... It's a tough choice then.
M: You choose. But you know I like action movies.
W: I know. But **why don't we watch** something that has a great story?
M: OK. **It's settled**. I'll check the show times.

남: Roger Robertson이 최고라고 뽑은 영화를 보러 가자.
여: Sun Times 지의 영화 평론가 말하는 거지?
남: 맞아. 난 대개 그가 뽑은 최고의 영화들을 좋아해. 이번 주말에 〈AvaAva World〉를 보러 가자. Roger가 별 다섯 개를 줬거든.
여: John, 난 그런 종류의 영화는 싫어. 공상과학 영화는 보고 싶지 않아!
남: 알겠어. 공상과학 영화는 안 보는 걸로.
여: 이봐, 〈About Melissa〉가 상영 중이네. Sandra가 그 영화 재밌다고 했는데. 너 Daniel Lee 좋아하잖아, 그렇지 않니?
남: Daniel Lee는 상관없어. 그런데 Roger가 그 영화에 고작 별 두 개만 줬네. 난 별 두 개짜리 영화는 안 볼 거야. Roger를 믿거든!
여: 음…. 그렇다면 선택이 쉽지 않네.
남: 네가 선택해. 그런데 내가 액션 영화를 좋아하는 건 알지.
여: 알아. 하지만 스토리가 훌륭한 영화를 보는 게 어때?
남: 좋아. 결정됐네. 내가 상영 시간을 확인할게.

어휘 **pick** 선택, 고르기; 고르다 / **critic** 비평가, 평론가 / **science fiction (SF)** 공상과학 영화[소설] / **flick** (구어) 영화 / **show time** (영화의) 상영 시간 | 선택지 어휘 | **genre** (예술 작품의) 장르, 유형, 형식

11 짧은 대화에 이어질 응답 | ⑤

▶ 남자가 여자에게 재킷의 두 가지 사이즈를 가져다 달라고 요청하며 둘 다 입어 볼 수 있는지 물었으므로 이에 가장 적절한 응답을 고른다.

① 옷이 제 몸에 안 맞네요.
② 이 재킷 멋지네요!
③ 라지 사이즈는 너무 딱 붙어요.
④ 문제없습니다. 75달러입니다.
⑤ 물론이죠. 잠시만 기다려 주세요.

M: Excuse me. Do you have this jacket in a larger size?
W: Yes, I'll bring you one. **What size do you need**?
M: Either a large or an extra large. **Can I try both**?
W: ______________________________

남: 실례합니다. 이 재킷 더 큰 사이즈로 있나요?
여: 네, 가져다 드릴게요. 어떤 사이즈를 원하시나요?
남: 라지나 엑스트라 라지요. 둘 다 입어 봐도 될까요?
여: ______________________________

12 짧은 대화에 이어질 응답 | ③

▶ 연극에 필요한 인원이 부족한 상황에서 관심이 있을 만한 사람이 생각나는지 물었다. 이에 적절한 응답을 찾는다.

① 우리 둘이서 충분해.
② 난 대본 쓰는 것부터 시작할게.
③ 몇 명 생각나는 사람이 있어.
④ 우리 부모님께서 연극을 보러 오실 거야.
⑤ 학교 연극이 모두 재밌는 건 아니야.

W: I'm not sure what to do for the talent show. Do you have any ideas?
M: We should **put on a play**, but we'll need more people.
W: Great idea. Can you think of anyone else **who might be interested**?
M: ______________________________

여: 장기자랑에서 뭘 해야 할지 모르겠어. 좋은 생각 있니?
남: 우린 연극을 해야 해. 하지만 사람이 좀 더 필요할 거야.
여: 좋은 생각이야. 관심 있을 만한 다른 누군가가 생각나니?
남: ______________________________

어휘 **put on** (연극 등을) 무대에 올리다, 공연하다

13 긴 대화에 이어질 응답 | ③

▶ 남자의 여자 친구가 남자와 여자와의 관계를 오해하고 있으므로 여자는 오해를 풀어주려고 할 것이다.

① 언니가 곧 아이를 출산해.
② 나도 그렇게 생각해. 우리는 결혼해야 해.
③ 원한다면 내가 그 애와 얘기해 볼게.
④ 나도 여자 형제 말고 남자 형제가 있으면 좋겠어.
⑤ 네 여자 친구는 정말 아름답고 똑똑해.

W: What's wrong, Brian?
M: My girlfriend **is really upset with me**.
W: Why? What happened?
M: Well, she doesn't like the fact that you and I are such good friends.
W: Oh, she's **jealous of our relationship**?
M: Yes, which is strange because you are like a sister to me.
W: And I think of you as a brother. Did you explain that to her?
M: I tried to. I told her that we have been friends since we were babies.
W: What did she say?
M: She said that we sounded like a match made in heaven! **How can I convince her** that she has the wrong idea about us?
W: ______________________________

여: 무슨 일이야, Brian?
남: 여자 친구가 내게 정말 화가 났어.
여: 왜? 무슨 일이 있었는데?
남: 음, 그 애는 너랑 내가 정말 친한 친구 사이라는 것을 좋아하지 않아.

여: 아, 그 애가 우리 관계를 질투하는 거니?
남: 응, 그게 이상해. 왜냐하면 너는 내게 여자 형제 같은 존재이거든.
여: 그리고 나도 너를 남자 형제로 생각하고, 그 애에게 그렇게 설명해 줬니?
남: 그렇게 하려고 노력했어. 우리가 아기 때부터 친구였다고 얘기했거든.
여: 그 애는 뭐라고 말했니?
남: 우리가 천생연분처럼 보인다고 말했어! 어떻게 하면 그 애가 우리 관계에 대해 잘못 알고 있다는 것을 납득시킬 수 있을까?
여: ______________________________

어휘 **a match made in heaven** 천생연분 / **convince** 납득시키다

14 긴 대화에 이어질 응답 | ⑤

▶ 딸이 조심성이 없다고 생각하는 여자(아내)에게 딸이 책임감 있는 행동을 한 것을 알게 된 남자(남편)가 할 수 있는 대답을 고른다.

① 그건 정말 이상한 일이군요.
② 다음번에는 그 애가 내 휴대전화를 쓰게 해야겠어요.
③ 여보, 차 안에서는 휴대전화를 사용하지 말아요.
④ 그 애가 왜 그렇게 책임감이 없는지 이해가 안 돼요.
⑤ 아마도 그 애는 당신이 생각하는 것보다 책임감이 강한 것 같군요.

W: Hi, everyone, I'm home.
M: Hi, honey.
W: Where's Jennifer?
M: She **hasn't come home yet**. I thought you knew where she is.
W: No, I don't.
M: Well, it's only 8:30.
W: She **isn't supposed to go anywhere** without telling us. She doesn't have a cell phone anymore.
M: Just buy her a new one.
W: She's too careless. Her last cell phone was only one week old and she lost it.
M: Maybe she's with Julie. Phone Julie's mom.
W: Oh! I **missed a message on my cell phone**. *[pause]* It's from Jennifer. She sent a message with Julie's cell phone.
M: Where is she?
W: Studying at Julie's house. And she also tried to call when I was driving.
M: ______________________________

여: 안녕, 나 왔어요.
남: 어서 와요, 여보.
여: Jennifer는 어디 있어요?
남: 아직 집에 오지 않았어요. 그 애가 어디 있는지 당신은 알 거라 생각했는데.
여: 아뇨, 몰라요.
남: 음, 아직 8시 30분밖에 되지 않았네요.
여: 그 애는 말없이 아무데도 가지 않기로 했잖아요. 휴대전화도 더 이상 가지고 있지 않고요.
남: 그냥 새로 사 줘요.
여: 그 아이는 너무 조심성이 없어요. 지난번 휴대전화는 일주일밖에 되지 않았는데 잃어버렸잖아요.
남: 아마 Julie와 함께 있을지도 몰라요. Julie의 어머니에게 전화해봐요.
여: 아! 문자 메시지 하나를 확인하지 않았어요. *[잠시 후]* Jennifer에게서 온 것이네요. Julie의 휴대전화로 문자 메시지를 보냈네요.
남: 어디 있대요?
여: Julie네 집에서 공부하고 있대요. 그리고 그 애는 내가 운전하고 있는 중일 때 전화도 하려고 했군요.
남: ______________________________

어휘 **be supposed to-v** v하기로 되어 있다 | 선택지 어휘 | **irresponsible** 책임감이 없는 (↔ responsible 책임감 있는)

15 상황에 적절한 말 | ⑤

▶ 자신의 출산휴가가 동료들에게 부담될까 봐 걱정하는 Sue를 안심시킬 수 있는 내용을 유추한다.

① 그러면 출산휴가를 신청하는 게 어때요?
② 당신 덕분에 그 프로젝트가 마침내 마무리되었어요.
③ 축하해요! 당신은 분명히 좋은 엄마가 될 거예요.
④ 직장에 다니는 엄마들은 남편의 도움이 절실히 필요하죠.
⑤ 추가 인력이 당신 팀원들의 업무량을 줄여줄 거예요.

W: Sue is an employee at a large company, and she is expecting a baby in five months. After going to human resources **to request time off for her pregnancy**, she returns to her desk. As the day passes, she begins to worry about what will happen to her project because it is important to the company. Because she is the director, she worries that **her absence might be a burden** to her teammates. On a break, she discusses this anxiety with Mr. Collins, her immediate supervisor. Mr. Collins listens carefully because he understands that Sue **is truly concerned about** her teammates. He wants to reassure Sue and relieve her worries. In this situation, what would Mr. Collins most likely say to Sue?

여: Sue는 대기업 직원으로 5개월 후면 출산할 예정이다. 그녀는 인사부에 출산휴가를 신청하고 자기 자리로 돌아온다. 시간이 지날수록 그녀는 자신이 진행하고 있는 프로젝트가 어떻게 될지 걱정이 되기 시작했는데 그것이 회사에 중요한 프로젝트이기 때문이다. 자신이 (프로젝트의) 책임자이기 때문에 그녀는 자신의 부재가 팀원들에게 부담이 될까 봐 걱정이다. 휴식 시간에 그녀는 이런 걱정에 대해 직속 상사인 Collins 씨와 의논한다. Collins 씨는 Sue가 자신의 팀원들을 진심으로 걱정하고 있다는 사실을 알기 때문에 그녀의 말을 주의 깊게 듣는다. 그는 Sue를 안심시키고 그녀의 걱정을 덜어주고자 한다. 이러한 상황에서 Collins 씨가 Sue에게 할 말로 가장 적절한 것은 무엇인가?

어휘 **expect a baby** 출산 예정이다, 임신 중이다 / **human resources** (회사의) 인사부; 인적 자원 / **pregnancy** 임신 / **reassure** 안심시키다 | 선택지 어휘 | **maternity leave** 출산휴가 / **manpower** 인력 / **lessen** 줄이다; 줄다 / **workload** 업무량, 작업량

16~17 세트 문항 | 16. ② 17. ⑤

▶ 16. 약간의 정리와 적당한 장식으로 작은 공간에서의 불편함에서 벗어나라고 하면서 작은 방에서 사는 것이 불편하지 않게 할 몇 가지 팁을 알려주고 있다.

① 작은 방에서 사는 것의 불리한 점
② 작은 공간을 더 살 만하게 만드는 법
③ 정기적인 집 청소의 필요성
④ 작은 방을 위한 가구 배치법
⑤ 방에서 자연광에 노출되는 것의 효과

▶ 17. 해석 참조

① 탁자 ② 소파 ③ 거울 ④ 커튼 ⑤ 책장

M: Small rooms are a reality for a lot of people. But just because you live in a small space it doesn't mean you have to feel uncomfortable. With a little organization and proper decorating, you can escape some of your frustration. First, make sure everything actually stays in its place. Keep small items like remote controls in storage baskets, and don't allow things like newspapers and books **to lie around on tables**. Also, just because your space is small, don't shy away from big furniture. **Try placing a big red sofa** in the middle of the room and keep the rest of the room simple. A lot of small furniture can make a room feel cluttered. Use a single color for the wall and use other colors for accents. Another important element is the mirror. Mirrors are **great for reflecting light** and creating the illusion of more space. Placing a large mirror near or across from a window is always effective. The natural light will make the room feel bigger and brighter. Hang curtains outside the window frame **to maximize natural light**. By following these guidelines, living in small spaces doesn't have to be so uncomfortable.

남: 작은 방은 많은 사람들에게 하나의 현실입니다. 그러나 여러분이 작은 공간에 살고 있다고 해서 여러분이 불편함을 느껴야 한다는 뜻은 아닙니다. 약간의 정리와 적당한 장식으로, 여러분은 일부 좌절에서 벗어날 수 있습니다. 먼저, 모든 것이 실제로 있어야 할 곳에 있는가를 확인하십시오. 리모컨 같은 작은 물건들은 보관 바구니에 넣어두고, 신문이나 책을 ① 탁자 위에 놓는 것을 피하십시오. 또한 당신의 공간이 작다고 해서 커다란 가구를 피하지는 마십시오. 시험 삼아 커다란 빨간 ② 소파를 방 가운데 한번 놓아보고 방의 나머지를 단순하게 두십시오. 많은 작은 가구는 방을 더 어수선한 느낌이 나게 할 수 있습니다. 벽에 한 가지 색을 사용하고 다른 색들은 강조를 위해 사용하십시오. 또 다른 중요한 요소는 ③ 거울입니다. 거울은 빛을 반사하여 더 넓은 공간의 환상을 만들어 내는 데 아주 좋습니다. 큰 거울을 창문 가까이나 창 건너편에 두는 것은 언제나 효과적입니다. 자연광은 방을 더 크고 더 밝게 만듭니다. 자연광을 극대화하기 위해 창틀 바깥에 ④ 커튼을 다십시오. 이러한 지침을 따름으로써 작은 공간에 사는 것이 그렇게 불편할 필요는 없을 것입니다.

어휘 **uncomfortable** 불편한, 불쾌한 / **proper** 적당한 / **storage** 보관 / **shy away from** ~을 피하다 / **cluttered** 어수선한 / **accent** 강조; 말씨 / **reflect** 반사하다 / **illusion** 환상, 환각 / **effective** 효과적인, 인상적인 / **maximize** 극대화하다 / **guideline** 지침 | 선택지 어휘 | **livable** 살 만한, 살기에 좋은

01. ① **02.** ③ **03.** ④ **04.** ② **05.** ③ **06.** ③ **07.** ② **08.** ⑤ **09.** ⑤ **10.** ①
11. ③ **12.** ⑤ **13.** ④ **14.** ① **15.** ③ **16.** ③ **17.** ④

01 화자가 하는 말의 목적 | ①

▶ 마지막 말에서 알 수 있듯이 개교 30주년 행사를 소개하면서 학부모에게 적극 참여해 달라고 부탁하는 것이 담화의 목적이다.

W: First of all, thank you so much for joining us today. We know it's not easy for parents **to take the time to attend meetings** during the school week. As some of you may already know, Virgil High School will be celebrating its 30th anniversary **in the following months** through a variety of events and activities. We'll be holding a sports event that will have teachers and students competing with each other. Also, our school will set up a bazaar **to raise money for the school** next month. All used items you donate to us will be part of our school yard sale. **We need all the support** of the parents to make our events a success!

여: 먼저, 오늘 저희와 함께해 주셔서 정말로 감사를 드립니다. 주중에 부모님들께서 회의에 참석할 시간을 내신다는 게 쉽지 않다는 것을 알고 있습니다. 몇몇 분들께서는 이미 알고 계시듯이, Virgil 고등학교는 앞으로 몇 달 동안 다양한 행사와 활동을 통해 개교 30주년을 기념할 것입니다. 선생님들과 학생들이 서로 겨루는 스포츠 행사를 개최할 것입니다. 또한, 저희 학교에서는 다음 달에 학교 기금 마련을 위한 바자회를 마련하려고 합니다. 여러분들께서 저희에게 기증해 주시는 모든 중고 물품이 학교 알뜰 시장의 일부가 될 것입니다. 저희 행사가 성공하기 위해서는 부모님들의 아낌없는 성원이 필요합니다!

어휘 **anniversary** 기념일 / **bazaar** 바자회; 시장 / **yard sale** 알뜰 시장, 마당 세일(개인 주택의 마당에서 사용하던 물건을 파는 것)

02 의견 | ③

▶ 여자가 받은 쿠키 선물의 포장을 보고 남자가 과대 포장을 염려하면서 그것이 환경문제가 되고 지구 온난화에도 영향을 준다고 말하고 있다.

W: Look at what I got from my sister! It's a box of premium brand cookies.
M: It's very impressive, but why do the cookies all need to be individually wrapped?
W: I think it's artistically done and pleasing to the eye.
M: That's true, but **I'm concerned about** the excessive packaging.
W: What do you mean?
M: It's terrible for our environment. In fact, **one third of all trash is made up of** packing materials.
W: Oh, my. I had no idea it was so much.
M: Producing packaging uses up natural resources, energy, and water. And **it can contribute to global warming**.
W: Oh, then we need to help manufacturers change their packaging habits.
M: Right! We can start by complaining and boycotting their products. Packaging is destroying our environment every day. It's a serious problem.

여: 내 여동생으로부터 받은 것 좀 봐봐! 고급 브랜드의 쿠키야.
남: 정말 멋지다. 그런데 왜 쿠키들이 모두 각각 따로 포장되어 있어야만 하는 거야?
여: 예술적으로 만들어서 눈을 즐겁게 하려고 그런 것 같아.
남: 그건 사실이지만, 과도한 포장이 걱정 돼.
여: 무슨 뜻이야?
남: 환경에 정말 안 좋거든. 사실, 모든 쓰레기의 3분의 1이 포장 재료들로 이루어져 있어.
여: 아, 이럴 수가. 그렇게 많았는지 몰랐어.
남: 포장재를 만들어내는 것은 천연자원과 에너지, 그리고 물을 다 써 버리거든. 그리고 그건 지구 온난화의 원인이 될 수 있어.
여: 아, 그러면 우리가 제조사들의 그런 포장 관습을 바꾸도록 해야겠구나.
남: 맞아! 항의하거나 그들의 상품 구매를 거부하는 것부터 시작할 수 있겠지. 포장재는 매일 우리의 환경을 파괴하고 있어. 그건 심각한 문제야.

어휘 **individually** 각각 따로, 개별적으로 / **artistically** 예술적으로 / **concerned** 걱정하는; 관심이 있는 / **excessive** 과도한, 지나친 / **packaging** 포장; 포장재 / **be made up of** ~로 구성되다 / **use up** 다 써버리다 / **contribute to** ~의 한 원인이 되다; ~에 기여하다 / **manufacturer** 제조사[업자] / **boycott** (항의의 표시로) 구매[사용]를 거부하다, 보이콧하다

03 관계 | ④

▶ 남자가 여자에게 파우더를 발라주고 눈에 아이라인을 그려주는 등 화장을 해주는 것으로 보아 메이크업 아티스트임을 알 수 있다. 여자는 결혼사진을 찍는다고 하고 웨딩드레스를 입어야 한다고 했으므로 예비 신부임을 알 수 있다.

M: Now tilt your head backwards.
W: Sure.
M: I need to put on some more powder. Close your eyes. I don't want the powder **to get into your eyes**.
W: Okay.
M: When does your wedding photo shoot start?
W: **It's supposed to start** at two o'clock.
M: We need to hurry then. You still need to put on your wedding dress, so we don't have much time. Now, close your eyes.
W: Sure.
M: I'm going to put on a heavy eyeliner since you need to take photos.
W: Are you going to put on false eyelashes?
M: Yes. Just a moment. *[pause]* I need to add some touches to your eyes. Alright, you're all set. **Take a look at yourself in the mirror**. What do you think?
W: I love it. *[laughing]* It doesn't look like me.

남: 이제 머리를 뒤쪽으로 젖혀주세요.
여: 네.
남: 파우더를 좀 더 발라야 해요. 눈을 감아주세요. 파우더가 당신의 눈에 들어가게 하고 싶지 않거든요.
여: 알겠어요.
남: 결혼사진 촬영을 언제 시작하나요?
여: 2시에 시작하기로 되어 있어요.
남: 그럼 서둘러야겠어요. 손님께선 웨딩드레스도 입어야 하니 시간이 많지 않아요. 이제 눈을 감아주세요.
여: 네.
남: 사진을 찍어야 하니 진한 아이라이너를 그릴 거예요.
여: 인조 속눈썹도 붙이실 건가요?
남: 네. 잠시만요. *[잠시 후]* 눈 손질 좀 더 할게요. 자, 다 됐습니다. 거울 좀 한번 보세요. 어떠세요?
여: 마음에 들어요. *[웃으면서]* 저 같아 보이지 않네요.

어휘 **tilt** 기울이다 / **eyelash** 《주로 복수형》 속눈썹 / **touch** 손질, 마무리; 만짐; 촉감

04 그림 불일치 | ②

▶ 남자는 선생님이 팔짱을 끼고 그냥 서 있기만 한다고 의아해했는데 그림에는 선생님이 붓과 종이를 들고 있으므로 일치하지 않는다.

W: Oh, Jack! I didn't expect to see you here. Are you here to participate in the art event?
M: Oh, hi, Miranda. My son has art lessons here, and **I stopped by to take a look**.
W: I see. My daughter has a lesson here once a week.
M: We can look at the kids through this big window here. Oh, look at my Daniel!
W: Oh, is he the boy **applying paint to the canvas** with his hands? He seems very creative.
M: He's quite naughty as you can see. I don't know why the teacher is letting him do that. She is just standing **with her arms crossed**.
W: I'm sure it's because she wants to make a creative environment for the kids. My daughter, Anna, is painting on the floor over there.
M: Oh, there's a cat sitting on the floor watching her paint.
W: Look at the boy on the right. He's drawing an airplane. He draws very well.
M: He looks very artistic.

여: 아, Jack! 여기서 당신을 볼 거라고는 예상 못 했어요. 미술 행사에 참가하러 여기 온 건가요?
남: 아, 안녕하세요, Miranda. 제 아들이 여기에서 미술 수업이 있는데, 저는 한 번 보려고 들렀어요.

여: 그렇군요. 제 딸도 여기서 1주일에 한 번 수업을 들어요.
남: 여기 이 큰 창문을 통해서 아이들을 볼 수 있겠네요. 아, 제 아들 Daniel 좀 보세요!
여: 아, 손으로 캔버스에 물감을 칠하고 있는 아이인가요? 정말 창의적인 것 같아요.
남: 보시다시피 그는 정말 장난꾸러기예요. 왜 선생님이 그가 저렇게 하는 걸 내버려두는지 모르겠네요. 그녀는 단지 팔짱을 낀 채로 서 있어요.
여: 그녀는 아이들을 위해 창의적인 환경을 만들어주고 싶어서일 거라고 확신해요. 제 딸 Anna는 저쪽 바닥에서 그림을 그리고 있네요.
남: 아, 그녀가 그림 그리는 걸 보면서 바닥에 앉아 있는 고양이가 있어요.
여: 오른쪽에 있는 남자아이 좀 보세요. 비행기를 그리고 있어요. 정말 잘 그리네요.
남: 그는 정말 예술적인 감각이 있어 보여요.

어휘 **apply** 바르다; 신청하다; 적용하다 / **naughty** 장난꾸러기의, 장난이 심한 / **artistic** 예술적 감각이 있는; 예술의

05 추후 행동 | ③

▶ 남자가 아이들은 자기가 돌볼 테니 친구와 밖에서 저녁을 같이하라고 하자, 여자가 이를 받아들인다. 따라서 여자는 친구를 만나러 외출 준비를 할 것이다.

W: George! Back so soon! **Didn't you take** the kids to the beach?
M: Yeah, they loved it.
W: Where are they now?
M: They're in the car. We're going to have pizza for dinner.
W: We're going out for pizza?
M: Not you. You're going to get dressed up and go out with Cathy and the girls.
W: But I can't! I **have to stay home and look after** the kids.
M: I'll take care of the kids. You go to dinner with Cathy tonight. Come on, her wedding is next week. She's your best friend. It's important.
W: Okay... if you insist....
M: I do! Now **go and get ready** before I change my mind!

여: George! 정말 빨리 돌아왔네요! 아이들 데리고 해변에 가지 않았어요?
남: 갔었죠. 아이들이 아주 좋아했어요.
여: 아이들은 지금 어디 있어요?
남: 차 안에 있어요. 저녁 식사로 피자를 먹으러 가려고요.
여: 우리 피자 먹으러 가는 거예요?
남: 당신은 아니고요. 당신은 옷을 입고 Cathy하고 친구들과 함께 외출해요.
여: 하지만 그럴 수 없어요. 집에서 아이들을 돌봐야 하는걸요.
남: 아이들은 내가 볼게요. 오늘 밤은 Cathy와 저녁 식사를 해요. 자, 그녀의 결혼식이 다음 주잖아요. Cathy는 당신의 제일 친한 친구고요. 그게 중요하지요.
여: 좋아요… 정 그렇다면….
남: 그렇게 해요! 마음 변하기 전에 얼른 가서 준비해요!

어휘 **get dressed** 옷을 입다 / **look after** ~을 돌보다 / **if you insist** 정 그렇다면

06 금액 | ③

▶ 하루에 40달러 하는 표준형 차를 8일간 빌리기로 했으므로 320달러를 내야하고, 추가 보험이 하루에 3달러씩 8일에 24달러이므로 합계 344달러를 지불해야 한다.

M: We'd like to rent a car. How much is it for a day?
W: We have a sedan for only 60 dollars a day.
M: Wow, that's expensive! **Can I get something much cheaper**?
W: A compact car is 30 dollars a day, and a standard-sized car is 40 dollars. We also have hybrid cars. As you know, hybrid cars have excellent gas mileage.
M: I'm not interested in hybrid cars. I think a compact will be too small because **there are four of us traveling together**. I want a standard-sized.
W: Okay. How many days will you need the car for?
M: We'd like to rent it for 8 days. Do we need to buy insurance, too?
W: **The rental fee automatically includes insurance**, but you can purchase extra coverage as well, if you'd like.
M: I want to purchase extra coverage.
W: It will cost you an extra 3 dollars per day. Can I see your driver's license?
M: Sure. Here you are.

남: 차를 빌리고 싶은데요. 하루에 얼마인가요?
여: 세단형 자동차는 하루에 60달러밖에 하지 않습니다.
남: 와, 비싸네요! 훨씬 더 싼 것으로 할 수 있을까요?
여: 소형 자동차는 하루에 30달러이고요, 표준형 자동차는 하루에 40달러입니다. 저희는 하이브리드 자동차도 보유하고 있습니다. 아시다시피, 하이브리드 자동차는 연비가 아주 좋아요.
남: 하이브리드 자동차에는 관심이 없어요. 네 명이 함께 여행하는 거라서 소형 자동차는 너무 작을 것 같아요. 표준형 자동차로 하고 싶어요.
여: 알겠습니다. 며칠 동안 차가 필요하신가요?
남: 8일 동안 빌리고 싶어요. 보험에도 들어야 하는 건가요?
여: 대여료에 보험료는 자동으로 포함되지만, 원하시면 추가 보험도 들 수 있습니다.
남: 추가 보험을 들고 싶어요.
여: 하루에 3달러의 추가 비용이 듭니다. 운전면허증 좀 볼 수 있을까요?
남: 물론이에요. 여기 있습니다.

어휘 **compact car** 소형 승용차 / **coverage** (보험의) 보상 범위; 보도, 취재

07 이유 | ②

▶ 여자는 미국의 대도시에서는 밤에 다니는 것이 무서운 데 반해 서울은 안전해서 좋다고 말하고 있다.

M: It seems like **you've done a lot of traveling**.
W: Not really. But I'd like to travel more.
M: So, how do you like Seoul?
W: I completely love it! I've only been here for two weeks, but I don't want to leave.
M: What do you like best? Do you like **many good places to go shopping**?
W: Well, no. But I was surprised lots of people shop on the streets till late at night. In American big cities, getting around at night can be scary sometimes.
M: What do you mean?
W: **The crime rate is high**, and there are a lot of scary people and violence.
M: Oh, that's right.
W: But here in Seoul, I don't feel any of that! I feel completely safe here, and not at all nervous! That's why I like Seoul.
M: That's wonderful to hear. I'm so glad that you're happy here. Seoul also has beautiful ancient palaces.
W: Yes, I know.

남: 당신은 여행을 많이 하신 것 같아요.
여: 별로 그렇지 않아요. 하지만 더 많이 여행하고 싶어요.
남: 그럼, 서울은 어떠세요?
여: 정말로 좋아요! 이곳에 2주밖에 있지 않았지만, 떠나고 싶지가 않아요.
남: 뭐가 가장 좋았나요? 쇼핑할 수 있는 좋은 여러 장소들이 마음에 드나요?
여: 음, 아니요. 하지만 많은 사람이 밤늦게까지 거리에서 쇼핑하는 것을 보고 놀랐어요. 미국의 대도시에서는 밤에 돌아다니는 게 때로 무서울 수 있거든요.
남: 무슨 뜻이에요?
여: 범죄율이 높고, 무서운 사람들과 폭력이 많아요.
남: 아, 그렇군요.
여: 하지만 여기 서울은 그런 느낌이 들지 않아요! 여기선 정말 안전하다는 느낌이 들고, 전혀 불안하지 않아요! 그게 제가 서울을 좋아하는 이유예요.
남: 그런 말을 들으니 좋네요. 당신이 이곳에서 행복하다니 기뻐요. 서울에는 아름다운 고궁들도 있어요.
여: 네, 알고 있어요.

어휘 **get around** 돌아다니다 / **crime rate** 범죄율

08 언급하지 않은 것 | ⑤

▶ 해석 참조

M: I need your advice regarding some colleges, Ms. Johnson.
W: How can I help?
M: **I got accepted into six colleges**, and I can't decide where I want to go.
W: First, you should think about **what you want to major in** and see which schools have the strongest department in that field. You wanted to major in math, right?
M: Initially, I did. But now I'd like to study economics.
W: Then let's see **what is ranked highest** in that major. Also, consider the tuition.
M: I cannot attend a school whose tuition is over $10,000.
W: And the location? Do you have to be close to home?
M: **Not necessarily**, but I can't be too far. Since most of my family is in Virginia, I don't want to go to the west coast like LA or San Francisco.

W: Let's see. Well, it looks like you have your answer.
M: Thank you so much for your help.

남: 몇몇 대학에 관련해서 조언이 좀 필요해요, Johnson 선생님.
여: 뭘 도와주면 되니?
남: 제가 여섯 개 대학에 입학 허가를 받았는데요, 어디를 가고 싶은지 결정을 못 내리겠어요.
여: 먼저, 네가 무엇을 전공하고 싶은지에 대해서 생각하고 그 분야에서 가장 실력 있는 학과가 어느 학교에 있는지 알아야 해. 너는 수학을 전공하고 싶어 했잖니, 그렇지?
남: 처음에는 그랬어요. 그런데 지금은 경제학을 공부하고 싶어요(① 전공).
여: 그러면 그 전공 분야에서 어느 학교가 상위를 차지하는지 보자꾸나(② 전공 학과의 학교 순위). 또, 수업료도 고려해야지.
남: 저는 수업료가 10,000달러가 넘는 학교에는 다닐 수 없어요(③ 수업료).
여: 그리고 위치는? 집에서 가까워야 하니?
남: 꼭 그럴 필요는 없지만, 너무 멀리는 갈 수 없어요. 가족 대부분이 Virginia에 있기 때문에, LA나 San Francisco 같은 서부 해안 쪽으로는 가고 싶지 않아요(④ 위치).
여: 어디 보자. 음, 네가 답을 찾은 것 같구나.
남: 도와주셔서 정말 감사합니다.

어휘 **initially** 처음에 / **rank** (등급, 순위를) 차지하다 / **tuition** 수업료

09 내용 불일치 | ⑤

▶ You can find it easily just outside the palace.라는 말로 보아 궁 밖에 선물 가게가 있음을 알 수가 있다

M: We welcome you to The Royal Palace in Bangkok. The Royal Palace is open to the public from 10:00 a.m. to 3:00 p.m., Wednesday to Sunday. **Please be mindful of certain areas** that are not open to the public. The entrance fee for adults is $12, and it's $7 for children over 7 years old. All children under the age of 7 **get free admission**. We have guides for various languages including English, Chinese, and Korean. If you'd like a guide during your visit, please contact us in advance and make a reservation. **All guides are free of charge**. Make sure to stop by our gift shop. You can find it easily just outside the palace. There are souvenirs, postcards, and plenty of books on the palace.

남: 방콕 The Royal Palace에 오신 여러분을 환영합니다. The Royal Palace는 수요일부터 일요일까지, 오전 10시부터 오후 3시까지 대중에게 공개됩니다. 대중에게 개방되지 않는 특정 장소들을 유념해 주시기 바랍니다. 성인 입장료는 12달러이고, 7세 이상 아동 입장료는 7달러입니다. 7세 미만의 모든 아동은 무료입장입니다. 저희는 영어, 중국어와 한국어를 포함해 다양한 언어의 안내원 해설이 있습니다. 방문하시는 동안 안내원 해설을 원하시면, 사전에 연락하셔서 예약해 주시기 바랍니다. 모든 안내원 해설은 무료입니다. 저희 선물 가게에 꼭 들러보십시오. 궁 바로 밖에서 쉽게 찾으실 수 있습니다. 기념품, 엽서, 그리고 궁에 관한 많은 책이 있습니다.

어휘 **mindful** 유념하는, 염두에 두는 / **free of charge** 무료로 / **souvenir** 기념품, 선물

10 도표 이해 | ①

▶ 남자가 택하려는 강의는 경영학 과목이 아닌 3학점짜리이며, 월요일과 수요일 수업이 아닌 것으로 첫 번째 여름학기에 개설되는 것이다.

M: I'm planning to register for a summer course.
W: What kind of course? Will it be a course for your business major?
M: No. I want to take something else. But I haven't decided what to take yet.
W: How many units **do you have in mind**?
M: I'd like something that's 3 units. I need to work this summer, so **that's all I can handle**.
W: When will you be working?
M: Monday and Wednesday, from 9 a.m. to 3 p.m.
W: It looks like you'll be very busy. **Summer school is divided into two semesters**. Which one will you take?
M: What are the dates for the two semesters?
W: The first semester begins on May 19 and ends June 26. The second semester begins on June 29 and ends August 7.
M: I'm planning to travel in July, so **my class needs to end in June**.
W: I guess this course is the one for you.
M: You're right. It seems like I don't have a choice.

남: 나는 여름 학기 강의에 등록하려고 계획 중이야.
여: 어떤 강의? 너의 경영학 전공을 위한 강의야?
남: 아니. 다른 걸 좀 들어보고 싶어. 그런데 아직 무엇을 들을지 정하지는 못했어.
여: 몇 학점짜리를 생각하고 있는데?
남: 3학점짜리면 좋겠어. 이번 여름에 일해야 해서, 그게 내가 감당할 수 있는 전부야.
여: 언제 일하는 거야?
남: 월요일과 수요일에, 오전 9시부터 오후 3시까지야.
여: 너 정말 바빠지겠구나. 여름학교는 두 학기로 나뉘잖아. 어떤 걸 들을 거니?
남: 두 학기 날짜가 어떻게 돼?
여: 첫 번째 학기는 5월 19일에 시작해서 6월 26일에 끝나. 두 번째 학기는 6월 29일에 시작해서 8월 7일에 끝나.
남: 7월에 여행갈 계획이어서, 수업이 6월에 끝나야 해.
여: 이 강의가 너에게 맞는 것 같아.
남: 네 말이 맞아. 선택의 여지가 없어 보이네.

어휘 **unit** (학과목) 학점; 단위

11 짧은 대화에 이어질 응답 | ③

▶ 쇼핑하러 나가는데 아들이 책을 사다 달라고 한다. 이에 대한 응답으로는 어떤 책을 원하는지 알려달라고 하는 것이 적절하다.

① 요령 피우려고 노력하지 마. 그저 열심히 공부해.
② 서점은 커피숍 바로 옆에 있어.
③ 물론이지. 내게 책 제목하고 저자를 알려주기만 하렴.
④ 나는 시험 결과가 걱정돼.
⑤ 맞아. 너는 책을 읽는 습관을 길러야 해.

M: Mom, I have a final exam next week. I'm very busy.
W: But **take a little break**. You look tired. Your dad and I are going shopping. Is there anything you need?
M: Yes, **could you stop by the bookstore** on Elm Street? I need some books for my sociology class.
W: ______________________________

남: 엄마, 저 다음 주에 기말고사가 있어요. 정말 바빠요.
여: 그래도 휴식 좀 취하렴. 피곤해 보이는구나. 너희 아빠와 나는 쇼핑하러 갈 거야. 혹시 필요한 거 있니?
남: 네. Elm 거리에 있는 서점에 잠시 들르실 수 있어요? 사회학 수업을 위한 책이 좀 필요해요.
여: ______________________________

어휘 **stop by** ~에 잠시 들르다 | 선택지 어휘 | **shortcut** 지름길; 손쉬운 방법

12 짧은 대화에 이어질 응답 | ⑤

▶ 식사에 초대받아 맛있다고 칭찬하자 한 그릇 더 먹겠느냐고 묻는다. 이에 대한 응답으로는 더 먹겠다고 수락하거나 그만 먹겠다고 사양하는 답변이 자연스럽다.

① 당신은 식당을 열어도 되겠어요.
② 쇠고기가 정말 부드럽고 육즙이 많아요.
③ 이건 저희 엄마의 비밀 요리법이었어요.
④ 지금까지 먹어본 것 중 가장 훌륭한 구운 쇠고기 스테이크예요.
⑤ 좀 먹고 싶지만 정말 배가 불러요. 고마워요.

W: **What did you think of** the grilled beef steak with garlic herb butter?
M: It was absolutely delicious. I didn't know **you were such a good cook**.
W: I'm glad you like it. Would you like a second helping?
M: ______________________________

여: 마늘 허브 버터와 함께 구운 쇠고기 스테이크가 어떠셨어요?
남: 정말로 맛있었어요. 당신이 이렇게 요리를 잘하시는지 몰랐어요.
여: 좋아하시니 다행이에요. 한 접시 더 드시겠어요?
남: ______________________________

어휘 **a second helping** 한 번 더 담는 음식, 두 그릇째 | 선택지 어휘 | **tender** (음식이) 부드러운, 연한 / **juicy** 즙이 많은

13 긴 대화에 이어질 응답 | ④

▶ 영화를 보는데 남자가 영화를 이해하지 못하고 계속 여자에게 엉뚱한 질문을 한다. 이에 대한 여자의 응답으로는 ④가 가장 적절하다.

① 괜찮아. 너를 방해하고 싶지 않아.
② 아니, 그건 내가 네게 물어보려던 게 아니야.
③ 너를 귀찮게 하고 싶지 않아. 내가 처리할 수 있어.
④ 아, 제발! 영화에 전혀 집중할 수 없잖아.
⑤ 너한테 화 안 났어. 그냥 나 자신한테 화가 난 거야.

M: Amber, sorry for interrupting, but do you know why the man is being chased?

W: It's because **he is suspected of murder**.
M: Really? I didn't know that. Who did he murder and why?
W: Actually, he didn't. Didn't you see that?
M: No, I didn't. It's not easy to understand. Uh... what's the short man's role? Is he a spy?
W: What are you talking about? There isn't a spy in this movie.
M: Oh, I mean the short man **who is wearing a black suit**.
W: He is just an extra. Nobody! Please stop asking questions.
M: Okay. I thought **he had an important role** in this movie. I have one more question. Why did that man's brother get angry?
W: ______________________________

남: Amber, 방해해서 미안한데, 왜 남자가 쫓기고 있는지 알아?
여: 그가 살해 혐의를 받고 있어서 그래.
남: 정말? 몰랐어. 그가 누구를 왜 살해했는데?
여: 사실, 그는 죽이지 않았어. 모르겠니?
남: 응, 모르겠어. 이해하기 쉽지 않아. 아… 키 작은 남자의 역할은 뭐야? 스파이야?
여: 무슨 말 하는 거야? 이 영화에 스파이는 없어.
남: 아, 나는 검은 정장을 입고 있는 키 작은 남자를 말한 거야.
여: 그는 그냥 엑스트라야. 아무도 아니라고! 질문 좀 제발 그만해 줘.
남: 알겠어. 나는 그가 이 영화에서 중요한 역할을 맡았다고 생각했어. 나 질문 하나만 더 할게. 저 남자의 형은 왜 화가 난 거야?
여: ______________________________

어휘 **be suspected of** ~의 혐의를 받다 / **murder** 살인하다; 살인(죄), 살해

14 긴 대화에 이어질 응답 | ①

▶ 일이 바빠 전화 연결을 하지 말라는 남자의 말에 대한 응답으로는 ①이 적절하다.

① 걱정하지 마요. 당신에게 오는 전화를 차단해 줄게요.
② 알겠어요. 당신이 보고서 준비하는 것을 도와줄게요.
③ 죄송하지만, 그는 잠시 자리를 비웠습니다.
④ 알겠어요. 오후에 다시 전화할게요.
⑤ 기다려 주세요. 그가 도착했는지 알아볼게요.

M: Good morning, Linda! How was your weekend?
W: Not bad. How about you?
M: Great. I went hiking near White Mountain.
W: Sounds great. By the way, are you busy right now?
M: Yeah. **I have to respond to all the emails** from our customers. And I should copy all these papers, too.
W: **When it rains, it pours**, doesn't it?
M: It sure does. Oh, Mr. Reed of MT Company just called and wanted you to call him back.
W: All right. I'll call him later. Seth, I need to finish up this report by 11. And I have to prepare a presentation. **I don't want to be bothered**.
M: I see. You're terribly busy, too.
W: No kidding. **Don't let anyone through**, please. If someone calls, tell him or her I stepped out of the office. OK?
M: ______________________________

남: 좋은 아침이에요, Linda! 주말 어땠어요?
여: 나쁘지 않았어요. 당신은요?
남: 좋았어요. White 산 근처로 하이킹을 갔거든요.
여: 좋았겠네요. 그런데 지금 바쁜가요?
남: 네. 고객들에게서 온 모든 이메일에 답변해야 해요. 그리고 이 서류들을 모두 복사도 해야 하고요.
여: 비만 왔다 하면, 꼭 쏟아붓네요(안 좋은 일은 겹쳐서 일어나기 마련이에요). 그렇지 않나요?
남: 정말 그래요. 아, MT Company의 Reed 씨가 방금 전화하셨는데 당신보고 전화해 달라고 했어요.
여: 알겠어요. 나중에 전화하죠. Seth, 저는 이 보고서를 11시까지 끝내야 해요. 그리고 발표도 준비해야 하고요. 방해받고 싶지 않네요.
남: 알겠어요. 당신도 엄청나게 바쁘군요.
여: 정말 그래요. 아무도 들어오게 하지 말아 주세요. 누가 전화하면, 사무실에서 나갔다고 말해 주세요. 알겠죠?
남: ______________________________

어휘 **No kidding.** 정말이야, 농담이 아니야 | 선택지 어휘 | **screen** 차단하다; 가리다

15 상황에 적절한 말 | ③

▶ 여행 가는 한 달 동안 고양이를 맡길 곳이 없어서 곤란을 겪는 Madison에게 이웃 Jonathan이 고양이를 돌봐주겠다고 하자 Madison이 감사를 표한다. 이 상황에서 할 말로는 ③이 가장 적절하다.

① 제 고양이들이 당신에게 너무 폐를 끼쳐서 죄송해요.
② 당신의 상황을 이해하지만, 도와드릴 수가 없어요.
③ 당신 고양이들이 사랑스럽잖아요. 이웃 좋다는 게 뭔가요?
④ 그러면 동물 보호소를 알아보는 게 어때요?
⑤ 제 고양이들을 돌봐줄 사람을 찾을 수가 없어요. 어떻게 해야 하죠?

W: Madison is planning to visit France and Italy for a month this summer. But she doesn't know what to do about her two cats. She obviously can't take them on her trip. So, she calls her friends **in hopes of finding someone** who will look after her cats, but to no avail. Some of her friends **are allergic to cats**, and some are taking off for vacations at the same time too. Then she runs into her neighbor, Jonathan, and tells him about her situation. Jonathan volunteers to look after her cats for a month. Madison **expresses her appreciation** for this kind offer. Afterward, what would Jonathan most likely say to Madison in return?

여: Madison은 이번 여름에 한 달간 프랑스와 이탈리아에 가려고 계획 중이다. 그러나 그녀는 자신의 고양이 두 마리에 대해 어떻게 해야 할지 모른다. 그녀는 분명 고양이들을 여행에 데려갈 수 없다. 그래서 그녀는 고양이들을 돌봐줄 누군가를 찾을 거라는 희망을 품고 친구들에게 전화하지만, 소용이 없다. 친구들 중 몇몇은 고양이에 알레르기가 있고, 몇몇은 그녀와 같은 시기에 휴가를 떠난다. 그러고 나서 그녀는 이웃인 Jonathan을 우연히 만나서, 그녀의 상황에 관해 이야기한다. Jonathan은 자진해서 한 달간 그녀의 고양이들을 돌봐주기로 한다. Madison은 이러한 친절한 제안에 대해 감사를 표현한다. 그 후, Jonathan이 Madison에게 답변으로 할 말로 가장 적절한 것은 무엇인가?

어휘 **to no avail** 도움이 되지 않고, 헛되이 / **in return** 대답[답례]으로서

16~17 세트 문항 | 16. ③ 17. ④

▶ 16. 영화가 정신 건강을 향상시키는 데 도움이 될 뿐만 아니라 교육적으로도 유용하다는 내용의 담화이므로 ③이 주제로 가장 적절하다.

① 영화의 교육적 활용 ② 영화 장르를 분류하는 방법 ③ 영화 감상의 다양한 장점
④ 오락거리로서의 영화 ⑤ 다큐멘터리의 높아지는 인기

▶ 17. 해석 참조

M: Movies are enjoyed and loved by all, and they have the ability to influence our lives. While movies offer great entertainment, they are also very useful for enhancing an individual's mental health. They **enable people to take time to really relax** and momentarily forget about their daily concerns and problems. Through watching a science-fiction movie or an adventure film, a person **can escape from his or her daily cares** by becoming absorbed in the characters in the movie. Movies are also highly informative, especially the ones that **are based on events that actually happened**. When you watch another person's life in a movie, you get more information concerning the current world we are living in. Documentaries also **provide educational benefits**, and they are generally very interesting to watch. Historical films offer vital data about how life was in the past. Watching historical movies can help you get more data concerning historical events, like the Civil War or World War 1 or 2. Through watching educational movies, individuals can also expand their vocabulary and further enhance their knowledge.

남: 영화는 모든 사람이 즐기고 사랑하며, 우리의 삶에 영향을 미칠 수 있는 능력이 있습니다. 영화가 큰 즐거움을 제공하는 한편 개인의 정신 건강을 향상시키는 데에도 매우 유용합니다. 영화는 사람들이 정말로 편히 쉴 수 있는 시간을 갖게 하고 일상의 걱정과 문제를 잠시 잊을 수 있게 합니다. ① 공상과학 영화나 ② 모험 영화를 보는 것을 통해, 영화에 나오는 등장인물들에 빠져들게 됨으로써 일상의 걱정에서 벗어날 수 있습니다. 영화는 또한 매우 유용한 정보를 주는데, 특히 실제 일어난 사건을 기반으로 한 영화들이 그렇습니다. 영화에서 다른 사람의 삶을 볼 때, 우리가 살고 있는 현실 세계에 관련해 더 많은 정보를 얻습니다. ③ 다큐멘터리 또한 교육적인 유익함을 제공하며, 보기에도 일반적으로 매우 재미있습니다. ⑤ 역사 영화는 과거에 삶이 어땠는지에 대해 필수 정보를 제공합니다. 역사 영화를 보는 것은 여러분이 남북 전쟁이나 제1차 세계 대전 또는 제2차 세계 대전과 같은 역사적인 사건에 관해 더 많은 정보를 얻는 데 도움이 됩니다. 교육 영화를 봄으로써, 개인은 또한 어휘를 확장하고 더 나아가 지식을 늘릴 수 있습니다.

어휘 **enhance** 향상시키다; 높이다 / **momentarily** 잠깐 / **informative** 유용한 정보를 주는 / **vital** 필수적인 / **expand** 확장하다 | 선택지 어휘 | **classify** 분류하다

01. ⑤ 02. ② 03. ② 04. ⑤ 05. ⑤ 06. ④ 07. ④ 08. ④ 09. ② 10. ③
11. ④ 12. ③ 13. ③ 14. ① 15. ② 16. ② 17. ⑤

01 화자가 하는 말의 목적 | ⑤

▶ 폐건전지가 환경에 미치는 부정적 영향과 그로 인해 실시되는 회사의 폐건전지 수거 정책에 대해 설명하고 있다.

M: Unfortunately, many of the devices at this company **are powered by batteries** that eventually end up in landfills. Experts say that discarding used batteries in this way may have potentially harmful effects on the environment. This is because batteries contain heavy metals and various toxic chemicals **that can get into the soil**, underground water supplies, and the sea. For this reason, we will begin collecting our used batteries for recycling. A box for used batteries will be set up in the supply room. When you have batteries **you want to dispose of**, simply place them in the box. When the box is full, **it will be taken to** a recycling center. Please remember to do this for the environment.

남: 유감스럽게도, 이 회사에 있는 많은 기기가 결국에는 쓰레기 매립장에 버려질 건전지로 작동됩니다. 전문가들은 다 쓴 건전지를 이런 방식으로 폐기하는 것이 잠재적으로 환경에 해로운 영향을 미칠 수도 있다고 합니다. 이것은 건전지에 중금속과 여러 가지 독성 화학 물질이 들어 있어 토양과 지하수 공급원, 그리고 바다로 흘러들어 갈 수 있기 때문입니다. 이런 이유로, 우리는 다 쓴 건전지를 재활용하기 위해 수거하기 시작할 예정입니다. 다 쓴 건전지를 담는 상자를 비품실에 놓아두겠습니다. 버리고 싶은 건전지가 있으면 그 상자에 그냥 넣어주십시오. 상자가 가득 차면, 재활용 센터로 보낼 것입니다. 환경을 위해 이렇게 할 것을 기억해 주십시오.

어휘 **landfill** 쓰레기 매립지 / **discard** 폐기하다, 버리다 / **potentially** 잠재적으로 / **heavy metal** 중금속; 헤비메탈(록 음악의 한 장르) / **supply room** 비품실 / **dispose of** 없애다, 처리하다

02 의견 | ②

▶ 여자는 성인 대상의 대중가요는 사랑 노래도 성인을 겨냥한 것이고 속어를 사용한다는 점에서 어린이들에게 적절하지 않다고 말하고 있다.

W: Hi, John. What's up?
M: Hi, Marie, I'm trying to find some songs Amy would like.
W: Ah, your brother's daughter. That's nice. How old is she now?
M: She's turning 7 next week. **I'll play these at** her birthday party. Good idea, right?
W: Hmm.... I don't think so. Many pop songs have adult themes.
M: Marie, I wouldn't pick anything advocating violence, **if that's what you mean**.
W: Of course, but love songs are also aimed at a mature audience.
M: That's true. How about Chris Black's new song? The one in the cola advertisement.
W: **I only heard it once**, but I remember there's a lot of slang in that song. She could pick up some bad speaking habits.
M: Good point. Then children's songs are my only choice.
W: That's an idea.

여: 안녕, John. 어쩐 일이야?
남: 안녕, Marie. Amy가 좋아할 노래 몇 곡을 찾고 있어.
여: 아, 네 형의 딸 말이구나. 친절하다. 그 애는 지금 몇 살이니?
남: 다음 주에 일곱 살이 돼. 그 애의 생일 파티에서 이 노래들을 틀 거야. 좋은 생각이지?
여: 음…. 난 그렇게 생각하지 않아. 많은 대중가요는 성인용 주제로 되어 있잖아.
남: Marie, 폭력을 옹호하는 노래는 고르지 않을 거야, 그게 네가 의미하는 거라면 말이야.
여: 물론 그렇겠지만, 사랑 노래 역시 성인인 청중을 겨냥하잖아.
남: 그건 맞는 말이야. Chris Black의 신곡은 어때? 콜라 광고에 나오는 것 말이야.
여: 한 번밖에 못 들어봤지만, 그 노래에는 속어가 많은 걸로 기억해. 그 애는 나쁜 말버릇이 생길 수 있어.
남: 좋은 지적이야. 그러면 동요가 내 유일한 선택이구나.
여: 괜찮은 생각이야.

어휘 **adult theme** 성인용 주제 / **advocate** 지지[옹호]하다; 지지[옹호]자; 변호사 / **aim at** ~을 목표로 하다 / **mature** 성숙한, 다 자란 / **slang** 속어, 은어 / **pick up** (습관 · 재주 등을) 들이게 되다; ~을 듣게[알게] 되다

03 관계 | ②

▶ 남자는 떠돌이 개를 보호하고 있다고 하였고 여자는 그 부상당한 떠돌이 개를 검진하고 깁스가 필요할 것이라고 하였으므로 두 사람은 떠돌이 개 보호자와 수의사이다.

M: Hello, I called you an hour ago. I'm Steve Dale.
W: Hi, Mr. Dale. **Can you put him on** the examining table? What happened? He's limping.
M: Yes, he can't walk and he's hardly eating.
W: Is he your dog or a stray dog?
M: He's a stray dog **but I'm taking care of him**.
W: He looks much thinner than dogs should be at his age.
M: Yes, I'm really worried about it.
W: Do you know **how he got injured**?
M: No, but I saw a hole in the yard this morning. He might have gotten his leg caught in that.
W: Hmm, I should take an X-ray. Could you bring him this way?
M: Sure. Do you think he'll be okay?
W: Well, just **by looking at his movements**, I think he needs a cast.
M: Oh, no! That's too bad.
W: Can you hold his leg here?
M: Okay.

남: 안녕하세요, 한 시간 전에 전화 드렸는데요. 저는 Steve Dale입니다.
여: 안녕하세요, Dale 씨. 그 개를 검진용 테이블 위에 놓아주시겠어요? 무슨 일이 있었나요? 다리를 절뚝거리네요.
남: 예, 걷지 못하고 거의 먹지도 않아요.
여: 당신 개인가요? 아니면 떠돌이 개인가요?
남: 떠돌이 개인데 제가 돌보고 있어요.
여: 자기 연령대 개들보다 훨씬 말라보이네요.
남: 예, 그게 정말 걱정돼요.
여: 어떻게 다쳤는지 아세요?
남: 아니오, 하지만 오늘 아침 마당에 구멍 하나를 봤어요. 거기에 다리가 걸렸을지도 모르겠네요.
여: 음, X레이를 찍어야겠어요. 이쪽으로 데려와 주시겠어요?
남: 그럼요. 개가 괜찮을까요?
여: 음, 움직임만 봐서는 깁스가 필요하겠어요.
남: 아, 이런! 너무 안됐어요.
여: 여기 다리를 붙잡아 주시겠어요?
남: 알겠습니다.

어휘 **limp** 절뚝거리다 / **stray dog** 떠돌이 개 / **cast** 깁스(붕대)

04 그림 불일치 | ⑤

▶ 여자는 큰 별을 크리스마스트리 꼭대기에 달아 놓았다고 말했다.

W: What do you think, Grandpa?
M: You decorated the living room for Christmas! It looks nice!
W: Yes, finally. Do you like the banner that says "Merry Christmas" on the wall?
M: It's great! Where did you get that candle **on the shelf above the fireplace**?
W: Actually, I got that from one of the old boxes in storage.
M: Oh, look at those cute socks hanging from the fireplace. They're wonderful!
W: I made the flower-patterned one in the middle, and Mom made the other two.
M: Wow! You did excellent work. And what are those on the floor?

W: Those are presents for you, Grandpa! They're a secret. You're **not supposed to open them** until Christmas Eve.
M: I know. Don't worry. I won't. By the way, did you use the big star I gave to you the other day?
W: Of course. I **put it on top of** the Christmas tree on the right side of the fireplace.
M: Oh, I found it. I think it's a perfect match with the tree!

여: 어때요, 할아버지?
남: 거실에 크리스마스 장식을 해 놓았구나. 멋지다!
여: 네. 드디어요. 벽에 있는 '메리 크리스마스'라고 쓰인 배너 맘에 드세요?
남: 훌륭하구나! 벽난로 위 선반에 있는 양초는 어디에서 구했니?
여: 실은, 창고에 있는 낡은 상자 중 하나에서 가져왔어요.
남: 오, 벽난로에 걸린 저 귀여운 양말들 좀 보렴. 아주 멋져!
여: 가운데 걸려 있는 꽃무늬 양말은 제가 만들었고요, 나머지 두 개는 엄마가 만드셨어요.
남: 와! 훌륭한 일을 해냈구나. 그런데 바닥에 있는 건 무엇이니?
여: 할아버지께 드릴 선물이요! 비밀이에요. 크리스마스이브가 되기 전까지는 열어 보실 수 없어요.
남: 알겠다. 걱정하지 말렴. 안 열어보마. 한데, 요전에 내가 너에게 주었던 큰 별은 사용했니?
여: 물론이죠. 벽난로 오른쪽에 있는 크리스마스트리 꼭대기에 달아 놓았어요.
남: 오, 찾았다. 트리와 완벽하게 잘 어울리는 것 같구나!

어휘 **decorate** 장식하다 / **fireplace** 벽난로 / **storage** 창고

05 추후 행동 | ⑤

▶ 여자가 엄마의 귀걸이를 잃어버려 찾고 있는데 수업에 들어가야 하므로 남자가 대신 찾아 주겠다고 했다.

M: Why are you **crawling around on the floor** when you should be in class, Mary?
W: One of my earrings fell out and is lost in this thick carpet.
M: That's terrible. Is it expensive?
W: It has a diamond in it and **belongs to my mother**.
M: She'll be really upset if you lose it.
W: Yes, especially since I didn't ask her permission to wear them.
M: Well, you **will get in more trouble** if you miss class too. I'll look for it while you are in class.
W: That would be really great. I **owe you one**.
M: Anything to keep you from getting grounded twice!

남: Mary야, 수업을 받고 있어야 할 시간에 왜 바닥을 기어 다니고 있니?
여: 귀걸이 한쪽을 이 두꺼운 카펫 속에 떨어뜨려 잃어버렸어.
남: 안됐다. 비싼 거니?
여: 안에 다이아몬드가 박혀 있고 우리 엄마 것이야.
남: 네가 그걸 잃어버리면 진짜 화내시겠다.
여: 응, 내가 그 귀걸이를 해도 되는지 허락을 구하지 않았기 때문에 특히.
남: 음, 수업도 빠지면 더 곤란해질 거야. 네가 수업 받는 동안 내가 찾아볼게.
여: 그렇게 해주면 정말 좋지. 내가 신세를 지는구나.
남: 네가 두 번이나 외출 금지를 당하지 않게 하려면 뭐든지!

어휘 **crawl** 기어가다 / **permission** 허락 / **get grounded** 외출 금지 당하다

06 금액 | ④

▶ 36장의 사진 인화비가 36달러이고 두 통의 필름 현상비가 20달러이므로 총 56달러를 지불해야 한다.

M: I found these rolls of film in a desk drawer and I want to **get them developed**.
W: We don't develop film here anymore. We will **have to send them out**.
M: That's fine. I'm not really in a hurry. I'm just curious to know **what is on them**.
W: It will take about 5 days and there is a processing fee plus a fee per photo.
M: And how much is that?
W: For each roll, it is $10 for processing plus $1 for each picture.
M: Well, there are 12 pictures on this roll and 24 on the other.
W: Yes, that will be $36 **for the pictures alone**. And then you have to add the processing fee.
M: Wow, for two rolls... that's expensive.

남: 책상 서랍에서 이 필름들을 발견했는데 현상하고 싶어요.
여: 저희는 더 이상 여기서 필름을 현상하지 않습니다. 다른 곳으로 보내야 할 겁니다.
남: 괜찮아요. 급한 건 아니니까요. 단지 거기에 무엇이 찍혀 있는지 궁금해서요.
여: 기간은 5일 정도 걸릴 것이고 현상비와 사진 한 장당 수수료가 있습니다.
남: 그럼 얼마인데요?
여: 필름 한 통마다 현상비가 10달러이고 사진 한 장당 1달러입니다.
남: 음, 이 필름 통에는 사진이 12장 있고 다른 통에는 24장이 있어요.
여: 네, 사진만 36달러군요. 그리고 현상비를 추가하셔야 해요.
남: 와, 두 통이면… 비싸군요.

어휘 **develop** (사진을) 현상하다 / **process** (필름을) 현상하다

07 이유 | ④

▶ 여자는 어머니를 병원에 모시고 가야 해서 저녁 식사에 함께할 수 없다고 말했다.

M: Nadia, did you hear that **several of us are going to have** dinner together to celebrate the end of the semester?
W: What a great idea! Where are you going?
M: We're meeting tonight at O'Sullivan's. You should come!
W: I'm afraid I can't, but thanks for inviting me.
M: This isn't because of your diet, is it?
W: Of course not! It's just that I have to go to the hospital tonight.
M: Oh? **Is this related to** your recent medical checkup?
W: No. My mother isn't feeling well, and she **asked me to take** her to the hospital tonight. I already promised.
M: That is important. I hope she feels better soon.
W: Thanks, and maybe we can have dinner together soon.
M: **I'd like that**.

남: Nadia, 우리 몇 명이 학기말 기념으로 함께 저녁 먹기로 한 것 들었니?
여: 좋은 생각인데! 어디로 갈 거니?
남: 우린 오늘 밤 O'Sullivan's에서 만날 건데. 너도 와!
여: 안타깝게도 못 가지만, 그래도 초대해줘서 고마워.
남: 다이어트 중이라서 그런 건 아니지, 그렇지?
여: 물론 아냐! 그저 오늘 저녁에 병원에 가야 하기 때문이야.
남: 그래? 최근에 네가 받은 건강검진과 관련된 거야?
여: 아니. 어머니가 몸이 좋지 않으셔서, 나에게 오늘 저녁 병원에 데려다 달라고 부탁하셨거든. 이미 약속을 했어.
남: 중요한 일이네. 어머니께서 곧 나아지시길 바라.
여: 고마워. 우린 조만간 함께 저녁을 먹을 수 있을 거야.
남: 그래 좋아.

08 언급하지 않은 것 | ④

▶ 해석 참조

W: The Hubble Space Telescope is surely the most successful space telescope of all time. Launched in 1990 from the space shuttle Discovery, the telescope **is about the size** of a double-decker bus — 13 m long, 4 m across, and weighing 11,000 kg. It has a 2.4-meter-wide mirror, several cameras, and electronic detectors **that are able to take clear images**. Hubble's power lies in the fact that it is **located above the atmosphere** — so its photographs are not distorted. Now that the telescope is getting old, its fate is uncertain. **Its equipment has been updated** for the last time, and NASA will soon end its program. At this time, NASA may crash it safely into the ocean or recover it for future study.

여: 허블 우주 망원경은 분명 역대 가장 성공적인 우주 망원경입니다. 1990년(① 발사 연도)에 우주 왕복선 Discovery 호로부터 발사된 이 망원경은 크기가 대략 이층 버스만한데, 길이가 13m, 폭이 4m(② 크기), 그리고 무게가 11,000kg에 이릅니다(③ 무게). 허블 우주 망원경은 2.4m 폭의 거울, 카메라 몇 대, 그리고 선명한 사진 촬영이 가능한 전자 감지기를 갖추고 있습니다. 허블 우주 망원경의 강점은 그것이 대기권 밖에 위치해 있다는 사실에 있는데, 이 때문에 촬영된 사진이 왜곡되지 않습니다. 이제 망원경이 노후화되고 있어 그 운명이 불확실합니다. 허블 우주 망원경의 장비는 마지막으로 새롭게 교체되었으며, NASA는 곧 그

프로그램을 종료할 것입니다. 현재로서는, NASA가 허블 우주 망원경을 안전하게 바다로 추락시키거나 향후 연구를 위해 회수할 수도 있습니다(⑤ 폐기 계획).

어휘 **launch** 발사하다; 시작하다 / **double-decker bus** 이층 버스 / **detector** 탐지기 / **distort** 왜곡하다 / **now that** ~이기 때문에 / **fate** 운명 / **recover** 되찾다; 회복하다

09 내용 불일치 | ②

▶ 마야인들은 현대적인 도구 없이도 60미터가 넘는 피라미드(pyramids that are over 60 meters tall)를 지을 수 있었다고 했다.

M: The ancient Mayan pyramids of Mexico and Central America **draw thousands of visitors** each year. The oldest of these structures was completed nearly 3,000 years ago. Without modern tools, the Mayans **were still able to build** pyramids that are over 60 meters tall. All of the pyramids have steep steps and a flat top. Some were used for religious ceremonies, and priests would stand on top where everyone could see them. Others **were built to honor** gods, and their steps were not to be used. Because they look so similar, even experts **have a hard time determining** what a particular Mayan pyramid was used for.

남: 멕시코와 중앙아메리카에 있는 고대 마야 피라미드는 매년 수천 명의 방문객을 끌어들입니다. 이 구조물 중 가장 오래된 것은 거의 3,000년 전에 완성되었습니다. 현대적인 도구 없이도 마야인들은 높이 60미터가 넘는 피라미드를 지을 수 있었습니다. 그 피라미드들은 전부 계단이 가파르고 꼭대기가 평평합니다. 일부는 종교의식을 위해 사용되었고, 사제들은 모든 사람이 자신들을 볼 수 있는 꼭대기에 올라서곤 했습니다. 다른 피라미드들은 신에게 경의를 표하기 위해서 지어졌고, 계단은 사용될 수 없었습니다. 이 둘은 매우 비슷하게 생겼기 때문에, 전문가들조차 특정 마야 피라미드가 어떤 용도로 사용되었는지 알아내는 데 어려움을 겪습니다.

어휘 **steep** 가파른, 급격한 / **religious** 종교의 / **ceremony** 의식 / **priest** 사제, 성직자

10 도표 이해 | ③

▶ 70달러가 넘지 않는 가격에 무선을 원했고 밝은색이 더 좋다고 했다. 이에 해당하는 ②, ③ 중에서 보증 기간이 1년보다 긴 것을 원했으므로 여자가 구입할 반죽기는 ③이다.

W: Jack, I'm looking for an electric mixer. I need to get one for my baking class.
M: You have a catalog. There are **so many to choose from**.
W: I know! I think the Hillcrest mixers are pretty reputable. But they have so many models.
M: First of all, how much are you willing to spend?
W: No more than 70 dollars. I think I can find **something reasonable for that price**.
M: I think you're right. You can buy something mid-range for that price. Would you like a cordless one?
W: I think that would come in very handy.
M: Well, that **narrows down your choices** a bit. Is there a particular color you'd like?
W: I don't want anything that's dark, so a brighter option is better.
M: Okay. You'll pay a little more but I think it'll **be worth it**. Well, it looks like you have two choices left.
W: I need more than a one-year warranty so I'll go for this one.
M: Good. That mixer fulfills all of your requirements.

여: Jack, 나는 전동 반죽기를 찾고 있어요. 제빵 수업을 위해서 하나 사야 해요.
남: 카탈로그를 갖고 있군요. 선택할 게 무척 많네요.
여: 그래요! Hillcrest 반죽기가 꽤 평판이 좋은 것 같아요. 하지만 모델이 너무 많아요.
남: 우선, 얼마를 기꺼이 쓸 건가요?
여: 70달러를 넘으면 안 돼요. 그 가격이면 적당한 것을 찾을 수 있을 것 같아요.
남: 당신 말이 맞는 것 같아요. 그 가격이면 중간급의 물건을 살 수 있을 거예요. 무선을 원하나요?
여: 그게 아주 편리할 거라고 생각해요.
남: 자, 당신의 선택이 조금 좁혀지네요. 특별히 좋아하는 색이 있어요?
여: 어두운 건 원하지 않으니 더 밝은 것을 선택하는 것이 낫죠.
남: 알겠어요. 조금 더 지불하겠지만 그만한 가치가 있다고 생각해요. 음, 두 개의 선택이 남은 것 같군요.
여: 전 1년보다 긴 보증 기간을 원하니까 이걸 택할게요.
남: 좋아요. 그 반죽기가 당신의 모든 필요조건을 충족하네요.

어휘 **mixer** 반죽[혼합]기 / **catalog** 카탈로그 / **reputable** 평판 좋은 / **be willing to-v** 기꺼이 v하다 / **reasonable** 적당한 / **mid-range** 중간급의 / **cordless** 코드가 없는 / **handy** 편리한 / **narrow down** 좁히다, 줄이다 / **worth it** 그만한 가치가 있는 / **warranty** (품질) 보증 / **go for** ~을 택하다 / **fulfill** 충족시키다 / **requirement** 필요조건, 요건

11 짧은 대화에 이어질 응답 | ④

▶ 얼룩진 셔츠를 맡기려고 세탁소의 위치를 묻는 여자의 말에 슈퍼마켓 뒤에 있다는 응답이 가장 적절하다.

① 예쁜 셔츠구나.
② 너무 비싸진 않을 거야.
③ 거기선 그 얼룩을 지울 수 없어.
④ 슈퍼마켓 뒤에 하나 있어.
⑤ 너는 더 조심했어야 했어.

W: Do you see this stain? I spilled grape juice all over this shirt!
M: Oh, isn't that your favorite shirt? **You'd better take it** to a laundry.
W: I think I have to. Do you know **where the nearest laundry shop is**?
M: ________________________________

여: 이 얼룩 보이니? 이 셔츠에 온통 포도 주스를 쏟았어.
남: 이런, 그거 네가 제일 좋아하는 셔츠 아니니? 세탁소에 맡기는 게 낫겠다.
여: 그래야 할 것 같아. 가장 가까운 세탁소가 어딘지 알고 있니?
남: ________________________________

어휘 **stain** 얼룩 / **laundry** 세탁소; 세탁(물)

12 짧은 대화에 이어질 응답 | ③

▶ 언제 이사 가는지 묻는 여자의 말에 이달 말 전에 이사 간다는 응답이 가장 적절하다.

① 너를 돕게 되어서 정말 기뻐.
② 가지러 갈 준비가 되면 전화해.
③ 이달 말 전에 이사 갈 거야.
④ 나의 새 아파트는 여기서 멀지 않을 거야.
⑤ 그 세탁기는 2년밖에 안 됐어.

M: The house that I'm moving into doesn't have a washing machine.
W: Instead of buying one, **why don't you take mine**? I won't need it after I move out.
M: **That would be amazing**. When are you moving out?
W: ________________________________

남: 내가 새로 이사 갈 집에는 세탁기가 없어.
여: 하나 사는 것 대신, 내 것을 가져가면 어때? 이사 가고 나면 나는 세탁기가 필요 없을 거야.
남: 그게 좋겠다. 언제 이사 가는데?
여: ________________________________

13 긴 대화에 이어질 응답 | ③

▶ 아직 기타를 칠 줄 모르는, 기타 강습 수강을 원하는 초보자에게 할 수 있는 대답을 고른다.

① 아마도 피아노로 바꾸셔야 할 것 같네요.
② 스스로 학습하는 것이 최선의 방법이에요.
③ 초급자 강습에 등록시켜 드릴 수 있어요.
④ 미안합니다, 저는 기타 치는 법을 몰라요.
⑤ 좋은 성적을 받기 위해서 더 노력하셔야 해요.

W: I bought a guitar last week, but I still can't play it.
M: Well, **it takes years to become** really good at an instrument.
W: I don't have years! I'm entering the talent show at my school in two months!
M: It sounds like you need some intensive lessons and a lot of practice.
W: When I asked my friend what was **the easiest instrument to learn**, he said the guitar!
M: For some people, it is easy. For me, it was very hard, but **the practice paid off**.
W: If I practice very hard, how good can I get in two months?
M: Well, the more you practice, **the better you will get**.
W: I'll practice really hard if you let me take lessons from you.
M: ________________________________

여: 지난주에 기타를 샀는데요, 여전히 치지를 못하겠어요.
남: 음, 악기를 정말 잘 다루려면 몇 년이 걸린답니다.
여: 몇 년을 기다릴 시간이 없어요! 두 달 뒤에 학교에서 열리는 장기자랑에 참가할 거예요!
남: 집중 강습과 많은 연습이 필요하신 것 같네요.
여: 친구에게 가장 배우기 쉬운 악기가 뭐냐고 물어보니 기타라고 했어요!
남: 어떤 사람에게는 쉽지요. 제게는 매우 어려웠어요. 하지만 열심히 연습했더니 성과가 있더군요.
여: 제가 정말 열심히 연습한다면 두 달 후에는 얼마나 잘 칠 수 있을까요?
남: 음, 연습을 더 많이 할수록 실력은 더 좋아지겠죠.
여: 선생님 수업을 듣게 해주신다면, 정말 열심히 연습할게요.
남: ______________________________

어휘 **intensive** 집중적인 / **pay off** 성과를 거두다 | 선택지 어휘 | **switch** 전환하다, 바꾸다

14 긴 대화에 이어질 응답 | ①

▶ 없어진 물건을 제대로 찾아보지 않고 친구를 의심한 남자에게 할 수 있는 말을 찾는다.

① 거봐, 성급하게 단정하면 안 돼.
② 그 애는 물건을 빌리기 전에 먼저 물어봐야 해.
③ 너를 의심해서 정말 미안해.
④ Jacob이 그것을 거기에 두지 말았어야 하는데.
⑤ 그것을 어디에서 찾았니?

M: Cathy, have you seen my new red pen?
W: No, I haven't seen it.
M: I'm sure I left it on my desk. Jacob **must have taken it**.
W: Huh? Why do you say that?
M: He was telling me how much he liked it. But he shouldn't take it **without asking**.
W: Hold on. You don't know he took it.
M: Look, it was on my desk and it's not there now. And he **was looking at it** today.
W: You're not **being fair**. Have you looked carefully for it?
M: Yeah. But, hmm, let me see. *[pause]* Oh, here it is.
W: Where was it?
M: **It had fallen off my desk** and into my bag.
W: ______________________________

남: Cathy, 내가 새로 산 붉은색 펜 봤니?
여: 아니, 못 봤는데.
남: 분명히 책상에 놓아뒀는데. Jacob이 가져간 게 틀림없어.
여: 뭐? 왜 그렇게 생각하니?
남: 그 애가 그 펜이 정말 마음에 든다고 말했거든. 하지만 물어보지도 않고 가져가면 안 되지.
여: 잠깐만. 그 애가 가져갔는지 모르잖아.
남: 봐, 내 책상 위에 있었는데 지금은 없다고. 그리고 그 애가 오늘 그 펜을 보고 있었고.
여: 넌 공정하지가 않아. 잘 찾아 본 거니?
남: 응. 하지만 음, 어디 보자. *[잠시 후]* 아, 여기 있다.
여: 어디 있었니?
남: 책상에서 떨어져서 가방에 들어가 있었네.
여: ______________________________

어휘 **fair** 공정한 | 선택지 어휘 | **jump to conclusions** 성급하게 단정하다 / **accuse** 혐의를 제기하다; 비난하다

15 상황에 적절한 말 | ②

▶ Simon은 공공장소에서 다른 사람을 고려하는 것이 중요하다고 생각하므로 식당에서 다른 사람을 방해하며 제멋대로 구는 아이들을 제지하도록 부탁할 것이다.

① 제 아이가 식사를 먼저 끝마치도록 도울게요.
② 자녀분들에게 예의 바르게 행동하라고 말해 주세요.
③ 자녀분들이 질문을 그만하게 해 주세요.
④ 좀 방해를 해야겠네요. 질문이 뭐였죠?
⑤ 자녀분들을 자리에 앉히세요. 쇼가 곧 시작합니다.

W: Simon **is out to dinner** at a restaurant with his son James. At the next table a couple have just finished dinner and are having a serious conversation. When Simon starts eating, two boys start running around the restaurant and making noises. Other people in the restaurant **look uneasy with the boys**. One of the boys calls "Mom." The woman at the next table answers, but does nothing to stop the kids from interrupting others who are still eating. Simon believes **considering others is very important** in public places, and he doesn't want his son to follow the other boys' example. He **decides to say something** to the couple at the next table. In this situation, what would Simon most likely say to the couple?

여: Simon은 아들 James와 함께 식당에 저녁을 먹으러 왔다. 옆 테이블에는 한 부부가 식사를 막 마치고 진지한 대화를 나누고 있다. Simon이 식사를 시작할 때, 두 남자아이가 식당을 뛰어다니며 소란을 피우기 시작한다. 식당에 있는 다른 손님들도 아이들 때문에 불편해하는 것 같다. 아이들 중 한 명이 '엄마'라고 부른다. 옆 테이블의 여성이 대답을 하지만 아이들이 아직 식사 중인 다른 손님들을 방해하지 못하도록 제지하지 않는다. Simon은 공공장소에서는 다른 사람을 고려하는 것이 매우 중요하다고 생각한다. 그리고 아들이 그 아이들을 본받는 것을 원하지 않는다. 그래서 그는 옆 테이블의 부부에게 무언가를 말하기로 결심한다. 이러한 상황에서 Simon이 그 부부에게 할 말로 가장 적절한 것은 무엇인가?

어휘 **uneasy** 불편한 / **interrupt** 방해하다 | 선택지 어휘 | **behave oneself** 예의 바르게 행동하다

16~17 세트 문항 | 16. ② 17. ⑤

▶ 16. 운동을 하다가 부상을 입을 수 있는 원인들을 설명함으로써 안전하게 운동할 수 있는 방법을 제시하고 있다.

① 적절한 스포츠 활동을 선택하기 위한 조언
② 운동으로 인해 발생 가능한 부상의 예방법
③ 운동의 장점에 대한 이해
④ 스포츠 활동에 참여하기 위한 연령 제한
⑤ 스포츠를 하기 전 준비운동의 중요성

▶ 17. 해석 참조

M: Thinking of starting a new physical activity program? If so, you **may be at risk** of a training injury. Training injury can happen **when you try to take on** too much physical activity too quickly. So before starting a new physical activity, find out what can cause injury and how to safely increase your activity level. First, a training injury typically **results from training incorrectly**. For example, among the most common factors causing injury in long distance runners and tennis players are training errors. Going too fast, exercising for too long, or simply doing **too much of one type of activity** can lead to a training injury. Wrong technique can also damage your body. If you use poor form as you do training exercises, for example, swinging a golf club or throwing a baseball, it can cause a training injury. Although a training injury can happen to anyone, you **may be more likely to be injured** if you have certain medical conditions. Training injuries are also more likely to occur as you get older. For these reasons, it's a good idea to talk to your doctor before starting a new activity. Your doctor may offer tips to **help make physical activity safer** for you.

남: 새로운 신체활동 프로그램을 시작하는 것을 생각하고 계십니까? 만약 그렇다면, 운동 부상 위험이 있을지도 모릅니다. 운동 부상은 너무 많은 신체 활동을 너무 빨리 떠맡을 때 일어날 수 있습니다. 그러므로 새로운 신체 활동을 시작하기 전에, 무엇이 부상을 일으킬 수 있는지와 어떻게 안전하게 활동 수준을 높일 수 있는지에 대해 알아보십시오. 첫째, 일반적으로 운동 부상은 운동을 부정확하게 하는 데서 기인합니다. 예를 들어 장거리 주자(① 장거리 달리기)와 테니스 선수들(② 테니스)에게 있어 부상을 일으키는 가장 흔한 요소는 훈련 오류들입니다. 너무 빨리 가거나, 너무 오랫동안 운동하는 것, 또는 단지 한 가지 유형의 운동을 너무 많이 하는 것이 운동 부상으로 이어질 수 있습니다. 잘못된 기술 역시 신체에 해를 줄 수 있습니다. 운동을 연습할 때, 예를 들어 골프채를 휘두르거나(③ 골프) 야구공을 던질 때(④ 야구) 잘못된 폼을 사용하면 운동 부상을 일으킬 수 있습니다. 운동 부상이 누구에게나 일어날 수 있지만, 특정한 질병이 있으면 부상을 입을 가능성이 더 클지도 모릅니다. 운동 부상은 또한 나이가 들면서 더 발생하기 쉽습니다. 이러한 이유들 때문에, 새로운 운동을 시작하기 전에 의사와 상담을 하는 것도 좋은 생각입니다. 의사는 더 안전한 신체 활동을 하도록 도와주는 조언을 당신에게 해줄 것입니다.

어휘 **be at risk** 위험하다 / **take on** 떠맡다 / **typically** 일반적으로; 전형적으로 / **swing** 휘두르다; 흔들다[흔들리다]

01. ③	02. ⑤	03. ②	04. ④	05. ⑤	06. ①	07. ①	08. ②	09. ③	10. ②
11. ④	12. ①	13. ④	14. ④	15. ②	16. ④	17. ④			

01 화자가 하는 말의 목적 | ③

▶ 긍정적 사고를 하는 것이 성공을 일구어내고, 질병을 이기고 공부를 하는 데에도 도움이 된다는 내용이다.

W: People who think they will be successful are successful. Those who think they will fail do fail! **These basic ideas are being supported** by lots of new research. Researchers have shown that positive thoughts **increase our ability to fight** diseases. In drug tests, positive thinkers who are given a worthless sugar pill often become as healthy as those actually taking medicine. Their positive thoughts help heal them. In life, you must think positively to be successful. If you think you can't understand advanced math, for example, you'll never be able to do it. And if you think speaking English is too hard, **you'll never be able to do it either**. The first step to success is saying "I can do it."

여: 자신이 성공할 것이라고 생각하는 사람들은 성공합니다. 실패할 것이라고 생각하는 사람들은 정말 실패합니다! 이런 기본적 생각들은 새로운 연구를 통해서 많이 입증되고 있습니다. 연구자들은 긍정적 사고가 질병과 싸우는 능력을 향상시킨다는 것을 증명했습니다. 약물 실험에서, 긍정적 사고를 하는 사람들에게 효과가 없는 설탕 성분의 알약을 투여하더라도 실제 약물을 섭취한 사람만큼 종종 건강해집니다. 그들의 긍정적 사고가 치료에 도움이 된 것입니다. 삶에서 성공하기 위해서는 긍정적으로 사고해야 합니다. 예를 들어 자신이 고등 수학을 이해 못할 거라고 생각하면, 앞으로도 결코 못할 것입니다. 그리고 영어로 말하는 것이 너무 어렵다고 생각하면, 그것 역시 절대 못할 것입니다. 성공의 첫 단계는 '나는 할 수 있다'라고 말하는 것입니다.

어휘 **support** 입증하다, 뒷받침하다 / **worthless** 가치 없는 / **heal** 치료하다, 고치다 / **advanced** 고등의, 고급의

02 대화 주제 | ⑤

▶ 여자는 대학교에 다니며 자취 생활을 하려는 남자에게 생활비를 줄일 수 있는 방법들을 알려주고 있다.

M: Jennifer, **can you take a look at** my budget for attending university?
W: Wow, that's a lot! Can you afford to spend that much?
M: No, but what can I do? It's only the essentials.
W: Well, **you could cut your rent in half** if you had a roommate.
M: I guess that would save a lot of money.
W: Also, **you've budgeted a lot** for eating out. Why don't you try cooking at home?
M: I don't know how to cook, and I don't have any pots or pans.
W: It would be cheaper to buy some kitchenware and a cookbook than to eat out every day.
M: I guess you're right. Can you suggest anything else?
W: You should consider buying used furniture and textbooks. It will **save you a lot of money**.

남: Jennifer, 내가 대학에 다니면서 필요한 생활비 예산 좀 봐줄래?
여: 와, 많은데! 그렇게 많이 쓸 여유가 있어?
남: 아니, 하지만 어쩔 수 없잖아? 필수적인 것들뿐인데.
여: 음, 룸메이트가 있다면 집세를 절반으로 줄일 수 있을 거야.
남: 그러면 돈이 많이 절약되겠다.
여: 또, 넌 외식에 예산을 많이 세웠어. 집에서 요리를 해보는 게 어때?
남: 난 요리할 줄 모르고, 냄비랑 팬도 없어.
여: 주방용품 몇 개랑 요리책을 사는 게 매일 외식하는 것보다 비용이 더 적게 들 거야.
남: 네 말이 맞는 것 같아. 다른 것도 제안해 줄 수 있니?
여: 중고로 가구와 교과서를 사는 것도 고려해 봐야 해. 돈을 많이 절약하게 될 거야.

어휘 **budget** 예산, (지출 예상) 비용; 예산을 세우다 / **essential** (주로 복수형) 필수적인 것 / **kitchenware** 주방용품

03 관계 | ②

▶ 과거에 상사와 인턴사원 관계였던 두 사람이 다른 회사의 면접에서 면접관과 지원자로 만나서 인터뷰를 하고 있다.

M: Ms. Evans, please come in and **have a seat**.
W: Thank you. Oh... Mr. Jenner, is that you?
M: Sarah!
W: Yes, you remember. You changed companies?
M: Yes, last year.
W: I didn't know you had left KS Media.
M: A good opportunity came up here. But **I'm supposed to be** interviewing you. What happened after your internship at KS ended?
W: **I've been studying full-time** for the last two years.
M: When do you graduate?
W: This summer. I hope to work in the global business department here at Big Top Corporation.
M: Well, when I was your supervisor at KS Media, I was really happy with your work. But working here in the global business department would be very different.
W: I know that. But **I am eager to learn**.
M: OK.

남: Evans 씨, 들어오셔서 자리에 앉으세요.
여: 감사합니다. 아… Jenner 씨 아니십니까?
남: Sarah 씨!
여: 네, 기억하고 계시는군요. 회사를 옮기셨습니까?
남: 네, 작년에요.
여: KS Media를 떠나신 건 모르고 있었습니다.
남: 여기에 좋은 기회가 있어서요. 하지만 Sarah 씨의 면접을 봐야 하는 입장이군요. KS에서 인턴직을 끝내고 나서 어떤 일이 있었나요?
여: 지난 2년간 열심히 공부했습니다.
남: 언제 졸업하나요?
여: 올여름입니다. 저는 여기 Big Top 사의 해외 사업부에서 일하고 싶습니다.
남: 음, 제가 KS Media에서 상사였을 때, 정말 만족스럽게 일해 주셨죠. 하지만 이곳의 해외 사업부에서 일하는 것은 많이 다를 거예요.
여: 잘 압니다. 하지만 열심히 배우겠습니다.
남: 알겠습니다.

어휘 **come up** (일이) 일어나다, 생기다 / **be supposed to-v** v하기로 되어 있다 / **internship** 인턴직 / **department** 부서, 부문 / **supervisor** 관리자, 감독관 / **be eager to-v** v하기를 갈망하다

04 그림 불일치 | ④

▶ 남자는 마녀와 빗자루를 그리려고 하다가 생각을 바꿔 빗자루만 그렸다고 했다.

W: What are you drawing?
M: I just finished drawing my invitation for our club's Halloween party.
W: It's so impressive! **What a great idea to draw** a spider and its web at the top!
M: Thank you! I also thought the big full moon in the center would be nice.
W: Good. The moon really makes the words, Halloween Party, stand out. You even drew **three bats flying below it**.
M: Bats are symbolic of Halloween. Do you like the flying broom near the bats?
W: Of course. **It's interesting that** you just drew a broom without a witch.
M: I wanted to draw a witch at first, but I changed my mind. Do you think I should draw one?
W: No, I like it. I think this is more suggestive.
M: I also drew three carved pumpkins on the bottom.
W: They're called jack-o-lanterns, right? You have everything that represents Halloween in this picture.
M: Thanks. I'm so **excited just thinking about the party**. I should show this to the other club members now.

여: 뭘 그리고 있니?
남: 우리 동아리의 핼러윈 파티 초대장 그리기를 막 끝냈어.
여: 아주 좋구나! 맨 위에 거미하고 거미줄을 그린 건 정말 훌륭한 아이디어야!

남: 고마워! 나는 또 중앙에 커다란 보름달도 멋질 거라고 생각했어.
여: 좋아. 달이 정말로 '핼러윈 파티'라는 문구를 두드러지게 한다. 넌 그 밑에 날고 있는 박쥐 세 마리도 그렸구나.
남: 박쥐는 핼러윈의 상징이지. 박쥐 가까이에 날아가는 빗자루는 마음에 드니?
여: 물론이지. 네가 마녀 없이 그냥 빗자루만 그린 게 흥미로워.
남: 난 처음에는 마녀를 그리려고 했지만 생각을 바꿨어. 내가 마녀를 그려야 한다고 생각하니?
여: 아니야. 난 이게 좋아. 이게 더 암시적인 것 같아.
남: 난 맨 아래 조각한 호박도 세 개 그렸어.
여: 그것들을 jack-o-lantern(호박등)이라고 하지, 맞지? 이 그림 안에 핼러윈을 나타내는 모든 게 있어.
남: 고마워. 파티에 대해 생각만 해도 너무 신나. 지금 이걸 다른 동아리 회원들에게 보여줘야겠다.

어휘 **web** 거미줄 / **stand out** 두드러지다 / **broom** 빗자루 / **witch** 마녀 / **suggestive** 암시적인 / **carve** 조각하다 / **pumpkin** (서양)호박 / **jack-o-lantern** 호박등(호박에 얼굴 모양으로 구멍을 뚫고 안에 촛불을 꽂은 등) / **represent** 나타내다, 상징하다

05 부탁한 일 | ⑤

▶ 여자는 남자의 친구가 자신에게 여분의 모기장을 빌려줄 수 있는지 물어봐 달라고 했다.

W: Seho, look at **these all over me**!
M: Ouch! The mosquitoes bit you all night long.
W: They sure did. **Don't they bother you**?
M: Not a bit.
W: What's your secret?
M: I usually use a special cream before I go to bed.
W: But I don't like the sticky feeling.
M: Then you should get a mosquito net. They're perfect **for keeping mosquitoes away**.
W: Where can I get one?
M: Actually, the other night, my friend Haesu said she had an extra one in her closet.
W: That's great. Will you ask Haesu if she can **lend me her spare one**?
M: No problem.

여: 세호야, 내 온몸에 이것들 좀 봐!
남: 아이쿠! 모기한테 밤새 물렸구나.
여: 그랬어. 너는 모기에 물리지 않니?
남: 전혀.
여: 비결이 뭐야?
남: 잠자리에 들기 전에 특수 크림을 주로 사용해.
여: 하지만 나는 그런 끈적거리는 느낌이 싫어.
남: 그럼 모기장을 사야겠네. 모기가 접근하지 못하게 하는 데 딱 좋아.
여: 어디서 구할 수 있지?
남: 사실, 요전 날 밤에 내 친구 해수가 자기 옷장에 하나 더 있다고 했어.
여: 잘됐다. 해수에게 여분의 모기장을 나에게 빌려줄 수 있는지 물어봐 줄래?
남: 알겠어.

어휘 **sticky** 끈적거리는 / **spare** 여분의, 예비의

06 금액 | ①

▶ 구매할 책의 합계는 70달러인데, 5달러짜리 상품권 3장을 사용해 15달러를 할인받고, 3달러 상당의 회원 카드 포인트를 사용한다고 했으므로 남자가 지불할 총액은 52달러이다.

W: Excuse me, sir. Are these books yours?
M: Yes, these three are mine.
W: OK. **I'll ring these up** for you now — $15, $35, and $20. Is that everything?
M: Yes. But I'd like a paper bag, please.
W: OK, it's **free of charge**, so the total is $70. How will you be paying?
M: Cash. But, oh, wait a minute. I have some gift certificates. Can I use them here?
W: Let me see.... Yes, you can. You have three $5 certificates. I'll **take these off your total**.
M: Oh, and here's my Readers' Book Club card. I want the points for this purchase.
W: No problem. Let me put it through the machine. Oh, it says you have 3,000 points before this purchase. **That's worth** $3. Do you want to apply those points to this purchase?
M: Yes, please.

여: 실례합니다, 고객님. 이 책들이 고객님의 것인가요?
남: 네, 이 세 권이 제 것입니다.
여: 알겠습니다. 이것들을 지금 계산해 드리겠습니다. 15달러, 35달러, 20달러입니다. 그게 전부인가요?
남: 네. 그런데 종이 봉투 하나 주세요.
여: 알겠습니다. 그것은 무료라서 총 70달러입니다. 어떻게 결제하시겠습니까?
남: 현금으로요. 아, 그런데 잠시만요. 상품권이 몇 장 있어요. 여기서 사용할 수 있나요?
여: 한번 볼게요…. 네, 사용하실 수 있습니다. 5달러짜리 상품권을 세 장 가지고 계시네요. 총액에서 할인해 드릴게요.
남: 아, 그리고 여기 Readers' Book Club 카드요. 이 구매품에 대한 포인트를 적립해주세요.
여: 문제없습니다. 기계에 긁어 볼게요. 아, 이번 구매 전에 3,000포인트가 있다고 하네요. 3달러 상당인데, 이번에 구매하실 때 그 포인트를 사용하시겠어요?
남: 네, 부탁해요.

어휘 **ring up** (금전 등록기에 상품 가격을) 입력하다 / **free of charge** 무료의 / **gift certificate** 상품권 ***cf.* certificate** 증명서; 자격증 / **purchase** 구매(품); 구매하다

07 이유 | ①

▶ 여자는 출장을 가야 해서 남자가 출연하는 영화의 시사회에 참석할 수 없다고 했다.

M: Hi, Aunt Sharon! Here is a ticket to my movie premiere. I hope you can come.
W: I'd love to. I can't believe you are in a movie!
M: I didn't **play a major role**. Don't expect too much, okay?
W: Still, I'm impressed. *[pause]* So, the place is the Twin Oaks Theater, right?
M: Yes, **it's not far from** your home.
W: And it's on Saturday at 7 p.m.? I think I have something on that day.... Let's see....
M: You don't have to work on the weekend, do you?
W: No. But I'll be away on a business trip. I'm so sorry.
M: **It can't be helped**. That's okay.
W: I heard that tickets for this movie premiere are very hard to get. It's a shame to lose this chance.
M: **It will be playing** in several theaters soon. You can see it later.
W: Okay. I promise I'll come to your next premiere.

남: 안녕하세요, Sharon 숙모님! 여기 제 영화 시사회 표예요. 꼭 오셨으면 좋겠어요.
여: 나야 좋지. 네가 영화에 나온다니 믿기지 않는구나!
남: 중요한 역할은 아니에요. 너무 많이 기대하지는 마세요, 아셨죠?
여: 그래도 감동적이구나. *[잠시 후]* 그러면, 장소는 Twin Oaks 극장 맞지?
남: 네, 숙모님 댁에서 멀지 않아요.
여: 토요일 저녁 7시구나? 그날은 일이 좀 있는 것 같은데…. 어디 보자….
남: 주말엔 일 안 하셔도 되잖아요, 그렇죠?
여: 그렇긴 하다만 출장 중일 거야. 정말 미안하다.
남: 어쩔 수 없죠. 괜찮아요.
여: 이 영화 시사회 표를 구하기가 매우 어렵다고 들었는데. 이 기회를 놓치다니 무척 아쉽구나.
남: 곧 몇 개 극장에서 상영될 거예요. 나중에 보실 수 있어요.
여: 그래. 다음 시사회에는 가겠다고 약속하마.

어휘 **premiere** 시사회; (영화의) 개봉; (연극의) 초연 / **it can't be helped** 어쩔 수 없다

08 언급하지 않은 것 | ②

▶ 해석 참조

M: Hi, Cindy. How are you?
W: Hi, Jim. **To be honest**, I'm nervous about my job interview.
M: That's understandable. I felt the same way before my first few interviews.
W: Really? Did you do well?
M: Actually, no. But I learned a few things. For instance, you should **remember to keep smiling**.
W: Okay. What else?
M: Even though you are nervous, be sure to speak loudly and clearly.
W: I'll try to give a good impression with my voice. And I should dress formally, right?
M: Yes, it's important to look your best. Make sure your hair and clothes are neat.
W: It's in the morning, so **I'd better wake up early** to give myself plenty of time.
M: Definitely. You don't want to be late. Interviewers look down on that.
W: Well, thanks. I feel **a bit more prepared now**.
M: No problem. Good luck.

남: 안녕, Cindy. 잘 지내?
여: 안녕, Jim. 솔직히 말하면, 취업 면접 때문에 긴장돼.
남: 그럴 만해. 나도 처음 몇 번의 면접을 보기 전에 똑같은 기분이었어.
여: 정말? 면접은 잘 봤니?
남: 실은, 그러지 못했어. 그렇지만 배운 것도 몇 가지 있어. 예를 들면, 미소를 유지하는 걸(① 표정) 명심해야 해.
여: 좋아. 그밖에 다른 것은?
남: 긴장이 되더라도 꼭 크고 분명하게 말해야 하고(③ 목소리).
여: 목소리로 좋은 인상을 주려고 노력할게. 그리고 정장을 입어야 하겠지?
남: 응, 최대한 좋은 모습으로 보이는 게 중요해. 머리와 옷은 꼭 단정히 하고(④ 복장).
여: 면접이 아침에 있으니까 일찍 일어나서 여유 시간을 충분히 갖는 게 좋을 것 같아.
남: 물론이야. 면접에 늦고 싶지는 않잖아. 면접관들은 면접에 늦는 걸 좋지 않게 보거든(⑤ 시간 엄수).
여: 음, 고마워. 이제 조금 더 준비된 기분이야.
남: 고맙긴. 잘되길 바라.

어휘 **job interview** 구직 면접 / **understandable** 당연한, 정상적인 / **dress formally** 정장을 차려입다 / **interviewer** 면접관 ***cf.*** **interviewee** 면접받는 사람 / **look down on** ~을 내려다보다; 깔보다, 얕보다

09 내용 불일치 | ③

▶ 이 배의 첫 출발지는 영국이 아니라 네덜란드이다.

M: What do you do with that ice-cream stick after eating an ice-cream bar? You **throw it away**, right? Well, Robert McDonald, a Hollywood stunt man, built a 15-meter long Viking ship from ice-cream sticks. **He plans to sail it** from the Netherlands to England and then from England to North America. On the way to America he will visit Iceland and Greenland as the Vikings also did long ago! The ship **was made from** 15 million ice-cream sticks and McDonald got the help of more than 5,000 children to build it. He said he wanted **to teach children** that anything is possible. So what could you build from 15 million ice-cream sticks?

남: 아이스크림 바를 먹고 난 후 아이스크림 막대기로 무엇을 하십니까? 그냥 버리시겠지요? 할리우드에서 스턴트맨으로 활약 중인 Robert McDonald 씨는 아이스크림 막대기로 15미터 길이의 바이킹 배를 만들었습니다. 그는 네덜란드에서 영국까지 그리고 나서 영국에서 북미까지 그것을 타고 항해할 계획입니다. 미국으로 가는 길에 그는 오래전에 바이킹들이 그랬던 것처럼 아이슬란드와 그린란드를 방문할 것입니다! 그 배는 천오백만 개의 아이스크림 막대기로 축조되었으며 McDonald 씨는 오천 명이 넘는 어린이들의 도움을 받아 그것을 완성했습니다. 그는 아이들에게 무엇이든 가능하다는 것을 가르쳐주고 싶었다고 말했습니다. 그렇다면 여러분은 천오백만 개의 아이스크림 막대기로 무엇을 만들겠습니까?

어휘 **throw away** 버리다 / **stunt man** 스턴트맨, 대역 배우 / **on the way to** ~로 가는 도중에

10 도표 이해 | ②

▶ 여자는 우선 스페인어를 쓰는 나라를 택했고 한 달이나 두 달 프로그램을 원하고 있다. 하고자 하는 일은 아이들에게 컴퓨터를 가르치는 일이고 6월에는 못 떠나고 7월에 떠난다고 했으므로 여자가 선택한 자원봉사 프로그램은 ②이다.

W: I want to sign up for some volunteer work this summer.
M: Wow, great. Where do you want to go?
W: Well, I **have to consider the language first**, so I'd like to go to a country that requires Spanish.
M: Then, you should probably head down to South America. How long do you plan to do this?
W: For about one month or two months. I think that would **give me enough time to get to know** the people and culture there.
M: That's a great idea. What kind of work do you want to do?
W: My major is computer science, so I'd like to teach kids computer skills. Would you like to come with me?
M: If I decide to go, I should participate in a home building project since I'm studying architecture. But I already signed up for summer school.
W: Oh, I see.
M: **When will you leave**?
W: I'll be busy in June, so I'll probably leave in July. So this program is my best option.
M: I really hope you have a wonderful experience.

여: 나는 올여름에 자원봉사 일에 좀 참가하고 싶어.
남: 와, 멋진데. 어디로 가고 싶니?
여: 글쎄, 우선 언어를 고려해야 하니까 스페인어를 필요로 하는 나라에 가고 싶어.
남: 그러면 아마 남미로 가야겠구나. 얼마나 할 예정이니?
여: 약 한 달이나 두 달쯤. 그러면 그곳 사람들과 문화를 알기에 충분한 시간일 거라고 생각해.
남: 좋은 생각이야. 어떤 종류의 일을 하고 싶니?
여: 내 전공이 컴퓨터 공학이니까 아이들에게 컴퓨터 기술을 가르치고 싶어. 나하고 함께 갈래?
남: 내가 가기로 한다면 난 건축학을 공부하고 있으니까 집짓기 프로젝트에 참여해야 할 거야. 하지만 난 이미 여름 학교에 등록했어.
여: 아, 알겠어.
남: 언제 떠날 거니?
여: 내가 6월에는 바쁠 거라 아마 7월에 떠날 거야. 그러니까 이 프로그램이 나의 최상의 선택이야.
남: 네가 정말 멋진 경험을 하기 바란다.

어휘 **sign up** 참가하다, 등록하다 / **participate** 참가하다 / **architecture** 건축학 / **option** 선택, 선택권

11 짧은 대화에 이어질 응답 | ④

▶ 어제 샌드위치를 먹은 여자가 오늘 또 먹고 싶다고 하자 남자가 질리지 않는지 물었다.

① 멀지 않아. 걸어가자.
② 난 점심을 아주 조금 먹었어.
③ 오늘 저녁은 밖에 나가서 먹기엔 너무 지쳤어.
④ 난 샌드위치를 매일이라도 먹을 수 있어.
⑤ 네가 만든 구운 쇠고기 샌드위치가 최고야.

M: I'm hungry. Do you **want to go to dinner soon**?
W: Sure. Let's go to the sandwich shop on the corner.
M: We had sandwiches yesterday. **Aren't you tired of** them?
W: ______________________________

남: 나 배고파. 바로 저녁 먹으러 갈래?
여: 물론이지. 모퉁이에 있는 샌드위치 가게에 가자.
남: 우리 어제 샌드위치 먹었잖아. 안 질리니?
여: ______________________________

어휘 **be tired of** ~에 싫증나다

12 짧은 대화에 이어질 응답 | ①

▶ 남자는 밤늦게 친구들을 초대하는 룸메이트 때문에 불편을 겪고 있다. 룸메이트에게 그 문제에 대해 말해보라는 여자의 조언에 가장 적절한 응답을 찾는다.

① 했지, 하지만 아무것도 변하지 않았어.
② 그 애 친구들이 날 정말 귀찮게 해.
③ 그건 분명히 규칙에 어긋나.
④ 나는 밤샘 파티하는 걸 즐겨.
⑤ 그 앤 그것에 대해서 아무 말도 안 했어.

W: **How are things going with** your new roommate?
M: Not well. He always invites his friends over late at night.
W: **Why don't you tell** him that it bothers you?
M: ______________________________

여: 새 룸메이트와는 어떻게 지내니?
남: 잘 지내지 못해. 그 앤 밤늦게 늘 친구들을 집으로 초대해.
여: 그것 때문에 성가시다고 그 애한테 말하는 게 어때?
남: ______________________________

어휘 **invite A over** A를 집으로 초대하다

13 긴 대화에 이어질 응답 | ④

▶ 여자는 만화책에 대해서는 부정적인 입장이며, 이미 많은 책을 추천한 상태이므로 책을 골라야 하는 남자에게 자신이 추천한 책을 살펴보자는 답변이 가장 적절하다.

① 만화책은 휴가 때 읽기에 정말 좋아요.
② 당신은 지금쯤 모든 것을 다 싸놓았어야 했어요.
③ 내 책을 먼저 골라야 해요.
④ 내가 추천한 것들을 찾아봐요, 알았죠?
⑤ 생각해봐요. 나는 이것들을 지불해야 해요.

W: Danny? There you are! Are you ready to go? I'm tired.
M: Hang on a second, will you? **I haven't found any good books** to take on our holiday.
W: But we've been in the bookstore for ages. And I gave you **lots of suggestions for good books**.
M: Sorry, I started reading comic books and forgot all your suggestions.

W: Comic books are too simple. Well, hurry up! I've already paid for my books.
M: What did you get?
W: *Gossip Girl* and *Sisterhood of the Traveling Pants*. You wouldn't like them.
M: Yeah, I don't think I'll enjoy those. **What should I get**?
W: ________________________________

여: Danny? 거기 있었어요! 갈 준비 되었어요? 난 피곤해요.
남: 기다려요. 우리 휴가 때 가지고 갈 좋은 책들을 아직 발견하지 못했어요.
여: 하지만 우린 서점에서 너무 오래 있었어요. 내가 좋은 책들을 많이 추천해 줬잖아요.
남: 미안해요. 만화책을 읽기 시작해서 당신이 추천한 것들을 모두 잊어버렸어요.
여: 만화책은 너무 단순해요. 음, 서둘러요! 난 이미 내 책값을 지불했어요.
남: 뭘 샀는데요?
여: 〈가십걸〉과 〈청바지 돌려입기〉요. 당신은 좋아하지 않을 거예요.
남: 그래요, 내가 그것들을 즐길 거라고 생각하지 않아요. 난 어떤 책을 사야 할까요?
여: ________________________________

어휘 **hang on** 기다리다; 꼭 붙잡다 / **suggestion** 추천, 제안

14 긴 대화에 이어질 응답 | ④

▶ 여자는 자신이 맡은 역할을 열심히 하겠다는 약속을 어기려 하고 있다.

① 문제없어. 네 역할은 별로 중요하지 않아.
② 〈웨스트 사이드 스토리〉에서 너는 훌륭히 해냈어.
③ 재미있게 놀고 있을 때는 시간이 빨리 지나가.
④ 너는 약속을 어겨서는 안 돼.
⑤ 그가 전혀 개의치 않으리라 확신해.

W: Hi, Bob.
M: Hi, Jessica. **What's bothering you**? You don't look so good.
W: It's the school play. It's too much work.
M: But you're the leading actress.
W: I know and I promised Mr. Hampton I'd do a great job.
M: Yes, you promised. He'll be angry if you don't **make a full effort**. He didn't want to give you the leading role at first.
W: Yes, I know. I **missed a lot of practices** when we were doing *West Side Story*, the previous play.
M: Betty also wanted the leading role?
W: Yes, but I am so busy with my classes. And I'm busy applying to universities, too.
M: I understand. You've got to try to use your time wisely.
W: I'll try, but honestly **I'm considering giving up my role**.
M: ________________________________

여: 안녕, Bob.
남: 안녕, Jessica. 무슨 걱정이 있니? 안색이 안 좋구나.
여: 학교 연극 때문에 그래. 할 일이 너무 많아.
남: 하지만 넌 주연 여배우잖아.
여: 알아. 그리고 Hampton 선생님께 잘하겠다고 약속도 드렸어.
남: 그래, 네가 약속했지. 네가 전력을 다해서 노력하지 않으면 선생님께서 화내실 거야. 선생님께서는 처음에 네게 주연을 주지 않으려고 하셨잖아.
여: 응, 나도 알아. 우리가 저번 연극 〈웨스트 사이드 스토리〉 할 때 내가 연습을 많이 빠졌지.
남: Betty도 역시 주연을 원했지?
여: 응, 하지만 나는 수업 때문에 너무 바빠. 그리고 대학을 지원하는 일도 바쁘고.
남: 이해해. 너는 시간을 현명하게 쓰려고 노력해야 해.
여: 노력할게. 하지만 솔직히 내 역할을 포기할까 고려 중이야.
남: ________________________________

어휘 **make an effort** 노력하다; 애쓰다 / **leading role** 주연, 주역 / **apply** 지원하다, 신청하다; 적용하다 / **consider** 고려하다 | 선택지 어휘 | **go back one's word** 약속을 어기다

15 상황에 적절한 말 | ②

▶ Diane은 사진기를 빌려주겠다고 말만 하고 완전히 잊어버리고 있었기 때문에 Owen에게 미안해할 것이다.

① 조심해, 그렇지 않으면 미끄러져 넘어질 수도 있어.
② 미안해, 완전히 잊고 있었어.
③ 물론이지, 내가 어떻게 도울 수 있을까?
④ 내 사진기를 좀 더 조심해서 다뤄 줘.
⑤ 안녕, 즐거운 휴가가 되기를 빌어.

W: Owen is Diane's good friend and co-worker. They have many good memories of each other. Owen needs to ask Diane for a favor. Diane has two digital cameras. She bought one and **won the other one in a contest**. This Saturday, Owen is going away and he wants to borrow one of Diane's cameras because last month he slipped and dropped her camera. **It no longer works**. On Monday, Owen asked Diane **if she would mind lending** him one of her cameras. Diane said it was not a problem. All week Owen kept expecting Diane to bring the camera to work. But Diane never did. She **had forgotten all about it**. On Friday, Owen asks Diane about the camera. In this situation, what is Diane most likely to say to Owen?

여: Owen은 Diane의 친한 친구이자 동료이다. 그들은 서로에게 좋은 추억을 많이 가지고 있다. Owen은 Diane에게 부탁을 할 필요가 있다. Diane은 디지털 사진기가 두 대 있다. 하나는 구입한 것이고 다른 하나는 대회에 참가하여 받은 것이다. 이번 토요일 Owen은 여행을 떠날 예정이라 Diane의 사진기 중 한 대를 빌리고 싶어 한다. 왜냐하면 지난달에 그는 사진기를 놓쳐 떨어트렸기 때문이다. 그 사진기는 더 이상 작동하지 않는다. 월요일에 Owen은 Diane에게 사진기를 빌려줄 수 있겠냐고 물었다. Diane은 문제없다고 말했다. 일주일 내내 Owen은 Diane이 회사로 사진기를 가져오기를 기다렸다. 하지만 Diane은 가져오지 않았다. 그녀는 그것에 대해 완전히 잊어버렸다. 금요일에 Owen은 Diane에게 사진기에 대해서 묻는다. 이러한 상황에서 Diane이 Owen에게 할 말로 가장 적절한 것은 무엇인가?

어휘 **co-worker** 동료 | 선택지 어휘 | **slip one's mind** 잊어버리다 / **assistance** 도움; 조력, 보조

16~17 세트 문항 | 16. ④ 17. ④

▶ 16. 어린이의 선물을 고르는 요령에 대해 설명하고 있다.

① 아이들에게 더 가까이 다가가는 방법
② 위험할 수 있는 장난감들
③ 어린아이들을 위한 창의적인 선물들
④ 아이들에게 적절한 선물을 고르는 방법
⑤ 유아용품에 포함된 유해 물질들

▶ 17. 해석 참조

M: Giving is **one of the best ways** to show you care, but it can be difficult to choose a gift for someone else's child. Children develop at different rates, and their interests can change from year to year. Fortunately, there are a few guidelines **that can help you out**. Most importantly, check with the parents first whenever possible. This will give you important clues about the child's likes and dislikes. Then check the gift-buying guides of your favorite online toy stores. But **no matter what you pick**, safety is most important. To begin with, avoid anything that a young child could choke on. Rubber balloons, for example, are especially dangerous. Also, be aware that metal jewelry may contain toxic materials. Similarly, be careful when selecting cotton products, since most cotton **has been exposed to** pesticides at one point. Even wooden blocks may contain poisonous chemicals from the factory. **All of the extra effort will be worth it** when you see the smiling face of the child who receives your gift.

남: 무언가를 주는 것은 여러분이 마음을 쓰고 있다는 것을 보여주는 가장 좋은 방법 중 하나이지만, 누군가의 아이를 위한 선물을 고르는 것은 어려울 수 있습니다. 아이들은 각기 다른 속도로 발달하며, 그들의 관심사도 해마다 바뀔 수 있습니다. 다행히도 당신에게 도움을 주는 지침이 몇 가지 있습니다. 가장 중요한 것은, 가능하면 언제든지 아이의 부모에게 먼저 물어보는 것입니다. 이렇게 하면 그 아이가 좋아하는 것과 싫어하는 것에 대한 중요한 정보를 알 수 있게 됩니다. 그러고 나서, 당신이 특히 좋아하는 온라인 장난감 가게의 선물 구매 지침을 확인해 보십시오. 하지만 당신이 무엇을 고르건, 안전이 가장 중요합니다. 우선, 어린 아이가 질식할 수도 있는 선물은 무엇이든지 피하십시오. 예컨대 ① 고무풍선은 (이 점에서) 특히 위험합니다. 또한, ② 금속 장신구는 독성 물질을 포함하고 있을 수도 있다는 것을 알아야 합니다. 마찬가지로, ③ 면제품을 고를 때도 주의해야 하는데, 대부분의 면직물이 한 단계에서는 살충제에 노출되어 왔기 때문입니다. 심지어 ⑤ 나무 블록도 공장에서 사용하는 독성 화학물질을 포함하고 있을지 모릅니다. 당신의 선물을 받은 아이 얼굴에 띤 미소를 보면 이런 모든 세심한 노력이 그만한 가치가 있을 것입니다.

어휘 **choke** 질식하다, 숨이 막히다 / **toxic** 유독한; 중독(성)의 / **be exposed to** ~에 노출되다 / **pesticide** 살충제 / **poisonous** 유독한, 독성의 | 선택지 어휘 | **substance** 물질; 재질, 재료

01. ④ **02.** ④ **03.** ④ **04.** ③ **05.** ⑤ **06.** ③ **07.** ③ **08.** ③ **09.** ③ **10.** ⑤
11. ③ **12.** ⑤ **13.** ① **14.** ① **15.** ② **16.** ③ **17.** ⑤

01 화자가 하는 말의 목적 | ④

▶ 항공 수하물이 분실되면 작성해야 하는 서식과 신고 시간 등에 관한 항공사의 안내 방송이다.

M: May I have your attention, please? This is an announcement for passengers of Interconnect Airlines. Making sure that **your baggage is properly handled** is extremely important to us. In the unfortunate event of lost property, however, you must fill out a Passenger Baggage Loss Claim form. A copy of this form may be obtained from an Interconnect Airlines employee, or you can download it from our website at www.ica.com. Please note that missing property **must be reported within 24 hours**. We strongly advise our passengers to do this **prior to leaving the airport**. Once we receive your form, we will do our best to return your luggage to you as soon as possible. Thank you very much.

남: 잠시 주목해주시겠습니까?. 이것은 Interconnect 항공사 승객을 위한 안내 방송입니다. 고객님의 수하물이 제대로 처리되도록 확실히 하는 것이 저희에게는 매우 중요합니다. 그러나 만일 물건이 분실되는 불상사가 생기면, 승객 수하물 분실 청구 서식을 작성해주셔야 합니다. 이 서식의 사본은 Interconnect 항공사 직원에게서 받으시거나 저희 웹사이트 www.ica.com에서 내려받으실 수 있습니다. 분실된 물건은 24시간 이내에 신고되어야 함을 유의해주시기 바랍니다. 승객 여러분께서 공항을 떠나시기 전에 신고하시기를 강력히 권고합니다. 일단 신고서가 접수되면, 고객님께 가능한 한 빨리 수하물을 돌려드리도록 최선을 다할 것입니다. 대단히 감사합니다.

어휘 **announcement** 공고, 발표 / **baggage** 수하물 (= luggage) / **in the event of** 만일 ~의 경우 / **fill out** 기입하다, 작성하다 / **prior to A** A에 앞서, 이전에

02 의견 | ④

▶ 여자는 자연식품과 달리 가공식품은 구성 성분이 몸에 미치는 영향을 확신할 수 없고 건강에 좋은 것에 관한 의견도 끊임없이 바뀌므로 차라리 자연을 믿는 게 좋다고 말했다.

M: Are you hungry? I have an extra energy bar that you can have.
W: Thanks, but I brought some snacks of my own. Plus, I try to avoid processed foods.
M: Oh, really? **Why do you avoid them**?
W: Unlike natural foods, I **can't be certain of** how the ingredients will affect my body.
M: I know what you are saying, but these energy bars have been developed for athletes. Surely they are good for us.
W: I understand your point, but doctors are constantly updating their views on **what is healthy and what is not**. I prefer to trust Mother Nature instead.
M: Well, don't hesitate to ask me later, if you change your mind.

남: 너 배고프니? 네가 먹어도 되는 에너지 바가 하나 더 있어.
여: 고맙지만 난 내 간식을 좀 가져왔어. 게다가, 가공식품을 피하려고 하고 있거든.
남: 아, 정말? 왜 그걸 피하는데?
여: 자연식품과 달리, 그 성분들이 내 몸에 어떤 영향을 미칠지 확신할 수 없으니까.
남: 무슨 말인지 알지만, 이 에너지 바들은 운동선수를 위해 개발되어 왔어. 분명 우리 건강에 좋을 거야.
여: 네 말은 이해해. 그렇지만 의사들은 무엇이 건강에 좋고 무엇이 그렇지 않은지에 대한 의견을 끊임없이 새롭게 하고 있어. 난 대신 대자연을 믿는 게 더 좋아.
남: 음, 나중에라도 마음이 바뀌면 주저하지 말고 내게 부탁해.

어휘 **processed food** 가공식품 / **natural food** 자연식품 / **ingredient** 성분, 재료 / **Mother Nature** (만물의 어머니 같은) 대자연

03 관계 | ④

▶ 남자는 여자에게 이야기를 조금 바꾸자고 제의했고, 여자는 본인이 각본을 쓴 사실을 언급하며 남자의 다큐멘터리 영화의 일원이 된 것이 영광이라고 한다. 또한 남자가 자신의 첫 연출이라고 말하는 것을 보아 두 사람은 다큐멘터리 감독과 작가이다.

M: Rachel, can I speak to you for a minute?
W: Sure. Is something wrong?
M: I feel that we should make some changes to the story.
W: Why do you think so?
M: I'm afraid our audience **will lose interest** if the narration continues this long.
W: I'm sorry you feel that way. Do you have any good ideas?
M: Why don't we put a few more interviews with scientists in the film?
W: Okay. There is a list of AI scientists I met while writing the script. **Why don't you choose** some of them to interview?
M: All right. Let's have a meeting tomorrow at 11 a.m. and talk about it. I hope my decision **doesn't bother you** too much.
W: No problem. It's an honor for me to be a part of your documentary film.
M: You've had a lot of experience with AI, so it's very helpful for my directing. And I'll call the camera director, Philip, to the meeting, too.
W: Okay.

남: Rachel, 잠깐 얘기 좀 할 수 있을까요?
여: 물론이죠. 뭐가 잘못되었나요?
남: 전 우리가 이야기를 조금 바꿔야 한다고 생각해요.
여: 왜 그렇게 생각하세요?
남: 만약 내레이션이 이렇게 길면 관객들이 흥미를 잃을 것 같아요.
여: 그렇게 느끼신다니 유감이네요. 좋은 생각 있으세요?
남: 영화에 과학자들과의 인터뷰를 몇 개 더 집어넣는 건 어때요?
여: 알겠어요. 각본을 쓰는 동안 제가 만났던 인공지능 과학자들의 목록이 있어요. 그들 중 인터뷰할 몇 명을 고르시는 게 어때요?
남: 좋아요. 내일 오전 11시에 회의를 열어서 그것에 대해 이야기해 봅시다. 제 결정이 당신을 너무 귀찮게 하지 않았으면 좋겠어요.
여: 문제없어요. 감독님의 다큐멘터리 영화의 일원이 된 것이 제게는 영광이에요.
남: 작가님이 인공지능에 많은 경험이 있으셔서 제 연출에 매우 도움이 돼요. 그럼 제가 카메라 감독 Philip도 회의에 부를게요.
여: 알겠어요.

어휘 **lose interest** 흥미를 잃다, 싫증이 나다 / **narration** 내레이션; 서술하기 / **AI** 인공지능 / **script** 각본, 대본, 원고 / **bother** 귀찮게 하다; 신경 쓰이게 하다 / **honor** 영광; 명예 / **directing** 연출

04 그림 불일치 | ③

▶ 남자는 아이가 토끼 모양의 풍선을 잃어버렸다고 말했다.

M: Hey, look at this photo of our family. It's pretty old. Maybe more than 10 years.
W: **How time flies**! Is that really your dad wearing the striped shirt on the left side of the picture? He looks so young!
M: Yes, it's him. And the shirt was a birthday gift from Mom.
W: It's cool. Hey, look at the dog **playing with a ball in front of you**.
M: Yeah, he was our dog, Spike. He really loved that ball!
W: I see. **Who is the girl in the middle**? Is it Susan, or Julie?
M: It's Susan. Julie was on a girl scout trip at that time.
W: Oh, yeah? But why does Susan look upset in this picture?
M: It was probably because she lost her rabbit-shaped balloon.
W: She must have loved that balloon. Why is your mom pointing at the watermelon on the table?
M: That's because it was so sweet!

남: 이야, 이 가족사진 좀 봐요. 무척 오래된 거네. 아마 10년도 넘은 것 같아요.
여: 시간 정말 빠르죠! 사진 왼쪽에 줄무늬 셔츠를 입고 있는 분이 정말 아버님이세요? 진짜 젊어 보이세요!
남: 네, 우리 아버지예요. 그리고 이 셔츠는 어머니가 생신 선물로 드린 거고요.
여: 멋진데요. 아, 당신 앞에서 공을 가지고 놀고 있는 개 좀 보세요.
남: 그래요. 우리 개 Spike예요. 그 공을 정말 좋아했어요!

여: 그렇군요. 가운데 여자애는 누구죠? Susan? 아니면 Julie인가요?
남: Susan이에요. Julie는 그때 걸스카우트 소풍을 갔거든요.
여: 아, 그래요? 근데 이 사진에서 Susan이 왜 화가 나 보이죠?
남: 아마 토끼 모양 풍선을 잃어버려서 그랬을 거예요.
여: 그 풍선을 참 좋아했던 게 틀림없어요. 어머님은 왜 테이블 위에 놓인 수박을 가리키고 계시죠?
남: 그 수박이 진짜 달았거든요!

어휘 **striped** 줄무늬의

05 추후 행동 | ⑤

▶ 가족 여행이 취소되어 남자의 DVD 파티에 갈 수 있게 된 여자는 엄마에게 전화해서 가도 되는지 허락을 구하겠다고 말했다.

W: Hi, Mark. What's up?
M: I've just rented some DVDs.
W: Yeah. I can see that. You've rented a bunch of Harry Potter movies.
M: Yeah. I've rented the first four movies. I'm having a Harry Potter DVD party at my house today. **Don't you remember**?
W: Oh, that's right.
M: I invited you last week, but you said your family would be traveling this weekend.
W: Oh, **my family cancelled the trip**.
M: Join us then. We're starting at three in the afternoon. My mom is cooking a lot of food. Lisa is bringing some drinks and Justin is bringing some snacks.
W: Can I bring some snacks, too?
M: **It's not necessary**. We'll have plenty of food.
W: OK. I'll phone my mom right now and **ask her if it's OK**.

여: Mark야 안녕. 무슨 일이야?
남: 방금 DVD를 몇 장 빌렸어.
여: 응. 그런 것 같네. Harry Potter 영화를 많이 빌렸구나.
남: 응. 처음 네 편을 빌렸어. 오늘 우리 집에서 Harry Potter DVD 파티를 할 거야. 기억 안 나니?
여: 아, 맞아.
남: 지난주에 널 초대했지만, 네가 이번 주말에 가족이 여행 갈 거라고 말했잖아.
여: 아, 우리 가족은 여행을 취소했어.
남: 그럼 우리와 함께해. 오후 3시에 시작할 거야. 엄마께서 많은 음식을 요리하는 중이셔. Lisa는 음료수를 좀 가져올 거고 Justin은 간식을 좀 가져올 거야.
여: 나도 간식을 좀 가져갈까?
남: 그럴 필요 없어. 음식이 많이 있을 거야.
여: 알겠어. 엄마께 지금 바로 전화해서 괜찮은지 여쭤볼게.

어휘 **a bunch of** 많은; 한 다발[송이, 묶음]의

06 금액 | ③

▶ 남자는 C구간에서 A구간으로 갈 것이므로 기본요금(2달러 50센트)에다 두 개 구간을 지나는 추가 요금(1달러)을 내야 한다. 따라서 3달러 50센트를 버스 요금으로 내야 한다.

M: How much is the bus fare?
W: It depends. The basic fare is $2.50. Then you add 50 cents more for **each additional zone you travel**.
M: Is there a map of the different zones at the bus stop?
W: Yes, there is. Look, there are four zones in the city. The downtown area is zone A, then zone B circles zone A.
M: Each zone **circles the previous zone**.
W: Yes. And we are here in zone C, the Eastside village.
M: And we want to go to the Art Museum downtown.
W: So you **must pay the basic fare**, $2.50, plus the additional fare for two zones.
M: What about you?
W: Oh, I have a monthly three-zone transit card. It's cheaper.

남: 버스 요금이 얼마야?
여: 경우에 따라 달라. 기본요금은 2달러 50센트이고 각 구간을 추가로 지나가면 50센트씩 추가돼.
남: 버스 정류장에 다른 구간의 지도가 있니?
여: 응, 있어. 봐, 도시는 네 개의 구간으로 되어 있어. 도심은 A구간인데 B구간이 A구간을 둘러싸고 있어.
남: 각 구간이 이전 구간을 둘러싸고 있구나.
여: 그래. 그리고 우리는 Eastside 마을인 여기 C구간에 있어.
남: 그리고 우리는 도심에 있는 미술관으로 가려고 하지.
여: 그럼 넌 기본요금 2달러 50센트를 내고 두 구간에 대한 추가 요금을 내면 되겠구나.
남: 너는?
여: 아, 난 3구간 월정액 통행 카드가 있어. 이게 더 싸거든.

어휘 **fare** 요금, 운임 / **zone** (교통 기관의) 동일 운임 구간 / **circle** ~의 둘레를 돌다, 우회하다 / **previous** 이전의, 앞의 / **additional** 추가의 / **transit** 통행, 통과

07 이유 | ③

▶ 여자가 바지를 반품하기 위해 영수증을 가지고 갔지만, 구매 당시 그 바지가 할인 상품이어서 반품할 수 없었다고 했다.

W: Hi, honey. What are you doing?
M: Oh, nothing. By the way, whose pants are in this bag?
W: Did you forget? Those are the ones I wanted to return because I **got a similar pair as a birthday present**.
M: Oh, right. You were going to do that yesterday, weren't you?
W: That was my plan, but I failed.
M: I guess you were **too busy with other things**.
W: No, I took them to the store, but they wouldn't accept them.
M: I don't understand. You kept the receipt, didn't you?
W: I did. The problem was that they were on sale at the time of purchase.
M: Now I get it. Sometimes, sale items **can't be returned or exchanged**.
W: Right. So, I'll just give them away to someone.
M: That's a good idea. At least they won't go to waste.

여: 안녕, 여보. 뭐 하고 있어요?
남: 아, 그냥 있었어요. 그런데, 이 가방 안에 바지는 누구 것인가요?
여: 잊었어요? 생일 선물로 비슷한 바지를 받아서 반품하길 원했던 거잖아요.
남: 아, 맞아요. 당신이 어제 반품하려고 했죠, 그렇지 않나요?
여: 그럴 계획이었지만, 못했어요.
남: 당신은 다른 일들로 너무 바빴던 거군요.
여: 아니에요. 상점에 바지를 가져갔지만 받아주지 않았어요.
남: 이해가 안 돼요. 당신은 영수증을 갖고 있었잖아요, 아닌가요?
여: 그랬죠. 문제는 구매할 때 바지가 할인 중이었다는 거였어요.
남: 이제 알겠어요. 때때로, 할인 상품은 반품이나 교환이 안 되죠.
여: 맞아요. 그래서 그 바지를 다른 누군가에게 선물로 주려고 해요.
남: 좋은 생각이에요. 최소한 그 바지가 쓸모없게 되진 않겠어요.

어휘 **receipt** 영수증; 수령, 받기 / **on sale** 할인[세일] 중인 / **purchase** 구매(하다) / **give A away** A를 선물로[거저] 주다 / **go to waste** 쓸모없이 되다; 낭비되다

08 언급하지 않은 것 | ③

▶ 해석 참조

W: Few things are more valuable than the experience of traveling abroad, but it can be expensive! Luckily, it's not impossible with the right planning. To begin with, you **need to pack with care**. Baggage fees are the worst. Bring only a carry-on to avoid baggage fees. Next, bring friends. **Traveling with a group** means splitting expenses, from your hotel room, to cabs, to food. Plus, you'll feel significantly safer. Also, traveler's checks and credit cards **can cost you a lot in fees**. Using local ATMs is a safer and cheaper option. Finally, your student status **can get you discounts** on flights, hotels, transportation, and other attractions. If you're staying in your home country, your college ID should work. But for travel overseas, consider an International Student ID Card.

여: 해외여행의 경험보다 더 가치 있는 것은 거의 없지만, 비용이 너무 많이 들 수 있습니다! 다행히도 올바른 계획을 세운다면 불가능하지 않습니다! 우선 신경 써서 짐을 꾸리세요. 수하물 요금이 가장 심각합니다. 수하물 요금을 피하려면 ① 기내 수하물만 가지고 가세요. 다음으로, ② 친구를 데려가세요. 여럿이서 여행하는 것은 호텔 방에서부터 택시, 음식에 이르기까지 비용을 나누는 것을 의미합니다. 게다가 당신은 상당히 더 안전하다고 느낄 것입니다. 또한, 여행자 수표와 신용카드는 당신에게 상당한 수수료 비용을 발생시킬

수 있습니다. ④ 현지의 현금 인출기를 이용하는 것이 더 안전하고 저렴한 선택입니다. 마지막으로 학생 신분이라는 것은 비행기, 호텔, 교통수단, 그리고 다른 관광명소들에서 할인을 받게 해줄 수 있습니다. 자신의 나라에 머무신다면, 대학교 학생증이 유효할 것입니다. 그러나 외국으로 여행하시려면 ⑤ 국제 학생증을 고려해 보십시오.

어휘 **fee** 요금; 수수료 / **carry-on** 기내 수하물 / **split** 나누다; 쪼개다 / **expense** 지출, 비용 / **significantly** 상당히, 크게 / **traveler's check** 여행자 수표 / **status** 신분, 지위; 상황 / **transportation** 수송, 운송; 교통수단 / **attraction** 명소, 명물; 매력

09 내용 불일치 | ③

▶ 투표를 하는 데 등록 카드가 반드시 필요한 것은 아니다.

M: If you're a registered voter, **you will receive a registration card** before the election date. It will indicate where your polling place is and when you can vote. Your polling place will probably be a nearby school or community hall. It will be open between 6 a.m. and 6 p.m. You can bring your registration card with you but **it's not necessary in order to vote**. If you have difficulty in getting to the polling place, contact the election commission to apply to vote by mail. And if you have a disability that makes it impossible to vote on ballot papers, **a special voting device is available**. Or ask for assistance from the election official.

남: 여러분이 등록된 선거인이라면 선거일 전에 등록 카드를 받을 것입니다. 카드에는 투표소의 위치와 투표할 수 있는 시간이 적혀 있을 것입니다. 여러분의 투표소는 가까운 학교나 마을회관이 될 것 입니다. 투표소는 오전 6시에서 오후 6시까지 개방될 것입니다. 등록 카드를 가지고 오셔도 되지만 투표를 하는 데 있어서 필수적인 것은 아닙니다. 투표소에 오시는 것이 어려우면 선거 관리 위원회에 연락을 하셔서 우편으로 투표하는 것을 신청하십시오. 그리고 장애가 있어서 투표용지에 투표하실 수 없는 분들은 특수한 투표 장치를 이용하시거나 선거 관리원에게 도움을 청하십시오.

어휘 **register** 등록하다 ***cf.*** **registration** 등록 / **indicate** 나타내다; 가리키다 / **polling place** 투표소 / **vote** 투표(하다) ***cf.*** **voting** 투표, 선거 / **election commission** 선거 관리 위원회 / **disability** 장애 / **ballot paper** 투표용지

10 도표 이해 | ⑤

▶ 호텔의 하루 숙박비로 300달러는 너무 비싸고, 아이들이 좋아하는 수영장이 필요하며, 남자가 일을 하기 위한 인터넷 접속과 공항 셔틀버스가 필요하므로 모든 조건을 충족시키는 것은 ⑤이다.

M: Julie, do you have any idea **where we should stay in** Los Angeles?
W: Sure. I found these hotels online. What do you think?
M: The Oasis 7 looks the best, but I'm a little **worried about the price**.
W: Me too. 300 dollars a night is a bit much. It would be nice to have a pool though.
M: I agree. **The kids really enjoyed** the swimming pool last time.
W: Right. You also need Internet access for work, don't you?
M: Yes, I do. I really need the Internet.
W: Okay, so there are two left to choose from. Do we need a shuttle to the airport?
M: That would **make it much easier to get** to the airport in the morning. I think we want a shuttle service.
W: There's only one choice then.

남: Julie, Los Angeles에서 어디에 머물지 생각해 봤어요?
여: 물론이죠. 온라인에서 이 호텔들을 찾았어요. 어떻게 생각하나요?
남: Oasis 7이 가장 멋져 보이지만, 가격이 약간 걱정돼요.
여: 저도 그래요. 하룻밤에 300달러는 좀 지나친 것 같아요. 그렇지만 수영장이 있으면 좋겠어요.
남: 저도 동의해요. 지난번에 아이들이 수영장에서 정말 즐거워했어요.
여: 맞아요. 당신은 일 때문에 인터넷 접속도 필요하죠, 그렇지 않나요?
남: 그럼요. 인터넷이 정말 필요하죠.
여: 좋아요. 그렇다면 선택할 수 있는 것이 두 개 남았네요. 공항으로 가는 셔틀버스가 필요할까요?
남: 셔틀버스는 아침에 공항에 도착하는 것을 훨씬 더 쉽게 만들어 줄 거예요. 우리는 셔틀버스 서비스가 필요할 것 같아요.
여: 그러면 단 한 개의 선택만이 남았네요.

어휘 **stay** (손님·방문객으로 어디에(서)) 머물다[묵다] / **access** 접속; 접근; 접속하다; 접근하다 / **get to A** A에 도착하다

11 짧은 대화에 이어질 응답 | ③

▶ 노트북 컴퓨터로 인터넷에 접속하는 것을 도와달라는 여자의 부탁에 가장 적절한 응답을 고른다.

① 물론이지. 좋은 노트북 컴퓨터를 추천해줄게.
② 네가 생일 선물로 또 어떤 걸 받았는지 궁금해.
③ 미안하지만 난 컴퓨터에 대해 잘 몰라.
④ 새로 업데이트된 프로그램을 설치하려고 기다리고 있어.
⑤ 너는 인터넷에 쓰는 시간을 제한해야 해.

W: Guess what? I got a new laptop computer as a birthday present.
M: Wow! **I really envy you**.
W: But **I can't seem to access** the Internet. Could you help me with that?
M: ______________________________

여: 있잖아, 나 생일 선물로 새 노트북 컴퓨터를 받았어.
남: 우와! 정말 부럽다.
여: 그런데 인터넷 접속이 잘 안 되는 것 같아. 좀 도와줄 수 있니?
남: ______________________________

어휘 **envy** 부러워하다; 부러움 | 선택지 어휘 | **install** 설치하다

12 짧은 대화에 이어질 응답 | ⑤

▶ 업무 경험을 쌓겠다는 여자의 말에 남자가 아르바이트를 할 것이냐고 물었다. 따라서 이미 몇 군데 지원했다는 응답이 가장 적절하다.

① 아니, 난 쉬는 게 더 좋아. ② 솔직히, 내 일은 아주 힘들어.
③ 응, 나는 아주 많은 관광 명소를 방문할 거야. ④ 해외 경험은 가치 있을 거야.
⑤ 응, 이미 몇 군데 지원했어.

M: I'm going to Europe during the summer to travel. **What about you**?
W: I think I'll stay here and **try to get some work experience**.
M: Does that mean you are going to have a part-time job?
W: ______________________________

남: 난 여름에 유럽으로 여행갈 거야. 너는?
여: 난 여기 머물면서 업무 경험을 쌓아보려고 해.
남: 아르바이트를 하겠다는 뜻이니?
여: ______________________________

어휘 | 선택지 어휘 | **tourist spot** 관광 명소 / **overseas** 해외의, 외국의

13 긴 대화에 이어질 응답 | ①

▶ 앞으로 무리하게 연습하지 않겠다는 여자의 말에 남자도 더 열심히 연습에 임하겠다는 의지를 보일 것이다.

① 최선을 다할게. 걱정하지 마.
② 그 카페는 자정에 문을 닫으니 빨리 가야 해.
③ 나는 이런 일을 하는 데 있어서 충분한 보상을 더이상 받지 못하고 있어.
④ 춤 대신에 노래로 바꿔야 해.
⑤ 우린 다른 춤 장면을 배웠어야 했는데.

W: Let's **go over it again**. The talent contest is in a month.
M: Exactly! A month. So let's relax and go see a movie or get a coffee.
W: How can we relax **when our dancing is so awkward**?
M: Easy. We put our coats on and walk down to the café!
W: You aren't committed to this show like I am.
M: I'm committed, but I'm exhausted. Nobody can learn a dance sequence when they are this tired.
W: Just one more time and then I promise, we'll take a break.
M: All right. But you have to **promise to take it easy** for the next few weeks.
W: I promise. But you have to promise to work extra hard when we do practice.
M: ______________________________

여: 다시 한 번 해 보자. 장기자랑이 한 달 뒤야.

남: 바로 그거야! 한 달. 그러니 쉬면서 영화도 보고 커피도 한 잔 마시자.
여: 우리 춤이 이렇게 서투른데 어떻게 쉴 수가 있니?
남: 진정해. 코트를 입고 카페로 내려가는 거야!
여: 넌 나만큼 이번 장기자랑에 전념하지 않는구나.
남: 전념하고 있어. 하지만 너무 지쳤어. 이렇게 피곤하면 누구도 춤 장면을 배울 수 없을 거야.
여: 한 번만 더 하자. 그러면 쉰다고 약속할게.
남: 알겠어. 하지만 앞으로 몇 주간은 무리하지 않겠다고 약속해야 해.
여: 약속할게. 하지만 너도 우리가 연습할 때는 더 열심히 할 거라고 약속해야 해.
남: ______________________________

어휘 **go over** 반복하다, 복습하다 / **awkward** 서투른, 어색한 / **committed** 전념하는, 헌신적인 / **exhausted** 지친 / **sequence** 장면; 일련의 연속, 순서 / **take it easy** 무리하지 않고 느긋하게 하다, 서두르지 않다

14 긴 대화에 이어질 응답 | ①

▶ 불법 복제 파일을 다운받는 것을 그만두기란 쉽지 않을 것이라는 남자의 의견에 유료 사이트를 이용하고 있는 여자의 적절한 답변을 찾는다.

① 나도 그렇게 생각해. 하지만 나는 노력 중이야.
② 법에 항상 위배되는 것은 아니야.
③ 우리 둘 중 하나가 먼저 그만둬야 해.
④ 난 다운받는 데는 문제가 없어.
⑤ 나는 우리가 MP3 플레이어를 사야 한다고 생각해.

M: I download a lot of MP3 files these days.
W: So do I.
M: It's **costing me a lot of money**. 99 cents a song and I download 30 or 40 files a month.
W: So you don't download the files of others for free?
M: No. **I used to**, but I stopped.
W: Me too. I always download from pay sites.
M: There's so much **illegal copying going on**. Movies, textbooks, computer programs.... It just doesn't feel right.
W: I know, but my friends are always offering me DVDs of new movies **which have been illegally downloaded**.
M: I don't think it's easy to stop playing or listening to illegally copied works.
W: ______________________________

남: 난 요즘 MP3 파일을 많이 다운받고 있어.
여: 나도 그래.
남: 돈이 정말 많이 들어. 노래 한 곡에 99센트인데 한 달에 30~40여 개의 파일을 다운받거든.
여: 다른 사람의 파일을 무료로 다운받는 게 아니야?
남: 응. 예전엔 그랬지. 하지만 그만뒀어.
여: 나도 그래. 항상 유료 사이트에서 다운받아.
남: 불법 복제가 너무 성행하고 있어. 영화나 교과서, 컴퓨터 프로그램까지…. 그건 옳지 않은 것 같아.
여: 맞아. 하지만 친구들이 나에게 불법으로 다운받은 새로 나온 영화의 DVD를 항상 제안해.
남: 불법으로 복제된 작품을 틀거나 듣는 것을 그만두기란 쉽지 않다고 생각해.
여: ______________________________

어휘 **for free** 무료로 / **pay site** 유료 사이트 / **illegal** 불법의 ***cf.* illegally** 불법적으로

15 상황에 적절한 말 | ②

▶ 상태가 악화되는 것을 원치 않으시는 선생님은 Angus의 상태를 검사받아 확인하고 싶어 하실 것이다.

① 속도가 충분히 빠르지 않아, Angus! 더 열심히 해 봐!
② 네 다리를 먼저 검사받아야 할 것 같구나.
③ 넌 그 메달을 모두 딸 자격이 있어. 잘했다!
④ 이 허들은 너무 높아. 내가 더 낮은 것을 가져오마.
⑤ 어제 좀 쉬었니? 드디어 오늘이구나.

W: Angus has been training hard for the inter-school sports next week. He **holds the school's record** in several track and field events, including high jump, long jump, and the 200 meter hurdles. The school's P.E. teacher, Ms. Foster, is very proud of Angus and thinks he has an excellent chance of winning several medals at the inter-school sports. However, she has noticed that he is limping now, **as if a leg is sore or injured**. Ms. Foster knows that Angus will ignore a slight injury and she **doesn't want it to get worse**. She thinks that if he's sore, he must rest. Angus approaches Ms. Foster and says he's ready to practice his long jumps. In this situation, what is Ms. Foster most likely to say to Angus?

여: Angus는 다음 주에 있을 학교 대항 체육대회를 위해 열심히 훈련 중이다. 그는 높이뛰기, 멀리뛰기, 200미터 장애물 경주 등을 포함한 여러 가지 육상 종목에서 학교 기록을 보유하고 있다. 체육 선생님이신 Foster 선생님은 Angus를 아주 자랑스러워하고 그가 학교 대항 체육대회에서 메달을 여러 개 획득할 수 있는 절호의 기회를 얻었다고 생각하신다. 그러나 선생님은 다리가 아프거나 다친 것처럼 Angus가 절뚝거리고 있다는 사실을 눈치채셨다. Foster 선생님은 Angus가 가벼운 부상 정도는 무시하리라는 것을 알고 계신다. 선생님은 상태가 악화되는 것을 원하지 않으신다. 선생님은 그가 아프면 반드시 휴식을 취해야 한다고 생각하신다. Angus는 Foster 선생님께 다가와서 멀리뛰기를 연습할 준비가 되었다고 말한다. 이러한 상황에서 Foster 선생님이 Angus에게 할 말로 가장 적절한 것은 무엇인가?

어휘 **track and field** 육상경기 / **P.E. (physical education**의 약자**)** 체육 / **limp** 절뚝거리다 / **sore** 아픈, 쓰린 / **injured** 상처 입은 / **ignore** 무시하다 | 선택지 어휘 | **deserve** ~할[받을] 자격이 있다 / **hurdle** 허들 (경기); 장애(물)

16~17 세트 문항 | 16. ③ 17. ⑤

▶ 16. 각 반려동물이 주는 장점들, 즉 위안감, 안전, 책임감 기르기, 즐거움 등을 나열하고 있다.

① 반려동물 선택에 관한 조언
② 스트레스를 없애는 방법들
③ 반려동물을 기르는 것의 장점들
④ 반려동물을 보살피는 노력
⑤ 다양한 반려동물들에 대한 비교

▶ 17. 해석 참조

① 개 ② 고양이 ③ 금붕어 ④ 햄스터 ⑤ 도마뱀

M: Have you heard about guide dogs for the blind? These animals **offer obvious benefits to humans**. However, the average pet also has much to offer. Dogs and cats in particular are **a source of comfort**. Even the most stressful day is no match for a happy puppy with a wagging tail. Dogs can also provide security for the home against robbers. Goldfish are another popular choice. By raising goldfish, children learn responsibility as they maintain the aquarium and keep up with feeding. Maintaining the goldfish tank can be an event **bringing the whole family closer together**. Hamsters are another alternative to the traditional cat or dog. They are cute little pets that **don't require a lot of care**. And it's fun to watch them climb through a series of tubes or run on an exercise wheel. There are many benefits to owning a pet rabbit, too. They're lovely, funny, quiet, and clean. But one thing many people may not realize is that rabbits are ecologically-friendly. They eat greens, which you can find in your own backyard. You can **kill two birds with one stone** and feed your bunnies your unwanted weeds. So, why not bring a pet into your life?

남: 시각장애인들을 위한 안내견에 대한 이야기를 들어본 적이 있으십니까? 이런 동물들은 인간들에게 명백한 편익을 제공합니다. 그러나 평범한 반려동물 역시 많은 것을 제공하지요. 특히 ① 개나 ② 고양이는 위안을 주는 원천입니다. 가장 스트레스를 받은 날도 꼬리를 흔드는 행복한 강아지와 겨룰 바가 되지 않지요. 개들은 또한 강도로부터 집을 안전하게 해줄 수 있습니다. ③ 금붕어는 또 다른 인기 있는 선택입니다. 금붕어를 기름으로써, 아이들은 수조를 관리하고 먹이를 정기적으로 줘야 하므로 책임감을 배웁니다. 금붕어 수조를 관리하는 것은 모든 가족들을 좀 더 가깝게 모이게 할 수 있는 이벤트가 될 수 있습니다. 전통적 반려동물인 고양이나 개에 비해 ④ 햄스터는 또 다른 대안입니다. 햄스터들은 그리 많은 보살핌이 요구되지 않는 귀엽고 작은 반려동물입니다. 그리고 햄스터들이 일련의 튜브를 기어서 통과하거나 운동하는 바퀴에서 달리고 있는 것을 보는 것은 재미있습니다. 반려 토끼를 기르는 것도 많은 혜택을 줍니다. 그것들은 사랑스럽고, 재미나며, 조용하고 깨끗합니다. 그러나 많은 사람들이 깨닫지 못하고 있을지도 모르는 한 가지가 있는데, 토끼들은 생태 친화적입니다. 그것들은 푸른 채소를 먹는데, 뒷마당에서 그런 풀들을 볼 수 있습니다. 일석이조로, 토끼에게 당신이 원하지 않는 잡초를 먹일 수 있습니다. 그러니, 생활에 반려동물을 한 마리 들여놓는 것은 어떠신가요?

어휘 **guide dog** 시각장애인을 위한 안내견 / **comfort** 위안, 위로 / **match** 필적할 만한 것; 경기; 성냥 / **wag** (꼬리를) 흔들다 / **security** 보안 / **robber** 강도, 도둑 / **keep up with** ~을 정기적으로 하다 / **alternative** 대안 / **ecologically-friendly** 생태 친화적인 / **green** (복수형) 푸른 채소 / **weed** 잡초

01. ④ 02. ① 03. ④ 04. ⑤ 05. ⑤ 06. ③ 07. ④ 08. ② 09. ④ 10. ①
11. ② 12. ④ 13. ④ 14. ⑤ 15. ⑤ 16. ③ 17. ②

01 화자가 하는 말의 목적 | ④

▶ 디지털 사진을 찍는 사진작가들을 대상으로 실재 사진 앨범을 제작하는 곳을 소개하고 이용법 등을 알리고 있다.

W: Attention, photographers! The last few years have seen an amazing change in digital photography. But do you ever feel that something is missing? **What about the feel of holding** a real photo album? Well, we're here to help. The Photo Den, located on the corner of Oak Street and Fourth Avenue, specializes in the creation of high-quality photo albums. There are **a variety of design options to choose from**. You can even choose the type of paper and size of the album. Just upload your photos and choose your style. We'll do the rest. Check out our prices online at photoden.com, or **give us a call** at 777-8383. Experience the joy of a quality photo album!

여: 사진작가 여러분, 주목해주세요! 지난 몇 년간 디지털 사진술에 놀라운 변화가 있어 왔습니다. 하지만 여러분은 뭔가 빠진 게 있다고 느낀 적이 한 번이라도 있나요? 실제 사진 앨범을 들고 있는 느낌은 어떨까요? 자, 저희가 도와드리겠습니다. Photo Den은 Oak 가와 Fourth 가 모퉁이에 위치하며, 고품질의 사진 앨범 제작을 전문으로 합니다. 고를 수 있는 다양한 디자인 선택사항들이 있습니다. 여러분은 용지 종류와 앨범 크기를 선택할 수도 있습니다. 단지 여러분의 사진을 업로드하고 스타일을 고르기만 하세요. 나머지는 저희가 하겠습니다. photoden.com에서 온라인으로 가격을 확인하시거나 777-8383으로 전화 주세요. 품질 좋은 사진 앨범이 주는 즐거움을 경험하세요!

어휘 **avenue** (도시의) –가, 거리 / **specialize in** ~을 전문으로 하다 / **a variety of** 다양한 / **check out** 확인[조사]하다; 살펴보다 / **quality** 품질 좋은, 고급(의); 품질

02 의견 | ①

▶ 남자는 딸 Kate를 자원봉사 단체에 함께 데려가자고 제안하며 어린 시절에 하는 자원봉사의 의의에 대해 말하고 있다.

M: Honey, how about taking Kate to our volunteer club this weekend?
W: Isn't she **too young to be volunteering**? I'm a little worried.
M: This time we're planning to help some elderly people who live alone. I'm sure she can do it if she **thinks of them as her grandparents**.
W: Yeah, that might be a good experience to have during childhood.
M: Right. I think more children need to learn the importance of volunteer work. It can be a valuable experience for them.
W: I agree. They can learn that volunteering is **a good way to help people in need**.
M: Besides, children can do a lot for others even though they're young.
W: You're right. I hope Kate learns a lot from volunteering.

남: 여보, 이번 주말 Kate를 우리 자원봉사 단체에 데려가는 게 어때요?
여: 자원봉사하기에는 Kate가 너무 어리지 않나요? 조금 걱정이 되네요.
남: 이번에는 독거노인들을 도울 계획이잖아요. Kate가 그분들을 자신의 조부모님이라고 생각한다면 분명 할 수 있을 거예요.
여: 그래요, 어릴 때 해보는 좋은 경험이 될 수도 있겠네요.
남: 맞아요. 나는 더 많은 아이들이 자원봉사의 중요성을 배울 필요가 있다고 생각해요. 그것은 아이들에게 값진 경험이 될 수 있어요.
여: 동의해요. 자원봉사가 어려움에 처한 사람들을 돕는 좋은 방법이라는 것을 아이들이 배울 수 있으니까요.
남: 게다가, 비록 아이들이 어리다 하더라도 다른 사람들을 위해 많은 걸 할 수 있어요.
여: 당신 말이 맞아요. Kate가 자원봉사를 하면서 많이 배우면 좋겠어요.

어휘 **in need** 어려움에 처한, 궁핍한

03 관계 | ④

▶ 여자는 집을 개조하고 설계를 하는 직업이므로 인테리어 디자이너라고 볼 수 있다. 그리고 남자는 난방비 절약에 대해 언급하고 설계에 대해 승인을 해 주는 위치에 있는 것으로 보아 고객(집주인)임을 알 수 있다.

W: So, Mr. Ross, are you happy with the overall concept?
M: Yes. I'm especially pleased about using environmentally friendly materials.
W: You do understand, however, the cost of those materials is **higher than for ordinary ones**.
M: Yes, but I will save hundreds of dollars on my home heating bills after this remodeling.
W: The recycled wood you've chosen for the flooring brings costs down too.
M: OK, what's the next stage?
W: Now, I **need to take detailed measurements** throughout your house.
M: And then when can I expect to see the first drawings?
W: The creative process can take several weeks, but I should **have initial plans for your approval** by September 1st.
M: OK, I got it.

여: Ross 씨, 전체적 구상은 마음에 드십니까?
남: 네. 친환경 소재를 쓰는 부분이 특히 만족스럽네요.
여: 그러시군요. 하지만 그 소재들이 기존 소재보다 가격이 더 높습니다.
남: 네, 하지만 이번 개조 후에는 난방비 수백 달러를 아끼게 될 거예요.
여: 바닥 재료로 재생 목재를 선택하셨기 때문에 비용이 또한 줄어들 것입니다.
남: 알겠습니다. 다음 단계는 뭔가요?
여: 이제, 집 전체를 자세히 측량해야 합니다.
남: 그러면 첫 도면은 언제쯤 볼 수 있을까요?
여: 창의를 요하는 과정은 수주일 걸릴 수 있지만, 고객님의 승인을 받기 위한 첫 도면은 9월 1일까지 될 겁니다.
남: 네, 알겠습니다.

어휘 **concept** 개념, 발상 / **environmentally friendly** 친환경적인 / **material** 소재, 재료 / **recycled** 재생된, 재활용된 / **flooring** 바닥재 / **measurement** 측량 / **plan** 도면, 설계도 / **approval** 승인, 동의

04 그림 불일치 | ⑤

▶ 여자는 시계가 2시를 가리키고 있다고 말했다.

M: Mom, I took a picture of the stage for our school play. I'd love to show you.
W: Okay. *[pause]* Wow, did you make everything by yourselves? I can't believe it!
M: Thanks, Mom. That big pumpkin on the left **will be turned into a carriage**.
W: Oh? How is that possible?
M: It's simple. We already placed the carriage behind the pumpkin. When the fairy touches the pumpkin, smoke will come out. Then **we just have to switch the two**.
W: What a clever idea!
M: How do you like the square-shaped well?
W: It's a perfect match for the play.
M: Do you see the rock behind the well? That's where I'll pop out during the play.
W: Great. The rock really looks real. And... where's the clock? You know it's important in this play.
M: I know. It's right there on the castle on the far right of the stage.
W: Yes, I see that **the clock says 2 o'clock**.

남: 엄마, 학예회 무대 사진 찍어왔어요. 보여드리고 싶어요.
여: 그래. *[잠시 후]* 우와, 너희들끼리 이 모든 걸 다 만들었단 말이지? 믿기지가 않네!
남: 고마워요, 엄마. 왼편에 저 커다란 호박은 마차로 변할 거예요.
여: 그래? 그게 어떻게 가능한데?
남: 간단해요. 호박 뒤에 미리 마차를 갖다놓았거든요. 요정이 호박을 건드리면 연기가 나올 거예요. 그때 우리는 두 개의 자리를 바꿔놓기만 하면 돼요.
여: 정말 영리한 생각이네!
남: 이 사각형 우물은 어떠세요?

여: 연극과 아주 잘 맞는구나.
남: 우물 뒤에 바위 보이세요? 거기서 제가 연극 중간에 튀어나올 거예요.
여: 훌륭해. 그 바위는 진짜처럼 보여. 그리고… 시계는 어딨니? 이 연극에서 중요하잖아.
남: 알아요. 무대 맨 오른쪽에 있는 성에 있어요.
여: 그렇구나. 시계가 2시를 가리키고 있는 게 보이네.

어휘 **by oneself** 혼자 힘으로 / **switch** 전환하다, 바꾸다 / **pop out** 튀어나오다

05 추후 행동 | ⑤

▶ 여자가 엄마의 생신 선물을 고르기로 하고 오늘 쇼핑몰에 가서 산다고 말하자 남자가 헬스클럽에 가는 길에 자동차로 데려다주겠다고 말했다.

W: It's Mom's 55th birthday next Friday.
M: Oh, that's right. Are we going to have a dinner party somewhere?
W: Yes, we're all going to a buffet restaurant. Do you have any idea **what we should give her**?
M: I don't know. I always leave that to you.
W: Well, I wish you'd come up with some ideas sometimes.
M: I don't know what she likes. You know I'm not good at buying gifts.
W: I guess **it's up to me again**. I think I should go shopping today. I have a busy week coming up.
M: Well, I can **take you to the shopping mall** by car right now. I'm going to work out at the gym and it's on the way.
W: Good idea. Give me five minutes to get ready.
M: OK. I need five minutes to pack my gym bag, too.

여: 엄마의 쉰다섯 번째 생신이 다음 주 금요일이야.
남: 아, 그러네. 어딘가에서 저녁 식사 파티를 할 예정이야?
여: 응, 우리 모두 뷔페 레스토랑에 갈 거야. 엄마께 무엇을 드려야 할지 뭐 좋은 생각 있니?
남: 모르겠어. 그건 항상 누나에게 맡기잖아.
여: 음, 가끔은 네가 아이디어를 몇 가지 생각해주면 좋을 텐데.
남: 엄마께서 무엇을 좋아하시는지 모르겠어. 내가 선물 사는 데 소질이 없는 걸 알잖아.
여: 또 (결정이) 나에게 달려 있는 것 같네. 오늘 쇼핑하러 가야 할 것 같아. 바쁜 한 주가 다가오고 있거든.
남: 음, 내가 지금 바로 누나를 자동차로 쇼핑몰까지 데려다줄 수 있어. 헬스클럽에 운동하러 갈 건데 가는 길에 있잖아.
여: 좋은 생각이야. 준비하게 5분만 줘.
남: 알았어. 나도 운동 가방을 싸려면 5분이 필요해.

어휘 **come up with** (아이디어 등을) 생각해내다 / **up to A** (결정 등이) A에게 달려 있는 / **work out** 운동하다; (문제 등을) 해결하다

06 금액 | ③

▶ 부사장을 위한 명함은 1,000장에 30달러, 영업사원 명함은 1,000장에 10달러이다. 부사장은 1,000장이 필요하므로 30달러가, 영업사원은 2,000장이 필요하므로 20달러가 든다. 원래 총액은 50달러인데 20% 할인을 해준다고 했으므로 여자가 지불할 금액은 40달러가 된다.

W: I need some business cards for the new vice president and a new salesperson.
M: You'll want the premium package for the new vice president. Premium cards have color, any illustration of your choice, and coating. They're 30 dollars for 1,000 cards.
W: And for the new salesperson?
M: The basic package. Black print on uncoated white cards **with no illustrations except the company logo**. 10 dollars for 1,000 cards.
W: OK. 1,000 cards for the vice president and 2,000 cards for the salesperson.
M: What color and illustration do you want for the vice president?
W: **I'll have to ask her**. I'll order hers tomorrow.
M: And the basic package?
W: I'll get it today. I have the salesperson's phone numbers here.
M: Good.
W: Do I **get our company's usual discount**?
M: Sure. 20% off.
W: Thanks.

여: 새로 오신 부사장님과 영업사원이 쓸 명함이 필요한데요.
남: 새로 오신 부사장님을 위해서라면 고급 패키지가 마음에 드실 겁니다. 고급 명함에는 색깔과 원하시는 그림이 들어가고 코팅도 됩니다. 1,000장에 30달러예요.
여: 그러면 새로 온 영업사원을 위한 건요?
남: 기본 패키지입니다. 회사 로고 외에는 다른 그림 없이 코팅이 안 된 하얀 명함 위에 검은색으로 인쇄됩니다. 1,000장에 10달러입니다.
여: 좋아요. 부사장님 건 1,000장, 영업사원 건 2,000장으로 하지요.
남: 부사장님 명함에는 어떤 색깔과 그림으로 하실 건가요?
여: 부사장님께 여쭤봐야겠네요. 부사장님 건 내일 주문할게요.
남: 그러면 기본 패키지는요?
여: 오늘 가져갈게요. 여기 그 영업사원 전화번호요.
남: 알겠습니다.
여: 우리 회사가 늘 받는 할인이 되나요?
남: 그럼요. 20% 할인됩니다.
여: 고마워요.

어휘 **business card** 명함 / **vice president** 부사장 / **salesperson** 영업사원 / **premium** 고급의, 값비싼 / **illustration** 그림, 삽화; 설명

07 이유 | ④

▶ 이사 포장을 도와야 했던 사람은 파티에 늦게 온 Brandon임에 유의한다. 회사 일로 바빴냐는 말에는 남자가 부정했고 아내가 장모님을 돌보러 시카고에 가있기 때문에 아이들을 돌보느라고 파티에 못 갔다고 말하고 있다.

W: Michael, you didn't come to the party last night. I missed you.
M: **I wish I could have**. Did you have fun at the party?
W: Brandon was late. We waited an hour for him since it was his farewell party. He's leaving for New York next week.
M: He **must have been working late**.
W: He said he had to help his sister move yesterday. Since there was a lot to pack, it took much longer than he thought.
M: Then the party must have finished later.
W: Yes, but we had a wonderful time. By the way, why didn't you come? Were you busy at work?
M: No, I had to take care of my kids at home because my wife went to Chicago.
W: For a business trip?
M: No. Her mother is in the hospital for heart problems, so she's taking care of her.
W: I'm sorry to hear that.
M: **Her mother is doing much better** now.

여: Michael, 어젯밤 파티에 오지 않았더군요. 보고 싶었어요.
남: 가고 싶었어요. 파티에서는 재미있었나요?
여: Brandon이 늦었어요. 그의 송별 파티였기 때문에 우리는 그를 한 시간 기다렸어요. 그는 다음 주에 뉴욕으로 떠나요.
남: 늦게까지 일했나 보군요.
여: 어제 그의 누나가 이사하는 것을 도와야 했다고 말했어요. 짐 쌀 게 많아서 생각했던 것보다 훨씬 더 오래 걸렸대요.
남: 그러면 파티가 더 늦게 끝났겠네요.
여: 예, 하지만 즐거운 시간을 보냈어요. 그런데, 왜 오지 않았어요? 직장에서 바빴나요?
남: 아뇨, 아내가 시카고에 갔기 때문에 집에서 아이들을 돌봐야 했어요.
여: 출장으로요?
남: 아뇨, 장모님이 심장 문제로 입원하셔서 아내가 돌봐드리고 있어요.
여: 유감이군요.
남: 지금은 장모님이 훨씬 더 좋아지셨어요.

어휘 **farewell party** 송별회 / **pack** 싸다, 포장하다

08 언급하지 않은 것 | ②

▶ 해석 참조

[Phone rings.]
W: Hello?
M: Hi, Mom. I'm really sorry, but I don't think **I'll be coming over for dinner**.
W: What's wrong, Steven? You sound sick.
M: I caught the flu. My entire body hurts.
W: Then you'd better get plenty of rest. That's the best way to recover.
M: Of course. I'll be staying home tonight. But I doubt if I'll get much sleep with this sore throat.
W: Try gargling with salt water. That always works when my throat is raw.

M: Thanks, Mom. I will **right after I take a hot bath**.
W: Oh, and please use the humidifier I bought for you. This dry winter air will only **make your symptoms worse**.
M: Good idea. I'd completely forgotten to turn it on. I also bought some aspirin for my fever.
W: Good. Get some rest, and I'll come check on you tomorrow.

[전화벨이 울린다.]
여: 여보세요?
남: 엄마, 정말 죄송하지만, 저녁 먹으러 못 갈 것 같아요.
여: 무슨 일이니, Steven? 어디 아픈 것 같구나.
남: 독감에 걸렸어요. 온몸이 아파요.
여: 그럼 충분히 쉬는 게 낫겠구나(① 휴식 취하기). 그게 회복하는 데 가장 좋은 방법이야.
남: 그럼요. 전 오늘 밤 집에 있을 거예요. 하지만 목이 이렇게 아파서 잠을 푹 잘 수 있을지 모르겠어요.
여: 소금물로 입을 헹궈 보렴(③ 소금물로 입 헹구기). 내 목이 따끔거릴 때 그 방법이 항상 효과가 있거든.
남: 고마워요, 엄마. 뜨거운 물로 목욕하고 나서 바로 해 볼게요.
여: 오, 그리고 내가 사준 가습기를 사용하렴(④ 가습기 사용하기). 이렇게 건조한 겨울 공기는 네 증상이 더 나빠지게만 할 거야.
남: 좋은 생각이에요. 그걸 켠다는 걸 완전히 잊고 있었어요. 전 열 때문에 아스피린(⑤ 약 복용하기)도 좀 샀어요.
여: 잘했어. 좀 쉬렴. 내일 들여다볼게.

어휘 **raw** 따가운, 쓰라린; 날[생] 것의 / **humidifier** 가습기 / **symptom** 증상, 증후

09 내용 불일치 | ④

▶ 투어는 두 가지 언어가 아니라 세 가지 언어(영어, 한국어, 중국어)로 할 수 있다고 말했다.

M: Welcome to the City of the Future Exhibition. Here you will see famous engineers' and architects' visions of the modern city. Room 1 features a model of Pyramid City. **It's an enclosed city shaped** like a 1 km-tall pyramid. This city will house up to 750,000 people. Room 2 features Tunnel City. It's an underground utopia for a future time when the sun and air **may become dangerous for us**. And finally, Room 3 shows Greenhouse City, which recreates a healthy Earth atmosphere completely under glass. Tours will be available in English, Korean and Chinese. In order to allow the most people to enjoy this great exhibit, **registration is required in the lobby**.

남: 미래 도시 전람회에 오신 것을 환영합니다. 이곳에서는 현대 도시에 대한 유명한 기술자들과 건축가들의 비전을 보실 수 있습니다. 1번 방은 피라미드 도시의 모형을 특색으로 삼고 있습니다. 이곳은 1킬로미터 높이의 피라미드 같은 모양을 하고 있는 밀폐형 도시입니다. 이 도시는 75만 명까지 수용할 것입니다. 2번 방은 터널 도시를 특징으로 하고 있습니다. 이곳은 태양과 공기가 우리에게 위험해질 수도 있는 미래를 대비한 지하 유토피아입니다. 그리고 마지막으로 3번 방에서는 온실 도시를 전시하고 있는데, 이 도시는 유리 아래로 건강한 지구 대기를 완벽하게 재현하고 있습니다. 투어는 영어와 한국어 그리고 중국어로 가능합니다. 대다수가 이 훌륭한 전시를 즐기게 하기 위해서 로비에서 등록하셔야 합니다.

어휘 **feature** 특징으로 삼다 / **enclosed** 단절된, 고립된; 둘러싸인; 동봉된 / **house** 수용하다 / **utopia** 유토피아, 이상향 / **recreate** 재현하다, 되살리다

10 도표 이해 | ①

▶ 여자는 서울에서 오전에 출발하며 중간 기착지에서 연결 항공편을 타기까지 15시간 넘게 남는 일정을 택하려고 한다. 그리고 너무 이른 아침, 또는 밤늦게 뉴욕에 도착하는 일정은 피하려고 한다.

W: My travel agent emailed this flight schedule to New York. I need to decide which flight to take.
M: Weren't there any non-stop schedules available?
W: No, it's high season, **they're sold out**.
M: What is the most important thing for you?
W: I don't want a flight that leaves Seoul in the afternoon.
M: You **prefer earlier flights**.
W: Yes. And I want to visit one of the stopover cities on the way there.
M: Then, you need more than 15 hours between connecting flights.
W: Right, but I'd love **to stop over in any of those cities**.
M: You don't want to arrive in New York too early in the morning or late at night, though.
W: You're right, I don't. **My decision is made**!

여: 여행사에서 이 뉴욕행 항공편 일정을 이메일로 보내왔어요. 어떤 항공편을 이용할지 결정해야 해요.
남: 직항 일정표는 없나요?
여: 네, 성수기여서 매진되었어요.
남: 당신에게 가장 중요한 사항은 뭐죠?
여: 서울에서 오후에 출발하는 항공편은 싫어요.
남: 일찍 출발하는 항공편을 선호하는군요.
여: 네, 그리고 그곳에 가는 도중에 중간 기착 도시들 중 한 곳을 방문하고 싶어요.
남: 그렇다면, 연결 항공편 사이에 15시간 넘게 필요할 텐데요.
여: 맞아요, 하지만 그 도시들 중 어느 곳에든 들르고 싶은걸요.
남: 그래도 뉴욕에 너무 이른 아침이나 밤늦게 도착하고 싶진 않겠죠.
여: 맞아요, 싫어요. 결정했어요!

어휘 **high season** 성수기 / **stopover** (비행기의) 중간 기착, (여행 도중에) 잠시 들르는 장소 ***cf.* stop over** (긴 여정 중에) 잠시 머무르다 / **connecting** (기차, 비행기 등이) 연결되는

11 짧은 대화에 이어질 응답 | ②

▶ 회의에서 누가 처음으로 발표를 할 것인지를 묻는 여자의 물음에 대한 가장 적절한 응답을 고른다.

① 15분간 휴식 후에요.
② Andrew가 곧 무대에 오를 거예요.
③ 직원 복리후생에 관한 거예요.
④ 당신의 발표는 정말 훌륭했어요.
⑤ 차 사고 때문에 길이 많이 막혔어요.

W: I'm so sorry. I'm late because **my previous meeting lasted too long**.
M: Don't worry, Jackie. The conference was postponed a little.
W: **That's a relief**. Who's going to give the first presentation?
M: ______________________

여: 정말 죄송해요. 이전 회의가 너무 오래 걸려서 늦었어요.
남: 걱정 말아요, Jackie. 회의가 조금 연기되었어요.
여: 다행이네요. 누가 처음으로 발표하나요?
남: ______________________

어휘 **postpone** 미루다, 연기하다 / **relief** 안심; (고통 · 불안 등의) 경감[완화] | 선택지 어휘 | **welfare benefits** 복리후생

12 짧은 대화에 이어질 응답 | ④

▶ 가장 가까운 슈퍼마켓이 문을 닫아 가지 못하는 상황이다. 남자가 근처에 다른 슈퍼마켓이 있는지 물었으므로 그 위치를 알려주는 응답이 가장 적절하다.

① 커피도 좀 사다 줘.
② 그 슈퍼마켓은 아주 커.
③ 근처에 카페가 몇 군데 있어.
④ 주유소 바로 지나서 하나 있어.
⑤ 난 그 편의점에서 아르바이트를 해.

M: I'm going to the convenience store. Do you want anything?
W: Some snacks, please. But you should go to the supermarket instead. It's **much cheaper**.
M: I know, but the nearest one is closed now. **Is there another near here**?
W: ______________________

남: 나 편의점 갈 거야. 뭐 사다 줄까?
여: 과자 몇 가지만 부탁해. 그런데 (편의점) 대신 슈퍼마켓으로 가. 훨씬 더 싸거든.
남: 알고 있지만, 가장 가까운 곳이 지금 문을 닫았어. 이 근처에 다른 데가 있니?
여: ______________________

어휘 **convenience store** 편의점

13 긴 대화에 이어질 응답 | ④

▶ 요리 학원에 쿠키를 만들어 가서 맛에 대한 평가를 받게 될 어머니께 자신이 도움이 될 거라고 말한 의미를 유추해 본다.

① 저를 위해서 쿠키를 좀 살 생각이에요.
② 어머니께서 좋은 성적을 받으실 수 있을 거라고 확신해요.
③ 여기 다양한 종류의 쿠키가 있어요.
④ 그것이 맛있는지 그렇지 않은지 어머니께 알려 드릴 수 있잖아요.

⑤ 정말 맛있어요. 더 먹어도 될까요?

M: Mom, what are you cooking?
W: Actually, I'm baking some cookies.
M: Great! **I can't wait**.
W: They aren't for you. It's kind of a test for me.
M: A test?
W: You know I'm taking that baking class at a cooking institute downtown.
M: Yes, I know that.
W: Well, I **am supposed to bake some cookies** and bring them to class tomorrow. The teacher is going to taste them and give me a grade.
M: You mean if the cookies taste great, you'll get a good grade?
W: That's right.
M: Then you really need my help.
W: Huh? **What do you mean**?
M: ____

남: 어머니, 무엇을 요리하고 계세요?
여: 사실, 쿠키를 굽고 있단다.
남: 좋아라! 기대돼요.
여: 너 줄 게 아니란다. 내겐 일종의 시험 같은 거야.
남: 시험이요?
여: 너도 알다시피 내가 시내에 있는 요리 학원에서 제빵 수업을 듣고 있잖니.
남: 네, 알아요.
여: 글쎄, 쿠키를 좀 구워서 내일 수업에 가져가기로 되어 있거든. 선생님께서 맛을 보시고 점수를 주실 거야.
남: 쿠키 맛이 좋으면 좋은 점수를 받을 수 있다는 뜻이죠?
여: 그렇단다.
남: 그럼 제 도움이 정말 필요하시겠어요.
여: 뭐? 무슨 뜻이니?
남: ____

14 긴 대화에 이어질 응답 | ⑤

▶ 남자의 마지막 말에서 할머니는 자기 관리를 잘하셔서 나이보다 젊어 보이신다는 사실을 유추할 수 있다.

① 아니, 할머니는 나랑 전혀 닮지 않으셨어.
② 응, 나는 내 나이보다 훨씬 더 나이 들어 보여.
③ 동감이야. 난 할머니를 더 잘 보살펴 드려야 해.
④ 맞아, 할머니는 재정적 도움은 필요 없으셔.
⑤ 응, 할머니는 나이보다 훨씬 젊어 보이셔.

M: Your apartment is nice, Susie. Can I look at those photographs over there?
W: Yes, of course. Look at this one. Everyone in my family is here. It was taken at my brother's wedding three years ago.
M: Hmm... three years ago, so you are 12 in the photograph. You **look a lot older now**.
W: Of course! I'm not a child anymore.
M: Hmm... your grandmother **looks young and healthy in this picture**.
W: She really takes care of herself. She walks in the park and eats healthy food.
M: Is she in her mid-50s?
W: No, she is 63 in that photograph. Look at this photograph of the two of us taken a few weeks ago.
M: Wow, **I see what you mean by saying** "she really takes care of herself."
W: ____

남: 아파트가 멋지구나, Susie. 저기 있는 사진들을 봐도 되니?
여: 응, 물론이지. 이것 좀 봐. 여기에 우리 가족이 모두 있어. 3년 전 오빠의 결혼식 날 찍은 거야.
남: 음… 3년 전이라, 그럼 사진에서 너는 열두 살이겠구나. 지금이 훨씬 더 나이 들어 보여.
여: 당연하지! 더 이상 어린애가 아니라고.
남: 음… 이 사진에서 네 할머니께서는 젊고 건강해 보이신다.
여: 할머니는 정말 자기 관리를 잘하셔. 공원에서 걷고 건강식을 드셔.
남: 50대 중반이시니?
여: 아니, 그 사진에서는 예순셋이셔. 몇 주 전에 할머니와 둘이 찍은 이 사진을 봐.
남: 와, 네가 '할머니는 정말 자기 관리를 잘하셔'라고 말한 것이 이해 가.
여: ____

어휘 **mid** 중간의 | 선택지 어휘 | **financial** 재정상의

15 상황에 적절한 말 | ⑤

▶ Nathan은 기숙사 방을 같이 쓰려면 Shawn이 방을 더 깨끗이 써야 한다고 생각한다.

① 내가 쓰레기를 갖다 버릴 차례니?
② 다른 사람을 초대하기 전에 나에게 알려줘.
③ 우리는 매주 일요일에 방을 청소해야 해.
④ 나를 초대하지 않고 파티를 열었니?
⑤ 네가 뒷정리를 잘해 주면 고맙겠어.

W: Shawn and Nathan share a dorm room at the university. Nathan is very careful **never to leave a mess** that may bother Shawn or look bad when he has friends over. Nathan recently took a trip home for the weekend. He cleaned up the room and took out the trash before he left for home on Friday. When he returns on Sunday night, **the room is a complete mess**. The garbage is overflowing, **dirty clothes are scattered around**, and there are empty pizza boxes and soda bottles everywhere. This isn't the first time Shawn has left a mess in the room. Nathan thinks Shawn needs to be more careful to stay together, and it is a good chance to tell him what he thinks. In this situation, what would Nathan most likely say to Shawn?

여: Shawn과 Nathan은 대학에서 기숙사 방을 함께 사용한다. Nathan은 Shawn에게 방해가 되지 않기 위해, 또는 친구들이 놀러 왔을 때 더럽게 보이지 않기 위해 방을 어지르지 않으려고 매우 조심한다. Nathan은 최근에 주말 동안 집에 다녀왔다. 금요일에 집으로 출발하기 전에 그는 방을 청소하고 쓰레기를 버렸다. 일요일 밤에 그가 돌아왔을 때 방은 완전히 어질러져 있었다. 쓰레기통은 넘치고 세탁물은 흩어져 있으며 빈 피자 상자와 음료수 병이 여기저기 놓여 있었다. Shawn이 방을 어지럽혀 놓은 것은 이번이 처음이 아니다. Nathan은 함께 지내기 위해서는 Shawn이 더 조심할 필요가 있으며 이번이 자신의 생각을 말할 좋은 기회라고 생각한다. 이러한 상황에서 Nathan이 Shawn에게 할 말로 가장 적절한 것은 무엇인가?

어휘 **mess** 어질러 놓은 것 / **overflow** 넘쳐흐르다 / **scattered** 흩어져 있는 | 선택지 어휘 | **appreciate** 감사하게 생각하다 / **clean up after** ~ 뒤를 청소하다

16~17 세트 문항 | 16. ③ 17. ②

▶ 16. 거짓말할 때 나타나는 행동에 대해 말하고 있다.

① 시선 맞춤의 중요성
② 사람들이 거짓말을 하는 흔한 이유
③ 거짓말의 흔한 증거
④ 직장에서의 효과적인 대화법
⑤ 지인과의 대화 예절

▶ 17. 해석 참조

M: Welcome back. We've spent a lot of time talking about the concept of truth, but what about the opposite? We believe someone who has an "honest face," and don't believe someone who has "nervous eyes," but why? In fact, a liar's body and voice do give clues that he or she is not telling the truth. When people are lying, they tend to **speak in a higher voice than usual**. And they tend to close their eyes or blink rapidly. This is considered to be a form of behavior that **goes back to their childhood habit** of closing their eyes so it cannot be seen that they're lying. Even though it's a very childlike behavior, a lot of us still do it in adulthood. Liars also **tend to stumble over their words**, saying "uh" and "er" a lot. People make forced smiles, if they smile at all, and they often avoid showing their hands. And yes, nervous eyes can indicate that a person is lying. Also, people telling a lie tend to **look away from the person** they are speaking to.

남: 어서 오세요. 우리는 진실의 개념에 대해 이야기하는 데 많은 시간을 할애했는데요, 그 반대의 것은 어떨까요? 우리는 '정직한 얼굴'을 한 사람은 믿고, '초조한 눈빛'을 한 사람은 믿지 않는데, 왜 그럴까요? 사실, 거짓말하는 사람의 신체와 목소리는 그 사람이 진실을 말하고 있지 않다는 단서를 실제로 제공합니다. 사람들은 거짓말하고 있을 때 ① 평소보다 더 높은 목소리로 말하는 경향이 있습니다. 그리고 그들은 눈을 감거나 빨리 깜박거립니다. 이는 거짓말을 하고 있다는 것을 볼 수 없도록 눈을 감는 어렸을 적 습관으로 거슬러 올라가는 행동의 한 가지 유형으로 간주됩니다. 매우 어린아이 같은 행동이지만, 많은 사람들이 어른이 되어서도 여전히 그렇게 합니다. 거짓말을 하는 사람들은 또한 '어'와 '저'를 많이 말하면서 말을 더듬거립니다. 웃는다고 하더라도 ③ 억지스러운 미소를 지으며, 보통 손을 드러내려고 하지 않습니다. 그리고 맞습니다, '수상쩍은', 즉 ④ 초조해하는 눈빛은 어떤 사람이 거짓말하고 있다는 것을 나타낼 수 있습니다. 거짓말하는 사람들은 ⑤ 이야기하고 있는 사람에게서 눈길을 돌리는 경향이 있습니다.

어휘 **blink** 눈을[눈이] 깜박이다 / **stumble over** 말을 더듬거리다 / **forced** 억지로 하는, 강요된 / **look away** 눈길[얼굴]을 돌리다 | 선택지 어휘 | **acquaintance** 지인, 아는 사람

01. ③ 02. ④ 03. ⑤ 04. ④ 05. ① 06. ④ 07. ② 08. ② 09. ② 10. ⑤
11. ② 12. ⑤ 13. ③ 14. ④ 15. ④ 16. ① 17. ⑤

01 화자가 하는 말의 목적 | ③

▶ 보안 위반 사건 조사로 인해서 일시적으로 공항 시설의 운영 및 업무를 중단한다는 내용의 안내 방송이다.

W: Attention passengers. There has been a security violation in the International Terminal. Mysterious packages have been left in Terminal B. We are sorry for the inconvenience, but we need to evacuate the airport immediately **due to the possible danger**. So we'll temporarily close the facilities and cease airport operations. All flights currently on the runways **will be allowed to take off**, but arriving passengers will not be allowed to leave their planes. We expect the delay **to last for at least one hour** while we are investigating. Please proceed to the nearest exit with all of your possessions. Walk, do not run. We will do our best to speed everyone through security when normal operations begin again. Thank you.

여: 승객 여러분께 안내 말씀 드리겠습니다. 국제선 터미널에서 보안 위반 사건이 발생했습니다. 내용물을 알 수 없는 짐 가방이 터미널 B에 버려져 있습니다. 불편을 끼쳐 드리게 되어 죄송합니다. 하지만 혹시라도 발생할 위험한 상황에 대비하여 즉시 공항에서 대피해야 합니다. 그러므로 일시적으로 공항 시설을 폐쇄하고 공항 업무를 중지할 것입니다. 현재 활주로에 있는 모든 항공편은 이륙이 허가될 것입니다. 하지만 도착한 승객들은 비행기를 떠나서는 안 됩니다. 저희가 조사하는 동안 적어도 한 시간 정도 업무의 지연이 있을 것으로 예상됩니다. 여러분의 소지품을 모두 가지고 가장 가까운 출구로 이동해 주십시오. 뛰지 말고 걸어가십시오. 업무가 재개되면 모든 분들이 신속히 보안 검색을 받을 수 있도록 최선을 다하겠습니다. 감사합니다.

어휘 **security** 보안, 안전 / **violation** 위반, 방해 / **inconvenience** 불편; 불편한 것 (↔ convenience 편리; 편리한 것) / **evacuate** (위험한 장소를) 떠나다; 대피시키다 / **temporarily** 일시적으로, 임시로 / **facility** (주로 복수형) 시설, 설비 / **cease** 중지하다 / **operation** 운행; 작동 / **runway** 활주로 / **investigate** 조사하다, 수사하다 / **proceed** 가다, 나아가다 / **possession** (주로 복수형) 소지품, 소유물

02 의견 | ④

▶ 남자는 안구 건조증, 흐린 시야 등 시력 교정 수술 후에 발생할 수 있는 부작용에 관해 이야기하며 시력 교정술을 받는 것에 대해 오랫동안 생각해 볼 것을 권하고 있다.

M: Hi, Megan. Where are you going?
W: Hi, Neal. I'm going to the eye clinic for a regular eye checkup.
M: Oh, are you having problems **with your eyesight**?
W: No, I just want to check if my eyes are fine.
M: You've been wearing glasses since you were very young, right?
W: Yes, it's pretty uncomfortable. So, I'm considering laser eye surgery.
M: But I heard about **some possible side effects of the surgery**, and I don't think it's a good idea.
W: Really? I also know about some problems that I might experience after the surgery, like dry eyes.
M: Some people have blurry vision afterward, so I think **you should take plenty of time** to think about it.
W: Okay, I see. Thanks!

남: 안녕, Megan. 어디 가니?
여: 안녕, Neal. 나는 안과에 정기 검진을 받으러 가는 길이야.
남: 아, 시력에 문제가 있는 거니?
여: 아니, 그냥 눈이 괜찮은지 확인해 보려고.
남: 너는 꽤 어렸을 때부터 안경을 써 왔지, 그렇지?
여: 응, 매우 불편해. 그래서 난 시력 교정 수술을 고려하고 있어.
남: 하지만 발생할 수 있는 부작용에 관해 들은 적이 있어서, 수술을 받는 게 좋은 생각 같지는 않아.
여: 정말? 나도 수술 후에 겪게 될 수도 있는 몇 가지 문제점에 대해 알고 있어, 안구 건조증 같은 것 말이야.
남: 어떤 사람들은 나중에 시야가 흐려지기도 해서, 내 생각엔 네가 수술을 받는 것에 대해서 오랫동안 생각해 봐야 할 것 같아.
여: 그래, 알았어. 고마워!

어휘 **side effect** 부작용 / **blurry** 흐릿한, 모호한 / **vision** 시야; 시력

03 관계 | ⑤

▶ 여자는 남자가 태어난 일시를 가지고 미래를 예언하고 있다.

M: So what do you want me to tell you?
W: For me your date of birth is important.
M: **Don't you need to look at** my hands or anything?
W: No, but **I would like you to write down** the exact date and time of your birth on this paper.
M: OK. Now what?
W: Now I need to check this chart. Hmm... I see.
M: What is it?
W: Well, according to my chart you have a very lucky period coming up.
M: Really? **I'm about to start** a new job overseas!
W: Yes, I see. I believe your luck will be in New York. I have a strong feeling about this.
M: A feeling?
W: Yes, of course. I don't just rely on my chart for this. I have a special gift.

남: 무엇을 알려 드릴까요?
여: 제게는 당신의 생일이 중요합니다.
남: 손이나 다른 것은 보실 필요가 없나요?
여: 네, 이 종이 위에 태어난 일시를 정확하게 적어 주십시오.
남: 네, 그럼 이제는 뭘 하나요?
여: 이제 이 표를 확인해야 합니다. 음… 그렇군요.
남: 뭔데요?
여: 음, 제 표에 따르면 당신에게 행운의 시기가 다가오고 있군요.
남: 정말입니까? 해외에서 새 일을 시작하려는 참이었어요!
여: 네, 그렇군요. 뉴욕에서 좋은 일이 있을 거예요. 아주 강한 느낌이 와요.
남: 느낌이요?
여: 네, 물론이죠. 이 일을 할 때 표에만 의존하는 것이 아니거든요. 제게는 특별한 능력이 있지요.

어휘 **be about to-v** 막 v하려 하다 / **overseas** 외국에, 외국으로 / **rely on A** A에 의지하다

04 그림 불일치 | ④

▶ 그림에선 남자의 삼촌이 손으로 사과를 따고 있는 모습이지만, 대화에선 긴 막대기를 사용한다고 했으므로 일치하지 않는다.

W: That's a great picture, Tom.
M: You think so? It was taken at my uncle Sam's apple farm last weekend. I went there with my family.
W: It looks like a good time. Is that your mother **sitting on the mat**?
M: Yes, she was setting out food for a picnic. We ate after taking this picture.
W: It looks like **someone had already started eating** beside her.
M: That's my younger sister, Susan. She was so hungry! It was really funny.
W: Is that your family's dog running around?
M: No, that's Max. He's my uncle's dog, but he looks just like ours.
W: They do look similar. And I'll guess that's your uncle **picking apples on the right**?
M: Right. He is using that long stick to reach high into the trees. You can only see three trees behind him, but it's a huge farm.
W: It must be a lot of work!

여: 멋있는 사진이구나, Tom.
남: 그렇게 생각하니? 지난 주말에 Sam 삼촌의 사과 농장에서 찍은 거야. 가족과 함께 그곳에 갔어.

여: 즐거운 시간을 보내는 것 같구나. 돗자리에 앉아 계신 분은 너희 어머니이셔?
남: 응. 소풍을 위해 음식을 차리고 계셨어. 우린 이 사진을 찍고 나서 먹었지.
여: 어머니 옆에서 누군가 이미 먹기 시작한 것처럼 보이는데.
남: 그건 내 여동생 Susan이야. Susan은 무척 배고팠거든! 정말 재미있었어.
여: 너희 집 강아지가 뛰어다니고 있는 거니?
남: 아니야. 저건 Max야. 삼촌네 강아지인데, 우리 집 강아지와 꼭 닮았어.
여: 그들은 정말로 비슷해 보이는구나. 그리고 오른쪽에서 사과를 따고 있는 분은 너희 삼촌이시지?
남: 맞아. 삼촌께서는 나무 높은 데까지 닿기 위해 저 긴 막대를 사용하고 계셔. 삼촌 뒤에 세 그루의 나무들만 보이지만, 이건 엄청 큰 농장이야.
여: 틀림없이 일이 많겠구나!

어휘 **mat** 돗자리 / **set out** ~을 진열하다[정리하다] / **run around** 뛰어다니다

05 부탁한 일 | ①

▶ 편지에 답장을 하는 데 몇 주가 걸릴 것이라는 남자의 말에 여자가 Not if you help me sort them out.이라고 말한 부분에서 답을 유추할 수 있다.

W: Wow. Ever since I was on that TV show, I have been getting so much fan mail.
M: There must be 500 letters here!
W: Yes, and that is only this week. I have another pile from last week, too.
M: Are you going to answer every letter?
W: Well, most of them. Some are from men **asking me to marry them**!
M: Even without those letters, it's still going to take weeks to answer the rest.
W: Not if you **help me sort them out**.
M: OK. Tell me **how to do it**.
W: First, make three piles. One is for letters from children, the next is from adults, and the third is for guys who want to marry me.
M: I think I know **which pile is going to be the biggest**!

여: 와. 그 TV 프로그램에 나온 이후로 나는 팬레터를 아주 많이 받고 있어.
남: 여기 편지가 분명 500통은 되겠다!
여: 응. 그리고 그건 이번 주에만 온 것들이야. 지난주에 온 편지 더미가 또 있어.
남: 모든 편지에 답장을 할 거니?
여: 글쎄, 대부분 해야지. 일부는 나에게 결혼해 달라는 남자들한테 온 거야!
남: 그런 편지를 빼고도 나머지에 답장을 하려면 몇 주는 걸리겠다.
여: 네가 그것들을 분류하는 것을 도와준다면 그렇게 걸리진 않겠지.
남: 좋아. 어떻게 하면 되는지 말해 줘.
여: 우선 세 더미로 만들어 줘. 하나는 아이들한테 온 편지고, 다음은 어른들, 그리고 세 번째는 나와 결혼하고 싶어 하는 남자들에게 온 것들이야.
남: 어떤 더미가 가장 클지 알 것 같아!

어휘 **fan mail** 팬레터 / **pile** 더미, 쌓아 올린 것 / **sort out** 분류[구분]하다; 처리하다

06 금액 | ④

▶ 남자는 여행객이므로 나중에 10%의 세금을 되돌려 받을 수 있지만, 이 가게에서는 세금을 포함한 모든 금액을 먼저 지불해야 한다.

W: Let's see... the total is $55.
M: Isn't this hat $20 and this T-shirt $30?
W: They are.
M: Then **why do I have to pay $5 more**?
W: You have to pay a 10% sales tax.
M: Really?
W: But I see that you're a tourist, so I am sure you can get a sales tax rebate.
M: Rebate? You mean **I won't have to pay** the sales tax, the 10% extra?
W: Yes.
M: Great. I'm from Singapore. Here's my passport.
W: I don't need your passport. You must pay the tax now, but you can **get it back later**. You apply at the airport **as you are leaving**.
M: OK.

여: 한번 볼까요… 총 55달러입니다.
남: 이 모자는 20달러이고 이 티셔츠는 30달러 아닌가요?
여: 그렇습니다.
남: 그럼, 제가 왜 5달러를 더 내야 하죠?
여: 판매세 10%를 지불하셔야 합니다.
남: 정말이요?
여: 하지만 여행객이신 것 같으니 손님은 판매세 환급을 받으실 수 있으리라고 봅니다.
남: 환급이요? 제가 추가로 10%의 판매세를 내지 않아도 된다는 말씀이신가요?
여: 그렇습니다.
남: 잘됐군요. 저는 싱가포르에서 왔고 여기 제 여권이 있습니다.
여: 여권은 필요 없습니다. 손님께서는 세금을 지금 내셔야 합니다만, 나중에 환급받으실 수 있습니다. 출국하실 때 공항에서 신청하시면 됩니다.
남: 알겠습니다.

어휘 **rebate** 환급, 환불 / **apply** 신청하다, 지원하다; 적용하다

07 이유 | ②

▶ 여자는 남자와 함께 촬영하기로 했던 여자 모델이 패션쇼 리허설 중 다리를 다쳐 사진 촬영이 연기되었다고 했다.

[Cell phone rings.]
M: Hello?
W: Mr. Smith, this is Jumi from Jamia Advertising. Do you have a few minutes to talk?
M: Yes, the photographer gave me a break before the next shoot.
W: Okay. It's about this weekend's photo shoot on Jeju Island.
M: Oh, I heard that **the weather won't be good** on Jeju Island this weekend. Was the location changed?
W: No, but the woman **you were supposed to shoot with** has a problem.
M: Lana Jacobs? Did something happen?
W: She hurt her leg on the runway while rehearsing for an upcoming fashion show.
M: I hope she will recover soon. What will happen to the shoot?
W: **It's been postponed**. We'll contact you after speaking with Ms. Jacobs' agency.
M: Okay. I understand.

[휴대전화 벨이 울린다.]
남: 여보세요?
여: Smith 씨, Jamia 광고회사의 Jumi예요. 잠깐 통화할 시간 있으세요?
남: 네, 사진사가 다음 촬영을 하기 전에 잠깐 휴식을 주었거든요.
여: 좋아요. 이번 주말에 제주도에서 있을 사진 촬영에 관한 거예요.
남: 아, 이번 주말에 제주도 날씨가 좋지 않을 거라고 들었어요. 장소가 바뀌었나요?
여: 아뇨, 그런데 함께 사진을 찍기로 한 여성분에게 문제가 생겼어요.
남: Lana Jacobs 씨요? 무슨 일이 생겼나요?
여: 곧 있을 패션쇼 리허설 도중에 무대에서 다리를 다쳤어요.
남: 빨리 회복되었으면 좋겠군요. 그럼 촬영은 어떻게 되나요?
여: 연기되었어요. Jacobs 씨의 소속사와 상의한 후 연락드릴게요.
남: 네. 알겠습니다.

어휘 **shoot** 사진[영화] 촬영 / **be supposed to-v** v하기로 되어 있다 / **runway** (패션쇼의) 무대 / **rehearse** 리허설을 하다, 예행연습을 하다 / **upcoming** 곧 있을, 다가오는 / **recover** 회복하다 / **postpone** 연기하다, 미루다

08 언급하지 않은 것 | ②

▶ 해석 참조

W: Danny, do you want to do something with me this weekend?
M: I'd love to, but I'm afraid my family already has plans to visit my sister this weekend.
W: Oh, she's a student at UC Berkeley, isn't she?
M: That's right. It's a large school, **with over 35,000 students in total**.
W: They've also had many famous professors over the years, including 70 Nobel Prize winners.
M: I didn't know that. I guess you have an interest in Berkeley then?
W: My father attended Berkeley and **I hope to go there as well**. I know all about its history, from its foundation in 1868 to the current day.
M: Then I guess you know that the annual football game versus Stanford will take place this weekend?
W: Of course. That's a famous rivalry that **goes back over a century**. I wish I could go with you.
M: At least I can tell you all about it when I get back.

여: Danny, 이번 주말에 나와 무언가를 함께하지 않을래?
남: 그러고 싶지만, 우리 가족은 이번 주말에 누나를 보러 가기로 이미 계획했어.
여: 오, 누나가 UC Berkeley에 다니는 학생이지?
남: 맞아. 총 35,000명(① 재학생 수)이 넘는 학생이 다니는 아주 큰 학교야.
여: 70명(③ 노벨상 수상자 수)의 노벨상 수상자를 포함해 오랫동안 많은 유명 교수들도 배출했어.
남: 그건 몰랐네. 그럼 너도 Berkeley에 관심이 있나 보구나?
여: 우리 아빠가 Berkeley에 다니셨어. 그래서 나도 거기에 가고 싶어. 난 1868년(④ 설립 연도) 설립부터 현재까지 그 학교의 역사에 대해 모두 알고 있어.
남: 그럼 Stanford와의 연례 축구전(⑤ 연례 축구전)이 이번 주말에 열린다는 것을 알고 있겠네?
여: 물론이지. 그건 백 년이나 된 유명한 대항전이잖아. 너랑 함께 가면 좋을 텐데.
남: 적어도 내가 돌아오면, 너에게 그것에 대해 모두 말해줄게.

어휘 **professor** 교수 / **attend** (학교에) 다니다; 출석하다 / **foundation** 설립, 창립; 기초, 토대 / **annual** 해마다의; 1년의 / **versus** (소송, 경기 등에서) ~ 대(對) / **rivalry** 대항, 경쟁

09 내용 불일치 | ②

▶ 기계를 직접 작동해 볼 수 있다는 내용은 없다.

M: Welcome to a tour of Green Factory. I'm James, your tour guide today. Everyone must sign out and carry a visitor badge. This badge **is equipped with** a locator device that can be activated in the event of an emergency. The machinery is actively producing cereal during your visit. It has many moving parts that could cause bodily injury. For your safety, please **follow the yellow line at all times**. The entire tour **takes a total of two hours**, and it will end at the parking lot. For a shorter version, use any of the three shortcuts. People with any type of heart trouble should consider using the shortcuts at difficult points of the tour.

남: Green Factory 견학에 오신 것을 환영합니다. 저는 오늘 견학을 안내해드릴 James라고 합니다. 모든 분들은 서명을 하시고 방문증을 휴대하셔야 합니다. 이 방문증에는 비상 시 작동될 수 있는 위치 탐지기가 내장되어 있습니다. 여러분이 방문하시는 동안에 기계는 곡물을 활발히 생산하고 있습니다. 기계에는 신체를 다치게 할 수 있는 많은 움직이는 부품들이 있습니다. 안전을 위해서 항상 황색 선을 따라오시기 바랍니다. 전체 견학은 총 2 시간이 걸리며 주차장에서 끝날 것입니다. 더 짧은 견학을 위해서 세 가지 단축 코스 중 어느 것이든 이용하시기 바랍니다. 어떤 종류라도 심장병을 앓고 계신 분들은 견학 중 어려운 지점에서 단축 코스의 이용을 고려하셔야 합니다.

어휘 **sign out** 서명을 하고 (물건을) 빌리다 / **badge** 증표, 배지 / **be equipped with** ~을 갖추고 있다 / **locator** 위치 탐지기 / **activate** 작동시키다 / **in the event of** 만일 ~의 경우에는 / **machinery** 기계(류) / **cereal** 곡물; 시리얼 / **shortcut** 지름길; 손쉬운 방법

10 도표 이해 | ⑤

▶ 여자는 일본어 외에 다른 것을 시도해 보고 싶고 휴가 때문에 14일부터 시작할 수 있다고 했다. 말하기 수업이 더 재밌을 것 같지만, 수요일과 금요일에 음악 수업이 있어서 들을 수 없으므로 ⑤가 적절하다.

M: Hi, Clara. What are you looking at?
W: It's a schedule of winter language courses. **I want to take one**, so I'm checking the course schedule.
M: I know you've been studying Japanese. So, **why not take another Japanese class**?
W: I'd like to try something different.
M: So, what about the dates? Can you start on the 7th?
W: Oh, I almost forgot **I'm going on vacation** that week. I can start on the 14th.
M: That leaves two. **If I were you**, I'd take speaking. That's always more fun.
W: I agree, but I'm afraid I have music lessons on Wednesdays and Fridays.
M: Sounds like the decision has been made then.
W: I guess so. I'll sign up today. Thanks for your help.

남: 안녕, Clara. 무엇을 보고 있니?
여: 겨울 어학 강좌의 시간표야. 수업 하나를 듣고 싶어서 강좌 시간표를 확인하고 있어.
남: 네가 일본어를 공부해 오고 있는 것을 알고 있어. 그러니 또 다른 일본어 수업을 수강하는 게 어때?
여: 난 다른 것을 시도해보고 싶어.
남: 그럼, 날짜는? 7일에 시작할 수 있니?
여: 아, 그 주에 휴가 가는 것을 하마터면 잊을 뻔했네. 난 14일부터 시작할 수 있겠어.
남: 그러면 2개가 남네. 내가 너라면, 말하기 수업을 들을 거야. 그게 항상 더 재미있거든.
여: 나도 동의하지만 안타깝게도 수요일과 금요일에 음악 수업이 있어.
남: 그러면 결정이 된 것 같구나.
여: 그런 것 같아. 오늘 등록해야겠어. 도와줘서 고마워.

어휘 **leave** 남기다; 떠나다; 그만두다 / **sign up** 등록[신청]하다; 참가하다

11 짧은 대화에 이어질 응답 | ②

▶ 31번 버스가 얼마나 자주 오는지 묻는 남자의 말에 가장 적절한 응답을 찾는다.

① 막차는 이미 떠났어요.
② 10분에 한 대씩이요.
③ 그건 당신이 어디로 가느냐에 따라 달라요.
④ 이 지역 버스 체계는 형편없군요.
⑤ 오전 6시에서 오후 11시 30분 사이에 있어요.

M: Excuse me, but has the number 31 bus passed by here?
W: Yes, **you just missed it**. There will be another one soon.
M: **How often does it come**?
W: ______________________________

남: 실례지만 31번 버스가 여길 지나갔나요?
여: 네, 방금 놓치셨네요. 다음 버스가 곧 올 거예요.
남: 그 버스는 얼마나 자주 오나요?
여: ______________________________

12 짧은 대화에 이어질 응답 | ⑤

▶ 유럽 여행을 다시 가고 싶어 하는 남자에게 여자는 그럴 수 있다면 어떤 점을 다르게 할 것인지 물었다. 이에 적절한 응답을 찾는다.

① 대신 베트남을 선택할 거야.
② 네가 직접 가서 확인해야 해.
③ 난 4개국에 가 봤어.
④ 문화 차이는 큰 의미가 없어.
⑤ 시간을 낭비하지 않도록 미리 계획을 세울 거야.

W: Richard, you spent a summer in Europe, didn't you?
M: I did, but it wasn't a very satisfying trip. **I wish I could go back**.
W: Really? If you could go again, **what would you do** differently?
M: ______________________________

여: Richard, 너 여름을 유럽에서 보냈지?
남: 그랬어, 하지만 매우 만족스러운 여행은 아니었어. 돌아갈 수 있다면 좋을 텐데.
여: 정말? 다시 갈 수 있다면, 뭘 다르게 할 거니?
남: ______________________________

13 긴 대화에 이어질 응답 | ③

▶ 여자는 사료를 사기 위해서 강아지의 주인인 여동생에게 강아지의 품종을 물어봐야 할 것이다.

① 제가 가서 그에게 바로 물어보겠습니다.
② 제가 그에 대해서 설명을 해 드릴까요?
③ 여동생에게 전화를 걸어서 바로 물어보겠습니다.
④ 저는 푸들에게 먹일 강아지 사료로 하겠습니다.
⑤ 개는 갈색이고 코에 흰 점이 있습니다.

M: May I help you find anything?
W: Yes, I am taking care of my sister's dog while she is **away on business**, and I need some food for it.
M: OK. Do you know what kind of dog it is?
W: It is a large brown dog. I don't know what kind of dog it is.
M: Do you know how old it is? If it's a puppy, we have special food for them.
W: He is just under one year old.
M: Hmm... **that puts him right between** being a puppy and an adult. It would really help to know the breed.
W: I said that it is big. Doesn't that help?
M: "Big" isn't **a good enough description**. Is there any way you can find

out?

W: ____

남: 찾는 게 있으신가요?
여: 네, 제 여동생이 출장 간 동안 그 애의 강아지를 돌보고 있는데요, 사료가 좀 필요해서요.
남: 알겠습니다. 어떤 종의 개인지 아십니까?
여: 큰 갈색 개입니다. 종이 무엇인지는 모릅니다.
남: 나이는 얼마나 되었는지 아십니까? 강아지라면 특수 사료가 있습니다.
여: 아직 한 살이 안 되었습니다.
남: 음… 그럼 강아지와 성견의 딱 중간쯤이 됩니다. 품종을 알면 정말 도움이 될 텐데요.
여: 제가 큰 개라고 말씀드렸는데요. 도움이 되지 않습니까?
남: '크다'는 것은 충분한 설명이 되지 않습니다. 알아볼 수 있는 방법이 없습니까?
여: ____

어휘 **on business** 사업차, 볼일로 / **breed** (동식물의) 품종, 종류 / **description** 설명, 기술 ***cf.* describe** 묘사하다, 설명하다 | 선택지 어휘 | **spot** 반점, 얼룩

14 긴 대화에 이어질 응답 | ④

▶ 남자는 수영이나 파도타기를 하고 싶어 하지만 여자의 아버지가 없어서 바다에는 가지 못한다. 그래서 여자는 파도타기가 가능한 워터 파크에 가자고 한다.

① 난 파도타기를 좋아하지 않아. 너무 무섭거든.
② 그냥 여기서 너희 아버지를 기다리자.
③ 너무 더워서 아무것도 못하겠어. TV나 보자.
④ 좋아! 어느 (워터) 파크였는지 기억하니?
⑤ 그럼 네가 말했던 그 해변에 가자.

M: Hey, Tara! Thanks for inviting me to your house again.
W: Hi, Justin. **What do you feel like doing** today?
M: It was so nice last week when your dad **took us surfing**.
W: Sorry, we can't go surfing today. Dad's playing golf all day.
M: Oh, my. I brought my swimsuit with me. I really wanted to swim or surf today.
W: Well, then, let's go to a water amusement park! I'll find one on the Internet.
M: Hmm, I don't really like crowds, especially at those big water parks.
W: It's not so hot today, so they **won't be very crowded**. And I heard one of them has big surfing waves.
M: ____

남: Tara야! 너네 집에 다시 초대해줘서 고마워.
여: 안녕, Justin. 오늘 무엇을 했으면 좋겠니?
남: 지난주에 너희 아버지께서 우리를 파도타기 하러 데리고 가 주셨을 때 정말 좋았어.
여: 미안. 오늘은 파도타기 하러 못 가. 아버지가 오늘 하루 종일 골프를 치시거든.
남: 이럴 수가. 나는 수영복도 가지고 왔는데. 오늘 정말 수영이나 파도타기를 하고 싶었거든.
여: 그럼, 워터 파크에 가자! 내가 인터넷으로 찾아볼게.
남: 음, 나는 사람이 많은 곳은 그렇게 좋아하지 않아. 특히 그런 대형 워터 파크들 말이야.
여: 오늘은 그다지 덥지 않아서 그렇게 붐비지는 않을 거야. 그리고 그중 한 곳에 큰 파도타기용 파도가 있다고 들었거든.
남: ____

15 상황에 적절한 말 | ④

▶ Robbie는 다음 경기에는 다른 골키퍼가 뛰게 될 것임을 Sean에게 조심스럽게 알려야 한다.

① 별일 아니야. 새로 온 친구는 잘 못하더라고.
② 너는 이번에 골키퍼로 뛰기에 충분히 잘해.
③ 플레이오프에 나가려면 우린 새로운 팀 주장이 필요해.
④ 유감스럽게도, 감독님께서는 다음 경기에 골키퍼를 교체하실 거야.
⑤ 프로 선수가 되는 것에 대해 생각해 본 적이 있니?

W: Robbie is the captain of the soccer team. His best friend, Sean, plays goalkeeper on the team. But a new player **has tried out for the position** and is even better than Sean at the goalpost, so the coach has decided to **let him play in the next game**. Sean has been the goalkeeper for two seasons now and **will be very upset when he finds out**. The coach thinks Robbie should tell Sean about the change in the lineup for the next game. Robbie doesn't want to do it, but the coach insists that **it is part of his role** as a team leader. In this situation, what is Robbie most likely to say to Sean?

여: Robbie는 축구팀의 주장이다. 그의 가장 친한 친구인 Sean은 팀에서 골키퍼를 맡고 있다. 하지만 새로 들어온 선수가 그 포지션에 지원했고 골대에서 Sean보다 훨씬 더 뛰어난 기량을 보였다. 그래서 감독님은 그를 다음 경기에 출전시키기로 결정하셨다. Sean은 지난 두 시즌 동안 골키퍼로 활약하여서 그가 알게 되면 아주 언짢아할 것이다. 감독님은 다음 경기의 선수 진용의 변화에 대해서 Robbie가 Sean에게 말해야 한다고 생각하신다. Robbie는 그렇게 하고 싶지 않지만, 감독님은 그것이 팀의 주장으로서 그의 역할의 일부라고 주장하신다. 이러한 상황에서 Robbie가 Sean에게 할 말로 가장 적절한 것은 무엇인가?

어휘 **goalpost** 골대 / **lineup** 선수 인원 구성 / **insist** 주장하다 | 선택지 어휘 | **playoff** 플레이오프, 결승 진출 결정전

16~17 세트 문항 | 16. ① 17. ⑤

▶ 16. 스테이케이션의 의미와 그것을 즐기는 방법을 나열하며 스테이케이션을 계획할 것을 제안하고 있다.

① 스테이케이션을 즐기는 몇 가지 방법들
② 우리 일상생활에서 휴가의 필요성
③ 휴가를 계획할 때 고려해야 할 것들
④ 스테이케이션의 장단점
⑤ 스테이케이션과 실제 휴가의 차이점

▶ 17. 해석 참조

① 놀이동산 ② 미술관 ③ 역사적인 장소 ④ 지역 박물관 ⑤ 극장

M: Many people dream of a wonderful vacation, but they can't have a vacation **due to certain reasons**. A staycation is the best option for people in such circumstances. A staycation is a kind of vacation **where you just relax at home**, take a whole day trip and get back to your place at night. In order to have a proper staycation, you need to plan things to do. First, turn off your alarm. A good vacation **has no set routine**. Also, find new and fun activities. You can visit an amusement park or an art gallery. You can also explore places such as historical sites or local museums around you. Turn off your phone. Pretend that you're half a world away **with little access to your phone**. Go to bed when you'd like and wake up when you'd like. The best part of vacationing is taking the time to truly relax with an afternoon snooze. Pull the shades down, put on some soothing music and spend your afternoon basking in **the luxury of nothing to do**. You can enjoy all these things without flying off to a Caribbean island. In a sense, a staycation is actually better than a real vacation. Plan your staycation today!

남: 많은 사람이 신나는 휴가를 꿈꾸지만, 그들은 어떤 이유로 휴가를 보내지 못합니다. 스테이케이션이 그러한 상황에 있는 사람들에게 최고의 선택입니다. 스테이케이션은 여러분이 그저 집에서 휴식을 취하고 온전한 하루의 여행을 떠나 밤에 여러분의 장소로 돌아오는 휴가의 유형입니다. 제대로 된 스테이케이션을 보내기 위해 여러분은 할 일들을 계획해야 합니다. 우선 알람을 끄세요. 좋은 휴가에는 정해진 틀이 없습니다. 또한 새롭고 재미있는 활동을 찾으세요. 여러분은 ① 놀이동산이나 ② 미술관에 방문할 수 있습니다. 여러분은 또한 여러분 주변의 ③ 역사적인 장소나 ④ 지역 박물관과 같은 장소들을 답사할 수 있습니다. 전화기를 끄세요. 여러분이 전화기에 거의 접근할 수 없는 채로 지구 반대편에 있다고 가정하세요. 원할 때 잠자리에 들고 원할 때 일어나세요. 휴가를 보내는 것의 가장 좋은 점은 오후의 낮잠으로 진정으로 휴식을 취하는 데 시간을 쓰는 것입니다. 빛 가리개를 내리고 마음을 달래는 음악을 틀고 할 일이 아무것도 없는 사치를 누리며 여러분의 오후를 보내세요. 여러분은 이 모든 것들을 카리브해의 섬으로 날아가지 않고도 즐길 수 있습니다. 어떤 의미에서 스테이케이션은 실제 휴가보다 정말로 더 낫습니다. 오늘 여러분의 스테이케이션을 계획하세요!

어휘 **certain** 어떤; 어느 정도의; 확신하는; 틀림없는 / **staycation** 스테이케이션(집이나 집 근처에서 보내는 휴가) / **circumstance** 상황; 형편 / **proper** 제대로 된, 적절한 / **set** 정해진; 위치한 / **routine** (지루한 일상의) 틀, (판에 박힌) 일상 / **pretend** ~라고 가정[상상]하다; ~인 척하다 / **snooze** 낮잠; (낮에) 잠깐 자다 / **shade** 빛 가리개; 그늘 / **soothing** 마음을 달래는, 진정시키는 / **bask in** ~을 누리다

16 Sense Up 듣기 모의고사
ANSWERS & COMPREHENSION

본문 p.98

01. ⑤ 02. ② 03. ④ 04. ① 05. ④ 06. ④ 07. ⑤ 08. ③ 09. ② 10. ③
11. ① 12. ② 13. ④ 14. ② 15. ② 16. ② 17. ④

01 화자가 하는 말의 목적 | ⑤

▶ 남자는 강의마다 관련 자료가 있다고 말하며 학교 홈페이지에서 그것을 다운로드 받는 방법을 알려주고 있다.

M: Welcome, freshmen! I'm Professor Nate Brunswick and I'll be teaching "Intro to Economics" this semester. For each lecture, there will be **some related materials**. Let me explain a bit more about this. First, you **must be logged on to** the school's homepage to see the files. Your ID is your school ID number and the password is your date of birth. Once you are on the homepage, you should find the "reference" section. Type our lecture's name into the search box to get the materials. Additionally, I strongly recommend that you change your initial password into something unique. I hope you will **get used to the system** soon.

남: 환영합니다, 신입생 여러분! 저는 Nate Brunswick 교수이며 이번 학기에 '경제학 입문'을 가르칠 것입니다. 강의마다 관련 자료가 있을 것입니다. 이에 대해 좀 더 설명해드리겠습니다. 우선, 파일을 확인하기 위해서는 학교 홈페이지에 로그인해야 합니다. 아이디는 학생증 번호(학번)이며 비밀번호는 여러분의 생년월일입니다. 홈페이지에 접속하면, '참조' 섹션을 찾아야 합니다. 자료를 받으려면 검색창에 우리 강의명을 입력하십시오. 또한, 저는 처음에 설정된 여러분의 비밀번호를 독특한 것으로 바꾸기를 강력히 권합니다. 여러분이 곧 이 시스템에 익숙해지기를 바랍니다.

어휘 **reference** 참조; 언급; 추천서 / **initial** 처음의, 초기의 / **get used to** ~에 익숙해지다

02 의견 | ②

▶ 남자는 등산로에 왜 쓰레기통이 없는지 의아해하고 여자는 쓰레기통이 없는 이유를 설명하며 쓰레기통이 있는 것이 오히려 결과가 더 나쁠 것이라고 이야기하고 있다.

M: Wow! This view is incredible!
W: It is. This trail is popular because it's easy and safe.
M: It's great. Thanks for inviting me. If you hadn't, I **would have played computer games** all weekend without seeing this.
W: I'm glad you're enjoying the hike. But we should head down because it'll be dark soon.
M: Alright, but I want to find a trash can first.
W: There aren't any. We **should take our garbage with us**.
M: Really? Why hasn't the local government installed trash cans?
W: Because someone would have to hike up here to empty them.
M: But now people leave their trash on the ground.
W: Even if there were trash cans, the cans would quickly fill up and spill over. The result might be even worse.
M: You may be right. It's **not too difficult to carry** our garbage.

남: 와! 경치가 정말 멋있다!
여: 그렇지. 이 등산로는 수월하고 안전해서 인기가 많아.
남: 아주 좋아. 날 초대해줘서 고마워. 그러지 않았다면 이 경치를 못 보고 주말 내내 컴퓨터 게임만 했을 거야.
여: 네가 하이킹을 즐기고 있다니 기뻐. 하지만 곧 어두워질 테니까 내려가야 해.
남: 알겠어, 그런데 먼저 쓰레기통을 찾고 싶어.
여: 여긴 쓰레기통이 없어. 우리는 쓰레기를 가져가야 해.
남: 정말? 왜 지방 정부가 쓰레기통을 설치하지 않았지?
여: 쓰레기통을 비우려면 누군가 여기에 올라와야 할 테니까.
남: 하지만 지금은 사람들이 쓰레기를 땅에 버리잖아.
여: 쓰레기통이 있더라도, 통이 금세 가득 차서 넘칠 거야. 결과는 훨씬 더 나쁠지도 몰라.
남: 네 말이 맞을지도 모르겠다. 쓰레기를 가져가는 게 아주 어렵지는 않지.

어휘 **trail** (산속의) 작은 길, 산길; 자국, 흔적 / **install** 설치하다 / **spill over** 넘치다

03 관계 | ④

▶ 남자는 TV로 Warm Heart 재단에 대한 프로그램을 보고 감동받아 도움을 주고 싶어 전화했고, 전화를 받은 여자는 이에 감사를 표하며 도울 방법으로 기부와 기증에 대해 알려주고 있다. 따라서 두 사람의 관계는 자선 재단 직원과 후원 신청자이다.

[Phone rings.]
W: Warm Heart Foundation. This is Katelyn Hudson.
M: Hello, my name is Joshua Miller and I watched the program about your foundation's Wheelchairs for Kids project on TV last night.
W: Oh, thank you for calling us. You watched the program that was aired yesterday.
M: Yes. **I was very touched by** your dedication to children in need.
W: I'm glad to hear it. We're hoping that more people take an interest in this project.
M: I hope so, too. I'm calling today because I wanted to know **if there was anything** I could do to help them.
W: Of course, there are many ways you can help. You can donate money or donate a wheelchair **you are no longer using**.
M: I see. I don't have any wheelchairs so I can help out financially.
W: That would be wonderful, too. You can make a donation through our foundation's website.
M: Okay. I will donate just twenty dollars since I'm a student. Is that okay?
W: Absolutely. Every little bit of help counts.

[전화벨이 울린다.]
여: Warm Heart 재단입니다. 저는 Katelyn Hudson입니다.
남: 여보세요, 제 이름은 Joshua Miller인데 어젯밤에 TV로 이 재단의 Wheelchair for Kids 프로젝트에 대한 프로그램을 봤습니다.
여: 아, 저희에게 전화 주셔서 감사해요. 어제 방송된 프로그램을 보셨군요.
남: 예, 어려움에 처한 어린이들을 위한 여러분의 헌신에 무척 감동받았어요.
여: 그 말씀을 들으니 기쁩니다. 더 많은 분들이 이 프로젝트에 관심을 가져주시기를 바라고 있어요.
남: 저도 그렇게 되기를 바랍니다. 오늘 전화 드린 이유는 제가 그들을 도울 수 있는 게 있을지 알고 싶었기 때문입니다.
여: 물론, 도우실 수 있는 많은 방법이 있습니다. 돈을 기부하시거나 더 이상 사용하고 있지 않는 휠체어를 기증해주실 수 있습니다.
남: 알겠습니다. 제가 휠체어는 없으니까 재정적으로 도울 수 있겠네요.
여: 그것 역시 훌륭합니다. 저희 재단의 웹사이트를 통해 기부를 하실 수 있습니다.
남: 알겠습니다. 제가 학생이기 때문에 20달러만 기부할 거라서요. 괜찮나요?
여: 그렇고말고요. 모든 작은 도움이 중요하답니다.

어휘 **foundation** 재단 / **air** 방송하다 / **touch** 감동시키다 / **dedication** 헌신 / **in need** 어려움에 처한 / **donate** 기부하다, 기증하다 / **financially** 재정적으로 / **count** 중요하다, 가치가 있다

04 그림 불일치 | ①

▶ 남자는 야자수들이 일렬로 늘어서 있다고 했다.

W: What a nice view!
M: Yeah, it really is! Do you see the palm trees **standing in a line over there**?
W: Oh, that looks so exotic!
M: We're lucky we could get this room. I can see the entire resort from here.
W: I know. Do you see the round swimming pool? **I can't wait to swim there**.
M: I'd prefer to lie down on one of the pool chairs on the right and read a book.
W: Good idea! I like the polka-dot patterned beach umbrellas next to the chairs. I think it's fitting.
M: **It's truly picture-perfect.**
W: Wait a minute. What's that sitting by the edge of the swimming pool? Is it some kind of animal?
M: I think it's a frog-shaped water fountain.
W: Oh, yeah. Now I can see water **coming out of its mouth**. How cute!

M: I think this vacation is just what we wanted.

여: 경치 진짜 좋네요!
남: 정말 그러네요! 저쪽에 한 줄로 늘어선 야자수가 보여요?
여: 아, 정말 이국적이에요!
남: 이 방을 얻은 건 정말 행운이에요. 여기서 리조트 전체가 보여요.
여: 그러게요. 동그란 모양의 수영장 보여요? 빨리 저기서 수영하고 싶어요.
남: 나는 오른쪽에 있는 수영장 의자 하나에 누워서 책을 읽으면 좋겠어요.
여: 좋은 생각이에요! 의자들 옆에 있는 물방울무늬 파라솔이 맘에 들어요. 잘 어울리는 것 같거든요.
남: 정말 그림 같이 완벽해요.
여: 잠깐만요. 수영장 가장자리에 앉아 있는 저건 뭐죠? 동물 같은 건가요?
남: 내가 보기엔 개구리 모양의 분수 같은데요.
여: 아, 그러네요. 지금 보니 입에서 물이 나오는 게 보여요. 귀여워라!
남: 이번 휴가는 정확히 우리가 원했던 거예요.

어휘 **palm tree** 야자수 / **stand in a line** 한 줄로 늘어서다 / **exotic** 이국적인 / **lie down** 눕다 / **polka-dot patterned** 물방울무늬의 / **fitting** 어울리는, 적합한 / **picture-perfect** 흠잡을 데 없이 완벽한 / **edge** 가장자리 / **water fountain** 분수

05 추후 행동 | ④

▶ 학생회장 선거 운동을 위한 포스터를 준비하는 상황으로, 여자가 그림을 그려줄 사람이 필요하다고 하자 남자가 그려줄 수 있다고 하였다.

W: Noah, I'm nervous about my campaign for student council president.
M: Why do you say that? You're definitely the best student for the job.
W: Thanks for saying so, but I don't think many students **even know I'm running**.
M: So, what are you going to do? Do you have an idea?
W: I suppose a few more campaign posters could help. I've got some paper here. Could you help me?
M: Of course. Do you need pens or decorations?
W: **I have all of that**. I just need someone to draw a few eye-catching pictures.
M: I can do that for you. I love to draw.
W: Great! Thank you so much.
M: I'm happy to help. **Have you already chosen a design**?
W: I haven't. So, I'll choose a design first.

여: Noah, 난 학생회장을 뽑는 선거 운동이 긴장돼.
남: 왜 그렇게 말하니? 너는 분명히 그 일에 최고로 적합한 학생이야.
여: 그렇게 말해줘서 고맙지만, 많은 학생들이 내가 입후보한 것도 모르는 것 같아.
남: 그렇다면, 무엇을 하려고 하니? 아이디어가 있어?
여: 선거 운동 포스터가 몇 장 더 있으면 도움이 될 거라고 생각해. 여기 종이가 좀 있어. 도와줄래?
남: 물론이지. 펜이나 장식물들이 필요하니?
여: 그건 내가 모두 갖고 있어. 단지 몇 가지 눈길을 끄는 그림을 그려줄 사람이 필요해.
남: 내가 널 위해 그려줄 수 있어. 난 그림 그리는 것을 정말 좋아하거든.
여: 좋아! 정말 고마워.
남: 돕게 되어서 기쁘다. 디자인은 이미 골랐니?
여: 아니. 그럼 우선 디자인을 고를게.

어휘 **campaign** 선거 운동; 캠페인 / **student council** 학생회 / **president** 회장; 대통령 / **definitely** 분명히 / **run** (선거에) 입후보[출마]하다 / **decoration** 장식물, 장식 / **eye-catching** 눈길을 끄는

06 금액 | ④

▶ 350달러에 판매하는 두 개의 은색 램프로 된 세트를 구매했는데, 250달러 이상 구매 시 10% 할인권이 사용 가능하므로 여자가 지불할 금액은 315달러이다.

M: Can I help you find anything?
W: Yes. I'm looking for a nice floor lamp for my new apartment.
M: We have several that you might be interested in. **This one here is on sale** for $120.
W: I like the simple design, but **I don't care for the color**. What about this silver one?
M: That is actually part of a two-lamp set that sells for $350.
W: Could I buy one **for half that price**?
M: I'm afraid not. However, we do have this similar lamp. It's currently $200.
W: I like it. I'll take it, and I'll use this 10% discount offer that I received in the mail.
M: I'm afraid **that only applies** if your total is over $250.
W: Oh. In that case, I'll take the set with two silver lamps.
M: Great choice.

남: 찾는 걸 도와드릴까요?
여: 네. 저는 새 아파트에 놓을 괜찮은 플로어 램프를 하나 찾고 있어요.
남: 관심 가지실 만한 것이 몇 개 있습니다. 여기 이것은 120달러에 판매 중입니다.
여: 단순한 디자인이 마음에 들지만, 그 색깔을 좋아하지 않아요. 이 은색으로 된 것은요?
남: 그것은 사실 350달러에 판매하는 램프 두 개로 된 세트 중 하나입니다.
여: 반값에 하나만 살 수 있나요?
남: 죄송하지만 안 됩니다. 하지만 이런 비슷한 램프도 있습니다. 지금 200달러이고요.
여: 그거 좋네요. 그걸로 할게요. 그리고 제가 메일로 받은 이 10% 할인권도 사용할게요.
남: 죄송하지만 그것은 총 구매 금액이 250달러가 넘는 경우에만 적용됩니다.
여: 아. 그러면 두 개의 은색 램프로 된 세트를 살게요.
남: 잘 선택하셨습니다.

어휘 **care for** ~을 좋아하다; ~을 돌보다 / **currently** 지금, 현재

07 이유 | ⑤

▶ 남자의 아내가 한국인인데, 그녀의 가족들과 가까워지고 싶어서 한국어를 배우려고 노력 중이라고 했다.

W: Hi, I'm Lucy.
M: Nice to meet you. My name's Parker. So, why did you **sign up for this class**?
W: My company is planning to send me to Seoul in a few months. I'll need to speak Korean to deal with clients. What about you?
M: My wife is Korean. I'm trying to learn the language so I can **get closer to her family**.
W: Oh, really? How did you meet her?
M: We met in university. We were both history majors.
W: That's interesting. Does your wife's family live here, in Chicago?
M: No, but they visit occasionally. We actually had the wedding in Busan. It was my first trip to Korea, and I really enjoyed it.
W: In that case, maybe **you can give me a few tips** about Korean culture.
M: I'd be happy to share what I know, but **I still have a lot to learn**.

여: 안녕하세요, 저는 Lucy입니다.
남: 만나서 반가워요. 제 이름은 Parker에요. 그런데 왜 이 수업에 등록하셨어요?
여: 제가 다니는 회사에서 몇 달 뒤 저를 서울로 보낼 예정이거든요. 고객들을 응대하려면 한국어를 할 필요가 있을 거예요. 당신은요?
남: 제 아내가 한국인이에요. 그녀의 가족들과 더 가까워지기 위해 한국어를 배우려고 노력 중이에요.
여: 아, 정말요? 그녀를 어떻게 만나셨어요?
남: 우린 대학에서 만났어요. 우리 둘 다 역사를 전공했어요.
여: 흥미롭네요. 아내분의 가족은 여기 시카고에 살고 있나요?
남: 아니요, 그렇지만 그들은 종종 방문한답니다. 우린 사실 부산에서 결혼식을 올렸어요. 그게 제가 처음으로 한국을 여행한 건데, 정말 즐거웠어요.
여: 그럼, 당신은 제게 한국 문화에 대해 몇 가지 조언을 주실 수 있겠네요.
남: 제가 아는 것을 공유한다면 기쁘겠지만, 전 아직 배울 게 많아요.

어휘 **occasionally** 때때로, 가끔

08 언급하지 않은 것 | ③

▶ 해석 참조

[Phone rings.]
M: Heller's Career Development Center, Rich speaking. How may I help you?
W: Hi. I recently graduated from university, and I'm having some trouble with my job search.
M: Then **you've called the right place**. We maintain a career-related website that is full of currently available positions.
W: That might help, but to be honest, **I've really struggled with** interviews.
M: Well, we also offer one-on-one interview training sessions.
W: Oh, and my friend mentioned that you help with résumé creation as

well.

M: Right. And you can **take an online aptitude test**. That will help you find the most suitable job.

W: Great. Then I'll call back later and make an appointment.

M: Why don't I send you an email with some further information?

W: Okay. That could be really helpful. Thanks.

[전화벨이 울린다.]

남: Heller 경력 개발 센터의 Rich입니다. 무엇을 도와드릴까요?

여: 안녕하세요. 저는 최근에 대학을 졸업하고 일자리를 구하는 데 어려움을 겪고 있어요.

남: 그렇다면 잘 전화하신 겁니다. 저희는 현재 지원 가능한 일자리로 가득한 직업 관련 웹사이트(① 구직 정보 사이트)를 보유하고 있습니다.

여: 그건 도움이 될 것 같지만, 솔직히, 전 면접 때문에 애를 먹어 왔거든요.

남: 음, 저희는 일대일 면접 교육(② 면접 교육)도 제공합니다.

여: 아, 그리고 제 친구가 여기서 이력서 작성도 도와준다고 말해줬어요(④ 이력서 작성 지원).

남: 맞습니다. 온라인 적성검사(⑤ 온라인 적성검사)도 치를 수 있으십니다. 그건 가장 적합한 직업을 찾는 것을 도와드릴 겁니다.

여: 좋아요. 그럼 나중에 다시 전화해서 약속을 잡도록 할게요.

남: 좀 더 상세한 정보를 이메일로 보내드리는 건 어떠세요?

여: 좋아요. 정말 도움이 될 것 같아요. 감사합니다.

어휘 **struggle** 분투[고투]하다; 몸부림치다 / **training session** 교육 (과정) / **aptitude** 적성, 소질

09 내용 불일치 | ②

▶ 15개국에서 89곳의 출판사가 이번 축제에 참여했다.

W: Welcome to the Children's Book Festival at the New York Exhibition Center. There are 89 publishers of children's books from 15 different countries **represented at this year's festival**. Your children are sure to have fun reading the books on display. Authors will also read their books for children. Some famous stories **will be acted out on the stage**. The festival is also for writers. There will be writing workshops for writers of children's stories. Many of the books on display **are also for sale**. Please ask if you are interested in purchasing a book. Enjoy the festival!

여: 뉴욕 전시관에서 열리는 어린이 도서 축제에 오신 것을 환영합니다. 올해 축제에는 15개국에서 89곳의 어린이 도서 출판사들이 참가했습니다. 여러분의 자녀들은 전시된 책을 읽으면서 분명 즐거운 시간을 보낼 것입니다. 작가들이 어린이들을 위해 자신의 책을 읽어주기도 할 것입니다. 몇몇 유명한 동화는 무대에서 상연될 예정입니다. 축제는 작가들을 위한 것이기도 합니다. 동화 작가들을 위한 집필 워크숍도 개최됩니다. 전시된 책들 중 상당수는 판매용입니다. 도서 구매에 관심이 있으신 분들은 문의해 주십시오. 즐거운 축제 되십시오!

어휘 **publisher** 출판사, 출판인 / **on display** 전시된 / **for sale** 판매용인 / **purchase** 구매(하다)

10 도표 이해 | ③

▶ 남자의 아버지는 회색을 좋아하시지 않고, 방수 기능은 필요하지 않다고 했다. 또한, 하이킹을 하고 자전거 타는 곳에 대해 계속 알고 계실 수 있도록 GPS 기능이 있어야 하며, 남은 두 개 중 더 저렴한 것으로 선택했으므로 ③이 적절하다.

W: Honey, what are you looking at?

M: I'm shopping for an activity tracker online. I thought **it might make a nice birthday gift** for my father.

W: That's a good idea. Which color do you want to buy?

M: I thought about the gray one first, but he doesn't like that color.

W: Does your father need one that's waterproof? **I don't think he's interested in** water sports.

M: I guess you're right. We don't need one that's waterproof.

W: But he definitely needs one with GPS.

M: Of course. With GPS, he can keep track of where he hikes and bikes.

W: Then, **you have two options left**. What do you think?

M: Hmm... I don't want to spend more than $60.

W: You're right. **Let's choose the cheaper one of the two**.

M: Okay. I'll order it now.

여: 여보, 무엇을 보고 있나요?

남: 온라인으로 활동량 추적기를 쇼핑하고 있어요. 아버지께 멋진 생일 선물이 될지도 모른다고 생각했어요.

여: 좋은 생각이네요. 어떤 색으로 사고 싶어요?

남: 처음엔 회색을 생각했지만, 아버지는 그 색을 좋아하지 않으세요.

여: 아버님이 방수되는 것을 필요로 하실까요? 수상 스포츠에 관심이 있으신 것 같진 않아요.

남: 당신이 맞는 것 같아요. 방수되는 게 필요하진 않죠.

여: 하지만 아버님은 GPS 기능이 있는 것을 분명히 필요로 하실 거예요.

남: 물론이죠. GPS 기능이 있다면, 아버지는 하이킹을 하고 자전거 타는 곳에 대해 계속 알고 계실 수 있어요.

여: 그러면, 선택할 수 있는 것이 두 개 남았네요. 어떻게 생각해요?

남: 음… 60달러 넘게는 쓰고 싶지 않아요.

여: 맞아요. 둘 중에 더 저렴한 것으로 선택합시다.

남: 좋아요. 지금 주문할게요.

어휘 **activity tracker** 활동량 추적기 / **waterproof** 방수의 / **definitely** 분명히, 틀림없이 / **keep track of** ~에 대해 계속 알고[파악하고] 있다; ~을 기록하다

11 짧은 대화에 이어질 응답 | ①

▶ 강의실이 다른 곳으로 바뀐 것을 듣지 못했냐는 남자의 마지막 말에 가장 적절한 응답을 찾는다.

① 난 몰랐어. 어서 가자.
② 이 캠퍼스는 정말 커.
③ 그건 여기서 아주 멀리 있지 않은 게 분명해.
④ 네가 만약 늦으면, 넌 무언가를 놓칠 거야.
⑤ 난 역사 수업 듣는 게 힘들어.

M: We'd better leave now for history class. I don't want to be late.

W: We still have ten minutes. **What's the hurry**?

M: **Didn't you hear** that it's been moved to the other side of campus?

W: ______________________________

남: 이제 역사 수업을 들으러 가는 게 좋겠어. 지각하고 싶지 않아.

여: 우리 아직 10분 남았어. 왜 그렇게 서둘러?

남: 강의실이 캠퍼스 반대편으로 바뀐 거 못 들었니?

여: ______________________________

12 짧은 대화에 이어질 응답 | ②

▶ 저녁을 준비하는 상황에서 여자가 자신이 샐러드를 만들 동안 남자에게 도와줄 것을 요청했으므로 승낙하는 응답이 가장 적절하다.

① 점심을 만들어 줘서 고마워요.
② 물론이죠. 내가 면을 삶을게요.
③ 음료도 주문할게요.
④ 당신을 가게에 데려다줄 수 있어요.
⑤ 채소 사는 걸 잊지 마세요.

W: Honey, I'm back from the store. What are you doing?

M: Nothing special. **What's for dinner tonight**?

W: I'm thinking pasta. **Why don't you give me a hand** while I'm preparing salad?

M: ______________________________

여: 여보, 나 가게에서 돌아왔어요. 뭐 하고 있어요?

남: 특별히 하는 거 없어요. 오늘 저녁 메뉴는 뭐예요?

여: 파스타를 생각 중이에요. 내가 샐러드를 준비하는 동안 나 좀 도와줄래요?

남: ______________________________

13 긴 대화에 이어질 응답 | ④

▶ 반려동물을 비행기에 태울 수 있느냐는 질문에 적절한 대답을 찾는다.

① 동물을 들여오려면 세금을 많이 내셔야 합니다.
② 죄송합니다만, 저희 호텔에는 동물을 데리고 오실 수 없습니다.
③ 괜찮습니다. 제가 경비원에게 그것을 알리겠습니다.
④ 가능합니다만, 반드시 (반려동물용) 이동가방에 넣어서 데리고 오셔야 합니다.
⑤ 집으로 데려가실 수 있게 강아지들을 이 바구니에 넣어 드릴게요.

W: Would you like to upgrade to a first class ticket?

M: Maybe. How much will that cost?

W: You can either use some of your air miles or you can pay $600 extra.

M: I think I will use my air miles. Will I still have sufficient miles to upgrade **on the way back**?

W: Let me check. Hmm... it looks like **you will have just enough** for an upgrade both ways.

M: I think **that is what I'll do**. And can I request a special meal?
W: Sure. We offer vegetarian, Muslim and low-fat.
M: I would like the vegetarian meal please.
W: All right. And is there anything else I can do for you today?
M: Yes, I was wondering **if I could bring my dog with me**.
W: ______________________________

여: 일등석 티켓으로 승격시켜 드릴까요?
남: 글쎄요. 그건 가격이 얼마죠?
여: 손님의 항공 마일리지를 사용하시거나 600달러를 추가로 내시면 됩니다.
남: 제 항공 마일리지를 사용할게요. 돌아오는 비행티켓도 승격시킬 수 있을 만큼 충분한 마일리지가 남아 있나요?
여: 확인해 보겠습니다. 음… 왕복 항공편을 모두 승격시키는 데 필요한 마일리지가 되는 것 같습니다.
남: 그렇게 하겠습니다. 그리고 특별식을 주문해도 되나요?
여: 물론입니다. 채식, 이슬람 음식, 저지방식이 제공됩니다.
남: 채식으로 하고 싶습니다.
여: 알겠습니다. 더 도와 드릴 일이 있습니까?
남: 네, 제 개를 데리고 갈 수 있을지 궁금합니다.
여: ______________________________

어휘 **upgrade** 승격시키다 / **sufficient** 충분한 / **Muslim** 이슬람(의) | 선택지 어휘 | **import** 들여오다, 수입하다 / **notify** 통지하다 / **carrier** 운반기

14 긴 대화에 이어질 응답 | ②

▶ 여자는 남자가 유행에 대해 잘 모르므로 옷을 고르러 같이 가주겠다고 말했다. 이때 남자의 적절한 반응을 찾아본다.

① 미안해. 이번에는 너를 도와줄 수가 없어.
② 그래서 네가 나랑 같이 가줬으면 하는 거야.
③ 나도 잘 몰라. 그러니까 더 돌아보자.
④ 그래, 정말 유행하는 옷들이구나.
⑤ 아니, 네가 돈이 많이 필요할 거라고 생각하지 않아.

M: My parents have given me some money to buy some new clothes.
W: Good. I think you need some new clothes.
M: You mean my clothes look old and unfashionable?
W: Well, I don't want to criticize, but **you could look better**.
M: So I am going clothes shopping this afternoon. Would you like to join me?
W: Hmm... but I don't have any money. And I'm sure my parents **won't give me any**.
M: Why is that?
W: They gave me money for new clothes a few weeks ago.
M: Oh? But **you don't have to buy anything**?
W: Hmm....
M: Actually, I need you to come to help me pick out clothes.
W: OK. You don't really know **what's in fashion**.
M: ______________________________

남: 우리 부모님이 새 옷을 사라고 돈을 좀 주셨어.
여: 잘됐구나. 네가 새 옷이 몇 벌 필요한 것 같았어.
남: 내 옷이 오래되고 유행에 뒤떨어져 보인다는 뜻이니?
여: 글쎄, 흠을 잡으려는 게 아니야. 하지만 너는 더 나아 보일 수도 있어.
남: 그래서 오늘 오후에 옷을 사러 가려고 해. 같이 갈래?
여: 음… 하지만 난 돈이 없는걸. 그리고 우리 부모님도 돈을 주시지 않을 거야.
남: 왜?
여: 몇 주 전에 새 옷 사라고 돈을 주셨거든.
남: 그래? 하지만 아무것도 살 필요가 없니?
여: 음….
남: 사실, 네가 옷을 고르는 걸 도와줬으면 해.
여: 알았어. 넌 어떤 것이 유행하고 있는지 잘 모르잖아.
남: ______________________________

어휘 **criticize** 흠을 잡다, 비판하다 / **pick out** 선택하다 / **in fashion** 유행하고 있는

15 상황에 적절한 말 | ②

▶ Janice는 하이킹을 처음 하기 때문에 모든 것이 힘들다. 하산길을 선택하는 것을 걱정하고 있을 때, 눈에 띄는 동호회 회원은 Bob뿐이다. 따라서 그에게 하산길을 동행해달라는 부탁을 할 것이다.

① 우리가 곧 정상에 도달할 것 같아요?
② 나와 같이 가주시겠어요? 그럼 고맙겠어요.
③ 그 사람들이 서로 헤어진다니 믿을 수가 없어요.
④ 하이킹 후에는 모두 보통 무엇을 하나요?
⑤ 왜 이 동호회 회원이 되었나요?

M: Janice hates exercising. But since she **has put on some weight**, she decides to start exercising. She'd like to do something outside, so she joins the hiking club at her office. The first hike she goes on is not an easy one. The trail is steep, rising quickly and sharply. But **she sticks it out**. She doesn't give up. Finally, she reaches the top. On the way down, however, the members of the hiking club form small groups. Each group **takes a different path down**. Janice is worried as the two hikers in front of her **go separate ways**. She stops and turns around. She sees Bob. He is the only member of her club she can see. In this situation, what would Janice most likely say to Bob?

남: Janice는 운동을 싫어한다. 그러나 체중이 좀 늘었기 때문에 운동을 시작하기로 결심한다. 그녀는 야외에서 뭔가를 하고 싶어서 회사의 하이킹 동호회에 가입한다. 처음 간 하이킹은 쉽지 않다. 길이 가파르고 급경사를 이룬다. 그러나 그녀는 계속한다. 포기하지 않는다. 마침내 그녀는 정상에 도달한다. 그러나 내려오는 길에 하이킹 동호회 회원들은 여러 개의 작은 무리를 짓는다. 각각의 무리마다 서로 다른 하산길을 택한다. Janice는 자기 앞의 두 명의 동호회 회원들이 각각 다른 길로 가자 걱정이 된다. 그녀는 멈춰 서서 뒤돌아본다. Bob이 보인다. 그는 그녀의 눈에 띄는 유일한 동호회 회원이다. 이러한 상황에서 Janice가 Bob에게 할 말로 가장 적절한 것은 무엇인가?

어휘 **put on weight** 체중이 늘다 / **trail** (산속의) 작은 길, 산길; 자국, 흔적 / **steep** 가파른, 비탈진; 급격한 / **sharply** 급격하게 / **stick out** (어려운 일 등을) 계속하다 | 선택지 어휘 | **peak** 정상, 산꼭대기; 절정, 최고점 / **stick with** ~와 함께 있다

16~17 세트 문항 | 16. ② 17. ④

▶ 16. 장거리 비행에 대비하여 좀 더 쾌적한 비행을 하기 위해 미리 준비하면 좋을 물품들을 소개하고 있다.

① 여행 가방을 꾸리는 방법
② 장거리 비행을 준비하는 방법
③ 장거리 비행의 부정적인 측면
④ 항공사 무료 서비스 이용하기
⑤ 철저한 여행 준비의 중요성

▶ 17. 해석 참조

W: Good preparation is the key to enjoying a comfortable flight. **The more ways you have prepared**, the better! First, bringing your own soft blanket and pillow can really **make your flight much more comfortable**. Though airlines usually offer them, it's wise to use your own. Having an eye mask will help you sleep and rest your eyes. Though the lights in a plane will be turned off on an overnight flight, you may still want **some extra protection for your eyes**. Similarly, ear plugs can help you block unwanted noise. You may get stuck near two people who talk constantly, so you want to protect yourself just in case. Again, some planes may offer ear plugs, but **it's best not to count on it**. If you're the kind of person who needs to brush his or her teeth after every meal, then it might be a good idea to bring a small toothbrush and toothpaste on the flight. Though it won't be super easy to brush your teeth in the tiny airplane bathroom, it's better than having bad breath.

여: 준비를 잘하는 것은 편안한 비행을 즐기기 위한 비결입니다. 더 많이 준비할수록 더 좋습니다! 첫 번째로 당신의 ① 부드러운 담요와 베개를 가지고 가는 것은 정말로 비행을 훨씬 더 편안하게 해줄 수 있습니다. 항공사에서 대개 그것들을 제공하기는 하지만 당신의 것을 쓰는 것이 현명합니다. ② 안대를 착용하면 당신이 잠을 자고 눈을 쉬게 하는 데 도움이 될 것입니다. 야간 비행 중에는 기내의 조명이 꺼지겠지만, 당신은 여전히 눈을 더 보호하고 싶어 할지 모릅니다. 마찬가지로, ③ 귀마개는 당신이 원하지 않는 소음을 차단하도록 도움을 줄 수 있습니다. 당신이 끊임없이 이야기하는 두 사람 근처에서 꼼짝 못 하게 될 수도 있으므로, 만약에 대비해 (소음으로부터) 자신을 보호하고 싶을 것입니다. 역시, 일부 비행기에서는 귀마개를 제공할지도 모르지만 그것에 의존하지 않는 것이 최상입니다. 만약 당신이 매 식사 후에 이를 닦아야 하는 사람이라면 ⑤ 작은 칫솔과 치약을 기내에 가져가는 것도 좋습니다. 기내의 조그만 화장실에서 양치하는 것이 그리 쉬운 일은 아니지만 구취가 나는 것보다는 나을 것입니다.

어휘 **get stuck** 꼼짝 못 하게 되다 / **(just) in case** (~할) 경우에 대비해서 / **count on** 의지하다, 믿다

17 Sense Up 듣기 모의고사 ANSWERS & COMPREHENSION

본문 p.104

01. ③ 02. ⑤ 03. ③ 04. ④ 05. ④ 06. ② 07. ③ 08. ④ 09. ② 10. ④
11. ② 12. ④ 13. ① 14. ④ 15. ④ 16. ③ 17. ④

01 화자가 하는 말의 목적 | ③

▶ This means no garbage ~와 후반부의 That's why we limit ~을 통해 여자가 주민에게 쓰레기를 지정된 날에 버릴 것을 당부하고 있음을 알 수 있다.

W: Dear residents: As you well know, every Monday morning the garbage truck comes and collects the garbage **that was put out the night before**. This means no garbage should be left out for collection on any other day of the week. Garbage that you put out on the wrong day causes many problems. Waste paper, including newspaper and milk cartons, **is the most problematic**. When it's windy, for example, it gets blown all over town and has to be picked up from lawns and parking lots. That's why we limit the time you can place garbage outside for collection from Sunday afternoon to early Monday morning! **I urge your cooperation** in our efforts to make our neighborhood a better place to live!

여: 주민 여러분, 잘 아시다시피, 매주 월요일 아침에 쓰레기차가 와서 전날 밤에 내놓은 쓰레기를 수거합니다. 이는 곧 나머지 요일에는 수거할 쓰레기를 내놓아서는 안 된다는 것을 뜻합니다. 엉뚱한 요일에 내놓은 쓰레기는 여러 가지 문제를 발생시킵니다. 신문이나 우유 팩을 포함한 종이 쓰레기가 제일 큰 골칫거리입니다. 예를 들어, 바람 부는 날이면, 종이 쓰레기가 마을 곳곳을 날아다녀 잔디 위나 주차장에 있는 쓰레기를 치워야만 합니다. 그래서 우리가 수거할 쓰레기를 내놓는 시간을 일요일 오후부터 월요일 이른 아침까지로 제한하는 것입니다! 우리 동네를 더욱 살기 좋은 곳으로 만들기 위한 노력에 협조해 주실 것을 촉구합니다!

어휘 **put out** 내놓다; (불 등을) 끄다 / **carton** (음식, 음료를 담는) 종이 상자 / **problematic** 골칫거리인, 문제가 되는 / **lawn** 잔디(밭) / **urge** 촉구[재촉]하다; 강하게 충고하다

02 의견 | ⑤

▶ 남자는 반려동물 유기 문제를 도덕적 관점에서 해결하는 것이 가장 좋지만 벌금 부과와 같은 엄격한 조치가 실제적인 변화를 가져올 것이라고 생각한다.

W: Honey, where did you get this cute little kitten?
M: I saw her wandering around the neighborhood and felt bad, so I decided to bring her home.
W: Oh, she **must have been abandoned**! How could someone do that?
M: People often don't realize that pets are a huge responsibility. **When they feel overwhelmed**, they abandon the animal.
W: But it's so sad. I wish people would learn to treat animals with respect.
M: Personally, I think it's a social issue and strict measures could discourage people from abandoning pets.
W: Well, I don't think that's a long-term solution. Instead, people need to **see it as an issue of morals**.
M: That would be the best, but **the fear of being fined** would lead to real change.
W: You have a point.

여: 여보, 이 귀여운 새끼 고양이를 어디서 데려왔어요?
남: 근처에서 방황하고 있는 걸 보고 안쓰러워서 집에 데려오기로 했어요.
여: 아, 분명 버려진 걸 거예요! 어떻게 그런 일을 할 수 있을까요?
남: 사람들은 종종 반려동물을 키우는 데 커다란 책임이 따른다는 사실을 깨닫지 못하거든요. 감당하지 못하겠다고 느끼면 동물을 버리죠.
여: 그렇지만 정말 슬픈 일이에요. 사람들이 동물을 존중하는 마음으로 대하는 법을 안다면 좋겠어요.
남: 개인적으로 나는 이걸 사회적 문제라고 생각해요. 엄격한 조치를 취하면 사람들이 반려동물을 버리는 것을 막을 수 있을 거예요.
여: 글쎄요, 내 생각에 그건 장기적인 해결책이 아닌 것 같아요. 대신에 사람들이 이 사안을 도덕적 문제로 볼 필요가 있어요.
남: 그러면 가장 좋겠지만, 벌금을 물어야 한다는 두려움이 실제적인 변화를 가져올 수 있을 거예요.
여: 당신 말도 일리가 있군요.

어휘 **abandoned** 버려진, 유기된 ***cf.* abandon** (돌볼 책임이 있는 것을) 버리다; 포기하다 / **overwhelmed** 감당하기 힘든; 압도된 / **moral** (사회의) 도덕; 도덕(상)의, 윤리의

03 관계 | ③

▶ 남자는 아들인 Tommy의 학교생활에 대해 궁금해하는 학부모이고, 여자는 Tommy의 학교생활에 대해 학부모에게 말해주는 담임 교사이다.

W: Thank you for coming, Mr. Brown. Did you have any trouble finding the classroom?
M: Not at all, Ms. Grey. I'm glad to meet you, and **I'm curious about** Tommy's school life.
W: He is adjusting well to school. You should be very proud.
M: That's good to hear. He says your lessons are quite enjoyable.
W: **I try to come up with** a variety of activities. Young students have a lot of energy and like to try new things.
M: I see. By the way, what are those posters on the wall?
W: That's from a group project the students did on ocean life. I had them research sea animals.
M: So that's why Tommy **won't stop talking about** whales. He sure learned a lot.
W: I'm glad to hear that. He is an active learner. I'm **impressed with** his participation.
M: That's wonderful. Do you have any of his work I could see?
W: Yes, I have some of Tommy's assignments right here. Let's look at a few together.
M: Great.

여: 와주셔서 감사합니다, Brown 씨. 교실을 찾는 데 문제없으셨나요?
남: 전혀요, Grey 선생님. 만나서 반갑습니다. 저는 Tommy의 학교생활이 궁금하네요.
여: 그 애는 학교에 잘 적응하고 있습니다. 참 자랑스러우시겠어요.
남: 다행이네요. 아들이 선생님의 수업이 참 즐겁다고 하더군요.
여: 다양한 활동을 제시하려고 노력하죠. 어린 학생들은 많은 에너지를 갖고 있고 새로운 것들을 시도하기를 좋아하거든요.
남: 그렇군요. 그런데 벽에 저 포스터들은 무엇인가요?
여: 저것은 해양 생물에 대해 학생들이 조별 과제로 한 거예요. 학생들에게 해양 동물을 조사하도록 했죠.
남: 그래서 Tommy가 고래에 대해 계속 얘기를 했군요. 그 애가 정말 많이 배웠어요.
여: 그렇다니 좋은데요. 아드님은 적극적인 학생이에요. 참여하는 것에 깊은 인상을 받았어요.
남: 훌륭하네요. 제가 볼 수 있는 아들의 작품이 있나요?
여: 네, 바로 여기에 Tommy의 과제물 일부가 있어요. 몇 가지를 같이 보시죠.
남: 좋습니다.

어휘 **have trouble v-ing** v하는 데 어려움을 겪다 / **adjust** 적응하다; 조정[조절]하다 / **come up with** ~을 제시하다[생각해내다] / **a variety of** 다양한 / **impressed** 깊은 인상을 받은; 감명을 받은 / **participation** 참여, 참가 / **assignment** 과제, 임무; 배정; 배치

04 그림 불일치 | ④

▶ 여자는 그림이 거꾸로 되어 있다고 말했다.

W: Brandon, your desk is messy. Why don't you clean up?
M: Sorry, Mom, but I like it the way it is.
W: But **the bookshelves are empty** and all the books are piled up on your desk. If you put them back on the bookshelves, you would have more space.
M: I know, but I **haven't finished using them yet**.
W: All right. What about those cups on the right corner of the desk? I think I have seen them there for three straight days.
M: I forgot. I'll take them to the kitchen in a minute.
W: And the picture on the wall looks like **it's upside down**.
M: Oh, no. I didn't know that. I'll fix it later.
W: Hmm... I'm glad to see that your model planes hanging from the ceiling **are well maintained at least**.
M: That's because they're my favorite.

여: Brandon, 네 책상이 엉망이구나. 좀 치우지 그래?
남: 죄송해요, 엄마. 그런데 전 이대로가 좋은 걸요.

여: 하지만 책장은 텅 비었는데 책은 전부 책상 위에 쌓여 있잖니. 책을 책장에 꽂아놓으면 공간을 넓게 쓸 수 있잖아.
남: 알아요. 그렇지만 그 책들 아직 다 안 봤는걸요.
여: 알았다. 책상 오른쪽 귀퉁이에 있는 저 컵들은? 사흘 내내 거기 있는 걸 본 것 같은데.
남: 잊어버렸어요. 곧 주방에 갖다 둘게요.
여: 그리고 벽에 걸린 저 그림은 거꾸로 걸린 것 같구나.
남: 아이고, 몰랐어요. 이따가 바로잡아 놓을게요.
여: 음… 적어도 천장에 달려있는 네 모형 비행기들은 잘 관리하고 있는 것 같아 다행이네.
남: 제가 가장 좋아하는 거니까요.

어휘 **messy** 엉망인, 지저분한 / **pile up** 쌓아두다 / **ceiling** 천장 / **maintain** 관리하다, 지속하다; 유지하다

05 추후 행동 | ④

▶ 마지막 부분의 Please stay with the dog에서 남자가 해야 할 일을 알 수 있다.

[Phone rings.]
W: Hello, Parkview Animal Hospital. How may I help you?
M: I have an emergency. I was driving down Main Street and **found an injured dog** lying on the street.
W: Is the dog conscious?
M: Yes, he is breathing very heavily and moaning a bit.
W: **Is the owner around**?
M: I'm afraid not. This neighborhood is very quiet at this time of day.
W: Then you're going to have to bring the dog in yourself.
M: I don't think I can. I am very allergic to dogs and if I touch him, I **won't be able to breathe**. And then we will both need a doctor.
W: OK. Please stay with the dog and we will send someone to pick him up.

[전화벨이 울린다.]
여: 여보세요, Parkview 동물 병원입니다. 무엇을 도와 드릴까요?
남: 응급 상황입니다. 제가 Main 가를 따라 운전하던 중에 다친 강아지가 길에 누워있는 것을 발견했어요.
여: 강아지가 의식이 있나요?
남: 네, 힘겹게 숨을 쉬고 있고 조금 끙끙거리고 있어요.
여: 주인이 주위에 있나요?
남: 그렇지 않은 것 같아요. 이 동네는 이 시간이면 매우 인적이 드물어요.
여: 그럼 강아지를 직접 데리고 오셔야 하겠습니다.
남: 안 될 것 같은데요. 제가 강아지에 심한 알레르기가 있어서 만약 제가 강아지를 만진다면 저는 숨을 못 쉴 거예요. 그럼 우리 둘 다 의사가 필요하게 돼요.
여: 알겠습니다. 강아지와 함께 있어 주세요. 그러면 저희가 강아지를 실어 올 사람을 보내겠습니다.

어휘 **emergency** 위급, 비상사태 / **conscious** 의식이 있는 / **moan** 끙끙거리다, 신음하다 / **neighborhood** 지역, 이웃, 구역 / **be allergic to A** A에 알레르기가 있다

06 금액 | ②

▶ 호텔의 200달러 패키지에 성인용 Super Saver 카드를 두 장 구입하면 추가로 30달러가 더 든다.

[Phone rings.]
M: Hepburn Springs Hotel.
W: Hi, I'd like to book a room for two adults and three children for March 21st and 22nd please.
M: We have a special weekend family package then; $200 for two days.
W: I see. **What's included in the package**?
M: Passes to the zoo and the children's museum, worth $90.
W: Sounds good.
M: We also sell a Super Saver card. With this card you can use local restaurants and the hot spring spas **at discounted prices**.
W: How much is that?
M: $15 per adult. It's **not available for children**.
W: Really? OK, great. I'll buy two cards then.
M: All right, to confirm: 21st and 22nd of March, $200 package plus the Super Saver cards for two adults.
W: Yes, that's right.

[전화벨이 울린다.]
남: Hepburn Springs 호텔입니다.
여: 안녕하세요. 성인 두 명과 어린이 세 명이 3월 21일부터 22일까지 묵을 수 있는 방을 예약하고 싶습니다.
남: 그러시다면 저희는 주말 가족 특별 패키지를 운영하고 있습니다. 이틀에 200달러입니다.
여: 그렇군요. 패키지에 무엇이 포함되나요?
남: 가격이 90달러인 동물원과 어린이 박물관 입장권입니다.
여: 좋네요.
남: 저희는 Super Saver 카드도 판매하고 있습니다. 이 카드로 지역 식당과 온천을 할인가에 이용하실 수 있습니다.
여: 그건 얼마인가요?
남: 성인은 15달러씩이고, 어린이는 이용할 수 없습니다.
여: 그래요? 좋습니다. 그럼 카드 두 장을 사겠습니다.
남: 그럼 확인해 드리겠습니다. 3월 21일과 22일이고, 200달러 패키지에 성인 두 명의 Super Saver 카드를 구입하시는 것입니다.
여: 네, 맞습니다.

어휘 **hot spring** 온천 / **confirm** 확인하다

07 이유 | ③

▶ 남자의 컴퓨터가 고장 나서 아침에 수리점에 맡겼는데 그것이 정오쯤 되어야 수리될 거라서 오전 회의에 가지 못한다고 말하고 있다.

[Cell phone rings.]
M: Hello.
W: Hi, Dan. What's up? Did something happen?
M: Yes, it did. **The meeting is supposed to start** at 10 this morning, right?
W: Yes, exactly. No specific changes have been made to the schedule yet. Is there something wrong with the test results?
M: I don't have them yet. My computer crashed last night and **I was working all through the night** to retrieve the file.
W: Oh, no. Please don't tell me that you've lost the entire file.
M: Well, not exactly. I did back it up.
W: Oh, **that's a huge relief**. You really scared me!
M: I took my computer to the shop first thing this morning. They say it will be ready by noon so I'm afraid I can't get to the meeting in time.
W: Well, **I am relieved** that you didn't lose the file.
M: I will print it out as soon as I get my hands on it.
W: Thank you. I'll put off the meeting until later this afternoon.

[휴대전화가 울린다.]
남: 여보세요.
여: 안녕, Dan. 무슨 일이에요? 무슨 일이 일어났어요?
남: 예, 그래요. 회의를 오늘 아침 10시에 시작하기로 했죠, 맞죠?
여: 예, 맞아요. 아직 일정에 특별한 변화가 생기지는 않았어요. 시험 결과에 잘못된 게 있나요?
남: 아직 그게 없어요. 내 컴퓨터가 어젯밤에 갑자기 고장 나서 파일을 복구하느라 밤새 일을 하고 있었어요.
여: 아, 안 돼. 파일을 몽땅 잃어버렸다고 말하지는 말아줘요.
남: 음, 꼭 그런 건 아니에요. 그걸 백업했거든요.
여: 아, 그건 천만다행이네요. 정말 깜짝 놀랐잖아요!
남: 오늘 아침에 제일 먼저 내 컴퓨터를 수리점으로 가져갔어요. 수리점에서 컴퓨터가 정오까지 준비될 거라고 해서 난 회의에 제시간에 갈 수 없을 것 같아요.
여: 음, 파일을 잃어버리지 않았다니 안심이에요.
남: 내가 그걸 손에 넣는 대로 바로 프린트할게요.
여: 고마워요. 내가 회의를 오늘 오후로 연기할게요.

어휘 **crash** 갑자기 고장 나다 / **retrieve** 복구[회복]하다; 되찾다 / **back up** (파일 · 프로그램 등을) 백업하다 / **relief** 안심 *cf.* **relieved** 안심[안도]하는 / **first thing** 맨 먼저 / **in time** 시간 맞춰 / **get one's hand on** (필요한 것을) 손에 넣다 / **put off** 연기하다

08 언급하지 않은 것 | ④

▶ 해석 참조

M: Nicole, do you have a minute?
W: Sure, Darren. What's up?
M: Well, the boss **has asked me to come up with a good way** to market our company's new line of printers.
W: TV commercials have been successful in the past. **Why not stick with what works**?
M: That was my first idea, too. But we don't have the money right now.

W: How about providing more training to our sales staff?
M: That could help. I'd also like to make some new brochures.
W: Good idea! The old brochures **fail to demonstrate** the features of our new printers.
M: Right. And I think a sale would attract some new customers.
W: I'll talk to Dave about that. He'll know **the lowest price we can offer**.
M: Thanks. I think we have a good plan.

남: Nicole, 시간 좀 있어요?
여: 그럼요, Darren. 무슨 일인가요?
남: 저, 상사가 제게 회사의 새 프린터 제품군을 판매할 좋은 방안에 대해 생각해내라고 하셨거든요.
여: 지금까지 TV 광고(① TV 광고 제작)가 성공적이었잖아요. 효과가 있는 것을 계속해보는 게 어때요?
남: 저도 처음에 그걸 생각해봤어요. 그런데 우린 지금 당장 자금이 없어서요.
여: 판매 사원 교육(② 판매 사원 교육)을 더 늘려 보는 건 어떤가요?
남: 도움이 될 수 있겠네요. 새 광고 책자도 만들고 싶어요(③ 광고 책자 제작).
여: 좋은 생각이에요! 기존 광고 책자는 새 프린터기의 특징을 제대로 보여주지 못해요.
남: 맞아요. 그리고 할인 판매(⑤ 할인 판매 행사)를 하면 신규 고객을 모을 수 있을 거예요.
여: Dave에게 그것에 관해 이야기해 봐야겠어요. 그는 우리가 제시할 수 있는 최저 가격을 알고 있을 거예요.
남: 고마워요. 좋은 계획을 세운 것 같군요.

어휘 **stick with** ~을 계속하다; ~의 곁에 머물다

09 내용 불일치 | ②

▶ 지원자는 언론과 관련된 분야를 전공해야만 한다고 했다.

M: The Sun Broadcasting Company is calling aspiring journalists. We offer a summer internship program every year, and it starts this July. For students who are thinking about a career in journalism, this internship is **an excellent chance to gain experience** in the broadcasting industry. But there are some things you should be aware of **before applying for the program**. First, applicants should be majoring in a related field of journalism. Second, the internship is available to college graduates as well as current college students, but when it comes to college students, only seniors can apply. Lastly, interested applicants should submit a résumé and a cover letter by April 26th. You **will be individually notified of the results** during the following week.

남: The Sun 방송국에서 패기 있는 기자를 모집하고 있습니다. 저희는 매년 여름 인턴십 프로그램을 제공하고 있으며, 이 인턴십은 올해 7월에 시작합니다. 언론 분야에서 일하고 싶은 학생들에게 이 인턴십은 방송 산업에서 경험을 쌓는 절호의 기회입니다. 단, 여러분이 이 프로그램에 지원하기 전에 알아야 할 몇 가지 사항이 있습니다. 첫째, 지원자는 언론과 관련된 분야를 전공해야만 합니다. 둘째, 인턴십 프로그램은 현재 대학을 다니는 학생뿐 아니라 대학 졸업생도 지원할 수 있습니다만, 대학 재학생의 경우에는 4학년만 지원할 수 있습니다. 끝으로, 관심 있는 지원자는 이력서와 자기소개서를 4월 26일까지 제출해야 합니다. 결과는 그다음 주에 개별적으로 통보해 드릴 것입니다.

어휘 **aspiring** 패기 있는, 야심이 있는 / **journalism** 언론계 / **résumé** 이력서 / **cover letter** 자기소개서

10 도표 이해 | ④

▶ 남자의 어머니는 힙합을 좋아하지 않고, 여성 가수를 선호하며, 더 오래된 곡이 좋을 것 같다고 했으므로 답은 ④이다.

M: Paige, you enjoy listening to music, don't you?
W: Of course. I love music.
M: Can you help me then?
W: Sure. What is it?
M: I made a video for my mom's birthday, and I was wondering if you could help me choose the background music for the video.
W: Oh, that's so sweet of you. I'd love to **help you choose something**. Wait a minute. *[pause]* Choose a song from the list of five songs here. They're all good.
M: Thanks. My mom isn't fond of hip hop, so we'll skip those two.
W: **What looks appealing to you**? Is there a particular artist that your mom likes?
M: She prefers listening to female artists.
W: Then you'll have to choose from these two.
M: I think **the older song would be better**. She might not know some of the new songs. I really appreciate your help.
W: It's my pleasure. I'm sure your mom is going to be thrilled.

남: Paige, 너 음악 듣는 거 좋아하지?
여: 물론이지, 난 음악을 매우 좋아해.
남: 그럼 나 좀 도와줄래?
여: 그럼. 무슨 일인데?
남: 어머니 생신을 위해 동영상을 제작했는데, 동영상에 쓸 배경 음악을 고르는 데 네가 날 도와줄 수 있을까 해서.
여: 오, 너 무척 자상하구나. 네가 선택하는 걸 돕고 싶어. 잠깐 기다려. *[잠시 후]* 여기 있는 다섯 곡 중에서 한 곡을 골라봐. 그것들은 전부 괜찮아.
남: 고마워. 우리 어머니는 힙합을 좋아하지 않으셔서 이 두 곡은 뺄 거야.
여: 무엇이 너에게 흥미로워 보이니? 어머니께서 특별히 좋아하시는 가수가 있니?
남: 어머니는 여성 가수의 노래를 듣는 것을 선호하셔.
여: 그럼 이 두 곡 중에서 선택해야 할 거야.
남: 더 오래된 곡이 더 좋을 것 같아. 어머니는 새로운 곡을 잘 모르실 것 같거든. 도와줘서 정말로 고마워.
여: 천만에. 분명 너희 어머니께서 감격하실 거야.

어휘 **be fond of** ~을 좋아하다 / **appealing** 흥미로운, 매력적인; 호소하는 / **female** 여성(의) (↔ male 남성(의)) / **thrilled** 황홀해하는, 아주 흥분한[신이 난]

11 짧은 대화에 이어질 응답 | ②

▶ 제출해야 할 기말 보고서를 교수님에게 이메일로 보냈으나 반송되었다는 남자의 말에 적절한 응답을 고른다.

① 내 보고서를 보낼 때 네 것도 보낼게.
② 그래? 왜 그런 일이 일어났는지 알아보자.
③ Holstein 교수님은 언제나 아주 늦게 답장하셔.
④ 네가 나한테 다시 보내주는 걸 깜빡한 게 틀림없어.
⑤ 그건 아마 내가 이메일 주소를 바꿨기 때문일 거야.

M: Bell, did you submit your term paper to Professor Holstein?
W: Yes, I **turned it in this morning**. Did you?
M: Actually, I just sent an e-mail, but **it was returned**.
W: ______________________________

남: Bell, Holstein 교수님께 기말 보고서 제출했니?
여: 응, 오늘 아침에 제출했어. 너도 제출했니?
남: 실은, 나는 방금 이메일로 보냈는데 반송됐어.
여: ______________________________

어휘 **submit** 제출하다 / **term paper** 학기말 보고서 / **turn A in** A를 제출하다

12 짧은 대화에 이어질 응답 | ④

▶ 영화의 주연 배우가 누구인지 묻는 말에 그 배우의 이름은 모르지만 멋지다는 응답이 가장 적절하다.

① 배우가 되는 것은 굉장히 힘들어.
② 그는 영화 마지막에 숨을 거둬.
③ 공포 영화는 썩 마음에 내키지 않아.
④ 이름은 모르지만, 멋진 배우야.
⑤ 내 남동생은 아역 배우였어.

W: Jay, *Vampire Horror* **is on in a few minutes**. Do you want to watch it?
M: I saw it before, but I'd love to watch it again.
W: Okay. By the way, do you know **who the leading actor is**?
M: ______________________________

여: Jay야, 〈Vampire Horror〉가 곧 시작해. 볼래?
남: 전에 봤어. 하지만 또 보고 싶어.
여: 알겠어. 그나저나, 주연 배우가 누구인지 알아?
남: ______________________________

13 긴 대화에 이어질 응답 | ①

▶ 한국에서 지낸 지 6개월이 되었지만 여전히 바닥에 앉는 것이 불편한 여자가 할 수 있는 말을 찾는다.

① 글쎄, 난 익숙해지지가 않아.
② 내가 어디에 앉으면 좋겠니?
③ 나는 네가 더 연습해야 한다고 생각해.
④ 나도 그래. 난 항상 바닥에 앉았어.
⑤ 어릴 때 그것들을 많이 사용했어.

M: You use chopsticks really well, Wendy.
W: Well, I **could use them well** before I came to Korea.
M: Oh? How did you learn to use them?
W: Well, when I was living in Canada, I used to go to many Asian restaurants. And in those restaurants I **always used chopsticks to eat**.
M: I see. But I'm sorry to say that you don't look too comfortable sitting on the floor.
W: Actually, I'm not. I never sat on the floor until I came here.
M: Really?
W: Yeah. And I've been here for six months, but when I sit on the floor, I **still don't feel comfortable**.
M: Oh, that's too bad. I grew up sitting on the floor. It's natural for me.
W: ____________________

남: 젓가락질을 정말 잘하는구나, Wendy.
여: 음, 한국에 오기 전부터 젓가락을 잘 사용했어.
남: 그래? 어떻게 사용법을 배우게 되었니?
여: 음, 캐나다에 살 때 아시아 식당에 많이 다니곤 했어. 그 식당들에서 항상 젓가락을 사용해서 음식을 먹었어.
남: 그렇구나. 그런데 미안한 말이지만 바닥에 앉아 있는 게 그다지 편안해 보이지는 않는구나.
여: 사실, 편하지 않아. 여기 오기 전에는 한 번도 바닥에 앉아 본 적이 없어.
남: 정말?
여: 응, 그리고 여기서 6개월을 살았는데도 바닥에 앉으면 여전히 불편해.
남: 아, 안됐구나. 난 좌식 생활을 하면서 자라서 나에겐 그것이 자연스러워.
여: ____________________

어휘 **grow up v-ing** v하면서 자라다 | 선택지 어휘 | **get used to A** A에 익숙해지다

14 긴 대화에 이어질 응답 | ④

▶ 아들이 열심히 하고 있는지 확신이 없던 어머니에게 최선을 다하고 있는 아들이 할 수 있는 적절한 대답을 찾는다.

① 죄송합니다만, 잘 안 들려요.
② 아니요, 제가 기억하는 한 그게 맞아요.
③ 괜찮아요. 작년에 정말 열심히 공부했거든요.
④ 걱정하지 마세요. 실망시키지 않겠다고 약속할게요.
⑤ 안됐네요. 할머니께서 빨리 나으시면 좋겠어요.

M: Good morning, Mom. When did you come home?
W: Around 2 a.m. You were sleeping then. Did you study last night?
M: Yes, I did. Don't worry.
W: I visited Grandma and Grandpa. They **are not doing so well these days**.
M: I know. How is Grandma's back?
W: Not good. But there is **not much she can do about it**. Is your school bag ready?
M: I just have to put the homework I was doing last night in it.
W: I'm glad to see you're working harder. Remember you promised **to raise your grades**.
M: I know. I didn't study much last year. But I'm doing my best now.
W: Well, that's good to hear. I **wasn't sure about that**.
M: ____________________

남: 안녕히 주무셨어요, 엄마. 언제 집에 오신 거예요?
여: 새벽 2시쯤. 넌 그때 자고 있더구나. 어젯밤에 공부는 했니?
남: 네, 했어요. 걱정 마세요.
여: 할머니와 할아버지를 찾아뵈었단다. 요즘 건강이 그렇게 좋지 않으시거든.
남: 알아요. 할머니는 허리가 좀 어떠세요?
여: 좋지 않으셔. 하지만 할머니가 하실 수 있는 것이 별로 없더구나. 책가방은 챙겼니?
남: 어젯밤에 하던 숙제만 넣으면 돼요.
여: 네가 더 열심히 공부하는 모습을 보니 기쁘구나. 성적을 올리겠다고 약속한 것을 잊지 마라.
남: 알아요. 작년에는 공부를 많이 안 했지만 지금은 최선을 다하고 있어요.
여: 음, 반가운 소리구나. 그것에 대해 확신이 없었거든.
남: ____________________

어휘 **do well** (건강 상태가) 양호하다 | 선택지 어휘 | **let A down** A를 실망시키다

15 상황에 적절한 말 | ④

▶ 맛있는 음식을 남기게 되어 아쉽다는 Stacy의 말에 동의하는 Kevin은 남은 음식을 포장해 가자는 말을 할 것이다.

① 우리가 음식을 너무 많이 주문한 것 같아요.
② 우리 다음번에는 그렇게 많이 요리해선 안 돼요.
③ 우리의 기념일을 위한 훌륭한 선택이었어요.
④ 종업원에게 음식을 싸달라고 해봐요.
⑤ 아마 나는 이따가 다시 배가 고플 거예요.

W: Today is Kevin and Stacy's third anniversary. To celebrate, the couple **made reservations for dinner** at a fancy restaurant. There, they ate, drank, and talked about their life together. They both had a wonderful time and greatly enjoyed the delicious food. Kevin ordered a steak and lobster dish, and Stacy had the baked salmon. **Both were surprised** by the size of the meals. Now as the evening **comes to an end**, there is still a lot of food remaining. Stacy mentions that it's a shame to waste such delicious food. Kevin agrees and thinks it would be a good idea to **take the food home to eat later**. In this situation, what would Kevin most likely say to Stacy?

여: 오늘은 Kevin과 Stacy의 세 번째 기념일이다. 이를 기념하기 위해, 둘은 고급 식당에 저녁 식사를 예약했다. 거기에서 그들은 먹고 마시며 삶에 관한 이야기를 함께 나누었다. 그들 둘 다 즐거운 시간을 보내고 맛있는 음식도 매우 즐겼다. Kevin은 스테이크와 바닷가재 요리를 주문하고, Stacy는 구운 연어를 먹었다. 둘은 주문한 요리의 엄청난 양에 놀랐다. 이제 저녁 시간이 끝나 가는데 여전히 많은 양의 음식이 남아있다. Stacy는 그렇게 맛있는 음식을 버리다니 아쉽다고 말한다. Kevin도 동의하며 나중에 먹을 수 있도록 음식을 집으로 가져가는 것이 좋겠다고 생각한다. 이러한 상황에서 Kevin이 Stacy에게 할 말로 가장 적절한 것은 무엇인가?

16~17 세트 문항 | 16. ③ 17. ④

▶ 16. 코골이의 원리와 원인을 설명하고 있다.

① 코골이에 대처하는 방법
② 숙면을 방해하는 요인
③ 사람들이 코를 고는 원리와 이유
④ 인간 코의 기능
⑤ 코골이가 건강에 미치는 영향

▶ 17. 해석 참조

M: Snoring is instantly recognizable. It's the loud sound that **some of us make when sleeping**. In the worst cases, the animal-like sounds of a person snoring can awaken even the heaviest sleeper in a nearby bed. But your noisy, dreaming roommate isn't trying to wake you on purpose. When we fall asleep, our muscles begin to relax. This causes our throats to contract. And a smaller throat has **less room for air to pass through**. In some people, this narrowing of the throat is extreme. When air is forced through such a tight throat, the back of the throat vibrates. The vibration is what produces **the sound we all know as snoring**. Some common causes of snoring include sleeping with your head up too high on pillows, illnesses and allergies that cause excess fluid in the throat, and obesity. Physical factors, such as an extraordinarily small jaw or short neck, **can also play a role**. Of course, some of these factors cannot be controlled, but others can, meaning there is some hope for the snorer's family.

남: 코를 고는 것은 즉각적으로 알 수 있습니다. 그것은 우리 중 몇몇 사람들이 잘 때 내는 큰 소리입니다. 최악의 경우에는, 코를 고는 사람이 내는 동물 같은 소리가 근처 침대에서 숙면을 취하고 있는 사람까지 깨울 수 있습니다. 하지만 시끄럽게 잠을 자는 당신의 룸메이트는 고의로 당신을 깨우려는 것이 아닙니다. 우리가 잠이 들 때, 근육이 이완하기 시작합니다. 이는 목구멍을 수축하게 합니다. 그리고 목구멍이 좁아지면 공기가 드나들 공간이 더 적어집니다. 어떤 사람들에게는, 이렇게 목구멍이 좁아지는 것이 심합니다. 공기가 그런 비좁은 목구멍을 억지로 통과하게 되면, 목구멍 뒤편이 진동합니다. 이 진동이 우리가 코골이로 알고 있는 소리를 만들어내는 것입니다. 코골이의 몇 가지 흔한 원인으로는 ① 높은 베개 베고 자기, 목에 과도한 분비액을 만드는 질병이나 ② 알레르기, ③ 비만이 있습니다. 이례적으로 작은 턱이나 ⑤ 짧은 목과 같은 신체적인 요소들도 원인으로 작용합니다. 물론 이러한 요소들 중 일부는 통제될 수 없지만, 다른 요인들은 통제될 수 있는데, 이는 코를 고는 사람의 가족들에게 희망이 있다는 것을 의미합니다.

어휘 **snore** 코를 골다 / **recognizable** 알아볼[분간할] 수 있는 / **on purpose** 고의로 / **contract** 수축하다; 계약하다 / **vibrate** 진동하다, 흔들리다 ***cf.* vibration** 진동 / **pillow** 베개 / **excess** 과도한 / **fluid** (동식물의) 분비액 / **obesity** 비만 / **extraordinarily** 이례적으로, 엄청나게 | 선택지 어휘 | **deal with** 처리하다; 대처하다 / **disturb** 방해하다

01. ②	02. ②	03. ③	04. ⑤	05. ④	06. ②	07. ②	08. ③	09. ⑤	10. ②
11. ⑤	12. ②	13. ②	14. ①	15. ⑤	16. ②	17. ④			

01 화자가 하는 말의 목적 | ②

▶ 학교 봄 축제 내용과 그중 가장 인기 있는 행사인 미술전을 상세히 소개하고 있다.

W: Good afternoon, students. I hope you are **adjusting to the new school year and new classes**. Following tradition, the spring school festival will begin next week. **All students are invited to participate**. There will be a play, music performances, and much more to enjoy. In past years, the most popular event has been the art show. It will be held from 9 a.m. to 5 p.m. with many works of art and festival pictures **on display**. Those who wish to set up an art booth should sign up now. Art booths will be located next to the gym, but space is limited. You are welcome to display any paintings, sculptures, drawings, or other artwork at your booth. We hope everyone enjoys the festival, and **don't forget to bring** your friends and family!

여: 안녕하세요, 학생 여러분. 여러분이 새 학년과 새로운 수업에 적응하고 있기를 바랍니다. 전통에 따라, 학교 봄 축제가 다음 주에 시작될 것입니다. 모든 학생이 참여하도록 초대합니다. 연극, 음악 공연 그리고 즐길 만한 훨씬 더 많은 것들이 있을 것입니다. 지난 몇 해 동안 가장 인기 있는 행사는 미술전이었습니다. 전시회는 오전 9시부터 오후 5시까지 열리며 많은 미술 작품과 축제 사진이 전시될 것입니다. 미술 부스를 설치하기 원하는 분들은 지금 신청해야 합니다. 미술 부스들은 체육관 옆에 위치할 것이지만 공간이 제한되어 있습니다. 여러분의 부스에 그림이나 조각, 소묘 또는 그 밖의 어떤 미술 작품이든 전시해도 좋습니다. 모두가 축제를 즐기길 바라며, 여러분의 친구들과 가족을 데려오는 것을 잊지 마세요!

어휘 **adjust to A** A에 적응하다 / **on display** 전시된, 진열된 / **set up** 설치하다; 세우다; 새로 시작하다 / **booth** 부스, (칸막이를 한) 작은 공간 / **sign up** 신청[참가]하다 / **sculpture** 조각(상) / **drawing** (색을 칠하지 않은) 소묘, 그림

02 의견 | ②

▶ 동네에 공원이 없어 먼 곳까지 와야 하고 동네 주민들이 운동하거나 놀 곳이 없으므로 새로운 공원 건설이 필요하다고 말하고 있다.

M: Hi, Hazel. I'm surprised to see you here.
W: Yes, well, I come here to play badminton when I can.
M: It's **a long way from your home**, right?
W: It takes about 25 minutes on the subway, but there aren't any parks in my neighborhood.
M: I guess this is **one of the few large parks** on this side of the city.
W: Right. The city was planning to build another park in my neighborhood, but the plans were cancelled.
M: I remember that. A new concert hall was built on that location instead.
W: Right. It's a shame because the concert hall is rarely used and the residents of my neighborhood have **nowhere to exercise or play**.
M: I agree. I hope the city reconsiders building some new parks.

남: 안녕, Hazel. 여기서 널 보다니 놀라운데.
여: 그래, 음, 난 올 수 있을 때 배드민턴을 치러 여기 와.
남: 너희 집에서 거리가 멀지?
여: 지하철로 25분 정도 걸리지만, 우리 동네에는 공원이 하나도 없거든.
남: 여기가 도시 이쪽 편에 있는 몇 안 되는 큰 공원 중 하나인 것 같아.
여: 맞아. 시(市)에서 우리 동네에 공원을 하나 더 지을 계획이었지만 취소됐지.
남: 기억나. 대신 새로운 공연장이 그 위치에 지어졌잖아.
여: 맞아. 그 공연장은 좀처럼 사용되지 않고 우리 동네 주민들은 운동하거나 놀 곳이 아무 데도 없으니 애석한 일이야.
남: 동의해. 시(市)에서 새로운 공원 건설을 재고하면 좋겠어.

어휘 **resident** 주민, 거주자 / **reconsider** 재고하다, 다시 생각하다

03 관계 | ③

▶ 남자는 바이올린을 구매하려는 고객이며, 여자는 악기를 추천해주고 영업시간을 말하는 것으로 보아 악기 판매원이다.

W: Excuse me, is there anything I can help you with?
M: Well, I'm actually shopping for my daughter. She's in a band.
W: You're a good father. What instrument does she play?
M: **She's been playing the piano** for years, and she also plays the guitar. She's so talented.
W: That's impressive. Maybe I should show you our selection of acoustic guitars.
M: Actually, she's been talking about learning the violin. That's why I'm here.
W: I see. Well, the violins you see here are all good quality.
M: **Can you recommend one** as a gift for her?
W: Hmm, the size can make a big difference. I could recommend one based on her age, but **it would be better to bring** your daughter to the store.
M: Oh, I hadn't thought of that. You've saved me from a big mistake. I'll return on a later date.
W: No problem. Come back anytime. We're open every day until eight.

여: 실례합니다, 제가 도와드릴 게 있을까요?
남: 음, 사실 저는 딸을 위해 쇼핑 중이에요. 딸아이는 밴드부에 속해 있죠.
여: 훌륭한 아버지시네요. 따님은 어떤 악기를 연주하나요?
남: 몇 년 동안 피아노를 쭉 치고 있고 기타도 연주합니다. 아주 재능이 있어요.
여: 굉장하네요. 저희가 엄선한 어쿠스틱 기타들을 보여드려야 할 것 같네요.
남: 사실, 딸아이는 바이올린을 배우는 것에 관해 얘기하고 있어요. 그래서 제가 여기 온 것입니다.
여: 알겠습니다. 음, 여기 보시는 바이올린들은 모두 품질이 좋아요.
남: 딸아이를 위한 선물로 하나 추천해 주시겠어요?
여: 음, 사이즈 때문에 큰 차이가 날 수 있어요. 따님의 나이를 기반으로 하나를 추천해 드릴 수 있지만, 가게로 따님을 데려오시는 게 더 나을 거예요.
남: 아, 그 생각을 못 했네요. 제가 큰 실수를 면하게 해주셨군요. 다음에 다시 오겠습니다.
여: 그렇게 하셔도 됩니다. 언제든 다시 오세요. 저희는 매일 8시까지 엽니다.

어휘 **instrument** 악기; 기구 / **talented** 재능이 있는 / **selection** 선택[선정/선발]된 것들[사람들] / **acoustic** 어쿠스틱, (악기가) 전자 장치를 쓰지 않는 / **based on** ~을 기반[바탕]으로; ~에 근거하여 / **save** (힘들거나 불쾌한 일을) 피하게 하다; 구하다

04 그림 불일치 | ⑤

▶ 여자는 스노보드가 벽에 기대어 있다고 말했다.

W: Come this way, Tyler. I guess this store is having a sale.
M: Oh, you're right. It says, "SALE 50% off," right up there.
W: Wow! **That's a bargain**! We can buy ski equipment at a reasonable price here.
M: That's right. I'm thinking about buying a helmet for skiing. I think the one the mannequin's wearing **would probably look good on me**.
W: I think so too. Oh, look at the mittens. I love them. That style with buckles is in fashion nowadays.
M: You mean the ones on the left?
W: Yes. **Those will perfectly match** with my ski jacket.
M: Great. That would be cool.
W: Oh. Didn't you say you needed ski boots? How about the ones next to the box? They look very comfortable.
M: Yes. Those look perfect. I should check if they have the right size for me.
W: I hope they do. Also, I need to check those snowboards **leaning against the wall**.
M: Okay, let's go inside the store to take a closer look.

여: 이리 와 봐요, Tyler. 이 가게가 할인 판매를 하는 것 같아요.
남: 아, 맞네요. 저 위에 '50퍼센트 할인'이라고 적혀 있어요.
여: 와! 정말 싸네요! 여기서 스키 장비를 싸게 살 수 있겠어요.
남: 그래요. 나는 스키용 헬멧을 살까 생각 중이에요. 마네킹이 착용하고 있는 헬멧이 나한테 잘 어울릴 것 같아요.

여: 그런 것 같네요. 아, 벙어리장갑 좀 봐요. 맘에 드는데요. 버클 달린 스타일이 요즘 유행이에요.
남: 왼쪽에 있는 거 말이에요?
여: 네. 저게 내 스키 재킷과 잘 어울릴 것 같아요.
남: 좋네요. 멋지겠네요.
여: 아, 스키 부츠 필요하다고 하지 않았어요? 저 상자 옆에 있는 건 어때요? 무척 편해 보여요.
남: 네. 딱 좋겠어요. 나에게 맞는 치수가 있는지 확인해봐야겠어요.
여: 있으면 좋겠어요. 그리고 나는 벽에 기대어 세워진 스노보드를 좀 봐야겠어요.
남: 좋아요. 가게 안으로 들어가서 자세히 보도록 하죠.

어휘 **bargain** 싼 물건, 특가품 / **equipment** 장비 / **mannequin** 마네킹 / **mitten** 벙어리장갑 / **buckle** 버클, 잠금장치 / **lean against** ~에 기대어 있다

05 부탁한 일 | ④

▶ 여자는 다른 아이들로부터 선물 살 돈을 모아 달라고 부탁했다.

W: Do you know that it's Wendy's birthday on Friday?
M: Oh, I forgot. How old will she be?
W: Fifteen, **the same age as us**.
M: I'll have to go and buy her a present.
W: I thought we could collect some money from everyone and then buy her one nice present.
M: Good idea. How much would you like everyone to give? Five dollars?
W: Yes, **that sounds reasonable**.
M: OK. *[pause]* Here's my money.
W: Actually, I was wondering **if you could do me a favor** and collect the money from everyone.
M: Oh? OK.
W: If you do that, I'll be the one who'll go and buy the gift.
M: I don't have a problem with that.

여: 금요일이 Wendy의 생일인 것 알고 있니?
남: 아, 잊고 있었다. 그 애가 몇 살이 되는 거지?
여: 열다섯 살. 우리랑 동갑이야.
남: 가서 선물을 사 줘야겠네.
여: 모두에게서 돈을 모아 좋은 선물 하나를 사 줬으면 하는 생각인데.
남: 좋은 생각이야. 모두 얼마씩 내면 좋겠니? 5달러?
여: 응, 그게 적당한 것 같다.
남: 알겠어. *[잠시 후]* 이건 내 몫이야.
여: 실은, 내 부탁을 들어줄 수 있는지 궁금해. 모두에게서 돈을 모아 주었으면 해.
남: 그래? 좋아.
여: 네가 그렇게 해 주면 선물은 내가 사러 갈게.
남: 그건 문제없어.

어휘 **do A a favor** A의 부탁을 들어주다, A에게 호의를 베풀다

06 금액 | ②

▶ 남자는 여자에게 역기와 DVD를 사기로 했다. 역기는 50달러이고, DVD는 원래 30달러인데 반값인 15달러에 주기로 했으므로 지불할 총 금액은 65달러이다.

[Phone rings.]
M: Hello.
W: Hello, Peter? This is Kelly. **You agreed to buy the weights** that I advertised on the gym's noticeboard for $50, right?
M: That's right. Is there a problem? You said you could deliver them tomorrow.
W: Yes, but, I just checked on the map and your house **is very far from mine**. I wonder if you could also pay me $10 for gas.
M: I beg your pardon, but we already agreed on a total price.
W: Yes, you're right. But **fuel costs are so high**. Okay forget it, same price.
M: Good. Umm.... Kelly, do you still have the weight training DVDs for $30?
W: Yes, I do. If you like, you can **have them half-price**.
M: Great. I'll buy them too. And you'll deliver both the weights and DVDs tomorrow?
W: Yes, I'll be there at 10.

[전화벨이 울린다.]
남: 여보세요.
여: 여보세요. Peter 씨? Kelly입니다. 당신이 제가 체육관 게시판에 광고한 역기를 50달러에 사기로 하셨죠?
남: 맞아요. 무슨 문제가 있나요? 내일 배달해 주실 수 있다고 말씀하셨잖아요.
여: 네. 하지만 방금 지도를 확인했는데 Peter 씨 집이 저희 집에서 매우 멀더군요. 기름값으로 10달러를 더 주실 수 있는지 궁금해서요.
남: 미안하지만, 우리는 이미 총 가격에 합의했잖아요.
여: 네, 맞습니다. 하지만 연료비가 너무 비싸서요. 알겠습니다. 잊어버리세요. 동일 가격으로 하겠습니다.
남: 좋아요. 음…. Kelly 씨, 근력 운동용 DVD를 아직 30달러에 파시나요?
여: 네, 팔아요. 원하신다면 반값에 드릴게요.
남: 좋아요. 그것도 살게요. 그러면 내일 역기와 DVD 둘 다 배달해 주실 거죠?
여: 네. 10시에 가겠습니다.

어휘 **weight** 역기; 무게 / **noticeboard** 게시판 / **weight training** 근력 운동

07 이유 | ②

▶ 여자가 사촌의 피아노 연주회에 가져가려고 주문한 꽃다발을 아들이 망가뜨려서 걱정하는 상황이다.

M: Jessica, is everything okay? You look stressed.
W: I am a little stressed. My cousin has a piano recital this evening.
M: That's amazing! **Shouldn't you be happy about that**? What's stressing you out?
W: Of course I am happy. So, I ordered a bouquet of flowers for her.
M: There's no flower shop around here, so **you needed to order it**.
W: Right, the bouquet was delivered by the florist this morning, and I put it in the refrigerator to keep it cool **until it was time to leave** for the recital.
M: What happened?
W: My little son found it and took it to his room and ruined it.
M: Oh, **he thought it was a toy**.
W: Yeah. The recital is in two hours, and I don't know what to do.
M: Your cousin will understand. Hmm.... Maybe there is a flower shop near the recital hall.

남: Jessica, 괜찮니? 힘들어 보여.
여: 난 조금 스트레스를 받은 상태야. 내 사촌이 오늘 저녁에 피아노 연주회가 있거든.
남: 굉장한데! 그거라면 기뻐해야 하지 않아? 뭐가 널 힘들게 하는데?
여: 물론 기쁘지. 그래서 그녀를 위해 꽃다발도 주문했는걸.
남: 이 근처에는 꽃집이 없어서 주문해야 했구나.
여: 맞아. 오늘 아침에 꽃집 주인이 꽃다발을 배달해줬어. 그리고 난 연주회에 갈 시간이 될 때까지 차갑게 보관하려고 그걸 냉장고에 넣어두었거든.
남: 어떻게 됐는데?
여: 내 작은 아들이 그걸 발견하고는 자기 방으로 가져가서 망가뜨렸어.
남: 이런, 그 애는 장난감이라고 생각했나 봐.
여: 맞아. 연주회가 두 시간 후에 있는데, 어떻게 해야 할지 모르겠어.
남: 네 사촌도 이해할 거야. 음…. 어쩌면 연주회장 근처에 꽃집이 있을지도 몰라.

어휘 **recital** 발표회, 연주회 / **bouquet** 부케, 꽃다발 / **florist** 꽃집 주인[직원]

08 언급하지 않은 것 | ③

▶ 해석 참조

W: Take a look at this picture, David.
M: That's the biggest flower I've ever seen. What is it?
W: It's a Rafflesia flower, and it's about 90 cm in diameter. I think we can use it for the topic of our report.
M: Good idea. So, what's the rest of the plant look like?
W: The flower is the whole plant. It can't **survive on its own**.
M: Then it's a parasite living on other plants?
W: Right. Another unusual thing is its smell. It smells like rotting meat!
M: That's disgusting. I'm glad there aren't any growing around here. So, **how does it reproduce**?
W: When it dies, it becomes a sticky pool of seeds and liquid. The seeds stick to the feet of animals and **get carried around**.
M: What an unusual plant!

여: David, 이 사진을 좀 봐.
남: 내가 본 꽃 중에서 가장 큰 꽃인데. 이건 무엇이니?

여: 라플레시아(Rafflesia) 꽃인데 지름이 약 90cm(① 크기)야. 내 생각엔 우리가 이 꽃을 리포트 주제로 쓸 수 있을 것 같아.
남: 좋은 생각이야. 그럼, 이 식물의 나머지 부분은 어떻게 생겼니?
여: 꽃이 그 식물의 전부야. 그 꽃은 혼자서는 생존할 수 없어.
남: 그럼 다른 식물에 들러붙어 사는 기생 식물(② 생존 방식)이란 말이야?
여: 맞아. 한 가지 더 특이한 점은 냄새야. 썩은 고기 냄새가 나(④ 냄새)!
남: 그거 끔찍하다. 이 주변에서 자라고 있는 것이 없어서 다행이다. 그런데 그건 어떻게 번식하지?
여: 그 꽃이 죽으면, 씨앗과 액체가 한데 모여 끈적거리는 상태로 변해. 씨앗은 동물의 발에 붙어서 여기저기 옮겨지지(⑤ 번식 방법).
남: 정말 특이한 식물이구나!

어휘 **diameter** 지름 / **parasite** 기생 동물[식물] / **rot** 썩다, 부패하다 / **reproduce** 번식하다; 복사하다; 재현하다

09 내용 불일치 | ⑤

▶ 이번 달까지 3개월 회원으로 등록하면 특별 할인을 해주는 이벤트를 제공한다고 했다.

M: Summer is coming, and that means it's time to lose some weight, get in shape, and look your best. So, **if you could use some help** fitting into that favorite swimsuit, why not join Wellbeing Fitness? Wellbeing Fitness is a newly-opened fitness center for improving your health. We provide various classes such as aerobics and Pilates. We have **more than 10 personal trainers** who can develop a customized program to help you meet your goals. The use of all facilities, including the shower room and the lockers, **is provided with your membership**. Until the end of this month, we are offering special discounts to those who register for a 3-month membership. Don't miss out on this incredible opportunity **to get fit**!

남: 여름이 다가오고 있습니다. 살을 빼고 몸매를 관리해서 최고의 모습을 보여야 할 때라는 것을 의미하는 거죠. 좋아하는 수영복이 (몸에) 잘 맞도록 도움을 받으시려면, Wellbeing 피트니스에 가입해 보시는 건 어떠세요? Wellbeing 피트니스는 귀하의 건강을 증진하기 위해 새로 개장한 헬스클럽입니다. 저희는 에어로빅과 필라테스 같은 다양한 강좌를 제공하고 있습니다. 귀하의 목표를 달성하도록 돕는 맞춤형 프로그램을 짜드릴 수 있는, 열 명이 넘는 개인 트레이너도 두고 있습니다. 회원으로 등록하시면 샤워실과 라커를 포함한 모든 시설을 이용하실 수 있습니다. 이번 달 말까지, 3개월 회원으로 등록하시는 분들께는 특별 할인을 제공해드리고 있습니다. 몸매를 탄탄하게 가꾸실 이 굉장한 기회를 놓치지 마세요!

어휘 **get in shape** 좋은 몸 상태[몸매]를 유지하다 / **customized** 개개인의 요구에 맞춘 / **miss out on** ~을 놓치다 / **fit** (몸이) 탄탄한, 건강한; 적합한

10 도표 이해 | ②

▶ 두 사람은 이른 아침에 출발하여 오후 5시까지 돌아오는 버스 투어 중에서 점심 식사를 포함하고 일인당 80달러를 넘지 않으며 시청에서 출발하는 것을 선택하기로 했다.

M: Let's take the 1-Day bus tour tomorrow. **I'm tired of walking around** the city.
W: Sounds good. I heard there are several city bus tours, so let's check the Internet.
M: Oh, here we go. There are **a few to choose from**. Let's first decide on the time.
W: We have dinner plans with the Johnson family, so we have to be back here no later than 5 p.m.
M: Then let's take a tour that leaves early in the morning.
W: I agree. How about lunch?
M: Since it's our first time, let's get **a tour that includes lunch**. But I don't want to spend more than $80 per person.
W: Got it. One tour leaves from Grand Station and the other from City Hall.
M: I heard Grand Station is far from here. **It takes an hour to get there**.
W: Then it looks like we have only one choice. It only takes 10 minutes to City Hall.
M: Okay. I think this is our best option.

남: 내일 일일 버스 투어를 하자. 도시를 걸어다니는 게 지겨워.
여: 좋아. 도시 버스 투어가 몇 가지 있다고 들었어. 그러니 인터넷을 확인해보자.
남: 자, 시작해 보자. 선택할 수 있는 게 몇 가지 있네. 먼저 시간을 정하자.
여: Johnson 씨 가족과 저녁 약속이 있으니, 늦어도 오후 5시까지는 이곳에 돌아와야 해.
남: 그러면 아침 일찍 출발하는 투어로 하자.
여: 동의해. 점심은 어떻게 하지?
남: 이번이 처음이니까 점심 식사를 포함하는 투어를 고르자. 하지만 일인당 80달러가 넘는 돈은 쓰고 싶지 않아.
여: 알겠어. 한 투어는 Grand역에서 출발하고 나머지 하나는 시청에서 출발해.
남: Grand역이 여기에서 멀다고 들었어. 거기에 가는 데 한 시간이 걸려.
여: 그러면 우린 한 가지만 선택할 수 있는 것 같은데. 시청까지는 10분밖에 안 걸려.
남: 좋아. 이게 우리에게 최고의 선택인 것 같아.

어휘 **be tired of** ~에 싫증나다 / **no later than** 늦어도 ~까지는 / **include** 포함하다

11 짧은 대화에 이어질 응답 | ⑤

▶ 엄마가 아침에 드시려고 남겨둔 머핀을 알려달라는 여자의 말에 가장 적절한 응답을 고른다.

① 원하면 내 것을 먹어도 돼.
② 어머니께 널 도와주라고 부탁드릴게.
③ 오늘 아침 식사를 만들어줘서 고마워.
④ 머핀을 좀 더 만들자.
⑤ 파란 점들이 있는 거야.

W: I'm hungry. Can I have **one of these muffins**?
M: Sure. Just don't take the blueberry one. Mom is saving it for her breakfast.
W: I can't tell which one that is. **Could you point it out for me**?
M: ______________________________

여: 배고파. 여기 있는 머핀 하나 먹어도 되지?
남: 그럼. 단 블루베리 머핀은 안 돼. 엄마가 아침에 드시려고 남겨두신 거야.
여: 그게 어느 건지 모르겠는데. 좀 알려줄래?
남: ______________________________

12 짧은 대화에 이어질 응답 | ②

▶ 이번 주 출연자가 누구인지 묻는 남자의 말에 가장 적절한 응답을 찾는다.

① 그건 매주 금요일 저녁 9시에 방송해.
② 같이 보면서 알아보자.
③ 최고의 무용수가 항상 우승하는 건 아냐.
④ 심사위원들은 매주 똑같아.
⑤ 내가 가장 좋아하는 배우가 출연하는 로맨틱 코미디 영화가 있어.

M: **Do you mind if I change** the channel? I want to watch a movie.
W: Actually, I was hoping to watch *Dancing with the Stars*. It starts in five minutes.
M: I like that show, too. **Who is on it this week**?
W: ______________________________

남: 채널을 바꿔도 되니? 나는 영화를 보고 싶어.
여: 사실 나는 〈Dancing with the Stars〉를 보고 싶어. 5분 후에 시작해.
남: 나도 그 방송 좋아해. 이번 주에는 누가 출연하지?
여: ______________________________

13 긴 대화에 이어질 응답 | ②

▶ 천장 누수로 보수 담당자를 부르겠다는 남자에게 여자는 그의 번호가 있는지 묻는다. 이에 대한 남자의 적절한 답변을 고른다.

① 걱정하지 마세요. 제가 수도꼭지를 고쳐 드릴 수 있어요.
② 고맙지만 이미 적어 두었어요.
③ 제가 방청소를 해야 하는 걸 어떻게 아셨어요?
④ 알겠어요. 바로 경비원을 부르겠어요.
⑤ 오래 걸리면 안 돼요. 수리공이 곧 도착할 거예요.

[Knock, knock, knock.] [Door opens.]
M: Hi! I'm Jake. I live downstairs from you.
W: Nice to meet you, Jake. I'm Allison. **What brings you up here**?
M: I noticed some water dripping from my bathroom ceiling and wondered if you could check where it's coming from.
W: Really? Let me run and check.
M: Yes, please hurry.
W: *[Pause]* Uh oh. I **left my bathwater running** while I was cooking and forgot about it. I turned the faucet off now.
M: I'm quite sure my ceiling is damaged. It might be expensive to fix.
W: I'm really sorry. I'll pay for the repair.
M: Well, I need to call the maintenance man first.
W: Do you have his number? **I can give it to you**.
M: ______________________________

[똑, 똑, 똑.] [문이 열린다.]
남: 안녕하세요! Jake라고 합니다. 아래층에 살아요.
여: 만나서 반가워요, Jake 씨. 저는 Allison이라고 해요. 무슨 일이시죠?
남: 제 욕실 천장에서 물이 떨어지는 것을 발견했어요. 그래서 물이 어디에서 떨어지는지 확인해주실 수 있을지 알아보려고 왔습니다.
여: 정말요? 빨리 가서 확인하고 올게요.
남: 네, 서둘러 주세요.
여: *[잠시 후]* 아, 이런. 요리하는 동안에 목욕탕 물을 틀어 놓고 잊고 있었어요. 수도꼭지를 방금 잠갔어요.
남: 저희 집 천장이 훼손된 게 분명해요. 수리하려면 비쌀 거예요.
여: 정말 죄송합니다. 제가 수리 비용을 지불할게요.
남: 음, 우선 보수 담당자에게 연락해야겠군요.
여: 그의 번호가 있으세요? 제가 번호를 드릴 수 있어요.
남: ____________________

어휘 **drip** (액체가) 똑똑 떨어지다 / **ceiling** 천장 / **faucet** 수도꼭지 / **maintenance man** (건물의) 보수[정비] 담당자

14 긴 대화에 이어질 응답 | ①

▶ 핑곗거리를 만들어서라도 친구의 전화를 대신 거절해 달라고 부탁하는 남자에게 여자가 할 수 있는 대답을 찾는다.

① 알겠습니다. 제가 처리할게요. 걱정하지 마세요.
② 그분께 선생님께서 수술 중이시라고 말씀드렸어요.
③ 환자분께 선생님을 방문하시라고 할게요.
④ 그분께 5분만 더 기다리시라고 전할까요?
⑤ 나머지 예약을 취소할까요?

W: Good morning, Doctor Silver.
M: Good morning, Judy. **Who am I seeing first** this morning?
W: Mrs. Jenkins is coming in for what she described as flu-like symptoms.
M: OK. And then who?
W: And then you have the Russell twins. Their mother said they are both coughing a lot.
M: Anyone else?
W: Oh, and your friend, Mr. Hill, called. He wants you to call him back **as soon as you get in**.
M: Oh boy. If he calls back, please tell him I'm busy. He **kept asking me to see someone**.
W: He was very insistent that you call him.
M: Well, please make up some kind of excuse. I really don't want to be disturbed by him today.
W: ____________________

여: 안녕하세요, Silver 선생님.
남: 안녕하세요, Judy. 오늘 아침 첫 번째로 진료할 환자는 누구죠?
여: Jenkins 부인이 독감과 비슷한 증상으로 오실 거예요.
남: 알겠습니다. 그 다음은 누구죠?
여: 그런 다음 Russell 씨 댁 쌍둥이입니다. 애들 어머니께서 둘 다 기침을 많이 한다고 하셨어요.
남: 다른 사람은요?
여: 아, 그리고 친구이신 Hill 씨께서 전화하셨습니다. 선생님께서 들어오시는 대로 전화해 달라고 말씀하셨어요.
남: 아, 이런. 그 친구가 다시 전화하면, 내가 바쁘다고 전해 주세요. 자꾸 누굴 만나보라고 해서요.
여: 꼭 전화해 달라고 부탁하셨는데요.
남: 음, 핑곗거리 좀 만들어 주세요. 오늘은 정말 그에게 방해받고 싶지 않아요.
여: ____________________

어휘 **symptom** 증상 / **insistent** 강요하는 / **make up** 꾸며내다 / **disturb** 방해하다

15 상황에 적절한 말 | ⑤

▶ 주문 착오로 이미 50분을 기다린 John은 30분을 더 기다려달라고 말하는 점장에게 불평을 할 것이다.

① 유감스럽게도 경기가 거의 끝난 것 같군요.
② 얼마나 더 오래 걸릴 것 같나요?
③ 저는 치즈 피자가 아니라 페퍼로니 피자를 주문했습니다.
④ 어쩌면 우린 그냥 치즈 피자를 먹어야 할 것 같아요.
⑤ 이미 50분 넘게 기다렸다고요!

W: John has invited some of his friends to his house to watch a football game. After the first half, his team is winning and everyone **is in good spirits**. John decides to order pizza for everyone. He calls the pizza shop and orders two large pepperoni pizzas. The manager tells John **it will take about 20 minutes**. After 30 minutes, the delivery man arrives with three cheese pizzas. John explains that the order is incorrect, and the delivery man returns to the shop. Another 20 minutes passes as everyone grows hungry. John calls to ask about his order. The manager explains that **the order was forgotten** and asks John to wait for 30 minutes. In this situation, what would John most likely say to the manager?

여: John은 그의 친구들 중 몇 명을 집으로 초대해 축구 경기를 보자고 했다. 전반전이 끝나고, 그가 응원하는 팀은 이기고 있으며 모두가 기분이 좋다. John은 모두가 먹을 피자를 주문하기로 한다. 그는 피자 가게에 전화해서 큰 페퍼로니 피자 두 판을 주문한다. 점장은 John에게 20분쯤 걸릴 거라고 말한다. 30분이 지나자, 배달원은 치즈 피자 세 판을 가지고 도착한다. John은 주문한 것과 다르다고 설명하고 배달원은 가게로 돌아간다. 20분이 더 지나자 모두가 배고파한다. John은 전화를 걸어 그가 주문한 것에 대해 묻는다. 점장은 주문을 깜박했다고 설명하고 John에게 30분을 기다려 줄 것을 요청한다. 이러한 상황에서 John이 점장에게 할 말로 가장 적절한 것은 무엇인가?

어휘 **in good spirits** 기분이 좋은

16~17 세트 문항 | 16. ② 17. ④

▶ 16. 독특한 각도와 다양한 시선 처리, 초점 등을 이용하여 인물 사진을 잘 찍을 수 있는 방법에 대해 말하고 있다.

① 풍경 사진을 찍는 방법
② 좋은 인물 사진을 찍는 것에 대한 조언
③ 풍경 사진을 위한 카메라 설정
④ 전문 사진작가가 되는 방법
⑤ 인물 사진과 풍경 사진의 차이점

▶ 17. 해석 참조

① 각도 ② 시선 처리 ③ 거리 ④ 배경 ⑤ 초점

M: On Monday, we discussed many ways of taking remarkable pictures of landscapes while traveling. Today, we're going to **learn to focus on something different**. When you use people as a focal point, it's important for you to create a certain wow factor. For example, instead of using the common method of placing a person in the center, try experimenting with different angles and perspectives. Some good methods are to get up high and shoot down on a person, or to get close to the ground and shoot up. **Another thing to consider** is eye contact. You can have the person look directly at the lens, or **look away from it**. The distance between you and your subject also has a huge impact on the feel of the picture. Don't be afraid to experiment with extreme close-ups. These have the power to capture the full force of an emotion. Also, **play around with the focus** a bit. Sometimes, the perfect way to highlight one subject is to blur out all the others. Hopefully, these strategies will help you **create pictures with varying moods**.

남: 월요일에는 여행할 때 멋진 풍경 사진을 찍을 수 있는 여러 방법들에 대해 이야기 나눴습니다. 오늘은 다른 것에 초점을 맞추는 것을 배울 겁니다. 인물을 (사진의) 초점으로 이용할 때, 어떤 '감탄할 만한 요소'를 만들어 내는 것이 중요합니다. 예를 들어, 인물을 가운데에 두는 흔한 방법을 사용하는 대신에, 다른 ① 각도와 관점으로 실험해 보십시오. 몇몇 괜찮은 방법들은 높이 올라가서 인물을 아래로 찍는 것, 또는 땅바닥에 가까이 다가가 (인물을) 올려 찍는 것입니다. 고려해야 할 또 한 가지는 ② 시선 처리입니다. 인물이 렌즈를 똑바로 바라보거나, 렌즈로부터 눈길을 돌리게 할 수 있습니다. 당신과 피사체 사이의 ③ 거리도 사진이 주는 느낌에 커다란 영향을 미칩니다. 두려워하지 말고 아주 가깝게 클로즈업해보세요. 이것은 감정을 최대한으로 잡아내는 힘이 있습니다. 또한 ⑤ 초점을 살짝만 응용해보세요. 때로 한 물체를 강조하는 제일 좋은 방법은 다른 모든 사물을 흐릿하게 만드는 것입니다. 부디 이 기술들로 여러분이 다양한 분위기의 사진을 만들어내는 데 도움이 되었으면 합니다.

어휘 **remarkable** 주목할 만한, 뛰어난 / **landscape** 풍경, 경치 / **focal point** (관심·활동의) 초점, 중심 / **wow factor** (사람의 마음을 끄는) 놀라운 요소, 감탄 요인 / **perspective** 관점, 시각; 원근법 / **shoot** (영화, 사진을) 찍다 / **highlight** 강조하다 / **blur out** ~을 흐릿하게 만들다 / **varying** 다양한, 변화하는 | 선택지 어휘 | **portrait** 인물 사진, 초상화

01. ① 02. ④ 03. ① 04. ⑤ 05. ⑤ 06. ③ 07. ④ 08. ④ 09. ⑤ 10. ④
11. ④ 12. ④ 13. ② 14. ① 15. ④ 16. ⑤ 17. ⑤

01 화자가 하는 말의 목적 | ①

▶ 다른 세제들의 문제점을 언급하면서 자사 제품의 장점을 말하고 있다. 또한, 웹사이트 방문 시 무료 샘플을 준다는 말을 통해 여자가 하는 말의 목적이 제품 홍보임을 알 수 있다.

M: Most modern household cleaning products contain unnecessary chemicals. **Not only do they cause allergies** and skin disorders in children and illnesses in adults, but they are also destroying our environment. Orange Magic company uses oil from 100 percent organically grown oranges to manufacture our unique cleaning products. Our laboratories conduct careful tests **to ensure product safety and effectiveness**. Our website, orangemagic.com, contains page after page of positive reviews from hundreds of customers. Leave your address when you visit the website and we'll send a free sample set of our bestselling cleaners, so you can **try before you buy**. Satisfaction guaranteed.

남: 대부분의 현대 가정용 세제들은 불필요한 화학 물질을 포함하고 있습니다. 그것들은 어린이에게 알레르기와 피부병을, 성인에게 질병을 일으킬 뿐만 아니라, 우리의 환경을 파괴하고 있습니다. 오렌지 매직 회사는 100퍼센트 유기농으로 재배한 오렌지로부터 얻은 기름을 사용하여 특별한 세제를 만듭니다. 저희 연구실은 제품 안전과 효과를 보장하기 위해 철저한 실험을 합니다. 저희 웹사이트인 orangemagic.com에는 수백 명의 고객이 남긴 긍정적인 후기가 여러 페이지에 걸쳐 담겨 있습니다. 웹사이트를 방문하실 때 주소를 남겨 주시면 가장 잘 팔리는 세제의 무료 샘플 세트를 보내드리오니, 구매 전에 사용해 보십시오. 만족하시리라 보장합니다.

어휘 **household** 가정용의; 가족, 가정 / **disorder** 병, 장애; 무질서, 혼란 / **organically** 유기농으로 / **manufacture** 제조[제작]하다; 제조, 제작 / **conduct** 처리하다, 수행하다 / **ensure** 보장하다 / **effectiveness** 효과, 유효(성) / **guaranteed** 보장된

02 의견 | ④

▶ 여자는 수업 중 질문 기회 및 교수님과 직접 이야기를 나누고 피드백을 받을 기회의 부족을 문제점으로 들며 수업 정원이 많으면 제대로 된 교육을 받을 수 없을 것이라고 말했다.

M: Well, the first day of school is over. How were your classes?
W: They seem alright, but I'm worried about the number of students.
M: My classes were fairly crowded also, but I still **managed to get a seat**.
W: It's not just a matter of getting a seat. For instance, almost everyone in my philosophy class wanted to speak, but **only half of us got the chance**.
M: I suppose it would be nice if classes were smaller.
W: Of course. We need opportunities to talk directly with our professors and get feedback from them.
M: So you think that we aren't getting **the education that we deserve**?
W: With as many students in a class as we have, I don't see how we possibly could be.

남: 자, 학교 첫날이 끝났어. 네 수업들은 어땠니?
여: 괜찮은 것 같았는데 학생 수가 걱정이야.
남: 내가 들은 수업들도 꽤 사람이 많았지만, 그래도 난 간신히 자리를 잡았어.
여: 그저 자리 잡는 것에 관한 문제가 아니야. 이를테면, 내가 들은 철학 수업에서는 거의 모든 학생이 말하고 싶어 했지만, 우리 중 절반에게만 기회가 있었어.
남: 수업 정원이 더 적다면 좋을 것 같아.
여: 당연하지. 우리에게는 교수님과 직접 이야기하고 교수님께 피드백을 받을 기회가 필요해.
남: 그럼 넌 우리가 받아야 마땅한 정도의 교육을 받고 있지 않다고 생각하니?
여: 우리가 듣는 수업의 정원만큼 한 수업에 많은 학생이 있다면, 도대체 (그 정도의 교육을) 어떻게 받을 수 있을지 모르겠어.

어휘 **fairly** 꽤, 상당히; 공정히 / **manage to-v** 간신히 v해내다 / **philosophy** 철학 / **feedback** 피드백, (정보 · 서비스 이용자 등의) 반응[의견]

03 관계 | ①

▶ 여자는 손님을 환영하자는 말로 시작해서 남자에게 계속 질문을 하며 대화를 이끌어 나가는 사회자이고, 남자는 여자의 질문에 자신이 득점을 내고 있고, 연습 도중 부상을 당했으며, 3점 슛 연습을 할 것이라고 답하는 것으로 보아 운동선수이다.

W: Now let's welcome today's guest, Steven Adams. Thank you for coming, Steven.
M: It's my pleasure, Sharon.
W: First off, congratulations on **a great start to the season**. You must be pleased.
M: Winning is a team effort, but yes, I've practiced hard, and I'm scoring points.
W: Now, I've heard a rumor **that you're injured**. Is that true?
M: Unfortunately, it is. It happened during practice when I was running for the ball.
W: Does that mean we won't see you on the court for a while? The fans will be disappointed.
M: Doctors say I can play again in a few weeks. Until then, I'll work on my 3-point shooting.
W: With over 22 points per game, **it's hard to imagine** you have much room for improvement.
M: I appreciate you saying so, but I want to give my best for the fans every time.
W: We hope you recover soon. Thanks for coming, Steven.
M: Thank you, Sharon.

여: 이제 오늘의 손님, Steven Adams를 환영합시다. 와 주셔서 감사합니다, Steven.
남: 천만에요, Sharon.
여: 우선, 이번 시즌의 출발이 좋은 것을 축하드립니다. 기쁘시겠군요.
남: 이기는 것은 팀의 노력이지만, 네, 전 열심히 연습해 왔고, 득점을 하고 있습니다.
여: 이번에 부상을 당했다는 소문을 들었습니다. 사실인가요?
남: 안타깝게도, 사실입니다. 연습 도중 공을 쫓아 달리다가 그 일이 일어났습니다.
여: 그 말은 당분간 코트에서 당신을 볼 수 없을 것이란 뜻인가요? 팬들이 실망할 거예요.
남: 의사 선생님들께서 제가 몇 주 후에는 다시 뛸 수 있다고 말씀하셨어요. 그때까지는 3점 슛 연습에 노력을 들일 거예요.
여: 게임마다 22점이 넘는 득점을 하시는데, 향상할 부분이 많다는 것은 상상하기 힘드네요.
남: 그렇게 말씀해주시니 감사합니다. 그렇지만 팬들을 위해 매 순간 최선을 다하고 싶습니다.
여: 곧 회복하시길 바랍니다. 와 주셔서 감사합니다, Steven.
남: 고맙습니다, Sharon.

어휘 **first off** 우선, 먼저 / **season** (운동 경기 등의) 시즌; 계절; 양념(하다) / **score points** 득점을 하다 / **injure** 부상을 입히다[입다] / **work on** ~에 노력을 들이다 / **appreciate** 감사하다; 감상하다; 진가를 인정하다

04 그림 불일치 | ⑤

▶ 여자는 크랜베리 소스 그릇이 칠면조 뒤에 놓여 있다고 했다.

M: Rebecca, it's about time. Are you done with the Thanksgiving dinner yet?
W: Almost done. Would you **like to take a look**?
M: Okay. *[pause]* Oh, everything looks perfect. And what's this? I've never seen this oval table before.
W: I borrowed it from next door.
M: It will be perfect for 6 people.
W: Honey, I think the turkey in the middle will taste delicious. I cooked it **the way I learned from my grandmother**.
M: It smells good. And what's on the square plate to the left of the turkey?
W: It's a pumpkin pie. The kids will like it.
M: That's my favorite, too. Is **the corn piled up in the basket** from uncle Bill's farm last week?
W: Yes, it's still very fresh.
M: I see. And what's in the bowl with a spoon in it?
W: Do you mean, the bowl behind the turkey? That's cranberry sauce. **It goes perfectly with** turkey.

남: Rebecca, 시간 다 됐는데. 추수감사절 만찬은 준비되었나요?
여: 거의 다 됐어요. 한번 볼래요?
남: 좋아요. *[잠시 후]* 아, 모든 게 완벽해요. 그런데 이건 뭐죠? 이 타원형 식탁은 전에 본 적이

없는데요.
여: 옆집에서 빌려왔어요.
남: 여섯 명이 사용하기에 알맞을 거예요.
여: 여보, 중간에 놓인 칠면조가 맛있을 거예요. 할머니께 배운 방법대로 요리했거든요.
남: 냄새 좋네요. 칠면조 왼쪽 옆에 놓인 사각 접시에 담겨진 건 뭐죠?
여: 그건 호박파이에요. 아이들이 좋아할 거예요.
남: 나도 그거 좋아해요. 바구니에 층층이 쌓여 있는 옥수수는 지난주에 Bill 아저씨 농장에서 가져온 건가요?
여: 네. 아직도 정말 싱싱해요.
남: 알겠어요. 스푼이 담긴 그릇 안엔 뭐가 들어 있죠?
여: 아, 칠면조 뒤에 놓인 그릇 말이에요? 그건 크랜베리 소스에요. 칠면조와 잘 어울리거든요.

어휘 **oval** 타원형의 / **pile up** 층층이 쌓다

05 추후 행동 | ⑤

▶ 여자(어머니)는 허리가 아프다고 했고 남자(아들)는 허리와 목을 주물러 주겠다고 했다.

W: Jimmy, would you **take out the trash**?
M: I think that's what Dad does every night.
W: There's a big bucket **full of food waste** here that he didn't take last night.
M: Actually, Dad said he would take it out tonight.
W: OK, then, I'm going to take a rest.
M: Mom, you look tired.
W: It's my back again. I carried heavy shopping bags home from the market today.
M: You should have a nice hot bath. **Shall I fill** the bathtub for you?
W: No, you need to eat your dinner. It's nearly ready.
M: Come sit down for just a few minutes, Mom. Let me rub your back and neck.
W: All right, Jimmy. But **don't leave your dinner too long**!
M: Don't worry, it won't get cold.

여: Jimmy야, 쓰레기를 밖에 내놓아 주겠니?
남: 그건 아빠가 매일 밤 하시는 일이잖아요.
여: 음식물 쓰레기가 가득 차 있는 큰 통이 여기 있는데, 아빠가 어젯밤에 치우지 않으셨구나.
남: 실은 아빠가 오늘 밤에 그것을 내놓으시겠다고 말씀하셨어요.
여: 알았다. 그럼 나는 좀 쉴게.
남: 엄마, 피곤해 보이세요.
여: 또 허리 때문이란다. 오늘 시장에서 집까지 무거운 장바구니를 들고 왔거든.
남: 뜨거운 물로 목욕하시는 게 좋겠어요. 제가 욕조에 물을 받아 드릴까요?
여: 아니다. 너는 저녁을 먹어야지. 준비가 거의 다 되었단다.
남: 오셔서 몇 분만 앉아 계세요, 엄마. 제가 허리와 목을 주물러 드릴게요.
여: 그래, Jimmy. 하지만 저녁 식사를 너무 오래 놔두어서는 안 돼!
남: 걱정하지 마세요. 식지 않을 거예요.

어휘 **bucket** 통, 양동이 / **bathtub** 욕조 / **rub** 주무르다, 문지르다

06 금액 | ③

▶ 하이힐은 표시된 가격인 200달러에서 30퍼센트 할인되므로 140달러이고, 캐주얼 슈즈는 50퍼센트 할인된 가격이 40달러라고 했으므로 여자가 지불할 금액은 180달러가 된다.

W: Excuse me, I like these two pairs of shoes, but I can't figure out **how much they are being discounted**. The sign in front of the store says, "Up to 50% off everything."
M: Hmm.... Can I see that pair?
W: The sticker on these high heels says $200. Are they 50% off?
M: No, I'm sorry. **They were on that rack** and the items there are only 30% off the sticker price.
W: **It's still a good deal**. I'll take them. I love the color and the brand. Now what about these casual shoes?
M: Oh, those are 50% off.
W: But they don't have a price sticker on them, so how much are they?
M: $40, ma'am.
W: You mean the sale price or the regular price?
M: The sale price, ma'am.
W: OK, I'll take them.

여: 실례합니다. 이 신발 두 켤레가 마음에 드는데 얼마나 할인 중인지 알 수가 없네요. 가게 앞 표지판에는 '전 품목 50퍼센트까지 할인'이라고 되어 있던데요.
남: 음…. 그 신발을 볼 수 있을까요?
여: 이 하이힐에 붙어 있는 스티커에는 200달러라고 쓰여 있어요. 그것이 50퍼센트 할인되나요?
남: 죄송하지만 아닙니다. 그것은 저 진열대에 있었고 거기에 있는 물품들은 표시된 가격에서 30퍼센트만 할인됩니다.
여: 그래도 괜찮은 가격이네요. 그것을 살게요. 색상과 브랜드가 마음에 들어요. 그럼 이 캐주얼 슈즈는 어떤가요?
남: 아, 그것은 50퍼센트 할인됩니다.
여: 그렇지만 가격표가 없어서요. 얼마인가요?
남: 40달러입니다, 손님.
여: 할인 가격인가요, 아니면 정가 말인가요?
남: 할인 가격입니다, 손님.
여: 알겠어요. 그것을 살게요.

어휘 **rack** 받침대, 선반 / **sticker price** 희망 소비자 가격 / **regular price** 정가

07 이유 | ④

▶ 남자가 망설인 이유는 나중에 수리와 도색하는 데 돈이 더 많이 들 것 같아서이다.

M: Hello, I'm here to buy a car. Can you show me the car you have for sale?
W: Yes, here it is. It's a Fiat 500L. What do you think of it?
M: How much mileage does the car have?
W: It has 14,582 miles. It's a 2015 model.
M: Well... It's **kind of on the small side**, isn't it?
W: It may be a little small, but I can assure you that **it's the fastest around**.
M: Has the car ever been involved in an accident?
W: No, I have an eight-year accident-free driving history.
M: Sounds good. What about its paint job? It's not very clean and shiny. **Has it been cared for well**?
W: I do maintenance checkups on it regularly. It runs very smooth!
M: What would be the final price of the car?
W: It's 12,500 dollars.
M: Well, **I'll have to pay more** later for repairs and new paint, so I'm not sure it's reasonable. Thanks, anyway.

남: 안녕하세요, 저는 차를 사고 싶어서 왔는데요. 판매하시는 차를 좀 보여주시겠어요?
여: 네, 여기요. Fiat 500L입니다. 어떠세요?
남: 주행 거리가 얼마나 됐나요?
여: 14,582마일입니다. 2015년 모델이에요.
남: 음…. 좀 작은 편이지 않나요?
여: 조금 작을지도 모르지만, 가장 빠르다고 장담할 수 있어요.
남: 사고가 난 적이 있나요?
여: 아니요, 8년간 무사고 운전 경력을 가지고 있어요.
남: 좋아요. 도색은요? 그다지 깨끗하지 않고 광택이 나진 않네요. 잘 관리되었나요?
여: 정비 검사를 정기적으로 해요. 매우 부드럽게 달린답니다!
남: 최종 가격이 얼마인가요?
여: 12,500달러입니다.
남: 음, 제가 나중에 수리와 새로 도색을 하려면 돈이 더 많이 들게 되니, 적당한 가격이 아닌 것 같아요. 어쨌든, 고맙습니다.

어휘 **mileage** (자동차의) 주행 거리 / **maintenance** 정비, 유지, 보수 / **reasonable** 타당한, 합리적인; 너무 비싸지 않은

08 언급하지 않은 것 | ④

▶ 해석 참조

[Phone rings.]
W: Hello. How may I help you?
M: Hi, I'm calling for information about Sunshine Hospital's 15th annual fundraiser.
W: Great. The fundraiser is a fun event that welcomes the entire community.
M: I see. And **it's being held at the hospital**?
W: No. The fundraiser will be at Memorial Park, located off exit 10 on Highway 95.
M: I'm hoping to bring my family in the afternoon. When does it finish?
W: It's open from 9 a.m. to 10 p.m., and the prize lottery begins at 2 p.m.
M: Is a lottery ticket **included with my entrance ticket**?
W: No. Entrance is $15, and lottery tickets are sold for $5 each.
M: Oh, I see. That's a little expensive.
W: **The prizes are worth it**. We're giving away TVs, digital cameras, and much more.
M: Well, thank you for your help.

[전화벨이 울린다.]
여: 안녕하세요. 도와드릴까요?
남: 안녕하세요. Sunshine 병원의 제15회 연례 기금 모금 행사에 관한 정보를 구하고자 전화드립니다.
여: 좋습니다. 기금 모금 행사는 전 지역민을 환영하는 즐거운 행사입니다.
남: 그렇군요. 행사는 병원에서 열릴 예정인가요?
여: 아니요. 모금 행사는 95번 도로의 10번 출구에서 가까운 곳에 위치한 추모 공원(① 장소)에서 열릴 거예요.
남: 오후에 가족과 함께 가고 싶은데요. 행사는 언제 끝나나요?
여: 오전 9시부터 저녁 10시까지(② 행사 시간) 개최되며, 경품 추첨(③ 추첨 행사)은 오후 2시에 시작합니다.
남: 추첨권은 입장료에 포함된 건가요?
여: 아니요. 입장료는 15달러(⑤ 입장료)이고, 추첨권은 한 매당 5달러에 판매합니다.
남: 아, 알겠습니다. 조금 비싸군요.
여: 상품이 그 값을 하거든요. TV, 디지털 카메라 등 많은 것들을 경품으로 드릴 겁니다.
남: 그렇군요. 도와주셔서 감사합니다.

어휘 **fundraiser** 모금 행사 / **lottery** 추첨; 복권

09 내용 불일치 | ⑤

▶ 아프리카 지역사회에 바이오 에너지를 공급할 가능성은 있지만, 현재 에너지원으로 사용되지는 않는다고 했다.

W: Elephant grass is a tall grass that is native to the savannahs of Africa. It requires little water or nutrients for its survival, and therefore **grows well in poor soils**. Traditionally, it has been used primarily for feeding domestic animals; however, it is now being used for pest management. Fields of elephant grass are planted **to eliminate harmful insects** from important crops like corn. This technique is especially effective against moths because moths are strongly attracted to it. This grass can also be used to fuel power stations and replace traditional sources of energy, such as coal. Furthermore, it can be processed into bio-oil or bio-gas. Although **this is not currently being done**, it has the potential to provide energy to African communities.

여: 코끼리풀(Elephant grass)은 아프리카 대초원이 원산지인 커다란 풀입니다. 생존하는 데 물이나 영양분을 거의 필요로 하지 않기 때문에 척박한 땅에서도 잘 자랍니다. 코끼리풀은 전통적으로 가축을 먹이는 데 주로 사용되었습니다. 하지만 지금은 해충 관리에 이용되고 있습니다. 옥수수 같이 중요한 작물에서 해충을 없애기 위해 코끼리풀밭을 가꿉니다. 나방이 코끼리풀에 잘 꼬이기 때문에 이 방법은 나방에 대해 특히 효과적입니다. 이 풀은 발전소에 연료를 공급하고, 석탄과 같은 전통적인 에너지원을 대체하는 데도 사용될 수 있습니다. 나아가 바이오 오일이나 바이오 가스로 가공될 수도 있습니다. 현재 시행되고 있지는 않지만, 아프리카 지역사회에 에너지를 공급할 가능성도 있습니다.

어휘 **native to** ~이 원산지인 / **savannah** (특히 아프리카의) 대초원, 사바나 / **domestic animal** 가축 / **pest** 해충 / **eliminate** 없애다, 제거[삭제]하다 / **moth** 나방 / **power station** 발전소 / **bio-oil** 바이오 오일 / **bio-gas** 바이오 가스《미생물의 작용에 의하여 생성되는 메탄가스로, 발전이나 열 에너지원으로 사용됨》

10 도표 이해 | ④

▶ 화장실과 샤워 시설이 있고 놀이터와 수영장이 있는 곳을 원했으며 애완동물을 데려갈 수 있어야 한다. 또한 하루 묵는 가격이 100달러를 넘지 않는 곳을 원했으므로 답은 ④이다.

W: How about going camping this weekend?
M: That's a great idea. Let's rent a camping van this time.
W: That'll be so much fun! The kids will love it.
M: Let's first make a reservation.
W: We need a place that has a restroom and a shower facility.
M: Right. The camping van **may not have those facilities** inside the car.
W: The kids will be rolling in the dirt and having fun, so we definitely need them to take a shower. A playground and swimming pool **would also be ideal**.
M: Of course.
W: Oh, we also need to think about our dog, Freya. Since we won't be at a hotel, I'd like to **take her along with us**.
M: Yes, we should. I'm sure the kids will like playing with Freya at the campground.
W: How much will everything cost? We can't spend more than $100 per night.
M: Don't worry. There's a campground that's perfect for us. I'll reserve a spot now.

여: 이번 주말에 캠핑가는 게 어때요?
남: 좋은 생각이에요. 이번엔 캠핑용 승합차를 빌립시다.
여: 정말 재밌겠어요! 아이들이 좋아할 거예요.
남: 우선 예약을 합시다.
여: 화장실과 샤워 시설을 갖춘 곳이 필요해요.
남: 맞아요. 캠핑용 승합차는 아마 내부에 그런 시설이 없을 거예요.
여: 아이들이 흙에 뒹굴며 재미있게 놀 테니 샤워하려면 그것들이 필요해요. 놀이터와 수영장도 좋겠어요.
남: 물론이죠.
여: 아, 우리 개 Freya도 생각할 필요가 있어요. 우린 호텔에 머물지 않을 거니까 함께 데려갔으면 좋겠어요.
남: 네, 그래야죠. 아이들이 Freya와 함께 캠핑장에서 노는 걸 분명 좋아할 거예요.
여: 모두 비용이 얼마나 들까요? 하룻밤에 100달러 넘게 쓸 수는 없어요.
남: 걱정 마요. 우리에게 딱 맞는 캠핑장이 있어요. 지금 예약할게요.

어휘 **make a reservation** 예약하다 / **facility** 시설, 설비

11 짧은 대화에 이어질 응답 | ④

▶ 동영상에 노래를 넣는 방법을 모르겠다고 말하는 남자의 말에 가장 적절한 응답을 고른다.

① 네가 날 도와줄 수 있을 것 같지 않아.
② 네가 딱 맞는 노래를 고르는 걸 도와줄게.
③ 현장 학습 전부를 촬영했다니 멋지다.
④ 전혀 어렵지 않아. 내가 가르쳐줄게.
⑤ 내일 있을 현장 학습이 정말 기대돼.

M: Hey, Kate! Can you **come and help me**?
W: Sure. Are these videos from the field trip last week?
M: Yes, but I don't know **how to insert a song** into the video clip.
W: ____________________

남: 저기, Kate! 와서 날 도와줄 수 있어?
여: 물론이지. 이 비디오는 지난주 현장 학습에서 찍은 거야?
남: 응, 그런데 동영상에 노래를 넣는 방법을 모르겠어.
여: ____________________

어휘 **insert** 끼워 넣다

12 짧은 대화에 이어질 응답 | ④

▶ 여자는 동아리의 새 회장이 된 남자에게 신규 회원 모집과 관련해서 자신의 도움을 원하는지 물었다. 이에 적절한 응답을 찾는다.

① 내 계획이 네 도움 덕분에 성공했어.
② 한가하면 우리가 가입할 수 있는 다른 동아리를 찾아줘.
③ 물론이지. 탁구는 건강을 유지하는 데 좋아.
④ 그래. 동아리 포스터 만드는 걸 도와줄 수 있어?
⑤ 유감이지만 우리는 이미 회원이 충분히 있는데.

W: Congratulations on becoming the new president of our table tennis club!
M: Thank you. **My first task as president** will be to recruit new club members.
W: **That won't be easy**. Would you like me to help you?
M: ____________________

여: 우리 탁구 동아리의 새 회장이 된 것을 축하해!
남: 고마워. 회장으로서의 내 첫 임무는 동아리 신규 회원을 모집하는 일일 거야.
여: 쉽지 않겠구나. 내가 도와줄까?
남: ____________________

어휘 **recruit** (신입 사원·회원 등을) 모집하다; 신입 사원[회원]

13 긴 대화에 이어질 응답 | ②

▶ 음식 종류를 가리지 않는 여자가 할 수 있는 대답을 고른다.

① 나는 중요한 결정을 잘 내려요.
② 전 까다롭지 않아요. 정말 상관없어요.
③ 스테이크로 주세요. 잘 익혀 주시고요.
④ 오늘 저녁은 제가 살게요.
⑤ 주문하시겠습니까?

M: Where will your company transfer you?
W: Los Angeles or New York. I can choose.
M: Which city do you prefer?
W: I **don't have a preference**.
M: Really? I think Los Angeles would be better because it's warmer.
W: I like cold weather, so it's OK. Hmm. You know **it doesn't really**

matter. But we've been talking a long time. Let's go to a restaurant to eat.

M: Sounds good. How about Chinese food?
W: Sure.
M: Oh, there is a good Italian place near here.
W: **Either of those is fine**. I like everything.
M: But tell me what you would like to have.
W: ________________________________

남: 회사에서 당신을 어디로 전근 보내나요?
여: 로스앤젤레스나 뉴욕이요. 제가 고를 수 있어요.
남: 어떤 도시를 더 좋아하세요?
여: 선호하는 곳은 없어요.
남: 정말이요? 저는 로스앤젤레스가 따뜻해서 더 좋을 것 같은데요.
여: 전 추운 날씨를 좋아해서 괜찮아요. 음, 당신도 알다시피 그것은 별로 중요하지 않아요. 우리가 오래 이야기를 나눈 것 같은데 식사하러 가죠.
남: 좋아요. 중국 음식은 어때요?
여: 좋아요.
남: 아, 이 근처에 괜찮은 이탈리아 음식점이 있어요.
여: 두 곳 모두 괜찮아요. 저는 다 좋아해요.
남: 하지만 무엇을 먹고 싶은지 알려주세요.
여: ________________________________

어휘 **transfer** 전근[전학] 가다[시키다]; 옮기다 / **prefer** 선호하다 *cf.* **preference** 선호(도), 애호 | 선택지 어휘 | **picky** 까다로운

14 긴 대화에 이어질 응답 | ①

▶ 부모님 생각보다는 자신이 원하는 전공을 선택해야 한다고 믿는 남자가 할 수 있는 말을 찾아본다.

① 그래도 부모님께 말씀드려야 해. 네 인생이잖아.
② 부모님이 네게 실망하실까 봐 걱정된다.
③ 그럼 의학으로 전공을 바꿔.
④ 그래, 너 자신만 생각하는 것은 무례한 일이겠지.
⑤ 괜찮아. 부모님도 건축가는 훈련이 필요한 것을 아셔.

M: So have you decided **what you want to major in** at university next year?
W: Well, my mother and father want me to study law, so I guess that's it.
M: What? You can't let them decide what you will do for the rest of your life!
W: They are my parents. I have to obey their wishes.
M: But what about your wishes?
W: It **doesn't matter what I want**.
M: Have you even thought about what you want?
W: Yes, I want to study architecture. I would like to design skyscrapers.
M: Did you tell your parents that?
W: No. I couldn't possibly tell them I don't want to become a lawyer.
M: Why not?
W: **What if they get disappointed**?
M: ________________________________

남: 내년에 대학에서 무엇을 전공할지 결정했니?
여: 글쎄, 부모님께서는 내가 법학을 공부하기를 원하셔. 그래서 그걸로 할 것 같아.
남: 뭐라고? 네가 평생 동안 할 일을 부모님이 결정하시게 해서는 안 돼!
여: 그분들은 내 부모님이신걸. 부모님이 바라시는 것을 따라야지.
남: 하지만 네가 원하는 것은 어쩌고?
여: 내가 원하는 것은 중요하지 않아.
남: 네가 뭘 원하는지 생각은 해 봤니?
여: 응, 건축을 공부하고 싶어. 고층 빌딩을 설계해 보고 싶거든.
남: 부모님께 그걸 말씀드렸니?
여: 아니, 변호사가 되고 싶지 않다고 도저히 말씀드릴 수가 없어.
남: 왜?
여: 실망하시면 어떻게 하니?
남: ________________________________

어휘 **obey** 따르다, 순종하다 / **skyscraper** 초고층 빌딩, 마천루 / **possibly** 도저히, 아무리 해도 | 선택지 어휘 | **medical science** 의학 / **disrespectful** 무례한, 실례되는

15 상황에 적절한 말 | ④

▶ 딸이 수업 과제를 위해 무엇을 준비해야 하는지 궁금해하는 학부모에게 할 수 있는 말을 고른다.

① Jane은 준비하는 데 필요한 시간을 좀 더 가질 수 있습니다.
② 저는 곧 내일 있을 수업 준비를 마칠 것입니다.
③ Jane의 고민거리를 저에게도 알려주셔서 감사합니다.
④ 내일 수업이 끝나면 제가 아이와 그것에 대해 이야기해 보겠습니다.
⑤ Jane이 건강해져서 곧 학교에 나올 수 있기를 바랍니다.

M: Mary is a teacher at a public elementary school. After the day's classes, she is about to leave her classroom, when she receives a phone call from a mother. The mother **is concerned because her daughter**, Jane, is very upset. Jane told her mother that she's scared about failing a class project. Jane says she **doesn't know what to do** because she was sick and missed some classes. Suddenly, Mary realizes that she **forgot to explain the project clearly** to Jane. So, Mary tells the mother that she will give Jane extra time to prepare for the project. The mother sounds relieved but still wonders what her daughter should do to prepare. In this situation, what would Mary most likely say to the mother?

남: Mary는 공립 초등학교의 선생님이다. 모든 수업을 마치고 그녀가 교실을 나가려고 할 때, 한 어머니로부터 전화 한 통을 받는다. 그 어머니는 자신의 딸 Jane이 매우 속상해하고 있다며 걱정한다. Jane은 어머니에게 수업 과제를 해내지 못할까 봐 두렵다고 말했다. Jane은 아파서 수업을 몇 번 빠졌기 때문에 무엇을 해야 할지 모르겠다고 말한다. 문득 Mary는 Jane에게 과제에 대해 명확히 설명해 줄 것을 잊어버렸음을 깨닫는다. 그래서 Mary는 Jane에게 과제를 준비할 시간을 좀 더 주겠다고 어머님께 말씀드린다. 어머니는 안도하는 것 같지만 여전히 자신의 딸이 무엇을 준비해야 하는지 궁금해한다. 이러한 상황에서 Mary가 Jane의 어머니에게 할 말로 가장 적절한 것은 무엇인가?

어휘 **relieved** 안도하는 | 선택지 어휘 | **shortly** 곧; 간단히

16~17 세트 문항 | 16. ⑤ 17. ⑤

▶ 16. 아파트 지하 주차장, 엘리베이터, 쓰레기장, 화단의 유지 보수와 청소, 소독 등의 일정을 안내하고 있다.

① 곧 있을 주차장 확장 공사
② 지정 주차 제도에 대한 안내
③ 최근 발생한 공사 소음에 대해 사과
④ 승강기 안전 예방 조치에 대한 안내
⑤ 아파트 유지 보수 일정 통보

▶ 17. 해석 참조

W: Good morning, residents. This is the security office for Health Village apartments. We **apologize for disturbing you** and promise to keep this message brief. Today, we want to remind you about the schedule for **cleaning and maintenance work** this week. On Monday and Tuesday, the underground parking area will be cleaned and repainted. Cleaning starts at 9 a.m. No cars may be parked in the parking areas during these times. Cars may return at 6 p.m. on the same day. On Wednesday and Thursday, **the elevators will be inspected**. Please use the stairs instead during these times. On Friday, the garbage collection and recycling areas will be cleaned. So **please use the temporary bins** that will be placed nearby. On Saturday, pesticide will be sprayed on all plants surrounding the apartments and throughout the gardens. Make sure to close your windows on this day and **keep children from playing outdoors**. Again, we apologize for the inconvenience. With your help, this work will go smoothly and we can all enjoy the benefits. Thank you for your cooperation.

여: 입주민 여러분, 안녕하십니까. 헬스 빌리지 아파트 경비실입니다. 폐를 끼치게 돼 사과드리며 안내방송은 짧게 하도록 하겠습니다. 오늘은 이번 주 청소 및 유지 보수 작업에 관한 일정을 다시 한 번 알려 드리고자 합니다. 월요일과 화요일에는 ① 지하 주차장을 청소하고 다시 페인트칠합니다. 청소는 오전 9시에 시작됩니다. 이 기간에는 주차장에 차를 주차해서는 안 됩니다. 차는 당일 오후 6시에 돌려놓으실 수 있습니다. 수요일과 목요일에는 ② 엘리베이터 점검이 있겠습니다. 이때에는 계단을 대신 이용해주시기 바랍니다. 금요일에는 ③ 쓰레기 수거장 및 재활용 구역 청소가 시행됩니다. 따라서 근처에 설치될 임시 쓰레기통을 사용해주시기 바랍니다. 토요일에는 아파트 주변의 모든 식물과 ④ 정원 전체에 살충제가 분사될 것입니다. 이날은 창문을 닫아주시고 아이들이 밖에서 놀지 않도록 해주시기 바랍니다. 다시 한 번 말씀드리지만, 불편을 겪게 해 드려 죄송합니다. 입주민 여러분께서 협조해주신다면, 이번 유지 보수 작업이 순조롭게 진행될 것이며 모든 분들이 그로 인한 혜택을 누리실 수 있을 것입니다. 협조에 감사드립니다.

어휘 **resident** 거주자, 주민 / **security office** 경비실 / **maintenance** 유지, 관리, 보수 / **inspect** 점검하다 / **temporary** 임시의; 일시적인 / **pesticide** 살충제 / **smoothly** 순조롭게, 부드럽게 / **cooperation** 협조; 협력 | 선택지 어휘 | **expansion** 확장, 확대 / **designated** 지정된, 정해진 / **precaution** 예방 조치 / **notification** 알림, 통고

01. ③ **02.** ② **03.** ⑤ **04.** ④ **05.** ⑤ **06.** ③ **07.** ④ **08.** ② **09.** ④ **10.** ⑤
11. ② **12.** ④ **13.** ④ **14.** ① **15.** ④ **16.** ② **17.** ⑤

01 화자가 하는 말의 목적 | ③

▶ 허리케인에 대비하는 방법을 알려주고 있다.

M: Now that the hurricane season is over, we should examine what we did wrong this year. In April, Hurricane Sally did little damage, but if she had been stronger, she **could have done** a lot more damage as residents were not ready. When a hurricane watch is issued, you must do several things to prepare for the coming hurricane. You must put tape on your house's windows. Then you must **nail wooden boards across them**. It's also important to bring outdoor furniture inside. If you can't bring it inside, you must tie it down. Then, you must **check your emergency supplies**: food, water, and a battery-powered radio.

남: 이제 허리케인의 계절이 끝났으니 올해 우리가 잘못 대처했던 점들을 검토해 보아야 합니다. 4월에 발생했던 허리케인 Sally의 경우는 피해가 거의 없었습니다. 하지만 그것이 더 강력했다면 지역 주민들이 준비가 되어 있지 않았던 터라 훨씬 더 큰 피해를 주었을 것입니다. 허리케인 주의보가 발효되면, 접근하는 허리케인에 대해 여러 가지 대비를 해야 합니다. 가옥의 유리창에 테이프를 붙이고 거기에 나무판자를 가로질러 못질을 해 두어야 합니다. 밖에 놓아둔 야외용 가구를 집안에 가져다 놓는 것도 중요합니다. 안에 가져다 놓을 수 없다면 잘 묶어 놓아야 합니다. 그런 다음, 음식과 물 그리고 배터리를 이용하는 라디오와 같은 비상 물품을 확인해야 합니다.

어휘 **examine** 검토하다, 조사하다 / **do damage** 손해를 끼치다 / **issue** 발표[공표]하다; 발행하다 / **nail** 못을 박다 / **tie down** ~을 묶어 놓다 / **supply** (복수형) 용품

02 대화 주제 | ②

▶ 온라인으로 수업을 듣기로 한 남자가 여자에게 온라인 기반 학습의 특징을 이야기해주고 있다.

W: Hi, Kevin. Are you going to be in Ms. Jackson's writing class?
M: No, I decided to take an online writing class instead.
W: I didn't know we had that option. Anyway, **wouldn't it be better** to take the class in person?
M: That's **what I thought at first**, but once I saw all the things that are available online, I changed my mind.
W: I guess it will be nice to be able to pause the lectures anytime you want.
M: Of course. Plus, I can listen to them on my own schedule.
W: What are the assignments like?
M: There are mini-quizzes and assignments just like in any class, but everything is graded immediately. There are even chat rooms **where we can discuss** the lectures and get help.
W: Wow, maybe I'll try that next time.

여: 안녕, Kevin. Jackson 교수님의 작문 수업을 들을 거니?
남: 아니, 그 대신 온라인 작문 수업을 듣기로 결심했어.
여: 그런 선택 사항이 있다는 걸 몰랐어. 어쨌든, 수업을 직접 듣는 게 더 좋지 않을까?
남: 처음에는 그렇게 생각했는데, 온라인에서 이용할 수 있는 모든 걸 보자마자 생각이 바뀌었어.
여: 원할 때마다 강의를 멈출 수 있다는 건 좋을 것 같아.
남: 물론이야. 게다가, 내 일정에 맞게 강의를 들을 수 있어.
여: 과제들은 어때?
남: 어떤 수업에서나 그렇듯이 미니 퀴즈랑 과제가 있지만, 모든 게 점수가 바로 매겨져. 강의에 대해서 토의하고 도움을 받을 수 있는 대화방도 있고.
여: 와, 다음에 나도 들어봐야겠는 걸.

어휘 **assignment** 과제, 임무 / **immediately** 즉시 / **chat room** (인터넷의) 대화방

03 관계 | ⑤

▶ 소비자의 의견을 설문을 통해 조사하는 사람과 행인의 대화이다.

W: Good afternoon. May I ask you a few questions?
M: How long will it take? I'm on my way to the bank.
W: Not long. And I can **give you this free gift**.
M: What is it?
W: A toiletry set for traveling: shampoo and conditioner, soap, and a toothbrush.
M: OK. I guess I have a few minutes.
W: I'd like to ask your opinion about electronics such as televisions, DVD players, and digital cameras.
M: OK.
W: **Which brand do you think has** the best reputation for quality?
M: KDT does! When I want to buy electronics, I always buy KDT stuff.
W: Why is that?
M: I know they are well made. **They won't break easily**.
W: OK. And I have a few more questions.
M: Go ahead.

여: 안녕하세요. 몇 가지 질문을 해도 될까요?
남: 얼마 정도 걸리나요? 은행에 가는 길이라서요.
여: 오래 걸리지 않아요. 그리고 이 선물도 무료로 드리고요.
남: 그게 뭔데요?
여: 여행용 세면용품 세트요. 샴푸, 린스, 비누 그리고 칫솔이 들어 있어요.
남: 좋아요. 몇 분 정도는 시간이 있어요.
여: 텔레비전이나 DVD 플레이어, 그리고 디지털 카메라와 같은 전자제품에 관한 의견을 묻고 싶어요.
남: 알겠어요.
여: 어떤 브랜드가 품질 면에서 가장 좋은 평가를 받는다고 생각하십니까?
남: KDT죠! 전자제품을 살 때는 항상 KDT 제품을 구입해요.
여: 왜 그렇지요?
남: 잘 만들어져서 쉽게 고장이 나지 않아요.
여: 알겠습니다. 그리고 질문이 몇 가지 더 있습니다.
남: 계속하세요.

어휘 **toiletry set** 세면용품 등의 세트 / **electronics** (복수형) 전자제품 / **reputation** 평판, 명성 / **quality** 품질

04 그림 불일치 | ④

▶ 대화에서는 중앙에 팝콘 통이 있고 그 주변을 탄산 음료가 둘러싸고 있다고 했지만, 그림에서는 팝콘 통 오른쪽에 탄산 음료가 있으므로 일치하지 않는다.

M: Alice, did you finish designing the new cinema discount coupons?
W: Sure, Bob. Take a look, and **tell me what you think**.
M: Oh, I like the font you chose for "Discount Coupon" in the top left!
W: That's good to hear. I was worried it might be too big.
M: Not at all. **It matches well with** the star under it advertising 30% off.
W: I hope it's not too small. I wanted to keep this image of a huge bucket of popcorn in the center.
M: I like what you've done. After all, the bucket in the center and the sodas all around it are the main attraction.
W: **I was thinking the same thing**.
M: And there was still plenty of room for the cinema's information in the bottom right corner.
W: Right. I included both the website and the address.
M: It looks like you thought of everything. Let's **get them printed**.
W: Great.

남: Alice, 새 영화관 할인 쿠폰 디자인하는 거 끝냈어?
여: 물론이지, Bob. 한번 보고 어떻게 생각하는지 말해줘.
남: 아, 왼쪽 상단에 네가 고른 '할인 쿠폰' 글씨체가 마음에 들어!
여: 그거 반가운 소리네. 너무 클까봐 걱정했어.
남: 전혀 아니야. 그 아래에 있는 30% 할인을 광고하는 별과 잘 어울려.
여: 난 이게 너무 작지 않았으면 해. 큰 팝콘 통의 이미지를 중앙에 유지하고 싶었거든.
남: 난 네가 한 게 좋아. 어쨌든, 중앙의 팝콘 통과 그걸 둘러싼 탄산음료는 가장 큰 매력이야.
여: 나도 똑같이 생각하고 있었어.
남: 그런데도 우측 하단 모서리에 영화관 정보를 위한 충분한 공간이 있었구나.
여: 맞아. 웹사이트 주소와 실제 주소 둘 다 포함시켰어.
남: 넌 모든 것을 고려한 것 같구나. 우리 이거 인쇄하자.
여: 좋아.

어휘 **font** 글씨체, 서체 / **advertise** 광고하다; 알리다 / **bucket** 통, 양동이 / **attraction** 매력; 끌림; 명소 / **plenty of** 충분한, 많은

05 추후 행동 | ⑤

▶ 여자는 주말 동안 부모님 댁에 가 있기로 했는데, 먼저 버스표를 알아보기 위해 버스 터미널에 전화해 보겠다고 했다.

[Phone rings.]

M: Hello?

W: Dad, it's Jenny. There's a problem. The boiler is broken. It's freezing and I haven't had hot water for two days.

M: Are you sure the gas valve is turned on?

W: Dad, I'm not that stupid.

M: Sorry, dear. Then, the pipe **might have frozen and burst**. Did you tell the landlady about it?

W: I did. But she said that if it froze and burst I should fix it by myself.

M: You should call the repair technician right now.

W: I already did. But, it's Friday night. He **may not come and fix it** until Monday morning. Dad, I need a hot shower. I'm coming home for the weekend.

M: If you do, we'll be happy. But I'm not sure **there are any tickets left**. It's already the weekend.

W: Yes, you're right. I should call the bus station first. Could you come and pick me up if there aren't any tickets left? I can't stay here for the whole weekend.

M: OK, I will. I'll tell your mother you're coming.

W: Thanks, Dad!

[전화벨이 울린다.]

남: 여보세요?

여: 아빠, 저 Jenny예요. 문제가 생겼어요. 보일러가 고장 났어요. 엄청 추운데다 이틀 동안 뜨거운 물이 안 나오고 있어요.

남: 가스 밸브가 열려 있는 게 확실하니?

여: 아빠, 저 그렇게 바보 같진 않아요.

남: 미안하다, 얘야. 그렇다면 파이프가 동파되었을지도 모르겠구나. 주인아주머니께 말씀은 드렸니?

여: 네. 그런데 동파된 거라면 제가 알아서 고쳐야 한다고 말씀하셨어요.

남: 지금 바로 수리기사를 불러야겠다.

여: 벌써 불렀어요. 하지만 지금은 금요일 밤이라 수리기사는 월요일 아침에야 와서 고칠지도 몰라요. 아빠, 저 뜨거운 물로 샤워하고 싶어요. 주말 동안 집에 가 있을게요.

남: 네가 그렇게 한다면 우리야 좋지. 그런데 표가 남아 있을지 모르겠구나. 벌써 주말이잖니.

여: 네, 그러네요. 버스 터미널에 먼저 전화해야겠어요. 만약에 표가 남아 있지 않다면 아빠가 차로 데리러 오시겠어요? 주말 내내 여기에 있을 순 없어요.

남: 그래, 그렇게 하마. 엄마한테 네가 온다고 말해줄게.

여: 고마워요, 아빠!

어휘 **burst** 터지다, 파열하다 / **landlady** 여자 집주인

06 금액 | ③

▶ 100달러에서 20달러를 할인받았는데 거기에 이름을 넣는 값 10달러를 추가하면 남자가 지불할 총액은 90달러이다.

W: How can I help you?

M: I want to buy my nephew something as a graduation gift. Could you recommend one? He's going to **graduate from high school**.

W: If that's the case, how about a nice wallet?

M: Good idea. How much are they?

W: This brown leather wallet is $90 and this fabric one is $40.

M: I think **a leather wallet is more durable**. I'll take that black leather wallet. Is it also $90?

W: It was originally $100 but it's 20 dollars off now.

M: Sounds great.

W: If you want, we can put your nephew's name on it since it's a personalized wallet.

M: Really? How much does it cost and **how long does it take to personalize**?

W: You just pay an additional $10 and it'll take about 30 minutes.

M: Okay. **I'll take it**. I hope my nephew will love it.

W: I'm sure it'll be a very special gift for him.

여: 뭘 도와드릴까요?

남: 제 조카에게 졸업 선물로 뭔가 사주고 싶어요. 하나 추천해주실 수 있나요? 조카는 고등학교를 졸업할 거예요.

여: 그런 경우라면 멋진 지갑이 어떨까요?

남: 좋은 생각이에요. 얼마죠?

여: 이 갈색 가죽 지갑은 90달러이고 이 천 지갑은 40달러예요.

남: 가죽 지갑이 더 오래 쓸 것 같군요. 저 검은 가죽 지갑을 살게요. 그것도 90달러인가요?

여: 그건 원래 100달러였는데 지금 20달러 싸게 드려요.

남: 그거 좋군요.

여: 그게 이름을 넣을 수 있는 지갑이라서 원하시면 조카분의 이름을 그 위에 넣어드릴 수 있어요.

남: 정말이요? 이름을 넣으려면 값은 얼마나 하고 얼마나 오래 걸리나요?

여: 추가로 10달러만 내시는 것이고 약 30분 걸릴 거예요.

남: 좋습니다. 그걸로 살게요. 제 조카가 그걸 좋아하길 바라요.

여: 분명히 조카분께 아주 특별한 선물이 될 거예요.

어휘 **fabric** 천, 직물 / **durable** 오래 견디는, 튼튼한 / **personalize** 자기의 이름을 넣다, (개인 소유물임을 나타내는) 표시를 하다 / **additional** 추가의

07 이유 | ④

▶ 여자는 자신의 우스꽝스러운 사진을 친구가 블로그에 마음대로 게시한 것에 화가 났다고 했다.

M: **Is something bothering you**, Kelly?

W: I'm just in a bad mood. Don't worry about it.

M: I'm your friend, and I'm always happy to listen.

W: Thanks, but it's just something Lydia did that really upset me.

M: Was she late for an appointment again? That really **gets on my nerves**.

W: I know what you mean, but no. She took some pictures of me that look ridiculous.

M: Well, that's not so bad. Just some funny faces, right?

W: Yes, but I look really bad in the photos, and she put them on her blog!

M: Oh, now I get it. That would make me mad too.

W: She **should have at least asked me** before uploading the pictures.

M: Why don't you ask her to delete the photos?

W: I will. Hopefully, she'll understand my point of view.

남: 뭐 신경 쓰이는 일이라도 있어, Kelly?

여: 그냥 기분이 안 좋아. 신경 쓰지 마.

남: 난 네 친구잖아. 그리고 네 얘기를 듣는 건 언제나 기뻐.

여: 고마워. 하지만 Lydia가 한 일이 나를 정말 화나게 했을 뿐이야.

남: Lydia가 약속에 또 늦었니? 그건 정말 내 신경을 건드리더라.

여: 무슨 말인지는 알겠지만, 아니야. 그 애가 우스꽝스러워 보이는 내 사진을 몇 장 찍었어.

남: 음, 그렇게 나쁜 것도 아니네. 그냥 우스운 얼굴 사진 몇 장이잖아, 그렇지?

여: 응, 그렇지만 사진이 정말 못 나왔고, 그 애가 그 사진들을 자기 블로그에 올렸어!

남: 아, 이제 알겠다. 그건 나라도 화가 날 거야.

여: 그 애는 최소한 사진들을 올리기 전에 나한테 물어봤어야 해.

남: Lydia한테 사진들을 지워달라고 요청하는 게 어때?

여: 그럴 거야. 바라건대, 그 애가 내 입장을 이해해 줬으면 해.

어휘 **get on A's nerves** A의 신경을 건드리다 / **ridiculous** 우스꽝스러운; 터무니없는

08 언급하지 않은 것 | ②

▶ 해석 참조

M: Rebecca, are these pictures from your trip to the United States?

W: They are. The one you are looking at right now was taken in Yellowstone National Park.

M: It looks beautiful. It's somewhere **in the middle of the country**, right?

W: It's mainly in the state of Wyoming, but parts of it are in Montana and Idaho.

M: I didn't know that. It **must be quite large then**.

W: It covers nearly 9,000 square kilometers, and much of it is volcanic.

M: Do you have any pictures of the volcanoes? I'd like to see them.

W: No. There aren't any active volcanoes in Yellowstone at the moment, but the entire park **will someday erupt**.

M: That's a scary thought. Oh, what about this picture? Is this a bear?

W: Yes, Yellowstone is home to many black bears, bison, mountain goats, and deer, but I was really lucky to get that picture.

남: Rebecca, 이 사진들은 미국 여행에서 찍은 거니?
여: 맞아. 네가 지금 보고 있는 사진은 Yellowstone 국립공원에서 찍은 거야.
남: 멋져 보이네. 그건 미국 중부 어딘가에 있지?
여: Yellowstone 국립공원은 주로 와이오밍 주에 있지만 부분적으로는 몬태나 주와 아이다호 주에 있어(① 위치).
남: 그건 몰랐네. 그럼 상당히 크구나.
여: 면적이 거의 9,000 평방 킬로미터(③ 크기)에 달하고, 상당 부분이 화산 지대야.
남: 화산을 찍은 사진들도 가지고 있니? 보고 싶어.
여: 아니. 지금은 Yellowstone에 활화산이 없지만 언젠가 그 공원 전체에서 화산이 폭발할 거야 (④ 화산 활동).
남: 그건 생각만 해도 무서운데. 오, 이 사진은 뭐야? 이건 곰인가?
여: 응, Yellowstone은 많은 흑곰, 들소, 산양, 사슴의 서식지야(⑤ 서식 동물). 그런데 그 사진을 찍다니 정말 운이 좋았어.

어휘 **mainly** 주로, 대개 / **volcanic** 화산(성)의; 화산이 있는[많은] ***cf.* volcano** 화산 / **entire** 전체의; 완전한 / **erupt** (화산이) 폭발하다; (화산재 등이) 분출하다 / **bison** 들소

09 내용 불일치 | ④

▶ 전망 2, 3층에 가기 위해서는 다른 엘리베이터로 갈아타야 한다고 말했다.

W: Welcome to I Tower. **While you're waiting** for the elevator, I'll tell you about I Tower. I Tower, which is 250 meters tall, was originally built in 1975 as a communications tower. Even now it sends and receives radio and TV signals. But these days, I Tower **is better known for** its scenic views. There are three observatory floors beginning at the 200-meter mark. You get off the main elevator at Observation Floor 1. Then you must take another elevator to go to either the café and bakery on Observation Floor 2 or the romantic Sky View restaurant on Observation Floor 3. The Sky View restaurant spins, **taking 50 minutes to make one complete circle**. Thank you. Please enjoy the view.

여: I Tower에 오신 것을 환영합니다. 엘리베이터를 기다리시는 동안 I Tower에 대해서 설명을 드리겠습니다. I Tower는 높이가 250미터이고, 1975년에 통신 탑으로 처음 세워졌습니다. 현재까지도 라디오와 TV의 전파를 송수신하고 있습니다. 하지만 오늘날 I Tower는 멋진 전망으로 더 잘 알려져 있습니다. 200미터 지점부터 세 개 층에 걸쳐서 전망대가 있습니다. 전망 1층의 중앙 엘리베이터에서 내리십시오. 전망 2층의 카페와 빵집이나 혹은 전망 3층의 낭만적인 Sky View 레스토랑에 가시려면 다른 엘리베이터로 갈아타셔야만 합니다. Sky View는 회전 레스토랑으로 한 바퀴를 도는 데 50분이 걸립니다. 감사합니다. 전망을 즐기시길 바랍니다.

어휘 **signal** 신호 / **scenic** 경치가 아름다운 / **observatory** 전망대

10 도표 이해 | ⑤

▶ 남자는 우선 거리가 너무 멀리 떨어져 있는 High Land Avenue에 있는 의사를 제외한 후 알레르기 전문의를 택했고 경력이 오래된 사람 중 남자 의사를 택하기로 했다.

M: Hi, Julia. The school nurse told me **to see a doctor for my cough**. But I don't know what to do since I'm an exchange student.
W: Do you have a doctor in mind?
M: She recommended five doctors in this area.
W: Let's take a look. The doctor on Highland Avenue is too far away from the school. It probably takes about an hour and a half to get there from here.
M: Well, since I don't have a car, I guess **that's not an option**. Which doctor is the closest?
W: All the other doctors are about 30 minutes away. Is your cough due to a cold or an allergy?
M: I don't have a cold. It's due to an allergy.
W: Then you should see a doctor **who specializes in allergies**.
M: You're right. And I'd like someone who's been in practice for at least 5 years.
W: Then you'll have to choose from these two doctors.
M: Hmm... I think I'll be more comfortable with a male doctor.
W: It looks like this doctor is the one for you.
M: Thanks. I'll call and **make a reservation** now.

남: 안녕, Julia. 양호 선생님이 기침 때문에 내가 병원에 가야 한다고 말씀하셨어. 그런데 난 교환학생이라서 어떻게 해야 할지 모르겠어.
여: 생각하고 있는 의사 선생님은 있니?
남: 양호 선생님이 이 지역의 의사 선생님 다섯 분을 추천해 주셨어.
여: 한번 보자. Highland Avenue에 있는 의사 선생님은 학교에서 너무 멀리 떨어져 있어. 여기서 거기에 가는 데 아마 한 시간 반은 걸릴 거야.
남: 음, 난 차가 없으니까 거긴 선택사항이 아닌 것 같아. 어느 의사 선생님이 가장 가깝니?
여: 다른 의사 선생님들은 모두 여기서 30분 정도 떨어진 곳에 계셔. 네 기침이 감기 때문이니 아니면 알레르기 때문이니?
남: 감기에 걸리지 않았어. 알레르기 때문이야.
여: 그러면 너는 알레르기를 전문적으로 다루시는 의사 선생님을 찾아봐야 해.
남: 네 말이 맞아. 그리고 난 적어도 5년간 진료를 봐오신 분이면 좋겠어.
여: 그러면 넌 이 두 분 중에서 선택해야만 해.
남: 음… 난 남자 의사 선생님이 더 편할 것 같아.
여: 이 분이 널 위한 의사 선생님인 것 같네.
남: 고마워. 지금 전화해서 예약할게.

어휘 **allergy** 알레르기 / **specialize** 전문적으로 다루다, 전공하다 / **practice** (의사·변호사 등 전문직 종사자의) 업무; 영업

11 짧은 대화에 이어질 응답 | ②

▶ 일반적으로 언제 결혼하는 것이 적절하다고 생각하는지 묻는 말에 가장 적절한 응답을 찾는다.

① 시내에 있는 예식장에서야.
② 내 생각엔 취업을 먼저 해야 해.
③ 결혼은 기본적인 사회 제도야.
④ 봄에 결혼하는 게 더 좋아.
⑤ 나이가 더 많은 사람들 대부분은 이미 결혼했어.

W: Robert and Sara **are going to get married** next month.
M: Wow, aren't they really young for that?
W: Maybe. **When do you think** people should get married?
M: ______________________________

여: Robert와 Sara가 다음 달에 결혼할 거야.
남: 와, 그러기엔 정말 어리지 않아?
여: 글쎄. 넌 사람들이 언제쯤 결혼해야 한다고 생각하니?
남: ______________________________

어휘 | 선택지 어휘 | **institution** 제도; 기관, 협회

12 짧은 대화에 이어질 응답 | ④

▶ 내일 휴가인 여자에게 보고서에 대해 질문이 있으면 어떻게 연락해야 하는지 묻고 있으므로 이에 적절한 응답을 찾는다.

① 걱정하지 마세요. 우리 보고서는 완벽해요.
② 답변은 이메일로 보내 드렸어요.
③ 드디어 휴가를 와서 기분이 아주 좋아요.
④ 여기요, 제 휴대전화 번호를 드릴게요.
⑤ 질의응답 시간이 있을 거예요.

M: Thanks for finishing this report. I'll ask you tomorrow if I have questions.
W: Actually, I'll **be on vacation** tomorrow. But I can still answer questions if you have any.
M: Okay, great. How can I **get in touch with** you?
W: ______________________________

남: 이 보고서를 다 끝내 주셔서 고맙습니다. 질문이 있으면 내일 여쭤보겠습니다.
여: 실은, 제가 내일 휴가예요. 하지만 질문이 있으시면 대답해 드릴 수는 있습니다.
남: 네, 잘됐네요. 어떻게 연락드리면 될까요?
여: ______________________________

어휘 **get in touch with** ~와 연락하다 | 선택지 어휘 | **session** (활동을 위한) 시간, 기간

13 긴 대화에 이어질 응답 | ④

▶ 대화 내용으로 보아 남자는 아이를 돌보느라 상당히 힘들었을 것으로 추측할 수 있다.

① 그렇지는 않아요. 당신은 집안일을 하지 않아요.
② 나는 5년간 매니저로 일했어요.
③ 네, 그 애가 〈곰돌이 푸〉를 정말 좋아해요.
④ 할 수는 있지만 정말 힘든 일이에요.
⑤ 당신이 여기에 없을 때 난 너무 행복했어요.

W: Hi, honey. I'm home.
M: Oh, hi. I'm happy to see you.
W: Happy? Why? Is anything wrong?
M: No, **I was fine by myself**. It's just nice that you're home. How was the manager's meeting?

W: OK. How was Ethan?
M: Everything was fine. I picked him up from daycare. And we played in the park for a while.
W: In the sandbox?
M: Yes, he loves that. Don't worry. I washed his hands when we came home.
W: **What did you have for dinner**?
M: Spaghetti. And we had some salad, too.
W: He ate a lot?
M: Yes, don't worry. Next we watched one of his DVDs. It was *Winnie the Pooh*. And then he went to bed.
W: Well done. **You can manage very well** without me.
M: ______________________________

여: 여보, 나 왔어요.
남: 아, 어서 와요. 당신을 보니 좋네요.
여: 좋다고요? 왜요? 무슨 안 좋은 일이라도 있었나요?
남: 아니요, 나 혼자서도 괜찮았어요. 그냥 당신이 집에 오니까 좋아서요. 매니저 회의는 어땠어요?
여: 잘됐어요. Ethan은 어땠어요?
남: 모든 게 좋았어요. 유아원에서 Ethan을 데리고 와서 공원에서 잠시 놀았어요.
여: 모래통에서요?
남: 그래요, 정말 좋아하더군요. 걱정하지 마요. 집에 돌아와서 손을 씻겼으니까요.
여: 저녁으로 무얼 먹었어요?
남: 스파게티요. 그리고 샐러드도 먹었어요.
여: 아이가 많이 먹던가요?
남: 그럼요, 걱정 말아요. 그런 다음 아이의 DVD 중 하나를 함께 봤어요. 〈곰돌이 푸〉였어요. 그 후 아이는 잠자리에 들었어요.
여: 잘했어요. 당신은 나 없이도 아주 잘 해낼 수 있군요.
남: ______________________________

어휘 **daycare** (낮 동안에 운영되는) 유아원 | 선택지 어휘 | **house chores** 집안일

14 긴 대화에 이어질 응답 | ①

▶ 예전에 금연 실패를 경험한 삼촌에게 여자는 이번에는 실패하지 말라는 용기를 주는 말을 할 것이다.

① 이번에는 굴복하지 마세요.
② 네, 딱 한 번만 더 해야지요.
③ 맞아요. 그건 아무 해가 없어요.
④ 아버지도 금연을 하실 수 있으면 좋겠는데.
⑤ 미안하지만 여기서는 담배를 피우면 안 됩니다.

M: Guess what, Sunny! I've quit smoking.
W: Congratulations, Uncle Bob! **Smoking is disgusting**, and bad for your health. When did you quit?
M: Almost three weeks ago. It's hard. I still have a strong desire to smoke.
W: Have you tried nicotine patches? Dad used them when he quit smoking.
M: Um, I should try them. I'll do anything to be successful this time.
W: So, you **tried to quit before**?
M: Four or five times. I started smoking a long time ago.
W: What happened when you tried to quit before?
M: I **got immediately addicted again** because I told myself "Go on, just one little cigarette won't hurt."
W: ______________________________

남: 들어봐, Sunny야! 내가 담배를 끊었단다.
여: 축하해요, Bob 삼촌! 담배를 피우는 것은 정말로 싫어요. 건강에도 나쁘고요. 언제 끊으셨어요?
남: 거의 3주 전에. 매우 힘들어. 난 아직도 담배를 몹시 피우고 싶단다.
여: 니코틴 패치는 사용해 보셨어요? 아버지는 담배를 끊으실 때 그것을 사용하셨어요.
남: 음, 나도 그것을 사용해 봐야겠다. 이번에는 성공할 수 있게 뭐든지 할 거야.
여: 그럼, 전에도 끊으려고 시도하셨어요?
남: 네다섯 번 정도. 난 오래전에 담배를 피우기 시작했거든.
여: 예전에 금연을 하려고 할 때는 어떤 일이 있었어요?
남: 곧 다시 담배에 빠지고 말았어. 왜냐하면 내 자신에게 "그냥 피워, 담배 한 개비는 괜찮을 거야."라고 했거든.
여: ______________________________

어휘 **disgusting** 정말 싫은, 역겨운 / **patch** 헝겊 조각; 반창고 / **addicted** ~에 빠져 있는, 중독된 | 선택지 어휘 | **give in** 굴복하다 / **do harm** 해가 되다, 손해를 끼치다

15 상황에 적절한 말 | ④

▶ 선생님은 수민에게 유인물을 나눠 줄 것을 부탁하려고 한다.

① 문을 잡아 줘서 고맙구나.
② 모두에게 복사를 해 줄래?
③ 질문 있니?
④ 모든 학생에게 유인물을 나눠 주겠니?
⑤ 매주 운동은 얼마나 하니?

M: As Mr. Fredricks comes into the classroom, the class stands up. Mr. Fredricks is carrying a lot of papers, so Sumin walks over and **asks if he needs help**. He says he doesn't. After putting all the papers down on the teacher's desk, Mr. Fredricks **tells the class to sit down**. He says that today's English grammar class will be about the present perfect tense. He has made copies of some exercises he typed up yesterday. While he writes an explanation on the board, he **wants a student to pass out** the exercises. He decides to ask Sumin to do this. In this situation, what would he most likely say to Sumin?

남: Fredricks 선생님이 교실 안으로 들어오시자 학생들은 자리에서 일어난다. Fredricks 선생님은 유인물을 많이 들고 오셨고, 수민은 다가가서 도움이 필요하신지 여쭤본다. 선생님은 괜찮다고 말씀하신다. 교탁에 유인물을 모두 내려놓으신 후 Fredricks 선생님은 학생들에게 자리에 앉으라고 하신다. 선생님은 오늘 영어 문법 수업은 현재완료시제에 대한 것이라고 말씀하신다. 선생님은 어제 작성한 연습문제를 복사해 오셨다. 선생님은 칠판에 설명을 적는 동안 학생 한 명이 연습문제를 나누어 주기를 원하신다. 선생님은 수민에게 이 일을 부탁하기로 결정하신다. 이러한 상황에서 선생님이 수민에게 할 말로 가장 적절한 것은 무엇인가?

어휘 **present perfect tense** 현재완료시제 / **make a copy** 복사하다 / **explanation** 설명, 해석 / **pass out** (물건을) 나눠 주다 | 선택지 어휘 | **handout** 유인물

16~17 세트 문항 | 16. ② 17. ⑤

▶ 16. 매일 조금씩 공부하기, 시험 칠 때 긴장 풀기, 그리고 시험 장소에 미리 가보는 것 등은 모두 시험을 더 잘 보기 위한 비결이라고 할 수 있다.

① 가장 좋은 공부법
② 시험을 더 잘 보는 비결
③ 기억력 향상법
④ 바쁜 일정 관리법
⑤ 스트레스를 받을 때 침착함을 유지하는 방법

▶ 17. 해석 참조

W: Let's say it's the middle of the school year and you are really busy. You have assignments, projects, and afterschool activities. Now a test is coming up and you have to do well on it. How should you study to get the best results? First, most people do better **when studying in small pieces** instead of large blocks. This should be obvious because it's easier to remember small amounts of information than large amounts. So, try to study a little every day. This can include many simple things like reading a little of your textbook, reviewing the day's notes, or researching online. **Once you are well prepared**, it's just a matter of staying calm during the test. If you are so nervous that you blank out, you might need a mini-break. Keep your eyes closed for a while and relax all of your muscles. Try to **empty your mind of all thoughts**, take a few deep breaths, or imagine yourself in a relaxing location. Finally, if you can, it's a good idea to spend some time in the testing location before the test. **This helps you to feel comfortable** when the big day arrives.

여: 지금 한창 학기 중이고, 매우 바쁘다고 해봅시다. 과제, 프로젝트, 방과 후 활동들이 있습니다. 이제 시험이 다가오고 있고, 잘 해내야만 합니다. 최고의 결과를 얻기 위해 어떻게 공부해야 할까요? 먼저, 사람은 대체로 큰 덩어리보다 작은 조각으로 공부할 때 더 잘합니다. 이 점은 분명할 것인데, 많은 양보다 적은 양의 정보를 기억하기가 더 쉽기 때문입니다. 그러므로 매일 조금씩 공부하려고 노력하세요. 여기에는 많은 간단한 것들이 포함되는데, 교과서 조금 읽기, 그날의 필기 복습하기, 또는 온라인 자료 조사 같은 것들입니다. 일단 만반의 준비가 되면, 시험 동안 침착함을 유지하는가의 문제일 뿐입니다. 너무 긴장해서 갑자기 아무것도 생각나지 않는다면, 짧은 휴식이 필요할지도 모릅니다. ① 잠시 눈을 감고 ② 모든 근육의 긴장을 풀라. ③ 마음속에서 모든 생각을 비우려고 노력하고, ④ 몇 번 심호흡하거나 편안한 장소에 있는 자신을 상상하세요. 마지막으로, 가능하다면 시험 전에 시험 장소에서 시간을 보내는 것도 좋은 생각입니다. 이는 시험 당일이 되었을 때 편안한 마음을 갖도록 도와줍니다.

어휘 **be in the middle of** 한창 (바쁘게) ~하는 중이다 / **obvious** 분명한, 확실한 / **blank out** 갑자기 (머릿속이) 텅 비다 / **empty A of B** A에서 B를 비우다

21 Sense Up 듣기 모의고사 ANSWERS & COMPREHENSION

본문 p.128

01. ② 02. ② 03. ③ 04. ③ 05. ④ 06. ④ 07. ② 08. ⑤ 09. ④ 10. ②
11. ⑤ 12. ④ 13. ⑤ 14. ② 15. ⑤ 16. ① 17. ②

01 화자가 하는 말의 목적 | ②

▶ 정수기의 좋은 점을 나열하고 저렴한 가격에 살 수 있다고 말하며 정수기를 광고하고 있다.

W: As you know, about 60 percent of your body is water, and you **must drink plenty of it every day**. The standard recommendation is to drink at least eight 8-ounce glasses a day. But while you're doing all this drinking, **make sure you're not adding new toxins** to your body. That's why I'm going to introduce the Pureit water purifier to you. It not only helps in purifying the water **but also removes harmful materials** and protects you from waterborne diseases. Plus, you can get hot and cold water anytime you want. This energy saving water purifier comes with a warranty of one year and is easily available at a small price. With Pureit, stay healthy and fit.

여: 여러분도 알다시피, 우리 신체의 약 60퍼센트가 물이라서 여러분은 매일 많은 물을 마셔야 합니다. 표준 권장량은 하루에 적어도 8온스 유리잔으로 8잔을 마시는 것입니다. 하지만 여러분이 이를 모두 마시면서 신체에 새로운 독소를 추가하지 않도록 하셔야 합니다. 이것이 제가 여러분에게 Pureit 정수기를 소개하려는 이유입니다. 그것은 물을 깨끗이 할 뿐만 아니라 해로운 물질을 제거하고 여러분을 수인성 질병으로부터 보호합니다. 게다가, 여러분은 원하는 어느 때든 뜨겁고 차가운 물을 얻을 수 있습니다. 이 에너지 절약 정수기는 1년 보증이고 얼마 안 되는 가격에 쉽게 구할 수 있습니다. Pureit으로 건강과 몸매를 유지하십시오.

어휘 **recommendation** 권고 / **toxin** 독소 / **water purifier** 정수기 ***cf.*** **purify** 깨끗이 하다 / **waterborne** 수인성의, 물에 의해 퍼지는 / **plus** 더욱이, 게다가 / **warranty** 보증

02 의견 | ②

▶ 여자는 신중하게 돈을 관리하는 방법으로 가계부 작성과 비상시에 대비한 여유 자금 보유하기 등을 이야기하고 있다.

W: Corey, we should buy a birthday present for Grandmother. Do you think you can **afford half of it**?
M: Gee, I'm afraid I can't. I've already used a lot of money this month for a new computer, a new phone, and some new clothes and shoes.
W: I'm afraid you spent too much money at once. Maybe you need to use your money more carefully.
M: You're right. But I don't know **how to budget my money**.
W: It's not difficult. You can record your income and expenses in a personal accounts book.
M: I guess it would **help me identify unnecessary spending**.
W: That's what I mean. You should always have some extra money in case of emergency.
M: OK. Thank you for your concern.

여: Corey, 우리 할머니 생신 선물을 사야 해. 네가 반을 부담할 수 있을 것 같니?
남: 이런, 못할 것 같아. 새 컴퓨터, 새 휴대전화, 새 옷 몇 벌과 신발을 사느라 이번 달에 이미 돈을 많이 써버렸거든.
여: 넌 한번에 돈을 너무 많이 쓴 거 같아. 어쩌면 좀 더 신중하게 돈을 써야 할지도 몰라.
남: 누나 말이 맞아. 하지만 돈을 규모 있게 쓰는 법을 모르겠어.
여: 어렵지 않아. 너의 수입과 지출을 지출 장부에 기록하면 돼.
남: 그러면 내가 불필요한 지출을 파악하는 데 도움이 되겠구나.
여: 내 말이 그 말이야. 너는 비상시를 대비해서 늘 여윳돈을 가지고 있어야 해.
남: 알겠어. 걱정해 줘서 고마워.

어휘 **budget one's money** 규모 있게 돈을 쓰다 / **identify** 알아보다, 파악하다

03 관계 | ③

▶ 남자는 Ronda 강을 보호하는 단체에 후원을 신청하려고 전화한 후원 신청자이고, 여자는 자신의 기관을 돕는 방법을 안내하는 환경 단체 직원이다.

[Phone rings.]
W: Greener World. This is Joan Stuart.
M: Hello, my name is Alan Kyle and I'm calling about a program that I watched on TV last night.
W: Oh, hello. That must be **in regards to the program** that was aired on TWBS.
M: Yes, I was very touched by the stories of your effort and dedication to preserve the Ronda River.
W: I'm happy to hear it. We're hoping that more people take an interest in the preservation of the Ronda River.
M: I hope so, too. I'm calling today because I wanted to help your organization.
W: There are many ways you can help the environment here at Greener World. You can **volunteer to clean up** the Ronda River.
M: Oh, unfortunately I live far away so I can't do that. But I can help out financially.
W: That would be wonderful, too. You can make a donation through our website. You can help us with a $50 or more donation.
M: **How can I find** your website?
W: Type "Greener World" in the search box. We really appreciate all your support.

[전화벨이 울린다.]
여: Greener World입니다. 저는 Joan Stuart입니다.
남: 안녕하세요, 제 이름은 Alan Kyle이고 어젯밤 TV에서 본 프로그램에 관해 전화를 걸었어요.
여: 아, 안녕하세요. 그것은 분명히 TWBS에 방송된 프로그램에 관한 것이겠군요.
남: 네, 저는 Ronda 강을 보존하기 위한 귀사의 노력과 헌신에 대한 이야기에 아주 감동을 받았습니다.
여: 그것을 들으니 좋군요. 저희는 더 많은 사람들이 Ronda 강을 보존하는 데 관심을 갖기를 희망하고 있습니다.
남: 저도 그러길 바랍니다. 전 오늘 당신의 기관을 돕고 싶어서 전화를 걸었습니다.
여: 여기 Greener World에서 환경을 도울 수 있는 많은 방법이 있습니다. Ronda 강을 청소하는 자원봉사 활동을 할 수 있고요.
남: 아, 안타깝지만 저는 멀리 살고 있어서 그것을 할 수 없습니다. 하지만 저는 재정적으로 도울 수 있어요.
여: 그것도 굉장히 좋습니다. 귀하는 저희 웹사이트에서 기부를 하실 수 있습니다. 50달러 이상의 기부로 저희를 도우실 수 있으세요.
남: 귀사의 웹사이트를 어떻게 찾을 수 있나요?
여: 검색창에 'Greener World'라고 치세요. 저희는 귀하의 모든 지원에 정말로 감사드립니다.

어휘 **in regards to** ~에 관해서 / **air** ~을 방송하다 / **dedication** 헌신 / **preserve** 보존[유지]하다 ***cf.*** **preservation** 보존, 유지 / **financially** 재정적으로, 재정상 / **make a donation** 기부[기증]하다

04 그림 불일치 | ③

▶ 여자는 두 개의 로봇이 서로 마주보고 있다고 했다.

W: James, **what's all this stuff** in here?
M: That's my hobby. I collect old things.
W: Interesting! Oh, look at the radio next to a fan. I've seen radios with antennas, just like that one, in old movies.
M: Yes, my parents said that was a very popular model at one time.
W: I see. So, where did you get that umbrella lying across the table? It looks very old.
M: My grandfather gave it to me. I like **its checkered pattern**.
W: It's great. Hey, I think I've seen these robots that are facing each other somewhere.
M: They are characters from a famous, animated TV show.
W: That's right! By the way, the clock **hanging on the wall** looks very old too. Does it still work?
M: Yes, it does. Every hour, the cuckoo comes out and announces the time.
W: That's unique. **What else do you have**?

M: This square table. It is also more than 50 years old.

여: James, 여기 이 물건들은 다 뭐예요?
남: 내 취미예요. 오래된 물건들을 수집하거든요.
여: 재밌네요! 아, 선풍기 옆에 있는 라디오 좀 보세요. 저것처럼 안테나 달린 라디오들은 옛날 영화에서 봤어요.
남: 네. 저희 부모님 말씀이 한때는 그게 아주 인기 있는 모델이었대요.
여: 그렇군요. 테이블을 가로질러 놓인 우산은 어디서 났어요? 아주 오래되어 보여요.
남: 할아버지가 주셨어요. 전 그 우산의 체크무늬가 맘에 들어요.
여: 훌륭한데요. 서로 마주 보고 있는 이 로봇들 어디선가 본 적 있는 것 같아요.
남: 유명한 TV 만화영화 캐릭터들이에요.
여: 맞아요! 근데 벽에 걸린 시계도 무척 오래되어 보여요. 아직 작동하는 거예요?
남: 그럼요, 작동하죠. 매 시간마다 뻐꾸기가 나와서 시간을 알려주는 걸요.
여: 독특하네요. 다른 건 뭐 없어요?
남: 이 사각형 테이블이요. 이것도 50년이 넘은 된 거예요.

어휘 **face each other** 서로 마주보다 / **animated** 만화영화로 된 / **cuckoo** 뻐꾸기

05 부탁한 일 | ④

▶ 남자는 여자에게 소포를 배달할 시간까지 기다려 달라고 부탁하고 있다.

[Phone rings.]
W: Hello?
M: Hi, is Mrs. Green there?
W: Not at the moment. **Can I take a message**?
M: No. But I talked to her an hour ago and she said she'd be home all afternoon. **I want to deliver a package**.
W: My mom told me to stay at home until you came.
M: Oh, OK. I had promised your mom I'd be there by now, but I am way behind schedule in my deliveries.
W: When will you drop off the package?
M: About 5:30. Could you be sure you're there at that time?
W: Yes, but please hurry. **Do you need directions**?
M: Well, I know the area around Ace Apartments very well.
W: OK.
M: I'll visit you around 5:30.

[전화벨이 울린다.]
여: 여보세요?
남: 안녕하세요. Green 부인 계십니까?
여: 지금 안 계세요. 전하실 말씀이 있나요?
남: 아니요. 하지만 제가 한 시간 전에 통화를 했는데 오후 내내 댁에 계실 거라고 하셔서요. 소포를 배달하려고 합니다.
여: 엄마가 배달하시는 분이 오실 때까지 저보고 집에 있으라고 하셨어요.
남: 아, 알겠습니다. 어머님께 지금쯤 도착할 것이라고 약속드렸는데요, 배달이 예정보다 훨씬 더 늦어질 것 같습니다.
여: 소포는 언제쯤 배달될까요?
남: 5시 30분 정도요. 그 시간에 확실히 거기 계실 수 있나요?
여: 네, 하지만 서둘러 주세요. 길을 알려드릴까요?
남: 음, Ace 아파트 부근 지역은 매우 잘 압니다.
여: 알겠습니다.
남: 5시 30분경에 방문하겠습니다.

어휘 **way** 훨씬 / **behind schedule** 예정보다 늦게 / **drop off** 도중에 내려놓다

06 금액 | ④

▶ 남자가 사려는 작은 봉지의 사료는 12달러이고, 6달러를 추가하면 살 수 있는 통조림 샘플도 사겠다고 했으므로 18달러를 지불하게 된다.

W: Can I help you with anything?
M: I'm not sure. I'm taking care of a friend's dog **while he is away**, and I need to buy some dog food.
W: First of all, I'd like to recommend this brand. It has all natural ingredients **that are proven to be healthier**.
M: The price tag says $45! I do want to get something healthy, but that's a lot.
W: That's the price for the largest size. A small bag is only $12.
M: Oh, that's only $3 more than this Happy Chow. **That seems reasonable**. I'll get that.
W: We are also offering two package deals. For an extra $7, you can get this chew toy, or for an additional $6, you can get these samples of canned food.
M: The toy **won't be necessary** but the canned food couldn't hurt. I'll take it.
W: Great. I'll ring you up at the counter.

여: 무엇을 도와드릴까요?
남: 잘 몰라서요. 친구가 자리를 비운 동안 친구의 개를 돌보고 있는데, 개 먹이를 좀 사야 해요.
여: 우선, 이 브랜드를 추천하고 싶네요. 더 건강에 좋다고 입증된 천연 성분만 들어있어요.
남: 가격표에 45달러라고 되어 있네요! 건강에 좋은 것을 정말로 사고 싶지만, 그건 비싸네요.
여: 그 가격은 제일 큰 용량이에요. 작은 봉지는 겨우 12달러랍니다.
남: 와, 이 Happy Chow보다 겨우 3달러만 더 비싸군요. 합리적 가격인 것 같아요. 그걸로 할게요.
여: 게다가 패키지 두 개 구매 정책을 제공하고 있습니다. 7달러를 추가하시면, 이 씹는 장난감도 드립니다. 아니면 6달러를 더 내시면 이 통조림 샘플을 드립니다.
남: 장난감은 필요하지 않겠지만, 통조림은 나쁘지 않네요. 그걸 살게요.
여: 좋습니다. 카운터에서 계산해 드릴게요.

어휘 **couldn't[wouldn't] hurt** 나쁠 것 없다, 손해 볼 것 없다 / **ring up** (금전 등록기에 상품 가격을) 입력하다; (특정 가치의 상품을) 팔다

07 이유 | ②

▶ 남자는 자신이 책을 빌려준 친구의 전화번호를 여자에게 묻고 있는데, 그 책이 숙제에 필요하기 때문이라고 했다.

M: Kim, do you know Ina's phone number?
W: I think **I have it saved** in my phone. Why?
M: I let her borrow a book from me, but now I realize that I need it for an assignment.
W: Well, I'm going to meet her for dinner soon. Want to join us?
M: Thanks, but I'm in a hurry. I have to finish this assignment by tomorrow morning, but **I'm only half-way done**.
W: Are you talking about the group project for history class? Because I think that was postponed.
M: You're right. It was. This is something for Mr. Gerson's class.
W: Oh. I've heard **he's quite strict**. Is that true?
M: It is. He won't accept anything that is even a minute late.
W: Well, in that case, here's the number. *[pause]* Good luck.
M: Thanks. Have a nice dinner.

남: Kim, Ina의 전화번호를 알고 있니?
여: 내 휴대전화에 저장해 놓았을 거야. 무슨 일이야?
남: 내 책을 그녀에게 빌려줬는데, 그게 숙제에 필요하다는 것을 지금 알았어.
여: 음, 내가 그녀와 저녁 먹으려고 곧 만날 예정이야. 같이 갈래?
남: 고맙지만, 내가 바빠서. 내일 아침까지 이 숙제를 끝내야 하는데 아직 반밖에 못 했어.
여: 역사 수업의 조별 과제를 말하는 거야? 왜냐하면 그게 연기된 것 같거든.
남: 맞아, 그랬어. 이건 Gerson 선생님의 수업이야.
여: 아. 그 선생님은 꽤 엄격하시다고 들었어. 정말이니?
남: 그래. 그분은 일 분 늦는 것조차도 용납하지 않으실 거야.
여: 음, 그렇다면, 번호 알려줄게. *[잠시 후]* 행운을 빌어.
남: 고마워. 저녁 맛있게 먹어.

어휘 **postpone** 연기하다, 미루다 / **strict** 엄한, 엄격한

08 언급하지 않은 것 | ⑤

▶ 해석 참조

W: Honey, have you given any thought to our vacation?
M: I have, and I think Aruba sounds perfect.
W: Aruba? That's an island in the Caribbean Sea, right?
M: Yes, it's 30 km north of Venezuela and about the size of Dokdo.
W: That's tiny! **Won't we get bored**?
M: Well, it's famous for water sports. We can try surfing, scuba diving, and even fishing.
W: Oh, that sounds fun! **When can we go**?

M: I heard that the average temperature is about 27 degrees year-round. **Any time will be perfect**.
W: Then we should start to prepare. I'd like to learn at least a few phrases in the local language.
M: Good idea. Dutch is the official language, but English and Spanish are also spoken.
W: Oh, this is going to be so much fun!

여: 여보, 휴가에 대해 생각해 봤어요?
남: 생각해 봤는데, 내 생각에는 Aruba가 좋을 것 같아요.
여: Aruba? 카리브해에 있는 섬(① 위치)이죠, 그렇죠?
남: 맞아요. 베네수엘라에서 북쪽으로 30킬로미터 떨어져 있고(① 위치) 독도의 크기와 비슷해요.
여: 작네요! 지루하지는 않을까요?
남: 글쎄요. 그곳은 수상스포츠로 유명해요. 서핑, 스쿠버 다이빙, 심지어 낚시(② 활동 가능 스포츠)까지 해 볼 수 있어요.
여: 와, 재밌겠네요! 언제 갈 수 있죠?
남: 연중 평균 기온이 약 27도(③ 평균 기온)라고 들었어요. 아무 때나 가도 좋을 거예요.
여: 그러면 준비를 시작해야겠네요. 현지 언어로 최소한 몇 개의 표현은 배우고 싶어요.
남: 좋은 생각이에요. 네덜란드어가 공식 언어(④ 공용어)지만, 영어와 스페인어도 사용한대요.
여: 아, 정말 재미있겠네요!

어휘 **year-round** 연중 계속되는 / **phrase** 구, 구절; 표현하다

09 내용 불일치 | ④

▶ 컴퓨터 칩이 접촉된 부분의 위치를 파악하여 그 접촉을 음성으로 바꾼다고 했다.

M: My invention, the "Intelligent Waistcoat," will give the power of speech to disabled children who have, until now, never been able to talk. It's made of a touch-sensitive cloth attached to an electronic speech machine, so that children wearing it can communicate simply **by pressing certain parts** of their waistcoat. The cloth is unique in that it can send and receive electricity. When the cloth is touched, a computer chip **identifies the location of the touch** and translates the touch into speech through the voice machine. Most importantly, the waistcoat can be produced in large quantities at a low cost and washed normally. These characteristics of the "Intelligent Waistcoat" will help disabled children to **express their thoughts and feelings** through sound.

남: 저의 발명품인 '지능형 조끼'는 지금까지 말을 전혀 할 수 없었던 장애 어린이들에게 말할 수 있는 능력을 줄 것입니다. 그것은 전자 음성 기계에 부착된, 손을 대면 감응하는 천으로 만들어졌습니다. 그래서 그것을 입은 어린이들은 단순히 조끼의 특정 부분을 누름으로써 의사소통할 수 있습니다. 그 천은 전기를 송신하고 수신할 수 있다는 점에서 독특합니다. 천을 만지면, 컴퓨터 칩이 접촉된 부분의 위치를 파악하여 음성 기계 장치를 통해 그 접촉을 음성으로 바꿉니다. 가장 중요한 것은, 조끼가 저렴한 가격에 대량 생산될 수 있고, 일반 세탁이 가능하다는 것입니다. '지능형 조끼'의 이런 특징들은 장애 어린이들이 자신의 생각과 감정을 소리를 통해 표현하는 데 도움이 될 것입니다.

어휘 **waistcoat** 조끼 / **disabled** 장애가 있는 / **sensitive** 반응하는; 민감한, 예민한 / **in that** ~라는 점에서 / **characteristic** 특징, 특질

10 도표 이해 | ②

▶ 우선 접을 수 있는 의자를 원했고, 컵 거치대가 최소한 2개 이상 있으며 가격은 70달러가 넘지 않는 것을 사려고 하고 있다. 마지막 남은 선택인 ②와 ③ 중 가격이 더 비싸더라도 빨간색이 아닌 의자를 원했으므로 두 사람이 주문할 낚시 의자는 ②이다.

M: Jennifer, we have to buy a fishing chair for our family trip next week. I'd like to order one online.
W: Good. **Make sure you order a foldable chair**.
M: Of course. Foldable chairs are easy to store and transport.
W: And we need a chair with cup holders.
M: I think so. Cup holders are **useful for holding** drinks, snacks, and phones.
W: Let's buy one with at least two cup holders.
M: Got it. What about the price?
W: I don't want to **spend more than** $70 on a fishing chair.
M: Okay. Now we should choose one of these two. Would you like to buy a cheaper one?
W: Well, since we already have a red fishing chair, I want **one in a different color** this time even if it's more expensive.
M: It's settled. Let's order it right away.

남: Jennifer, 다음 주 우리 가족 여행을 위해 낚시 의자를 사야 해요. 온라인으로 하나 주문하고 싶어요.
여: 좋아요. 반드시 접을 수 있는 의자로 주문하도록 해요.
남: 물론이죠. 접이식 의자는 보관과 운반이 쉽잖아요.
여: 그리고 우리는 컵 거치대가 있는 의자가 필요해요.
남: 나도 그렇게 생각해요. 컵 거치대는 음료와 간식, 전화기를 보관하는 데 유용하죠.
여: 컵 거치대가 적어도 두 개 있는 걸로 사요.
남: 알았어요. 가격은요?
여: 난 낚시 의자에 70달러 넘게 쓰고 싶지는 않아요.
남: 좋아요. 이제 이 둘 중 하나를 선택해야 해요. 가격이 더 싼 걸 살래요?
여: 음, 우리가 이미 빨간 낚시 의자를 갖고 있기 때문에 더 비싸더라도 이번엔 다른 색의 의자를 원해요.
남: 결정됐군요. 지금 바로 그걸 주문합시다.

어휘 **foldable** 접을 수 있는 / **store** 보관하다 / **transport** 운반하다 / **settle** 결정하다, 결심하다

11 짧은 대화에 이어질 응답 | ⑤

▶ 피로한 눈을 위해 무엇을 할 수 있는지를 묻는 남자의 말에 가장 적절한 응답을 고른다.

① 내 시력이 예전에 그랬던 만큼 좋지 않아.
② 네가 쓰는 모니터는 신형이 아니야.
③ 모니터 설정을 조절하는 법을 알려줄게.
④ 당근을 먹는 게 시력을 좋아지게 하는 것 같진 않아.
⑤ 모니터로 작업할 때 눈을 자주 쉬게 해줘.

M: I can't see the letters on the monitor clearly.
W: Oh, your eyes **must be tired** from working so much.
M: **I guess so**. Is there anything I can do for my eyes?
W: ______________________________

남: 모니터의 글씨가 또렷하게 안 보여.
여: 아, 일을 너무 많이 해서 네 눈이 피로한 게 틀림없어.
남: 그런 것 같아. 내 눈을 위해 할 수 있는 게 있을까?
여: ______________________________

12 짧은 대화에 이어질 응답 | ④

▶ 더 큰 사이즈의 재킷이 있는지 물어보겠다고 말하며 남자에게 어떤 사이즈를 입는지 묻는 여자의 말에 가장 적절한 응답을 고른다.

① 나는 캐주얼한 스타일이 더 좋아.
② 라지 사이즈는 너에게 너무 커.
③ 갈색은 내게 어울리지 않을 것 같아.
④ 미디엄 사이즈가 딱 맞을 것 같아.
⑤ 유감이지만 더 큰 사이즈가 하나도 없습니다.

W: **Why don't you try on** the brown jacket?
M: I don't think **it will fit**. It's only a small.
W: I'll ask the clerk for a larger size. What do you wear?
M: ______________________________

여: 그 갈색 재킷을 입어보는 게 어때?
남: 맞을 것 같지 않아. 스몰 사이즈야.
여: 점원에게 더 큰 사이즈가 있는지 물어볼게. 무슨 사이즈를 입니?
남: ______________________________

13 긴 대화에 이어질 응답 | ⑤

▶ 합당하지 않은 근거로 자신을 뽑아달라는 남자에게 할 수 있는 대답을 고른다.

① 내가 너의 선거 참모가 되어 줄까?
② 네 말이 맞아. 그녀가 훨씬 더 자격이 있어.
③ 말도 안 돼. 너는 더 나은 대우를 받을 자격이 있어.
④ 그녀는 그 위치에 만족하지 않을 거야.
⑤ 그런 식의 선거운동으로는 내 표를 얻을 수 없어.

M: I hope **you'll vote for me** as class president.
W: I didn't know you were running. Good luck.

M: Does that mean you're going to vote for me?
W: My best friend Susan is **running for class president** too.
M: I thought I was your best friend.
W: You are my best guy friend. Susan is my best girl friend.
M: Anyway, **I'm much more qualified** to be president than her.
W: Based on what?
M: Based on the fact that I'm more popular than her.
W: ____________________

남: 나를 학급 회장으로 뽑아주기를 바라.
여: 네가 출마한 걸 몰랐어. 행운을 빌어.
남: 나에게 투표하겠다는 뜻이니?
여: 내 가장 친한 친구인 Susan도 학급 회장에 출마했어.
남: 내가 너의 가장 친한 친구라고 생각했는데.
여: 넌 가장 친한 남자 친구고 Susan은 가장 친한 여자 친구지.
남: 어쨌든, 그 애보다는 내가 학급 회장에 훨씬 더 적임이야.
여: 어떤 근거에서?
남: 내가 그 애보다 더 인기 있다는 사실을 근거로 해서야.
여: ____________________

어휘 **run** 입후보하다 / **qualified** 적격의 | 선택지 어휘 | **ridiculous** 터무니없는

14 긴 대화에 이어질 응답 | ②

▶ 약속이 겹치는 상황에서 남자가 자기에게 한 가지 생각이 있다고 했고, 여자가 그것이 무엇인지 물었으므로 해결 방안을 제안하는 응답이 적절하다.

① 그분은 오늘 저녁 식사를 하고 싶지 않으실 거라고 생각해요.
② 우리 모두 저녁 식사를 함께하면 어떨까요?
③ 그분이 전화하기 전에 제가 먼저 했어야 했어요.
④ 그분께 언제나 환영한다고 말씀해주세요.
⑤ 다음에 데이트할 수 있나요?

[Cell phone rings.]
M: Hello, Jane. What time do you want to meet?
W: Hi. Well, I have to wait for a phone call, so I'm not sure.
M: Can't you just **have the person call you** on your cell phone?
W: Yes, but if I get this phone call, I will have to go somewhere else.
M: You mean, you have another appointment? We have been planning this date for a week!
W: **It's my work**. One of my clients is in town. I may have to have dinner with him.
M: But our date is also important.
W: I know. Then what should I tell him **if he calls**?
M: I've got an idea.
W: What's that?
M: ____________________

[휴대전화 벨이 울린다.]
남: 여보세요, Jane. 몇 시에 만났으면 좋겠어요?
여: 안녕하세요. 음, 전화를 기다려야 해서 확실히 모르겠어요.
남: 그냥 그분이 당신 휴대전화로 연락하게 할 수 없나요?
여: 할 수 있지만 이 전화를 받으면 다른 곳에 가야 할 거예요.
남: 그 말은, 다른 약속이 있다는 거예요? 이번 데이트를 일주일 동안 계획했잖아요!
여: 일 때문에 그래요. 제 고객 중 한 분이 시내에 계세요. 그분과 저녁 식사를 같이 해야 할지도 몰라요.
남: 하지만 우리 데이트도 중요하잖아요.
여: 알아요. 그럼 그분이 전화하시면 뭐라고 말해야 할까요?
남: 나에게 한 가지 생각이 있어요.
여: 그게 뭐예요?
남: ____________________

15 상황에 적절한 말 | ⑤

▶ Sara는 Jake가 의사의 지시를 듣지 않고 축구를 한 것이 잘못이라고 생각한다고 했으므로 이를 나무라는 말이 적절하다.

① 더 심해지기 전에 의사에게 가야 해.
② 완전히 회복하려면 충분히 휴식을 취하는 게 중요해.
③ 네가 이번 달에 축구를 다시 할 수 있다고 생각하지 않아.
④ 나라면 너처럼 다리가 부러진 상태로 경기할 수 없었을 거야.
⑤ 너는 의사의 지시를 따랐어야 해.

W: Sara and Jake are good friends. Jake plays soccer for a small local team, and Sara often comes to the games. A few months ago, however, **Jake was injured while playing**. He broke his leg and was unable to play for two months. On the third month, Jake **went to see his doctor**. His doctor told Jake to rest for another two months. Jake didn't listen though. He was anxious to play and couldn't wait. But just ten minutes into his first game, Jake fell in pain. His injury **had gotten worse**. Now Jake is on the phone with Sara. He's complaining that he can't play soccer for another two months. Sara is annoyed by this. She thinks it's Jake's fault **for ignoring his doctor.** In this situation, what would Sara most likely say to Jake?

여: Sara와 Jake는 친한 친구이다. Jake는 작은 지역팀에서 축구를 하고, Sara는 종종 경기를 보러 온다. 하지만 몇 달 전에 Jake는 경기 중 부상을 당했다. 그는 다리가 부러졌고 두 달 동안 경기를 할 수 없었다. 세 번째 달에, Jake는 의사를 방문했다. 의사는 Jake에게 두 달을 더 쉬라고 말했다. 하지만 Jake는 그 말을 듣지 않았다. 그는 축구를 하려는 생각이 간절했고 기다릴 수 없었다. 그러나 Jake는 그의 첫 경기에서 10분 만에 아파서 쓰러졌다. 그의 부상은 더 심해졌다. 지금 Jake는 Sara와 통화 중이다. 그는 두 달 더 축구를 못 하게 된 것을 불평하고 있다. Sara는 이 말에 화가 난다. 그녀는 Jake가 의사의 말을 무시한 것이 잘못이라고 생각한다. 이러한 상황에서 Sara가 Jake에게 할 말로 가장 적절한 것은 무엇인가?

16~17 세트 문항 | 16. ① 17. ②

▶ 16. 해마, 부엉이, 치타, 토끼, 개구리의 예를 들며 위장술을 사용하는 동물들에 대해 말하고 있다.

① 주변 환경과 섞이는 동물들
② 육지 동물과 바다 동물의 차이점
③ 경쟁이 진화를 이끄는 방법
④ 혹독한 기후에서 생존하는 동물들
⑤ 다양한 동물을 찾아내고 확인하는 방법

▶ 17. 해석 참조

① 해마 ② 나비 ③ 치타 ④ 토끼 ⑤ 개구리

M: Last time, we talked about how animals in nature are **in constant competition with one another**. And we learned that this has caused animals to evolve some truly amazing abilities. These abilities help them survive in harsh climates, escape predators, and find food. One particularly fascinating adaptation is the ability to blend with the environment. This can be seen everywhere in the oceans. For example, the pigmy seahorse attaches itself to the coral it lives with and **becomes almost invisible**. On land, hiding oneself is just as popular. Most owls, for instance, are a shade of grey **that can hardly be seen** against the grey trunks of trees. In the grasslands of Africa, a cheetah's brown coat hides it well in the dry plants of its surroundings. High in the mountains, a white rabbit disappears into the snow. And in tropical jungles, a green frog is almost impossible to spot. **Just take a moment** to think of how your favorite animal has adapted to its surroundings.

남: 지난 시간에는 자연 속 동물들이 어떻게 서로 끊임없이 경쟁하는지에 대해 이야기 나눴습니다. 그리고 우리는 이것이 동물들로 하여금 정말 놀라운 능력을 진화시키게 했다는 것을 알게 되었지요. 이런 능력들은 동물들로 하여금 혹독한 기후에 살아남고 포식자들로부터 도망가고 먹이를 찾게 해줍니다. 한 가지 특별히 놀라운 적응력은 주변 환경과 섞이는 능력입니다. 이것은 바다 모든 곳에서 볼 수 있습니다. 예를 들어 피그미 ① 해마는 자신이 살고 있는 산호초에 몸을 밀착시켜 거의 보이지 않습니다. 땅에서도 자신을 숨기는 것은 아주 흔합니다. 예를 들어 대부분의 부엉이들은 회색 나무줄기에 대비되면 잘 보이지 않는 회색 색조입니다. 아프리카 초원에서 ③ 치타의 갈색 털은 주변 환경인 마른 식물들 속에 잘 숨게 해줍니다. 높은 산속에서 하얀 ④ 토끼는 눈 속으로 사라집니다. 그리고 열대 정글에서 초록색 ⑤ 개구리는 찾아내기 거의 불가능하죠. 이제 잠시 시간을 내어 여러분이 좋아하는 동물들이 각자의 환경 속에 어떻게 적응해왔는지를 생각해보세요.

어휘 **evolve** 진화시키다 ***cf.*** **evolution** 진화 / **harsh** 혹독한 / **predator** 포식자 / **fascinating** 대단히 흥미로운, 매력적인 / **adaptation** 적응(력) ***cf.*** **adapt** 적응하다 / **attach to** ~에 들러붙다 / **coral** 산호초 / **invisible** 보이지 않는 / **shade** 음영, 그늘 / **trunk** 나무의 몸통 / **coat** (동물의) 털; 외투 / **tropical** 열대지방의 / **spot** 찾아내다

22 Sense Up 듣기 모의고사 ANSWERS & COMPREHENSION

본문 p.134

01. ⑤ 02. ③ 03. ② 04. ② 05. ① 06. ④ 07. ④ 08. ⑤ 09. ⑤ 10. ⑤
11. ② 12. ② 13. ④ 14. ③ 15. ④ 16. ① 17. ⑤

01 화자가 하는 말의 목적 | ⑤

▶ 교육 프로그램의 마지막 단계인 UCC 비디오 제작 프로젝트를 수행하는 방법에 관해 안내하고 있다.

W: Good morning, everyone. Congratulations to all of you for **making it to the last step** of the training program. Today, you're going to work in teams to make a UCC video to promote our shoes. Your team **will be made up of** six members. Each team can choose any one of our products and then ask for a sample of the product from our design team. You may cast anyone in the video, but the main character must be one of your team members. You should make two versions of the film — a one-minute video and a thirty-second video. Please upload your video file to our company's website by 12 p.m., **so that it can be voted on** tomorrow. Enjoy the project.

여: 좋은 아침이에요, 여러분. 교육 프로그램의 마지막 단계까지 오신 것에 대해 여러분 모두에게 축하를 드립니다. 오늘, 여러분은 팀을 이루어 자사의 신발을 홍보하기 위한 UCC 비디오를 제작해 볼 것입니다. 팀은 여섯 명으로 구성됩니다. 각 팀은 자사의 제품 중 어느 것이든 하나를 선택할 수 있으며 그 후 디자인 팀에 샘플 제품을 요청하면 됩니다. 비디오에는 누구든지 출연시킬 수 있지만, 주인공은 여러분의 팀원 중 한 사람이어야 합니다. 영상은 두 가지 버전으로 만들어야 하는데 하나는 1분짜리, 다른 하나는 30초짜리입니다. 내일 투표할 수 있도록, 여러분이 만든 비디오 파일을 오후 12시까지 우리 회사 웹사이트에 올려 주십시오. 즐거운 프로젝트가 되기를 바랍니다.

어휘 **make it** (모임 등에) 가다, 도착하다; 성공하다 / **UCC** 사용자 제작 콘텐츠(User Created Content의 약어) / **promote** 홍보하다; 촉진하다; 승진시키다 / **upload** 업로드하다(더 큰 컴퓨터 시스템으로 데이터를 보내다) / **vote on** ~에 대해 투표하다

02 대화 주제 | ③

▶ 두 사람은 지역 내에서 이용할 수 있는 문화 시설이 설립되기를 바란다고 이야기하고 있다.

W: Hi, Jack. How was your trip?
M: It was great! I had such a good time. I visited public art galleries, live performances in the parks, weekend street fairs, and so on.
W: **I wish there were more to enjoy** here, too.
M: You know, there is a proposal to increase funding for cultural facilities in our town. I really **want it to pass**.
W: That's pleasing to hear. We really need facilities such as museums, stadiums, and public concert halls.
M: That's right. We **get to vote on it** next month.
W: I'd be very happy if the proposal is passed.
M: Of course.

여: 안녕, Jack. 여행 어땠니?
남: 정말 좋았어! 아주 즐거운 시간을 보냈어. 공공 미술관, 공원에서의 라이브 공연, 주말 거리 축제 등 여러 곳에 갔었거든.
여: 이곳에도 즐길 거리가 더 많았으면 좋겠어.
남: 있잖아, 우리 시에 문화 시설을 위한 자금을 늘리자는 제안이 있어. 그게 꼭 통과되면 좋겠어.
여: 반가운 소식이네. 우린 박물관, 경기장, 공공 콘서트홀과 같은 시설이 정말 필요해.
남: 맞아. 우리는 다음 달에 그것에 관해 투표하게 돼.
여: 그 제안이 통과하면 정말 기쁠 거야.
남: 당연하지.

어휘 **proposal** 제안, 제의; 프러포즈, 청혼 / **funding** 자금 (제공) / **facility** 시설, 설비

03 관계 | ②

▶ 잇몸 염증과 충치가 있다고 하면서 치료를 위해 접수 담당자에게 예약하고 가라는 내용으로 미루어 두 사람은 치과 의사와 환자임을 알 수 있다.

W: I'll recline your chair. *[pause]* Can you move a little upward?
M: I see. Is that okay?
W: All right. **Does it hurt when I touch it**?
M: Ah, yes, it does.
W: Look at this monitor. There is some inflammation of the gums. You also have **a few cavities as well**.
M: That's not good news.
W: I'll move your chair up again. Don't worry. There are just two and they are superficial.
M: Then I won't need surgery?
W: No, I'll just get these two fillings drilled and taken care of.
M: Oh, okay. Can you do it now?
W: No, you'll need to **book an appointment with** the receptionist on the way out. You should get it done as soon as possible.
M: Yes, I'll do that.

여: 의자를 눕히겠습니다. *[잠시 후]* 조금 위로 이동하실 수 있나요?
남: 알겠습니다. 됐나요?
여: 좋아요. 제가 건드리면 통증이 있나요?
남: 아, 예, 그래요.
여: 이 모니터를 보세요. 잇몸에 염증이 좀 있어요. 게다가 충치도 몇 개 있군요.
남: 그건 좋은 소식이 아니군요.
여: 의자를 다시 위로 올릴게요. 걱정 마세요. 단지 두 개뿐이고 표면에 있어요.
남: 그러면 수술이 필요하지 않은 거죠?
여: 네, 그냥 이 두 개의 봉을 박아 넣고 처리할 거예요.
남: 아, 알겠습니다. 지금 그걸 해줄 수 있나요?
여: 아니오, 나가시는 길에 접수 담당자와 예약을 해야 할 겁니다. 가능한 한 빨리 치료해야 해요.
남: 예, 그렇게 하겠습니다.

어휘 **recline** 눕히다 / **upward** 위쪽으로 / **inflammation** 염증 / **gum** 잇몸 / **cavity** 충치, 구멍 / **superficial** 표면의 / **surgery** 수술 / **filling** (치아의) 충전재 / **receptionist** 접수 담당자

04 그림 불일치 | ②

▶ 남자는 자전거가 바닥에 쓰러져 있다고 했다.

M: **I've been thinking**. Why don't we clear out some of the junk in the backyard and plant some trees?
W: That's a great idea. We need some shade anyway.
M: Since we don't use that barbecue grill next to the fence, let's remove it.
W: But that spot doesn't get much sunshine. I don't think it's good for trees.
M: Good point. Oh, look at **the bicycle lying on the ground**. Whose is it?
W: That's mine. I don't have any other place to keep it.
M: Okay, then. How about the slide next to the bicycle? The kids are grown up. I don't think they use it anymore.
W: We **could give it to the neighbors**. They have two kids.
M: That would be nice. What else? *[pause]* The swing in front of the bench looks very old.
W: Yeah, but I like to sit on it and drink coffee.
M: Okay. We'll leave the swing. But I think the duck beside the swing isn't necessary.
W: You're right. Let's move it and plant some trees.

남: 생각을 해봤는데요, 뒷마당에 쓸모없는 물건을 좀 없애고 나무를 심는 게 어때요?
여: 좋은 생각이에요. 어쨌든 그늘이 좀 필요하니까요.
남: 울타리 옆에 있는 바비큐그릴을 사용하지 않으니까 그걸 없애요.
여: 그렇지만 그 자리는 햇빛이 많이 들지 않잖아요. 나무들한테는 안 좋은 자리인 것 같아요.
남: 좋은 지적이에요. 땅에 쓰러져 있는 자전거 좀 봐요. 누구 거죠?
여: 내 것이에요. 다른 데 둘 데가 없어요.
남: 좋아요, 그럼. 자전거 옆에 있는 미끄럼틀은요? 애들도 다 컸고, 더 이상은 쓰지 않는 것 같은데요.
여: 이웃집에 주면 되겠어요. 애들이 둘 있거든요.

남: 그거 좋겠어요. 그 밖에 뭐가 있죠? *[잠시 후]* 벤치 앞에 있는 그네가 무척 오래되어 보이네요.
여: 맞아요. 하지만 나는 거기 앉아서 커피 마시는 게 좋아요.
남: 좋아요. 그네는 그냥 둡시다. 그런데 그네 옆에 있는 오리는 필요가 없을 것 같네요.
여: 맞아요. 그걸 옮기고 나무를 심어요.

어휘 **junk** 쓸모없는 물건, 쓰레기 / **slide** 미끄럼틀

05 추후 행동 | ①

▶ 숙제를 같이하게 된 두 사람이 일을 분담하고 있다. 시각 자료를 위해 필요한 것들을 언급하며 여자가 자신은 담요가 없다고 하자 남자가 가져오겠다고 했다.

W: I don't like our homework topic. Scientific terms like "static electricity" are difficult.
M: Don't worry, Jisu. We just need to find some websites about it.
W: But the teacher said we need pictures and a visual to show **how it works**.
M: Then why don't we start by searching for pictures?
W: I suppose pictures showing static electricity **won't be too hard to find** online.
M: Right. And for the visual, we need a sweater and a small blanket.
W: I'll bring the sweater tomorrow, but I'm afraid I don't have a blanket.
M: No problem. **I'll bring one**. Now, what else is there to do for this assignment?
W: That just leaves the writing. I'll call you later **to decide on a time for that**.
M: Sounds good. Don't forget to bring everything tomorrow.
W: Okay. See you later.

여: 난 우리 숙제 주제가 맘에 들지 않아. '정전기' 같은 과학 용어는 어려워.
남: 걱정하지 마, 지수야. 그것에 관해 홈페이지 몇 군데를 찾아보면 돼.
여: 하지만 선생님께서 어떻게 정전기가 작용하는지 보여주는 사진들과 시각 자료가 필요하다고 말씀하셨어.
남: 그러면 사진부터 찾는 거로 시작하면 어떨까?
여: 정전기를 보여주는 사진을 인터넷에서 찾는 게 그리 어려울 것 같진 않아.
남: 맞아. 그리고 시각 자료를 위해서 우리는 스웨터랑 작은 담요가 필요해.
여: 내가 내일 스웨터를 가져올게. 그런데 담요는 없는데.
남: 괜찮아. 내가 담요를 가져올게. 자, 이 숙제를 위해 해야 할 다른 일이 뭐가 있지?
여: 글쓰기만 남았어. 글쓰기 시간을 정하기 위해 내가 나중에 전화할게.
남: 그래 좋아. 내일 모든 것을 가져오는 것 잊지 마.
여: 그래. 다음에 보자.

어휘 **term** 용어; 학기; 기간 / **static electricity** 정전기 / **visual** 시각 자료; 시각의; (눈으로) 보는 / **suppose** 생각하다; 추정[가정]하다 / **blanket** 담요 / **assignment** 숙제; 과제, 임무 / **leave** 남기다; (사람 · 장소에서) 떠나다; (직장 · 학교 등을) 그만두다

06 금액 | ④

▶ 남자는 부품 교체에 80달러, 인건비로 160달러가 든다고 했으므로 여자가 지불할 금액은 240달러이다. 남자의 마지막 말에 언급된 100달러는 제때 수리하지 않았을 때의 추가적인 비용이므로 지불할 금액에 포함하지 않도록 한다.

W: Were you able to **locate the problem**?
M: Yes. It seems the leak is coming from some old pipes connected to your upstairs bathroom.
W: All right. **How much will it cost to fix it**?
M: The parts will cost $80. That doesn't include labor.
W: How much do you think the labor will be?
M: It will probably take around 4 hours to complete the job. That's $160.
W: So $240 in total? **That seems like a lot**. Maybe I should check with someone else.
M: I guarantee that any plumber in this city will charge at least $200.
W: Still, **I'd like to ask around first**.
M: Suit yourself, but if you don't take care of that leak soon, you're going to find yourself with an additional $100 in floor damage.
W: Okay. Then I'll take care of it now.

여: 문제가 된 곳을 찾아내실 수 있었나요?
남: 네. 위층 화장실과 연결된 오래된 배관에서 누수되는 것 같습니다.
여: 그렇군요. 수리하려면 얼마가 들까요?
남: 부품은 80달러입니다. 인건비는 제외하고요.
여: 인건비는 얼마가 될 것 같나요?
남: 일을 끝마치는 데 아마 4시간 정도가 걸릴 겁니다. 160달러예요.
여: 그럼 총 240달러요? 너무 비싼 것 같아요. 아마도 다른 분에게 문의해 봐야겠어요.
남: 이 시에 있는 어떤 배관공도 최소 200달러는 청구할 거라고 확신해요.
여: 그래도 먼저 이리저리 알아보고 싶어요.
남: 좋으신 대로 하세요. 하지만 새는 곳을 빨리 처리하지 않는다면 바닥 손상으로 100달러가 추가적으로 청구될 겁니다.
여: 알겠습니다. 그러면 지금 그걸 수리할게요.

어휘 **locate** ~의 정확한 위치를 찾아내다 / **leak** (액체 · 기체가) 새는 곳; 누출; (액체 · 기체가) 새다 / **labor** 노동 / **check with** ~에게 문의[조회]하다 / **guarantee** 확신하다; 보장하다; 보증 / **plumber** 배관공 / **ask around** 이리저리 알아보다 / **suit oneself** 자기 마음대로 하다 / **additional** 추가의

07 이유 | ④

▶ 여자는 지금의 머리를 관리하는 것이 힘들다고 했다.

M: What can I do for you today?
W: I haven't made up my mind, but I think I might want to **have my hair cut short**.
M: That is the style this season, and many actresses are choosing short hair.
W: True, but I've never been one to follow trends.
M: Yes, I know. Anyway, your hair looks very healthy. You must **take great care of it**.
W: That's the thing. It's so difficult to maintain. I'm so tired of washing it and waiting for it to dry.
M: I can imagine. Well, you do have the perfect face for short hair.
W: **You've never led me wrong** in the past, so I guess there is no reason not to trust you.
M: Alright. Then I'll get started.

남: 오늘은 어떻게 해드릴까요?
여: 아직 결정은 못했는데, 머리를 짧게 잘라도 괜찮을 것 같아요.
남: 그게 이번 시즌에 유행하는 스타일이어서 많은 여배우들이 짧은 머리를 택하고 있어요.
여: 맞아요. 하지만 전 유행을 따른 적은 없었어요.
남: 네, 알아요. 어쨌든 손님의 머리는 아주 건강해 보이네요. 관리를 잘하시는 게 틀림없어요.
여: 그게 문제예요. 유지하는 건 정말 힘든 일이거든요. 머리를 감고 마르기까지 기다리는 게 정말 지겨워요.
남: 알 만해요. 음, 손님은 정말이지 짧은 머리에 잘 어울리는 얼굴이에요.
여: 이전에 저를 잘못된 쪽으로 이끄신 적은 없으니 이번에도 믿지 못할 이유가 없겠네요.
남: 좋아요. 그럼 시작할게요.

어휘 **trend** 유행; 경향 / **maintain** 유지하다; 지속하다

08 언급하지 않은 것 | ⑤

▶ 해석 참조

M: You've probably never heard of the Swedish village of Jukkasjarvi because it's really only famous for one thing: its Ice Hotel. The Ice Hotel is **exactly what it sounds like** — it's a hotel made entirely of ice and snow! The hotel is huge, measuring around 5,000 square meters, and it contains more than 30,000 cubic meters of snow and 3,000 tons of ice. **It includes sixty guest rooms** with beds made of ice. As you might expect, the hotel isn't very warm. The indoor temperature is kept between –5 and –8 degrees Celsius. Luckily, guests have plenty to distract them from the cold. The Ice Hotel features an ice restaurant, an ice bar, and a wide variety of winter activities. If you're feeling adventurous, **why not give it a try**?

남: 여러분은 아마 스웨덴의 유카스야르비 마을에 대해 들어본 적이 없으실 것입니다. 이곳은 정말 단 한 가지, 얼음 호텔로만 유명하기 때문입니다. 얼음 호텔은 말 그대로 완전히 얼음과 눈으로 만들어진 호텔입니다! 이 호텔은 약 5천 제곱미터로 거대하고, 3만 세제곱미터가 넘는 눈과 3천 톤이 넘는 얼음이 있습니다(① 규모). 이 호텔은 얼음으로 만들어진 침대가 있는 60개의 객실(② 객실 수)을 포함합니다. 예상하다시피, 이 호텔은 별로 따뜻하지는 않습니다. 실내 온도는 섭씨 영하 5도에서 영하 8도 사이(③ 실내 온도)로 유지됩니다. 다행히도 고객들에겐 추위에서 주의를 돌릴 만한 것들이 많습니다. 얼음 호텔은 얼음 레스토랑, 얼음 바(④ 부대시설), 그리고 매우 다양한 겨울 활동을 특징으로 합니다. 만약 모험을 하고 싶은 기분이 든다면, 한번 시도해 보는 게 어떤가요?

어휘 **entirely** 완전히, 전적으로 / **measure** ~의 길이[폭, 높이]이다 / **square meter** 《넓이의 단위》 제곱미터(m^2) ***cf.*** **cubic meter** 《부피의 단위》 세제곱미터(m^3) / **distract from** (주의 등을) 다른 곳으로 돌리다 / **feature** 특징으로 삼다 / **adventurous** 모험심이 강한; 흥미진진한

09 내용 불일치 | ⑤

▶ 오늘날 우리가 보는 것은 예전 모습의 4분의 1이라고 했으므로 4분의 3이 소실된 셈이다.

W: Stonehenge is a circular arrangement of huge stones in southern England, and it was built between 3,500 and 5,000 years ago. No one knows exactly why Stonehenge was built, but **popular explanations include it** being a place of worship or a sacred burial ground. It consists of two types of stone: sandstone and a bluish stone called "bluestone." Over the years, many of this monument's stones **were transported to other sites** and used to make bridges, dams, or flood walls. And some of the smaller stones have been damaged by visitor contact. So, visitors have been prohibited from approaching the monument since 1978. Thus, what we see today are only the ruins of Stonehenge, about one-fourth of **what it once was**.

여: 스톤헨지는 영국 남부에 둥글게 배열된 거석(巨石)이고 3,500년에서 5,000년 전 사이에 지어졌습니다. 스톤헨지가 왜 만들어졌는지는 아무도 정확히 알지 못하지만, 일반적인 설명은 그것이 예배당이거나 신성한 묘지라는 것을 포함합니다. 그것은 두 종류의 암석으로 이루어져 있는데, 사암(砂巖)과 '청석'으로 불리는 푸르스름한 암석입니다. 수년간, 이 기념물의 많은 암석이 다른 지역으로 옮겨져 다리, 댐, 또는 홍수 방벽을 건설하는 데 쓰였습니다. 그리고 더 작은 암석의 일부는 관광객의 접촉으로 훼손되었습니다. 그래서 1978년부터 관광객이 이 기념물에 접근하는 것은 금지되어 왔습니다. 따라서 오늘날 우리가 보는 것은 예전 모습의 약 4분의 1인 스톤헨지의 잔해일 뿐입니다.

어휘 **circular** 원형의, 둥근 / **arrangement** 배치; 준비, 마련; 합의 / **worship** 예배; 예배하다 / **sacred** 성스러운; 신성시되는 / **burial ground** 묘지 / **consist of** ~로 구성되다 / **bluish** 푸르스름한 / **monument** (건물 등의) 기념물 / **prohibit A from B** A가 B하는 것을 금하다[못하게 하다] / **ruin** 잔해; 폐허로 만들다

10 도표 이해 | ⑤

▶ 두 사람은 경유하지 않으며, 14일 이후에 출발하고, 일주일 넘게 뉴욕에서 체류할 수 있는 항공편을 선택하기로 했다.

W: Honey, were you able to find any flights for our trip to New York?
M: Well, **most of the flights had already been booked**, but I did find these five.
W: Oh, let me take a look at that.
M: I don't know about you, but I'd really prefer a nonstop flight.
W: Of course. Let's avoid a stopover if we can. But don't forget that I have to work until the 14th.
M: Right. **That narrows it down**. So, how many days would you like to spend in New York?
W: It's a big city with many famous attractions, but I think 7 days should be enough.
M: You might be right, but we probably **won't have another chance to travel** to the U.S. soon.
W: On second thought, I agree. Longer is better.
M: Then we've decided. I'll make the reservations.

여: 여보, 뉴욕 여행을 위한 항공편은 찾을 수 있었나요?
남: 음, 대부분의 항공편은 이미 예약되었어요. 하지만 이 다섯 개를 찾아냈어요.
여: 아, 한번 보죠.
남: 당신은 어떨지 모르겠지만, 난 정말 직항편을 타고 싶어요.
여: 물론이죠. 가능하다면 경유하는 항공편은 피하도록 해요. 하지만 내가 14일까지 일을 해야 한다는 걸 잊어선 안 돼요.
남: 맞아요. 그러면 범위가 좁혀지는군요. 그런데 뉴욕에서는 며칠이나 보내고 싶어요?
여: 볼거리가 매우 많은 큰 도시지만, 내 생각에 7일이면 충분할 것 같아요.
남: 당신 말이 옳을지도 모르지만, 우리가 조만간 미국을 다시 여행할 기회는 아마 없을 거예요.
여: 다시 생각해보니 그 말이 맞네요. 길수록 더 좋겠죠.
남: 그럼 결정되었군요. 예약할게요.

어휘 **stopover** 단기 체류; 잠깐 들르는 곳 / **narrow down** 좁히다[줄이다]

11 짧은 대화에 이어질 응답 | ②

▶ CD를 빌려준 James의 말처럼 CD가 자동으로 로딩되지 않고 비밀번호를 요구한다는 여자의 말에 대한 가장 적절한 응답을 고른다.

① 그 보고서는 이틀 후가 마감일이야. ② 그 애가 너에게 엉뚱한 CD를 빌려준 것 같아.
③ 네 비밀번호를 변경해야 해. ④ 맞아. James는 컴퓨터를 잘해.
⑤ 원하면 내 노트북 컴퓨터를 빌려줄 수 있어.

W: James lent me this CD for my report, but **it requires a password**.
M: Didn't you get the password from him?
W: No, he said **it would load automatically** after I insert it.
M: ______________________________

여: James가 내 보고서 때문에 이 CD를 빌려줬는데, 비밀번호가 필요해.
남: 그 애한테서 비밀번호 받지 않았어?
여: 안 받았어. CD를 넣으면 자동으로 로딩될 거라고 했거든.
남: ______________________________

어휘 **load** (프로그램을) 로딩하다 / **automatically** 자동으로; 기계적으로 / **insert** 끼우다, 삽입하다 | 선택지 어휘 | **due** ~하기로 되어 있는[예정된] / **laptop** 노트북 컴퓨터

12 짧은 대화에 이어질 응답 | ②

▶ 수업에 관한 어려움을 김 선생님에게 이야기하라는 남자의 제안에 가장 적절한 응답을 찾는다.

① 나는 김 선생님의 기분을 상하게 하고 싶지 않아. ② 차라리 내가 직접 해결하겠어.
③ 그분은 정말 지루한 선생님이야! ④ 너도 돕기 위해 네 역할을 해야 해.
⑤ 나는 모든 일을 직접 하는 것이 지겨워.

M: I'm looking forward to Mr. Kim's lab class. It's always so much fun.
W: **I couldn't disagree more**. My lab partner is so lazy!
M: That's too bad. **Why don't you talk to** Mr. Kim about it?
W: ______________________________

남: 김 선생님의 실험 수업이 기대돼. 늘 정말 재미있어.
여: 나는 절대 동의할 수 없어. 내 실험 파트너는 진짜 게을러!
남: 안됐구나. 김 선생님께 그것에 대해서 말해 보는 게 어때?
여: ______________________________

어휘 **lab** (laboratory의 약자) 실험실 | 선택지 어휘 | **deal with** (문제 등을) 처리하다 / **instructor** 교사, 강사 / **be tired of v-ing** v하는 것이 지겹다

13 긴 대화에 이어질 응답 | ④

▶ 남자친구와 헤어진 줄도 모르고 Mia에게 남자친구의 안부를 물었던 여자에게 해 줄 수 있는 조언을 고른다.

① 그 남자가 누구였는지 그냥 그 애에게 물어봐.
② 그에게 데이트 신청을 하지 그래?
③ 그 애에게 다시 한번 기회를 줘야 할 때인 것 같아.
④ 가서 사과해. 지금이 좋은 기회야.
⑤ 나도 모르겠어. Chuck이 그랬을 리 없을 텐데.

W: Oh, no! There she is!
M: Who? Mia?
W: Yes. She **must have been really mad at me**.
M: Why? What did you do?
W: I saw her last weekend at the movies with some guy. I assumed it was her brother because she has been dating Chuck for so long.
M: Oh, no! You asked her about Chuck?
W: Yes, I asked her **where her boyfriend was** and if this was her brother or cousin.
M: That wasn't very tactful. What did she say?
W: Nothing. She started crying and left the theater immediately.
M: You didn't know what happened to her and Chuck, did you?
W: I had no idea at that time. But only today I found out she doesn't see Chuck anymore.
M: That's too bad.
W: I don't know **what I should do**.
M: ______________________________

여: 이런! 그 애가 저기 있어!
남: 누구? Mia?
여: 응. 나에게 단단히 화가 났을 거야.
남: 왜? 네가 어떻게 했는데?
여: 지난 주말에 영화관에서 그 애가 어떤 남자와 있는 것을 봤어. 난 남동생일거라 생각했어. 왜냐하면 그 애는 Chuck이랑 오랫동안 사귀었으니까.
남: 아 이런! 그 애에게 Chuck에 대해서 물어봤니?
여: 응. 남자친구는 어디에 있는지 그리고 그 남자가 동생이나 사촌이냐고 물었지.
남: 그건 별로 적절하지 못했네. 그 애가 뭐라고 했어?
여: 아무 말도 하지 않았어. 울기 시작하더니 바로 영화관에서 나갔어.
남: 너는 그 애와 Chuck에게 무슨 일이 있었는지 몰랐구나?
여: 그때는 전혀 몰랐지. 하지만 오늘에서야 더 이상 Chuck과 만나지 않는다는 사실을 알게 되었어.
남: 안됐구나.
여: 어떻게 해야 할지 모르겠어.
남: ______________________________

어휘 **assume** (사실일 것으로) 추정하다 / **tactful** 적절한, 재치 있는 / **immediately** 즉시

14 긴 대화에 이어질 응답 | ③

▶ 고장 난 세탁기를 고치도록 수리 기사를 부르는 것이 어떠냐는 남자(아들)의 말에 가장 적절한 대답을 찾는다.

① 나가서 축구 유니폼을 새로 사자.
② 좋은 생각이야. 그렇지 않으면 그가 나에게 전화를 하지 않을 거야.
③ 이미 했단다. 하지만 기사분이 내일에나 오실 수 있대.
④ 마르게 그냥 걸어 놓으렴. 밖에 햇빛이 좋단다.
⑤ 걱정하지 마라. 이미 수리했단다.

M: Mom, where is my soccer uniform?
W: It's in the laundry basket. I **haven't washed it yet**.
M: But I need it for the game tomorrow morning.
W: Can you wash it by hand, please? I have to go to work now.
M: OK. But **why can't I use** the washing machine?
W: It broke this morning. The water **won't drain out of it**.
M: Will my uniform be dry in time for the game?
W: Yes, of course. Use the automatic clothes dryer.
M: OK. And how about calling a repair technician?
W: ______________________________

남: 엄마, 제 축구복이 어디 있어요?
여: 세탁 바구니에 있단다. 아직 세탁하지 않았어.
남: 그렇지만 내일 아침 경기가 있어서 필요해요.
여: 네가 손으로 빨래? 지금 일하러 가야 해서 말이야.
남: 알겠어요. 하지만 왜 세탁기를 사용하면 안 되나요?
여: 오늘 아침에 고장이 났단다. 물이 빠지지를 않아.
남: 운동복이 경기 전에 마를까요?
여: 그럼, 물론이지. 자동 건조기를 사용하렴.
남: 알겠어요. 그런데 수리 기사분을 부르는 것은 어때요?
여: ______________________________

어휘 **drain** 배수하다 / **automatic** 자동식의, 자동의 / **technician** 기술자, 기사

15 상황에 적절한 말 | ④

▶ 오랫동안 노력해 왔지만 또다시 오디션에 낙방한 딸이 포기하지 않도록 아버지가 격려할 수 있는 말을 유추해 본다.

① 너의 목표에 대해서 다시 생각해볼 시간일지도 몰라.
② 네가 다음 오디션을 준비하는 것을 도와줄게.
③ 나는 네가 너무 무리해온 것 같아서 걱정이야.
④ 나는 네 모든 노력이 언젠가는 결실을 맺을 거라고 확신해.
⑤ 아마 너는 더 많은 시간을 연습해야 할 거야.

M: Kate works at a coffee shop part time, but her real passion is acting. She takes acting classes at a nearby college, **takes part in a local theater group**, and practices night and day. Whenever there are auditions for a professional movie or play, Kate goes. Unfortunately, Kate has been unsuccessful for almost a year, and today was no different. After failing an afternoon audition, she comes home to find her father in the kitchen. **She is obviously upset**, and her father is worried. He has seen how hard she works, and he's worried that too many experiences of failure **might cause her to give up**. He wants to say something to encourage her. In this situation, what would Kate's father most likely say to Kate?

남: Kate는 커피숍에서 파트타임으로 일하지만, 그녀가 정말 열정적으로 하는 활동은 연기이다. 그녀는 근처의 대학에서 연기 수업을 듣고, 지역 연극부에 참여하며, 밤낮으로 연습한다. 전문적인 영화나 연극의 오디션이 있을 때마다 Kate는 간다. 안타깝게도 Kate는 거의 일 년 동안 성공적이지 못했고, 오늘도 다르지 않았다. 오후에 있었던 오디션에서 떨어진 후, 그녀는 집에 와 부엌에 계신 아버지를 만난다. 그녀는 분명히 속상해하고 있고 그녀의 아버지는 걱정스럽다. 그는 딸이 얼마나 열심히 하는지 보아왔고, 너무 많은 실패의 경험이 딸로 하여금 포기하게 할까 봐 걱정한다. 그는 딸을 격려하기 위해 무슨 말을 하고 싶다. 이러한 상황에서 Kate의 아버지가 Kate에게 할 말로 가장 적절한 것은 무엇인가?

어휘 **passion** 열정적으로 하는 활동[취미]; 열정 / **unsuccessful** 성공하지 못한 / **obviously** 분명히, 명백히 / **encourage** 격려하다; 장려하다 | 선택지 어휘 | **struggle** 노력, 고투; (~하려고) 싸우다 / **pay off** 성공하다, 성과를 올리다

16~17 세트 문항 | 16. ① 17. ⑤

▶ 16. 사전에 등재된 인터넷 속어, 변화된 발음, 어원, 삽화, 어법 등의 특징을 열거하고 7일간의 무료 사용 혜택을 안내하면서 신간 사전을 홍보하는 내용이다.

① 신간 영어 사전 홍보
② 영어 사전의 편찬 역사
③ 단어를 암기하고 발음하는 효율적인 방법들
④ 온라인 영어 사전 활용법 안내
⑤ 어린아이들을 위한 영어 사전 할인 판매

▶ 17. 해석 참조

W: Language lovers can rejoice because Oxford's **latest has finally arrived**. And it's been updated to include Internet slang, such as "onliner." Since the first dictionary was published over 250 years ago, new words not only have been added over time, but the pronunciation of words has also changed. In fact, only a few hundred years ago, "mice" was pronounced "mace." **Changes like these happened slowly** and for fascinating reasons. Oxford has done a wonderful job of following these changes while providing current pronunciation information. The origins of words have also been included in the most interesting cases. For example, did you know that "jumbo," meaning "very large," was originally an African word for "elephant"? Plus, there are now even more full-color illustrations **to grab your attention**. These are combined with notes on common usage to aid your learning, **making it the ideal gift** for any student. With this well-respected dictionary, you can feel the amazing evolution of the English language. Free 7-day online trials will be offered for the next three days. Don't miss this chance!

여: 언어를 사랑하는 분들은 즐거워하셔도 좋습니다. 옥스퍼드의 최신판이 드디어 나왔으니까요. 이번 사전은 '온라이너(온라인 서비스 사용자)' 같은 ① 인터넷 속어도 포함하도록 업데이트 되었습니다. 250년도 더 전에 최초의 사전이 출간된 이래 시간이 지나면서 새로운 단어들이 등재되었을 뿐만 아니라 단어들의 발음도 변화해 왔습니다. 사실상, 몇 백 년 전만 해도 'mice'는 'mace'로 발음되었답니다. 이런 변화들은 천천히 그리고 대단히 흥미로운 이유로 생겨난 것들입니다. 옥스퍼드 사전은 현재 사용하는 ② 발음 정보를 제공하면서 이런 변화를 따라가는 훌륭한 일을 해내었습니다. 단어들의 ③ 어원도 가장 흥미로운 사례 속에 포함되었습니다. 예를 들어, '매우 큰'을 의미하는 'jumbo'라는 단어가 원래는 아프리카 단어 '코끼리'를 의미했다는 것을 아시나요? 게다가 이제 더 많은 전면 컬러 ④ 삽화가 여러분의 시선을 사로잡을 것입니다. 이 삽화들은 자주 쓰이는 용법에 대한 주석과 결합하여 여러분의 학습을 도와줄 것이며 어떤 학생에게든 이상적인 선물이 되어줄 겁니다. 높은 평가를 받고 있는 이 사전과 함께라면 여러분은 영어의 놀라운 진화를 느끼실 수 있습니다. 앞으로 사흘 동안 온라인에서 7일간의 무료 사용 기회를 드립니다. 이 기회를 놓치지 마세요!

어휘 **rejoice** 크게 기뻐하다 / **slang** 속어, 은어 / **fascinating** 매우 흥미로운; 매력적인 / **current** 현재의, 지금의 / **full-color** 전면 컬러의 / **illustration** 삽화 / **grab** (관심을) 끌다; (와락) 붙잡다 / **combine A with B** A와 B를 결합하다 / **usage** 어법; 용법 / **aid** 돕다 / **ideal** 이상적인 / **well-respected** 높이 평가되는 / **evolution** 진화 | 선택지 어휘 | **compilation** 편찬, 편집(본)

23 Sense Up 듣기 모의고사 ANSWERS & COMPREHENSION

본문 p.140

01. ⑤ 02. ① 03. ② 04. ④ 05. ④ 06. ② 07. ② 08. ③ 09. ④ 10. ③
11. ③ 12. ④ 13. ⑤ 14. ③ 15. ③ 16. ③ 17. ③

01 화자가 하는 말의 목적 | ⑤

▶ 여자는 컬러 프린터에 문제가 발생하지 않도록 두 대의 흑백 프린터 중 한 대를 사용해 줄 것을 요청하고 있다.

W: Good afternoon, everyone. I know it's been a long meeting, but I have one final thing to add. As many of you know, my team is **up against a tight deadline** with our current project. All this week, we're going to be printing samples for the fall fashion catalog. Because fall colors are important to the theme, we're relying on the office's sole color printer for our samples. Last week, this led to a major problem when **it ran out of ink**. To avoid this and ensure everything runs as smoothly as possible, please use one of the two black-and-white printers for other business. With any luck, the catalog will be completed soon and **this will no longer be an issue**. Thanks for your time, everyone.

여: 안녕하세요, 여러분. 회의가 길었다는 것을 알지만, 마지막으로 덧붙일 것이 한 가지 있습니다. 많은 분이 알고 계시듯이, 저희 팀은 현재 작업 중인 프로젝트의 빠듯한 마감일에 직면해 있습니다. 이번 주 내내, 저희는 가을 패션 카탈로그를 위해 견본을 인쇄할 것입니다. 가을 색깔은 카탈로그의 테마에 중요해서, 저희는 견본을 (만드는 데) 회사의 유일한 컬러 프린터에 의존하고 있습니다. 이는 지난주, 컬러 프린터의 잉크가 떨어졌을 때 큰 문제를 가져왔습니다. 이 같은 일을 피하고 모든 일이 가능한 한 순조롭게 돌아가도록 하기 위해, 다른 업무에는 두 대의 흑백 프린터 중 한 대를 사용해 주십시오. 일이 잘 풀리면, 카탈로그는 곧 완성될 것이고 이는(프린터 사용은) 더 이상 문제가 되지 않을 것입니다. 시간을 내주신 모든 분께 감사드립니다.

어휘 **up against** 직면하여, 당면하여 / **catalog** (물품 · 책 등의) 목록, 카탈로그 / **rely on** ~에 의존하다 / **sole** 유일한; 혼자[단독]의 / **ensure** 반드시 ~하게 하다, 보장하다 / **smoothly** 순조롭게 / **with any luck** 잘 되면, 뜻대로 된다면

02 의견 | ①

▶ 남자는 휴대전화 때문에 발생한 교통사고 현장을 언급하며, 안전을 위해 길을 걸으면서 휴대전화를 사용해서는 안 된다고 이야기하고 있다.

M: I just saw an accident right outside our building.
W: Really? What happened?
M: A car **had to turn quickly** to avoid hitting a woman who was crossing the street, but there wasn't enough space so it hit another car.
W: Wow, was anyone injured?
M: Fortunately, no one was hurt. The woman was extremely lucky. She was playing with her phone and not paying attention at all.
W: I think that is becoming more common these days. Usually, people simply **bump into one another** on the street while paying attention to their phones, but serious accidents do happen.
M: After seeing what I just saw, I don't think people should use their phones while walking anymore for everyone's safety.
W: You're right. **Safety is the most important thing**.

남: 우리 건물 바로 밖에서 방금 사고를 목격했어요.
여: 정말이요? 무슨 일이었어요?
남: 차 한 대가 길을 건너고 있던 여자를 치지 않으려고 급히 방향을 틀어야 했는데, 충분한 공간이 없어서 다른 차를 들이받았어요.
여: 와, 누군가 다쳤나요?
남: 다행히 아무도 다치지 않았어요. 그 여자는 운이 정말 좋았지요. 휴대전화를 가지고 놀면서 전혀 주의를 기울이고 있지 않았거든요.
여: 그런 일이 요즘 더 흔해지고 있는 것 같아요. 대개는, 사람들이 자신의 휴대전화에 집중하느라 길에서 서로 부딪칠 뿐이지만, 심각한 사고는 정말 일어나요.
남: 방금 목격한 것을 보고 나니, 모든 사람의 안전을 위해 이젠 걸어 다니면서 휴대전화를 사용해서는 안 된다는 생각이 들어요.
여: 맞아요. 안전이 가장 중요한 거니까요.

어휘 **injure** 다치게 하다 / **extremely** 극히, 극도로 / **bump into** 부딪치다; 우연히 마주치다

03 관계 | ②

▶ Tom이라는 배우를 자신의 다음 영화에 출연시킬 예정이라는 내용으로 보아 남자는 영화감독임을 알 수 있으며, 영화감독에게 여러 가지 질문을 하며 대화를 이끄는 것으로 보아 여자는 기자임을 알 수 있다.

W: I'd like to ask about working with Tom.
M: Well, Tom is a great guy, **really easy to work with**.
W: He's my favorite star, but it was reported in the newspaper that he was really demanding during the filming.
M: Don't believe **everything you read in the press**. He never demanded this or that on the set. And he did all of his own stunts: even that amazing one where he jumped from the helicopter to the train.
W: So you'd work with him again.
M: Yes, I hope to direct him in my next film. Because of the positive reaction from audiences and people like yourself, the studio has already asked me about continuing the story.
W: Really? My viewers will be excited to hear that.
M: It's true.
W: Then I can't wait to go and see your next film.
M: Well, wait for **about a year and a half**.
W: It'll be hard, but I'll try.

여: Tom과 함께 일했던 것에 관해 물어보고 싶어요.
남: 음, Tom은 멋진 친구예요. 함께 일하기 정말 편하죠.
여: 그는 제가 제일 좋아하는 배우예요. 그런데 영화를 찍는 동안 그가 상당히 까다로웠다고 신문에 보도되었던데요.
남: 신문에서 읽은 걸 다 믿지는 마세요. Tom은 촬영장에서 절대 이러니저러니 하며 요구하지 않았어요. 그리고 그는 위험한 연기를 모두 직접 했어요. 심지어 헬리콥터에서 기차로 뛰어내리는 그 놀라운 연기까지도 해냈어요.
여: 그래서 당신이 그와 다시 일하고 싶어 하는 거군요.
남: 네, 저는 그를 제 다음 영화에 출연시키고 싶어요. 관객들과 당신 같은 사람들의 긍정적인 반응 때문에, 스튜디오에서는 이미 다음 이야기를 계속해달라고 요청했답니다.
여: 정말이에요? 제 시청자들이 들으면 아주 신이 날 거예요.
남: 사실입니다.
여: 그러면 당신의 다음 영화를 보러 가는 게 정말 기다려지네요.
남: 음, 약 일 년 반 정도는 기다리셔야 합니다.
여: 기다리기 힘들겠지만 노력해 볼게요.

어휘 **demanding** 요구가 많은; (일이) 부담이 큰 / **press** 《the-》 신문, 언론; 누름; 인쇄기 / **set** (영화) 촬영장 / **stunt** (특히 영화에서의) 고난도 연기, 스턴트

04 그림 불일치 | ④

▶ 여자는 칠판 위에 국기가 있다고 했다.

W: Hello, Principal Dawson.
M: Hi, Christine. I stopped by to ask **how your first day is going**.
W: It's going well. I'm setting up my classroom. I just finished attaching the TV to the wall to the left of the blackboard.
M: You put it on the wall? It used to be on the table below the window, right?
W: Right. But the TV was too low, so students in the back couldn't see it.
M: Good job. Then where's the table?
W: The table is still there, but I put **some flower pots on it**.
M: They'll get plenty of sunshine there. Great idea!
W: And I left the national flag above the blackboard.
M: Yes, **that's school policy**.
W: But I moved the map of the world to the right side of the blackboard.
M: Oh, and you took down the picture that was there before. Good, it was old anyway.

여: 안녕하세요? Dawson 교장 선생님.
남: 안녕하세요, Christine 선생님. 오늘 첫날이 어땠는지 물어보려고 들렀어요.

여: 잘되고 있어요. 지금 교실을 정리하고 있는 중이에요. 지금 막 TV를 칠판 왼쪽 벽에다 붙이는 작업을 마쳤어요.
남: 벽에 붙였다고요? 전에는 창가 아래 탁자 위에 있었죠, 맞나요?
여: 맞아요. 근데 TV가 너무 낮아서 뒤에 있는 학생들이 TV가 안 보이더라구요.
남: 잘했어요. 그러면 그 탁자는 어디 있어요?
여: 탁자는 그대로 있는데 제가 그 위에 화분을 몇 개 놓았어요.
남: 거기 있으면 햇빛을 충분히 받겠네요. 좋은 생각이에요!
여: 그리고 국기는 칠판 위에 그대로 두었어요.
남: 네. 그게 학교 규칙이에요.
여: 그런데 세계지도는 칠판 오른쪽으로 옮겼어요.
남: 아. 그러면 그 자리에 있던 그림은 없앴네요. 잘했어요. 어차피 오래된 거니까요.

어휘 **stop by** ~에 들르다 / **national flag** 국기 / **take down** (구조물 등을 해체하여) 없애다, 치우다

05 부탁한 일 | ④

▶ 여자는 더 좋은 좌석을 구하려고 오케스트라석 대기자 명단에 이름을 올려 달라고 했다.

[Phone rings.]
M: Thank you for calling Ticket Box. How may I help you?
W: I need to buy two tickets to a show for Saturday.
M: What show **are you interested in seeing**?
W: Do you have any tickets left for *Cats* or *42nd Street*? I want great seats.
M: OK. I can tell you right now that *Cats* and *42nd Street* are both sold out.
W: How about *Rent*?
M: There are only balcony seats left.
W: Can you **put me on a waiting list** for orchestra seats then?
M: Yes, we can. Sometimes people do cancel. Which show?
W: I would like to see the Saturday night show of any of the three we discussed.
M: All right. We will call you **if anything becomes available**.

[전화벨이 울린다.]
남: Ticket Box에 전화해 주셔서 감사합니다. 무엇을 도와드릴까요?
여: 토요일에 있는 공연의 표를 두 장 구입하고 싶습니다.
남: 어떤 공연을 관람하고 싶으신가요?
여: 〈캣츠〉나 〈42번가〉 표가 남아 있나요? 좋은 좌석을 원해요.
남: 알겠습니다. 현재 〈캣츠〉와 〈42번가〉는 모두 매진되었습니다.
여: 〈렌트〉는 어떤가요?
남: 발코니석만 남아 있습니다.
여: 그럼 오케스트라석 대기자 명단에 올려주시겠어요?
남: 네, 그렇게 하겠습니다. 관객분들이 가끔 취소를 하시거든요. 어떤 공연으로 할까요?
여: 토요일 저녁 공연이라면 얘기했던 세 공연 중 어떤 것이라도 좋습니다.
남: 알겠습니다. 어느 공연이라도 좌석이 생기면 전화를 드리겠습니다.

어휘 **sold out** 표가 매진된 / **waiting list** 대기자 명단

06 금액 | ②

▶ 남자는 왼쪽의 카메라가 과분하다고 했으므로 오른쪽의 카메라(400달러)를 살 것이며, 이와 함께 여분의 메모리 카드 한 개(40달러)만 사겠다고 했으므로, 남자가 지불할 금액은 440달러이다.

W: Can I help you find anything?
M: Well, I'm interested in these two cameras. Could you **explain the differences to me**?
W: I'd be happy to. The one on the left has twice the memory and comes with an extreme wide-angle lens.
M: So that's why it costs an extra $250. I think that is more camera than I need.
W: I see. Then how about the camera on the right? It is a great value at $400.
M: **Now that I think about it**, I would like an extra memory card.
W: Good idea. Each memory card costs $40. However, we are offering a package deal that includes a tripod.
M: A package deal?
W: Yes. It includes the camera, one additional memory card, and a $70 tripod, **with all items at a 10% discount**.
M: I already have a tripod that I love, so I'll just get the camera and the memory card.
W: Great choice.

여: 뭐 찾으시는 것 있으세요?
남: 음, 이 두 카메라에 관심이 있는데요. 차이점을 설명해주실 수 있나요?
여: 기꺼이요. 왼쪽에 있는 이 카메라는 메모리가 두 배이고 초광각 렌즈가 딸려 있습니다.
남: 그래서 250달러가 추가로 드는 것이군요. 그건 제가 필요로 하는 것보다 과분한 카메라인 것 같아요.
여: 그렇군요. 그러면 오른쪽에 있는 카메라는 어떠세요? 그것은 400달러로 큰 값어치를 하죠.
남: 생각해보니, 여분의 메모리 카드가 있어야겠어요.
여: 잘 생각하셨어요. 메모리 카드는 각각 40달러입니다. 그런데 저희가 삼각대를 포함하는 패키지 상품을 제공해 드리고 있어요.
남: 패키지 상품이요?
여: 네. 카메라, 추가 메모리 카드 한 개, 그리고 70달러짜리 삼각대를 포함하고, 모든 상품이 10퍼센트 할인됩니다.
남: 제가 아끼는 삼각대가 이미 있거든요. 그러니 카메라와 메모리 카드만 할게요.
여: 잘 선택하셨어요.

어휘 **come with** ~이 딸려 있다 / **wide-angle** (사진기의 렌즈가) 광각(廣角)인 / **tripod** 삼각대

07 이유 | ②

▶ 여자는 주말에 수영 수업에 등록해서 영화표를 취소했다고 말했다.

W: Hi, Will.
M: Hi, Clair.
W: What are you going to do this weekend?
M: I'm going to **volunteer at the senior center**, like I usually do. You're planning to see a movie, right?
W: I was going to see *Hidden Dragon*, but I cancelled the tickets.
M: Oh, really? Then I guess you have time to come with me to the senior center.
W: I'm afraid not. I **signed up for a swimming class**. It's every Saturday and Sunday at 5 p.m.
M: That sounds like a lot of fun. Besides, I've heard that *Hidden Dragon* is really long and boring anyway.
W: Really? I know it's **almost 3 hours in length**, but I've read some good reviews.
M: Not me. I'll probably avoid it. Anyway, have a good weekend.

여: 안녕, Will.
남: 안녕, Clair.
여: 이번 주말에 뭐 할 거야?
남: 양로원에 자원봉사하러 갈 거야. 내가 대개 그러는 것처럼 말이야. 너는 영화 보러 갈 계획이지, 맞아?
여: 나는 〈Hidden Dragon〉을 보러 가려고 했는데, 표를 취소했어.
남: 아, 정말? 그러면 나랑 같이 양로원에 갈 시간이 있을 것 같은데.
여: 그렇진 않아. 수영 수업에 등록했거든. 매주 토요일과 일요일 오후 5시야.
남: 무척 재밌겠다. 게다가, 어쨌든 〈Hidden Dragon〉은 정말 길고 지루하다고 들었어.
여: 그래? 거의 3시간 길이라는 건 알지만, 난 좋은 후기를 몇 개 읽었거든.
남: 난 아니었어. 난 아마 그 영화는 안 볼 것 같아. 어쨌든, 좋은 주말 보내.

어휘 **sign up for** (강좌에) 신청하다, 등록하다

08 언급하지 않은 것 | ③

▶ 해석 참조

W: Honey, do you have any other puzzle books? Lisa finished the one you gave her.
M: She finished the whole book in two hours?
W: Yes, and now she's bored again. Every parent thinks **they're raising a genius**, but we really might be.
M: Maybe she should join Mensa. It's the high-IQ society **that was founded by two lawyers** in 1946.
W: Well, she'd have to take an IQ test and score in the top 2% to join.
M: I think she'd pass. And Mensa could do a lot to foster her intelligence. That's the purpose of the society, after all.
W: By the way, can children join? What would she do there?

M: Of course. They provide activities and games **for the younger members as well**.
W: Then, let's talk to her about membership tonight.
M: All right.

여: 여보, 다른 퍼즐 책 가지고 있어요? Lisa가 당신이 준 책을 끝냈어요.
남: 그 애가 그 책 전부를 두 시간 만에 끝냈다고요?
여: 네, 그리고 지금 그 애는 다시 지루해하고 있어요. 모든 부모가 천재를 키우고 있다고 생각하는데, 우리는 정말 그럴지도 모르겠네요.
남: 어쩌면 딸아이는 멘사에 가입해야겠어요. 거긴 1946년(① 창설 연도)에 두 명의 변호사가 설립한, 높은 IQ를 가진 사람들의 모임이에요.
여: 음, 그 애가 가입하려면 IQ 테스트를 하고 상위 2퍼센트 안에 들어가는 점수를 받아야 할 거예요(② 회원 자격).
남: 그 애는 통과할 것 같아요. 그리고 멘사가 그 애의 지능 발달을 위해 많은 것을 해줄 수 있을 거예요. 결국은 그게 그 단체의 목적이거든요(④ 운영 목표).
여: 그런데 아이들도 가입할 수 있나요(⑤ 아동 가입 가능 여부)? 그 애가 거기에서 무엇을 하죠?
남: 물론이죠. 나이가 어린 회원들을 위한 활동과 게임도 제공해요.
여: 그러면 오늘 밤 딸아이에게 회원 가입에 관해 얘기해봐요.
남: 좋아요.

어휘 **society** 모임, 단체; 사회 / **foster** 발전시키다, 조성하다

09 내용 불일치 | ④

▶ 해충 대부분에 비교적 잘 견딘다고 했다.

M: Aloe vera is a stemless or nearly stemless plant **with thick green leaves**. It can grow to a height of 100 cm, and it produces flowers in the summer. Its natural range is unclear, as the species has been widely cultivated throughout the world for its medical uses. Furthermore, it's commonly grown as a decorative plant in many households. The aloe vera is relatively **resistant to most insect pests** but requires well-drained sandy potting soil and bright sunny conditions. However, these plants can burn under too much sun or die **if pots are not drained properly**. Large-scale agricultural production of aloe vera is undertaken in many countries to supply the cosmetics industry with aloe vera gel.

남: 알로에 베라는 두꺼운 녹색 잎을 가진, 줄기가 없거나 거의 없는 식물입니다. 그것은 100센티미터까지 자랄 수 있으며 여름에 꽃이 핍니다. 이 종(種)은 의료 목적으로 전 세계에서 널리 재배되어 왔기 때문에, 본래의 분포 범위는 확실치 않습니다. 더욱이, 이것은 많은 가정에서 관상용 식물로 흔히 기릅니다. 알로에 베라는 해충 대부분에 비교적 잘 견디지만 배수가 잘 되는 모래로 된 화분용 흙과 햇빛이 잘 드는 밝은 환경이 필요합니다. 하지만 이 식물은 너무 강한 햇빛 아래서는 탈 수 있으며, 또는 화분에서 물이 제대로 빠지지 않으면 죽을 수 있습니다. 알로에 베라의 대규모 농업 생산은 화장품 산업에 알로에 베라 젤을 공급하기 위해 여러 나라에서 이뤄지고 있습니다.

어휘 **stemless** 줄기가 없는 / **cultivate** 재배하다, 경작하다 / **furthermore** 뿐만 아니라, 더욱이 / **decorative** 장식용의; 장식이 된 / **relatively** 비교적으로 / **resistant** 잘 견디는, 저항력 있는; 저항[반대]하는 / **pest** 해충; 성가신 사람 / **drain** 물을 빼내다, 배수하다 / **large-scale** 대규모의 / **agricultural** 농업의, 농사[농예]의 / **undertake** (책임을 맡아서) 착수하다; 약속하다 / **cosmetics** 화장품

10 도표 이해 | ③

▶ 여자는 1월 10일 이후의 수업을 들을 수 있고 두 사람 모두 활동적인 것을 하고 싶다고 했으므로 요가 수업을 선택할 것이다. 수강료가 비싼 스키는 가장 먼저 제외되었다.

W: Do you have any plans for the winter holiday?
M: No. I hope it's not too boring. What about you?
W: I'm thinking about **taking one of these winter-school classes**. Why don't you join me?
M: That could be fun. Hey, let's try skiing!
W: Look at the price. I can't afford $150.
M: I didn't see that. Well, you're always saying that **you want to learn an instrument**. Guitar lessons?
W: I'm sorry, but I'm going to stay with my grandparents at the beginning of January. I'll be back on the 10th.
M: Then I guess David's class is not an option either.
W: Right. We could study Chinese, but **I'd rather do something active**.
M: I completely agree with you. I also need to exercise.
W: Great. I'll sign us up.

여: 겨울 방학 때 특별한 계획 있니?
남: 아니, 너무 지루하지 않으면 좋겠다. 넌 어때?
여: 난 겨울 학교 수업 중 하나를 신청할 생각인데, 너도 함께하지 않을래?
남: 그거 재밌겠다. 아, 스키 타러 가자!
여: 비용을 좀 봐. 난 150달러를 낼 형편이 못 돼.
남: 그건 미처 못 봤네. 음, 넌 늘 악기를 배우고 싶다고 말했으니까, 기타 수업은 어때?
여: 미안한데, 난 1월 초에는 조부모님과 함께 할 예정이거든. 그달 10일에 돌아올 거야.
남: 그럼 David 선생님의 수업도 고려할 필요가 없겠구나.
여: 그러게. 함께 중국어를 공부해 볼 수도 있겠지만, 활동적인 것을 하고 싶어.
남: 나도 전적으로 동의해. 나도 운동 좀 해야겠어.
여: 그래 좋아. 내가 우리 둘 다 등록해 놓을게.

11 짧은 대화에 이어질 응답 | ③

▶ 교수님을 뵈어야 해서 강당에 갈 수 없을 거라는 남자에게 여자가 무슨 일이 그렇게 중요하냐고 물었으므로 이에 가장 적절한 응답을 고른다.

① 넌 정말로 수업에 빠지면 안 돼.
② 알았어. 다음 강의에서 보자.
③ 나도 잘 모르지만, 교수님께서 보자고 하셨어.
④ 너에게 그 강의에 관해 얘기하고 싶어.
⑤ 네가 거기에 없으면 교수님께서 화를 내실 거야.

W: Should I **save you a seat** in the lecture hall?
M: Sorry, I have to meet with my professor, so I **won't be there**.
W: Really? What's so important?
M: ______________________________

여: 강당에 네 자리를 맡아 놓아야 해?
남: 미안, 교수님을 뵈어야 해서 거기에 못 갈 거야.
여: 정말? 뭐가 그렇게 중요한데?
남: ______________________________

어휘 **lecture hall** 강당

12 짧은 대화에 이어질 응답 | ④

▶ 드럼을 치고 싶어 하는 여자는 남자의 여동생이 밴드의 리더이며 드럼 연주자를 구하고 있다는 사실을 알게 된다. 이에 가장 적절한 응답을 고른다.

① 네 여동생의 밴드는 멋진 것 같아.
② 네 여동생의 공연을 놓치고 싶지 않아.
③ 네 여동생의 드럼 연주에 정말 감탄했어.
④ 그것에 관해 네 여동생에게 당장 얘기해야겠어.
⑤ 내가 네 밴드의 오디션을 볼 수 있게 해줘서 고마워.

M: Hi, Cindy. **Is that an audition notice** for a rock band?
W: Yes, I've always wanted to play the drums.
M: Really? My sister is the leader of a band and **she's looking for a drummer**.
W: ______________________________

남: 안녕, Cindy. 그거 록 밴드의 오디션 공고문이야?
여: 맞아, 난 항상 드럼을 치고 싶었거든.
남: 정말? 내 여동생이 밴드의 리더인데 드럼 연주자를 찾고 있어.
여: ______________________________

13 긴 대화에 이어질 응답 | ⑤

▶ 남자는 농구 경기 때문에 수요일 저녁에는 일을 할 수가 없는데, 여자는 남자가 수요일에도 일해 주기를 바란다. 이때 남자가 할 수 있는 대답을 고른다.

① 그럼 직원 농구 시합 날짜는 다시 잡도록 할게요.
② Sarah는 근무를 그렇게 많이 해선 안 돼요.
③ 그 애를 대신할 사람을 찾을 수가 없었어요.
④ 그 자리는 모두에게 항상 열려 있어요.
⑤ 시간이 되는 친구를 소개해 드릴까요?

M: Bye, Mrs. Reade. See you next Saturday!
W: Oh, Corey, before you leave, **can I have a word with you**?
M: Sure, Mrs. Reade. What is it?
W: I need you to take on Sarah's Wednesday shift. She starts college next month.
M: Yes, she does. **What are the hours**?
W: 6 p.m. to around 10:30 p.m., depending on how busy we are.

M: I'm sorry, but I can't. I have basketball on Wednesdays at 8.
W: But you're my best worker here at Ollie's Fried Chicken.
M: I like working for you, too, but I can't quit my basketball team.
W: Will you think about it, please? **I'm desperate for junior staff**.
M: ______________________________

남: 안녕히 계세요, Reade 씨. 다음 주 토요일에 뵙겠습니다!
여: 아, Corey, 가기 전에 얘기 좀 나눌 수 있겠니?
남: 물론이죠, Reade 씨. 무슨 일인가요?
여: 네가 Sarah의 수요일 근무를 맡아 주면 좋겠는데. 그 애가 다음 달부터 대학을 다니잖아.
남: 네, 그렇죠. 근무 시간은요?
여: 얼마나 바쁘냐에 달려 있지만, 오후 6시부터 10시 30분 정도까지야.
남: 죄송하지만 할 수가 없네요. 매주 수요일 8시에 농구 경기가 있어요.
여: 하지만 너는 여기 Ollie's Fried Chicken의 최고의 직원이잖니.
남: 저도 일하는 것이 좋아요. 하지만 농구팀을 그만둘 수는 없어요.
여: 생각해 보겠니, 응? 부하 직원이 정말 필요하단다.
남: ______________________________

어휘 **take on** 떠맡다 / **shift** 교대 근무, 변화; 이동하다 / **desperate** 절박한, 필사적인 / **junior** 하급의; 아랫사람 | 선택지 어휘 | **reschedule** 일정을 변경하다 / **spot** 자리, 곳; 얼룩

14 긴 대화에 이어질 응답 | ③

▶ 이미 나온 음식은 먹을 수가 없고 그렇다고 음식을 다시 주문할 시간도 없는 남자에게 여자가 할 수 있는 말을 고른다.

① 이 음식을 드셔도 돼요. 땅콩은 해롭지 않아요.
② 이렇게 음식을 많이 주문하지 말았어야 했는데! 배가 불러요!
③ 그럼, 음식을 바꾸는 게 어때요? 여기 제 음식을 드세요.
④ 제 음식을 서둘러서 가져다 달라고 해야겠어요.
⑤ 당신에게 땅콩은 주지 말라고 요리사에게 주의를 줬어요.

M: It took quite a long time to get here, sorry. Thanks for inviting me to lunch, anyway.
W: Well, you said you wanted to try Malaysian food.
M: It smells so good in here! **What did you order for me**?
W: The coconut rice meal. I'm having spicy shrimp soup with noodles.
M: And here it is! Uh-oh. Mary, are these peanuts in my food?
W: Yes, why?
M: I'm sorry, but I can't eat this dish. **I'm allergic to peanuts**.
W: But there aren't many. Can't you take them out?
M: No, even the tiniest trace of a peanut will nearly kill me.
W: Really? I had no idea! **I'll order another dish** for you.
M: We don't have time. I only have 30 minutes left for my lunch break.
W: ______________________________

남: 여기 오는 데 꽤 오래 걸렸어요, 미안해요. 어쨌든 점심 식사에 초대해 주셔서 고마워요.
여: 음, 말레이시아 음식을 먹어보고 싶다고 하셨잖아요.
남: 여기는 정말 좋은 냄새가 나는데요! 제 걸로 어떤 음식을 주문하셨어요?
여: 코코넛 쌀 요리요. 전 매운 새우 수프에 국수를 곁들인 음식을 먹을 거예요.
남: 와 여기 나오네요! 이런, Mary 씨, 제 음식에 들어 있는 이것들이 땅콩인가요?
여: 네, 왜요?
남: 미안하지만 이 요리를 못 먹겠어요. 땅콩에 알레르기가 있거든요.
여: 하지만 많이는 없어요. 땅콩을 덜어낼 수는 없나요?
남: 네, 아주 작은 땅콩 조각이라도 제겐 생명의 위협이 될 수도 있어요.
여: 정말이요? 몰랐어요! 다른 음식을 주문해 드릴게요.
남: 시간이 없어요. 점심시간이 30분밖에 남지 않았네요.
여: ______________________________

어휘 **be allergic to** ~에 알레르기가 있다 / **trace** 미량, 극소량 | 선택지 어휘 | **swap** (남과) 바꾸다 / **chef** 요리사, 주방장

15 상황에 적절한 말 | ③

▶ Peter는 영어로 하는 대화를 이해하는 데 시간이 좀 필요하다고 생각한다. 따라서 Chris에게 좀 더 천천히 말해달라고 부탁할 것이다.

① 미안해, 정말 피곤한 하루였어.
② 여러분 모두를 만나게 되어서 정말 기뻐요.
③ 좀 더 천천히 말해줄래?
④ 너에게 독일에 관한 모든 것을 말해주고 싶어.
⑤ 이해가 안 되면 나에게 알려줘.

W: Peter is an exchange student from Germany. Today, he arrives in Canada, where **he meets his host family**. Although Peter has studied English for several years, this is only the second time he has spoken with native English speakers. He has also just gotten off a long flight, and he's a bit tired and nervous. Meanwhile, his host family is very excited to meet Peter. The boy, Chris, is especially **eager to get to know** Peter. He's asking many questions, one after another, and he seems disappointed in Peter's answers. Peter is doing his best but can't understand **everything that is being said**. He thinks he just needs a bit more time to process the conversation. In this situation, what would Peter most likely say to Chris?

여: Peter는 독일에서 온 교환학생이다. 오늘, 그는 캐나다에 도착하고, 그곳에서 자신의 주인집 가족들을 만난다. 비록 Peter는 수년간 영어를 공부해왔지만, 이번이 영어를 모국어로 하는 사람과 이야기해보는 두 번째일 뿐이다. 그는 또한 장시간의 비행에서 막 내려서, 약간 피곤하고 긴장해 있다. 한편, 그의 주인집 가족은 Peter를 만나게 되어 매우 들떠 있다. Chris라는 소년은 Peter를 특히 알고 싶어 한다. 그 아이는 잇따라서 많은 질문을 하고 있지만, Peter의 대답에 실망한 것 같다. Peter는 최선을 다하고 있지만 (Chris가) 말하고 있는 전부를 이해할 수는 없다. 그는 대화를 처리하려면 좀 더 많은 시간이 필요하다고 생각한다. 이러한 상황에서 Peter가 Chris에게 할 말로 가장 적절한 것은 무엇인가?

어휘 **exchange student** 교환학생 / **meanwhile** 한편; 그동안에 / **be eager to-v** v하고 싶어 하다

16~17 세트 문항 | 16. ③ 17. ③

▶ 16. 범죄 예방을 위해 주차장, 상점, 엘리베이터, 거리 등에 설치된 CCTV의 긍정적 측면과 범죄자 체포의 어려움, 비용, 사생활 노출 등의 부정적 측면에 대해 이야기하고 있다.

① CCTV의 목적
② 집에 CCTV를 설치하는 방법
③ CCTV의 장점과 단점
④ CCTV 화질을 개선하는 방법
⑤ CCTV와 범죄율의 상관관계

▶ 17. 해석 참조

M: These days, CCTVs can be seen almost everywhere. They **serve as warnings to potential criminals** and protect businesses. They're also a cheap alternative to a full-time security guard. They work especially well in low-traffic areas. For example, many parking garages rely on CCTVs to protect the cars and their owners. Shops place them in hard-to-see locations to prevent theft. And they're in many elevators **for the protection of riders**. They're also useful on busy and dangerous streets. By recording license-plate numbers from cars, they allow police to identify reckless drivers and issue fines. Still, there are drawbacks that must be considered. Their low-quality cameras offer terrible image quality. Even when criminals are filmed, the videos capturing their actions often **fail to lead to an arrest**. Then there is the price. Someone must be paid to watch the cameras or some form of video storage must be purchased. Over thousands of hours, this really adds up. Finally, there is the cost we all pay through loss of privacy. After all, it isn't only the criminals **who are being filmed**.

남: 요즘, CCTV는 거의 모든 곳에서 볼 수 있습니다. CCTV는 잠재적 범죄자에게 경고하거나 사업체를 보호하는 역할을 합니다. 또한 종일 근무하는 경비 인력을 대체하는 값싼 대안이 되기도 합니다. 특히 통행이 적은 구역에 효과가 좋습니다. 예를 들어, 많은 ① 주차장들이 차와 차주를 보호하기 위해 CCTV에 의존합니다. ② 상점들은 절도를 막기 위해 잘 보이지 않는 자리에 CCTV를 설치합니다. 그리고 탑승자를 보호하기 위한 목적으로 많은 ④ 엘리베이터들 안에 설치됩니다. CCTV는 복잡하고 위험한 ⑤ 거리에서도 유용합니다. 차량 번호판을 녹화함으로써, 경찰이 난폭한 운전자를 식별하고 벌금을 부과하게 합니다. 그럼에도 불구하고, 고려해야 할 문제점이 있습니다. 저화질 CCTV 카메라는 형편없는 화질을 보여줍니다. 범죄자가 촬영되었을 때도, 그들의 (범죄) 행위를 담은 비디오가 종종 체포로 이어지지 못합니다. 게다가 가격의 문제가 있습니다. 누군가가 돈을 받고 카메라를 관찰하든지, 비디오를 저장하는 매체를 구매하든지 해야 합니다. 많은 시간이 흐르면서 이 비용은 실제로 늘어나게 됩니다. 끝으로, 사생활 침해로 인해 우리 모두가 치르는 대가도 있습니다. 결국, 촬영되고 있는 것은 범죄자만은 아니니까요.

어휘 **criminal** 범인; 범죄의 / **alternative** 대안, 대체물 / **security guard** 경비원, 보안 요원 / **theft** 절도 / **rider** 탑승자 / **license-plate** 차량 번호판 / **reckless** 난폭한; 무모한, 신중하지 못한 / **issue** (표 등을) 발부[교부]하다 / **drawback** 문제점, 결점 / **film** 녹화하다 / **arrest** 체포(하다) / **storage** 저장, 보관 / **add up** (조금씩) 늘어나다 | 선택지 어휘 | **footage** 화면, 장면

01. ② 02. ① 03. ⑤ 04. ④ 05. ④ 06. ① 07. ⑤ 08. ③ 09. ④ 10. ③
11. ① 12. ④ 13. ② 14. ④ 15. ③ 16. ④ 17. ④

01 화자가 하는 말의 목적 | ②

▶ 정부의 유류세 인하 정책에 대해 말하고 있다.

M: Almost every day, the price of oil **hits a record high**. So the government has announced plans to reduce the gasoline tax for the summer months. The purpose of this tax break is **to allow people to continue** to drive their vehicles and use their car air conditioners during the hottest time of the year. The gasoline tax will reduce the cost of gas by an average of $6 for each tank full of gasoline. An average driver will save up to $120 for the three-month period. Since working families are the backbone of the economy, the government **expects the plan to directly help** them in this time of difficulty.

남: 거의 매일 유가가 최고치를 경신하고 있습니다. 그래서 정부는 여름철에 유류세를 낮추는 방안을 발표했습니다. 이번 감세 조치는 시민들이 연중 가장 더운 시기에 차량을 운전하고 차량의 에어컨 이용을 계속할 수 있도록 하기 위한 목적입니다. 유류세의 인하로 연료탱크를 가득 채웠을 때 평균 6달러의 연료비용을 절감할 수 있게 될 것입니다. 일반 운전자는 3개월간 최대 120달러를 절감하게 될 것입니다. 일하는 가족들이 경제의 중추인 까닭에 정부는 (유류세 인하) 조치가 이번 어려운 시기에 직접적인 도움이 될 것으로 기대하고 있습니다.

어휘 **tax break** 세금 우대 조치 / **average** 일반적인, 보통의; 평균 / **up to** ~까지 / **backbone** 중추(中樞), (사물의) 중요 요소, 등뼈

02 의견 | ①

▶ 여자는 다른 사람들이 반대표를 던질 것이므로 자기는 투표할 필요가 없다는 생각으로 투표도 하지 않고 불평하는 남자의 태도를 지적하면서 반드시 투표해야 한다고 말하고 있다.

M: Hi, Susan. **Where are you off to**?
W: I'm going to vote for student council president.
M: Oh, that's right. Today is the last day. I'll certainly be glad when Tony is no longer our president.
W: Yeah, **I've had enough of his biased behavior**. So I guess you already voted?
M: Not this semester. I don't need to vote, because Tony is too unpopular to ever get re-elected.
W: Jim! That's exactly how he got elected the first time. Everyone assumed that he couldn't win, so very few people actually voted against him.
M: That could never happen again. Besides, I'm really busy.
W: You should vote. I'm not going to spend next semester **listening to you complain** about the student council if you don't even vote.
M: Okay, I'll come with you.

남: 안녕, Susan. 어디 가는 길이니?
여: 학생회장 투표하러 가고 있어.
남: 아, 맞아. 오늘이 마지막 날이지. Tony가 더 이상 회장이 아니라면 분명 기쁠 거야.
여: 그래, 그의 편파적인 행동은 진절머리 나. 그럼 넌 이미 투표했겠구나?
남: 이번 학기는 안 했어. Tony는 너무 인기가 없어서 재선되지 않을 테니 난 투표할 필요 없어.
여: Jim! 바로 그렇게 그가 처음에 당선된 거야. 모두 그가 당선되지 못할 거라고 생각해서 실제로 극소수만 반대표를 던졌지.
남: 그런 일은 두 번 다시 일어날 수 없을 거야. 게다가, 난 정말 바빠.
여: 넌 투표해야 해. 투표조차 안 한다면, 난 네가 학생회에 대해 불평하는 걸 들어주면서 다음 학기를 보내진 않을 거야.
남: 알겠어, 너와 함께 갈게.

어휘 **have had enough (of)** (~라면) 진절머리 난다 / **biased** 치우친, 편견을 지닌 / **re-elect** 다시 선출하다

03 관계 | ⑤

▶ 경찰이 정지시킨 버스에 타고 있던 두 승객 사이의 대화이다.

W: What's going on, sir?
M: An officer **pulled us over**.
W: What for?
M: I guess because the driver didn't stop at the sign back there.
W: Maybe you're right. It's hard to see that stop sign, with the tree branches hanging over it.
M: I'm already late for a meeting. I wish **he wouldn't stop us** for so long.
W: Oh, the driver is getting off.
M: Isn't the officer going to give him a ticket?
W: I think something is wrong with the bus.
M: Yes, the officer is looking into the engine compartment.
W: Oh no. Can you see the smoke coming out of it?
M: The driver is **gesturing to us**.
W: People are starting to get off.
M: I need to find a taxi. Today is not my day.

여: 무슨 일인가요?
남: 경찰관이 우리 차를 세웠어요.
여: 왜요?
남: 운전기사가 저 뒤에 있는 정지 신호에서 서지 않았기 때문일 거예요.
여: 그렇겠군요. 저 정지 신호는 보기가 힘들어요. 나뭇가지가 그 위로 늘어져 있어서요.
남: 전 이미 회의에 늦었어요. 경찰이 우릴 오래 잡아 두지 않으면 좋으련만.
여: 아, 기사가 내리고 있어요.
남: 경찰이 딱지를 떼려는 게 아닌가요?
여: 버스에 문제가 있는 것 같아요.
남: 네, 경찰이 엔진 부분을 들여다보고 있어요.
여: 아, 이럴 수가. 저기서 연기가 나오고 있는 거 보이세요?
남: 기사가 우리에게 손짓하고 있네요.
여: 사람들이 내리기 시작했어요.
남: 택시를 찾아봐야겠어요. 오늘은 운이 좋지 않은 날이네요.

어휘 **pull over** 차를 길가에 세우다 / **hang** (아래로) 늘어지다 / **compartment** 칸, 구획

04 그림 불일치 | ④

▶ 보통은 트럭으로 캠핑을 가서 텐트에서 잠을 자지만 이번에는 캠핑카를 가져왔다고 했으므로 그림에 캠핑카가 있어야 하는데 트럭과 텐트가 있으므로 이 부분은 내용과 일치하지 않는다.

W: What are you looking at?
M: This is a photo from our family camping trip last weekend. Take a look.
W: Oh, it's you sitting on the dock of the pond and fishing. It must have been taken at **the moment you were catching** a fish! Your fishing rod is bent.
M: Yes, that's right. I was so happy to catch a big fish.
W: Good. The woman stirring the pot over the fire is your mother, right?
M: Yes, she is preparing lunch. My father **is standing behind her**.
W: You mean the man who is holding a bunch of firewood?
M: Right. He got it all for the fire.
W: He seems like a camping expert. I see a camping car near your father. Is it yours?
M: We rented it. Usually **we go camping** in my father's truck and sleep in a tent, but this time we rented a camping car. It was fantastic!
W: Sounds great! I also like the two chairs on the right. They look very comfortable.
M: Exactly. We rented them at the same camping gear shop.
W: It looks like you had a wonderful time. **I wish I could go camping** with my family, too.

여: 뭘 보고 있니?
남: 이건 지난 주말에 우리 가족 캠핑 여행에서 찍은 사진이야. 봐.
여: 아, 네가 연못의 선착장에 앉아 낚시하고 있구나. 네가 물고기를 잡으려는 순간에 찍은 게 분명하네! 네 낚싯대가 휘어졌어.

남: 응, 맞아. 큰 물고기를 잡아서 너무 행복했어.
여: 좋네. 불 위에 있는 냄비를 휘젓고 있는 여자분이 네 어머니구나, 맞지?
남: 응, 어머니는 점심을 준비하고 계셔. 우리 아버지는 어머니 뒤에 서 계셔.
여: 장작 한 무더기를 안고 있는 남자분 말이니?
남: 맞아. 아버지는 불을 떼려고 그걸 모두 구하셨어.
여: 네 아버지는 캠핑 전문가이신 것 같다. 네 아버지 근처에 캠핑카가 보이네. 너희 것이니?
남: 렌트했어. 보통 우리는 아버지 트럭으로 캠핑을 가서 텐트에서 자는데 이번에는 캠핑카를 렌트했어. 환상적이었어!
여: 멋진 것 같아! 나는 오른쪽의 의자 두 개도 마음에 든다. 아주 편안해 보여.
남: 정말 그래. 우리는 그것도 같은 캠핑 장비 가게에서 렌트했어.
여: 좋은 시간을 보낸 것 같구나. 나도 우리 가족과 캠핑을 가고 싶어.

어휘 **dock** 선착장, 부두 / **fishing rod** 낚싯대 / **bend** 구부리다 / **stir** 휘젓다 / **firewood** 장작, 땔나무 / **expert** 전문가 / **gear** 장비

05 추후 행동 | ④

▶ 남자는 여자가 만든 인형을 벼룩시장에서 파는 것이 어떨지 제안하였고 인터넷으로 판매자 협회에 등록해야 한다고 알려주었다. 이에 여자는 노트북을 가져오겠다고 했으므로 인터넷으로 판매자 등록하는 일을 할 것이다.

M: You made these puppets yourself? They're really cool.
W: Thanks. My son loves these animal characters.
M: You're very artistic.
W: I can **teach you how to make them**.
M: Well, I'm not very good with my hands. But I think these are so good that people will buy them.
W: Buy them?
M: Sure. Try selling them at the flea market in your area. You can go there next Saturday. **All you have to do** is register with the sellers' association.
W: Could you tell me how to register?
M: You can register online.
W: But my computer isn't working. It has a virus.
M: You can register by phone then.
W: Oh, I can use Larry's laptop. I'll get it right now.
M: And **you'd better make** a lot more before the weekend.

남: 이 인형들 당신이 직접 만드신 건가요? 인형들이 정말 멋지네요.
여: 고마워요. 우리 아들이 이 동물 캐릭터들을 좋아하거든요.
남: 상당히 예술적 감각이 있으시네요.
여: 어떻게 만드는지 가르쳐 드릴 수 있어요.
남: 음, 전 그다지 손재주가 없어서요. 하지만 이 인형들은 정말 멋져서 사람들이 살 것 같아요.
여: 산다고요?
남: 물론이죠. 당신이 사는 지역의 벼룩시장에서 한번 팔아보세요. 다음 주 토요일에 갈 수 있어요. 당신이 할 일은 판매자 협회에 등록하는 것뿐이에요.
여: 등록하는 법을 알려주시겠어요?
남: 온라인으로 등록할 수 있어요.
여: 하지만 컴퓨터가 고장 났어요. 바이러스에 걸렸거든요.
남: 그러면 전화로 등록하세요.
여: 아, Larry의 노트북을 쓸 수 있어요. 바로 가져와야겠어요.
남: 그리고 주말 전에 인형을 더 많이 만들어 놓는 게 좋을 거예요.

어휘 **puppet** (인형극에 쓰는) 꼭두각시, 인형 / **be good with A's hands** 손재주가 있다 / **register** (공식 명부에 이름을) 등록하다 / **association** 협회; 연관

06 금액 | ①

▶ 통화료는 미국에서 다음 청구서에 모두 나오므로 지금 지불하지 않아도 되고, 주당 임대료는 45달러이다. 여기서 남자가 낸 보증금 10달러는 돌려받아야 하므로 남자는 최종적으로 35달러를 내면 된다.

M: I am returning my cell phone. I'd like to **pay the rental bill**. My name is Howard Wright.
W: Just a minute, Mr. Wright.
M: The daily rental rate is $7, but a weekly rate is $45, right?
W: Yes, you're right. Here's your bill.
M: I don't see any charges for the calls I made.
W: Well, you signed up for the global roaming service. All your call charges **will be on your next bill** in America.
M: Oh? Hmm... but my bill shouldn't be $52.
W: Oh, really?
M: I had the phone for a week, seven days, not eight days. And when I rented this cell phone, I paid a $10 refundable deposit.
W: Hmm... let me check. Yes, you're right. You rented the phone for only one week, and your deposit **should be returned**. I'll change the bill.

남: 제 휴대전화를 반납하려고요. 임대료를 내고 싶습니다. 제 이름은 Howard Wright입니다.
여: 잠시만요, Wright 씨.
남: 하루 임대료는 7달러이지만 주당 임대료는 45달러지요?
여: 네, 맞습니다. 여기 손님의 청구서가 있습니다.
남: 제가 걸었던 전화의 통화료가 보이지 않는군요.
여: 음, 손님께서는 국제 로밍 서비스를 신청하셨네요. 손님의 통화료는 미국에서 다음 청구서에 모두 나올 것입니다.
남: 어? 음… 하지만 요금이 52달러일 리가 없어요.
여: 아, 그렇습니까?
남: 전 일주일, 즉 7일간 전화기를 빌렸어요. 8일이 아니고요. 그리고 이 휴대전화를 빌릴 때 반환 보증금 10달러를 냈어요.
여: 음… 확인해 보겠습니다. 네, 손님 말씀이 맞으시네요. 휴대전화를 일주일간만 빌리셨군요. 그리고 보증금을 돌려받으셔야 하고요. 청구서를 바꿔 드리겠습니다.

어휘 **return** 돌려주다 / **rental** 임대의 / **sign up** 가입하다 / **deposit** 보증금

07 이유 | ⑤

▶ 남자는 Kensington 대학의 생물학 과정이 유명하기 때문에 선택했다고 했다.

W: Jack, did you **decide on a university to attend**?
M: I did, Ms. Flint. I chose Kensington University over my other option.
W: What was it that finally made up your mind?
M: Well, I started by comparing some basic points, like the distance from my home.
W: They are both relatively close.
M: Yes, that **didn't make much of a difference**. So I looked at tuition.
W: Kensington is the more expensive of the two, I think.
M: Right, and then I looked at scholarships, but I was still confused.
W: Did you give any thought to the majors offered by each school?
M: Actually, that's what finally made a difference. Kensington's biology program is renowned.
W: They also have fewer students per teacher.
M: I **hadn't even considered** that.
W: Anyway, you made a great decision.

여: Jack, 다닐 대학교는 결정했니?
남: 네, Flint 선생님. 다른 선택 사항보다는 Kensington 대학교를 택했어요.
여: 최종적으로 결정하게 된 이유가 무엇이었니?
남: 음, 집에서의 거리 같은 몇 가지 기본적인 사항들을 비교하면서 시작했어요.
여: 두 대학 모두 비교적 가깝지.
남: 네, 그건 별로 큰 차이가 없었어요. 그래서 등록금을 고려해 봤어요.
여: 내 생각으로는, Kensington 대학이 둘 중엔 더 비싼 것 같구나.
남: 맞아요, 그러고 나서 장학금을 살펴봤지만, 여전히 혼란스러웠어요.
여: 각 학교가 제공하는 전공은 좀 생각해 봤니?
남: 실은, 그것이 결정적인 차이를 만들었어요. Kensington 대학의 생물학 과정은 유명하거든요.
여: 교수 한 명당 학생 수도 더 적지.
남: 그것까진 생각해 보지 못했네요.
여: 어쨌든, 좋은 결정을 내렸구나.

어휘 **relatively** 비교적 / **tuition** 수업(료) / **give thought to** ~을 생각해보다 / **biology** 생물학; 생명 작용[활동] / **renowned** 유명한, 명성 있는 ***cf.* renown** 명성

08 언급하지 않은 것 | ③

▶ 해석 참조

M: Heather, have you thought of anyone to write our report about?
W: I think we should write about Henri Matisse because I've always loved his paintings.
M: That sounds good. To start with, I know that he was born in 1869 in France, and **his work is similar to** Picasso's.
W: Picasso and Matisse were actually very close. They met in 1906 and remained lifelong friends.

M: I know that they were both Impressionists. Did Matisse learn his technique from Picasso?
W: No. Picasso **was 12 years younger than** Matisse. Matisse learned to paint primarily from Gustave Moreau at an academy in Paris.
M: It looks like we already have several good details for our report. By the way, what's your favorite Matisse?
W: I think *The Plum Blossoms*, which he painted in 1948 and is now kept in New York's Museum of Modern Art, is my favorite because of its deep reds.
M: I **might just have to agree with you**.

남: Heather, 누구에 대해 우리 리포트를 쓸지 생각해봤니?
여: 내 생각에 우리는 앙리 마티스에 대해 쓰는 게 좋겠어. 왜냐하면 나는 늘 그의 그림을 좋아했거든.
남: 좋은데. 우선, 난 그가 1869년에 프랑스(① 출생 국가)에서 태어났고 그의 작품이 피카소의 작품들과 비슷하다는 것을 알아.
여: 피카소와 마티스는 사실 매우 친했어. 그들은 1906년에 만나서 평생 친구였지.
남: 그들은 둘 다 인상파(② 화풍) 화가였지. 마티스는 피카소에게 화법(畵法)을 배웠니?
여: 아니. 피카소는 마티스보다 12살 어려. 마티스는 주로 파리에 있는 학교에서 귀스타브 모로(④ 스승)에게 그림 그리는 것을 배웠어.
남: 우린 이미 리포트에 쓸 몇 가지 괜찮은 세부사항을 알고 있는 것 같은데? 그런데 네가 가장 좋아하는 마티스의 작품은 뭐야?
여: 강렬한 빨간 색채 때문에 〈The Plum Blossoms〉(⑤ 작품명)를 가장 좋아하는데, 그것은 1948년에 그려졌고 현재 뉴욕 현대 미술관에 있어.
남: 동감이야.

어휘 **lifelong** 일생의, 평생의 / **Impressionist** 인상파 예술가 / **primarily** 주로; 본래

09 내용 불일치 | ④

▶ 대출 카운터는 1층 정문 근처뿐 아니라 지하 주차장 입구 근처에도 있다.

W: Attention library patrons. We **will be closing in 15 minutes**. Please make all of your selections and take them to one of the checkout counters or the self-checkout scanners just to the right of the main counters. For your convenience, we **have extra staff on hand** to allow you to avoid long lines. Checkout counters are located on the first floor near the main entrance and on the basement level near the parking garage entrance. Remember, if you do not have your library card with you, your driver's license or passport **will be accepted**. Thank you for using the Parkview Public Library and have a pleasant evening.

여: 도서관 이용객 여러분께 알립니다. 15분 뒤에 도서관이 폐관합니다. 책 선택을 모두 마치시고 대출 카운터 중 한 곳이나 혹은 중앙 카운터 바로 오른쪽에 있는 셀프 대출 스캐너로 책을 가지고 오십시오. 여러분의 편의를 위해서 저희는 직원을 추가로 투입하여 여러분이 긴 줄에서 기다리시지 않도록 도와드리고 있습니다. 대출 카운터는 1층 정문 근처와 지하의 주차장 입구 근처에 위치하고 있습니다. 도서관 카드가 없으신 분들은 운전면허증이나 여권으로도 대출이 가능하다는 것을 기억해 주십시오. Parkview 공공 도서관을 이용해 주셔서 감사드립니다. 그럼 즐거운 저녁 되시길 바랍니다.

어휘 **patron** 고객, 단골손님 / **on hand** 바로 곁에, 출석해서 / **garage** 차고

10 도표 이해 | ③

▶ 우선 두 사람의 딸이 8세이므로 ①은 수강할 수 없다. 그리고 월요일 오후 수업을 제외하고 남은 3개의 강좌 중 가장 긴 경력의 강사를 택하려고 했으나, 수업료가 50달러가 넘지 않기를 원했으므로 두 사람이 선택한 강좌는 ③이다.

W: Honey, look at this flyer. The Rinx is open for the winter season.
M: Good news! They offer great ice skating lessons for children. Olivia wants to **learn how to skate**.
W: Here's a chart of what they offer.
M: Since Olivia is 8 years old, she shouldn't take this class.
W: Yeah. And she has to attend a dance class on Monday afternoon, so **any time other than that is fine**.
M: Now we have three options. I think we should think about the instructor's amount of experience.
W: I agree with you. **The more experience an instructor has**, the better.
M: Then I think we'll go with this class.
W: Wait a minute! We should consider the fees. I don't want to spend more than $50.
M: Then let's choose the second most experienced instructor among the three.
W: Okay. Let's sign up right now.

여: 여보, 이 전단지를 봐요. The Rinx가 겨울 시즌 동안 문을 열어요.
남: 좋은 소식이에요! 그들은 어린이들을 위해 훌륭한 아이스 스케이트 수업을 제공하는군요. Olivia는 스케이트 타는 법을 배우고 싶어 해요.
여: 여기 그들이 제공하는 것의 도표가 있어요.
남: Olivia가 여덟 살이기 때문에, 이 수업은 들을 수 없어요.
여: 네. 그리고 그 애는 월요일 오후에 댄스 수업에 참석해야 하니까 그 외에는 아무 때나 괜찮아요.
남: 이제 세 가지 선택 사항이 있군요. 우리는 강사의 경력에 대해 생각해봐야 할 것 같아요.
여: 당신 말이 맞아요. 강사는 경험이 많을수록 더 좋으니까요.
남: 그러면 이 강좌를 골라야겠네요.
여: 잠깐만요! 수업료를 고려해봐야 해요. 난 50달러 넘게 쓰고 싶진 않아요.
남: 그러면 셋 중에 두 번째로 경험이 많은 강사를 선택합시다.
여: 좋아요. 바로 등록합시다.

어휘 **flyer** 전단, 광고쪽지 / **chart** 도표 / **go with** 고르다, 선택하다

11 짧은 대화에 이어질 응답 | ①

▶ 사물함의 위치 때문에 불편을 겪는 상황에서 여자가 사물함을 바꾸자고 제안했으므로 이에 가장 적절한 응답을 찾는다.

① 그거 좋겠다. ② 중간에서 만나자.
③ 나는 사물함을 바꿀 거야. ④ 내 사물함 자물쇠 여는 것 좀 도와줘.
⑤ 이 사물함은 이미 주인이 있어.

W: Oh, I can't reach my locker, because it's too high.
M: Yeah? Well, mine is on the bottom. It's so **uncomfortable to use**.
W: I have an idea. **Why don't we switch**?
M: ______________________________

여: 아, 사물함이 너무 높이 있어서 손이 닿지 않아.
남: 그래? 음, 내 건 제일 아래쪽에 있어서 쓰기 아주 불편해.
여: 좋은 생각이 떠올랐어. 우리 (사물함을) 바꾸는 게 어때?
남: ______________________________

어휘 **switch** 바꾸다, 전환하다 | 선택지 어휘 | **occupied** 사용(되는) 중인

12 짧은 대화에 이어질 응답 | ④

▶ 아침에 근무를 해야 하고 위치도 멀어서 소풍을 갈 수 없다는 여자에게 남자는 자신이 데리러 가면 어떻겠냐고 물었다. 이에 적절한 대답을 찾는다.

① 넌 소풍을 취소하는 게 낫겠어. ② 하지만 난 주말에는 근무하지 않아.
③ 고마워, 하지만 걸어가기에는 너무 멀어. ④ 그렇다면, 함께하고 싶어.
⑤ 내 차에 공간이 충분하기만 하다면야.

M: **I'm having a picnic** by the river tomorrow. You should come.
W: Unfortunately, I work tomorrow morning, and my office is far from the river.
M: Your office isn't far from my house. **What if I come** and pick you up?
W: ______________________________

남: 내일 강가로 소풍 갈 거야. 너도 와.
여: 안타깝게도, 난 내일 아침에 근무하고 내 사무실은 강에서 멀어.
남: 네 사무실이 우리 집에서는 멀지 않잖아. 내가 차로 널 데리러 가면 어때?
여: ______________________________

13 긴 대화에 이어질 응답 | ②

▶ 강아지의 상태가 더 나빠지는지 지켜보고 후속 조치를 취하라는 여자의 요구에 대한 적절한 응답이 필요하다.

① 제 아이도 장난감을 삼켜서 아픕니다.
② 강아지의 상태가 더 나빠지는지를 지켜보겠습니다.
③ 저는 아이들에게 플라스틱 장난감을 사주지 않습니다.
④ 강아지에게 물어 올 것을 던져 주십시오.

⑤ 그 병원의 응급실은 너무 붐빕니다.

[Phone rings.]
W: This is the Willow Creek Pet Hospital, how may I help you?
M: My dog is sick. I'm really worried about him.
W: That's too bad. What are your dog's symptoms?
M: He started vomiting last night, and he **has not eaten or drunk** anything today.
W: OK. It sounds like he may have eaten something bad, like a piece of plastic or metal.
M: Well, he is still very young and curious.
W: Take a look around your home and tell me if there is **anything missing or chewed up**.
M: OK. Wait a minute. *[pause]* Yes, I found something. Part of a plastic toy that belongs to my child. **Half of it has been bitten off**.
W: Well, if he gets worse, I think you should contact us or bring him in.
M: ______________________________

[전화벨이 울린다.]
여: Willow Creek 동물 병원입니다. 무엇을 도와 드릴까요?
남: 제 강아지가 아파요. 정말 걱정이 되네요.
여: 안됐군요. 강아지의 증상이 어떻습니까?
남: 어젯밤에 토하기 시작했고 오늘은 아무것도 먹지 않고 마시지도 않았습니다.
여: 네. 플라스틱이나 금속 조각과 같은 나쁜 것을 삼켰을 수도 있는 것 같네요.
남: 음, 아직 매우 어리고 호기심이 많아서요.
여: 집을 두루 살펴보시고 사라진 것이나 씹어 놓은 게 있으면 말씀해 주십시오.
남: 네. 잠시만요. *[잠시 후]* 네, 뭔가 발견했어요. 제 아이의 플라스틱 장난감의 일부요. 반이 물어 뜯겼네요.
여: 그럼, 강아지의 상태가 더 나빠지면 저희에게 연락 주시거나 데리고 오셔야 할 것 같습니다.
남: ______________________________

어휘 **symptom** 증상, 징후 / **vomit** 구토하다 / **chew** 씹다 / **contact** 연락하다 | 선택지 어휘 | **fetch** (가서) 가지고[데리고] 오다 / **emergency room** 응급실

14 긴 대화에 이어질 응답 | ④

▶ 할인이 된다는 말에 손님이 남동생을 위해 한 벌 더 사겠다고 했으므로 그에 적절한 답변을 유추해 보면 된다.

① 손님은 매장 신용카드를 신청하실 수 있습니다.
② 그는 할인을 얼마 받을 수 있나요?
③ 제가 손님의 동생분을 전에 만난 적이 있습니까?
④ 동생분도 손님과 같은 사이즈의 옷을 입나요?
⑤ 중간 정도로 익혀 드릴까요, 아니면 완전히 익혀 드릴까요?

M: Excuse me, **can you find me a medium** in this sweater?
W: This one? Sure. It's a lovely sweater.
M: Yes, I like the color and the pattern.
W: Well, it's funny, but I **can't seem to find** a medium. I'll check in the back.
M: Please hurry, I'm late for lunch.
W: *[pause]* OK. Here it is. I finally found a medium.
M: It's $45, right?
W: Yes, but with a store credit card you can get a 10% discount. It's our Wild Wednesday sale. Everything is 10% off.
M: Well, I'll buy another one for my brother then. Maybe he'll **forgive me for being late** for lunch.
W: ______________________________

남: 실례합니다만 이 스웨터 중간 사이즈를 찾아 주시겠습니까?
여: 이것 말씀이세요? 물론이죠. 이것은 예쁜 스웨터예요.
남: 네. 색과 무늬가 맘에 들어요.
여: 음, 중간 사이즈를 찾을 수 없다니 이상하네요. 제가 뒤쪽에서 찾아보겠습니다.
남: 서둘러 주세요. 점심 약속에 늦겠어요.
여: *[잠시 후]* 좋아요. 여기 있네요. 중간 사이즈를 드디어 찾았어요.
남: 45달러이지요?
여: 네, 하지만 매장 신용카드로 10% 할인을 받으실 수 있습니다. 오늘이 화끈한 수요일 세일이거든요. 모든 것이 10% 할인입니다.
남: 그럼, 제 남동생 것으로 하나 더 사겠어요. 점심 약속에 늦어도 그 애가 아마 용서할 거예요.
여: ______________________________

15 상황에 적절한 말 | ③

▶ Cole은 쓰레기를 함부로 버리는 것을 좋지 않게 생각하기 때문에 친구에게 그렇게 하지 말라고 충고할 것이다.

① 더 이상 너를 무안하게 만들고 싶지 않아.
② 네가 하지 않은 행동인데도 비난받을 수 있어.
③ 쓰레기를 버리지 마. 우리 둘 다 나빠 보이잖아.
④ 부모님께서 더 이상 아이스크림을 먹지 말라고 말씀하셨어.
⑤ 너는 교장 선생님께 이번 쓰레기 투기 행위를 알려 드려야 해.

W: Todd and Cole walk home from school together each day. Todd often buys an ice cream from the corner store **on his way home** and eats it. When he is done, Todd throws the wrapper on the ground **no matter where he is**. Sometimes, there may be a trash can nearby, but he won't bother to put it in the can. Cole **was taught by his parents** that littering is bad and that litterers look ignorant. Sometimes people shake their heads when they see Todd litter. This embarrasses Cole. In this situation, what would Cole most likely say to Todd?

여: Todd와 Cole은 매일 방과 후에 함께 걸어서 집으로 간다. Todd는 집에 가는 길에 모퉁이에 있는 가게에서 종종 아이스크림을 사 먹는다. 다 먹은 후, Todd는 어디에서건 포장지를 땅에다 버린다. 때로 근처에 휴지통이 있어도 그는 휴지통에 버리려고 애쓰지 않는다. Cole은 쓰레기를 버리는 것은 나쁜 짓이며 쓰레기를 버리는 사람들은 무식해 보인다고 부모님께 배웠다. 때때로 Todd가 쓰레기를 버리는 것을 보고 사람들이 머리를 가로젓기도 한다. 이것은 Cole을 무안하게 한다. 이러한 상황에서 Cole이 Todd에게 할 말로 가장 적절한 것은 무엇인가?

어휘 **wrapper** 포장지 / **bother to-v** v하려고 애쓰다, 일부러 v하다 / **litter** (쓰레기를) 버리다; 쓰레기 / **ignorant** 무식한, 무지한 / **embarrass** 무안하게 하다, 당황하게 하다 | 선택지 어휘 | **be blamed for** ~로 비난받다

16~17 세트 문항 | 16. ④ 17. ④

▶ 16. 건강보조제의 종류와 기능에 대해 설명하고 있다.

① 종합비타민의 이점
② 영양 부족의 위험성
③ 잘못된 식습관과 관련된 질병들
④ 건강보조제의 종류와 효능
⑤ 건강보조제 오용으로 인한 부작용

▶ 17. 뼈의 건강 유지는 영양제가 아니라 미네랄 보조제 중 칼슘의 효능으로 언급되었다.

M: It's hard for our bodies to get **the ideal amounts of nutrients** from regular food. For this reason, many people take special pills called health supplements. Because health supplements affect the body, it's important to talk to your doctor before starting a new supplement. **Keeping that in mind**, let's talk a bit about them. First, there is one supplement that almost everyone should be taking, and this is a basic multivitamin. Multivitamins **are designed to give** us the extra nutrients that our bodies need. Then there are mineral supplements. Among them, calcium is the most important for maintaining healthy bones. Nutritional supplements form a third category of supplements. In fact, they are really specialty supplements **prepared for specific reasons** such as making your muscles stronger, losing weight, preventing hair loss, maintaining healthy skin, and a number of other reasons.

남: 우리의 몸은 일상 음식에서 이상적인 양의 영양소를 얻기가 힘듭니다. 이 때문에 많은 사람이 건강보조제라고 하는 특수한 알약을 복용합니다. 건강보조제는 몸에 영향을 미치기 때문에 새로운 보조제 복용을 시작하기 전에 의사와 상담하는 것이 중요합니다. 이를 명심하고 보조제에 관해 이야기를 좀 해보겠습니다. 첫째로 거의 모든 사람이 복용하고 있어야 하는 한 가지 보조제가 있는데, 이것은 기본 종합비타민입니다. 종합비타민은 우리 몸이 필요로 하는 영양소를 추가로 공급해 주도록 만들어져 있습니다. 다음으로는 미네랄 보조제가 있습니다. 그중에서 칼슘은 건강한 뼈를 유지하는 데 가장 중요합니다. 영양제는 건강보조제 중 세 번째 범주를 이룹니다. 사실 영양제는 특정한 이유 때문에 조제되는 정말 특수한 보조제인데, 예를 들면 ① 근육 강화, ② 체중 감량, ③ 탈모 방지, ⑤ 건강한 피부 유지 외에도 다른 많은 이유가 있습니다.

어휘 **nutrient** 영양분 ***cf.*** **nutritional** 영양상의 / **supplement** 보충(물) / **be designed to-v** v하도록 만들어지다[설계되다] / **mineral** (영양소로서의) 광물질, 미네랄 / **calcium** 칼슘 / **category** 범주 / **specialty** 특수성; 전문 / **prepare** (약 등을) 조제하다; 준비하다 / **specific** 특정한; 구체적인 | 선택지 어휘 | **side effect** 부작용 / **misuse** 오용, 남용

01. ②	02. ②	03. ③	04. ①	05. ④	06. ③	07. ②	08. ②	09. ③	10. ③
11. ②	12. ⑤	13. ②	14. ②	15. ⑤	16. ①	17. ①			

01 화자가 하는 말의 목적 | ②

▶ 청소년들에게 응급 처치를 가르치는 것이 필수적이라고 하면서 교과 과정에 포함시켜야 한다고 말하고 있다.

W: First aid is an essential life skill that equips young people with the confidence, **willingness and ability to step in and act** in a first aid emergency. Children as young as six can learn basic first aid, including how to recognize an emergency and call for help. It could help thousands of people a year. For example, I heard of a 12-year-old who **saved her best friend from choking** during lunchtime. Yet first aid isn't usually part of the curriculum. The Red Cross has tirelessly campaigned for years that all schools should teach first aid. It makes perfect sense to **make it a necessary part of school life**. All students should be taught what to do in an emergency. It would help keep them safer.

여: 응급 처치는 청소년들에게 응급 처치 위급 상황에서 돕고 나서서 행동하기 위한 자신감과 기꺼이 하려는 마음과 능력을 갖추게 하는 필수적인 생존 기술입니다. 6살 어린 나이의 아이들도 위급 상황을 인식하고 도움을 요청하는 법을 포함한 기본적인 응급 처치를 배울 수 있습니다. 그것은 한 해 수천 명의 사람을 도와줄 수 있습니다. 예를 들어, 저는 12살짜리가 점심시간에 친한 친구가 질식하지 않게 구했다고 들었습니다. 그러나 응급 처치는 통상 교과 과정에 들어있지 않습니다. 적십자가 수년간 꾸준하게 모든 학교가 응급 처치를 가르쳐야 한다고 운동을 해왔습니다. 그것을 학교생활의 필수 부분이 되도록 하는 것은 일리가 있습니다. 모든 학생들은 위급 상황에 무엇을 해야 할지를 배워야 합니다. 그것이 그들이 더 안전하도록 도울 것입니다.

어휘 **first aid** 응급 처치 / **equip** 갖추게 하다, ~할 능력을 기르다 / **confidence** 확신 / **willingness** 기꺼이 하기, 자진해서 하기 / **step in** 돕고 나서다, 개입하다 / **emergency** 비상 (사태), 위급 / **choke** 질식시키다 / **curriculum** 교과 과정 / **tirelessly** 꾸준하게 / **campaign** 운동을 하다

02 의견 | ②

▶ 여자는 대화 시 말하고 있는 사람을 쳐다보지 않으면, 상대방이 듣고 있는지 알 수 없고 이런 행동은 무례하므로 대화할 때 서로 눈을 마주쳐야 한다고 말하고 있다.

W: Chris, you need to listen to me. I'm trying to tell you something important.
M: I am listening, Mom.
W: Maybe you are, but **I can't tell if you aren't looking at me**. Just put down your phone for a few minutes.
M: I'm just checking my messages. I can **do two things at once**.
W: I'm sure you can, dear. But it's impolite not to look at someone who is talking to you.
M: Okay, I'm sorry. I guess **I didn't think it was a big deal**.
W: Maybe your friends don't mind, but there are plenty of people who agree with me.
M: You're right. I'm paying attention now.

여: Chris, 내 말을 귀담아들어야 해. 중요한 이야기를 하려고 하잖니.
남: 듣고 있어요, 엄마.
여: 아마 그렇겠지, 하지만 네가 나를 쳐다보고 있지 않으면 알 수 없단다. 잠깐 동안 휴대전화 좀 내려놓으렴.
남: 메시지를 확인하고 있을 뿐이에요. 전 두 가지 일을 동시에 할 수 있어요.
여: 물론 할 수 있겠지, 얘야. 그렇지만 너에게 말하고 있는 사람을 쳐다보지 않는 것은 무례하단다.
남: 알겠어요, 죄송해요. 별일이 아니라고 생각했나 봐요.
여: 네 친구들은 개의치 않을지도 모르지만, 내 말에 동의하는 사람들이 많이 있단다.
남: 엄마 말씀이 맞아요. 이제 주의를 기울일게요.

어휘 **impolite** 무례한, 버릇없는 / **big deal** 아주 중요한 것[일]

03 관계 | ③

▶ 남자가 택시 예약을 하려는 것을 보고 택시 콜센터에 전화를 한 것으로 생각할 수 있지만, hotel lobby, wake-up call 등의 표현이 등장한 것으로 보아 호텔 직원과 투숙객 사이의 대화임을 알 수 있다.

W: Good evening.
M: Hello. I need to be at the Korean Embassy at 9 a.m. tomorrow. Can you book a taxi for me, please?
W: I'm sorry sir, but traffic in the morning is very bad. A taxi to the embassy **could take an hour or more**.
M: Oh. Then what should I do?
W: Take the Sky Train. It's very convenient and fast.
M: Great. **Where do I catch that**?
W: Exit the hotel lobby, turn right, and you'll see City Hall Station. Catch a train from there to Embassy Station.
M: Excellent. **What time should I leave here** in the morning?
W: Well, the train trip takes about 15 minutes. Therefore, 8:30 will be fine. Would you like a wake-up call?
M: No, but thank you!

여: 안녕하세요.
남: 안녕하세요. 제가 내일 아침 9시까지 대한민국 대사관에 가야 하는데요. 택시 예약 좀 해주시겠어요?
여: 죄송하지만 고객님, 아침에는 차가 아주 많이 막힙니다. 택시를 타고 대사관에 가려면 한 시간 이상 걸릴 수 있습니다.
남: 아, 그러면 어떻게 하는 것이 좋을까요?
여: 스카이 전철을 이용하세요. 매우 편리하고 빠릅니다.
남: 좋아요. 어디에서 탈 수 있죠?
여: 호텔 로비에서 나가셔서 오른쪽으로 도세요. 그러면 시청역이 보일 겁니다. 거기서 대사관역으로 가는 전철을 타세요.
남: 잘됐군요. 아침에 몇 시쯤 여기서 나가야 할까요?
여: 음, 전철로 15분 정도 걸려요. 그러니까 8시 30분이 좋겠네요. 모닝콜을 해드릴까요?
남: 아니오. 고맙지만 괜찮습니다!

어휘 **embassy** 대사관 / **wake-up call** (호텔 등의) 모닝콜

04 그림 불일치 | ①

▶ 여자는 커다란 기타가 지붕 위에 있다고 했다.

[Cell phone rings.]
W: Hi, Eric. It's me, Jessica.
M: Hi, Jessica. Are you there yet?
W: Not yet. I'm passing by a music store **with a big guitar on the roof**.
M: Then you're almost there. Do you see the sign that says "Dr. Cho's Dental Clinic" on the 2nd floor?
W: Just a minute. Oh, right there. I think I found it.
M: It's on the 1st floor of the same building.
W: You mean the one with **the coffee cup on the window**?
M: That's right.
W: Okay. *[pause]* Now I'm here. How long will it take for you to get here?
M: Actually, **I'm stuck in heavy traffic**. But I'll be there in 15 minutes.
W: Take your time. I'll sit on the bench in front of the restaurant. There's a menu board standing beside the entrance. Why don't I select the menu to save time?
M: That's a good idea. Dinner is on me.

[휴대전화 벨이 울린다.]
여: 안녕하세요, Eric. 저예요, Jessica.
남: 안녕하세요, Jessica. 다 왔어요?
여: 아직요. 지붕 위에 커다란 기타가 있는 악기점을 지나고 있어요.
남: 그럼 거의 다 온 거예요. 2층에 'Dr. Cho's Dental Clinic'이라고 쓰인 간판 보여요?
여: 잠깐만요. 아, 저기 있네요. 찾은 것 같아요.
남: 같은 건물 1층에 있어요.

여: 창문에 커피 잔 그려진 데 말이에요?
남: 맞아요.
여: 알았어요. *[잠시 후]* 지금 도착했어요. 여기 오는 데 얼마나 걸릴 것 같아요?
남: 사실 지금 교통 체증에 걸려서요. 그렇지만 15분 인에는 도착할 거예요.
여: 천천히 와요. 식당 앞에 있는 벤치에 앉아있을게요. 입구 옆에 메뉴판이 세워져 있네요. 시간 절약을 위해 제가 음식을 골라 놓을까요?
남: 그거 좋은 생각이에요. 저녁은 제가 살게요.

어휘 **pass by** ~을 지나가다 / **be stuck in heavy traffic** 교통 체증에 걸리다

05 추후 행동 | ④

▶ 남자는 수학 문제를 여자에게 물어보려고 했으나 여자가 Carol의 집에 갈 것이라고 하자 자신도 그곳에 가도 될지 Carol에게 전화해서 물어보겠다고 했다.

[Phone rings.]
W: Hello.
M: Hi, Olivia. This is Jerry. Are you studying math?
W: I was. I studied for two hours.
M: Well, I've just started. And **I can't figure out a few questions**.
W: Jerry, it's too late. I can't help you. And I'm going out now.
M: Where are you going?
W: To Carol's house. She and I made a plan to study for the history test together.
M: That's what I studied first. **I should have studied math first**.
W: I'll help you tomorrow morning. Get to school as early as you can.
M: **Can't I just come over** to Carol's too?
W: You must phone and ask her first.
M: OK. I'll do that.
W: Good. Let me know what she said after that.

[전화벨이 울린다.]
여: 여보세요.
남: 안녕, Olivia. 나 Jerry야. 지금 수학을 공부하고 있니?
여: 했어. 두 시간 동안 공부했어.
남: 음, 난 막 시작했어. 그리고 몇 문제를 잘 모르겠어.
여: Jerry, 너무 늦었어. 너를 도와줄 수 없어. 그리고 나는 지금 나가는 길이야.
남: 어디를 가는데?
여: Carol네 집에. 그 애랑 나는 역사 시험 공부를 같이 하기로 계획했어.
남: 그건 내가 첫 번째로 공부한 과목이야. 수학을 먼저 공부했어야 했는데.
여: 내일 아침에 도와줄게. 할 수 있는 한 일찍 학교에 오도록 해.
남: 나도 그냥 Carol네 집으로 가면 안 될까?
여: 네가 Carol에게 전화해서 먼저 물어봐야 해.
남: 알겠어. 그렇게 할게.
여: 좋아. 그러고 나서 그 애가 뭐라고 했는지 내게 알려줘.

어휘 **figure out** 계산하다; 이해하다; 해결하다 / **come over** (**to**) (~에) 들르다

06 금액 | ③

▶ 이코노미석보다 가격이 50달러 비싼 이코노미 플러스석($810)을 선택하였으므로 두 사람이 지불할 금액은 1,620달러이다.

M: Honey, do you have a minute?
W: Of course. What's up?
M: I'm looking at plane tickets for our trip to Canada, and I'd like your opinion.
W: Okay. **What have you found so far**?
M: Well, the cheapest option is $690 per ticket, but we would have to transfer twice.
W: That sounds inconvenient. How much for a direct flight?
M: For weekend flights, each ticket is $980. We could save a little bit **by traveling during the week**.
W: That would be fine with me. *[pause]* It looks like there are two options. What's the difference?
M: The $760 ticket is for economy class. For $810 we can sit in economy plus, **which has more legroom**.
W: I'm willing to pay an extra $50 for that.
M: Great. Then it's settled.

남: 여보, 시간 좀 있어요?
여: 그럼요. 무슨 일이에요?
남: 우리의 캐나다 여행을 위해 비행기 표를 구하고 있는데, 당신의 의견이 필요해요.
여: 그래요. 지금까지 찾은 게 뭐예요?
남: 음, 가장 저렴하게 선택할 수 있는 것이 일인당 690달러짜리 표인데 두 번 갈아타야 해요.
여 불편하겠네요. 직항으로 가는 표는 얼마예요?
남: 주말 티켓은 일인당 980달러예요. 주중에 가면 돈을 조금 아낄 수 있어요.
여: 그게 좋겠네요. *[잠시 후]* 두 가지 선택사항이 있는 것 같군요. 무슨 차이예요?
남: 760달러짜리 표는 이코노미석이에요. 810달러짜리 표로는 이코노미 플러스석에 앉을 수 있는데, 다리를 뻗을 수 있는 공간이 더 넓어요.
여: 그렇다면 기꺼이 50달러를 더 내겠어요.
남: 좋아요. 그럼 결정됐네요.

어휘 **transfer** 갈아타다, 환승하다; 옮기다

07 이유 | ②

▶ 부모님과 버지니아주에 2년간 계속 살고 있어야 하지만, 남자는 작년에 이사 와서 장학금을 신청할 수 없다.

M: Excuse me. I'm here to apply for the Moore scholarship this semester.
W: Are you aware of all the requirements?
M: I'm not quite sure.
W: The Moore scholarship is not available to first-year students. Students starting from the second year **are eligible for this scholarship**.
M: I'm a sophomore.
W: You must have maintained a B average or better for the past two semesters.
M: My grades are **in pretty good shape**. I received mostly As in all my classes.
W: You also need a recommendation from one of your professors, and you need some experience in volunteer work.
M: I see. I think **I fulfill all the requirements**.
W: One more thing, since it's for Virginia residents, you and your parents must have lived in Virginia continuously for 2 years.
M: Really? I moved from New Hampshire last year.
W: Well, I'm sorry, but you can't apply for this scholarship then.

남: 실례합니다. 이번 학기 Moore 장학금을 신청하러 왔습니다.
여: 모든 자격요건은 알고 계신가요?
남: 잘 모르겠어요.
여: 1학년생은 Moore 장학금을 받을 수 없습니다. 2학년 때부터 이 장학금을 받을 자격이 있습니다.
남: 전 2학년이에요.
여: 지난 두 학기 동안 평균 B학점 이상을 유지했어야 합니다.
남: 제 성적은 꽤 괜찮아요. 모든 수업에서 대부분 A를 받았어요.
여: 교수님 중 한 분의 추천도 필요하고, 자원봉사 활동 경력이 좀 필요합니다.
남: 알겠습니다. 전 모든 자격요건을 충족시킨 것 같네요.
여: 한 가지 더요. 버지니아주 거주자들을 위한 것이기 때문에, 본인과 부모님이 버지니아주에 2년 동안 계속 살고 있어야 합니다.
남: 정말요? 전 작년에 뉴햄프셔주에서 이사 왔어요.
여: 음, 죄송하지만, 그렇다면 이 장학금에 신청하실 수 없어요.

어휘 **scholarship** 장학금 / **requirement** 필요조건, 요건 / **be eligible for** ~에 자격이 있다 / **sophomore** 2학년생 / **maintain** 유지하다; 지속하다 / **fulfill** (요구, 조건 등을) 만족시키다; 이행하다, 실행하다 / **continuously** 계속해서, 연속적으로

08 언급하지 않은 것 | ②

▶ 해석 참조

W: Honey, don't you think **we have far too much stuff**?
M: I couldn't agree more. I guess we could have a garage sale.
W: Great idea! My family would have them when I was young, so I know a few tips.
M: Oh, really? Like what?
W: To begin, we want to attract the most customers. So, a non-holiday weekend is perfect.
M: Makes sense. I suppose we also want to **advertise with some signs**.
W: It's even better to advertise in a newspaper.
M: Okay. And I guess we want to put our nicest items out by the street to grab attention.
W: Of course. Now, **pricing can be tricky**. Usually, around 25% of the

item's original cost is best.
M: Great. I think this will be a fun way to make some money.

여: 여보, 우리 너무 많은 물건을 가지고 있다고 생각하지 않아?
남: 정말 그래. 우리 차고에서 중고 물품 판매를 해도 되겠는 걸.
여: 좋은 생각이야! 어렸을 적에 우리 가족이 중고 물품 판매를 하곤 해서 몇 가지 비결을 알고 있어.
남: 아, 정말? 예를 들면?
여: 우선, 최대한 고객을 끌어모아야 해. 그래서 공휴일이 끼지 않은 주말(① 상품 판매 시기)이 가장 적절하지.
남: 일리 있네. 표지판 몇 개를 가지고 광고도 할 수 있을 거야(③ 판매 광고 방법).
여: 신문에 광고를 내면 훨씬 더 효과적이야(③ 판매 광고 방법).
남: 알겠어. 그리고 관심을 끌기 위해서 길옆에 가장 좋은 물품들을 내놓아야겠지(④ 상품 진열 방법).
여: 물론이지. 이제, 가격을 매기는 게 까다로울 거야. 보통, 물품의 원래 가격에서 25% 정도가 적절해(⑤ 가격 결정 방법).
남: 그래. 이렇게 하면 재미있게 돈을 벌 수 있을 것 같아.

어휘 **garage sale** (자기 집 차고에서 하는) 중고 물품 세일 / **grab attention** 관심을 끌다 / **tricky** 까다로운, 곤란한

09 내용 불일치 | ③

▶ 인구의 4분의 3이 농어업에 종사한다고 했다.

M: Located northeast of Australia and east of Papua New Guinea, the Solomon Islands are a group of nearly 1,000 islands in the Pacific Ocean. Humans have lived on the islands for over 30,000 years, but the first visit by a European was in 1568. During the Second World War, the Solomon Islands were **the site of intense fighting**, but afterward, the islands were relatively peaceful until a civil war broke out in 1998. Today, around three-quarters of its population **is involved in farming or fishing**. Tourism is also an important source of income for the islands, and scuba diving is especially popular with visitors. The islands have suffered two major earthquakes in 2007 and 2013. Each resulted in a 5 to 10 meter tsunami that **destroyed much of the nation**.

남: 호주의 북동쪽과 파푸아뉴기니의 동쪽에 위치한 솔로몬제도는 태평양에 있는 거의 1,000개나 되는 섬의 무리입니다. 사람들은 그 군도에 30,000년이 넘는 시간 동안 살아왔지만, 1568년이 되어서야 유럽인이 최초로 방문하였습니다. 제2차 세계대전 동안 솔로몬제도는 격렬한 전투의 현장이었지만, 그 후 1998년에 내전이 발발할 때까지 비교적 평화로웠습니다. 오늘날, 인구의 약 4분의 3이 농업이나 어업에 종사합니다. 관광업 또한 솔로몬제도의 중요한 수입원이며, 스쿠버 다이빙은 관광객들에게 특히 인기 있습니다. 솔로몬제도는 2007년과 2013년에 두 번의 대지진을 겪었습니다. 각각의 지진은 이 나라의 많은 것을 파괴한 5에서 10미터에 달하는 쓰나미를 초래했습니다.

어휘 **intense** 치열한; 극심한, 강렬한 / **relatively** 상대적[비교적]으로 / **civil war** 내전 / **result in** (결과적으로) ~을 초래하다[야기하다]

10 도표 이해 | ③

▶ 두 사람은 저녁에 시작하는 영화를 보기로 하였고, 공포 영화는 크리스마스에 보기에는 적절하지 않다고 했으며, 남은 두 영화 중에서 더 일찍 상영하는 영화를 보기로 했다.

W: Oh, look! The Jasper Cinema is having a Christmas special.
M: That's nice. Why don't we watch a movie later?
W: I was thinking the same thing. *Love and Hate* is romantic. What do you think?
M: Don't forget that we promised to have lunch with your parents at 12 today.
W: Oh, right. Well, I know you like *Space Shuttle,* but 162 minutes is just too long.
M: I agree. And **I'd prefer to go at night**. But a horror film just doesn't seem appropriate for Christmas.
W: **That leaves two options**. I say we go to the earlier one. Then we can have dinner afterward.
M: Are you sure? I've never seen *Broken* before.
W: Yes, I do not want to get back home too late.
M: Okay, then. **It's settled**.

여: 어, 이것 봐요! Jasper 영화관이 크리스마스 특집을 해요.
남: 그거 좋네요. 이따 함께 영화 보는 게 어때요?
여: 저도 같은 생각을 하고 있었어요. 〈Love and Hate〉는 로맨틱 영화인데, 어때요?
남: 오늘 12시에 당신 부모님과 함께 점심 식사하기로 한 걸 잊지 말아요.
여: 아, 맞아요. 음, 당신이 〈Space Shuttle〉을 좋아하는 걸 알지만, 상영시간 162분은 너무 길어요.
남: 나도 그렇게 생각해요. 그리고 난 저녁에 영화를 보러 가고 싶어요. 그런데 공포영화는 크리스마스에 보기에 적절하지 않겠어요.
여: 그럼 둘만 남았네요. 둘 중에 더 일찍 시작하는 것을 보러 가요. 그리고 나서 저녁을 먹을 수 있잖아요.
남: 정말요? 난 〈Broken〉을 아직 못 봤는데요.
여: 네, 난 집에 너무 늦게 돌아가고 싶지 않거든요.
남: 알겠어요. 그럼, 결정됐네요.

어휘 **appropriate** 적절한, 알맞은

11 짧은 대화에 이어질 응답 | ②

▶ 날씨가 추워서 스웨터를 빌린 여자에게 왜 스웨터를 가져오지 않았는지 묻고 있다. 이에 가장 적절한 응답을 찾는다.

① 일기예보에서 내일은 따뜻할 거래.
② 집에서 나올 때는 춥지 않았어.
③ 이 매운 수프를 먹으면 몸이 따뜻해질 거야.
④ 내 생각엔 우린 오늘 저녁에 집에서 먹어야겠어.
⑤ 고마워, 내가 스웨터를 가져오는 걸 깜빡하다니.

M: I'm hungry. Let's go outside and get something to eat.
W: Okay, but it's really cold. Do you **have a sweater I could borrow**?
M: I probably do, but **why didn't you bring one**?
W: ______________________________

남: 배고프다. 밖에 나가서 뭘 좀 먹자.
여: 그래, 하지만 너무 추워. 스웨터 좀 빌릴 수 있을까?
남: 빌려줄 수 있지만, 왜 네 스웨터는 가져오지 않았니?
여: ______________________________

12 짧은 대화에 이어질 응답 | ⑤

▶ 약의 복용법을 읽었는지 묻는 질문에 대한 가장 적절한 응답을 고른다.

① 응, 그 약은 내가 푹 잘 수 있게 도와줄 거야.
② 집에 도착하자마자 약을 먹을게.
③ 내일은 네 몸이 분명 나아질 거야.
④ 의사의 지시를 따르는 게 중요해.
⑤ 한 번에 두 알 넘게 복용하지 말라고 쓰여 있어.

W: Are you still sick? Maybe you should go home and rest.
M: **It's not too severe**. I'll just take some of these pills that I bought.
W: Those can make you sleepy. **Have you read the directions**?
M: ______________________________

여: 아직도 아프니? 집에 가서 쉬어야겠는걸.
남: 그렇게 심각하진 않아. 그냥 내가 사온 이 약을 먹을게.
여: 그걸 먹으면 졸릴 수 있어. 복용법은 읽었니?
남: ______________________________

어휘 **severe** 심각한, 극심한 / **direction** 사용법; 방향

13 긴 대화에 이어질 응답 | ②

▶ 남자는 정원에 채소를 심으려고 여자에게 흙을 갈아엎어 달라고 요청했다. 이 상황에서 여자가 할 수 있는 대답을 찾는다.

① 가서 정원에 심을 채소를 좀 사 오죠.
② 도와줄게요. 옷을 갈아입고요.
③ 당신이 그 나무들을 먼저 심는 것이 좋겠어요.
④ 모든 것이 준비되면 내가 다시 전화할게요.
⑤ 내가 이틀이 지나도 돌아오지 않으면, 나 없이 시작해요.

W: Where did all those potted vegetable plants come from?
M: I went to the garden center and bought them.
W: What do you plan to do with them?
M: I thought we could plant a garden with some vegetables.

W: That sounds like a good idea.
M: First I'm going to draw up **a plan for how we will plant them**.
W: I forgot you have a degree in landscape architecture.
M: **I have also been gardening** since I was very little.
W: Really? Anything you want me to do for you?
M: Yes. Maybe you could **turn over the soil** for me with a shovel.
W: ______________________________

여: 화분에 심은 저 채소들은 모두 어디에서 가져온 거예요?
남: 원예 용품점에 가서 사 왔어요.
여: 그것들로 무엇을 할 계획이에요?
남: 정원에 채소를 심을 수 있겠다고 생각했어요.
여: 좋은 생각인 것 같군요.
남: 먼저 그것들을 어떻게 심을지 계획을 세워야겠어요.
여: 당신이 조경학 학위가 있는 것을 잊고 있었군요.
남: 나는 또한 아주 어렸을 때부터 정원을 가꾸어 왔어요.
여: 정말이요? 내가 도와줬으면 하는 일이 있나요?
남: 네. 삽으로 흙을 갈아엎는 일을 해주면 되겠네요.
여: ______________________________

어휘 **potted** 화분에 심은 / **garden center** 원예 용품점 / **draw up** (계획을) 짜다 / **degree** 학위 / **landscape architecture** 조경술, 도시 계획술 / **turn over** 뒤집어엎다

14 긴 대화에 이어질 응답 | ②

▶ 매진된 공연을 볼 수 있게 남자의 이름을 초대 손님 목록에 올리겠다는 여자의 말에 적절한 대답을 찾는다.

① 죄송해요. 아직 손님이 너무 많이 계셔서요.
② 정말이요? 그렇다면 이 헤어컷은 무료입니다!
③ 초대 손님의 구성이 인상적이군요.
④ 지금은 머리 모양을 바꾸기엔 너무 늦었어요.
⑤ 죄송해요. 당신이 그렇게 하도록 제가 설득하지 않았어야 했어요.

M: OK, Julia, here's a mirror for you, so you can see the back.
W: Wow, it looks great! You are a genius hair stylist!
M: A shorter haircut really suits you, don't you think?
W: Yes, I'm glad **you talked me into it**.
M: Always a pleasure, Julia, and not just because you're a big star!
W: Thank you, Adrian! I have to run! I'm on stage at the Concert Hall at 8!
M: I wish **I could come and see you sing tonight**.
W: Well, why don't you? Do you have to work late?
M: No, you're my last client today, but your show tonight is sold out.
W: But that's no problem! I'll **have your name put on my guest list**!
M: ______________________________

남: 자 Julia 씨, 여기 거울이 있으니 뒤쪽을 보세요.
여: 와, 멋지군요! 정말 천재적인 솜씨의 헤어 디자이너세요!
남: 짧은 머리가 정말 잘 어울리는군요, 그렇지 않아요?
여: 네, 그렇게 하라고 설득해 주셔서 감사해요.
남: 항상 영광이죠, Julia 씨. 대스타라서 드리는 말씀은 아니에요!
여: 감사해요, Adrian 씨! 서둘러야겠어요! 8시에 Concert Hall 무대에 올라야 해요!
남: 오늘 밤에 노래하시는 것을 가서 볼 수 있으면 좋을 텐데요.
여: 음, 왜 안 되나요? 늦게까지 일하셔야 해요?
남: 아니요, 오늘 Julia 씨가 마지막 손님이세요. 하지만 오늘 밤 공연이 매진이어서요.
여: 하지만 그건 문제없어요! 초대 손님 목록에 당신의 성함을 올려놓을게요!
남: ______________________________

어휘 **suit** (머리, 옷 등이) 어울리다 / **talk A into B** A를 설득하여 B하게 시키다 / **on stage** 무대 위에서 | 선택지 어휘 | **impressive** 인상적인 / **line-up** 인원 구성

15 상황에 적절한 말 | ⑤

▶ 돌발 상황에 대비하여 월급 관리를 현명하게 하길 바라는 누나가 할 수 있는 말로 가장 적절한 것을 찾는다.

① 휴대폰을 잃어버리다니 부주의했어.
② 네가 현명하게 지출 계획을 세워서 기쁘다.
③ 도움이 필요할 땐 언제든 나에게 찾아와도 돼.
④ 너는 휴대전화비에 돈을 다 쓰면 안 돼.
⑤ 너는 돌발 상황에 대비해 돈을 저금하는 습관을 길러야 해.

W: Luke just started his first job two months ago. After his first paycheck, Luke **created a budget**. The budget divided all of his money among rent, food, entertainment, clothing, and transportation. He was proud of this budget and **stuck to it**. Unfortunately, one week before his second paycheck, Luke lost his phone and needed to buy another. **Not having extra money for this emergency**, Luke went to his older sister. Luke's sister was happy to help and gave him some money. But she worried that Luke wasn't planning for emergencies. She felt he could be smarter about **how he spent his salary**, and she wanted to offer some advice. In this situation, what would Luke's sister most likely say to Luke?

여: Luke는 두 달 전에 처음으로 일을 시작했다. 첫 월급을 받은 후, Luke는 지출 계획을 세웠다. 그의 월급 전액은 집세, 식비, 여가비, 의복비, 교통비로 나뉘어 계획되었다. 그는 이 계획이 만족스러웠고 굳게 지켰다. 유감스럽게도, 두 번째 월급을 받기 일주일 전에 Luke는 휴대폰을 잃어버려서 새로 사야 했다. 이런 돌발 상황에 대비할 여윳돈이 없었던 Luke는 누나에게 찾아갔다. Luke의 누나는 그를 도울 수 있어서 기뻤고 그에게 약간의 돈을 주었다. 하지만 그녀는 Luke가 돌발 상황에 대비하지 않는 것을 걱정했다. 그녀는 Luke가 월급을 사용하는 방식에 관해 더 현명해질 수 있으리라 생각했고, 조언을 해주고 싶었다. 이러한 상황에서 Luke의 누나가 Luke에게 할 말로 가장 적절한 것은 무엇인가?

어휘 **paycheck** 급료, 봉급 / **budget** 예산; 가계(家計), 생활비 / **stick to** 굳게 지키다, 고수하다 | 선택지 어휘 | **sensible** 현명한; 분별 있는

16~17 세트 문항 | 16. ① 17. ①

▶ 16. 베트남전 반대, 소말리아와 에티오피아의 기아 구호, 미국 농민 지원 등 사회적 이슈에 대한 음악의 사회적 영향력에 대해 말하고 있다.

① 음악이 사회에 미쳐온 영향
② 대중의 관심을 이끌어내는 효과적인 방법들
③ 성공한 음악가가 되는 방법
④ 세계의 가난한 사람들을 돕는 방법들
⑤ 다양한 음악을 듣는 것의 중요성

▶ 17. 해석 참조

① 프랑스 ② 베트남 ③ 소말리아 ④ 에티오피아 ⑤ 미국

M: Are you a music lover who is only interested in your favorite musician's music? I think that is unlikely, but if you are, I hope you will take a minute to think about all the social issues that music has brought to public attention and helped with. In the 1960s, musicians from Europe and North America sang songs **encouraging people to protest against** the Vietnam War. And these protests greatly helped to end the war. In the 1980s, famine in Somalia was raised as a global issue, and rock musicians held concerts **to raise money for famine relief**. Similar efforts brought food to thousands of hungry people suffering in Ethiopia. Millions of people watched, donated money, and learned about the famine, and results followed. Country stars like Willie Nelson have also gotten involved. In 1985, Nelson and others launched Farm Aid, a concert **to benefit struggling farmers** in the United States. Worldwide, musicians and their music are **doing more than just entertaining crowds**. They are bringing awareness to real issues and providing hope.

남: 당신은 오직 자신이 좋아하는 음악가의 음악에만 관심이 있는 음악 애호가인가요? 그렇지 않을 거라고 생각하지만, 만약 그렇다면, 음악이 대중의 주목을 이끌어서 도움을 주었던 모든 사회적 쟁점들에 대해 당신이 잠시 생각할 시간을 가졌으면 합니다. 1960년대에, 유럽과 북아메리카 음악가들은 사람들이 ② 베트남 전쟁에 반대하도록 촉구하는 노래를 불렀습니다. 그리고 이러한 반대 운동들은 전쟁을 끝내는 데 큰 도움이 되었습니다. 1980년대에는 ③ 소말리아의 기아가 세계적 쟁점으로 떠올랐고, 록 음악가들은 기아 구호를 위한 기금을 모으기 위해 콘서트를 열었습니다. 유사한 노력들이 ④ 에티오피아에서 어려움을 겪는 수천 명의 배고픈 사람들에게 음식을 가져다주었습니다. 수백만 명의 사람들이 관람했고, 기부했으며, 기아에 대해 알게 되면서, 결실이 따라왔습니다. Willie Nelson과 같은 컨트리 뮤직 스타들도 가담하였습니다. 1985년 Nelson과 다른 음악가들은 Farm Aid를 시작했는데, 이는 ⑤ 미국의 어려운 농부들에게 혜택을 주는 콘서트였습니다. 세계적으로, 음악가들과 그들의 음악은 단지 군중들을 즐겁게 하는 일 이상의 것을 하고 있습니다. 그들은 실질적인 이슈들에 대해 (사람들이) 인식하게 해주고 희망을 가져다주고 있습니다.

어휘 **bring A to B's attention** A에 대해 B의 주목을 이끌다 / **protest (against)** (~에 대해) 항의하다, 반대하다; 반대[항의] (운동) / **famine** 기근, 기아, 굶주림 / **raise** (문제를) 제기하다; (돈을) 마련하다 / **relief** 구호(품); 안심 / **donate** 기부하다 / **launch** 시작[착수]하다 / **benefit** 혜택을 주다 / **struggling** 분투하는, 발버둥치는 / **entertain** 즐겁게 하다 / **awareness** (무엇의 중요성에 관한) 인식, 의식

26 Sense Up 듣기 모의고사 ANSWERS & COMPREHENSION

본문 p.158

01. ① 02. ④ 03. ④ 04. ⑤ 05. ① 06. ④ 07. ⑤ 08. ③ 09. ⑤ 10. ③
11. ① 12. ④ 13. ② 14. ② 15. ④ 16. ⑤ 17. ④

01 화자가 하는 말의 목적 | ①

▶ 미래를 두려워하지 말고 졸업 후 다가올 도전과 기회를 받아들이라는 내용으로 보아 졸업생을 격려하는 것이 목적이다.

M: All of you are probably eager to start a new chapter in your life. Many of you will soon encounter many opportunities. Some of you may be **reluctant to take on new challenges**. Once you enter the real world, you will meet people from all walks of life and have a variety of experiences. You may feel that **what you've learned in school** is not relevant to your future needs. But you'll realize later that everything you've learned will be useful and important. Do not be afraid of your future, but be ready to take on the upcoming challenges and opportunities after this graduation. We are very proud of all of you and **have faith in each and every one of you**.

남: 여러분 모두 인생의 새로운 장을 시작하기를 고대하고 계실 겁니다. 여러분 중 많은 분들은 곧 많은 기회들을 접하게 될 것입니다. 어떤 분들은 아마 새로운 도전을 하는 것을 주저할지도 모릅니다. 일단 실제 세상에 들어서게 되면 여러분은 각계각층의 사람들을 만나고 다양한 경험을 하게 될 것입니다. 여러분이 학교에서 배운 것이 미래를 위해 필요한 것들과 관련이 없다고 생각할지도 모릅니다. 하지만 여러분이 배운 모든 것이 유용하고 중요하다는 것을 나중에 깨닫게 될 것입니다. 미래를 두려워하지 말고, 이 졸업식 이후에 다가올 도전과 기회를 잡으려는 준비를 하십시오. 우리는 여러분 모두가 자랑스럽고 여러분 모두를 믿습니다.

어휘 **be eager to-v** v하고 싶어 하다 / **encounter** 만나다, 마주치다; (위험, 곤란 등에) 부딪히다 / **reluctant to-v** v하길 꺼리는, 마지못해 v하는 / **relevant to** ~에 관련된 / **upcoming** 다가오는, 곧 있을 / **faith** 믿음, 신뢰

02 의견 | ④

▶ 남자는 집중력 향상 등을 예로 들며 규칙적으로 아침 식사를 하는 것의 장점에 대해 이야기하고 있다.

M: Hi, Kelly. Where are you going? **First period is starting soon**.
W: Hey, Chuck. I'm going to the cafeteria. I'm so hungry!
M: You're going now? Didn't you have breakfast?
W: No. I never wake up early enough.
M: That's why you're always hungry in the morning. I think you **should set your alarm a little earlier** and have breakfast.
W: You're right, but it's hard to get out of bed in the morning.
M: Yes it is, but eating breakfast will increase your ability to concentrate. It might improve your grades.
W: That's true. I've also read that eating breakfast regularly can **help with maintaining** a healthy weight.
M: Then, you know what you have to do from tomorrow.
W: Okay. You win. I'll start tomorrow.

남: 안녕, Kelly. 어디 가니? 1교시가 곧 시작할 거야.
여: 안녕, Chuck. 나는 매점에 가는 중이야. 무척 배고프거든!
남: 지금 간다고? 아침밥 안 먹었니?
여: 안 먹었어. 난 결코 (아침 식사를 할 만큼) 충분히 일찍 일어나지 않아.
남: 그래서 네가 오전에 늘 배가 고픈 거야. 알람시계가 좀 더 일찍 울리도록 맞추고 아침밥을 먹어야 한다고 생각해.
여: 네 말이 옳지만, 아침에 침대에서 빠져나오기가 힘들어.
남: 그건 그래. 하지만 아침 식사를 하면 네 집중력이 향상될 거야. 그렇게 하는 것이 네 성적을 올려줄지도 몰라.
여: 맞아. 나도 규칙적인 아침 식사를 하면 건강한 체중을 유지하는 데 도움이 될 수 있다는 걸 읽은 적이 있어.
남: 그러면, 넌 내일부터 무엇을 해야 하는지 알고 있겠구나.
여: 좋아. 네가 이겼어. 내일 시작할게.

03 관계 | ④

▶ runway outfits나 The main colors of this season 등의 말에서 두 사람이 말하는 쇼가 패션쇼임을 알 수 있다. 남자는 쇼 의상의 디자인을 담당하고 있고 여자는 그 의상에 맞는 메이크업과 헤어스타일을 담당하고 있으므로 두 사람의 관계는 패션 디자이너와 미용 전문가이다.

M: Kayla, I think we need to talk about the show now.
W: Sure. Did you finish the final runway outfits?
M: **I'm almost done**.
W: Can I see them?
M: Sure. These are photos of them. The main colors of this season are deep turquoise and navy blue.
W: Wow, great! Your designs are always stunning! You said the theme of this show is "water," didn't you?
M: Yes, I really **want the models' style to flow**.
W: Then I think I'll have to put something bright, like gold or green eyeshadow, on their eyelids. Is that okay with you?
M: That sounds beautiful. How about their hair?
W: I guess long soft wavy hair **will suit the dresses of your show**.
M: I trust your judgment. You'll do wonderfully!

남: Kalya, 우린 지금 쇼에 관해 얘기를 좀 나눠야겠어요.
여: 그래요. 최종 무대 의상을 끝마쳤나요?
남: 거의 끝나가요.
여: 볼 수 있을까요?
남: 물론이죠. 이게 그 사진들이에요. 이번 시즌의 주요 색상은 짙은 청록색과 짙은 남색이에요.
여: 와, 훌륭해요! 당신의 디자인은 언제나 멋져요! 이 쇼의 주제가 '물'이라고 했죠?
남: 네, 전 정말 모델의 스타일이 물이 흐르는 느낌이면 좋겠어요.
여: 그럼 금색과 녹색 아이섀도와 같이 밝은 걸 모델의 눈꺼풀에 발라야겠네요. 괜찮나요?
남: 그럼 아름다울 것 같아요. 머리는 어떻게 하나요?
여: 길고 부드러운 웨이브 머리가 당신의 쇼 의상들과 잘 어울릴 거예요.
남: 전 당신의 판단을 믿어요. 당신은 멋지게 해낼 거예요!

어휘 **runway** (패션쇼 등의) 무대; 활주로 / **outfit** (한 벌로 된) 옷, 복장 / **turquoise** 청록색 / **navy blue** 짙은 남색 / **stunning** 굉장히 아름다운; 깜짝 놀랄 / **eyelid** ((주로 복수형)) 눈꺼풀 / **wavy** 웨이브가 있는, 물결 모양의 / **judgment** 판단(력); 재판

04 그림 불일치 | ⑤

▶ 개 앞의 바닥에는 꽃바구니가 아니라 트로피가 있다고 했다.

M: What's this photo?
W: It's a picture of Loy, a dog that won Best in Show in last year's dog show.
M: Who's the person holding Loy? The long-haired woman who has a white strap around her arm **with a number on it**.
W: That's my sister. She's a trainer. The number on her arm is the participant number.
M: Oh, I see. Your sister looks really cool. Is the man who's holding the encased ribbon your father?
W: No, he's the head of the dog-show committee. And the woman **who's holding a metal plate** is also a committee member.
M: You're talking about the woman who's wearing a long dress, right?
W: Yes.
M: Then who's the lady on the other side who has short hair and is holding a bouquet of flowers?
W: She's also a committee member. All of the things they were holding were given to Loy.
M: There's **a trophy on the floor in front of** Loy. I guess he got that, too.
W: Yeah. As far as I remember, my sister was even interviewed by the local newspaper after this picture was taken.

남: 이건 무슨 사진이야?
여: 지난해 반려견 대회에서 Best in Show를 수상한 Loy의 사진이야.
남: Loy를 붙잡고 있는 사람은 누구야? 숫자가 쓰인 흰색 완장을 팔에 차고 있는 긴 머리의 여자 말이야.
여: 내 여동생이야. 그녀는 조련사야. 팔에 있는 숫자는 참가자 번호야.
남: 아, 알겠어. 네 여동생은 정말 멋져 보인다. 액자에 든 리본을 들고 있는 남자는 너희 아빠니?
여: 아니, 그분은 반려견 대회의 위원회장이야. 금속 상패를 들고 있는 여자분도 위원회 임원이야.
남: 긴 드레스를 입고 있는 여자분 말하는 거지?
여: 응.

남: 그럼 반대쪽에 짧은 머리에 꽃다발을 들고 있는 여자분은 누군데?
여: 그분도 위원회 임원이야. 이 사람들이 들고 있는 것들이 모두 Loy가 받은 거야.
남: Loy 앞의 바닥에 트로피가 있네. 그것도 Loy가 받은 거겠지.
여: 응. 내 기억으로는 이 사진을 찍은 뒤에 내 여동생은 지역신문과 인터뷰도 했어.

어휘 **strap** (가죽으로 된) 끈[줄, 띠] / **encase** (상자 등에) 넣다; 싸다 / **committee** 위원회

05 추후 행동 | ①

▶ 남자(아버지)가 잡초를 뽑으면 용돈을 주겠다고 했고, 여자(딸)는 좋다고 말했다.

W: Dad, **could you increase** my allowance? I seem to go over my budget every month.
M: I think you're getting enough money.
W: Come on, Dad. Don't I deserve more now that I'm older?
M: Then how about this? I won't increase your allowance, but you can earn money **by doing some work around the house**.
W: Is there any work I can do today? I need to go see a movie tonight, but I'm $10 short.
M: Well, the house needs to be vacuumed and cleaned and there are dirty dishes piled up in the sink, but I guess **you can start by helping me** in the garden.
W: Are we going to plant flowers?
M: Yes, but we need to get rid of the weeds first. I'll pay you $10 an hour.
W: $10 an hour? Okay.

여: 아빠, 용돈 좀 올려주시겠어요? 매달 예산이 초과되는 것 같아요.
남: 너는 충분한 용돈을 받고 있는 것 같다만.
여: 제발요, 아빠. 더 컸으니까 더 많이 받을 만하지 않나요?
남: 그럼 이건 어떠니? 용돈을 올려주진 않을 거지만, 네가 집안일을 좀 해서 돈을 받을 수 있단다.
여: 오늘 할 수 있는 일이 있나요? 오늘 밤에 영화를 보러 가야 하는데 10달러가 부족해요.
남: 글쎄, 진공청소기로 집 청소도 해야 하고, 싱크대에는 설거지거리가 쌓여 있단다. 그렇지만 정원에서 나를 돕는 것부터 시작할 수 있을 것 같구나.
여: 꽃을 심는 건가요?
남: 그렇단다. 하지만 잡초부터 먼저 없애야 한단다. 1시간에 10달러를 주마.
여: 1시간에 10달러요? 좋아요.

어휘 **allowance** 용돈; 허용량 / **over budget** 예산을 초과한 / **now that** ~이므로, ~이기 때문에 / **short** 부족한, 모자라는 / **pile up** ~을 쌓아 올리다

06 금액 | ④

▶ 택시비 60달러에 시외할증 20%를 더하면 72달러이다. 여기에 팁으로 8달러를 주겠다고 했으므로 여자가 지불할 금액은 80달러이다.

W: Just a minute. Is this the right street?
M: Didn't you say you wanted to go to Sandy Elementary School?
W: Yes, but this area **doesn't look at all familiar to me**. I've been here before, but I don't remember this area.
M: Don't worry. **I'm taking a shortcut**. Do you see the school over there?
W: Oh, I see. Wow, that was really fast. You really know your way around here.
M: I've been a taxi driver in this area for the past 19 years. Okay, here we are.
W: I see that the fare is exactly $60.
M: But we're **out of the downtown area**, so there is an extra 20% charge to the total fare.
W: Oh, I totally forgot about that. I don't have any cash with me, so is it okay to pay by credit card?
M: Of course.
W: Please add another $8 for your tip.
M: Thank you so much, ma'am. Hold on. Here's your card.

여: 잠시만요. 이 길로 가는 게 맞나요?
남: Sandy 초등학교로 가신다고 하지 않으셨나요?
여: 네, 그런데 이곳은 전혀 낯익어 보이지 않아서요. 저는 전에 여기 와 본 일이 있는데, 이곳은 기억이 나지 않네요.
남: 걱정하지 마세요. 지름길로 가고 있답니다. 저쪽에 학교가 보이세요?
여: 아, 보여요. 와, 정말 빨리 왔어요. 정말 이곳 지리에 밝으시네요.
남: 저는 이 지역에서 지난 19년간 택시 운전을 했어요. 자, 다 왔습니다.
여: 요금이 정확히 60달러네요.
남: 그런데 시외 지역이기 때문에 총 요금에 할증 요금 20%가 붙습니다.
여: 아, 완전히 잊고 있었네요. 제가 현금이 전혀 없는데, 신용카드로 내도 괜찮을까요?
남: 물론이죠.
여: 8달러는 팁으로 추가해 주세요.
남: 정말 감사합니다, 손님. 잠시만요. 여기 카드 드릴게요.

07 이유 | ⑤

▶ 여자는 할머니의 장례식에 다녀오는 길인데 할머니를 더 이상 볼 수 없다는 생각에 눈물이 났다고 했다.

M: Excuse me, I believe this is my seat.
W: Oh, sorry about my bag. Let me move it. I was a little preoccupied.
M: No worries. You **seemed deep in thought**. Hi, my name is Mr. Doolittle.
W: I'm sorry? Is that really your name?
M: Haha. No, I was just **hoping to get a laugh**. My real name is Matthew Ruben.
W: Hi, I'm Kate.
M: I hope you found that funny because you seemed so very sad.
W: Is it that obvious? How embarrassing.
M: There's nothing to be embarrassed about. We all get sad from time to time.
W: Actually, I am on my way home from my grandmother's funeral. The thought of not seeing her anymore **brought me to tears**. She meant a lot to my family.
M: I'm really sorry to hear that. Losing someone is always heartbreaking. But I hope you get over your sorrow soon.
W: Thanks.

남: 죄송하지만, 여긴 제 자리인 것 같습니다.
여: 아, 제 가방 때문에 죄송해요. 치울게요. 잠시 딴생각을 하고 있었네요.
남: 괜찮습니다. 깊은 생각에 잠긴 듯 보였어요. 안녕하세요, 제 이름은 Doolittle이에요.
여: 뭐라고요? 정말 당신의 이름인가요?
남: 하하. 아니요, 그냥 웃기게 해드리고 싶었어요. 제 진짜 이름은 Matthew Ruben입니다.
여: 안녕하세요, 전 Kate예요.
남: 매우 슬퍼 보이셔서 재미있어 하시기를 바랐어요.
여: 그랬나요? 창피하네요.
남: 창피해하실 거 없습니다. 우리 모두 때로 슬프잖아요.
여: 사실, 저는 할머니 장례식에 갔다가 집에 가는 길이에요. 할머니를 더 이상 볼 수 없다는 생각에 눈물이 났어요. 우리 가족에게 정말 소중한 분이셨거든요.
남: 정말 유감이네요. 누군가를 잃는다는 건 언제나 가슴 아픈 일이지요. 하지만 슬픔을 곧 극복하길 바랄게요.
여: 감사합니다.

어휘 **preoccupied** 몰두한, 정신이 팔린 / **deep in thought** 깊은 생각에 잠겨 / **get a laugh** 웃기다 / **obvious** 분명한, 명백한 / **embarrassing** 창피[당황]하게 하는 ***cf.*** **embarrassed** 창피한, 당황한

08 언급하지 않은 것 | ③

▶ 해석 참조

W: Come this way. This is the living room.
M: It's very nice and spacious.
W: Yes, as you already know, there are two big bedrooms in this apartment.
M: How about heating? Is it central heating?
W: No, you can **control the temperature inside your unit**.
M: I see. Does the rent include utility bills?
W: It includes water and gas but not electricity. Of course, you're responsible for telephone and Internet service.
M: Does the apartment building offer security?
W: Yes, it has 24-hour security **along with a security guard on site**.
M: Good. I like it.
W: I guarantee **you won't find anything for this price** in this part of town.

여: 이쪽으로 오세요. 여기가 거실입니다.
남: 매우 멋지고 넓네요.
여: 네, 이미 아시다시피, 이 아파트에는 두 개의 큰 침실(① 침실 개수)이 있습니다.
남: 난방은 어떤가요? 중앙 난방인가요?
여: 아니요, 가구별로 실내 온도를 조절하실 수 있어요(② 난방 방식).
남: 알겠습니다. 임대료에 공과금이 포함되나요?
여: 수도세와 가스 요금은 포함되지만 전기세는 포함되지 않습니다(④ 공공요금). 물론, 전화와 인터넷 서비스 요금은 고객님이 부담하셔야 합니다.

남: 아파트 건물이 보안을 제공합니까?
여: 네, 보안 요원이 대기하며 24시간 보안을 제공합니다(⑤ 보안).
남: 좋아요. 마음에 드네요.
여: 이곳 시내에서 이 가격으로 다른 곳은 찾을 수 없으실 거라 확신합니다.

어휘 **spacious** 넓은, 훤히 트인 / **unit** (아파트 같은 공동 주택 내의) 한 가구 / **utility bills** 공과금, 공공요금

09 내용 불일치 | ⑤

▶ 회원 가입 시 등록비는 5달러라고 했다.

W: To all customers of Borders Bookstore: we'd like to remind you of our popular Borders Book Club. This month's book club meeting will be at 5 p.m., Sunday, May 10th. Please pick up this month's book, *The History of Food* by Anthony Boyl and **be ready to share your thoughts** regarding the book. Due to the popularity of our book club, the club **is divided into several groups**. If you're interested, sign up today to join one of our groups. The sign-up sheet is located at the information desk on the first floor. Anyone aged 15 or older may join the club. In case you want to bring your children along, we also offer a book reading for them. So make this a family affair. There is a one-time registration fee of $5 that **you must pay when you sign up**. For further information, please check out our website at www.bordersbooks.com.

여: Borders 서점의 전 고객 여러분께 알립니다. 저희 서점의 인기 있는 Borders 독서 클럽에 대해 다시 한 번 알려드립니다. 이번 달 독서 클럽 모임은 5월 10일, 일요일 오후 5시입니다. 이달의 책인 Anthony Boyl의 〈음식의 역사〉를 구입하셔서 그 책에 관한 여러분의 감상을 공유할 수 있도록 준비해 오시기 바랍니다. 저희 독서 클럽은 인기 때문에 몇 개의 소모임으로 나누어집니다. 관심이 있으시다면, 오늘 소모임 중 하나에 가입하십시오. 가입 신청서는 1층 안내데스크에 비치되어 있습니다. 15세 이상이라면 누구나 클럽에 가입하실 수 있습니다. 여러분의 자녀를 데려오길 원하시는 경우, 저희는 또한 아이들을 위한 책 낭독을 제공해 드리고 있으니 이번 기회를 가족 행사로 만들어보시기 바랍니다. 가입하실 때 내셔야 하는 1회 등록비 5달러가 있습니다. 더 많은 정보를 원하신다면, 웹사이트 www.bordersbooks.com을 확인하십시오.

어휘 **remind A of B** A에게 B를 생각나게 하다[다시 한 번 알려주다] / **affair** 행사, 모임; 사건, 일 / **registration** 등록

10 도표 이해 | ③

▶ 가격대가 300달러 이하이고 광학 줌이 24배가 넘으며 색은 흰색, 그리고 LCD 스크린이 3인치 이상인 것을 원한다고 했다.

W: Matthew, I'd like to get a compact digital camera for my summer trip. I was wondering if you could help me choose the right one.
M: I'd love to help. First, I need to know **how much you're willing to spend** on the camera.
W: I was thinking of spending around $200-$300. No more than that.
M: Got it. How about a zoom lens?
W: Sure. **Something standard would be fine**.
M: Then more than 24X optical zoom would be enough.
W: All right. And I like bright colors.
M: So you **prefer white to black**. And I'm sure you want a large LCD screen, right?
W: Oh, yes, I want something larger than 3 inches because I'd like something easy to see.
M: Okay. I think this is the one you want.
W: Yes, I think so. Thanks for helping me.

여: Matthew, 여름에 여행 가는데 소형 디지털 카메라를 사고 싶어. 괜찮은 것을 고르는 데 네가 도와줄 수 있는지 궁금해.
남: 기꺼이 도와줄게. 먼저, 네가 카메라를 사는 데 돈을 얼마쯤 쓸 생각인지 알아야 돼.
여: 난 200에서 300달러 정도를 쓸 생각이었어. 그걸 넘으면 안 돼.
남: 알겠어. 줌 렌즈도 생각하는 거지?
여: 물론이지. 표준형이면 괜찮을 거야.
남: 그럼 24배가 넘는 광학 줌이면 충분할 거야.
여: 좋아. 그리고 난 밝은 색깔을 원해.
남: 그러면 검정색보다 흰색을 더 좋아하겠네. 그리고 LCD 스크린이 큰 것을 원하지?
여: 아, 맞아. 난 보기 편한 게 좋아서 3인치보다 큰 것을 원해.
남: 알았어. 이게 네가 원하는 거겠다.
여: 응, 그런 것 같아. 도와줘서 고마워.

어휘 **zoom** 영상의 급격한 확대[축소]; (렌즈가) 줌의 / **optical** 광학(光學)(상)의; 시각적인

11 짧은 대화에 이어질 응답 | ①

▶ 자동차가 시동이 안 걸려서 정비 서비스를 요청하려는 여자가 휴대폰 배터리가 없다고 했으므로 자신의 휴대폰을 건네주며 사용하라고 응답한 ①이 적절하다.

① 그럼 제 휴대폰을 쓰세요. 여기 있습니다.
② 무엇을 해야 할지 모르겠어요. 우리는 도시 밖에 있잖아요.
③ 주의하세요. 다음번에 당신 차는 견인될 겁니다.
④ 맞아요. 배터리를 자주 충전하는 게 좋아요.
⑤ 네, 이건 정말 긴급한 상황이거든요!

W: Excuse me. **Would you do me a favor**? My car won't start. I don't know why.
M: Oh, I'm sorry to hear that. Why don't you call an auto repair service?
W: The problem is that **my cell phone battery is dead**.
M: ______________________

여: 실례합니다. 좀 도와주시겠어요? 제 차가 시동이 안 걸려요. 이유를 모르겠어요.
남: 아, 유감이네요. 자동차 정비 서비스를 부르시는 게 어때요?
여: 문제는 제 휴대폰 배터리가 다 닳았다는 거예요.
남: ______________________

어휘 **auto repair** 자동차 수리 | 선택지 어휘 | **tow** (차, 배 등을) 견인하다 / **charge** 충전하다; 청구하다 / **frequently** 자주, 종종

12 짧은 대화에 이어질 응답 | ④

▶ 학교에서 동물을 사랑하는 사람들의 동아리를 만든 여자에게 남자가 자신도 가입해도 되는지 묻고 있다. 이에 대한 응답으로는 ④가 적절하다. 더 많은 회원을 찾고 있다고 했으므로 ⑤는 답이 될 수 없다.

① 넌 가입하지 않을걸. 넌 동물을 정말 싫어하잖아.
② 나는 나중에 아픈 동물들을 위해 병원을 열 거야.
③ 맞아. 개를 산책시키는 건 내 일이야.
④ 넌 동물을 정말 좋아하는 것 같구나. 네가 가입하는 걸 환영해!
⑤ 미안해. 회원을 더 받을 자리가 없어.

M: I heard you started a new club for people **who love animals at school**.
W: Yes, we've got seven members so far, but we're always looking for more!
M: **Do you think I could join**? I've got a dog at home, and I want to be a vet.
W: ______________________

남: 네가 학교에서 동물을 사랑하는 사람들을 위한 새 동아리를 시작했다고 들었어.
여: 응, 지금까지 일곱 명의 회원을 받았지만, 우린 늘 회원을 더 찾고 있어!
남: 내가 가입해도 될까? 난 집에 개를 한 마리 키우고, 수의사가 되고 싶거든.
여: ______________________

13 긴 대화에 이어질 응답 | ②

▶ 교수님과 저녁 약속이 있는 날 파티에 와달라고 부탁하는 친구에게 할 수 있는 가장 적절한 응답을 고른다.

① 멋진 파티였어. 초대해줘서 고마워.
② 정말로 안 돼. 네가 더 일찍 전화했다면 좋았을 텐데.
③ 멋진 주말을 보낸 것 같구나. 부럽다.
④ 너희를 빨리 만나고 싶어. 내일 보자!
⑤ 너에게 실망했어! 네가 약속을 취소한 게 이번이 세 번째야!

[Cell phone rings.]
W: Hello, Joseph. This is Olivia.
M: Oh, Olivia. Long time, no see. How have you been?
W: Good. I'm enjoying school life these days. How about you?
M: **Same as usual**. I'm usually in the lecture hall, research lab, or in the library. I recently started a new project with one of my professors.
W: I knew it. Do you have some time tomorrow?
M: Tomorrow? It's Friday, right? What time?
W: Seven in the evening. **I'm throwing a party** and I want you to come.
M: Oh, I can't. I have other plans. Professor Morgan invited me over for dinner.
W: You have to come! Tyler, Alex, Victoria, and Harry are all coming. I told them that you would be coming.
M: I'm sorry, but I can't. I already promised the professor that I would be coming.
W: Can't you **make some sort of excuse**? How often do we get together like this?

M: ____________________

[휴대전화 벨이 울린다.]
여: 안녕, Joseph. 나 Olivia야.
남: 아, Olivia. 오랜만이다. 어떻게 지냈니?
여: 잘 지냈어. 요즘 학교생활이 즐거워. 너는 어때?
남: 늘 똑같지. 주로 강의실이나 연구실, 도서관에 있어. 난 최근에 내 교수님들 중 한 분과 새 프로젝트를 시작했거든.
여: 알고 있어. 내일 시간 좀 있니?
남: 내일? 금요일 맞지? 몇 시에?
여: 저녁 7시에. 내가 파티를 여는데 네가 왔으면 해.
남: 아, 갈 수 없어. 다른 계획이 있거든. Morgan 교수님이 나를 저녁 식사에 초대하셨어.
여: 넌 꼭 와야 해! Tyler, Alex, Victoria, Harry가 올 거야. 애들한테 네가 올 거라고 말했단 말이야.
남: 미안하지만, 난 못 가. (저녁 식사에) 가기로 이미 교수님과 약속했어.
여: 핑계를 좀 댈 수 없을까? 우리가 얼마나 자주 이렇게 모이겠어?
남: ____________________

어휘 **throw a party** 파티를 열다

14 긴 대화에 이어질 응답 | ②

▶ 길을 묻는 남자에게 여자가 태워주겠다고 제안한다. 여자가 가려던 방향과 다를까 봐 걱정하는 남자에게 여자가 할 수 있는 응답을 고른다.

① 난 이해해, 그리고 네가 어떤 기분일지 알아. ② 아니야. 가는 길이니 걱정하지 마.
③ 네 말이 맞아. 걷는 게 건강에 좋아. ④ 다시 말해줄게. 받아 적으렴.
⑤ 폐를 끼쳐서 미안하지만, 급한 일이야.

W: Hi, Minsu. What are you doing here?
M: Oh, Megan, hi. I didn't expect to meet you here. What are you doing here?
W: I live around here. I'm **on my way to** the gym. I thought you lived in the school dormitory.
M: I do. I'm just looking for the Moore Career Center. I heard that they offer free classes for foreigners.
W: Oh, Moore Career Center is **quite a distance from here**.
M: Really? I guess I got off at the wrong stop. Can you tell me how to get there?
W: Sure. You go straight down this street and make a right at the next traffic light. And....
M: Please wait. I want to write it down or else I'll forget.
W: **Why don't you hop in**? I'll give you a ride. It'll only take us ten minutes.
M: That'd be great. I hope **it's not out of your way**.
W: ____________________

여: 민수야, 안녕. 여기서 뭐 해?
남: 아, Megan, 안녕. 여기서 널 만나다니 뜻밖이다. 너는 여기서 뭐 해?
여: 난 이 근처에 살아. 체육관에 가는 길이야. 나는 네가 학교 기숙사에 사는 줄 알았는데.
남: 맞아. 난 단지 Moore 진로 센터를 찾고 있어. 외국인들을 위한 무료 강좌를 제공한다고 들었거든.
여: 아, Moore 진로 센터는 여기서 꽤 멀어.
남: 정말? 내가 엉뚱한 정류장에서 내렸나 보네. 그곳까지 어떻게 가는지 말해줄 수 있니?
여: 물론이지. 이 길로 쭉 가서 다음 신호등에서 오른쪽으로 돌면 돼. 그리고….
남: 잠시만. 받아 적어야지 그렇지 않으면 잊어버릴 거야.
여: (내 차에) 타는 게 어때? 내가 태워다 줄게. 10분밖에 안 걸릴 거야.
남: 그래 주면 고맙지. 네가 가는 길에서 벗어나지 않으면 좋겠다.
여: ____________________

어휘 **dormitory** 기숙사 / **or else** 그렇지 않으면 / **hop in** (자동차에) 뛰어 올라타다 / **out of one's way** (사람이 가는) 길에서 벗어나서; 불가능하여 | 선택지 어휘 | **urgent** 긴급한

15 상황에 적절한 말 | ④

▶ GPS가 작동하지 않아 길을 잃는 바람에 식당에 늦게 도착해 예약이 취소된 상황이다. GPS를 미리 점검하지 않은 것을 자책하는 Austin에게 Nicole은 위로의 말을 할 것이다.

① 차를 대고 길을 물어보는 게 어때?
② 난 어두워진 후에 밖에 있는 것을 싫어해. 집에 가자.
③ GPS를 고쳐줘서 고마워. 이제 우린 길을 잃지 않을 거야.
④ 너무 속상해하지 마. 다른 식당으로 가자.
⑤ 넌 너무 고집이 세. 너 때문에 저녁 식사에 늦은 거야.

M: Nicole and Austin want to have dinner at a nice restaurant outside the city, and they reserve a table for 7 p.m. While driving to the restaurant, the GPS in his car stops working and they get lost. Since it's getting dark, they're **having trouble reading the street signs**. They try to ask someone for directions, but there is nothing outside. After half an hour, they find someone, and the person gives very nice directions. But they arrive late at the restaurant and **miss their reservation**. Austin isn't very happy about it and blames himself for not checking the GPS beforehand. But Nicole **doesn't think it's his fault**. In this situation, what would Nicole most likely say to Austin?

남: Nicole과 Austin은 시 외곽에 있는 멋진 식당에서 저녁을 먹고 싶어서 저녁 7시에 자리를 예약한다. 차를 몰고 식당에 가는 동안, 차에 있는 GPS가 작동하지 않아서 길을 잃는다. 날이 점점 어두워져서, 도로 표지판을 읽기 힘들다. 그들은 누군가에게 길을 물어보려고 하지만, 밖에는 아무것도 없다. 30분 후에 누군가를 발견하고, 그 사람은 길을 아주 잘 알려준다. 하지만 그들은 식당에 늦게 도착해서 예약을 놓친다. Austin은 기분이 매우 좋지 않아서 GPS를 미리 점검하지 않은 자신을 탓한다. 그러나 Nicole은 그것을 그의 잘못이라고 생각하지 않는다. 이러한 상황에서 Nicole이 Austin에게 할 말로 가장 적절한 것은 무엇인가?

어휘 **reserve** 예약하다 ***cf.* reservation** 예약 / **blame A for B** B를 A의 탓으로 돌리다 / **beforehand** 사전에; ~전에 미리 | 선택지 어휘 | **pull over** (길 한쪽으로) 차를 대다 / **stubborn** 고집 센, 완고한

16~17 세트 문항 | 16. ⑤ 17. ④

▶ 16. 자원봉사가 관심 있는 분야에서의 경험과 기술까지 쌓을 수 있는 좋은 방법임을 강조하고 있다.

① 자원봉사를 시작하는 것에 관한 조언 ② 적절한 자원봉사 기회를 찾는 방법
③ 대인 관계 기술을 향상하는 방법으로서의 자원봉사 ④ 자원봉사의 장단점
⑤ 경력 개발 기회로서의 자원봉사

▶ 17. 해석 참조

W: With busy lives, it can be hard to find time to volunteer. However, volunteering is **the perfect way to develop a new skill**. If you're considering a new career, volunteering can help you get experience in your area of interest. Even if you're not planning on changing careers, volunteering gives you the opportunity to practice **important skills used in the workplace**, such as teamwork, communication, problem solving, project planning, task management, and organization. In some fields, you can volunteer directly at an organization that does **the kind of work you're interested in**. For example, if you're interested in nursing, you could volunteer at a hospital or a nursing home. Just because volunteer work is unpaid does not mean the skills you learn are basic. Many volunteering opportunities provide extensive training. For example, you could become an experienced environmental activist while volunteering for an environmental organization or a knowledgeable art historian while donating your time as a museum guide. Volunteering can also help you **develop skills you already have** and use them to benefit the greater community. Now can you set aside the time for volunteering?

여: 바쁜 삶으로 인해, 자원봉사할 시간을 찾기 어려울 수 있습니다. 하지만 자원봉사는 새로운 기술을 익힐 완벽한 방법입니다. 새로운 직업을 생각하고 있다면, 자원봉사가 여러분의 관심 분야에서 경험을 쌓도록 도와줄 수 있습니다. 직업을 바꾸려고 계획하고 있지 않더라도 자원봉사는 팀워크, 의사소통, 문제 해결, 프로젝트 기획, 업무 관리, 조직화처럼 직장에서 사용되는 중요한 기술을 연습할 수 있는 기회를 줍니다. 어떤 분야에서는, 여러분이 관심 있는 종류의 업무를 하는 기관에서 바로 자원봉사를 할 수 있습니다. 예를 들면, 만약 간호에 관심이 있다면, ① 병원이나 ② 요양원에서 자원봉사를 할 수 있습니다. 자원봉사가 급여를 받지 않는 일이라고 해서 여러분이 배우는 기술이 기초적이라는 것을 의미하지는 않습니다. 많은 자원봉사의 기회가 광범위한 교육을 제공합니다. 예를 들어, ③ 환경단체에서 자원봉사를 하면서 경험이 풍부한 환경운동가가 되거나 ⑤ 박물관 안내원으로 지내면서 박식한 미술사학자가 될 수 있습니다. 자원봉사는 또한 여러분이 이미 가지고 있는 기술을 연마시키고 더 넓은 지역사회를 이롭게 하는 데 그 기술들을 사용하도록 도와줄 수 있습니다. 이제 자원봉사를 위한 시간을 따로 마련해보시겠습니까?

어휘 **workplace** 직장, 일터 / **nursing home** 요양원 / **extensive** 넓은, 광범위한 / **experienced** 경험[경력]이 있는, 숙련된 / **knowledgeable** 아는 것이 많은; 총명한 / **set aside** 따로 떼어 두다; ~을 한쪽으로 치워 놓다

01. ② 02. ⑤ 03. ② 04. ④ 05. ② 06. ③ 07. ④ 08. ⑤ 09. ① 10. ④
11. ② 12. ④ 13. ① 14. ④ 15. ③ 16. ② 17. ①

01 화자가 하는 말의 목적 | ②

▶ 바이러스 백신 업데이트와 P2P 사용을 자제하는 등의 신종 컴퓨터 바이러스 감염 예방법을 알려주고 있다.

W: Hi, this is Karen James with *Today's Technology Report* on KWSC radio. Well, there is a new virus **floating around cyberspace at an amazing speed**. One million computers have been infected in the last week alone. Once downloaded, the virus allows thousands of advertisements to pop up. Today, I want to **remind you to do the simple things**. First of all, update your anti-virus software. If it's not scanning your computer automatically, then turn on this feature. Secondly, avoid peer-to-peer networks. The recent virus **is being spread that way**. So you should not download movies or songs from these networks. They could be hiding viruses.

여: 안녕하세요. KWSC 라디오 〈오늘의 과학 기술 리포트〉의 Karen James입니다. 신종 바이러스가 사이버 공간에서 놀라운 속도로 퍼지고 있습니다. 지난주에만 백만 대의 컴퓨터가 감염되었습니다. 일단 다운로드되면, 바이러스는 수천 개의 광고가 갑자기 뜨게 만듭니다. 오늘은 제가 여러분께 몇 가지 간단한 방법을 알려 드리고자 합니다. 먼저, 바이러스 백신 소프트웨어를 갱신하십시오. 백신 소프트웨어가 컴퓨터를 자동으로 검사하지 않는다면 이 기능(자동 검사 기능)을 켜 놓으십시오. 두 번째로, P2P 네트워크 사용을 피하십시오. 최근의 바이러스는 이러한 경로를 통해서 확산되고 있습니다. 그러므로 이런 네트워크에서 영화나 음악을 다운로드해서는 안 됩니다. 그것들이 바이러스를 숨기고 있을 수도 있습니다.

어휘 **float** 떠돌다; 뜨다 / **infect** 감염시키다 / **pop up** 튀어 나오다, 불쑥 나타나다 / **remind** 생각나게 하다 / **update** 갱신하다 / **scan** (데이터를) 훑다 / **automatically** 자동적으로 / **feature** 특징 / **peer-to-peer** P2P(개인 PC끼리 직접 연결해서 파일을 공유하는) 방식의 / **spread** 퍼뜨리다, 유포시키다

02 대화 주제 | ⑤

▶ 장래 직업을 찾아보는 숙제와 관련해 직업 결정 시 고려할 사항에 관해 이야기하고 있다.

M: Did you finish the homework of searching for your future job?
W: Not yet. I need more time to think. There are so many jobs in the world.
M: Would you like some tips **to help you sort it all out**?
W: Sure, what are they?
M: Start **by finding out your personality type**. If you are social, it is a good idea to find a job interacting with people.
W: Like a consultant or a marketer?
M: Right.
W: So, we should know our talents. For example, if someone is gifted in art, they might want to be an art teacher or a painter. What else?
M: Well, the most important thing is to find a job you enjoy.
W: **That makes sense**. I hope these tips help me find the right career.
M: I think they will.

남: 장래 직업을 찾아보는 숙제 다 했어?
여: 아직 못 했어. 생각할 시간이 더 필요해. 세상엔 직업이 정말 많이 있잖아.
남: 골라내는 걸 도와줄 몇 가지 조언들을 알려줄까?
여: 좋지, 그게 뭔데?
남: 성격 유형을 알아보는 것부터 시작하는 거야. 네가 사교적이라면, 사람들과 교류하는 직업을 찾아보는 게 좋은 생각이지.
여: 상담가나 마케팅 담당자 같은 직업 말이지?
남: 맞아.
여: 그럼, 우리 재능을 알아야겠다. 예를 들어, 미술에 재능이 있는 사람이라면 미술 교사나 화가가 되고 싶어 할 수도 있잖아. 그 밖에 또 뭐가 있을까?
남: 음, 가장 중요한 건 네가 즐길 수 있는 직업을 찾는 거야.
여: 맞는 말이야. 이러한 조언들이 내게 맞는 직업을 찾는 데 도움이 되면 좋겠어.
남: 도움이 될 거야.

어휘 **sort out** 선별하다 / **consultant** 상담가, 컨설턴트 / **marketer** 마케팅 담당자 / **gifted** 재능이 있는 / **make sense** 타당하다, 말이 되다 / **career** 직업; 경력

03 관계 | ②

▶ 여자는 집을 팔려고 하고 있고, 남자는 집값을 알아보고 구매자를 소개하는 직업을 가진 사람이다.

W: How's the housing market nowadays?
M: Prices are really low right now.
W: Yes, it's really too bad. I wish we had a choice but we don't.
M: Everyone says prices will go up next year.
W: I know, but my husband's company is transferring him to Chicago.
M: Have you found a new house in Chicago?
W: Yes, we have. But we can't buy it **until we sell this one**.
M: OK. I understand. If we set a low price for your house, it will sell quickly.
W: How much **can we get for it**?
M: I will do some research and phone you tomorrow.
W: Thank you. You can show buyers the house **anytime you want**.
M: OK. I'll put ads in the paper tomorrow.

여: 요즘 주택 시장은 어떤가요?
남: 현재는 가격이 많이 떨어져 있습니다.
여: 네, 정말 곤란하게 되었어요. 선택의 여지가 있으면 좋겠지만 그렇지 못해요.
남: 다들 내년에는 가격이 상승할 거라고 하더군요.
여: 알아요. 하지만 남편이 시카고로 전근을 가게 되어서요.
남: 시카고에 집을 새로 구하셨습니까?
여: 네, 구했어요. 그렇지만 저희가 이 집을 팔아야 그 집을 살 수 있어요.
남: 예, 이해합니다. 집을 낮은 가격에 내놓으면 빨리 팔릴 겁니다.
여: 얼마나 받을 수 있죠?
남: 조사를 좀 해보고 내일 전화 드리겠습니다.
여: 고맙습니다. 원하시면 언제든지 구매자들에게 집을 보여주셔도 돼요.
남: 알겠습니다. 내일 신문에 광고를 내겠습니다.

어휘 **transfer** 전임시키다, 옮기다 / **do research** 조사를 하다

04 그림 불일치 | ④

▶ 벽장 위에 놓여 있는 것이 왕관이라고 했는데 그림에는 가발이 있으므로 일치하지 않는다.

M: What photo is this? It looks like a make-up room.
W: You're right. It's a picture of me in the make-up room **when I performed** in the school theater last year.
M: The mirror in front of you with all the light bulbs around the edge is really cool.
W: It's because we need a lot of lighting when applying make-up.
M: **Did you play the role** of a witch? There's a broom and pointed hat on the shelf on top of the mirror.
W: No. There was a witch in the play, but I played the princess. Do you see the dress with all the lace in the closet on the right? That was **the dress I wore**.
M: Wow, how beautiful! Did you wear the crown on top of the closet?
W: Yeah. I had to wear the crown.
M: What was inside the two large pieces of luggage next to the mirror?
W: Some costumes and accessories for the play. We borrowed them from a professional theater company.
M: Sounds like fun. It's too bad I missed the play.
W: We're doing another play this year, so I'll let you know in advance.

남: 이거 무슨 사진이니? 분장실 같아 보이는데.
여: 맞아. 내가 작년에 학교 극단에서 공연할 때 분장실에 있는 내 사진이야.

남: 네 앞에 있는, 테두리 주변에 온통 전구가 있는 거울이 정말 멋지다.
여: 왜냐하면 우리가 분장을 할 때에 조명을 많이 사용하는 게 필요하거든.
남: 네가 마녀 역할을 했니? 거울 위의 선반에 빗자루하고 뾰족한 모자가 있구나.
여: 아니야. 연극에 마녀가 있었지만 난 공주를 연기했어. 오른쪽에 있는 벽장 안에 레이스가 가득 달린 드레스가 보이니? 그게 내가 입은 드레스야.
남: 와, 정말 아름답다! 벽장 위에 있는 왕관은 네가 쓴 거니?
여: 응, 내가 왕관을 써야 했어.
남: 거울 옆에 있는 두 개의 커다란 짐 가방 안에는 뭐가 들어 있니?
여: 연극을 위한 의상들하고 장신구들이야. 우리는 그것들을 전문 극단에서 빌렸어.
남: 재밌겠다. 내가 연극을 못 봐서 아쉽네.
여: 우리는 올해 다른 연극을 할 거니까 내가 미리 알려줄게.

어휘 **make-up** 분장, 화장 / **light bulb** 전구 / **edge** 테두리, 가장자리 / **lighting** 조명 / **apply make-up** 화장을 하다 / **witch** 마녀 / **broom** 빗자루 / **pointed** 뾰족한 / **in advance** 미리, 사전에

05 추후 행동 | ②

▶ 여자가 할 일이 많다면서 내일 침대가 배달되어 오기 때문에 카펫 청소를 해야겠다고 하자 남자가 자기가 지금 하겠다고 했다.

M: Caroline, what are you doing? You said you have a headache.
W: I'm boiling Harper's bottles.
M: I'll do that. You don't look yourself. **Why don't you lie down** for a while?
W: I'm all right. And it's almost done. I just need to place the bottles to dry upside-down on a drying rack.
M: Is it necessary to boil baby bottles?
W: Absolutely. **If you don't make baby bottles completely clean**, viruses and bacteria can gather on them.
M: I see. Are you really okay? I bought a bag of oranges on the way home. I'll make some fresh-squeezed orange juice for you.
W: No, thanks. I'm really okay, and I have a ton of things to do. The carpet in our room needs to be cleaned.
M: Oh, Caroline. I vacuumed the carpet last Saturday.
W: But **the new bed is being delivered** tomorrow, so I'd like to do it again before the bed arrives.
M: Okay. I'll do that now. You need a rest.

남: Caroline, 뭐 하는 거예요? 두통이 있다고 했잖아요.
여: Harper의 우유병을 끓이고 있어요.
남: 내가 할게요. 당신 안 좋아 보여요. 좀 누워 있지 그래요?
여: 괜찮아요. 그리고 거의 다 했어요. 우유병을 말리기 위해 건조대에 거꾸로 두기만 하면 돼요.
남: 우유병을 끓이는 게 필요한가요?
여: 그럼요. 우유병을 완전히 깨끗하게 하지 않으면 바이러스와 세균이 생길 수 있어요.
남: 알겠어요. 당신 정말 괜찮은 거예요? 집에 오는 길에 오렌지 한 봉지를 샀어요. 당신을 위해 갓 짠 오렌지주스를 만들게요.
여: 고맙지만 됐어요. 난 정말 괜찮고 할 일이 너무 많아요. 우리 방 카펫도 청소해야 해요.
남: 아, Caroline. 지난 토요일에 내가 카펫을 진공청소기로 청소했어요.
여: 하지만 내일 새 침대가 배달될 거라서 침대가 도착하기 전에 청소를 다시 하고 싶어요.
남: 알겠어요. 내가 지금 할게요. 당신은 휴식이 필요해요.

어휘 **upside-down** 거꾸로[뒤집혀] / **rack** 선반, 걸이 / **absolutely** 정말 (그렇다), 그렇고말고 / **squeeze** 짜다 / **vacuum** 진공청소기로 청소하다

06 금액 | ③

▶ 가격이 8달러씩인 색깔 있는 티셔츠를 두 장 사고 한 장은 공짜로 받았으므로 16달러이고, 마지막에 흰색 티셔츠도 한 장 샀으므로 5달러를 추가하여 21달러를 지불해야 한다.

M: Excuse me, how much are these T-shirts right here?
W: The colored ones or the plain white ones?
M: The colored ones.
W: They are $8 each.
M: Are the plain white ones less expensive?
W: Yes, they are. They are $5 each. But **we are having a special sale** right now. If you buy two T-shirts, you **get the third one for free**.
M: On both types?
W: Yes. The offer applies to both colored and plain white T-shirts.
M: Great. I'll take a red one, a blue one and, hmm... a black one.
W: OK, three colored T-shirts. Do you want any plain white T-shirts, too?
M: Well, I don't really need any right now, but I will take one.

남: 실례합니다. 여기에 있는 이 티셔츠들은 얼마죠?
여: 색깔 있는 것 말씀이십니까, 아니면 무늬 없는 흰색 말씀이십니까?
남: 색깔 있는 것들이요.
여: 8달러씩입니다.
남: 무늬 없는 흰색은 더 싼가요?
여: 네, 그렇습니다. 5달러씩입니다. 그런데 저희는 지금 특별 세일 중입니다. 셔츠 두 장을 사시면 한 장은 공짜로 드립니다.
남: 두 종류 모두 말씀이신가요?
여: 네. 특별 세일은 색깔 있는 티셔츠와 무늬 없는 흰색 티셔츠 모두에 해당됩니다.
남: 좋은데요. 붉은색과 푸른색 한 장씩 주세요. 음…, 검은색도요.
여: 알겠습니다. 색깔 있는 티셔츠 3장요. 무늬 없는 흰색 티셔츠도 원하세요?
남: 글쎄요. 지금 당장은 별로 필요가 없지만, 하나 살게요.

어휘 **plain** 장식, 무늬 등이 없는 / **for free** 무료로 / **apply to A** A에 적용[해당]되다

07 이유 | ④

▶ 여자는 자신의 근무시간을 직접 정할 수 있어서 Dolby Industries를 선택했다고 말했다.

M: You look happy! What's up?
W: I just got a call from Dolby Industries. They offered me a job!
M: That's great! You **seem like a perfect match** for that company.
W: You think so? I know the commute won't be easy, but I'm really excited to start.
M: Then **what about your upcoming interview** with Jeoffrey Laboratories? You mentioned they were offering a high salary.
W: I will cancel that interview. The position at Dolby will let me choose my own hours, and it has the potential to become a career for me.
M: That sounds like a wise decision. **Why don't I take you out** for dinner to celebrate?
W: I'd love that. You're the best friend!

남: 너 즐거워 보인다! 무슨 일 있니?
여: 방금 Dolby Industries 사(社)에서 전화가 왔어. 나를 채용하겠대!
남: 잘됐다! 넌 그 회사에 정말 잘 어울리는 것 같아.
여: 그렇게 생각해? 출퇴근하는 게 편하지 않겠지만 정말 기대돼.
남: 근데 곧 있을 Jeoffrey 연구소의 면접은 어떻게 해? 넌 그 회사가 더 급여가 높다고 했잖아.
여: 나는 그 면접을 취소할 거야. Dolby에서는 내가 일할 시간을 정할 수 있고, 내 경력에 있어서 큰 잠재력을 갖고 있어.
남: 현명한 선택인 것 같네. 내가 축하하는 의미에서 저녁을 사는 게 어때?
여: 그래 좋아. 넌 정말 좋은 친구야!

어휘 **commute** 통근[통학] / **upcoming** 다가오는, 곧 있을 / **potential** 잠재력; 가능성

08 언급하지 않은 것 | ⑤

▶ 해석 참조

M: Amy, I'm **surprised to see you**! How was Italy?
W: It was great. I stayed with my grandmother in Rome and visited my cousin who works inside Vatican City.
M: That's a separate Italian-speaking country inside the city of Rome, right?
W: Right. It's incredibly small. There are only around 500 permanent residents.
M: Then I guess your cousin doesn't live inside the Vatican?
W: The Vatican **is controlled by** the Pope, and only Catholic officials can become citizens. My cousin works there, but she lives in Rome.
M: Most of the countries in that part of Europe use the Euro as their currency. Is the Vatican the same?
W: Yes. It's so small that **most of its income comes from** tourism and church fundraising.
M: That's really interesting. I'd like to visit there sometime.

남: Amy, 너를 만날 줄이야! 이탈리아는 어땠어?
여: 아주 멋졌어! 나는 로마에 계신 할머니와 함께 있었고 바티칸시국에서 일하는 내 사촌을

방문했어.
남: 그곳은 로마시 안에 있는(① 위치) 이탈리아어를 사용하는 독립된 국가잖아, 맞지?
여: 맞아. 그곳은 놀라울 정도로 작아. 500여 명(② 인구)의 영주권자들만이 있을 뿐이야.
남: 그럼 너의 사촌은 바티칸 안에서 살지 않겠네?
여: 바티칸은 교황에 의해 통치되고 오직 카톨릭 관계자들만이 시민이 될 수 있어. 내 사촌은 거기서 일하지만, 로마에 살고 있어.
남: 대부분의 그곳 유럽 국가들은 화폐로 유로를 사용하잖아. 바티칸도 똑같니(③ 화폐)?
여: 응. 그곳은 매우 작아서 대부분의 수입이 관광업과 교회 모금(④ 주 수입원)에서 나오고 있어.
남: 정말 흥미롭다. 나도 언젠가 그곳에 가보고 싶어.

어휘 **separate** 독립된, 분리된; 개별적인 / **permanent** 영구적인, 불변의 / **resident** 거주자, 주민 / **pope** 교황 / **official** 관계자; 공무원; 공식적인 / **citizen** 시민 / **currency** 화폐, 통화(通貨) / **income** 수입, 소득 / **fundraising** 모금

09 내용 불일치 | ①

▶ 인솔자가 여행객들에게 제시간에 버스로 돌아와 주어서 감사하다고 하고 남은 일정을 즐기라고 한 것으로 보아 지금 처음 모인 것은 아니다.

M: Well, everyone **looks to be seated**. Thank you for getting back on the bus right on time. Now we'll be going to Shindong Market, which is famous for **the variety of items you can buy**. You can buy anything from a pet dog to a sofa or a new suit. You should remember to bargain hard at the market. You can **spend two hours shopping** in the market. On the way there we'll pass the city's central plaza with its famous water fountain. You don't have to worry about taking pictures now. We'll return to look around the plaza tomorrow. I hope you enjoy the second half of the day's tour.

남: 음, 모두 자리에 앉으신 것 같군요. 시간에 맞춰 버스로 돌아와 주셔서 감사합니다. 이제 우리는 신동 시장으로 이동할 것인데, 그곳은 다양한 품목을 구매할 수 있다는 점으로 유명합니다. 여러분들은 반려견에서 소파나 새 옷까지 무엇이나 구입하실 수 있습니다. 시장에서는 적극적으로 흥정해야 한다는 점을 기억하세요. 여러분들은 시장에서 두 시간 정도 쇼핑하실 수 있습니다. 시장으로 가는 도중에 우리는 분수로 유명한 중앙 광장을 지나게 될 것입니다. 지금은 사진 찍는 것에 대해 신경 쓰실 필요가 없습니다. 광장을 둘러보러 내일 다시 방문할 예정입니다. 오늘 남은 일정을 즐겁게 보내시길 바랍니다.

어휘 **on time** 시간에 맞게 / **variety** 다양(성), 변화; 품종, 종류 / **bargain** 흥정하다; 싼 물건 / **fountain** 분수

10 도표 이해 | ④

▶ 조개가 초급 세트보다 많이 들어 있고, 가격이 50달러 미만이며, 은구슬이 20개가 넘는 세트는 두 가지이다. 그중 여자는 철사의 길이가 가능한 한 긴 것을 원했다.

W: I'm finally going to order the necklace kit my mom **has been promising me**.
M: That sounds neat.
W: I need to choose from these kits on the list.
M: But it really **isn't my thing**.
W: I'll make you something "manly" that you can wear.
M: Like a shell necklace that surfers wear?
W: For a shell necklace I'll need more shells **than the beginner set has**.
M: And you should make something nice for your mom to thank her.
W: I was thinking of something with a lot of silver.
M: Like the one with 50 silver beads?
W: No, that's too expensive. It should be under $50. But more than 20 silver beads, definitely.
M: And you could make birthday presents!
W: So I'll need a set with as much wire as possible.
M: Then you should get this one.

여: 엄마가 내게 사주시기로 한 목걸이 재료 세트를 드디어 주문하려고 해.
남: 멋지다.
여: 이 목록에 있는 세트 중에서 골라야 해.
남: 하지만 그런 건 정말 나랑은 안 맞아.
여: 네가 하고 다닐 수 있게 '남자다운' 것으로 만들어 줄게.
남: 서핑하는 사람들이 하는 조개 목걸이 같은 거?
여: 조개 목걸이를 만들려면 초급 세트에 있는 것보다 더 많은 조개가 필요해.
남: 그리고 너희 어머니께 감사의 표시로 좋은 것을 만들어 드려야 하잖아.
여: 은이 많이 들어 있는 것을 생각하고 있어.
남: 은구슬이 50개 있는 것 같은?
여: 아니, 그건 너무 비싸. 50달러 미만이어야 해. 하지만 분명히 은구슬은 20개가 넘어야 하고.
남: 그러면 생일 선물도 만들 수 있겠다!
여: 그래서 가능한 한 긴 철사가 든 세트가 필요해.
남: 그럼 이걸로 해야겠구나.

어휘 **kit** 재료 한 벌 / **manly** 남자다운 / **bead** 구슬

11 짧은 대화에 이어질 응답 | ②

▶ 핫소스가 몇 봉지 필요한지 묻는 여자에게 할 수 있는 대답을 찾는다.

① 다음번에 먹어볼게요. ② 네다섯 봉지면 될 것 같아요.
③ 유통 기한은 10개월입니다. ④ 피자는 이미 매워요.
⑤ 저희는 피자 4판만 시켰어요.

W: Okay, here are the five large pizzas you ordered. Enjoy.
M: Thanks so much. Oh, **could I have some extra packets** of hot sauce?
W: That's no problem. **How many would you like**?
M: ______________________________

여: 자, 여기 주문하신 라지 피자 5판입니다. 맛있게 드세요.
남: 정말 감사합니다. 아, 핫소스를 몇 봉지 더 얻을 수 있을까요?
여: 그럼요. 몇 봉지 드릴까요?
남: ______________________________

어휘 **packet** (보통 1회분의 액체 · 가루가 든) 봉지; 소포, 꾸러미 | 선택지 어휘 | **shelf life** (식품 등의) 유통 기한

12 짧은 대화에 이어질 응답 | ④

▶ 이전 룸메이트가 지저분했다는 여자의 말에 남자가 예를 들어달라고 했다.

① 널 그 애에게 소개해 줄게. ② 그 애를 위해 청소하는 게 좋아.
③ 새 룸메이트는 아주 좋아. ④ 그 앤 젖은 수건을 여기저기 놔뒀어.
⑤ 그게 그 애의 장점 중 하나인 것 같아.

M: Anna, why did you **decide to change roommates**?
W: I changed because my last roommate was too dirty.
M: I don't understand. **Could you give me an example**?
W: ______________________________

남: Anna, 왜 룸메이트를 바꾸기로 결정했니?
여: 이전 룸메이트가 너무 지저분해서 바꾸게 됐어.
남: 이해가 잘 안 돼. 예를 들어줄 수 있니?
여: ______________________________

13 긴 대화에 이어질 응답 | ①

▶ 소방관들이 언제 도착하느냐는 질문에 대한 적절한 답변을 찾는다.

① 소방차가 지금 가고 있습니다.
② 아이들은 불장난을 하면 안 됩니다.
③ 가족과 함께 불을 꺼 보세요.
④ 직장에서 해고되셨다니 유감이네요.
⑤ 지구 온난화는 자연의 비상사태입니다.

[Phone rings.]
M: Hello, you have reached the fire department. What is **the nature of your emergency**?
W: The house next door to mine is on fire.
M: Can you give me the address, please?
W: Yes, it's 1001 Maple Street.
M: Do you know if anyone is home? Are there any children or elderly people living there?
W: A young couple lives there with their grandmother and their small baby.
M: Can you see the flames from your house?

W: No. So far, **all I see is** thick, black smoke.
M: If you think it is safe, please **go knock on the door** to see if anyone answers.
W: OK. I'll do that now. When can you get here?
M: ______________________________

[전화벨이 울린다.]
남: 여보세요, 소방서입니다. 어떤 응급 상황인가요?
여: 저희 이웃집에 불이 났어요.
남: 주소를 알려주시겠습니까?
여: 네, Maple가 1001번지입니다.
남: 집에 누가 있는지 아십니까? 아이들이나 노인분들이 그곳에 살고 있습니까?
여: 젊은 부부가 할머니와 아기와 함께 살고 있습니다.
남: 집에서 불길이 보이십니까?
여: 아니요, 지금까지 보이는 것이라고는 자욱한 검은 연기뿐입니다.
남: 만약 안전하다고 생각되시면 대답하는 사람이 있는지 가서 문을 두드려 보시겠습니까?
여: 알겠습니다. 지금 해볼게요. 소방관들은 여기 언제 도착하십니까?
남: ______________________________

어휘 **reach** (전화 등으로) 연락하다 / **nature** 본질, 특징; 자연 / **emergency** 비상 / **on fire** 불타고, 불이 나서 / **flame** 불꽃, 화염 | 선택지 어휘 | **fire engine** 소방차 / **on the way** 진행 중의, ~하는 도중에 / **put out** (불 등을) 끄다 / **fire** 해고하다 / **global warming** 지구 온난화

14 긴 대화에 이어질 응답 | ④

▶ 드라마를 보는 것은 시간 낭비라는 남자의 말에, 드라마를 즐겨 시청하는 여자는 반대 의견을 내는 것이 자연스럽다.

① 나도 그 책을 가장 좋아해.
② 정보를 주는 TV 프로그램을 봐.
③ 너는 드라마를 너무 많이 봐서는 안 돼.
④ 하지만 모든 사람이 조금은 즐길 필요가 있어.
⑤ 난 그렇게 생각하지 않아. 저 책은 읽기가 쉬워.

M: What's that magazine you're reading?
W: It's a TV guide. Do you know what the most popular TV show here is?
M: Umm, is it the BBC news?
W: No, it's *Neighbours*. It says here that *Neighbours* **has been shown twice a day** in the U.K. since 1986. And it has **an average daily audience** of 11 million people!
M: Wow. That's billions of hours wasted on a TV soap opera. I don't believe it.
W: I love *Neighbours*. It's great. I watch it every day.
M: That's terrible. If you need a break, do some exercise, or read a good book.
W: ______________________________

남: 네가 읽고 있는 잡지가 무엇이니?
여: 이건 TV 가이드야. 여기서 가장 인기 있는 TV 프로그램이 무엇인지 아니?
남: 음, BBC 뉴스니?
여: 아니, 〈Neighbours〉야. 이 책에 따르면 〈Neighbours〉는 1986년부터 영국에서 하루에 두 번씩 방영되고 있대. 그리고 하루 평균 시청자가 천백만 명이고!
남: 와, 한 TV 드라마에 수십억 시간이 낭비된 것이구나. 믿을 수가 없어.
여: 난 〈Neighbours〉를 좋아해. 재밌어. 매일 시청하고 있어.
남: 맙소사. 쉬고 싶으면 운동을 하거나 좋은 책을 읽도록 해.
여: ______________________________

어휘 **average** 평균의, 보통의 / **soap (opera)** 연속극 | 선택지 어휘 | **informative** 정보를 주는, 유익한

15 상황에 적절한 말 | ③

▶ Paul은 지금 면접에 대해 말하고 싶지 않은 상태이다.

① 너를 귀찮게 하고 싶지 않아.
② 다음 면접이 언제니?
③ 어떻게 되었는지 묻지 말아줘.
④ 미안, 너에게 너무 실망했어.
⑤ 개인적인 질문을 해도 되니?

M: Paul is graduating and looking for a job. He has had a few job interviews but **hasn't been offered a job yet**. He has been disappointed a few times because he thought the interview had gone well. But today Paul had a terrible interview. He was asked questions **he hadn't prepared for**, so he answered poorly. On the bus going home, Paul meets a friend, Ted. He asks Paul **why he is dressed up**. Paul says he had a job interview. Paul knows Ted will ask him about the interview. But he is disappointed and **doesn't want to talk about it** right now. In this situation, what is Paul most likely to say to Ted?

남: Paul은 졸업을 앞두고 일자리를 찾는 중이다. 그는 몇 개의 면접이 있었지만 아직 일자리를 구하지는 못했다. 그는 면접을 잘 보았다고 생각했기 때문에 몇 번 실망한 적도 있다. 하지만 오늘 Paul은 면접을 완전히 망쳤다. 그는 준비하지 못한 질문을 받았고 형편없이 답변했다. 집으로 돌아오는 버스에서 Paul은 친구인 Ted를 만난다. 그는 Paul에게 옷을 차려입은 이유를 묻는다. Paul은 면접이 있었다고 말한다. Paul은 Ted가 면접에 관해 물어볼 것을 안다. 하지만 그는 실망한 상태라서 지금은 그것에 관해 이야기하고 싶지 않다. 이러한 상황에서 Paul이 Ted에게 할 말로 가장 적절한 것은 무엇인가?

어휘 **graduate** 졸업하다 / **poorly** 형편없이, 좋지 못하게 | 선택지 어휘 | **bother** 귀찮게 하다, 성가시게 하다

16~17 세트 문항 | 16. ② 17. ①

▶ 16. 비용을 절감하고 환경을 살릴 수 있는 에너지 절약법을 소개하고 있다.

① 물 소비량 줄이기
② 가정 내 에너지 절약법에 관한 조언
③ 중고 가전제품 구매로 인한 경제적 이득
④ 에너지 효율이 높은 기술 개발의 필요성
⑤ 실내 적정 온도 유지하기

▶ 17. 해석 참조

W: If you do the following things you can save up to $1,500 per year, and you'll be saving the environment. Less oil will be burnt and the carbon footprint **left by your activities** will be smaller. To begin with, go around your house and replace 100 watt light bulbs with energy efficient 60 watt bulbs, substituting longer-lasting LED bulbs wherever possible. It's also time to change a few of your bad habits: turn off the computer **when it's not in use**; use the washing machine only when you have a full load; and turn down the heat in your house. It is recommended that you keep indoor temperatures around 20°C, not 24°C or 25°C. If you feel cold, wear a sweater, and **don't forget to turn off the heat** in rooms your family is not using. Lastly, think about replacing old, inefficient appliances. New ones are expensive, but **the energy savings will add up**.

여: 여러분은 이제부터 소개해 드릴 것들을 하면 해마다 1,500달러까지 절약할 수 있으며 환경을 살리게 됩니다. 기름 연소가 줄 것이며 여러분이 활동함으로써 생기는 탄소 발자국이 줄어들 것입니다. 우선 여러분의 집을 둘러보고 100와트짜리 전구를 에너지 효율이 높은 60와트 전구로 교체하십시오. 그리고 가능한 곳이라면 더 오래가는 ② LED 전구로 교체하십시오. 여러분의 몇 가지 나쁜 습관을 바꾸어야 할 때이기도 합니다. ③ 사용하지 않을 때는 컴퓨터를 꺼두십시오. ④ 세탁물이 꽉 찼을 때에만 세탁기를 사용하십시오. 그리고 집안 온도를 낮추십시오. ⑤ 실내 온도를 섭씨 24도나 25도가 아니라 20도 정도로 유지할 것을 권장합니다. 춥다고 느껴지면 스웨터를 입고, 가족이 사용하지 않는 방은 난방을 꺼두는 것을 잊지 마십시오. 마지막으로 낡고 비효율적인 가전 기기를 교체하는 것을 고려해 보십시오. 새것은 가격이 비싸지만 에너지 절약은 늘어날 것입니다.

어휘 **carbon** (화학) 탄소 *cf.* **carbon footprint** 탄소 발자국(온실 효과를 유발하는 이산화탄소의 배출량) / **replace** 대신하다, 대체하다 (= substitute) / **efficient** 효율적인 (↔ inefficient 비효율적인) / **long-lasting** 오래 지속되는 / **load** 짐; (사람 · 기계의) 작업량 / **appliance** (가정용) 기기, 전기 제품

01. ③ **02.** ③ **03.** ⑤ **04.** ③ **05.** ③ **06.** ③ **07.** ④ **08.** ④ **09.** ③ **10.** ①
11. ② **12.** ① **13.** ④ **14.** ① **15.** ④ **16.** ⑤ **17.** ⑤

01 화자가 하는 말의 목적 | ③

▶ 국제 학생 클럽에서 주최하는 국제 학생 교류의 밤 행사를 홍보하고 있다.

M: The International Student Club of Maple University is an organization consisting of all the international students at the university. **Its main goal and purpose is** to learn more about the lifestyle and culture of the United States as well as other countries. The International Student Club also hosts the annual International Night. It is a magical event **filled with the sharing of cultures**, excellent food, and entertainment. This year it will be held at the Maple Theater at 6 p.m. on May the 13th. Doors open at 5:30 p.m. and **tickets will be sold at the door**. Tickets will cost $5 for adults and $3 for children under the age of 12.

남: Maple 대학교의 국제 학생 클럽은 이 대학에 재학 중인 모든 유학생으로 구성된 단체입니다. 클럽의 주된 목표는 다른 국가뿐만 아니라 미국의 생활방식과 문화에 대해 더 많이 배우고자 하는 것입니다. 또한, 국제 학생 클럽은 매년 국제 학생 교류의 밤 행사를 개최합니다. 이는 문화를 공유하고 훌륭한 음식을 즐기며, 즐거움을 만끽할 수 있는 멋진 행사입니다. 올해는 5월 13일 오후 6시에 Maple 극장에서 행사가 개최될 것입니다. 입장은 5시 30분부터이며 표는 출입구에서 판매될 것입니다. 성인 표는 5달러이며 12세 미만 어린이 표는 3달러입니다.

어휘 **organization** 단체, 조직, 기구 / **consist of** ~로 구성되다

02 의견 | ③

▶ 5시간 계속 운전하다가 잠깐 졸았던 남자에게 여자는 졸음 운전자는 음주 운전자만큼이나 나쁘다며 잠을 깨고 운전할 것을 권하고 있다.

W: Watch out! **Keep your eyes on the road**!
M: I'm sorry. I think I just dozed off for a second there.
W: Oh, dear. It's because you've been driving for five hours straight.
M: It's fine. I think I'll be okay.
W: Do you know **how dangerous it is to drive** when you're sleepy? I'll take over.
M: Let me roll down the window and play some loud music. That'll help.
W: Yes, but be careful. A sleepy driver is **about as bad as a driver** who's drunk.
M: It's really not so bad. Just keep talking to me and I'll be all right.
W: I think you should either pull over and get some rest or let me drive.
M: Okay. How about getting some rest at the next rest stop area?
W: Great idea. A ten-minute nap can do wonders.
M: Okay, I'll take your advice.

여: 조심해요! 도로를 잘 보라고요!
남: 미안해요. 거기서 잠깐 졸았던 것 같아요.
여: 오, 이런. 당신이 5시간 연속으로 운전해서 그래요.
남: 괜찮아요. 난 괜찮을 거 같아요.
여: 졸릴 때 운전하는 게 얼마나 위험한지 알아요? 내가 운전할게요.
남: 창문을 내리고 시끄러운 음악을 좀 틀게요. 그러면 도움이 될 거예요.
여: 네, 하지만 조심해요. 졸음 운전자는 술을 마신 운전자만큼이나 나빠요.
남: 정말로 그 정도는 아니에요. 나에게 계속 말을 걸어주면 괜찮아질 거예요.
여: 내 생각에는 당신이 차를 세우고 휴식을 취하거나 내가 운전해야 할 것 같아요.
남: 좋아요. 다음 휴게소에서 좀 쉬는 게 어때요?
여: 좋은 생각이에요. 10분간 낮잠을 자면 큰 효과가 있을 거예요.
남: 알았어요. 당신의 충고를 받아들이죠.

어휘 **doze off** (특히 낮에) 잠이 들다 / **take over** 인계받다; (기업 등을) 인수하다 / **roll down** 내리다[열다] / **pull over** 길 한쪽으로 차를 대다 / **do wonders** 놀라운 일을 하다

03 관계 | ⑤

▶ 남자는 씹을 때 통증이 심하다고 말하고, 여자는 남자에게 충치가 심해 뿌리를 뽑아야 한다고 말하는 것으로 보아 치과 의사와 환자의 대화임을 알 수 있다.

W: How long have you had this problem?
M: Well, it's been quite a while. And recently it started to really bother me.
W: I wish **you had come earlier**. It looks pretty serious.
M: I've been so busy with work.
W: I won't be able to treat it in one visit. I'll have to work on it for several weeks. Is that okay with you?
M: I guess I have no choice. I'm in so much pain right now. I can't eat anything **which involves jaw movement**. If I bite something, it sends a painful shockwave down one side of my head.
W: Your cavity has gotten so bad that we'll have to pull out your roots.
M: Really? Doesn't that hurt?
W: Yes, it will be a painful treatment, but it **will be worth it in the end**.
M: I see. When should I make the appointment?
W: You can check with the receptionist.

여: 얼마나 오랫동안 이 문제가 있었나요?
남: 글쎄요. 꽤 오래되었어요. 그리고 최근에 저를 애먹이기 시작했어요.
여: 좀 더 일찍 오셨으면 좋을 텐데요. 매우 심각해 보이거든요.
남: 일 때문에 정말 바빴어요.
여: 한 번 오셔서는 치료할 수가 없겠는데요. 몇 주 동안 치료를 해야 할 거예요. 괜찮으시겠어요?
남: 선택의 여지가 없는 것 같은데요. 지금 너무나 아픕니다. 턱을 움직여서 어떤 것도 먹을 수가 없어요. 무언가를 씹으면 머리 한쪽에 아픈 충격이 전해져요.
여: 환자분의 충치가 너무 심해서 뿌리를 뽑아야 할 거예요.
남: 정말요? 아프지 않나요?
여: 아프죠. 고통스러운 치료가 될 거예요. 하지만 결국 그럴 만한 가치가 있을 겁니다.
남: 알겠어요. 예약은 언제로 하나요?
여: 접수 담당자와 확인해 보십시오.

어휘 **jaw** 턱 / **shockwave** 충격파 / **cavity** 충치 / **receptionist** 접수 담당자

04 그림 불일치 | ③

▶ 여자는 케이크 옆에 아이의 나이에 맞게 두 개의 화분이 있다고 했다.

W: John! Come and have a look!
M: Wow! Did you decorate all this for Tracy? It's absolutely lovely.
W: The concept for the party is butterflies. **If you look closely** at the number 2 on the wall, it's all made with butterflies.
M: It's amazing. Did you make those paper butterflies by yourself?
W: I sure did. And look at those balloon butterflies, two on each side. **Aren't they cute**?
M: I'll say. The cake in the middle is also decorated with a butterfly.
W: You know that Tracy loves butterflies.
M: I see that you decorated the little flower pots next to the cake with butterflies, too.
W: Since Tracy is turning two, I placed two pots.
M: Great. You also have butterfly mobiles **hanging from the ceiling**. What a great idea!
W: Take a look at the front of the decorated table.
M: Oh, you hung a banner with Tracy's name on it. You really are the best mom.

여: John! 이리 와서 좀 보세요!
남: 와! Tracy를 위해 이 모든 걸 꾸민 거예요? 굉장히 멋져요.
여: 파티의 콘셉트는 나비예요. 벽에 있는 숫자 2를 가까이서 보면, 그게 전부 나비로 만들어져 있어요.
남: 놀라워요. 혼자서 그 종이 나비를 전부 만든 거예요?
여: 물론이죠. 그리고 양옆에 두 개씩 붙어 있는 나비 풍선을 보세요. 귀엽지 않나요?
남: 그럼요. 가운데의 케이크도 나비로 장식되어 있군요.
여: Tracy가 나비를 좋아한다는 걸 알잖아요.
남: 케이크 옆에 있는 작은 화분들도 나비로 꾸민 것 같군요.
여: Tracy가 두 살이 되니까, 두 개의 화분을 놓아두었지요.
남: 훌륭해요. 천장에 나비 모양 모빌도 걸어두었네요. 좋은 생각이에요!
여: 장식된 탁자 앞을 봐주세요.

남: 아, 배너 위에 Tracy의 이름을 써서 걸어두었군요. 당신은 정말 최고의 엄마예요.

어휘 **decorate** 꾸미다, 장식하다 / **absolutely** 전적으로, 틀림없이 / **concept** 콘셉트, 기본적 테마; 개념 / **by oneself** 홀로; 도움을 받지 않고

05 추후 행동 | ③

▶ 남자는 부엌에서 채소를 썰 것이다.

M: Do you have everything you need?
W: Almost. **I forgot to pick up some things** for dessert. But we have plenty of homemade ice cream in the refrigerator.
M: I'm sure they'll like your ice cream. But I could go to the grocery store if you'd like.
W: No, thank you. Oh, did you clean the living-room bathroom for the guests?
M: Sure. I did that in the morning.
W: You're the best. I hope your colleagues like my cooking. Frankly, I'm a little nervous.
M: Don't worry about a thing. You're the best cook around.
W: If it's okay with you, **I would like your assistance** in the kitchen.
M: What can I do?
W: It'd be a great help if you could chop some vegetables for me.
M: No problem! **I can handle that**.

남: 필요한 건 전부 있나요?
여: 거의 다 있어요. 디저트로 먹을 것들을 산다는 걸 잊어버렸네요. 하지만 냉장고에 집에서 만든 아이스크림이 많이 있어요.
남: 손님들이 당신이 만든 아이스크림을 분명 좋아할 거예요. 하지만 당신이 원한다면 식료품점에 다녀올 수도 있어요.
여: 아녜요, 고마워요. 아, 손님들을 위해 거실에 있는 화장실을 청소해 두었나요?
남: 그럼요. 오전에 청소했어요.
여: 당신이 최고예요. 당신의 직장 동료들이 내 요리를 좋아하면 좋겠어요. 솔직히, 약간 불안해요.
남: 아무것도 걱정하지 마요. 당신은 최고로 요리를 잘하거든요.
여: 당신이 괜찮다면, 부엌에서 당신의 도움을 받고 싶은데요.
남: 내가 무엇을 할 수 있죠?
여: 당신이 채소를 좀 썰어준다면 큰 도움이 될 거예요.
남: 문제없어요! 내가 할게요.

어휘 **colleague** 동료 / **frankly** 솔직히 / **assistance** 도움, 원조, 지원 / **handle** 처리하다, 다루다

06 금액 | ③

▶ 여자는 브레이크 수리(450달러), 차량 점검(40달러), 그리고 타이어 2개 교체(160달러)를 하겠다고 한다. 따라서 여자가 지불할 금액은 650달러이다.

W: What's going on? What is that horrible sound?
M: It's from the car's brakes. **They're wearing down**. That's the sound of metal rubbing on metal.
W: That's incredibly dangerous!
M: Yes, it's dangerous. A brake job costs $450.
W: That's very expensive. But **better safe than sorry**. I think I need to have an inspection to make sure everything else is okay.
M: Okay. It costs $40. And we'll give you an oil change free of charge.
W: Great. Anything else?
M: Hmm.... You need to change the two back tires. Tires cost $80 each.
W: I see. Well, **how much does it cost** if I install a new stereo system?
M: It's around $1,000.
W: Really? Oh, forget about it. Just the brakes, an inspection, and tires.
M: Okay.

여: 무슨 일이죠? 저 끔찍한 소리는 뭔가요?
남: 자동차의 브레이크에서 나는 소리예요. 브레이크가 마모되고 있어요. 금속끼리 부딪치는 소리죠.
여: 그건 매우 위험하잖아요!
남: 맞아요, 위험하지요. 브레이크 수리는 450달러입니다.
여: 정말 비싸군요. 하지만 나중에 후회하는 것보다 조심하는 게 낫지요. 다른 것도 전부 괜찮은지 검사를 해봐야 할 것 같아요.
남: 네. 그건 40달러예요. 그리고 오일은 무료로 교체해 드리겠습니다.
여: 좋아요. 다른 건요?
남: 음…. 뒤쪽의 타이어 두 개를 교체해야겠군요. 타이어는 개당 80달러입니다.
여: 알겠어요. 그럼, 새 오디오 장치를 설치하면 비용이 얼마나 들죠?
남: 약 1,000달러 정도 듭니다.
여: 정말이요? 이런, 그건 됐어요. 브레이크 수리, 차량 점검, 그리고 타이어 교체만 하겠어요.
남: 알겠습니다.

어휘 **wear down** 마모되다; 마모시키다 / **rub** 비비다, 마찰하다 / **incredibly** 믿을 수 없을 정도로, 엄청나게 / **inspection** 정밀 검사[조사]; 검열 / **free of charge** 무료로 / **install** 설치하다

07 이유 | ④

▶ 남자가 옷차림에 신경 쓰는 이유는 오늘 밤 오랜만에 고등학교 친구들을 만나기로 했기 때문이다.

W: Arnold, are you still standing in front of the mirror? Isn't it time for you to leave?
M: I'll be done in a few minutes. Does my jacket go well with my pants?
W: Are you going to a fancy party? **Why are you so preoccupied** with the way you look?
M: No, there's no party.
W: Oh, you're attending the orchestra concert? Is it today?
M: The concert **is being held next week**. Mom, I want your honest opinion.
W: The jacket looks great on you. Oh, you're going out on a date? I didn't know you had a girlfriend.
M: Mom, you know that I don't have a girlfriend. I'm getting together with some friends from high school tonight.
W: Oh, so you want to look good in front of them.
M: I **haven't seen them in several years**.
W: Don't worry, you look very handsome. Have fun!

여: Arnold, 아직도 거울 앞에 서 있어? 가야 할 시간 아니니?
남: 곧 다 될 거예요. 제 재킷이 바지와 잘 어울리나요?
여: 화려한 파티에 가는 거니? 왜 그렇게 외모에 신경을 쓰고 있어?
남: 아녜요, 파티는 없어요.
여: 아, 관현악 공연에 참석하려고? 그게 오늘이니?
남: 그 공연은 다음 주에 열려요. 엄마, 저는 엄마의 솔직한 의견을 원해요.
여: 그 재킷은 너에게 아주 잘 어울리는구나. 아, 오늘 데이트하러 가는 거니? 너에게 여자 친구가 있는 줄은 몰랐구나.
남: 엄마, 아시다시피 전 여자 친구가 없어요. 오늘 밤에 고등학교 친구들 몇 명과 함께 만날 거예요.
여: 아, 그럼 그 애들 앞에서 잘 보이고 싶은 거로구나.
남: 몇 년 동안 그 애들을 보지 못했어요.
여: 걱정하지 마, 넌 매우 멋져 보여. 재미있게 놀렴!

어휘 **go with** ~와 어울리다 / **preoccupied** 몰두한, 정신이 팔린

08 언급하지 않은 것 | ④

▶ 해석 참조

W: Excuse me, I'd like to park here. What should I do?
M: You can **park in the vacant spot** over there.
W: I just learned how to drive, and I'm not sure if I can park in that small space. Do you think you could park my car for me?
M: Sure, I can do that for you.
W: Thank you so much. Should I leave my keys in the car?
M: Yes, please. For how long will you park your car? We're open from 6 a.m. to 10 p.m.
W: **I'll be gone for about** two hours. How much is the parking fee?
M: It's $15 for the first hour and $5 for every 30 minutes thereafter.
W: Wow, that's expensive. Are there **any other services you provide**?
M: If you'd like, we offer a quick car wash. Of course, we charge for that service.
W: I'm all right then. Thank you for parking my car.
M: Here's your stub. Please don't lose it.

여: 실례합니다. 여기에 주차하고 싶은데요. 무엇을 해야 하나요?
남: 저쪽 빈자리에 주차하시면 됩니다.
여: 이제 막 운전하는 법을 배워서 저렇게 좁은 공간에 주차할 수 있을지 잘 모르겠습니다. 절 대신해서 제 차를 주차해주실 수 있나요(① 주차 대행 여부)?
남: 물론이죠, 제가 해드릴게요.

여: 정말 감사합니다. 열쇠를 차 안에 두어야 하나요?
남: 네, 그렇게 해주세요. 얼마나 오래 주차하실 건가요? 저희는 오전 6시부터 오후 10시까지 영업합니다(② 주차장 이용 시간).
여: 두 시간 정도 볼일 보러 갈 겁니다. 주차 요금은 얼마인가요?
남: 첫 한 시간은 15달러이고 그 이후에는 30분마다 5달러입니다(③ 주차 요금).
여: 와, 비싸군요. 제공하시는 다른 서비스가 있나요?
남: 원하신다면, 저희가 빠른 세차를 해드립니다(⑤ 세차 서비스). 물론, 그 서비스에는 요금을 청구합니다.
여: 그럼 알겠습니다. 주차를 해주셔서 감사해요.
남: 여기 보관용 표를 드릴게요. 잃어버리지 마세요.

어휘 **vacant** 빈, 비어 있는 / **spot** 곳, 장소; 점; 얼룩 / **fee** 요금 / **thereafter** 그 후에 / **charge** 요금을 청구하다; 요금 / **stub** (표 · 수표 등에서 한 쪽을 떼어 주고) 남은 부분

09 내용 불일치 | ③

▶ 입장권은 성인 6달러, 12세 미만 어린이는 2달러에 판매된다고 했다.

W: Attention please. I'd like to **make an announcement regarding** the upcoming winter concert at Venice High School. We will be holding the concert on Thursday, December 21 at 6:30 p.m. in the school auditorium. **The concert will feature** a Christmas musical by our award-winning choral group. Also, our very own rock band, Metal, will showcase some of their own songs for us. So don't miss this event. Tickets are $6 for adults and $2 for children under the age of 12. All students of Venice High School **are admitted free of charge**. All money will go to the Venice High Scholarship fund, so please come and support our school.

여: 안내 말씀드리겠습니다. Venice 고등학교에서 곧 열릴 겨울 공연에 관하여 알려드리고자 합니다. 우리는 12월 21일 목요일, 오후 6시 30분에 학교 강당에서 공연을 개최할 것입니다. 이번 공연에는 수상 경력을 가진 교내 합창단이 공연하는 크리스마스 뮤지컬이 포함될 것입니다. 또한, 우리 학교의 록 밴드인 Metal이 일부 자작곡을 우리에게 선보일 것입니다. 그러니 이번 행사를 놓치지 마십시오. 입장권은 성인 6달러, 12세 미만 어린이는 2달러입니다. Venice 고등학교의 모든 학생은 무료로 입장합니다. 전체 수익금은 Venice 고등학교 장학 기금으로 모이게 되니, 오셔서 우리 학교를 후원해 주십시오.

어휘 **announcement** 공고; 발표 / **regarding** ~에 관하여 / **feature** 특별히 포함하다, 특징으로 삼다; 특색, 특징 / **choral group** 합창단 / **showcase** 소개하다; 전시하다; 전시

10 도표 이해 | ①

▶ 여자는 한 번에 최소한 10잔을 추출할 수 있고 120달러 이하의 가격대이며, 보온 기능과 내장 그라인더를 포함한 커피 추출기를 원한다고 했다.

W: I'm looking for a coffee machine.
M: What kind do you prefer, an espresso machine or a drip coffee maker?
W: I'd like a drip coffee maker. I like drip coffee and the machines **are less expensive than** espresso machines.
M: All right. How many cups do you need to make at once?
W: I have to make at least 10 cups at once because I have a big family.
M: **How much are you willing to pay**?
W: I can pay up to 120 dollars. But the cheaper the better.
M: Well, the cheapest coffee maker doesn't have a heater.
W: No, I want a coffee maker **which can keep coffee warm**. And I also want a machine with a built-in grinder.
M: Okay. Then this is exactly what you want, I think. It does a nice job keeping coffee hot for at least three hours and has a grinder which has 5 grind settings.
W: That would be great. I'll take it.

여: 저는 커피 기계를 찾고 있습니다.
남: 무슨 종류를 선호하시나요? 에스프레소 기계인가요, 아니면 드립 커피 추출기인가요?
여: 드립 커피 추출기를 원합니다. 제가 직접 내려 마시는 커피를 좋아하기도 하고 또 기계도 에스프레소 기계보다 덜 비싸니까요.
남: 알겠습니다. 한 번에 몇 잔의 커피를 만드셔야 하나요?
여: 식구가 많아서 한 번에 최소한 열 잔의 커피를 만들어야 해요.
남: 비용은 얼마까지 쓸 생각이신가요?
여: 저는 120달러까지 지불할 수 있어요. 하지만 저렴할수록 더 좋지요.
남: 음, 가장 저렴한 커피 추출기는 보온 기능이 없습니다.
여: 안 돼요. 전 커피를 따뜻하게 유지할 수 있는 커피 추출기를 원해요. 그리고 그라인더가 내장된 기계가 좋겠어요.
남: 알겠습니다. 그러면 이게 바로 손님께서 원하시는 것인 듯해요. 이건 적어도 3시간 동안 커피를 뜨겁게 유지할 수 있고 5단계로 조절이 되는 그라인더를 장착하고 있어요.
여: 그게 좋겠어요. 그걸로 할게요.

어휘 **drip coffee** 드립 커피(커피 가루에 뜨거운 물을 부어 여과시켜서 만든 드립식 커피) ***cf.* drip** (액체가) 떨어지다 / **built-in** 내장된; 붙박이의 / **grinder** 가는[빻는] 기구 ***cf.* grind** 갈다, 빻다 / **setting** (기계 장치 등의) 조절 눈금, 설정

11 짧은 대화에 이어질 응답 | ②

▶ 남자는 여자의 커트 머리가 잘 어울린다고 했으므로 미용사의 의견에 동의하는 말을 할 것이다.

① 기운 내. 자신감을 가져.
② 그녀 말이 맞아. 그 커트 머리가 너에게 딱 어울려 보여.
③ 아, 이런! 넌 머리를 자르지 말았어야 했어.
④ 너 정말 변했구나. 나는 너인 줄 몰랐어!
⑤ 넌 그렇다고 말하지만, 넌 날 신경 쓰지 않잖아.

W: What do you think of my hair, Clark?
M: **You got a new hair cut**. It looks really cute. You look great.
W: My stylist said my face **would look brighter** with this cut.
M: ______________________________

여: Clark, 내 머리 어떠니?
남: 새로 머리를 잘랐구나. 정말 귀여워 보여. 멋지다.
여: 미용사가 그러는데 이렇게 자르면 내 얼굴이 좀 더 밝아 보일 거래.
남: ______________________________

어휘 | 선택지 어휘 | **confidence** 자신감; 신뢰 / **recognize** 알아보다; 인정하다

12 짧은 대화에 이어질 응답 | ①

▶ 아들과 함께 앉을 수 있도록 자리를 한 칸 옮겨달라는 남자의 요청에 가장 적절한 응답을 고른다.

① 물론이죠. 제가 다른 자리로 옮길게요.
② 알겠습니다. 자리를 맡아드릴게요.
③ 네, 당신들의 좌석은 5열에 있군요.
④ 아니요, 현재 모든 자리가 다 찼습니다.
⑤ 죄송합니다만, 그 의자를 가져가실 수 없습니다.

M: Excuse me. **Will someone be using this seat**?
W: No, you can take it. I'll move my bag.
M: Thanks. Also, **would you mind moving over** one seat so my son and I can sit together?
W: ______________________________

남: 실례합니다. 누군가가 이 자리를 사용하실 건가요?
여: 아니요, 앉으셔도 됩니다. 제 가방을 옮기겠습니다.
남: 고마워요. 그리고 제가 아들과 함께 앉을 수 있도록 자리를 한 칸 옮겨주실 수 있나요?
여: ______________________________

13 긴 대화에 이어질 응답 | ④

▶ 대화 중에 여자가 잠시 전화를 받고 난 후 어디까지 이야기했는지 남자에게 묻고 있다. 이런 상황에서 남자가 할 수 있는 말을 유추해 본다.

① 조금 전에 당신 사무실에 왔어요.
② 그건 책상 옆의 문서 보관함에 있어요.
③ 이게 전부 무엇에 필요한 것인지 알아내려고 노력해야 해요.
④ 필요하신 정보에 관해 이야기하던 중이었어요.
⑤ 이 문제를 해결하는 걸 도와주실 수 있을지 궁금해요.

M: **Here are the results** from the survey.
W: All right, Chris. This is what I want.
M: I'm glad you like it.
W: So, can you get more information for me?
M: No problem. I can get more information for you. This... *[Phone rings.]*
W: Excuse me. *[Answering the phone]* Hello? *[pause]* Oh, yes! I'm sorry. I'm **in the middle of something important**. Can I call you back later? *[pause]* Thank you.
M: **Is now a bad time**?
W: Not at all. I'm very **sorry to keep you waiting**.

M: That's all right.
W: Now, where were we?
M: ____

남: 조사 결과를 가져왔습니다.
여: 좋아요, Chris. 이게 제가 원하는 겁니다.
남: 마음에 드신다니 기쁩니다.
여: 그럼, 더 많은 정보를 구해주시겠어요?
남: 문제없습니다. 더 많은 정보를 구해드리죠. 이건… *[전화벨이 울린다.]*
여: 잠시만요. *[전화를 받으며]* 여보세요? *[잠시 후]* 아, 네! 죄송해요. 지금 중요한 일을 하는 중이에요. 나중에 다시 전화드려도 될까요? *[잠시 후]* 고마워요.
남: 지금 얘기 나누는 게 곤란하신가요?
여: 전혀요. 기다리게 해서 정말 미안해요.
남: 괜찮습니다.
여: 자, 우리 어디까지 이야기했죠?
남: ____

어휘 **survey** (설문) 조사 | 선택지 어휘 | **file cabinet** 문서 보관함

14 긴 대화에 이어질 응답 | ①

▶ 과제를 함께하는 친구와 마음이 맞지 않아 속상해하는 딸에게 아버지는 먼저 상대의 의견을 존중하는 모습을 보여줄 것을 조언하고 있다. 이에 이어질 응답으로 아버지의 조언을 받아들이겠다는 말이 가장 적절하다.

① 옳은 말씀이에요. 아버지의 조언대로 해 볼게요.
② 음, 전 그렇게 생각하지 않아요. 그 애는 진정한 신사에요.
③ 이해해요. 전 그 애도 아버지를 존경할 거라고 확신해요.
④ 맞아요. 선생님께 제가 짝을 바꿀 수 있는지 여쭤볼게요.
⑤ 네. 그건 대부분의 조별 과제가 갖고 있는 흔한 문제예요.

M: What's wrong, Chloe? You look worried.
W: It's because of the project for Mr. Nelson's class.
M: Did something happen?
W: I **can't stand my partner**, Jason. We don't get along very well. I really want a new partner.
M: What's the problem?
W: **He's too stubborn**. He refuses to listen to anything I have to say.
M: Well, did you listen to any of Jason's ideas?
W: They're not that great. I think **my ideas are much better than his**.
M: Chloe, I'm sure Jason feels the same way about his ideas. You need to put yourself in his shoes.
W: Oh! I didn't think about that.
M: Why don't you show respect for his opinion first? That way you can do the best job possible.
W: ____

남: Chloe, 무슨 일이니? 걱정스러운 얼굴을 하고 있구나.
여: Nelson 선생님 수업의 과제 때문이에요.
남: 무슨 일 있었니?
여: 제 짝인 Jason을 도저히 참지 못하겠어요. 우리는 잘 지내지 못해요. 전 정말 새로운 짝을 원해요.
남: 문제가 뭐니?
여: 그 애는 너무 고집이 세요. 제가 말하려는 건 들으려 하지 않아요.
남: 음, 넌 Jason의 의견 중에 들어준 게 있니?
여: 그 애의 의견은 그다지 좋지 않아요. 제 의견이 그 애의 의견보다 훨씬 더 괜찮은 것 같은데요.
남: Chloe, 아빠는 Jason도 자신의 의견에 관해서 똑같이 느끼고 있을 거라고 생각해. 너도 그 애의 입장이 되어 볼 필요가 있단다.
여: 아! 그것에 대해선 생각해보지 않았어요.
남: 그 애의 의견을 먼저 존중하는 모습을 보여주지 그러니? 그렇게 하면 너희는 과제를 가능한 최고로 잘 해낼 수 있을 거야.
여: ____

어휘 **stubborn** 완고한, 고집스러운 / **refuse to-v** v하기를 거절[거부]하다 / **put oneself in another's shoes** 다른 사람의 입장이 되어 보다

15 상황에 적절한 말 | ④

▶ 접시를 사고 싶지만 비싸서 망설이는 Lauren은 행상인에게 할인해달라는 말을 할 것이다.

① 얼마나 오랫동안 그것을 가지고 계셨나요? 그건 얼마나 오래되었죠?
② 저는 그것의 색깔과 디자인이 마음에 듭니다. 얼마인가요?
③ 여기 35파운드 드릴게요. 선물용으로 포장해주실 수 있나요?
④ 조금 비싸군요. 가격을 좀 깎아주실 수 있나요?
⑤ 가장 가까운 쇼핑몰이 어디에 있는지 말씀해주시겠어요?

M: Lauren has decided to visit her best friend in London during the summer vacation. This is her first visit to England, so she's anxious to fill her days **with as many activities as possible**. She likes antiques, so she decides to check out the biggest flea market in London. Vendors **are selling everything and anything**. She quickly takes notice of some antique plates at a stand. She asks the vendor **how much the plates cost**. They're thirty-five pounds, which she thinks is too expensive. She doesn't want to spend that much money for plates. But she **also doesn't want to let them go** without asking for a possible discount. In this situation, what would Lauren most likely ask the vendor?

남: Lauren은 여름 방학 동안 런던에 사는 가장 친한 친구 집에 방문하기로 했다. 이번이 영국에 처음 가는 것이어서, 그녀는 자신의 일정을 가능한 한 많은 활동으로 채우고 싶어 한다. 그녀는 골동품을 좋아해서 런던에서 가장 규모가 큰 벼룩시장을 둘러보기로 한다. 행상인들은 무엇이든지 다 팔고 있다. 그녀는 재빨리 좌판에 놓인 고풍스러운 접시 몇 개를 주목한다. 그녀는 행상인에게 접시가 얼마인지 묻는다. 접시는 35파운드이고, 그녀가 생각하기에 너무 비싸다. 그녀는 접시를 사는 데 그렇게 많은 돈을 쓰고 싶지 않다. 하지만 할인해달라고 요구하지 않고서 이대로 접시 사는 것을 포기하고 싶지도 않다. 이러한 상황에서 Lauren이 행상인에게 물어볼 말로 가장 적절한 것은 무엇인가?

어휘 **be anxious to-v** v하고 싶어 하다 / **antique** 골동품; 골동의; 고풍스러운 / **vendor** (거리의) 행상인 / **take notice of** ~을 알아차리다 / **stand** 가판대, 좌판 | 선택지 어휘 | **gift-wrap** 선물용으로 포장하다

16~17 세트 문항 | 16. ⑤ 17. ⑤

▶ 16. 바다에 버려지는 쓰레기와 기름 유출 등을 예로 들면서 해양 오염의 심각성에 대해 경고하고 있다.

① 플라스틱이 해양 생물에 미치는 영향들
② 해양 자원이 개발되어야 하는 이유
③ 해양 오염에 대처하는 방안들
④ 해양 오염이 인간의 건강에 연결되어 있는 이유
⑤ 해양 오염의 심각성에 대한 경고

▶ 17. 해석 참조

W: Did you know that there is a man-made island in the middle of the Pacific Ocean? That island **is made completely of trash** that people have thrown into the sea. All of the currents meet in this place, and **on them is carried** all of our litter and trash, such as bottles and styrofoam pieces. It's disgusting, isn't it? Every day, we drive ships and boats over the surface of the sea, polluting the seas with litter. According to the National Academy of Sciences, fishermen lose or throw away an estimated 150,000 tons of plastic fishing gear each year. This plastic trash **affects marine life in the ocean**. And then there are oil spills, some of the most dangerous events of all. When a large-scale oil spill happens in the ocean, hundreds of thousands of animals are killed or injured. Our oceans are one of the world's most precious resources, but **we as humans are ruining them**. We have to do something to protect the oceans, or we will lose them forever.

여: 여러분은 태평양 한가운데 인공 섬이 있다는 것을 알고 계셨나요? 그 섬은 온전히 사람들이 바다에 버린 쓰레기로 만들어졌습니다. 모든 해류가 이곳에서 만나게 되는데, ① 병이나 ② 스티로폼 조각처럼 우리가 버리는 모든 쓰레기가 그 해류를 타고 옮겨집니다. 끔찍하군요, 그렇지 않습니까? 매일, 우리는 바다 위에서 배를 몰며 바다를 쓰레기로 오염시킵니다. 국립 과학원에 의하면, 어부는 매년 십오만 톤으로 추정되는 ③ 플라스틱 낚시 장비를 잃어버리거나 폐기합니다. 이 플라스틱 폐기물은 바다에 사는 해양 생물에 영향을 끼칩니다. 그 다음으로는 모든 사고 중에 가장 위험한 사고 축에 속하는 ④ 기름 유출이 있습니다. 대규모의 기름 유출이 바다에서 발생할 때, 수십만의 동물이 죽거나 해를 입습니다. 바다는 세계의 가장 소중한 자원 중 하나입니다만 우리 인간은 바다를 파괴하고 있습니다. 우리는 바다를 보호하기 위해 무언가를 해야 합니다. 그렇지 않으면 우리는 바다를 영원히 잃게 될 것입니다.

어휘 **man-made** 인공의, 사람이 만든 / **current** 해류, 기류; 현재의, 지금의 / **litter** 쓰레기; (쓰레기 등을) 버리다 / **styrofoam** 스티로폼 / **gear** 장비; 장치 / **marine** 해양의, 바다의 / **spill** 유출, 엎지름; 엎지르다 / **ruin** 망치다, 엉망으로 만들다 | 선택지 어휘 | **seriousness** 심각함; 진지함

01. ④ 02. ④ 03. ④ 04. ③ 05. ⑤ 06. ③ 07. ④ 08. ③ 09. ⑤ 10. ④
11. ④ 12. ① 13. ① 14. ② 15. ① 16. ⑤ 17. ⑤

01 화자가 하는 말의 목적 | ④

▶ 남자는 대중교통 수단 이용, 자동차 함께 타기, 차량 정비, 적정 속도 유지 등 배기가스를 줄이기 위한 방법들을 설명하고 있다.

M: Your car is responsible for emitting as much carbon dioxide a year as your entire house is. These emissions **damage our crops and drinking water**, and cause smog. One of the easiest ways to reduce emissions is simply to change our mindset about driving. **Consider using public transportation** rather than private automobiles. Most forms of public transportation have lower pollutant emissions per passenger than private vehicles. If you must drive, consider carpooling. **Keep your vehicle well-maintained** as that will minimize emissions. Drive at a steady speed and avoid rapid acceleration, which increases fuel consumption and pollutant emissions. Avoid idling for long periods. If purchasing a new car, choose a fuel-efficient model.

남: 여러분의 자동차는 한 가구가 연간 배출하는 양만큼이나 많은 이산화탄소를 배출하는 것의 원인이 됩니다. 이러한 배기가스는 우리의 농작물과 식수에 해를 끼치며, 스모그를 유발합니다. (배기가스의) 배출을 줄이는 가장 쉬운 방법 중 하나는 단지 운전에 대한 우리의 사고방식을 바꾸는 것입니다. 자가용 대신에 대중교통을 이용하는 것을 고려해보십시오. 대부분의 대중교통 수단은 자가용보다 승객 한 명당 오염 물질 배출이 더 적습니다. 만약 꼭 운전을 해야 한다면, 자동차를 함께 타는 것을 고려해보십시오. 배기가스를 최소화하도록 여러분의 차량을 잘 정비하십시오. 일정한 속도로 운전하며, 연료 소모와 오염 물질 배출을 증가시키는 급가속을 피하십시오. 장시간 공회전(空回轉)하는 것을 피하십시오. 새 차를 구매하신다면, 연료 효율이 높은 모델을 선택하십시오.

어휘 **emit** (빛, 열, 향기 등을) 내다 ***cf.* emission** 배기가스; 배출 / **carbon dioxide** 이산화탄소 / **crop** 농작물, 수확물 / **mindset** 사고방식; 마음가짐 / **pollutant** 오염 물질 / **carpool** 카풀을[승용차 함께 타기를] 하다 / **minimize** 최소화하다 / **steady** 꾸준한; 안정된 / **acceleration** 가속; 《물리》 가속도 / **fuel** 연료; 연료를 공급하다 / **consumption** 소모, 소비 / **idle** (엔진 등이) 공회전하다; 빈둥거리다 / **fuel-efficient** 연료 효율이 좋은

02 의견 | ④

▶ 여자는 대학생인 아들에게 책임감을 가지고 학업을 최우선시하며 스스로를 통제하고 자제할 줄 알아야 한다고 말하고 있다.

[Phone rings.]
W: Hello?
M: *[yawning]* Hello.
W: Andy, are you still in bed? Do you have any idea what time it is?
M: Hey, Mom. What's wrong? Why are you calling me so early in the morning?
W: Early in the morning? It's noon right now!
M: Noon? It can't be! I have a paper **that is due in an hour**, and I haven't finished yet!
W: Oh, Andy, why did you **put off finishing your paper** until the last minute?
M: I didn't have time to work on it this past week.
W: You're a college student and you need to be more responsible from now on.
M: I understand. I'm doing my best.
W: Your school work should be a top priority. You need to be able to **control yourself and set limits**.
M: I know. I'll try harder next time.

[전화벨이 울린다.]
여: 여보세요?
남: *[하품하면서]* 여보세요.
여: Andy, 너 아직도 자고 있는 거니? 넌 지금이 몇 시인지 알기나 하니?
남: 저, 엄마. 무슨 일이세요? 왜 이렇게 아침 일찍 전화하셨어요?
여: 아침 일찍이라고? 지금 12시야!
남: 12시라고요? 그럴 리가! 1시간 후에 마감인 보고서가 있는데, 아직 못 끝냈단 말이에요!
여: 아, Andy, 왜 마지막까지 보고서 쓰는 것을 미뤘니?
남: 지난주에 그걸 할 시간이 없었어요.
여: 넌 대학생이고 이제부터 더 책임감을 가질 필요가 있어.
남: 알겠어요. 전 최선을 다하고 있어요.
여: 너의 학업이 최우선이 되어야 해. 너 자신을 통제하고 자제할 수 있어야 해.
남: 알겠어요. 다음엔 더 열심히 노력할게요.

어휘 **due** ~하기로 되어 있는; ~로 인한 / **priority** 우선해야 할 일

03 관계 | ④

▶ 다섯 명이 식사할 자리와 채식주의자를 위한 식사가 있냐고 묻는 것으로 보아 식당 손님과 식당 직원의 대화임을 알 수 있다.

M: Can I park in front here?
W: No, you can't. If you give us your key, we'll park your car for you.
M: Okay. Do you **have a table for five people**?
W: Do you have a reservation?
M: No, I don't. **Are there any tables available**?
W: Yes. Since it's a weekday, you're lucky.
M: Great. Would you happen to have a table by the window?
W: I'm sorry, but all those tables are reserved.
M: Oh, okay. I have another question. Do you have dishes for a vegetarian?
W: Absolutely. We **pride ourselves on** our special vegetarian dishes. Wait here for a second.
M: Sure.

남: 이 앞에 주차해도 될까요?
여: 아니요, 안 됩니다. 저희에게 열쇠를 주시면, 손님의 차를 주차해 드리겠습니다.
남: 알겠어요. 다섯 명이 앉을 자리가 있나요?
여: 예약하셨습니까?
남: 아니요. 자리가 있나요?
여: 네. 평일이라 다행이시네요.
남: 좋아요. 혹시 창가 쪽 자리가 있나요?
여: 죄송하지만, 그 자리는 모두 예약이 되어 있습니다.
남: 아, 알겠습니다. 질문이 하나 더 있는데요. 채식주의자를 위한 요리가 있나요?
여: 물론이죠. 저희는 특별한 채식 요리들을 자랑합니다. 여기서 잠시만 기다려 주십시오.
남: 알겠습니다.

04 그림 불일치 | ③

▶ 침대 바로 옆의 옷장 위에는 곰인형이 놓여 있다고 했다.

[Cell phone rings.]
W: Dave, are you at home?
M: Yes, Grandma! Is something wrong?
W: I just arrived at the community center and realized that I left my reading glasses at home. Do you think **you can bring them to me**?
M: Of course. Where did you put them?
W: They should be in my bedroom. First look at the nightstand on the left side of my bed.
M: You mean the table **where the potted plant is placed**? They're not there.
W: Then look on top of the dresser that's right next to the bed.
M: No, there's just a teddy bear on it. They're **also not on the bench** at the foot of the bed.
W: Where did I put them? Oh, why don't you look on top of the drawers by the window with the TV on top?
M: No, they're not there.
W: Wait. *[pause]* They're in my bag!
M: Oh, that's great!

[휴대전화 벨이 울린다.]
여: Dave, 집에 있니?
남: 네, 할머니! 무슨 일 있으세요?
여: 지금 막 지역주민 센터에 도착했는데 집에 독서용 안경을 두고 온 걸 알았단다. 네가 그걸 가져다줄 수 있겠니?
남: 물론이죠. 어디에 두셨어요?
여: 내 침실에 있을 거다. 내 침대 왼쪽에 있는 침대 탁자를 먼저 보렴.
남: 화분이 놓여있는 탁자를 말씀하시는 거지요? 거기에는 없어요.

여: 그럼 침대 바로 옆에 있는 옷장 위를 보렴.
남: 아니요, 거기에는 곰인형 하나만 있어요. 침대 발치에 있는 긴 의자에도 없고요.
여: 내가 그걸 어디에 두었더라? 아, 창문 옆에 TV가 놓인 옷장 위를 볼래?
남: 아니요, 거기에 없어요.
여: 잠깐. *[잠시 후]* 내 가방에 있어!
남: 오, 잘됐네요!

어휘 **nightstand** 침실용 탁자 / **potted** 화분에 심은 / **foot** (의자 · 테이블 등의) 다리 끝 부분

05 추후 행동 | ⑤

▶ 여자는 남자에게 부동산 중개인인 자신의 친구 전화번호를 문자 메시지로 알려주겠다고 했다.

[Cell phone rings.]
W: Hello?
M: Hi, Aunt Jane. It's Paul. Guess what!
W: **Did you get into a university**?
M: Yes! I just got a call from the University of Washington. I've been accepted!
W: Congratulations! I'm so proud of you. What are you going to do before school starts?
M: Well, I need to find a place to stay **that is close to the school**.
W: Why don't you stay with me? My place is only fifty minutes from the university.
M: I appreciate the offer, but I want to live closer. I'll do some research online.
W: If you say so. You know, I have a friend who is a real estate agent. **I'm sure she'd offer you** a good deal.
M: That would be incredible. Could you give me her number?
W: Of course. I'll send it via text message.
M: Thanks, Aunt Jane.

[휴대전화 벨이 울린다.]
여: 여보세요?
남: 여보세요, Jane 이모 저 Paul이에요. 있잖아요!
여: 너 대학에 들어갔니?
남: 네 방금 워싱턴 대학교에서 전화를 받았어요. 입학 허가를 받았다고요!
여: 축하한다! 네가 정말 자랑스럽구나. 학교가 시작하기 전에 뭘 할 거니?
남: 음, 학교 근처에 지낼 곳을 찾아야 해요.
여: 나와 지내는 게 어떻겠니? 우리 집은 워싱턴 대학에서 50분밖에 안 걸린단다.
남: 제안은 감사하지만, 더 가까운 곳에 살고 싶어요. 온라인으로 조사해 보려고요.
여: 하는 수 없구나. 있잖니, 내게 부동산 중개인인 친구가 한 명 있단다. 분명히 네게 좋은 집을 알려줄 거야.
남: 정말 좋겠는데요. 그분의 전화번호를 주실 수 있어요?
여: 물론이지. 문자 메시지로 보내주마.
남: 감사해요, Jane 이모.

어휘 **real estate agent** 부동산 중개인 / **deal** 거래; 물건 / **via** (특정한 사람 · 시스템 등을) 통하여; (어떤 장소를) 경유하여[거쳐]

06 금액 | ③

▶ 여자가 사기로 한 것은 Cat Woman 의상으로 원래 90달러였으나 50% 할인 중이라고 했으며, 거기에 장갑을 더 사서 10달러를 추가한다. 따라서 여자는 총 55달러를 지불할 것이다. 남자가 지불할 금액인 58달러를 여자가 지불할 돈으로 착각하지 않아야 한다.

W: Wow, it's really fantastic!
M: It really is. I heard this is **the best place to buy costumes** for Halloween.
W: Yeah, but it's very expensive. I'd like to buy an Elsa costume from the movie *Frozen*, but it's $87. I can't afford it.
M: They have some sale items. Come this way. *[pause]* Look! It's a Wonder Woman costume. It was originally 80 dollars, but it's 60% off now.
W: But **it's too old-fashioned**. I want something new.
M: Then how about this Black Widow costume? It's also on sale.
W: Well, I like this Cat Woman costume. This cat hood and black eye mask **would go perfectly with** the black jump suit.
M: Let's see. It was originally 90 dollars, and it's 50% off now.
W: Great. And I'd like to buy these long black gloves, too. They're 10 dollars.
M: They're not on sale.
W: That's okay. What are you going to get?
M: I'm going to get the Spider-Man costume. It's 58 dollars altogether.
W: It looks great.

여: 와, 정말 멋지다!
남: 정말 그러네. 난 여기가 핼러윈 의상을 사기에 최고의 장소라고 들었어.
여: 응, 근데 너무 비싸다. 난 영화 〈Frozen〉에 나오는 Elsa 의상을 사고 싶은데, 87달러야. 그걸 살 형편이 안 돼.
남: 할인 상품도 좀 있어. 이리 와봐. *[잠시 후]* 봐! Wonder Woman 의상이야. 원래 80달러였는데, 지금 60퍼센트 할인 중이네.
여: 하지만 그건 너무 유행이 지났어. 난 새로운 것을 원해.
남: 그렇다면 이 Black Widow 의상은 어때? 이것도 할인 중이야.
여: 음, 난 이 Cat Woman 의상이 마음에 들어. 이 고양이 모양의 두건과 검은색 눈가리개는 그 검은색 점프 수트와 완벽하게 어울릴 거야.
남: 어디 보자. 그건 원래 90달러였는데, 지금 50퍼센트 할인 중이네.
여: 잘됐다. 그리고 난 이 검은색 긴 장갑도 사고 싶어. 이건 10달러야.
남: 그건 할인 중이 아니네.
여: 괜찮아. 너는 뭘 살 거야?
남: 난 Spider-Man 의상을 살 거야. 모두 합해서 58달러야.
여: 근사해 보여.

어휘 **old-fashioned** 유행에 뒤떨어진; 구식의 / **hood** (흔히 외투에 달린) 두건 / **go with** ~와 어울리다, 조화되다 / **jump suit** 점프 수트《바지와 상의가 하나로 붙어 있는 여성복》

07 이유 | ④

▶ 여자는 요리사가 되는 꿈을 이루기 위해 직장을 그만둔다고 했다.

M: I just heard from Brian that you're leaving us. Is that really true?
W: I'm afraid so. I **put in my letter of resignation** a few days ago.
M: Is it because you didn't get a promotion last quarter?
W: Honestly, I was disappointed, but that's not the reason.
M: I know our boss gives you a hard time sometimes. But **don't take it personally**.
W: I didn't like him at first, but I do have great respect for him now.
M: Well, then it must be the salary. You're not happy with your salary.
W: Actually, I'm fine with what I receive.
M: Then I don't understand **why you want to quit**.
W: It's no one's fault. It's just that this 9-to-5 job doesn't suit me very well. I've always wanted to be a chef, so I've **decided to pursue my dreams**.
M: Wow, I'm impressed. It takes a lot of courage to make such a big change. I wish you the best of luck.

남: Brian에게 방금 들었는데 네가 우리 회사를 그만둔다며. 그게 사실이니?
여: 안타깝지만 그래. 며칠 전에 사직서를 제출했어.
남: 네가 지난 분기에 승진하지 못한 것 때문이니?
여: 솔직히, 난 실망했지만, 그게 이유는 아니야.
남: 우리 상사가 너를 가끔 힘들게 한다는 걸 알고 있어. 하지만 그걸 사적으로 받아들이지 마.
여: 난 처음엔 그분이 싫었지만, 지금은 매우 존경해.
남: 음, 그럼 봉급 때문인 게 틀림없겠네. 넌 네 봉급이 마음에 들지 않잖아.
여: 사실, 내가 받는 봉급은 괜찮아.
남: 그럼 왜 네가 그만두길 원하는지 이해할 수가 없어.
여: 그건 누구의 잘못도 아니야. 단지 9시부터 5시까지 근무하는 일이 나에게 잘 맞지 않을 뿐이야. 난 항상 요리사가 되길 원했고, 그래서 내 꿈을 좇기로 결심했어.
남: 와, 감동받았는 걸. 그렇게 크게 전향하는 데는 많은 용기가 필요한데. 행운을 빌게.

어휘 **put in** (요구, 서류 등을) 제출하다, 신청하다 / **resignation** 사직(서), 사임 / **promotion** 승진; 촉진; 판촉 / **quit** 그만두다; 떠나다 / **9-to-5** 《구어》 (회사에서) 9시에서 5시까지 일하는; 회사원의 / **pursue** 추구하다; 뒤쫓다, 추적하다

08 언급하지 않은 것 | ③

▶ 해석 참조

W: Mr. Martin, could you help me find some books to read over the summer?
M: Of course. I'm happy to help you.
W: I've asked some friends, and they gave me **some great suggestions for books**.
M: That's a great way. Another thing you can do is to try book reviews. You can read them in newspapers and also online.
W: Right. Book reviews are definitely helpful, but sometimes there are so many different opinions that it's hard to choose.
M: I can understand. If you have a favorite author, check out **other books written by the same author**.
W: I didn't think of that.

M: Another thing you could do is to pick up a book and get a rough idea about it by reading a page or two in the beginning. Then, read a page in the middle of the book.
W: Oh, what a great idea. Thank you so much for **guiding me in the right direction**, Mr. Martin.
M: My pleasure, and happy reading!

여: Martin 선생님, 제가 여름 동안에 읽을 만한 책을 찾는 걸 도와주시겠어요?
남: 물론이지. 기꺼이 도와주마.
여: 제 친구들에게 물어봤는데, 좋은 책을 몇 권 추천해 주었어요(① 친구의 추천 받기).
남: 그건 좋은 방법이구나. 네가 시도해볼 수 있는 또 다른 것은 서평을 한번 읽어보는 거야(② 서평(書評) 읽어보기). 신문이나 온라인에서도 그걸 읽어볼 수 있단다.
여: 네, 서평은 분명 도움이 되겠지만, 가끔 다른 의견들이 너무 많아서 선택하기 힘들어요.
남: 이해가 가는구나. 좋아하는 작가가 있다면, 같은 작가가 쓴 다른 책들도 찾아보렴(④ 좋아하는 작가의 다른 작품 찾아보기).
여: 그건 생각 못했어요.
남: 네가 할 수 있는 또 다른 방법은 책을 고른 다음에 처음 한두 페이지를 읽어 봄으로써 그 책을 대강 알아보는 거야. 그러고 나서, 책의 중반부를 읽어보렴(⑤ 책의 앞부분과 중반부 훑어보기).
여: 아, 기발한 생각이에요. 옳은 방향으로 이끌어 주셔서 감사해요, Martin 선생님.
남: 천만에, 즐겁게 책을 읽으렴!

어휘 **rough** 대강의, 대충의; (촉감이) 거칠거칠한; 서투른

09 내용 불일치 | ⑤

▶ 장학금 신청서 마감은 10월 15일이고 장학생 선발 통지는 연말이므로 2개월 이후에 수령자를 발표하는 것이다.

W: We have an exciting announcement to make. The generous people of the Green Acre Club are giving away a $4,000 scholarship to 3 high-school students. Students who have a financial need along with exceptional grades will be qualified for the scholarship. If you meet these requirements, pick up an application form from the Green Acre's main office right now. Please note that **all applications must be submitted** to the Green Acre Club office by October 15, 2024. The application **must be accompanied by transcripts** from your high school. You will be contacted for an interview a few weeks after **the deadline for the application**. A second interview will be held for finalists. Award notifications will be sent out at the end of the year. Check out their website at www.greenacre.com for more information.

여: 한 가지 기쁜 소식을 알려드립니다. Green Acre 클럽의 너그러운 분들께서 3명의 고등학생에게 4,000달러의 장학금을 기부하실 것입니다. 경제적 도움이 필요한 우수한 성적의 학생들은 장학금을 받을 자격이 있습니다. 이러한 자격 요건을 충족시킨다면, 지금 바로 Green Acre의 본사에서 신청서를 가져가십시오. 신청서는 2024년 10월 15일까지 Green Acre 클럽의 사무실에 제출하셔야 합니다. 신청서와 함께 여러분의 고등학교 성적표가 첨부되어야 합니다. 신청이 마감되고 몇 주 후에 면접을 위해 연락을 드릴 것입니다. 최종 후보를 대상으로 2차 면접이 있을 것입니다. 수령자 발표는 연말에 공지될 것입니다. 더 자세한 정보를 보시려면 웹사이트 www.greenacre.com을 확인해 주십시오.

어휘 **give away** 기부하다; 수여하다 / **scholarship** 장학금 / **exceptional** 뛰어난; 특별한; 예외적인 / **qualified** 자격 있는, 적격의 / **requirement** 자격[필요] 조건; 요구, 필요 / **submit** 제출하다 / **accompany** 동반하다 / **transcript** (미) 성적 증명서; 사본 / **finalist** 결승전 진출자 / **notification** 알림, 통지

10 도표 이해 | ④

▶ 조절이 가능한 핸들이 달려 있고, 바퀴는 3개가 아니며, 무게는 20파운드를 넘지 않아야 한다. 또한 큰 보관용 주머니가 좌석 밑에 있고 가격은 500달러 미만인 것을 원한다.

W: We need to buy a stroller for our baby.
M: Look at this one. It has curved handles like an umbrella. It's lightweight, compact, and easy to fold.
W: But it's not comfortable for the baby. I want a standard stroller **that has adjustable handles**.
M: Okay. How about a three-wheel stroller? Its wheels are bigger and look stronger.
W: That's a jogging stroller. We can **take our child with us** when we run. But doctors recommend not using it until the baby is about 6 months old.
M: Then we can't buy it, because our baby is a newborn.
W: Right. And we should think about the weight. I think we need one that weighs less than 20 pounds.
M: Good point.
W: I also want **one which has a large storage bag** beneath the seat.
M: You're right. That's ideal for holding diaper bags and purses. Let's get the lighter one.
W: I'd like to stay under $500. **That's beyond our budget**.
M: Okay. Then I think this is what we want. Let's get it.

여: 우리 아기를 위한 유모차를 사야 해요.
남: 이거 봐요. 우산처럼 구부러진 핸들이 달렸어요. 가볍고, 아담하면서, 접기 쉬워요.
여: 하지만 아기한테는 불편하겠네요. 나는 조절 가능한 핸들이 달린 표준형 유모차를 원해요.
남: 알겠어요. 바퀴가 세 개 달린 유모차는 어때요? 그 바퀴가 더 크고 견고해 보여요.
여: 그건 조깅용 유모차에요. 우리가 달릴 때 아기와 함께할 수 있겠어요. 하지만 의사들은 아기가 6개월이 될 때까지 그것을 사용하지 말래요.
남: 그럼 우리 아기는 신생아니까 그걸 살 수 없겠군요.
여: 맞아요. 그리고 우린 무게도 생각해야 해요. 무게가 20파운드를 넘지 않는 것이 필요한 것 같아요.
남: 좋은 지적이에요.
여: 나는 좌석 밑에 큰 수납용 주머니도 있는 것을 원해요.
남: 당신 말이 맞아요. 기저귀 가방과 핸드백을 담기에 적합하네요. 더 가벼운 것을 구매해요.
여: 난 500달러 미만으로 구매하고 싶어요. 그건 우리 예산을 초과하잖아요.
남: 알겠어요. 그럼 이게 우리가 원하는 거네요. 이걸 삽시다.

어휘 **stroller** 유모차; 한가히 거니는 사람 / **curved** 구부러진, 곡선 모양의 / **lightweight** 가벼운 / **compact** 소형의; 빽빽한 / **standard** 표준의; 일반적인 / **adjustable** 조절[조정]할 수 있는 / **beneath** 아래[밑]에 / **diaper** 기저귀 / **beyond** ~을 넘어서

11 짧은 대화에 이어질 응답 | ④

▶ 취업이 되어 좋아하는 남자에게 여자가 축하하자고 하고 있다. 이에 대한 남자의 응답은 좋다고 하면서 나가서 저녁을 사겠다고 말하는 ④가 가장 적절하다.

① 와! 훌륭해! 정말 잘했어.
② 괜찮아. 난 걱정하지 않을 거야.
③ 그렇지 않아. 그건 전혀 큰 의미가 없어.
④ 그게 좋겠어. 밖에 나가자. 내가 저녁 살게.
⑤ 천만에. 그것쯤은 당연히 할 수 있는 일이었어.

W: Ethan, **how did your job interview go**? Oh, you're smiling.
M: Yes! I got the job. I'll start work next week.
W: Congratulations! I knew it. **Let's celebrate**!
M: ______________________________

여: Ethan, 면접은 어땠니? 아, 너 미소 짓네.
남: 응! 나 거기 취직했어. 다음 주부터 일을 시작할 거야.
여: 축하해! 그럴 줄 알았어. 우리 축하하자!
남: ______________________________

12 짧은 대화에 이어질 응답 | ①

▶ 번지 점프를 한 번도 안 해본 여자에게 남자가 번지 점프를 하러 같이 가자고 권하고 있다. 여자는 위험해 보인다고도 말했으므로 완곡하게 거절하는 응답이 적절하다.

① 글쎄, 지금은 말고, 다음번에 시도해 볼게.
② 응, 그게 사람들이 번지 점프를 좋아하는 이유야.
③ 그건 걱정하지 마. 넌 분명 그것을 할 수 있어.
④ 그냥 한번 해봐. 그건 분명 재미있을 거야.
⑤ 어서. 참여하는 건 무료니까 잃을 게 없잖아.

M: I'm going to go to the Tana River and try bungee jumping. How about going together?
W: I've never been bungee jumping. It looks dangerous because **you rely on only a rope**.
M: As far as I know, the rope has never broken. **Let's try it together**!
W: ______________________________

남: 나는 Tana 강에 가서 번지 점프를 해볼 거야. 함께 가는 게 어때?
여: 난 한 번도 번지 점프를 해본 적 없어. 오직 줄에만 의지하기 때문에 위험해 보여.
남: 내가 아는 한, 그 줄은 결코 끊어진 일이 없어. 같이 한번 해보자!
여: ______________________________

어휘 **rely on** ~에 의지[의존]하다 / **as far as** ~하는 한; ~에 관한 한

13 긴 대화에 이어질 응답 | ①

▶ 신혼여행을 다녀온 남자가 저녁 식사에 여자와 Evan을 초대하겠다고 하자 여자가 Evan과 이야기해 보고 오늘 밤에 전화하겠다고 한다. 이에 가장 적절한 응답을 찾는다.

① 좋아요. 그러면 당신 전화를 기다릴게요. 안녕히 계세요.
② 그게 좋겠네요. 저는 내일 바쁘지 않을 것 같아요.
③ 물론이죠. 언젠가 다시 만나기를 바라요.
④ 맞아요. 전 당신을 전적으로 지지해요.

⑤ 알겠어요. 시간과 장소 조율은 당신에게 맡길게요.

W: William, you're finally back! We've missed you! You've been away for too long.
M: Is everything alright here?
W: Everything is just fine. How was your honeymoon in Spain?
M: It was incredible! My wife and I bought you a little souvenir. Here you go. It's a traditional hand-painted plate.
W: You didn't have to! It's absolutely lovely. **It's so thoughtful of you**.
M: Do you and Evan have any plans for this Saturday evening?
W: Saturday? I'll have to check with Evan, but I'm pretty sure we have nothing special planned. **What do you have in mind**?
M: You and Evan did so much for us at the wedding, so we'd like to **have you over for dinner** this Saturday.
W: Oh, how sweet! Let me check with Evan, and I'll give you a ring tonight and let you know.
M: ______________________________

여: William, 드디어 돌아왔군요! 우린 당신이 보고 싶었어요! 당신은 너무 오랫동안 떠나 있었어요.
남: 별일 없지요?
여: 잘 지내고 있어요. 스페인에서의 신혼여행은 어땠나요?
남: 굉장했어요! 제 아내와 제가 당신을 위해 작은 기념품을 샀어요. 여기요. 손으로 직접 그린 전통 접시에요.
여: 그러실 필요 없었는데! 정말 근사하네요. 정말 사려깊으시군요.
남: 당신과 Evan은 이번 주 토요일 저녁에 어떤 계획이 있나요?
여: 토요일이요? Evan과 확인해 봐야겠지만, 특별히 계획한 게 없을 거라 확신해요. 뭐 생각해 둔 거 있으세요?
남: 당신과 Evan이 저희의 결혼을 위해 정말 수고해 주셨으니, 이번 주 토요일 저녁 식사에 초대하고 싶어요.
여: 아, 자상하셔라! Evan과 확인해보고, 오늘 밤에 전화로 알려드릴게요.
남: ______________________________

어휘 **souvenir** 기념품 / **thoughtful** 사려 깊은 / **have A over** A를 초대하다 | 선택지 어휘 | **arrangement** 조정; 준비; 배열

14 긴 대화에 이어질 응답 | ②

▶ 새로 이사한 아파트가 시끄러워서 집에서 집중할 수 없다는 여자의 말을 듣고 남자는 늦게까지 도서관에 있는 이유가 그것 때문이라고 추측했다. 이에 가장 적절한 여자의 응답을 찾는다.

① 맞아. 그냥 내버려두고 그만 싸워.
② 응. 우리 집보다 여기 있는 게 훨씬 나아.
③ 아니, 네가 그 모든 소음을 내는 것 같아.
④ 물론이지! 위층 테라스에서 보는 경치는 굉장해!
⑤ 너무 시끄러워. 소리 좀 줄여 줘.

M: Allison! You're still here in the library? Do you have an exam tomorrow?
W: No, I'm just reading a novel. I just don't want to go home early.
M: Why is that? Did you argue with your family?
W: No, it's not that. Did I say **we moved into a new apartment**?
M: Yes, you said it's a newly-renovated, spacious apartment.
W: But the problem is that **it's located on a busy street** and extremely noisy.
M: Really? That's annoying and stressful.
W: **I can't stand it**. The windows and walls are not properly soundproofed, so I can hear car engines, buses, and garbage trucks.
M: Oh, that's terrible.
W: I can't concentrate on anything at home.
M: So **that's why you are here so late**.
W: ______________________________

남: Allison! 너 아직도 여기 도서관에 있는 거야? 내일 시험이 있니?
여: 아니, 난 소설을 읽고 있을 뿐이야. 그냥 집에 일찍 가기 싫거든.
남: 어째서? 가족들이랑 다투었니?
여: 아니, 그런 게 아니야. 우리 가족이 새 아파트로 이사했다고 내가 말했니?
남: 응, 새롭게 개조된 넓은 아파트라고 말했잖아.
여: 그런데 복잡한 길가에 있어서 너무 시끄럽다는 게 문제야.
남: 정말? 짜증나고 스트레스 받겠구나.
여: 참을 수가 없어. 창문과 벽의 방음이 잘 되지 않아서, 자동차 엔진, 버스, 쓰레기 수거차의 소리가 다 들려.
남: 아, 그건 심하다.
여: 집에서는 어떤 것에도 집중할 수가 없어.
남: 그래서 네가 늦게까지 여기에 있는 거구나.
여: ______________________________

어휘 **renovate** 새롭게 하다, 수리하다 / **spacious** 넓은 / **soundproof** 방음 장치를 하다

15 상황에 적절한 말 | ①

▶ Logan은 약속 시간을 자주 어기는 Ashley에게 약속 시간을 지킬 것을 상기시키고 있다. 이에 Ashley는 Logan을 안심시키는 말을 할 것이다.

① 내 걱정은 마. 역에 제시간에 갈게.
② 늦어서 미안해. 기차를 놓친 게 아니라면 좋겠다.
③ 이번 주에 늦은 게 이번이 세 번째야.
④ 잠시만 기다려! 그걸 네게 바로 가져다줄게.
⑤ 모든 게 다 고마워. 네가 정말 그리울 거야.

M: Logan and Ashley are friends. They plan to go on a picnic tomorrow. They plan to go to Bear Mountain, a mountain located outside the city. Because they don't have a car, they booked train tickets to Bear Mountain. It will **take a couple of hours to get there**. The train runs only twice a day, once in the morning and once in the evening. If they miss the 7:30 train in the morning, they can't go to the picnic. Logan is concerned because Ashley is **often late for appointments**. He tells Ashley that their plans will be ruined if she's late. Logan reminds Ashley again that **she has to be on time**. In this situation, what would Ashley most likely say to Logan?

남: Logan과 Ashley는 친구다. 그들은 내일 소풍을 가려고 한다. 시외에 있는 산인 Bear Mountain에 갈 계획이다. 그들은 차가 없어서 Bear Mountain으로 가는 기차표를 예매했다. 그곳까지 가는 데 두세 시간이 걸릴 것이다. 기차는 아침과 저녁에 한 번씩, 하루 두 번만 운행된다. 만약 그들이 아침 7시 30분 기차를 놓치면, 그들은 소풍을 갈 수 없다. Logan은 Ashley가 약속에 종종 늦기 때문에 걱정이 된다. 그는 Ashley에게 만약 그녀가 늦는다면 그들의 계획이 무산될 것이라고 말한다. Logan은 Ashley에게 제시간에 올 것을 다시 한 번 상기시킨다. 이러한 상황에서 Ashley가 Logan에게 할 말로 가장 적절한 것은 무엇인가?

어휘 **ruin** 망치다; 파멸시키다 / **remind** 상기시키다, 생각나게 하다

16~17 세트 문항 | 16. ⑤ 17. ⑤

▶ 16. 야영 시 사소한 사고라도 적절히 대처하지 않으면 생명에 위험을 줄 수 있다고 말하면서 야영객이 생존 기술을 배워야 할 필요성에 대해 이야기하고 있다.

① 야외 여가 활동의 종류
② 캠핑이 인기 있는 이유
③ 일상생활의 스트레스를 없애는 방법
④ 캠핑 장비를 고를 때 고려할 점
⑤ 야영객이 생존 기술을 배워야 할 필요성

▶ 17. 해석 참조

W: More and more people are releasing stress and finding peace of mind in nature, even if it's only for the weekend. People enjoy back-packing, simply walking, or even cycling along back-country roads. Similarly, the popularity of camping has increased greatly in the last few years. People head to stores to purchase camping gear so they can **enjoy nature whenever possible**. New equipment has **made it possible for anyone to go camping** with little difficulty. In fact, people have become so dependent on the gear that they have forgotten the importance of learning basic survival skills in case of an emergency. A simple accident could be life-threatening if not handled carefully. So, campers need to learn some basic skills. If you're going on a short hike in the mountains, you need to learn how to handle insect bites or possible burns. And, if you decide to visit a more isolated area, you **must be able to deal with** fevers, infections, or minor injuries, such as a sprained ankle, on your own. By preparing yourself, you can **prevent minor mistakes from turning into** life-threatening scenarios.

여: 주말 동안만이라도, 점점 더 많은 사람이 자연 속에서 스트레스를 해소하고 마음의 평온을 찾고 있습니다. 사람들은 배낭여행, 단순히 걷는 것, 또는 구석진 시골길을 따라 자전거 타기도 즐깁니다. 마찬가지로, 야영의 인기는 지난 몇 년간 대단히 증가해 왔습니다. 사람들은 가능할 때마다 자연을 만끽하기 위해서 야영 장비를 사려고 상점으로 향합니다. 최신 장비는 누구라도 어려움 없이 야영하는 것을 가능하게 합니다. 사실, 사람들은 그런 장비에 너무 의존하게 되어서 응급상황에 대비한 기본적인 생존 기술을 배우는 것의 중요성을 잊어버렸습니다. 사소한 사고라도 주의 깊게 대처하지 않으면 생명에 위협적일 수 있습니다. 그래서 야영하는 사람들은 몇 가지 기본적인 기술을 배울 필요가 있습니다. 만약 산에서 가벼운 등산을 할 거라면, ① 벌레 물림이나 발생 가능한 ② 화상에 대처하는 방법을 배울 필요가 있습니다. 그리고 더욱 외진 지역을 방문하기로 결정한다면, ③ 열병, ④ 감염, 또는 발목을 접질리는 것과 같은 경미한 부상에 스스로 대처할 수 있어야 합니다. 여러분 스스로 대비함으로써, 사소한 실수가 생명을 위협하는 상황이 되는 것을 막을 수 있습니다.

어휘 **back-country** 시골의, 오지의 / **gear** 장비, 장치 (= equipment) / **dependent** 의지[의존]하는 / **life-threatening** 생명을 위협하는 / **infection** 감염 / **minor** 작은[가벼운], 중요치 않은 / **sprain** (손목, 발목 등을) 삐다[접질리다] | 선택지 어휘 | **get rid of** ~을 없애다, 처리하다 / **consideration** 고려 사항; 사려, 숙고

01. ④ 02. ⑤ 03. ③ 04. ⑤ 05. ③ 06. ② 07. ③ 08. ④ 09. ③ 10. ④
11. ④ 12. ① 13. ① 14. ② 15. ⑤ 16. ① 17. ⑤

01 화자가 하는 말의 목적 | ④

▶ 준결승전과는 다르게 치러지는 결승전의 경기 방식을 자세히 설명하고 있다.

W: Thank you all for coming down here. I'm really excited about today's results. Now, all contestants, please listen carefully. You will soon find out that at the finals the game will be played differently **compared to the semi-finals**. You don't need to press your buzzers when answering a question anymore. I'll **give each of you different questions** individually. And the game will consist of three rounds instead of two. The most significant difference is the third round. The winner will be the first player to answer correctly in a set of questions. **Are we all clear about this**?

여: 여기 오신 모든 분들께 감사의 말씀을 드립니다. 오늘의 결과가 정말 기대되는군요. 이제 참가자들은 모두 주의 깊게 들어 주시기 바랍니다. 결승전 경기는 준결승전과는 다르게 치러진다는 것을 곧 알게 되실 겁니다. 문제에 답을 하실 때 더 이상 버저를 누르실 필요가 없습니다. 저는 여러분들에게 각기 다른 문제를 출제할 것입니다. 그리고 경기는 2라운드가 아니라 3라운드로 구성될 것입니다. 가장 두드러진 차이점은 세 번째 라운드입니다. 일련의 문제에서 가장 먼저 정확하게 대답한 사람이 우승자가 될 것입니다. 이에 대해 모두 이해가 되셨습니까?

어휘 **contestant** 경기자, 경쟁자 / **final** (복수형) 결승전 *cf.* **semi-final** 준결승 / **compared to** ~와 비교해서 / **individually** 개별적으로 / **significant** 현저한; 중요한

02 의견 | ⑤

▶ 남자는 성공하려면 타고난 능력보다 연습이나 굳은 의지와 같은 후천적인 노력이 더 필요하다고 생각한다.

M: Which singer is your sister?
W: That's her on the left. She just finished singing her solo.
M: Wow, I'm really impressed. She's as good as a professional singer.
W: She would be very happy to hear that. She practices her singing every day in hopes of becoming a famous singer.
M: Practice is the key. **Anything can be accomplished** if you have enough determination.
W: Actually, I don't think she needs to practice that much.
M: Really? What makes you say that?
W: She has always had a good voice. Some people **seem to be born with** amazing talents.
M: Yeah, they may fulfill their dreams more easily, but I think **it takes more than natural ability** to succeed.

남: 어느 성악가가 네 언니니?
여: 왼쪽에 있는 사람이야. 방금 독창을 끝냈어.
남: 와, 정말 인상 깊어. 언니가 전문 성악가만큼 잘하시는구나.
여: 그 말을 들으면 아주 기뻐할 거야. 언니는 유명한 성악가가 되기 바라면서 매일 노래 연습을 하거든.
남: 연습이 (성공의) 비결이야. 굳은 의지가 충분히 있다면 무엇이든 해낼 수 있지.
여: 사실, 언니는 그렇게 많이 연습할 필요가 없는 것 같아.
남: 정말? 왜 그런 말을 하는데?
여: 언니는 항상 목소리가 좋았어. 몇몇 사람들은 놀라운 재능을 타고나는 것 같아.
남: 맞아, 그 사람들은 꿈을 좀 더 쉽게 이룰지도 몰라. 하지만 내 생각에 성공하려면 타고난 능력 이상의 것이 필요해.

어휘 **determination** 결심, 결단(력); 결정 / **fulfill** (꿈 · 목표 등을) 달성하다; (책임 · 임무 등을) 수행하다

03 관계 | ③

▶ 마음에 드는 천을 고르고 벽에 칠할 페인트 색깔을 추천해달라고 하는 사람(여자)은 집주인이고, 천 샘플을 가져와 거실 디자인에 대해 조언하고 창문 치수를 재는 사람(남자)은 인테리어 디자이너이다.

W: Thanks for coming over. Would you like something to drink?
M: Just a glass of water, please.
W: No problem.
M: So, I looked at the living room pictures you sent via e-mail and brought some matching fabric samples.
W: They look beautiful. **Are those for the curtains**?
M: Yes. Is there anything you like?
W: I really like the blue one.
M: Great choice! The blue **will go well with** your white sofa and other furniture.
W: I also need help in picking paint colors for the wall. Would you recommend one?
M: Sure, but first, let me measure the windows for the curtain.
W: Oh, **I can't wait until everything's done**. With your help, this place is going to look fabulous!

여: 와 주셔서 감사해요. 마실 것 좀 드릴까요?
남: 물 한 잔만 주세요.
여: 알겠습니다.
남: 자, 고객님께서 이메일로 보내주신 거실 사진을 보고 그에 어울리는 천 샘플들을 가져왔습니다.
여: 멋져 보이네요. 커튼에 쓰일 것들인가요?
남: 네. 마음에 드시는 게 있습니까?
여: 파란색 천이 정말 마음에 들어요.
남: 탁월한 선택입니다! 파란색은 당신의 하얀 소파 및 다른 가구들과 잘 어울릴 거예요.
여: 벽에 칠할 페인트 색을 고르는 데도 도움이 필요해요. 색을 추천해주시겠어요?
남: 물론이죠. 그렇지만 먼저 커튼을 위해 창문의 치수를 재겠습니다.
여: 아, 모두 완성되는 게 무척 기다려져요. 당신의 도움으로 여기가 굉장히 멋져 보일 거예요!

어휘 **via** ~을 통해서 / **fabric** 직물, 천 / **go well with** ~와 잘 어울리다 / **fabulous** 굉장히 멋진, 좋은

04 그림 불일치 | ⑤

▶ 케이크는 선물과 학사모 사이에 놓여 있다고 했다.

M: Hi, honey. What's this? Are these the decorations for Jim's graduation party?
W: That's right. What do you think?
M: Everything looks great! I especially like the photos **attached to this board**.
W: They're all pictures from his school life. He looks so happy, doesn't he?
M: He does. Did you **have any trouble hanging** the arch-shaped banner that says "Happy Graduation!"?
W: No, I just stood up on a chair. The balloons above the banner were **harder to reach though**.
M: You did a good job. I like that there are round ones and heart-shaped ones.
W: Thanks. I also brought in the rectangular table from the kitchen to set things on.
M: Good idea. The cake smells delicious, too.
W: And it looks nice between his present and graduation cap. Oh, I think he'll be excited when he sees this.
M: Me too, honey. Let's get lots of pictures.
W: Of course!

남: 안녕, 여보. 이게 뭐예요? 이것들이 Jim의 졸업 파티를 위한 장식들인가요?
여: 맞아요. 어떻게 생각해요?
남: 모든 게 다 좋아 보여요! 특히 이 게시판에 붙어 있는 사진들이 좋네요.
여: 그 사진들은 Jim의 학교생활을 찍은 사진들이에요. 매우 행복해 보이지 않나요?
남: 그래 보여요. '졸업 축하해!'라고 쓰인 아치형의 현수막을 다는 데 힘들지 않았어요?
여: 아뇨, 그냥 의자 위에 올라갔어요. 그런데 현수막 위의 풍선들이 손이 닿기에 더 힘들었어요.
남: 잘했어요. 난 둥근 풍선과 하트 모양 풍선이 있는 게 마음에 들어요.
여: 고마워요. 물건들을 놓기 위해 부엌에서 직사각형 탁자도 가져왔어요.

남: 좋은 생각이에요. 케이크도 맛있는 냄새가 나네요.
여: 그리고 그것이 선물과 학사모 사이에 있으니 멋져 보이죠. 아, 아이가 이걸 보면 신날 것 같아요.
남: 나도 그래요, 여보. 사진을 많이 찍읍시다.
여: 물론이죠!

어휘 **decoration** 장식 / **graduation** 졸업 ***cf.*** **graduation cap** 학사모 / **attach** 붙이다, 첨부하다 / **arch-shaped** 아치형의 / **banner** 현수막, 플래카드 / **heart-shaped** 하트 모양의 / **rectangular** 직사각형의; 직각의

05 부탁한 일 | ③

▶ 여자가 학교 웹사이트에서 방과 후 수업 정보를 알아볼 수 있다고 하자 남자가 오늘 해달라고 부탁했다.

M: How is Karen doing with her French class?
W: **She's really struggling**. I think we should do something to help.
M: Does she need a dictionary? I could look for an electronic one at the store.
W: No, she already has one.
M: Maybe we could enroll her in an after-school program.
W: That's a good idea, but is there **one that works with her schedule**?
M: I'm not sure. We should get details from her school.
W: I think we can get information about it on the school website.
M: Right. Could you check today?
W: Sure. I'll do that. And **we can find a free online lecture** for Karen if we can't find a good program.
M: Sounds good.

남: Karen은 프랑스어 수업을 잘 받고 있어요?
여: 무척 고생하고 있어요. 우리가 도움 될 만한 뭔가를 해야 할 것 같아요.
남: 그 애가 사전이 필요한가요? 내가 상점에서 전자사전을 찾아볼 수 있어요.
여: 아니요, 이미 하나 가지고 있어요.
남: 아마도 그 애를 방과 후 프로그램에 등록시킬 수 있을 거예요.
여: 그거 좋은 생각이에요, 그런데 그 애의 일정에 맞는 것이 있을까요?
남: 확실치는 않아요. 학교로부터 자세한 사항을 알아봐야 해요.
여: 학교 웹사이트에서 그것에 관한 정보를 얻을 수 있을 거예요.
남: 알겠어요. 당신이 오늘 확인해줄 수 있어요?
여: 물론이죠. 내가 할게요. 그리고 만약 좋은 프로그램을 찾지 못한다면 Karen을 위해 무료 온라인 강의를 찾아줄 수 있어요.
남: 좋은 생각이에요.

어휘 **struggling** 분투하는, 발버둥치는 / **electronic** 전자의 / **enroll** 등록시키다

06 금액 | ②

▶ 산악자전거 두 대를 하루 동안 빌리는 가격은 30달러이고 4시간 이하로 빌리면 반값이다.

W: My son and I **want to rent bikes**.
M: Well, we're offering a special discount today to encourage more people to exercise.
W: Great. How much?
M: Mountain bikes **are on special** for $15 for the day, and we will give you a free water bottle for each bike.
W: Is that it?
M: We have 10-speed bikes for $11 for the day instead of the usual $20 rental fee.
W: **What if I rent a bike** only for a couple of hours?
M: For less than 4 hours you'll need to pay half of the full-day rate.
W: Then we'll take two mountain bikes. We'll **go for a ride** only for a couple of hours.
M: OK.

여: 아들과 제가 자전거를 빌리려고 하는데요.
남: 저희는 더 많은 분들이 운동을 하시도록 독려하기 위해 오늘 특별 할인행사를 합니다.
여: 잘됐네요. 얼마지요?
남: 산악자전거는 특가로 하루 동안 빌리는 데 15달러이고 자전거 한 대당 물병 하나를 무료로 제공합니다.
여: 그게 다인가요?
남: 평소 하루 20달러에 임대하던 10단 자전거를 하루 11달러에 빌려 드립니다.
여: 제가 자전거를 두세 시간만 빌리면 어떻게 되나요?
남: 4시간 이하로 빌리실 경우는 하루 가격의 반만 내시면 됩니다.
여: 그럼 산악자전거 두 대로 하겠습니다. 두세 시간만 탈 거예요.
남: 알겠습니다.

어휘 **rent** 임대하다 / **on special** 특가로 / **rate** 요금; 비율; 평가하다

07 이유 | ③

▶ 남자가 성적을 나쁘게 받을 것이라고 걱정하자 여자가 여러 이유를 대며 묻고 있다. 공부도 열심히 했는데 알람시계가 망가져서 시험에 지각해 시험 시간의 반을 놓쳤다고 했으므로 답은 ③이다.

W: Hi, Ben!
M: Oh, hi.
W: What happened? You look very upset.
M: I met Mr. Brown, my biology teacher. I will **get a bad grade on that exam**.
W: Why? Didn't you study hard for the exam?
M: Yes, I did. I studied for several days for that exam. I even practiced with all of the old exams from the previous semester.
W: Then why are you worried about it? I know **you'd never think of cheating on a test**. Oh, did you study the wrong chapter for the test?
M: No, my alarm clock broke and I was late for the exam. **I missed the first half** of the test.
W: Really? I think you should talk to the teacher.
M: I did. I just met with him, but he said it's my fault. Actually, he's right.
W: Oh, boy!
M: I don't know what to do.

여: 안녕, Ben!
남: 오, 안녕.
여: 무슨 일이야? 너 매우 기분이 안 좋아 보여.
남: 나는 내 생물학 담당이신 Brown 선생님을 만났어. 나는 그 시험에서 나쁜 성적을 받을 거야.
여: 왜? 너는 그 시험을 위해 열심히 공부하지 않았니?
남: 열심히 했어. 나는 이 시험을 위해 며칠을 공부했어. 나는 심지어 지난 학기의 모든 기출 문제도 공부했어.
여: 그러면 왜 걱정하는 거야? 나는 네가 시험을 칠 때 절대 부정행위를 할 생각을 하지 않는다는 걸 아는데. 아, 시험 범위가 아닌 다른 챕터를 공부한 거야?
남: 아니, 내 알람시계가 고장 나는 바람에 시험에 늦었어. 나는 시험의 앞 절반을 놓쳤어.
여: 정말이야? 난 네가 선생님께 말씀드려야 한다고 생각해.
남: 했어. 난 방금 선생님을 만났는데 내 잘못이라고 하셨어. 사실, 선생님이 옳아.
여: 이런!
남: 어떻게 해야 할지 모르겠어.

어휘 **biology** 생물학 / **cheating** (시험에서의) 부정행위

08 언급하지 않은 것 | ④

▶ 해석 참조

M: Hi, Jenna. What are you doing?
W: I'm searching for a packaged tour to the Philippines.
M: You speak English fluently. So, why do you want a packaged tour?
W: Well, it's convenient. Plus, it's **safer than traveling alone**.
M: I suppose so, but you can go anywhere you want when you travel alone.
W: That's true, but how would I find the best restaurants and attractions?
M: There's plenty of information on the Internet, and actually, traveling alone is a great chance to find hidden attractions and authentic local cuisine.
W: Hmm.... It would be nice to avoid some of the tourist traps.
M: Exactly. Also, **traveling on your own can be much cheaper** than a packaged tour.
W: Then I could use the extra money for souvenirs. You know, I might do that.
M: Trust me. **You won't regret it**.

남: 안녕, Jenna. 뭐 하고 있어?
여: 필리핀 패키지여행에 대해 검색하고 있어.
남: 너 영어 잘하잖아. 그런데 왜 패키지여행을 하려고 해?
여: 글쎄, 그게 편하거든. 거기다 혼자 여행하는 것보다 안전하기도 하고.

남: 그럴 수도 있겠지만, 혼자 여행하면 가고 싶은 곳은 어디든 갈 수 있어(① 이동의 자유).
여: 맞아. 하지만 최고의 식당과 명소는 어떻게 찾니?
남: 인터넷에 정보가 무척 많아. 그리고 실제로 혼자 여행하는 건 숨어 있는 명소(② 숨은 명소 방문)와 진정한 현지 음식을 찾는 좋은 기회(③ 현지 음식 향유)지.
여: 음…. 관광객에게 바가지 씌우는 곳을 피할 수 있다면 좋겠어.
남: 맞아. 그리고 혼자 여행하는 건 패키지여행을 하는 것보다 돈이 훨씬 덜 들기도 해(⑤ 저렴한 경비).
여: 그러면 남는 돈을 기념품 사는 데 쓸 수도 있겠네. 그럼 그렇게 할까 봐.
남: 날 믿어. 후회하지 않을 거야.

어휘 **package(d) tour** 패키지 여행(비용 일체를 일괄해서 내고 하는 (단체) 여행) / **fluently** 유창하게 / **attraction** (사람을 끄는) 명소, 명물; 매력(적인 요소) / **authentic** 진정한, 진짜의 / **cuisine** (보통 비싼 식당의) 요리; 요리법 / **tourist trap** (비격식) 관광객들에게 바가지를 씌우는 곳 / **souvenir** 기념품

09 내용 불일치 | ③

▶ Singapura는 익힌 닭고기나 햄을 특히 좋아한다고 했다.

M: The Singapura is **one of the smallest cats** in the world, with large eyes, a black-tipped tail, and brown or gray coloring. In 1990, the Singapore Government adopted it as their national mascot and later declared it to be a National Treasure. The Singapura is small but muscular, and its back legs are slightly longer than its front legs. Singapuras typically weigh between 5 and 8 pounds, and **there is little difference in size** between males and females. Their diet is typical, but they especially enjoy treats of cooked chicken or ham. Despite their size, Singapuras are surprisingly warm and can feel very pleasant on the lap; just one of many reasons Singapuras **make excellent pets**. They are lively and extremely curious, and they are not afraid of humans.

남: 싱가푸라는 커다란 눈과 끝 부분이 검은 꼬리, 갈색 혹은 회색 털을 가진, 세계에서 가장 작은 고양이 중 하나입니다. 1990년 싱가포르 정부는 그것을 국가 마스코트로 채택했으며 나중에는 국보로 선언했습니다. 싱가푸라는 몸집이 작지만 근육이 발달했으며, 뒷다리가 앞다리보다 조금 더 깁니다. 싱가푸라는 보통 몸무게가 5~8파운드 정도 나가며 수컷과 암컷의 크기 차이는 별로 없습니다. 주식은 특별할 게 없지만 익힌 닭고기나 햄 특식을 특히 좋아합니다. (작은) 크기에도 불구하고, 싱가푸라는 놀랍도록 따뜻해서 무릎 위에 올려놓고 있으면 느낌이 매우 좋습니다. 그리고 이것은 싱가푸라가 반려동물로 좋은 여러 이유 가운데 한 가지일 뿐입니다. 싱가푸라는 활달하고 호기심이 대단하며, 사람을 두려워하지 않습니다.

어휘 **black-tipped** 끝 부분이 검은 / **adopt** 채택하다 / **declare A (to be) B** A를 B로 선언[공표]하다 / **muscular** 근육의; 근육이 발달한 / **treat** 특별한 것[선물]; 대접; 대(우)하다

10 도표 이해 | ④

▶ 재질이 나무이며 접히는 다리와 옆 핸들이 있고, 검정색이 아닌 것을 골랐다.

M: What are you doing, Rose?
W: I'm looking at bed trays online. My mother **injured herself recently**, so she has to remain in bed for a few weeks.
M: I'm sorry to hear that. A bed tray would be really useful for her. Let me help you choose.
W: Sure. Do you already have a bed tray?
M: Yeah, I have a plastic bed tray, but it's not good. I **recommend a wooden tray**.
W: Got it. I think a tray with legs is more convenient.
M: Exactly. Why don't you choose a tray with foldable legs? You can **put it away easily when you don't need it**.
W: Good idea. What about side handles?
M: They are very useful! A tray with side handles is **easy to carry**.
W: Okay! I'll get one of these two. Hmm, My mother doesn't like black.
M: Then it's settled. This is what you want.
W: All right. Thanks for helping me.

남: 뭐 하고 있니, Rose?
여: 온라인으로 침대 트레이를 보고 있어. 최근에 우리 어머니가 다치셔서 몇 주간 침대에 계셔야 하거든.
남: 그거 안되셨구나. 베드트레이가 네 어머니께 정말로 유용할 거야. 내가 선택을 도와줄게.
여: 그래. 넌 이미 베드트레이를 가지고 있니?
남: 응, 난 플라스틱 베드트레이를 갖고 있는데, 그거 좋지 않아. 나무 트레이를 추천해.
여: 알았어. 다리가 있는 트레이가 더 편할 것 같아.
남: 맞아. 접을 수 있는 다리가 있는 트레이를 고르는 것은 어때? 필요 없을 때 쉽게 치워둘 수 있잖아.
여: 좋은 생각이야. 옆 손잡이는 어떠니?
남: 그것은 매우 유용해! 옆 손잡이가 있는 트레이는 나르기 쉽거든.
여: 알았어! 난 이 둘 중 하나를 살게. 음, 우리 어머니는 검은색을 좋아하지 않으셔.
남: 그러면 결정됐네. 이게 네가 원하는 거야.
여: 좋아. 도와줘서 고마워.

어휘 **injure** 다치게 하다 / **wooden** 나무로 된 / **foldable** 접을 수 있는 / **put away** (보관 장소에) 치우다, 넣다 / **settle** 결정하다; 해결하다

11 짧은 대화에 이어질 응답 | ④

▶ 여자가 영화 보기 전에 팝콘을 사면서 남자에게 탄산음료도 마실 것인지 물었다. 이에 적절한 응답을 찾는다.

① 둘 다 합쳐서 7달러야.
② 우리 좌석을 찾아볼게.
③ 여기 돈이 좀 있어.
④ 팝콘만 있으면 돼.
⑤ 영화가 점점 비싸지네.

W: Before we enter the theater, **let's buy some popcorn**.
M: I spent all my money on the tickets. **Can you afford it**?
W: Of course. Do you want some soda, too?
M: ______________________________

여: 영화관에 들어가기 전에 팝콘을 사자.
남: 난 표 사는 데 돈을 다 써버렸어. 네가 낼 수 있니?
여: 물론이지. 탄산음료도 마실래?
남: ______________________________

12 짧은 대화에 이어질 응답 | ①

▶ 도서관에 잠시 들러야 한다는 여자의 말에 남자는 얼마나 걸릴 것 같은지 물었다. 이에 적절한 응답을 찾는다.

① 몇 분밖에 안 걸릴 거야.
② 거기에서 하루 종일 공부할 거야.
③ 공연 후에 분명히 시간이 있을 거야.
④ 도서관은 평일 오후 9시까지 문을 열어.
⑤ 내가 여태껏 가본 것 중 가장 긴 공연이었어.

M: I'm ready to go to the concert. How about you?
W: Almost. I just **need to stop by the library**, and then I'll be ready.
M: You're going to the library? **How long do you think that will take**?
W: ______________________________

남: 난 공연 갈 준비 다 됐어. 넌 어때?
여: 거의 다 됐어. 도서관에 잠시 들르기만 하면 돼. 그러고 나면 준비가 끝나.
남: 도서관에 갈 거라고? 얼마나 걸릴 것 같니?
여: ______________________________

13 긴 대화에 이어질 응답 | ①

▶ 주말에 하이킹을 계획했으나 날씨가 나쁠 것이라는 여자의 말에 남자는 아마도 계획을 취소할 것이다.

① 이번에는 가지 않는 것이 좋겠군.
② 내일 아침 7시가 어때?
③ 다행히 너는 경험이 있구나.
④ 다음 쉼터까지 거리가 얼마나 되니?
⑤ 주말 날씨를 확인했니?

W: Kurt, come on. **Let's get out of** this dorm room. It's Friday night! Time for some fun!
M: Just let me shut my computer down.
W: *[pause]* So, **what are you up to this weekend**?
M: I'm going hiking tomorrow.
W: I've never been hiking.
M: Really? Come with me!
W: Tomorrow? I'd love to! What time and where?
M: I'm planning to do the Tara Trail.
W: What is that?
M: It's an easy 8 km walk. Is 7 a.m. **too early for you to start out**?
W: Hang on. Isn't the weather supposed to be bad this weekend?
M: Is it? I hadn't bothered to check. It's been so good lately.

W: I'm pretty sure they said heavy rain was expected all weekend.
M: ______________________________

여: Kurt, 어서, 기숙사에서 나가자. 금요일 밤이잖아! 좀 즐길 시간이야!
남: 그럼, 컴퓨터 좀 끄고.
여: *[잠시 후]* 이번 주말에 무엇을 할 거니?
남: 내일 하이킹을 할 거야.
여: 난 하이킹을 해 본 일이 없어.
남: 정말? 같이 가자!
여: 내일? 좋아! 몇 시에, 어디서?
남: 난 Tara 산길로 갈 계획이야.
여: 그게 뭔데?
남: 8킬로미터 길이의 걷기 쉬운 산책로야. 아침 7시에 출발하는 것은 너무 이르니?
여: 잠깐. 이번 주말 날씨가 나쁘다고 하지 않았니?
남: 정말? 확인 안 해봤어. 최근에 정말 날씨가 좋아서 말이야.
여: 주말 내내 많은 비가 예상된다고 했던 게 확실해.
남: ______________________________

어휘 **trail** 산길, 산책로 / **start out** 출발하다, 떠나다 / **bother** 신경 쓰다; 괴롭히다 | 선택지 어휘 | **give A a miss** A를 하지 않기로 결정하다 / **shelter** 쉼터, 피난처

14 긴 대화에 이어질 응답 | ②

▶ 최근에 필요할 때마다 자신의 이어폰을 여자가 사용하고 있었다는 남자의 말에 오늘 이어폰이 꼭 필요한 여자가 할 수 있는 답변을 유추해 본다.

① 정말 고마워. 나를 도와준 것을 정말 고맙게 생각해.
② 마지막으로 오늘 밤에만 네 것을 사용하면 어떻겠니?
③ 잘됐다. 그것을 찾아줘서 정말 고마워.
④ 엄마가 아시면 너에게 정말 소리 지르실 거야.
⑤ 너는 새 이어폰을 살 여유가 없어.

M: What's wrong, Jenny?
W: I can't seem to find my earphones for my cell phone. I've looked everywhere, but I can't find them.
M: You ought to buy a new pair.
W: I can't afford a new pair.
M: They can't be that expensive.
W: I went to a shop two weeks ago. They're 20,000 won.
M: You could save some of the money you get from Mom and Dad each week.
W: That's not easy to do. I need to spend that money on other stuff.
M: Then ask Mom and Dad for more money so that you can buy a new pair.
W: Mom will just yell and tell me how irresponsible I am.
M: Yeah. I know.
W: And you rarely use yours. I really need them tonight.
M: But lately whenever I want to use them, you've got them.
W: ______________________________

남: 무슨 일이야, Jenny 누나?
여: 휴대전화의 이어폰을 찾을 수가 없어. 다 둘러봤는데 찾을 수가 없어.
남: 새것을 사야겠네.
여: 새것을 살 여유가 없어.
남: 그렇게 비싸지는 않을 텐데.
여: 2주 전에 가게에 갔었는데 2만원 하더라고.
남: 매주 엄마, 아빠에게 받는 돈의 일부를 저금할 수도 있잖아.
여: 그렇게 하기가 쉽지 않아. 다른 곳에도 돈을 써야 한다고.
남: 그럼 엄마, 아빠에게 새 이어폰을 사게 돈을 더 달라고 말씀드려 봐.
여: 엄마는 소리치며 내가 책임감이 없다고 말하실 거야.
남: 응. 나도 알아.
여: 너는 네 이어폰을 거의 사용하지 않잖아. 난 오늘 이어폰이 정말 필요하단 말이야.
남: 하지만 최근에 내가 이어폰을 쓰려고 할 때마다 누나가 가지고 있었는데.
여: ______________________________

어휘 **irresponsible** 책임감이 없는 / **rarely** 좀처럼 ~하지 않는 | 선택지 어휘 | **appreciate** 감사하게 생각하다

15 상황에 적절한 말 | ⑤

▶ David는 Jack이 사는 곳을 알고 있으니 자신이 Jack에게 가보고 Lisa는 원래대로 봉사 활동을 하러 가는 게 좋을 거라 생각한다.

① Jack의 전화번호가 올바른 것이 확실하니?
② 노숙자를 위한 자원봉사를 몇 번이나 해봤니?
③ 우리가 Jack의 집으로 가서 차를 태워 주어야 해.
④ 왜 자원봉사 동아리에 가입했는지 말해줄 수 있니?
⑤ 내가 Jack이 어떤지 확인할 테니까 너는 무료 급식소에 가는 게 어때?

W: It is Saturday morning, and David is with his friend Lisa. They have both been waiting for an hour for Jack, another good friend of theirs, to arrive. The three of them had gotten acquainted with each other at the school volunteer club and had planned to go to a local soup kitchen to serve meals to the homeless. David and Lisa have both tried calling Jack several times, but he is not picking up the phone. It is unlike Jack to be so late without calling, and Lisa is worried that something might have happened to him. Since David knows where Jack lives, he thinks that Lisa should go ahead with the original plan while he goes to Jack's house to see if everything's okay. In this situation, what would David most likely say to Lisa?

여: 토요일 아침, David는 친구 Lisa와 함께 있다. 그들은 둘 다 또 다른 친한 친구인 Jack이 도착하기를 한 시간 동안 기다리는 중이다. 그들 세 명은 학교 자원봉사 동아리에서 서로 알게 되었고 지역 무료 급식소에 가서 노숙자에게 음식을 나누어 줄 계획이었다. David와 Lisa는 둘 다 Jack에게 여러 번 전화를 걸었지만, Jack은 전화를 받지 않는다. 전화도 없이 이렇게 늦다니 Jack답지 않아서 Lisa는 어쩌면 그에게 무슨 일이 생겼을지도 모른다고 걱정한다. David는 Jack이 사는 곳을 알고 있어서, 자신이 Jack의 집으로 가서 무슨 일이 있는지 알아보고, Lisa는 원래 계획대로 해야 한다고 생각한다. 이러한 상황에서 David가 Lisa에게 할 말로 가장 적절한 것은 무엇인가?

어휘 **get acquainted with A** A와 아는 사이가 되다 / **soup kitchen** (빈민을 위한) 무료 급식소 | 선택지 어휘 | **check up on** ~을 확인하다

16~17 세트 문항 | 16. ① 17. ⑤

▶ 16. 남자는 BookCrossing에 관해 소개하고 사람들의 관심을 유발하고 있다.

① 독특한 도서 클럽 홍보
② 개인 도서관을 구축하는 것에 관한 조언
③ 이웃과 도서를 공유하는 것의 이점들
④ 사람들이 자선단체에 책을 기부해야 하는 이유
⑤ 여행 클럽 신입 회원 모집

▶ 17. 해석 참조

M: On your shelves you probably have lots of books gathering dust. Why not share them with others? Select one of your favorite books that nobody is reading at the moment. Then register it on the BookCrossing website, and start its journey into the unknown. BookCrossing is a global book club for book-lovers that crosses time and space. It has 300,000 members, sharing 1.5 million books, all over the world. And it's completely free. A BookCrossing member leaves a book somewhere for others to pick up and read, and registers this book on the BookCrossing website. The person who finds the book reads it and passes it on again. This continues until it gets lost or someone doesn't pass it on. Each reader can also put their comments about the book on the BookCrossing website. This way, the person who originally supplied the book can keep track of its journey.

남: 당신의 책꽂이에는 분명 먼지가 수북이 쌓인 많은 책이 있을 겁니다. 그것을 다른 사람들과 함께 나누는 것은 어떠신지요? 당신이 좋아하는 책 중에서 지금 아무도 읽지 않는 책을 한 권 고르세요. 그러고 나서 그것을 BookCrossing 웹사이트에 등록하신 후, 책을 미지(未知)의 장소로 떠나보내세요. BookCrossing은 책을 사랑하는 사람을 위한, 시간과 공간을 넘나드는 세계적인 규모의 도서 클럽입니다. 전 세계에 걸쳐 삼십만 명의 회원(① 회원 수)을 보유하고 있으며 백오십만 권의 책(② 공유 도서 수)을 공유합니다. 그리고 완전히 무료입니다(③ 이용 비용). BookCrossing의 회원은 다른 사람이 가져가서 읽을 수 있도록 책 한 권을 놓아둔 다음, 그 책을 BookCrossing 웹사이트에 등록합니다. 책을 발견한 사람은 읽고 나서 다른 사람에게 다시 전달합니다(④ 이용 방법). 이러한 과정은 책이 분실되거나 누군가가 더 이상 전달하지 않을 때까지 계속됩니다. 책을 읽는 사람은 각자 그 책에 관한 의견을 BookCrossing 웹사이트에 남길 수도 있습니다. 이런 식으로, 처음 책을 제공했던 사람은 책의 이동 경로를 추적할 수 있습니다.

어휘 **register** 등록하다 / **pass on** 넘겨주다, 전달하다 / **supply** 공급하다, 주다 / **keep track of** ~을 추적하다; 파악하다 | 선택지 어휘 | **promotion** 홍보; 촉진 / **recruitment** 신회원[신병] 모집

ANSWER

정답 모음

01회 모의고사

01. ④ 02. ③ 03. ① 04. ② 05. ②
06. ② 07. ⑤ 08. ⑤ 09. ③ 10. ①
11. ① 12. ① 13. ⑤ 14. ① 15. ④
16. ① 17. ④

02회 모의고사

01. ④ 02. ⑤ 03. ④ 04. ② 05. ④
06. ③ 07. ⑤ 08. ② 09. ④ 10. ②
11. ② 12. ④ 13. ④ 14. ① 15. ②
16. ⑤ 17. ⑤

03회 모의고사

01. ③ 02. ③ 03. ④ 04. ③ 05. ③
06. ③ 07. ② 08. ④ 09. ④ 10. ③
11. ⑤ 12. ③ 13. ① 14. ② 15. ⑤
16. ③ 17. ④

04회 모의고사

01. ② 02. ① 03. ② 04. ③ 05. ④
06. ② 07. ③ 08. ④ 09. ④ 10. ④
11. ① 12. ③ 13. ③ 14. ⑤ 15. ④
16. ② 17. ①

05회 모의고사

01. ② 02. ④ 03. ⑤ 04. ④ 05. ①
06. ③ 07. ④ 08. ④ 09. ⑤ 10. ③
11. ④ 12. ② 13. ⑤ 14. ② 15. ①
16. ⑤ 17. ②

06회 모의고사

01. ④ 02. ③ 03. ④ 04. ② 05. ⑤
06. ③ 07. ④ 08. ② 09. ② 10. ③
11. ③ 12. ③ 13. ② 14. ② 15. ④
16. ② 17. ⑤

07회 모의고사

01. ④ 02. ② 03. ④ 04. ④ 05. ③
06. ② 07. ⑤ 08. ⑤ 09. ② 10. ②
11. ② 12. ② 13. ⑤ 14. ③ 15. ⑤
16. ④ 17. ④

08회 모의고사

01. ② 02. ③ 03. ③ 04. ② 05. ⑤
06. ④ 07. ⑤ 08. ② 09. ③ 10. ③
11. ② 12. ③ 13. ③ 14. ③ 15. ⑤
16. ② 17. ⑤

09회 모의고사

01. ④ 02. ① 03. ⑤ 04. ④ 05. ③
06. ② 07. ⑤ 08. ④ 09. ③ 10. ④
11. ⑤ 12. ③ 13. ③ 14. ⑤ 15. ⑤
16. ② 17. ⑤

10회 모의고사

01. ① 02. ③ 03. ④ 04. ② 05. ③
06. ③ 07. ② 08. ⑤ 09. ⑤ 10. ①
11. ③ 12. ⑤ 13. ④ 14. ① 15. ③
16. ③ 17. ④

11회 모의고사

01. ⑤ 02. ② 03. ② 04. ⑤ 05. ⑤
06. ④ 07. ④ 08. ④ 09. ② 10. ③
11. ④ 12. ③ 13. ③ 14. ① 15. ②
16. ② 17. ⑤

12회 모의고사

01. ③ 02. ⑤ 03. ② 04. ④ 05. ⑤
06. ① 07. ① 08. ② 09. ③ 10. ②
11. ④ 12. ① 13. ④ 14. ④ 15. ②
16. ④ 17. ④

13회 모의고사

01. ④ 02. ④ 03. ④ 04. ③ 05. ⑤
06. ③ 07. ③ 08. ③ 09. ③ 10. ⑤
11. ③ 12. ⑤ 13. ① 14. ① 15. ②
16. ③ 17. ⑤

14회 모의고사

01. ④ 02. ① 03. ④ 04. ⑤ 05. ⑤
06. ③ 07. ④ 08. ② 09. ④ 10. ①
11. ② 12. ④ 13. ④ 14. ⑤ 15. ⑤
16. ③ 17. ②

15회 모의고사

01. ③ 02. ④ 03. ⑤ 04. ④ 05. ①
06. ④ 07. ② 08. ② 09. ② 10. ⑤
11. ② 12. ⑤ 13. ③ 14. ④ 15. ④
16. ① 17. ⑤

16회 모의고사

01. ⑤ 02. ② 03. ④ 04. ① 05. ④
06. ④ 07. ⑤ 08. ③ 09. ② 10. ③
11. ① 12. ② 13. ④ 14. ② 15. ②
16. ② 17. ④

17회 모의고사

01. ③ 02. ⑤ 03. ③ 04. ④ 05. ④
06. ② 07. ③ 08. ④ 09. ② 10. ④
11. ② 12. ④ 13. ① 14. ④ 15. ④
16. ③ 17. ④

18회 모의고사

01. ② 02. ② 03. ③ 04. ⑤ 05. ④
06. ② 07. ② 08. ③ 09. ⑤ 10. ②
11. ⑤ 12. ② 13. ② 14. ① 15. ⑤
16. ② 17. ④

19회 모의고사

01. ① 02. ④ 03. ① 04. ⑤ 05. ⑤
06. ③ 07. ④ 08. ④ 09. ⑤ 10. ④
11. ④ 12. ④ 13. ② 14. ① 15. ④
16. ⑤ 17. ⑤

20회 모의고사

01. ③ 02. ② 03. ⑤ 04. ④ 05. ⑤
06. ③ 07. ④ 08. ② 09. ④ 10. ⑤
11. ② 12. ④ 13. ④ 14. ① 15. ④
16. ② 17. ⑤

ANSWER

정답 모음

21회 모의고사

01. ② 02. ② 03. ③ 04. ③ 05. ④
06. ④ 07. ② 08. ⑤ 09. ④ 10. ②
11. ⑤ 12. ④ 13. ⑤ 14. ② 15. ⑤
16. ① 17. ②

22회 모의고사

01. ⑤ 02. ③ 03. ② 04. ② 05. ①
06. ④ 07. ④ 08. ⑤ 09. ⑤ 10. ⑤
11. ② 12. ② 13. ④ 14. ③ 15. ④
16. ① 17. ⑤

23회 모의고사

01. ⑤ 02. ① 03. ② 04. ④ 05. ④
06. ② 07. ② 08. ③ 09. ④ 10. ③
11. ③ 12. ④ 13. ⑤ 14. ③ 15. ③
16. ③ 17. ③

24회 모의고사

01. ② 02. ① 03. ⑤ 04. ④ 05. ④
06. ① 07. ⑤ 08. ③ 09. ④ 10. ③
11. ① 12. ④ 13. ② 14. ④ 15. ③
16. ④ 17. ④

25회 모의고사

01. ② 02. ② 03. ③ 04. ① 05. ④
06. ③ 07. ② 08. ② 09. ③ 10. ③
11. ② 12. ⑤ 13. ② 14. ② 15. ⑤
16. ① 17. ①

26회 모의고사

01. ① 02. ④ 03. ④ 04. ⑤ 05. ①
06. ④ 07. ⑤ 08. ③ 09. ⑤ 10. ③
11. ① 12. ④ 13. ② 14. ② 15. ④
16. ⑤ 17. ④

27회 모의고사

01. ② 02. ⑤ 03. ② 04. ④ 05. ②
06. ③ 07. ④ 08. ⑤ 09. ① 10. ④
11. ② 12. ④ 13. ① 14. ④ 15. ③
16. ② 17. ①

28회 모의고사

01. ③ 02. ③ 03. ⑤ 04. ③ 05. ③
06. ③ 07. ④ 08. ④ 09. ③ 10. ①
11. ② 12. ① 13. ④ 14. ① 15. ④
16. ⑤ 17. ⑤

29회 모의고사

01. ④ 02. ④ 03. ④ 04. ③ 05. ⑤
06. ③ 07. ④ 08. ③ 09. ⑤ 10. ④
11. ④ 12. ① 13. ① 14. ② 15. ①
16. ⑤ 17. ⑤

30회 모의고사

01. ④ 02. ⑤ 03. ③ 04. ⑤ 05. ③
06. ② 07. ③ 08. ④ 09. ③ 10. ④
11. ④ 12. ① 13. ① 14. ② 15. ⑤
16. ① 17. ⑤

절대평가 대비 수능 문제풀이 감각

SENSE UP